SPORT LEADERSHIP

in the 21st Century

SECOND EDITION

Laura J. Burton, PhD
Professor
Department of Educational Leadership
University of Connecticut
Storrs, CT

Gregory M. Kane, PhD
Associate Professor
Department of Health and Physical Education
Eastern Connecticut State University
Willimantic, CT

John F. Borland, PhD
Associate Professor
Department of Sport Management and Recreation
Springfield College
Springfield, MA

JONES & BARTLETT
LEARNING

World Headquarters
Jones & Bartlett Learning
5 Wall Street
Burlington, MA 01803
978-443-5000
info@jblearning.com
www.jblearning.com

Jones & Bartlett Learning books and products are available through most bookstores and online booksellers. To contact Jones & Bartlett Learning directly, call 800-832-0034, fax 978-443-8000, or visit our website, www.jblearning.com.

16256-1

Production Credits

VP, Product Management: Amanda Martin
Director of Product Management: Cathy L. Esperti
Product Manager: Sean Fabery
Product Assistant: Andrew LaBelle
Project Specialist: Nora Menzi
Project Specialist: Jamie Reynolds
Digital Project Specialist: Rachel Reyes
Director of Marketing: Andrea DeFronzo
VP, Manufacturing and Inventory Control: Therese Connell

Composition and Project Management: Exela Technologies
Cover Design: Theresa Manley
Text Design: Kristin E. Parker
Rights & Media Specialist: John Rusk
Media Development Editor: Troy Liston
Cover Image: © Aleks Kend/Shutterstock
Printing and Binding: McNaughton & Gunn
Cover Printing: McNaughton & Gunn

Library of Congress Cataloging-in-Publication Data

Names: Burton, Laura J., author. | Kane, Gregory M., author. | Borland, John F., author.
Title: Sport leadership in the 21st century / Laura J. Burton, Gregory M. Kane, John F. Borland.
Other titles: Sport leadership in the twenty-first century
Description: Second Edition. | Burlington, Massachusetts : Jones & Bartlett Learning, [2018] | First edition published in 2015 with John F. Borland as principal author. | Includes bibliographical references and index.
Identifiers: LCCN 2018038125 | ISBN 9781284149586 (Paperback : alk. paper)
Subjects: LCSH: Sports administration. | Leadership. | Teamwork (Sports) | Sports teams.
Classification: LCC GV713 .B665 2018 | DDC 796.06/9–dc23 LC record available at https://lccn.loc.gov/2018038125

6048

Printed in the United States of America
23 22 21 20 19   10 9 8 7 6 5 4 3 2

Brief Contents

© Gorilla Images/Shutterstock

Contents

Chapter 10   Team Leadership and Group Dynamics 203

Peter Bachiochi
Wendi Everton

Chapter 11   Shepherding Sport for Development Organizations 223

Jennifer (Bruening) McGarry
Nadia Moreno
Brooke Page Rosenbauer

Chapter 12   Addressing the Gender Gap in Sport Leadership 243

Heidi Grappendorf

Chapter 13 Lingering Issues in Race and Leadership 261

Jacqueline McDowell
Algerian Hart
Emmett Gill

Chapter 14 Leading Athletes with Disabilities 283

Mary A. Hums
Eli Wolff
David Legg

Chapter 15 Real World Applications and Career Paths 301

Tim Liptrap

Preface

As we complete the second edition of this text, the contributors and editors are reminded that the original edition of this book was among the first sport management textbooks to address the topic of leadership. To date, there are still very few textbooks available to students, professors, and practitioners that focus on sport leadership. Prior to the publication of our book, many sport management professors had to rely on books written by sport leaders—which are not comprehensive—or textbooks that discuss leadership in general, forcing them to teach sport management students from a general leadership perspective, outside of the context of sport. We helped to fill that gap with the first edition of the book and are so pleased to provide the sport management community with the second edition of *Sport Leadership in the 21st Century*. We believe that this textbook provides a significant contribution to our discipline and reinforces the importance of sport leadership instruction in academic programs.

The text defines leadership in this way:

Leadership is an influence relationship aimed at moving organizations or groups of people toward an imagined future that depends on alignment of values and establishment of mutual purposes.

The significance of this conceptualization of leadership is its ability to capture three important elements: Influence, future, and mutuality. In sport organizations, there will always be a need for leaders to influence and motivate employees in positive ways to work toward organizational goals and future success. With the aging and retirement of the Baby Boomer generation, millennials are moving into organizations while Generation Z is learning and developing the skills to become leaders. These young people do not have the seasoned leadership experience of the people retiring. They may not know how to best influence their leaders and learn leadership concepts. Academic departments can address this need for leadership knowledge. We feel that this leadership definition—and this textbook—can give them a leg up. Furthermore, sport organizations—whether for-profit or not-for-profit—have the desire to be successful well into the future. This success is measured in the ability to reach established organizational goals. These organizations need people who can imagine what that successful future may look like through analyses of internal and external factors. Finally, no leader can do it alone. Leaders must establish mutual benefits for organization and employees and help followers to understand the value of work not only from an organizational standpoint but also from a personal standpoint. Leaders, if transformational, can establish mutual purposes by articulating how an organization's success connects to the personal success of individual employees.

This textbook is intended for upper-level undergraduate sport management students and sport management graduate students who are interested in learning about or leading sport organizations in the 21st century. Entry-level employees and other sport practitioners will also benefit from reading this book. Our purpose in developing the second edition is to provide foundational instruction on the construction of leadership in sport management based on the most current leadership scholarship and practices in the domain of sport management. We have provided two new chapters in this updated edition, one on motivation and leadership and another on leadership communication and crisis management. In addition, all chapters were updated to reflect content that relies on the most current research and sport industry practices of leadership, new case studies, interviews with a new group of leaders in a variety of sectors in the sport industry, and discussion questions that build critical thinking skills.

In many cases, the research utilized in these chapters is drawn from other disciplines, including psychology, business, sociology, and, of course, management; however, we are pleased to note that there is a robust and developing line of research specific to sport leadership that is reflected in the second edition. As in the previous edition, you will notice that there are similar leadership concepts that surface across multiple chapters. We did this by design, as we believe that repetition of these concepts will allow readers to recognize the most important information regarding leadership. For example, Chapter 2, "Positive Leadership Theory: Transformational, Transactional, and Servant Leadership," examines the characteristics of transformational leadership, but transformational leadership is a concept that finds its way into many chapters because it connects to many other concepts, such as communication and organizational change.

▶ New to the Second Edition

As noted above, in this new edition, we have added two important chapters that provide a more complete exploration of the various skills required by leaders. The first is Chapter 4, "Motivation and Leadership." This chapter explores the concepts of motivation, how leaders can effectively motivate employees and volunteers, and the motivational needs of the millennial generation and the newest generation to enter the workforce, Generation Z. Chapter author and co-editor of this textbook, John Borland of Springfield College, includes interviews with millennials working in sport organizations who share firsthand experiences of leadership that have effectively motivated them during their early careers. The other new entry is Chapter 5, "Leadership Communication and Crisis Management." This chapter examines the critical importance of communication and how leaders must utilize effective communication strategies, including the importance of trust in the communication process. The chapter also addresses conflict, the role of communication in the conflict process, and the leader's role in effective communication during times of organizational crisis. As noted by the chapter author, Michael Mudrick of York College, leaders must develop communication strategies that allow for a rapid response to crisis given the role of social media in the 21st century.

As we noted in the first edition and is still relevant today, readers must pay close attention to Chapter 6 and the topic of ethical leadership in sport. In "Applying a Principled and Ethical Approach to Sport Leadership," Meg Hancock and Mary Hums of the University of Louisville have written a comprehensive account of the importance in having leaders that exercise values and principles in their stewardship of 21st century sport organizations. As we also noted in the first edition, sport industry observers will agree that at every turn there is the potential for unethical behavior from sport organizations. The recent ethical scandals involving the cover-up by USA Gymnastics and Michigan State University of sexual abuse of athletes are but a few of the more egregious examples of failures of leadership. The contributors provide several examples, both historic and current, documenting unethical behavior, and they suggest pathways that leaders can use to make better decisions. We continue to advocate that leadership and ethics go hand in hand, and ethical leadership is a crucial competency for 21st century leaders, particularly in sport.

The second edition of the textbook continues to rely on industry perspectives in the form of case studies and interviews with leaders in the sport industry. These featured pieces help to bring additional voices into each chapter by providing real-world experiences for readers to consider. We also continue to strive for a balance between theory and practice in this revised edition, with an introductory chapter that delves into the importance of the theoretical development of leadership in the 20th century. The remaining 14 chapters are also rich in researched knowledge about best practices in leadership. The case studies and interviews allow readers to *apply* these theories and leadership paradigms. We have included case studies that range from effective team leadership for the popular e-sports team, Team Liquid (Chapter 10, "Team Leadership and Group Dynamics") to the continued under representation of women in international sport leadership (Chapter 12, "Addressing the Gender Gap in Sport Leadership"). Furthermore, industry interviews include information from the brave new world of social media (Chapter 5, "Leadership Communication and Crisis Management"), to how leaders of athletes with disabilities can hasten their full integration into media coverage and Olympics governance structures (Chapter 14, "Leading Athletes with Disabilities").

How to Use This Book

Each chapter of the second edition of *Sport Leadership in the 21st Century* includes a number of pedagogical elements designed to aid in the mastery of the material, including case studies, key terms, and discussion questions. The following explanations outline these key resources, which will assist you in grasping the key concepts at hand.

Clearly defined **Chapter Objectives** open each chapter and highlight the key concepts presented.

CHAPTER OBJECTIVES

- Differentiate the leadership styles of transactional, transformational, and servant leadership.
- Identify contexts that are appropriate for each type of leadership style.
- Understand and describe the behaviors associated with transactional, transformational, and servant leadership.
- Describe organizational outcomes associated with each type of leadership style.
- Explore positive leadership research in sport and sport organizations.

Interesting **Case Studies** are found in each chapter and bring real world experiences into the classroom.

CASE STUDY

Leadership and the Response to NFL Athlete Activism

During the 2016 NFL preseason, San Francisco 49ers quarterback Colin Kaepernick remained seated during the playing of the national anthem. Kaepernick made this decision as a way of bringing attention to allegations of police brutality and the killing of unarmed black men by police, which led to the Black Lives Matter movement. He told NFL Media in August of 2016 that "I am not going to stand up to show pride in a flag for a country that oppresses black people and people of color; to me, this is bigger than football and it would be selfish on my part to look the other way. There are bodies in the street and people getting paid leave and getting away with murder." (Wyche, 2016, n. p.)

As attention around the Kaepernick protest increased, other teammates joined and they began kneeling during the national anthem. At the end of the 2016 season, Kaepernick's contract with the 49ers was not renewed and he was not signed by another NFL team for the 2017 season. Despite his absence from the field, other NFL players from the league continued the protest against unjust police practices, including Michael Bennett of the Seattle Seahawks. In September of 2017, President Trump spoke about the NFL players protests in a campaign-style rally. President Trump conveyed his disagreement with the protests and called on the NFL and team owners to fire those who were protesting. These statements led to more player protests and subsequent responses, both positive and negative, by fans on both sides of this issue. Following the President's remarks, the NFL issued statements not only indicating support for the players but it also issued an appeal for all players to stand for the national anthem before games (for a timeline of the protests, see Riley, 2018).

In an attempt to quell dissent from players, owners of the NFL teams, and fans who supported the players' protests and those who were against the protests, the NFL partnered with the players and committed approximately $100 million to a fund that would support causes that were important to the African-American Black community (Trotter & Reid, 2017). Many members of the NFL Players Coalition were skeptical of this NFL fund, yet others felt that it was an important step by the league and its owners to recognize the players' concerns (Trotter & Reid, 2017).

During the NFL owners' meetings in May of 2018, the owners and the league office, without consultation with the NFL Players' Union, implemented a new rule regarding the national anthem for the 2018 to –2019 season. The new rule stipulates that any player on the field during the playing of the

Questions for Discussion

1. How would you describe the NFL owners' collective leadership on the players' protests? Read and review the chapter before answering this. Provide specific examples from the case study to support your answer.
2. Do you believe that this type of leadership will be effective in supporting the success of the NFL for the 2018–2019 season? Provide specific information to support your response.
3. What other type(s) of leadership would you recommend for owners of the NFL? Why would you recommend that type of leadership?
4. What type of leadership could be used by the NFL Players' Union to best resolve the apparent conflict between the players and the owners over the player protests? Provide specific information to support your response.

Important **Questions for Discussion** follow each case study and ask students to think critically about topics presented in the case.

▶ **Introduction**

Most scholars agree that there is a relationship between leadership and an organization's success or failure (Klimoski & Koles, 2001). At the most basic level, leaders will establish the direction of an organization by developing a vision of the future, and then, after forming influential relationships, will align people by communicating this vision and inspiring them to overcome any obstacles (Robbins & Judge, 2003). Leaders are individual actors who display personal behaviors. In this chapter, we examine the domain of positive leadership, including transformational and servant leadership. Positive leadership behaviors focus on interpersonal dynamics that support the development of followers' (e.g., employees, volunteers, interns) self-confidence, resulting in positive outcomes for the organization. Positive leadership theories emphasize outcomes beyond what is best for the organization, look to motivate followers beyond task expectations, and seek to increase followers' individual development and prosocial behaviors (Hannah, Sumanth, Lester, & Cavarretta, 2014).

A thorough **Introduction** sets the stage for each chapter and incorporates the topics discussed in the related case study.

Leadership Perspective boxes include engaging interviews with leaders in the sport industry who discuss interesting experiences and best practices in leadership.

LEADERSHIP PERSPECTIVE

Courtesy of Frank Rossi

Michael Capiraso

Michael Capiraso is the President and CEO of the New York Road Runners (NYRR), the organization that is responsible for the world's largest marathon in 2016 and 2017, the New York Marathon. Prior to joining the NYRR in 2010 and leading since 2015, Capiraso was a leader in brand marketing and organizational strategy for the National Football League and Major League Baseball. Among his initiatives have been key alignments with partners to enhance both the technological experiences on and off the race course as well as serving more than 600,000 participants throughout the country.

Q: What is your role in leadership? How long? Prior experiences?
Since May of 2015, I have served as the President and CEO of New York Road Runners. Before entering this role, I served as NYRR's COO. Prior to NYRR, I've held strategic, marketing and operational roles at the NFL, Cole Haan, Major League Baseball Productions, and Calvin Klein.

Additional **Discussion Questions** close out each chapter and are ideal for homework assignments and in-class discussion.

▶ **Discussion Questions**

1. Considering the leadership theories presented in this chapter, identify a leader in the field of sport and describe whether he or she uses transactional, transformational, servant, or authentic leadership.

2. Given the scandals facing professional sport (e.g., use of performance-enhancing drugs, illegal behavior by coaches and athletes), what type of leadership could best support organizations that are trying to move past such scandals? Use information from the chapter to support your answer.

3. Describe the most significant differences between transformational and servant leadership.

4. What are some of the noted outcomes reported in research that have examined servant leadership in sport organizations?

5. Which type of leadership behavior do you think is best to utilize within a sport organization? Provide details from the chapter to support your answer.

Acknowledgments

We are again deeply indebted to the contributors who have provided us with significant assistance in putting together this textbook. The expertise of the chapter authors ranged from large research universities to smaller teaching colleges. Some of our contributors are practitioners working in the field, which made them uniquely qualified to find and use content in the chapters that confirmed their leadership ideas and experiences.

In the case of Chapter 11, "Shepherding Sport for Development Organizations," the three contributors are practitioners in the sport-for-development field. In addition to founding and managing Husky Sport with the help of her graduate students, Jennifer (Bruening) McGarry is also a department chair and sport management professor at the University of Connecticut. In Chapter 11, she teamed with Nadia Moreno and Brooke Rosenbauer, who develop programming for A Ganar, a youth workforce development program that utilizes soccer and other team sports to help youth in Latin America and the Caribbean, ages 16-24, to find jobs. We think that, in order for our discipline to grow, we need to form more of these practitioner-professor relationships and shine the light on professors acting as practitioners. Chapter 11 is a result of such collaboration.

This is only one example of the valuable information put forth by the diversity of contributors to this book. We are so grateful to the contributors for their efforts and patience during the editorial process. As editors, we continue to learn more about sport leadership from the insights of the collaborators, and we thank them for finding time for this project given their already busy research and teaching schedules. We believe we have chosen the best people in our field to contribute to this textbook on sport leadership.

Further, we would like to thank the prospectus and chapter reviewers for helping guide the topic selection process and thoughtful feedback on how to improve the second edition of this textbook. We also thank everyone at Jones and Bartlett Learning for their patience. The steadfastness of Product Manager Sean Fabery and Product Assistant Andrew LaBelle were greatly appreciated as we endeavored to produce this second edition.

About the Authors

Laura J. Burton, PhD

Laura J. Burton is a professor of sport management in the Department of Educational Leadership within the Neag School of Education at the University of Connecticut. Her research interests include understanding leadership in organizations (particularly sport organizations) and exploring development, access, and success in leadership. In her work, Laura focuses on issues of gender in leadership contexts and specifically how stereotypes and discrimination impact women in sport leadership. She has served as the editor of the *Journal of Intercollegiate Sport* and serves on the editorial board of the *Journal of Sport Management* and *Women in Sport and Physical Activity Journal*. She has published in the *Journal of Sport Management*, *Sport Management Review*, and *Sex Roles*. She is co-editor of *Women in Sport Leadership: Research and Practice for Change*, published in 2017, and also co-wrote the textbook *Organizational Behavior in Sport Management*, published in 2018.

Gregory M. Kane, PhD

Gregory M. Kane is an associate professor and chair in the Department of Kinesiology and Physical Education at Eastern Connecticut State University. After completing his graduate degrees in exercise physiology (MA) and sport management (PhD) from the University of Connecticut, Dr. Kane went on to teach courses in sport sociology, research methodology in sport, and leadership and problem solving in sport. In addition, Dr. Kane has presented both nationally and internationally on the pedagogy and assessment of leadership. Currently, Dr. Kane maintains several leadership positions within the university, is the chair of the Association of Department Chairs, and serves on several advisory boards throughout the country.

John F. Borland, PhD

John Borland is an associate professor in the Sport Management and Recreation Department at Springfield College, where he teaches courses in sport communication, venue and personnel management, budgeting, and event management. He was a newspaper copy editor for nine years prior to returning to school to obtain his masters (Georgia State University) and his doctorate (University of Connecticut) in sport management. His research interests include sport for development, gender and race in sport, and the socialization of marginalized groups in sport.

Reviewers

Beth Easter, PhD
Professor and Program Director, Sport
  Management
Department of Health, Human Performance,
  and Recreation
Southeast Missouri State University
Cape Girardeau, MO

Richard Fabri, MS, CRSS
Assistant Professor and Sport Management
  Program Manager
School of Hospitality, Sport, and Tourism
  Management
Husson University
Bangor, ME

P. Graham Hatcher, PhD
Professor
Department of Kinesiology
Howard Payne University
Brownwood, TX

Lana L. Huberty, PhD
Assistant Professor
Department of Kinesiology
Concordia University,
St. Paul, MN

Jordan Kobritz, JD
Professor and Chair
Sport Management Department
SUNY Cortland
Cortland, NY

Merry Moiseichik, REd, JD
Professor and Program Coordinator
Department of Health, Human Performance,
  and Recreation
University of Arkansas
Fayetteville, AR

Justin K. Nichols, EdD
Lecturer
Department of Kinesiology and Health
  Promotion
University of Kentucky
Lexington, KY

Kathryn Shea, PhD
Assistant Professor and Program Director
School of Management and Communications
Fisher College
Boston, MA

CHAPTER 1

Leadership Theories

Gregory M. Kane

CHAPTER OBJECTIVES

- Develop an appreciation for the breadth and depth of leadership theory.
- Develop a foundational understanding of leadership.
- Identify and describe sources of power in the context of sport.
- Describe the ways in which would-be leaders assume the role of leader.

CASE STUDY

Warren Miller, Filmmaker, Author, Icon

Warren Miller, the self-described ski bum turned filmmaker and author, died on January 24, 2018, at the age of 93. His legacy is one of passion, storytelling, sport, and freedom. From humble beginnings of living out of a trailer to being called the single greatest influence in the action-sports film industry, Warren Miller's film contributions from the 1950s to 2004 were important contributions to the winter sports culture. His films were widely recognizable as being part documentary and part comedy. His company, Warren Miller Entertainment (WME), now under new management, continues to produce winter sports movies that are an annual event, often serving as a pep rally for the ski season. Their 69th film is scheduled to be released in the fall of 2018.

Miller, born in Hollywood, California, in 1924, took up skiing and surfing as a child. After his discharge from the Navy in 1946, he bought a camera and while living in a trailer in the parking lot of Sun Valley ski resort, began to film his friend Ward Baker and himself in an effort to improve their skiing technique ("In Memoriam"). At first, Miller would show the films and narrate to friends. Friends turned into parties, and parties turned into crowds. Before long, Miller had pieced together a full-length feature and would be touring in 130 cities a year. In reference to his prolific career, Miller wanted to "tell stories and have the film to back it up." It was a "labor of love" for Miller, whose first experience on snow was transformational. "It was total freedom but absolutely no control over it." (Channel, 2012) In the years that followed,

(continues)

CASE STUDY   (continued)

Miller would be recognized 10 times for the CINE Golden Eagles Award, eight times for the IFPA Award, and the International Documentary Achievement award, to name a few.

The filmmaker and ski icon was committed to his unique craft of documenting ski culture, its evolving action, and, of course, humor. His recognizable monotone voice and dry wit created a pallet for which skiing, nature, and freedom could be experienced through film. Despite his wide recognition, more than 500 film credits, and many awards, Warren Miller was never in the Academy of Motion Picture and Sciences. A close friend explained, "Warren, they don't think you make "real" movies." To which Miller responded, "...I don't." (Galbraith, 2018) Doing things Warren's way was as much about being headstrong as it was about telling the story. At a time when corporate sponsors, big budgets, and larger staff were the norm, Miller focused on small budgets, intimate relationships, and family. At one point, as Miller describes it, after becoming frustrated with partners and the lack of meaningful relationships, he sold the company to his son yet remained active in the company for another 15 years (Galbraith, 2018).

Off of the slopes, Miller and WME committed to being benefactors for more than just skiing. In 2009, Miller and others opened the Warren Miller Performing Arts Center in Big Sky, Montana ("Warren Miller Performing Arts Center," 2018). In addition, Miller helped develop the Warren Miller Freedom Foundation's Young Entrepreneur Program ("In Memoriam"). This program was designed to give children from grades 6 through 12 introductory experiences in business management, building relationships, and customer service. In 2012, and in partnership with former Vice President Al Gore's Climate Reality Project, WME began to tackle climate change from a unique perspective. The initiative, Pro Snow, focuses on the preservation of winter sports through protecting against environmental changes ("In Memoriam").

Warren Miller, while credited with creating the genre of action sports filmmaking, discovered this untapped market because of a passion for the sport. Often, doing what he loved rather than doing what made strong business sense, Miller developed a brand that is synonymous with outdoors, skiing, and freedom. This passion, with 1,200 columns and 11 books to his credit, developed into an industry that is loved by many today ("In Memoriam").

Questions for Discussion

1. Consider the different types of leadership described in Chapter 1. What types of leadership behavior did Warren Miller display?
2. Describe the traits that Warren Miller possessed that lend themselves to his being an effective leader? Use examples from the case study to support your answer.
3. How did Miller become the leader and innovator of an industry?
4. By using The Managerial Grid, where would you place Miller? Why?
5. What do you think are the challenges for this industry? How will action sport filmmaking transform in the next 10 years?

▶ Introduction

Thoughts on leadership and the qualities of a leader have existed for thousands of years, and many of these ideas have stood the test of time. Ancient Chinese philosopher and military tactician Sun Tzu is credited with several written works on leadership, most notably, *The Art of War*. After more than 2,500 years, his leadership philosophy and tactics are still employed by military leaders. Tzu's teachings are also finding an audience among contemporary business managers. In 2000, *Sun Tzu and the Art of Business* was published, connecting Tzu's thinking to modern business strategy. Like Tzu, today's leaders need to be adept at sizing up their competition and looking for perceived weaknesses that they can exploit to gain a marketplace advantage—if, indeed, this is one of their organization's goals.

Emanating from ancient Greece, Plato's *Republic* discussed the qualities of a just man and how these are needed for idealistic leadership in a just city-state (Brickhouse & Smith, 2009). Some leaders in sport are revered and respected because of their sense of fairness and impact on their organizations. Dan Rooney, former chairman of the Pittsburgh Steelers who passed away in 2017, is credited with suggesting the NFL's Rooney Rule that has attempted to pave the way for more diversity in hiring head coaches, comes to mind when considering Plato's sense of fairness. Although this text is predominantly focused on leadership in contemporary times—the 21st century—and equipping future leaders of sport with the skills and perspectives needed to lead both for-profit and not-for-profit sport organizations, it is crucial and instructive to glimpse the evolution of leadership and its theoretical development. Today's leaders have much to learn from past leaders and past theories of leadership because organizational challenges encountered today are often variations on situations encountered in the past.

Theories of leadership are a useful way for students learning about leadership to compare different perspectives at different points in history in different contexts. Furthermore, theories offer frameworks of analysis by providing explanations about why certain relationships exist between units (e.g., leader and follower) in the empirical—or observed—world. **Leadership** is a prolific area of study with several theories, many reaching back decades. For students who may have little formal education in leadership concepts, this chapter serves as an introduction. It is certain that you have observed leaders in society and sport, on your campus, or even at your workplaces; it is quite possible that you, as a sport management student, have already engaged in leadership opportunities on campus, in your community, in a group project in class, or at a sporting event where you have volunteered or worked. This chapter serves as a primer for what is going on between leaders and followers with regard to leadership styles and sources of power. The mechanisms for leadership ascendancy are also discussed. Finally, some of the prominent leadership theories of the 19th and 20th centuries are briefly explained. The theories included in this chapter are likely to reappear in your further study of leadership and were carefully selected for their contribution to the development of leadership thinking for the 21st century.

▶ Leader and Leadership Defined

In his seminal work, *Handbook of Leadership* (1974), Ralph Stogdill writes a brief account of the origins of the words **"leader"** and "leadership." This account is repeated in Bass's (1981) revision of Stogdill's original work. It appears as though "lead" and "leader" have been part of European languages since about 1300. The notable exception is French, in which the word "leader" had no clear translation, even into the late 20th century (Blondel, 1987). It is not until Webster's *An American Dictionary of the English Language* from 1828 that a definition of "leadership" appears. Likewise, in Europe, the word "leadership" did not appear until the first half of the 19th century in writings about political influence and control of the British Parliament (Bass, 1981). Curiously, *Webster's* omitted any definition of "leadership" from subsequent dictionaries until 1965, when several definitions are listed in the third edition of the *New International Dictionary of the English Language*.

The foundational starting point in the study of leadership is an understanding of the parts that make up the word. The word "leadership" can be broken down into three parts: *lead*, *-er*, and *-ship*. The first part, *lead*, is likely derived from the Middle English *lede*, which means to come first or go first

(Dictionary com, n.d.a). The use of *-er* denotes one who performs a task or is employed in a role, such as baker—one who bakes (Dictionary.com, n.d.b). Therefore, a leader is someone who is employed in a role in which he or she is at the forefront of a group; thus, the one who defines the path. The use of *-ship* denotes a skill or craft, as in the word "scholarship" (Dictionary.com, n.d.c). Based on this interpretation, leadership is the skill set needed in the craft of defining the path for a group by one who is employed in such a position.

A more modern interpretation of leadership is less concrete. Similar to the idea that there is no single model of the perfect leader, there is no perfect definition of leadership. However, there are some common elements to oft-quoted leadership definitions. Northouse (2012) defines leadership as a "process whereby an individual influences a group of individuals to achieve a common goal" (p. 5). Russell (2005) suggests that leadership is the "interpersonal influence exercised by a person or persons, through the process of communication, toward the attainment of an organization's goals" (p. 16). Furthermore, Rue and Byars (2009) define leadership as "the ability to influence people to willingly follow one's guidance or adhere to one's decisions" (p. 465).

There appear to be some similarities among these definitions. Influence is a common element in all of the definitions; goal setting and a relationship between the leader and the group being led are also alluded to in the definitions. The operational definition for this leadership text must then consider these important elements agreed upon by leadership scholars. The definition that this text will use throughout, developed through a closer examination of the differences between leadership and management and aligned well with the three definitions presented in the previous paragraph, is:

> Leadership is an influence relationship aimed at moving organizations or groups of people toward an imagined future that depends upon alignment of values and establishment of mutual purposes.

This definition builds on the works of others and includes several important ideas. First, leadership is more than just a role. It is the behaviors that one exhibits in this role. Some scholars have referred to leadership as a process; however, this loses the human element, the person-centered approach at investigating leadership. Leadership is interactive and dynamic, calling upon both actions and mannerisms to influence followers or subordinates. Second, power is an essential component of leadership in that it will alter the type of influence one has with one's followers (i.e., the group). Finally, alignment between leaders and followers on values and mutual purposes—or outcomes that benefit both the organization and the people involved—is necessary for leadership to be successful. Followers need to understand why a certain action is required.

▶ Power

An appreciation of power enables an effective leader to influence a group to achieve common goals. Thus, **power** is a condition that allows for influence over a group or individual and provides the ability to change another person's behavior, actions, or attitude (Raven, 2008). Therefore, a leader is in a state (power) to offer guidance, direction, incentive, or punishment to his or her subordinates. ("Subordinates" and "followers" are used interchangeably throughout this chapter.) Drawing upon this power allows the leader to obtain the desired goals by motivating the group.

In their seminal work, French and Raven (1959) discuss the five sources of leader power—reward, coercive, legitimate, referent, and expert—and how they relate to social systems. These provide a framework for this discussion of power and leadership in sport. A sixth source of power—informational power—was identified after the French and Raven work (Raven, 1992; Raven, Schwarz-wald, & Koslowsky, 1998).

Reward

Reward power is the state or condition in which a leader has the ability or authority to provide rewards to subordinates. In this instance, the leader is able to motivate the group to perform based on the promise of some type of reward. This would be the carrot that motivates the mule to move forward in the famous carrot-or-stick approach to motivation. The reward provides an incentive for production. In sport, this is a common tactic for motivating a team or group. For example, a marketing/sales director may reward an employee with a bonus based on going above and beyond a quota for group ticket sales. This power is especially effective if the employees themselves are motivated extrinsically (i.e., motivated by salary, vacations, pay bonuses, or promotions). The National Hockey League (NHL) instituted a performance-based pay system in 2009 that largely avoided guaranteed salary increases in favor of bonuses based on a league employee's fulfillment of annual goals. The system works this way: Before the start of a season, each league employee compiles a list of goals that he or she hopes to accomplish for the year, and the employee's ability to meet those goals determines the size of the pay bonus that he or she can receive at the end of the season (Mickle, 2009).

Coercive

Similar to reward power in that a leader has the ability to give something, with **coercive power**, the leader distributes punishments. This would be the stick in the carrot-or-stick approach. Coercive power is the condition in which a leader has the ability to distribute a negative consequence as the result of failing to meet expectations. In the previous NHL example, not fulfilling the goals that a league employee sets forth means not receiving a

salary bonus at the end of the season. This power is often used in sport. Given the competitive marketplace in sport, failure to reach revenue quotas or organizational goals tends to mean longer work hours or, if profits are not achieved over several quarters, a company staff "restructuring" plan that leads to layoffs can occur. The threat of punishment becomes the motivating factor to obtaining goals.

Legitimate

Legitimate power is rooted in the rights, responsibilities, and values of cultural groups. Social structure and learned hierarchy establish an order in which those at the top are awarded privileges and duties that those at the bottom follow. By now in your sport management studies, you have likely encountered an organizational chart, which shows the progression of power from the top (e.g., an athletic director) to the bottom (an intern). This implicit respect and acknowledgment of different levels of job titles provides an opportunity for power to influence interactions among members of the organization. Legitimate power is present when social and cultural norms exist that provide one with the right to influence others. Put another way, legitimate power is the power of a formal position or title. A general manager, an athletic director, or a league commissioner has implicit power that is associated with his or her position in the organization. Those within the group recognize that these people have a leadership role because of the title/role they possess.

Referent

Often compared with charisma, with **referent power**, the relationship between a leader and a subordinate is based on the personal qualities and characteristics exhibited by the leader. In this instance, the leader commands such a presence of personality that group members are compelled to follow. The late Bill Veeck, who owned three baseball teams and created many of the tenets on which modern-day sport marketing and customer service are based, had a commanding presence of personality. Veeck's propensity for needling baseball's conservative governance between the 1940s and 1980s with his off-the-wall promotions provided him with many loyal supporters. It was Veeck's enthusiasm and ingenuity that compelled his employees to line up behind him (Dickson, 2012). Furthermore, with referent power, the subordinate receives satisfaction by avoiding "discomfort," by complying with the wishes of the leader. The notion of avoiding discomfort applies less to Veeck, who welcomed new ideas, and more to the late George Steinbrenner, who owned the New York Yankees from 1973 to 2010. He maintained a large presence in the Yankees organization through his authoritarian leadership. His referent power was apparent by his nickname, "The Boss."

Expert Power

Power that is derived from having great knowledge, skill, or expertise is said to be **expert power**. This power materializes when a subordinate is in a position of need, and the leader has desirable information. A relationship is created in which the needs of the subordinate are satisfied while the leader provides some type of service. For example, a sport information director has desirable knowledge that an intern or an assistant sport information director desires. Thus, a relationship is created that satisfies the needs of both leader and subordinate. It is not necessary for this relationship to be a formal one; rather, this association may be created when a situation arises in which expertise or knowledge is needed. One sees a doctor for his or her expertise, visits a personal trainer to learn his or her skills, or enrolls in a course to seek the professor's knowledge.

Informational Power

Finally, **informational power** refers to a leader explaining to a subordinate how a job or task should be done differently. The leader puts forth persuasive reasons why the suggested change would be a more effective way of doing things (Raven, 2008). The subordinate agrees that the way described by the leader is better and changes his or her behavior accordingly. The information provided by the leader seems to be congruent in addressing the issue, thus influencing the supervisee's attitude or behavior (Gabel, 2011). Informational power may seem similar to expert power, but expert power refers more to a leader's accumulated knowledge, skills, and expertise whereas informational power is isolated to a single situation. A new baseball scout may seek to create a mentee/mentor relationship with the team's general manager (GM) so he or she can take advantage of the GM's expertise, which was acquired over 20 years of work (expert power). In contrast, that same GM can suggest new ways of doing work to his or her scouts through new sources of information. Oakland Athletics General Manager Billy Beane recommended that his scouts use different information to look for undervalued players who had a knack for getting on base and scoring runs (informational power) (Lewis, 2004) rather than the old-school way of scouting that places value on possession of the five tools of baseball: hitting for average, hitting for power, fielding, throwing, and base running.

It must be noted that although the six sources of power have been identified in different contexts, they can exist simultaneously within an individual. An athletic director can exhibit more than one source of power: (1) having the ability to reward coaches with contract renewals, (2) being able to punish with termination, (3) having the power that is embedded within the group from their title, (4) having charisma, (5) having expertise in coaching and administration, and (6) going to conferences and talking to fellow athletic directors to acquire new information on how to change job functions. The sources of power need not be mutually exclusive; rather, they enable a leader to draw upon power to meet a particular circumstance. The effective leader uses these sources of power dynamically as the need changes for different leadership styles.

▶ The Dynamics of Leadership Styles

The leader, whether he or she is leading one or many, amateurs or pros, children, teens, or adults, will find that no two situations are the same. As such, the leadership style must also change to fit the needs of the situation. Imagine the coaching style of Division I basketball coaches and how that style must change if he or she is coaching his or her son's or daughter's youth basketball team. Likewise, administrators of a top flight, highly competitive Division I program may lead the program differently from a competitive Division III program that emphasizes student-athlete development over competition. Which elements might alter leadership styles? When might a leader consider changing leadership style?

There are three elements to weigh when considering a leadership style: the leader, the subordinates, and the situation (environment) [Mondy, Holmes, & Flippo, 1980], as depicted in **FIGURE 1.1**. The interaction between the leader, the subordinate/group, and the environment will impact the resulting leadership

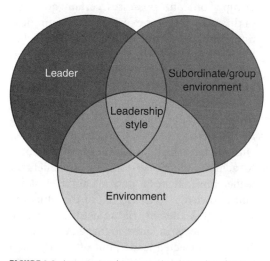

FIGURE 1.1 Interaction between leader, subordinate/group, and environment impact leadership style.

style. Thus, leadership styles are dynamic and depend on the characteristics of these three variables.

Up until this point we have discussed power as part of the leader's role. The leader is also a person with experiences, skills, and needs that are unique to that individual. Therefore, individual leadership styles can change as the leader's experiences change, as they gain skills, or as their personal needs change. Using Billy Beane of the Oakland A's again as an example, his leadership style changed as rival American League teams' payrolls ballooned and his team's payroll stayed relatively low in comparison. He sought more information about player assessment and asked his scouts to adjust their thinking to the Athletics' financial realities (Lewis, 2004). Thus, leadership styles need not be static; they can change as the leader matures, takes on new responsibilities, or self-evaluates and deems change necessary.

The subordinates or followers will contribute to the leadership style. The ages, abilities, skill levels, and knowledge of the subordinates will necessitate an alteration in one's leadership style. A GM for a Minor League Baseball team will lead his executive staff differently from a group of interns. Although the GM's knowledge does not change, the followers are altered. The leadership style must adapt to this changing subordinate group. The language that a leader uses will change, the emphasis on development of followers may change, and the skill-directed activities may change. Effective leaders evaluate and adjust their leadership to meet the needs of subordinates.

Likewise, the situation in which the leader is attempting to lead will exert an influence on the leadership style. Factors like the type of organization (e.g., not-for-profit or for-profit), the group's goals, and the actions of the group will influence the leadership style; for example, a difference in leadership style is needed for leading a recreational sport league versus a Division I athletic department, and each group of participants is not the only consideration. Leadership styles, in this situation, must reflect differences in levels of organization, commitment to competition, and drive for success.

▶ Paths to Leadership

The savvy individual who seeks a leadership role will be aware of the ways in which he or she can rise to this position. Understanding the route to achieving leadership status empowers an individual with a plan for action. Thus, having a firm understanding of the ways one might assume the role of leader becomes important. According to Shivers (1980), four paths exist: appointment, election, emergence, and charisma. Taking on leadership roles early on—particularly while you are still in school—can help put you in a position to take advantage of one of these four paths later in your career.

Appointment

In sport contexts, individuals are often appointed to positions of leadership. As in the case in which a marketing director may appoint a team leader on an account, appointment to the leadership position is a common occurrence. Interestingly, there are unique relationships that exist with this method of leadership attainment. A person is selected because he or she is thought to possess some qualities that align with those who are making the appointment. For instance, a marketing director may appoint a team leader because he or she has proven him- or herself in the past. Appointment suggests a relationship, responsibility, and perhaps shared values among the person who is selected and those who appointed him or her.

Election

The elected leader assumes a leadership role as the result of a process, formal or otherwise, which identifies an individual by popular decision.

In this case, the elected leader has appealed to the electorate, those people who are designated as having the right to vote, and received a majority of votes. This can exist in a formal environment such as the election of a new league commissioner by a vote of team owners. As in the appointment situation, a relationship is then developed with the electorate, in this case the team owners. Popularity existed and so a responsibility to those who elected the leader may be present. Often, this relationship between the owners and commissioner causes a rift between the commissioner and players union during times of labor strife (i.e., lockouts and player strikes). This is a time when a leader has many followers and has to rely on different leadership styles to work with opposing sides.

Emergence

The **emergent leader** is said to spontaneously rise from a group that is in need of leadership. For example, imagine a pick-up basketball game in which there are no captains. No captains are appointed; none is elected from the group. Yet, teams need to be balanced, the informal rules need to be agreed upon, and the game needs to be initiated. What follows is the process of emergent leadership. Someone possesses certain qualities, in this case, perhaps experience, communication, problem-solving abilities, and the ability to take control of the situation. Thus, that individual becomes the emergent leader. Children in informal play environments naturally engage in this type of leadership role process often, with the two best players emerging as the leaders. This is not to be confused with dictatorships, where leaders use force to achieve their leadership goals; emergent leadership matches a person's abilities, skills, and knowledge to the needs of the situation. Emergent leadership is sometimes seen in group projects in sport management classes. Nobody is elected leader, but often, a person with high standards for the quality of work to be submitted emerges as a guiding force.

Charisma

Charisma is the metaphysical force of one's personality that compels others to follow. Some people possess characteristics that are likable and entertaining, and have a belief that they are infallible, thus making them attractive to others. This attraction provides an avenue to leadership. The relationship that is developed is complacency (i.e., self-satisfaction), based on both the avoidance of displeasing the charismatic leader and the potential of pleasing the leader. Although this form of assuming the role of the leader is well established and commonly observed, it should be noted that this form of leadership depends on the strength of the leader's personality, not his or her knowledge, experience, or skill. This form of leadership can be dangerous to wield and even more dangerous to follow (Raelin, 2003). Simply having charisma is not enough; leaders must also possess substance in the form of knowledge and skills and the ability to form meaningful relationships with subordinates. Charismatic leaders cannot do it all on their own. The values shared between leaders and followers must be mutually beneficial.

▶ Leadership Theories

The theoretical underpinnings of leadership have had a distinctive history. Sun Tzu, Socrates, Plato, Lao Tzu, St. Thomas Aquinas, Niccolo Machiavelli, and Mahatma Gandhi are some of the classical names in the literature. Throughout the ages, leadership theories and philosophies moved from a focus on religious, military, and political matters to behavioral, optimal performance, and capitalist-like movements. The following are selected theories and their brief histories and philosophies.

Great Man Theory

The **great man theory** of leadership was a popular 19th-century belief that leaders are born, not made. According to this theory, popularized by Scottish writer Thomas Carlyle in the 1840s, leaders are both born with leader characteristics and born out of social, political, or economic circumstance. Thus, it was the innate qualities of individuals that allowed for their rise to leadership positions. The middle of the 20th century saw this theory fall from favor as behavioral theories began to take over. However, some held onto this belief. In 1980, Indiana basketball coach Bobby Knight (former basketball analyst on ESPN) said, "The first thing you people need to know about leadership is that most of you simply don't have it in you" (Organ, 1996). Contrary to the great man theory is the idea that individuals can develop knowledge, skills, and behaviors of leadership.

Trait Theory

In the 20th century, a systematic approach to studying leadership abilities emerged. Studies identified certain characteristics that might predispose someone as a great leader. These "traits" or factors were identified by comparing leaders and followers and by identifying the characteristics an effective leader possesses. In his meta-analysis of 124 leadership studies, Stogdill (1948) identified five factors that predispose leadership effectiveness: capacity, achievement, responsibility, participation, and status. Over the passing decades, others have contributed to the literature by offering their own meta-analyses (Lord, De Vader, & Alliger, 1986; Mann, 1959; Stogdill, 1974). Northouse (2012) reduced many of these analyses into five major leadership traits: intelligence, self-confidence, determination, integrity, and sociability. Leadership studies at two Midwest universities also laid some of the groundwork to ascertain leader traits.

The Ohio State Studies

The Ohio State Studies, initiated in 1945 and continuing into the 1950s, represented a turning point in the investigation of leadership behaviors (Stogdill & Coons, 1957).

Despite early pressure to simply look at case studies of successful leadership, the Ohio State Studies took a quantitative approach to investigating leadership (Shartle, 1979). Although criticized for their lack of theory development, the Ohio State Studies were successful in developing a multidimensional approach to leadership. Central to these studies were two dimensions of leadership behavior: Initiating structure and consideration. Initiating structure refers to developing goals, outlining tasks, and setting expectations; consideration refers to leader-subordinate relations and fellowship. This extensive body of research led to leadership measurements such as the Leadership Behavior Description Questionnaire-Form XII (LBDQ-Form XII) (Stogdill, 1963) and, later, the Leadership Scale for Sports (LSS) (Chelladurai & Saleh, 1980).

The University of Michigan Studies

Ohio State's gridiron rival to the north, the University of Michigan, also took a behavioral approach to identifying leadership qualities in the 1950s. However, unlike the Ohio State Studies, greater theory-based explanations of leader behavior were developed. Most importantly, the studies created a continuum of employee orientation/production orientation leadership behaviors. Whereas one end of the continuum was anchored by employee orientation—the leader's focus on creating a strong relationship with subordinates—the other end was anchored by production orientation—the leader's focus on the specific tasks.

Likert's System of Management

Perhaps outshined by the scale that bears his name (Likert Scale), Rensis Likert's system of management was an important contribution to the research and application of leadership theory and motivation. Like the foundational University of Michigan Studies, a continuum was developed from **autocratic** to **participative** (Likert, 1961). The four classifications follow:

1. *Exploitive authoritative:* This type of leadership is exemplified by the leader who has little trust in his or her subordinates and thus makes all of the decisions for the group. The group in this environment is motivated by threats and coercion.

2. *Benevolent authoritative:* Again, the leader has relatively low trust in his or her subordinates and makes decisions for the group. However, in this situation, the leader uses a system of rewards to motivate the subordinates.

3. *Consultative:* The leader has an enhanced level of trust in the subordinates and thus calls upon them to aid in decision making. The group is motivated by their ability to be involved with decision making.

4. *Participative team:* The leader displays a high degree of trust in the subordinates. Responsibility for success rests throughout the organization and motivation rests with achievement.

Situational Theory

Based on the work of Hersey and Blanchard (1969), situational leadership theory, later called **situational leadership**, suggested that leadership styles were dependent on the environment or "situation" in which a leader needs to act. This theory implies that leadership styles need to change as the situation and needs of the subordinates change. Essential to this is the idea that there are two dimensions that coexist to change the leader's behavior: supportive behavior and directive behavior (Blanchard, Zigarmi, & Nelson, 1993). Supportive behavior refers to showing socio-emotional concern for subordinates whereas directive behavior refers to the need for leaders to delegate tasks and watch over subordinates. Hersey and Blanchard (1982) note that these behaviors change depending on the skills and maturity of the workforce. If subordinates are mature and responsible, a large amount of supportive and directive behaviors may not be needed. The leader plays more of a background role, only providing socio-emotional support when necessary. However, for a group of subordinates that is insecure, immature, or lacks experience, more supportive and directive behaviors are needed until they grow and gain experience.

Lewin, Lippitt, and White Studies

In 1939, Lewin, Lippitt, and White created their highly regarded foundational work on "social climate" (Lewin, Lippitt, & White, 1939). This groundbreaking social science investigation focused on leadership behaviors in boys' hobby clubs (Edginton, Hudson, Scholl, & Lauzon, 2011). The authors developed an interesting experimental stimulus that the boys would be exposed to during their 3-month investigation. The three leadership styles were **authoritarian**, **democratic**, and **laissez-faire** (Lewin et al., 1939).

Authoritarian leadership was exemplified by a dictator-like style. All of the boys' activities were organized and directed by the leader. Praise and criticism were given to each individual, and the leader did not openly engage the group. This style of leadership led to enhanced levels of aggression, boys seeking approval and attention from the leader, and domination within the peer group. This reaction was significant enough that a "scapegoat" role resulted within the group, and boys opted out of the investigation (Lewin et al., 1939, p. 278).

Democratic leadership was characterized by the leader facilitating the group's activities in consultation with the group. Thus, the activities of the group were discussed and decided upon by full group input. The leader was "objective" and frequently participated in the activities of the group. Group members could choose with whom they wanted to work and which tasks each would do. This leadership style resulted in interactions between the boys that were "friendly" and more "spontaneous" (Lewin et al., 1939, p. 277). Furthermore, boys under this type of leadership style developed and exercised collective planning and individual decision making.

The laissez-faire style of leadership was the last group investigated. This style was characterized by lack of adult participation. Thus, all group decisions were generated by the boys, and they only interacted with the leader when technical questions arose. Furthermore, little to no praise or criticism was offered by the leader. The outcome of this environment was less productive than the other groups. However, in the absence of a leader, the group maintained its productivity, unlike in the authoritarian lead group.

The Lewin, Lippitt, and White studies remain an important, classic contribution to leadership theory. The lasting impact of their research is seen in modern applications of Lewinian theory to economics (Diamond, 1992), mathematics, biology, and social psychology (Scheidlinger, 1994).

Blake and Mouton's Managerial Grid

First developed in the 1960s, the managerial grid has been through many iterations (Blake & Mouton, 1964, 1978, 1985, 1994). It is widely accepted as a critical and important analysis of leadership behavior. It is similar in some respects to the Ohio State Studies, which combined a focus on tasks and a focus on the relationship with the subordinate. However, the managerial grid develops these concepts further by quantifying the degree to which the focus is on tasks or "concern for production/results," and the focus is on the relationship with the subordinate or "concern for people." The one to nine scale in **FIGURE 1.2** allows for discernment among the various responses regarding concern for production or people, where one represents a low concern and nine represents a high concern.

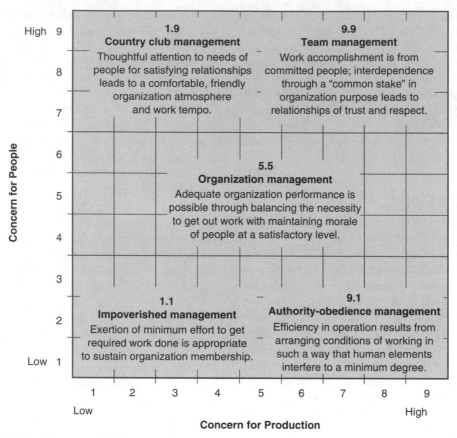

FIGURE 1.2 The Managerial Grid.

Reproduced from Blake, R. Moulton, J. (1964). *The Managerial Grid: The Key to Leadership Excellence*. Houston, TX: Gulf Publishing Company.

Blake and McCanse (1991) postulated that there were five leadership types:

1.1—Impoverished Management: Emphasizes a situation in which there is both low concern for results and for people. The apathetic nature of this leader results in behavior that is withdrawn from subordinates and indifferent to success.

1.9—Country Club Management: This combination of low concern for results with high concern for people results in a leader who is more interested in pleasing people than in the performance of tasks. This leader attempts to create an environment that is friendly and welcoming.

9.1—Authority-Compliance Management: This represents a high concern for results but a low concern for people. This controlling leadership style is characterized by dictating instructions to subordinates in a way that does not show concern or compassion.

5.5—Middle of the Road Management: This style of compromise is evident in leaders who balance concern for results with satisfying relationships. The group is functioning; however, there is potential for greater success.

9.9—Team Management: Great emphasis is placed on production and on people.

This optimal balance of developing human relationships and effective results attainment provides the most satisfying work environment.

▶ Path–Goal Theory of Leadership

Inspired by the work of Georgopoulous, Mahoney, and Jones (1957) and later Evans (1970), House (1971) developed the motivation-rich **path-goal theory**. The theory was later refined into the theory that we have come to understand today (House, 1996). According to the theory, leaders will change the path to attain a goal based on the motivation of their subordinates. Chellandurai & Saleh (1980) confirms the need for motivational factors similar to path-goal theory for coaching in the Leadership Scale for Sports. House (House & Mitchell, 1974) examined four approaches:

1. *Directive leadership:* Characterized by leaders who set clear expectations and goals for their subordinates. Thus, it is fundamentally satisfying to have clear and obtainable goals to achieve.
2. *Supportive leadership:* Exemplified by a leader who shows concern for the well-being of subordinates. This supportive behavior motivates the subordinate to achieve through mutual respect.
3. *Participative Leadership*: Leaders who actively consult with their subordinates and request shared decision making. Buy-in is achieved with this leadership style as well as satisfaction with the consultation.
4. *Achievement-Oriented Leadership*: Leaders who set high expectations and goals can motivate subordinates to achieve those goals. Goals need to be realistic yet far reaching to push subordinate to succeed.

▶ Summary

This chapter focused on pre–21st-century leadership perspectives. The information on leadership presented provides sport management students with a theoretical base of support with which to confidently begin their journey into the study of leadership. Understanding the evolution of leadership theories and ideas from Sun Tzu and Plato to Blake and McCanse provides future sport professionals with the understanding of how long philosophers and researchers have considered the importance of leadership. Undoubtedly, given the competitive nature of sport business and the difficulties not-for-profit and for-profit organizations face to remain competitive and solvent, leadership has become even more important for organizations in the 21st century. This chapter provides students learning about leadership with the ability to conceptualize leader-follower experiences in sport and understand what it might be like for them as an entry-level employee as they pursue internships and their first jobs. The information presented in this chapter allows the sport management student to begin to reflect on his or her practical sport experiences—as they happen—and provide scope to their exposure to leadership styles. Ultimately, the goal is to develop reflective perspectives on your own leadership abilities, styles, and behaviors as you develop them.

LEADERSHIP PERSPECTIVE

Michael Capiraso

Michael Capiraso is the President and CEO of the New York Road Runners (NYRR), the organization that is responsible for the world's largest marathon in 2016 and 2017, the New York Marathon. Prior to joining the NYRR in 2010 and leading since 2015, Capiraso was a leader in brand marketing and organizational strategy for the National Football League and Major League Baseball. Among his initiatives have been key alignments with partners to enhance both the technological experiences on and off the race course as well as serving more than 600,000 participants throughout the country.

Q: What is your role in leadership? How long? Prior experiences?
Since May of 2015, I have served as the President and CEO of New York Road Runners. Before entering this role, I served as NYRR's COO. Prior to NYRR, I've held strategic, marketing and operational roles at the NFL, Cole Haan, Major League Baseball Productions, and Calvin Klein.

Q: What skills are required to be an effective leader?
There are many skills required to be an effective leader, and I really try to focus on the following in my own leadership role:
Listening: It's critical to always listen to your customers (runners) and, of course, the team that supports you in your leadership role. The value of having an environment of listening is immeasurable.
Being Inquisitive: This supports listening. An effective leader will have an incredible thirst for knowledge and information. That desire to inquire and ask questions of both your team and the population you serve will create a constant cycle of listening and learning.
Leadership: This sounds obvious, but simply put, you need to have the skill to lead groups and individuals. People want and need leadership from people in these roles, and it is so important to be both that person who can inspire and that person on whom people can count to step up and lead.
Vision: All great leaders need a vision of what they hope to accomplish for and with their organization. You cannot lead effectively if you do not have vision of what you and your team is working toward. That vision should expand and change as the organization and the wider industry grows and changes alongside it. Being able to envision success and innovation for your team and your organization is a crucial leadership skill.

Q: What is your strength as a leader?
My strength as a leader reflect the leadership skills that I value most: Being inquisitive and a good listener, being a visionary, and taking initiative. I could not serve as a good leader without the amazing

support of my great team. Gaining my team's support means building personal relationships; listening to, questioning, and challenging your team members; and giving my team the support that they need to take on new initiatives in support of the organization. My ability to trust, support, and encourage my team members are the foundation of leadership. However, I also needed to cultivate my own vision and put forth my own initiatives to become a strong leader. I constantly challenge myself to think about how New York Road Runners can grow, improve, and have a greater impact on the running communities we serve. Whether that's through investing in new technology, finding ways to reach more kids in our free youth running programs, fostering partnerships with other mission-aligned organizations, working to improve the workplace for the NYRR staff, or any other number of initiatives, I have to constantly focus on creating and evolving for the organization or the group of people whom I lead. I strive to do just that each day.

Q: What changes has your industry gone though in recent years? How have you as a leader led your organization through these changes?
The advances in the digital space have made running a more accessible sport to people of all backgrounds around the world. With the launch of our Virtual Training and Virtual Racing initiatives, New York Road Runners has been a leader in this space, giving people of all ages and abilities around the world the opportunity to transform their lives through running. Access and inspiration are always two keys to success for us at NYRR, and through the advancements in our runner products and services, and, of course, the TCS New York City Marathon experience, we can continue to serve as a pioneer in the running industry. We also continue to see more initiatives to support communities. NYRR supports communities across New York City through our many free, weekly programs, including: Our Rising New York Road Runners youth program, weekly NYRR Open Runs in 16 parks, NYRR Striders sessions for the senior population, coach-lead history running tours and fun runs from our community *RUN*CENTER, weekly yoga and strengthening classes, and so much more. As a year-round community running organization, it is our mission to help and inspire community members to get moving, and we try to make that as easy and accessible as possible through these free programs.

Q: What lessons would you give to students to be future leaders? Experiences? Internships?
My biggest advice would be to take initiative…and get involved in things that excite, inspire, and challenge you. You learn to be a good leader by both observing the leaders who surround you in your school, community, home, or elsewhere, and then throwing yourself into roles to learn and grow. Take on internships and experiences that come your way and use those opportunities to ask questions, listen, and absorb what other leaders can teach you. Your initiative will drive your happiness and success.

▶ Key Terms

Authoritarian	Great man theory	Path-goal theory
Autocratic	Informational power	Power
Charisma	Laissez-faire	Referent power
Coercive power	Leader	Reward power
Democratic	Leadership	Situational leadership
Emergent leader	Legitimate power	Theories
Expert power	Participative	

▶ Discussion Questions

1. What role might power play in the leadership of a Major League Baseball team? A Minor League Baseball team? A Division I athletic department? Look at the six sources of power and compare and contrast the different scenarios.

2. Think about the six major professional team sport leagues in the United States (the WNBA, NHL, MLS, MLB, NFL, and NBA). Which ways exist in which one might assume the role of a leader (i.e., commissioner, coach, general manager, club president, players' representative)?

3. Pick a leader in sport or business whom you admire and would like to model yourself after. What type of leadership style do they exhibit based on the managerial grid shown in Figure 1.2?

4. What traits do you possess at this moment that you feel will enable you to become an effective leader?

5. What sources of power do you have as a sport management student? Think about your dream leadership job in sport. What sources of power will you need in that job?

For a full suite of assignments and additional learning activities, use the access code found in the front of your book. If you do not have an access code, you can obtain one at www.jblearning.com.

▶ References

Bass, B. M. (1981). *Stogdill's handbook of leadership*. New York: Free Press.

Blake, R. R., & McCanse, A. A. (1991). *Leadership dilemmas—Grid solutions*. Houston, TX: Gulf.

Blake, R. R., & Mouton, J. S. (1964). *The managerial grid: The key to leadership excellence*. Houston, TX: Gulf.

Blake, R. R., & Mouton, J. S. (1978). *The new managerial grid: Strategic new insights into a proven system for increasing organization productivity and individual effectiveness, plus a revealing examination of how your managerial style can affect your mental and physical health*. Houston, TX: Gulf.

Blake, R. R., & Mouton, J. S. (1985). *The managerial grid III: A new look at the classic that has boosted productivity and profits for thousands of corporations worldwide*. Houston, TX: Gulf.

Blake, R. R., & Mouton, J. S. (1994). *The managerial grid*. Houston, TX: Gulf.

Blanchard, K. H., Zigarmi, D., & Nelson, R. B. (1993). Situational leadership® after 25 years: A retrospective. *Journal of Leadership and Organizational Studies, 1*(1), 21–36.

Blondel, J. (1987). *Political leadership*. Beverly Hills, CA: Sage.

Bowers, D. G., & Seashore, S. E. (1966). Predicting organizational effectiveness with a four-factor theory of leadership. *Administrative Science Quarterly, 11*(2), 238–263.

Brickhouse, T., & Smith, N. D. (2009). Plato (427–347 BCE). *Internet Encyclopedia of Philosophy*. Retrieved from http://www.iep.utm.edu/plato

Channel, S. (Producer). (2012, June 27th, 2018). An Evening with: Warren Miller. Retrieved from https://www.youtube.com/watch?v=3EM_NWs86FU

Chelladurai, P., & Saleh, S. (1980). Dimensions of leader behavior in sports: Development of a leadership scale. *Journal of Sport Psychology, 2*(1), 34–45.

Diamond, G. A. (1992). Field theory and rational choice: A Lewinian approach to modeling motivation. *Journal of Social Issues, 48*(2), 79–94.

Dickson, P. (2012). *Bill Veeck: Baseball's greatest maverick*. New York: Walker.

Dictionary.com. (n.d.a). lead. Retrieved from http://dictionary.reference.com/browse/lead

Dictionary.com. (n.d.b). -er. Retrieved from http://dictionary.reference.com/browse/-er

Dictionary.com. (n.d.c). -ship. Retrieved from http://dictionary.reference.com/browse/-ship

Edginton, C. R., Hudson, S. D., Scholl, K. G., & Lauzon, L. (2011). *Leadership for recreation, parks, and leisure services*. Champaign, IL: Sagamore.

Evans, M. G. (1970). The effects of supervisory behavior on the path-goal relationship. *Organizational Behavior and Human Performance, 5*(3), 277–298.

French, J. R. P., & Raven, B. (1959). The bases of social power. In D. Cartwright (Ed.), *Studies in social power* (pp. 150–167). Ann Arbor, MI: Institute for Social Research.

Gabel, S. (2011). The medical director and the use of power: Limits, challenges and opportunities. *Psychiatric Quarterly, 82*(3), 221–228.

Galbraith, J. (2018). Warren Miller Memoriam. *The Ski Journal.* Retrieved from www.theskijournal.com /exclusive/warren-miller/

Georgopoulous, B. S., Mahoney, G. M., & Jones, N. W. (1957). A path-goal approach to productivity. *Journal of Applied Psychology, 41*(1), 345–353.

Hersey, P., & Blanchard, K. H. (1969). Life cycle theory of leadership. *Training and Development Journal, 23*(5), 26–34.

Hersey, P., & Blanchard, K. H. (1982). Leadership style: Attitudes and behaviors. *Training and Development Journal, 36*(5), 50–52.

House, R. J. (1971). A path goal theory of leader effectiveness. *Administrative Science Quarterly, 16*(3), 321–339.

House, R. J. (1996). Path-goal theory of leadership: Lessons, legacy, and a reformulated theory. *Leadership Quarterly, 7*(3), 323–352.

House, R. J., & Mitchell, T. R. (1974). Path-goal theory of leadership. *Contemporary Business, 3*, 81–98.

In Memoriam Retrieved from https://warrenmiller.org/

Lewin, K., Lippitt, R., & White, R. K. (1939). Patterns of aggressive behavior in experimentally created "social climates." *Journal of Social Psychology, 10*(2), 271–299.

Lewis, M. (2004). *Moneyball.* New York: W.W. Norton.

Likert, R. (1961). *New patterns of management.* New York: McGraw-Hill.

Lord, R. G., De Vader, C. L., & Alliger, G. M. (1986). A meta-analysis of the relation between personality traits and leadership perceptions: An application of validity generalization procedures. *Journal of Applied Psychology, 71*(3), 402–410.

Mann, R. D. (1959). A review of the relationships between personality and performance in small groups. *Psychological Bulletin, 56*(4), 241–270.

Michelson, M. (2018). Iconic Ski Director Warren Miller Dies. *Outside.* Retrieved from https://www .outsideonline.com/2277451/iconic-director-warren -miller-dies

Mickle, T. (2009, November 23). NHL starting performance-based pay system. *Street and Smith's Sports Business Journal.* Retrieved from https://www .sportsbusinessdaily.com/Journal/Issues/2009/11/23 /This-Weeks-News/NHL-Starting-Performance -Based-Pay-System.aspx?hl=NHL%20starting%20 %20performance-based%20pay%20system

Mondy, R. W., Holmes, E. B., & Flippo, E. B. (1980). *Management: Concepts and practices.* Newton, MA: Allyn and Bacon.

Northouse, P. G. (2012). *Leadership: Theory and practice.* Thousand Oaks, CA: Sage.

Organ, D. W. (1996). Leadership: The great man theory revisited. *Business Horizons, 39*(3), 1–4.

Raelin, J. A. (2003). The myth of charismatic leaders. *Training and Development, 57*(3), 46–51.

Raven, B. H. (1992). A power/interaction model of interpersonal influence: French and Raven thirty years later. *Journal of Social Behavior and Personality, 7*(2), 217–244.

Raven, B. H. (2008). The bases of power and the power/ interaction model of interpersonal influence. *Analyses of Social Issues and Public Policy, 8*(1), 1–22.

Raven, B. H., Schwarzwald, J., & Koslowsky, M. (1998). Conceptualizing and measuring a power/interaction model of interpersonal influence. *Journal of Applied Social Psychology, 28*(4), 307–332.

Rue, L. W., & Byars, L. L. (2009). *Management: Skills and application.* New York: McGraw Hill/Irwin.

Russell, R. V. (2005). *Leadership in recreation* (3rd ed.). New York: McGraw-Hill.

Scheidlinger, S. (1994). The Lewin, Lippitt and White study of leadership and "social climates" revisited. *International Journal of Group Psychotherapy, 44*(1), 123–127.

Shartle, C. L. (1979). Early years of the Ohio State University leadership studies. *Journal of Management, 5*(2), 127–134.

Shivers, J. S. (1980). *Recreational leadership: Group dynamics and interpersonal behavior.* Hightstown, NJ: Princeton Book Company.

Stogdill, R. M. (1948). Personal factors associated with leadership: A survey of the literature. *Journal of Psychology, 25*(1), 35–71.

Stogdill, R. M. (1963). *Manual for the leader behavior description questionnaire—Form XII.* Columbus: Ohio State University, Bureau of Business Research.

Stogdill, R. M. (1974). *Handbook of leadership: A survey of theory and research.* New York: Free Press.

Stogdill, R. M., & Coons, A. E. (1957). *Leader behavior: Its description and management.* Columbus, OH: Ohio State University, Bureau of Business Research.

Warren Miller Performing Arts Center. (2018). *Warren Miller Performing Arts Center.* Retrieved from http:// warrenmillerpac.org/about-wmpac/

CHAPTER 2

Positive Leadership Theory: Transformational, Transactional, and Servant Leadership

Laura J. Burton
Jon Welty Peachey
Zachary J. Damon

CHAPTER OBJECTIVES

- Differentiate the leadership styles of transactional, transformational, and servant leadership.
- Identify contexts that are appropriate for each type of leadership style.
- Understand and describe the behaviors associated with transactional, transformational, and servant leadership.
- Describe organizational outcomes associated with each type of leadership style.
- Explore positive leadership research in sport and sport organizations.

CASE STUDY

Leadership and the Response to NFL Athlete Activism

During the 2016 NFL preseason, San Francisco 49ers quarterback Colin Kaepernick remained seated during the playing of the national anthem. Kaepernick made this decision as a way of bringing attention to allegations of police brutality and the killing of unarmed black men by police, which led to the Black Lives Matter movement. He told NFL Media in August of 2016 that "I am not going to stand up to show pride in a flag for a country that oppresses black people and people of color; to me, this is bigger than football and it would be selfish on my part to look the other way. There are bodies in the street and people getting paid leave and getting away with murder." (Wyche, 2016, n. p.)

As attention around the Kaepernick protest increased, other teammates joined and they began kneeling during the national anthem. At the end of the 2016 season, Kaepernick's contract with the 49ers was not renewed and he was not signed by another NFL team for the 2017 season. Despite his absence from the field, other NFL players from the league continued the protest against unjust police practices, including Michael Bennett of the Seattle Seahawks. In September of 2017, President Trump spoke about the NFL players' protests in a campaign-style rally. President Trump conveyed his disagreement with the protests and called on the NFL and team owners to fire those who were protesting. These statements led to more player protests and subsequent responses, both positive and negative, by fans on both sides of this issue. Following the President's remarks, the NFL issued statements not only indicating support for the players but it also issued an appeal for all players to stand for the national anthem before games (for a timeline of the protests, see Riley, 2018).

In an attempt to quell dissent from players, owners of the NFL teams, and fans who supported the players' protests and those who were against the protests, the NFL partnered with the players and committed approximately $100 million to a fund that would support causes that were important to the African-American Black community (Trotter & Reid, 2017). Many members of the NFL Players Coalition were skeptical of this NFL fund, yet others felt that it was an important step by the league and its owners to recognize the players' concerns (Trotter & Reid, 2017).

During the NFL owners' meetings in May of 2018, the owners and the league office, without consultation with the NFL Players' Union, implemented a new rule regarding the national anthem for the 2018 to –2019 season. The new rule stipulates that any player on the field during the playing of the national anthem must stand. If players do not want to stand during the anthem, they must remain in the locker room. According to the rule, which was not voted on by owners but was agreed to during the meeting, each NFL team can institute a fine against players who do not stand for the anthem. The league can also impose a fine on players. At least two owners (Jed York of the San Francisco 49ers and Mark Davis of the Oakland Raiders) were not supportive of this policy (D'Andrea & Stites, 2018). The NFL Players' Union has also threatened to legally challenge any aspects of the policy that are inconsistent with the collective bargaining agreement (Anapol, 2018).

Questions for Discussion

1. How would you describe the NFL owners' collective leadership on the players' protests? Read and review the chapter before answering this. Provide specific examples from the case study to support your answer.
2. Do you believe that this type of leadership will be effective in supporting the success of the NFL for the 2018–2019 season? Provide specific information to support your response.
3. What other type(s) of leadership would you recommend for owners of the NFL? Why would you recommend that type of leadership?
4. What type of leadership could be used by the NFL Players' Union to best resolve the apparent conflict between the players and the owners over the player protests? Provide specific information to support your response.

▶ Introduction

Most scholars agree that there is a relationship between leadership and an organization's success or failure (Klimoski & Koles, 2001). At the most basic level, leaders will establish the direction of an organization by developing a vision of the future, and then, after forming influential relationships, will align people by communicating this vision and inspiring them to overcome any obstacles (Robbins & Judge, 2003). Leaders are individual actors who display personal behaviors. In this chapter, we examine the domain of positive leadership, including transformational and servant leadership. Positive leadership behaviors focus on interpersonal dynamics that support the development of followers' (e.g., employees, volunteers, interns) self-confidence, resulting in positive outcomes for the organization. Positive leadership theories emphasize outcomes beyond what is best for the organization, look to motivate followers beyond task expectations, and seek to increase followers' individual development and prosocial behaviors (Hannah, Sumanth, Lester, & Cavarretta, 2014).

What makes an effective 21st-century leader? Murray and Mann (2006) suggest that leaders must delegate and nurture, empower subordinates, relate to all people within the organization, encourage ownership, pursue learning opportunities for all members, build teamwork, and have fun at their jobs. Leadership experts Kouzes and Posner (1993) believe that highly effective leaders must inspire a shared vision, set an example for employees, enable others to act, encourage the heart by connecting with employees and building relationships, and challenge the process. Twenty-first century leaders must pay attention to relationship building and participatory decision making. As a result, over the past 20 years, a majority of the research in management, and also in other fields, including sport management, has examined the transformational style of leadership (Antonakis, 2012; Welty Peachey, Zhou, Damon & Burton, 2015).

The following sections of this chapter will explore **transformational** and **transactional leadership**, how these leadership behaviors are measured, and importantly, how transformational leadership has been studied in sport management. We will also explore pseudo transformational leadership, which is considered the darker side of transformational leadership. Pseudo transformational leadership describes a leader who uses a transformational type of leadership but is also exploitative, self-consumed, and focused on power and manipulating power (Bass & Riggio, 2006). In addition, we will describe **servant leadership**, an area of leadership that is gaining more interest within the context of sport management. Servant leadership as a leadership behavior will be described and a model to understand how servant leadership may work will also be presented. We will also explore new developments in how servant leadership is measured and discuss emerging research examining servant leadership in sport organizations. After reading this chapter, we hope that students considering careers in sport management will understand the different behaviors and characteristics associated with different types of leadership so that they can begin to develop these leadership tendencies while working toward their sport management degrees.

▶ Transformational and Transactional Leadership

James MacGregor Burns (1978) was the first to introduce the concepts of transformational and transactional leadership. Burns was interested in understanding what leaders and followers offered one another. Transformational leaders try to motivate followers to change or to transform themselves. Transformational leaders are responsive to the individual needs of followers; inspire followers; and align the goals of the organization, leader, group, and individuals. Transformational leaders—given their interest in the growth of their followers—set challenging expectations for them. In contrast, transactional leaders try to motivate their followers by exchanging resources and offering payment for doing work. Within transformational leadership, followers identify with the needs of the leader, and leaders will motivate their followers to achieve more than the followers believe is possible (Bass, 2008). A transactional leader is expected to give subordinates something they desire in exchange for something the leader wants (Kuhnert & Lewis, 1987). Transactional leaders emphasize exchanges made between leaders and followers (Bass, 2008). Whereas transactional leadership is viewed as similar to "old" approaches to leadership, focused on role and task requirements, transformational leadership is seen as a "new" approach focused on the charisma and vision of leaders (Antonakis, 2012; Bryman, 1992; Doherty, 1997). The model of transformational/transactional leadership developed by Bass (1985) is presented in **FIGURE 2.1** as the Full Range Leadership Model (Avolio & Bass, 1991) and includes the concepts of transformational, transactional, and laissez-faire leadership. Each leadership type is discussed in this chapter.

Transformational Leadership

Based on the work of Burns (1978) and Kuhnert and Lewis (1987) in the development of transformational leadership and the concept of charismatic leadership as developed by House (1977), Bass (1985) developed a more refined model of transformational leadership.

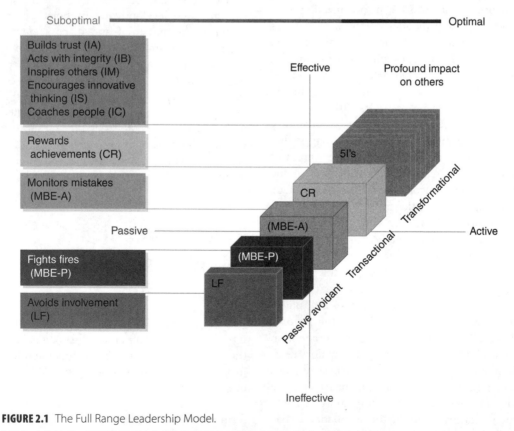

FIGURE 2.1 The Full Range Leadership Model.

Modified from Avolio, B. J., & Bass, B. M. (1991). *Full-range leadership development*. Binghamton, NY: Bass, Avolio & Associates.

He describes leaders as those who inspire followers to achieve extraordinary outcomes while also helping to develop the individual leadership skills of their followers (Bass, 2008). Mentor-coaches, such as Pat Summitt, Mike Krzyzewski, and Tony Dungy, have created coaching lineages that indicate their ability to equip their assistant coaches and former players with leadership skills. Transformational leadership is visionary and appeals to the higher-order psychological needs of employees of feeling valued and worthwhile in the organization (Bryman, 1992). Transformational leaders understand that these needs, along with esteem needs that recognize a follower's unique contributions, are necessary to distinguish themselves from transactional leaders.

Transformational leadership has four dimensions: (1) **idealized influence** (behaviors of leaders and attributes of leaders), (2) **inspirational motivation**, (3) **intellectual stimulation**, and (4) **individualized consideration** (Bass & Riggio, 2006). Idealized influence has two elements: The charismatic behaviors of the leader and the elements of leadership that are attributed to the leader by his or her followers. It is also described as the emotional component of leadership (Antonakis, 2012; Northouse, 2016). Leaders are trusted, admired, and respected by their followers because these leaders often demonstrate high levels of moral and ethical behavior (Bass & Riggio, 2006). As a result, leaders are highly respected by their followers and, in turn, followers seek to emulate the leaders' behaviors. For example, followers may view an intercollegiate athletic director as trustworthy, honest, and charismatic, attributes that would then engender respect and pride among athletic department employees who may, in turn, seek to emulate these behaviors. This athletic director may also be an excellent communicator, consistently conveying the values and mission of intercollegiate athletics to employees and other stakeholders. Furthermore, as noted by Northouse (2016), charismatic leaders develop connections with their followers

by "emphasizing the intrinsic rewards of work and deemphasizing the extrinsic rewards."

Inspirational motivation captures how leaders will set high expectations for followers and motivate and inspire their followers to meet these high expectations. Leaders set clear expectations for their followers and demonstrate that they are committed to these shared goals. Leaders will display enthusiasm and optimism to help followers meet these high expectations and provide support to help followers achieve more than they would in their own self-interest (Bass & Riggio, 2006). An intercollegiate athletic director may serve as a "cheerleader" during times when the teams are not doing well or when athletic departments have suffered sanctions and keep the department—particularly the marketing specialists who have to encourage spectators to still attend games—excited about future possibilities. This cheerleading can inspire employees to give their best efforts to the department, even in a year when performance is suffering and perceptions about athletics might be negative.

Intellectual stimulation describes the processes that leaders will use to stimulate followers to be creative and innovative. In addition, leaders will encourage followers to question assumptions and challenge the way things are done within an organization. Followers are encouraged to think on their own and leaders provide an open environment in which all ideas are encouraged and where followers are not criticized if their ideas differ from those of the leaders (Bass & Riggio, 2006). This is demonstrated when a marketing director of a minor league baseball team provides opportunities for undergraduate interns to develop and carry out new promotions to increase attendance at games. Furthermore, the executive director of a youth-based sport for development and peace (SDP) program can demonstrate intellectual stimulation by encouraging staff members to think creatively to solve problems, welcome innovative suggestions, and support risk taking when meeting objectives. This creative problem solving is sometimes seen in adaptive sports for athletes with disabilities. One of the difficulties in disability sports is addressing the fact that the limited number of participants in a particular sport will also have a wide variety of disabilities. To manage these sports, leaders of these organizations employ disability points. Athletes are given a point rating based on the degree of their disability. Teams in volleyball and wheelchair basketball can only have a set amount of points on the court at any time.

Finally, individualized consideration captures how leaders create a supportive environment, paying attention to their followers' needs for growth and achievement. Leaders recognize followers' needs and desires and provide environments that support these differences. Leaders designate tasks to followers in an effort to develop followers' leadership skills. In addition, leaders serve as advisors or mentors to help support followers as they carry out their assigned tasks (Northouse, 2016).

Before discussing transactional leadership, the concept of pseudo transformational leadership must be addressed. Those leaders who are described as pseudo transformational leaders have violated the moral foundations of acting ethically (Bass & Steidlmeier, 1999). Pseudo transformational leaders exploit the behaviors of being transformational leaders to serve their own self-interests and status within their organizations. This type of leader encourages or demands unconditional loyalty from followers and makes followers dependent on them. As a result, followers of pseudo transformational leaders are, therefore, more likely to comply with the directions or orders of their leaders (Lin, Huang, Chen, & Huang, 2017). There has been a call for research to examine pseudo transformational leadership in sport organizations (Cruickshank & Collins, 2016; Welty Peachey et al., 2015), as there is limited research on this type of leadership in sport management.

Transactional Leadership

A transactional leader motivates by contract and reward, promising followers rewards for good performance and focusing on rules and procedures (Bass, 1990). Transactional leadership includes the following four dimensions: (1) **contingent reward**, (2) **active management** by exception, (3) **passive management** by exception, and (4) **laissez-faire**. Using contingent rewards, leaders assign tasks for followers to fulfill with the understanding that a reward will be provided to the followers after successful completion of the task. Leaders try to gain agreement from the followers regarding which tasks must be completed and the reward for completing the tasks. An example of contingent reward would be a fitness club manager establishing a minimum number of new membership sales in conjunction with input from the staff of the fitness club. When the staff meets that sales goal, they will receive a previously agreed -upon performance bonus. Given the large percentage of sales jobs in the sport management field, it would not be surprising to find that contingent reward is a prevalent leadership technique.

Active management by exception occurs when leaders look for mistakes or deviations from normal standards when monitoring followers' work. Leaders then take actions to correct mistakes that are noticed. An example of management by exception would be when a facility manager reviews an event risk management plan developed by his or her staff member and makes changes to the plan prior to its implementation during the event. Or, when the facility manager inspects the setup for a basketball game, notices chairs and tables that are not set up correctly, and takes action to rectify the situation.

Leaders following passive management by exception wait for mistakes or deviations from normal standards. Only after these standards have not been met will the leader intervene to address the problem. Both active and passive management by exception use more negative reinforcement behaviors than positive reinforcement behaviors followed in contingent reward. Using the same example of a facility manager, if following passive management by exception, this leader would wait until an accident occurred during the event as a result of the faulty risk management plan before making changes to the plan. The facility manager would also not correct the faulty setup at the basketball game but would wait until a problem occurred before corrections were made. Figure 2.1 explains the contrast between active and passive leadership through the Full Range Leadership Model (Avolio & Bass, 1991).

Laissez-faire leadership is the absence of leadership. Leaders do not make necessary decisions and actions are not taken. An example of this type of leadership would be an athletic director who calls no meetings with his leadership team, has no strategic plan for the department, and has little contact with the athletic department staff.

▸ Transformational Leadership in Sport Management

Research has shown that leaders who demonstrate transformational leadership are considered by followers to be more effective compared with leaders using transactional or laissez-faire leadership behavior. Employees report more job satisfaction (Judge & Piccolo, 2004) and higher levels of engagement in their work when led by transformational leaders (Breevaart, Bakker, Hetland, Demerouti, Olsen, & Espevik, 2014). Additionally, transformational leadership was more effective in achieving increased employee work-team performance and effectiveness than transactional leadership (Stewart, 2006), and studies have shown that transformational leadership leads to higher-quality relationships with employees (Krishnan, 2005; Lee, 2005; Tse & Lam, 2008). Transformational leadership has also been shown to improve the performance of both employees working in groups and employees working alone (Strang, 2005; Wang & Huang,

2009) and to improve internal communication among employees in an organization (Men, 2014). Employees working for transformational leaders are also less likely to leave their jobs (Martin & Epitropaki, 2001; Tse & Lam, 2008). This is an important point considering the high cost of replacing employees with regard to job training and interviewing. In addition, transformational leaders have been shown to be more effective than transactional leaders in guiding and implementing significant organizational change (Eisenback, Watson, & Pillai, 1999). Finally, some work has also suggested that employees evaluate female leaders more favorably than male leaders when female leaders demonstrate transformational rather than transactional leadership behaviors. This more favorable evaluation of women as transformational leaders is linked to the view that this type of leadership is congruent with nurturing and communal characteristics, which are associated with women. In contrast, male leaders are expected to exhibit more transactional leadership qualities (Eagly & Carli, 2003; Powell, Butterfield, & Bartol, 2008; Vinkenburg, Van Engen, Eagly, & Johannesen-Schmidt, 2011).

In a comprehensive review of leadership research in the domain of sport management, Welty Peachey and his colleagues (2015) noted that transformational leadership was the most highly researched area of leadership in the field. Within sport management, researchers have found that, overall, transformational leadership is associated with more positive outcomes for sport organizations. A study with NCAA Division II head coaches revealed that although transactional leadership positively affected followers' behavior and action toward organizational goals, transformational leadership more broadly impacted followers' behavior in a positive manner beyond the effects of transactional leadership (Kim, 2009). Also, Division III athletic directors believed that leaders demonstrating transformational leadership motivated extra effort among followers. Additionally, these athletic directors believed that employees would be more satisfied working for transformational leaders. Transformational leadership was preferred overall, regardless of whether this style was displayed by a male or female leader (Burton & Welty Peachey, 2009; Welty Peachey & Burton, 2011). Leaders who demonstrated charisma and individualized consideration dimensions of transformational leadership were considered most effective. However, leaders who demonstrated passive management by exception and laissez-faire behaviors, characteristics of transactional leadership, were seen as least effective (Burton & Welty Peachey, 2009; Doherty & Danylchuk, 1996).

When intercollegiate coaches evaluated athletic directors, they indicated that their levels of job satisfaction were positively related to athletic directors demonstrating transformational leadership (Choi, Sagas, Park, & Cunningham, 2007; Yusof & Mohd Shah, 2008). Intercollegiate coaches were also less likely to consider leaving their jobs when working for athletic directors who had demonstrated transformational leadership (Wells & Welty Peachey, 2011). Also, transformational leadership of the athletic director resulted in higher levels of employee commitment to the athletic department. Employees reported feeling more attached to and more involved in the athletic department. Employees also reported feeling a closer sense of identification with the athletic department (Kent & Chelladurai, 2001). In addition, although transformational leadership of the athletic director was positively related to organizational commitment of department employees, it was even more strongly related to commitment to the supervisor (the athletic director) than to the organization (Andrew, Kim, Stoll, & Todd, 2011).

Transformational leadership is critical to successfully guiding and leading organizational change in sport organizations (Amis, Slack, & Hinings, 2004; Welty Peachey, Bruening, & Burton, 2011) in the 21st century. Employees and stakeholders of an organization typically resist organizational change, whether it is a change in leadership or new marketing initiatives. Transformational leaders are generally considered to have the qualities and skills necessary to help overcome employee resistance to change (Phelan, 2005; Slack & Hinings, 1992). Transformational leaders are active in the change process, visible to employees, and good communicators. They have the ability to align employees around a new vision. These leadership behaviors all serve to mitigate employee resistance. Transformational leaders also serve as "cheerleaders" during organizational change, which can motivate and inspire followers to embrace new ideas and routines (Ott, 1996).

Within a Division I athletic department, Welty Peachey, Bruening, and Burton (2011) found that the transformational leadership of the athletic director was a major factor in organizational change success and in mitigating resistance and ambivalence to change among employees over time. In another study, Welty Peachey and Burton (2012) discovered that Division I athletic directors displaying transformational leadership during organizational culture change were perceived by their employees as more effective and better able to stimulate extra effort than transactional leaders. Also, employees were more satisfied with transformational leaders. In the campus recreation department setting, leaders demonstrating more transformational leadership were able to implement culture-building activities and change the culture more effectively than those leaders demonstrating less transformational leadership (Weese, 1995). In a study of Canadian YMCA organizations, leaders demonstrating more transformational leadership behaviors also produced more positive organizational change outcomes than leaders displaying less transformational leadership (Wallace & Weese, 1995). Furthermore, employees perceived transformational leaders, compared with transactional leaders, as managing major structural realignment more effectively in Canada's National Sport Organizations (Amis, Slack, & Hinings, 2004; Slack & Hinings, 1992).

Transformational leadership was an essential ingredient for changing team cultures within professional sport franchises in the United States (Frontiera, 2010). Finally, Division I college head coaches who demonstrated transformational leadership were able to change team cultures by articulating and reinforcing shared visions and values (Schroeder, 2010).

Work by Wells and Welty Peachey (2011) found that both transformational and transactional leadership behaviors were associated with less voluntary turnover intentions of softball and volleyball assistant coaches within the National Collegiate Athletic Association (NCAA). In other research, scholars found that transformational leadership did not have a significant impact on job satisfaction for NCAA football conference athletic department employees, but this type of leadership did have an influence on employees' commitment at an organizational and individual level (Kim, Magnusen, Andrew, & Stoll, 2012). Transformational leadership, as demonstrated by athletic directors, was also found to impact the athletic administrators' commitment to their athletic departments, but the culture of the athletic department (i.e., values, norms, ways of doing) had an impact on this influence. Cultures that valued teamwork, employee development, and involvement that also had athletic directors who used transformational leadership had a positive impact on employee commitment to the department (Burton & Welty Peachey, 2014).

▶ Servant Leadership

Servant leadership focuses on the interaction between leader and follower and emphasizes how leaders can be attentive to the needs of followers, show concern for their followers, and nurture and emphasize the needs of their followers. Servant leaders place the interests, needs, and aspirations of others before their own (Greenleaf, 1977). The primary objective of the servant leader is first to serve and then to lead.

Servant leadership is different from other approaches to leadership because it emphasizes the ideal of service in the relationship between leader and follower (van Dierendonck, 2011). Servant leadership is a people-centered approach to leadership that also includes an ethical and moral component (Sendjaya, Sarros, & Santora, 2008). Additionally, whereas transformational leadership emphasizes leading for organizational objectives, servant leadership gives greater emphasis to serving followers (Stone, Russell, & Patterson, 2004). Considering the increasing interest in corporate social responsibility within sport organizations (both in the United States and internationally), servant leadership is an appealing and relevant form of leadership to examine within sport. Also, as national and international professional sport organizations and intercollegiate athletic departments suffer ethical breaches, servant leadership offers a needed perspective on leadership (Burton & Welty Peachey, 2013).

Although there is currently no consensus on a definition or theoretical framework for servant leadership, Robert K. Greenleaf is widely credited with the development of the concept of servant leadership and has written extensively about it. The most popular servant leadership definition comes from his writings (1977):

> It begins with the natural feeling that one wants to serve . . . The difference [is] the care taken . . . to make sure that other people's highest-priority needs are being served. The best test . . . is: Do those served grow as persons? Do they . . . become healthier, wiser, freer, more autonomous, and are they more likely to become servants themselves? And, what is the effect on the least privileged in society? Will they benefit, or at least not be further deprived? (p. 13).

Greenleaf credits the formation of the concept of servant leadership to *Journey to the*

A study of YMCA organizations in Canada showed that transformational leadership had a positive effect on organizational change behavior.

© Kevin Wolf/AP Images.

East, a novel by Hermann Hesse (1956). In this story of a band of men on a mythical journey, Hesse describes a servant, Leo, who works for the group. Leo does menial chores for the men but also sustains the men through his songs and his spirit. Leo is an extraordinary presence in the group. When Leo disappears, the group falls into disarray and the journey ends. Later, the men come to know that Leo, whom they had known as a servant, was actually a great and noble leader (Greenleaf, 1977).

With servant leadership, serving and leading become interchangeable, because being a leader implies that a person serves, and being a servant allows a person to lead (van Dierendonck, 2011). Servant leaders are defined by the character they display while serving others (Parris & Welty Peachey, 2012). Greenleaf (1977) noted that servant leadership is demonstrated whenever those served by such leaders are positively transformed in multiple dimensions (e.g., emotionally, intellectually, socially, and spiritually) into servant leaders themselves (Sendjaya et al., 2008).

A challenge to the study of servant leadership has been how to take the writings of Greenleaf and attempt to develop a theory to explain this concept of leadership. To build a theory of servant leadership, scholars have made numerous attempts to describe and classify the characteristics of servant leadership (van Dierendonck, 2011). Spears (2002) attempted to describe the characteristics of leadership in an effort to clarify servant leadership for practitioners (Northouse, 2016).

Model of Servant Leadership

In an effort to develop a more complete understanding of servant leadership, van Dierendonck (2011) provides a model to better understand and explain the complexities of this concept. This model of servant leadership takes into account antecedents to leadership behavior, the interaction of leader and follower, and the outcomes of servant leader behavior. The antecedent conditions, or existing conditions, that influence servant leadership behavior include the context and culture of the organization, the attributes of the leader, and the receptivity of followers (van Dierendonck, 2011). Servant leadership could best support the mission of intercollegiate athletics, which is to serve the needs of student-athletes (Burton & Welty Peachey, 2013). In addition, servant leadership could also be a beneficial type of leadership for SDP organizations, as the mission of SDP organizations is to help marginalized individuals. Servant leadership can also support building trust between groups experiencing high degrees of conflict, another goal of SDP organizations (Welty Peachey Burton, & Wells, 2017).

The middle part of the model describes a set of behaviors that characterize servant leadership, the leader/follower relationship, and the climate created by the leader. The final section of the model includes the outcomes associated with servant leadership, which include follower performance and growth, organizational performance, and societal impact.

Antecedent Conditions
Context and Culture of the Organization

The behaviors of a servant leader are influenced by the context and culture of the organization. As an example, a professional sport organization would foster a highly competitive context and would support a norm of competition among its employees. A recreation-based sport organization would more likely foster a cooperative environment and support collaboration among employees. These different norms could influence how servant leadership is performed in those organizations (Northouse, 2016). In addition, the culture in which the organization operates can also influence servant leadership. In a more collective culture (e.g., Japan), where the benefits to the group are valued above the interests of the individual, servant leadership would be more common. This may be quite different from a more individualistic culture (e.g., the United States), where individual accountability and effort are encouraged over the accountability of the group. In this type of culture, servant leadership may be challenged.

Leader Attributes

Each leader brings individual needs and qualities to the relationship with followers. These individual needs and qualities influence the process of servant leadership. Effective leaders, regardless of style of leadership, have a desire for power. Within the context of servant leadership, leaders would seek out a positive use of power; that is, servant leaders would desire power as a means to help others and care for others. In addition, individual traits, such as emotional intelligence, self-determination, and moral development, will have an influence on the behaviors of servant leaders (van Dierendonck, 2011). An additional trait has been added to servant leadership: that of compassionate love (van Dierendonck & Patterson,

2015). Compassionate love is described by Sprecher and Fehr (2005) as:

> ". . . an attitude toward other(s), either close others or strangers or all of humanity; containing feelings, cognitions, and behaviors that are focused on caring, concern, tenderness, and an orientation toward supporting, helping, and understanding the other(s), particularly when the other(s) is (are) perceived to be suffering or in need" (p. 630; as cited in van Dierendonck & Patterson, 2015).

Characteristics

Six characteristics of servant leadership, which are similar to those described by Spears (2002) earlier in **TABLE 2.1**, are included in the model of servant leadership (van Dierendonck, 2011).

1. *Developing people:* Servant leaders foster an empowering attitude in followers, which generates self-confidence and provides followers with a sense of personal power. This type of leadership behavior encourages information sharing with followers, encourages self-directed decision making, and provides support and coaching for innovative performance. Servant leaders fundamentally believe in the intrinsic value possessed by each follower, recognizing and acknowledging each person's abilities and what the person can learn (Greenleaf, 1998).

2. *Humility:* Servant leaders acknowledge that they can benefit from the expertise of others, and, therefore, actively seek out the contributions of followers. Servant leaders put their own accomplishments and talents in perspective. Demonstrating humility, the servant leader puts followers' interests first, provides them with support, and facilitates their performance. A servant leader also demonstrates humility by retreating into

TABLE 2.1 Characteristics of Servant Leadership

Characteristic	Description
Listening	Servant leaders communicate by listening first.
Empathy	Servant leaders demonstrate that they understand what followers are thinking and feeling.
Healing	Servant leaders—in caring for followers—help them to overcome personal problems.
Awareness	Servant leaders are attuned to and receptive to their social, physical, and political environments—and are, therefore, able to understand the greater context of situations.
Persuasion	Servant leaders influence change through clear and persistent communication that is nonjudgmental.
Conceptualization	Servant leaders are visionary—thinking about the long-term objectives of the organization and responding to problems in creative ways.
Foresight	Servant leaders have the ability to reasonably predict what is going to occur in the future.
Stewardship	Servant leaders take up the responsibilities of leading followers and the organization.
Commitment to growth	Servant leaders make a commitment to each follower, helping each person grow personally and professionally.
Building community	Servant leaders foster community, allowing followers to feel a part of something greater than themselves.

Data from Spears, L. C. (2002). Tracing the past, present, and future of servant leadership. In L. C. Spears, M. Lawrence, & K. Blanchard (Eds.), *Focus on leadership: Servant-leadership for the twenty-first century* (pp. 1-10). New York: John Wiley and Sons.

the background when a task has been successfully accomplished.

3. *Authenticity:* Servant leaders demonstrate authenticity by being true to oneself, both in public and in private. Authenticity is about expressing oneself in ways that are consistent with inner feelings and thoughts. A servant leader demonstrates authenticity by being honest, doing what was promised, and showing vulnerability.

4. *Interpersonal acceptance:* Servant leaders are able to create an environment in which followers feel safe and trust that they are able to make mistakes and still feel that they will be accepted. Servant leaders understand the perspectives of others and are able to "walk in another's shoes." Servant leaders show empathy, compassion, and forgiveness, even when confronted with arguments, personal offenses, or mistakes.

5. *Providing direction:* Servant leaders clearly demonstrate to followers what is expected of them. Within the context of servant leadership, leaders provide an appropriate amount of accountability for followers. Also, leaders customize directions based on followers' abilities, needs, and input. This type of leadership allows for new ways of getting things accomplished and creates new ways to meet old problems, with consistent reliance on values and convictions when accomplishing tasks.

6. **Stewardship**: Servant leaders are willing to take responsibility for the entire organization and put the interests of the organization over and above their own self-interests. Servant leaders act as role models and caretakers. By acting as role models and setting an example for followers, leaders can inspire others to act in the common interests of all. The characteristics of stewardship are closely linked to the concepts of teamwork, social responsibility, and loyalty.

Servant Leader/Follower Relationship

An important component of the model of servant leadership is an understanding of the quality of the relationship between the servant leader and the follower. Servant leaders will build this high-quality relationship with followers by striving for consensus among their followers. They will use persuasion through consultation, appeals, and use of explanation. When fostering such a relationship, a servant leader will voluntarily lead followers "because they are persuaded that the leader's path is the right one for them" (Greenleaf, 1998, p. 44). Furthermore, servant leaders understand the perspectives of their followers and are able to "walk in another's shoes." Servant leaders demonstrate compassion and show empathy

and forgiveness, even when confronted with arguments, personal offenses, or mistakes (van Dierendonck & Patterson, 2015).

In addition, a safe psychological climate is necessary to foster the servant leader and follower relationship. Servant leaders focus on empowerment of followers so that followers feel safe to use their knowledge, make mistakes, reflect on their actions, and continually learn and develop. In order for this to occur, interpersonal trust within a safe psychological climate is necessary.

Outcomes

Follower growth and development are central outcomes to a model of servant leadership. Followers' **self-actualization** is an expected outcome in the model of servant leadership. Self-actualization refers to the continual development of oneself and the realization of one's potential. An additional expected outcome of servant leadership is a positive attitude toward work, which would include job satisfaction, organizational commitment, and engagement (van Dierendonck, Stam, Boersma, De Windt, & Alkema, 2014). Another expected outcome is the potential development of servant leader behaviors in followers. When followers are cared for and empowered by servant leaders, they begin treating others in the same way (Northouse, 2016). Servant leadership is also linked to supporting and sustaining positive interactions among employees of an organization and higher perceptions of an ethical climate at work (Jaramillo & Noboa, 2015).

Organizational performance can also be impacted by servant leadership, and is, therefore, another outcome of the servant leadership model. Sustainable business practices and corporate social responsibility may be better served in an organization led by a servant leader. Organizations with a focus on corporate social responsibility will practice ethical behavior, care for people, recognize their responsibilities outside of the organization, and emphasize creativity in business practices. These characteristics are closely linked to servant leaders (Hind, Wilson, & Lenssen, 2009).

▶ Contrasting Servant and Transformational Leadership

Although there appear to be similarities between the behaviors of transformational leaders and servant leaders, the primary distinction between these leadership styles is that servant leaders emphasize the personal growth of their followers first, while also contributing to the community. In addition, servant leaders hope to inspire their followers to enact servant leadership behaviors. Servant leaders set the following priorities in their leadership focus: Followers first, organizations second, their own needs last (Graham, 1991). In contrast, the role of the transformational leader is to inspire followers in an effort to pursue the goals and objectives of the organization (Sendjaya et al., 2008). **TABLE 2.2** summarizes transactional, transformational, and servant leadership differences.

TABLE 2.2 Transactional, Transformational, and Servant Leadership Behaviors

Transactional	Transformational	Servant
Contingent reward ■ Provide external reward after successful completion of task Active management by exception ■ Takes corrective action when mistakes are noticed Passive management by exception ■ Only takes corrective action after mistakes occur Laissez-faire ■ No decision making, no actions taken	Idealized influence ■ Demonstrate high levels of moral and ethical behavior ■ Inspire followers to emulate ethical and moral behavior Inspirational motivation ■ Set high expectations and motivate followers to meet those expectations Intellectual stimulation ■ Encourage creativity and innovation in addressing challenges Individualized consideration ■ Create a supportive environment serving followers' needs for growth and development	Empower and develop ■ Share information with followers and encourage self-direction Humility ■ Put followers' interests first, provide support, and facilitate their performance Authenticity ■ Express oneself in ways consistent with inner thoughts and feelings Interpersonal acceptance ■ Demonstrate empathy, compassion, and forgiveness to followers Provide direction ■ Customize directions to followers' needs, abilities, and input ■ Provide an appropriate amount of accountability Stewardship ■ Take responsibility for entire organization—inspire followers to act in the common interest for all

Data from Bass, B. M., & Riggio, R. E. (2006). *Transformational leadership*. Mahwah, NJ: Lawrence Erlbaum Associates; Spears, L. C. (2002). Tracing the past, present, and future of servant leadership. In L. C. Spears, M. Lawrence, & K. Blanchard (Eds.), *Focus on leadership: Servant-leadership for the twenty-first century* (pp. 1-10). New York: John Wiley and Sons; van Dierendonck, D. (2011). Servant leadership: A review and syntheses. *Journal of Management, 37,* 1228-1261.

▶ Servant Leadership in Sport Management

In contrast to the extensive amount of research examining transformational leadership in sport management, there has not been a comparable amount of work examining servant leadership. However, there has been a noted increase in interest in servant leadership in sport management, both in research and in teaching practices (Robinson, Neubert, & Miller, 2018).

One area of research in sport that has noted the benefits of servant leadership is within the sport psychology literature, specifically examining coaches' use of servant leadership (Kim, Kim, & Wells, 2017). There has been a noted shift in the understanding of effective coaching behavior, as athletes seek out coaches offering more democratic approaches to leading, greater empowerment of athletes, and a shift away from autocratic fear-based models of coaching (Hammermeister, Burton, Pickering, Chase, Westre, & Baldwin, 2008). If the primary objective and motivation for coaches is success for their athletes, coaching offers an interesting context for the study of servant leadership (Hammermeister et al., 2008). Outcomes noted by coaches who adopt servant leadership behaviors included athletes who were more intrinsically motivated, demonstrated more mental toughness, and were more satisfied with their sport experiences (Hammermeister et al., 2008; Rieke, Hammermeister, & Chase, 2008). In addition, athletes playing for coaches with servant leader characteristics also performed better as a team and individually compared with athletes playing for non–servant leader coaches (Rieke et al., 2008). Servant leadership has also been proposed as a valuable leadership approach for strength and conditioning coaches in the intercollegiate sport setting (Schary, 2017).

In the management context of sport, researchers have explored the characteristics and behaviors of the leader of a nonprofit sport organization who demonstrated servant leadership. The servant leadership demonstrated by this leader influenced the development of long-term volunteers, who then went on to become servant leaders (Parris & Welty Peachey, 2013). Within the context of nonprofit sport organizations, servant leaders can positively influence the motivation of their volunteers by developing a shared vision to serve others, building a loving and open community and creating a context in which followers can become servant leaders (Parris & Welty Peachey, 2013).

Burton and Welty Peachey (2013) proposed servant leadership as a form of leadership that would support the mission of and potentially better address ethical issues in intercollegiate athletics. Initial work in this area seems to support this proposition, as those working in intercollegiate athletic departments (i.e., athletic administrators) reported working in a more ethical climate when their athletic director demonstrated the characteristics of servant leadership (Dodd, Achen, & Lumpkin, 2018). Furthermore, athletic directors who demonstrated servant leadership behaviors also fostered trust in their employees, which led to perceptions of a positive ethical climate in their athletic departments (Burton, Welty Peachey, & Wells, 2017). There has also been a call for researchers to explore servant leadership in the SDP context (Wells & Welty Peachey, 2016; Welty Peachey & Burton, 2017). Work by Wells and Welty Peachey revealed that the founder and regional coordinators of an SDP organization displayed servant leadership behaviors as perceived by those working in the organizations. Those leaders demonstrated authenticity; empowered and developed people; showed humility, interpersonal acceptance, provided direction, and stewardship to those employees. Additionally, to support the mission of this SDP organization, the founder and regional coordinators attended to employees' needs, by building and developing relationships with their volunteers and players and demonstrating an attitude of genuine care and concern. These findings support the call for servant leadership as a useful form of leadership to implement and guide SDP initiatives.

In other research, individuals working and leading both international and US-based SDP organizations described leaders using servant leadership behaviors. Furthermore, those using servant leadership helped to meet important psychological needs, including the need for autonomy, relatedness, and connectedness, of employees in those organizations. Servant leadership was also used as a way for leaders of those SDP organizations to set the mission and vision of their organizations (Welty Peachey, Burton, Wells & Chung, 2018).

In the realm of professional sports, there has been interesting work examining the leadership behaviors of athletes who demonstrate servant leadership behaviors (Crippen & Nigel, 2014; Crippen, 2017). The National Hockey League Vancouver Canucks players Daniel and Henrik Sedin demonstrated servant leadership in their roles as integral members of their team. Those attributes included, among others, being a person of character, putting the needs of others first, and being compassionate collaborators that helped build community and creating a culture of accountability on their team (Crippen & Nagel, 2014). This work provides an interesting approach to understanding how leaders, coaches, and team members can use servant leadership in the context of high performance sport.

Because research within sport management examining the concept of servant leadership is still in its infancy, there appear to be many opportunities for scholars to gain greater understanding of the influences of servant leadership on organizational outcomes and employee outcomes within the context of sport organizations. Another area garnering interest within sport management research is exploring ways in which servant leadership can be measured (Trail, Hanold, & Cuevas, 2012). The development of a valid and reliable instrument to study servant leadership in sport will

be necessary to advance our understanding of the influence of this type of leadership in sport organizations.

▶ Summary

One of the most widely studied leadership behaviors in sport management is transformational leadership. Leaders who demonstrate transformational leadership are responsive to the individual needs of their followers by empowering them and by aligning the goals of the organization, the leader, the group, and the individual (Bass, 2008). Transformational leaders are visionary and appeal to the higher-order psychological needs of employees for feeling valued and worthwhile in the organization (Bryman, 1992). In contrast, transactional leaders motivate followers by contract and reward. Transactional leaders focus on rules and procedures and promise followers rewards for good performance (Bass, 1990).

Research in sport management has found that transformational leaders are considered more effective leaders, achieve better outcomes for their organizations, create greater employee commitment and satisfaction, and are better able to lead organizations through significant change.

Servant leadership is related to transformational leadership, but is a distinct form of leadership. Servant leaders first serve their followers and empower followers, but not for organizational objectives. Servant leaders emphasize the personal growth of their followers first. In contrast, transformational leaders also want to empower followers, but they do so in order to better serve the objectives of the organization. There is growing interest in the use of servant leadership both in business and in sport management contexts, and as scholars continue to develop and refine valid and reliable measures of servant leadership, the influence of servant leadership in sport management will continue to develop.

LEADERSHIP PERSPECTIVE

Lawrence Cann
Lawrence Cann is the Founder and CEO of Street Soccer USA (SSUSA), a leading organization in the use of sport for social change. In 2012, Lawrence was selected as one of 15 AMEX Ashoka Emerging Leaders in Social Entrepreneurship. He has also been honored by People Magazine, being named a Hero Among Us in 2009 and as the 2010 winner of the Kuykendall Award for Community Service, his alma mater, Davidson College. Lawrence is a recent MBA graduate of Columbia University, where he has planned the growth and development of the SSUSA social enterprise.

Data from http://www.streetsoccerusa.org/leadership/

Q: Within the leadership literature, there are studies to support multiple types of leadership behavior as beneficial to organizational outcomes. Can you describe the leadership behaviors that you find to be most effective for you in supporting the outcomes you seek for SSUSA?

Having been a part of the organization from the time that it was a volunteer organization to today, where we are managing several programs across the US, it has been different as there is a need for different types of leadership across each stage of growth. A flexible approach to leadership is important. In the early days of the organization, it was more about entrepreneurial approaches to leadership and leadership by example; now, it is really about maintaining our culture. Our culture really drives the product that we deliver. It is really providing leadership that curates and demonstrates those values that we need to exhibit. We have a number of different values, but the behaviors that we want our staff to exhibit include craftsmanship with regard to coaching; an emphasis on effective time management, including being good stewards of the money that we have; and being results oriented. When we get involved in a community that is facing adverse circumstances, we can all come together and play and have a good time, but what is the impact? We want to be results oriented because we want to make a difference, while we also cultivate fun and empathy. We have to be leaders and the program has to lift people up. The program has to be joyful and we have to have fun while also realizing that we have to be empathetic and sensitive to the individuals we are serving.

We certainly use the approach of servant leadership. I am now in the role of helping our team to be successful. I pay attention to the culture and our employees look to our leaders to set the culture because that really filters down to the rest of the organization.

Q: What leadership behavior do you see as detrimental to or a hindrance when trying to support those outcomes?

We need to be cognizant of our outcomes and our results and what shows up on reports to our various funders. We also need to be focused on systems and processes as our organization grows;

(continues)

however, that has to be balanced with flexibility. We have to realize that although it is good to have policies in place, as a result of the population we serve, those without homes, access to transportation, and other resources; we must stay flexible and not allow those policies to dictate the program and undercut the unique things that make the program successful. As we become more formalized, we don't want our program to become formulaic. We have to be business focused; however, that cannot be our only focus.

Q: How do you work to develop your leadership skills? Recognizing that there is only so much time in the day and resources are always limited.

I realized that I was going to need to develop my skillset further based on the ambitions that I had for the organization in the role that I had. The leadership skills that had brought the organization and me to where we were was not going to be the same skillset that would be required to get us to our next phase and beyond.

I enrolled in an Executive MBA program. If we, as an organization, wanted to go from small grants of $1,000–10,000 to $100,000–$1,000,000 grants, we needed to demonstrate that we had the leadership skills to manage those funds. So having my MBA was critical to our growth as an organization.

To me, that was a leadership decision, to go and get that degree and figure out how to manage getting the degree while continuing to lead the organization. But I also do not want to fall into the trap of confusing leadership with management. I have gotten better at that, as leadership is quite different as we anticipate what is coming and catch the next growth cycle. Fortunately, we have gathered a set of advisors in each city and having that network of people to reach out for tips on leadership has been very helpful. And just reading in general—finding time in my day or on weekends to read about topics that relate to our work or outside of our work I think is the genesis of a lot of ideas and flexibility.

Q: What behaviors do you believe are most important for leaders to use in the Sport for Development and Peace domain?

When we first started this organization, we were based in a soup kitchen in North Carolina, and we were exposed to a lot of the aspects of servant leadership, so it isn't something that I think about or use that term on a regular basis. But that is the approach to leadership that we use. That certainly is on the direct-to-participant level—our coaches are servant leaders—even if we don't use that specific term. It is not about our coaches; it is about our participants; it is about getting out of the way. We let our participants solve the problems or challenges during participation; it is really about leading by getting out of the way. Your leadership is doing the things that allow others to be successful.

I think there can also be a lot of ego and competitiveness in the general approach to sports—so you have to be thoughtful about the design of your programs, what your philosophy is in terms of coaching in order to make sure that we are actually doing sport for development and not just sport. We have been most successful with staff that come to us, not those who we go out and recruit. We look for people who reflect our communities, who are committed long term and care about the cause. We match those people and their skills to the positions as opposed to recruiting for certain skill sets. You don't come to SDP for the money, so there is a certain way to support, reward, and encourage that type of person—having the ability to be creative, to feel as though they are doing meaningful work; having integrity and keeping that front and center is important. People can also give a lot, have a lot of passion, and as a result, can suffer from burnout. So, we have to be aware of that and support those employees in the best way possible.

▶ Key Terms

Active management
Authentic leadership
Contingent reward
Idealized influence
Individualized consideration

Inspirational motivation
Intellectual stimulation
Laissez-faire
Passive management
Self-actualization

Servant leadership
Stewardship
Transactional leadership
Transformational leadership

▶ Discussion Questions

1. Considering the leadership theories presented in this chapter, identify a leader in the field of sport and describe whether he or she uses transactional, transformational, servant, or authentic leadership.

2. Given the scandals facing professional sport (e.g., use of performance-enhancing drugs, illegal behavior by coaches and athletes), what type of leadership could best support organizations that are trying to move past such scandals? Use information from the chapter to support your answer.

3. Describe the most significant differences between transformational and servant leadership.

4. What are some of the noted outcomes reported in research that have examined servant leadership in sport organizations?

5. Which type of leadership behavior do you think is best to utilize within a sport organization? Provide details from the chapter to support your answer.

▶ References

Amis, J., Slack, T., & Hinings, C. R. (2004). Strategic change and the role of interests, power and organizational capacity. *Journal of Sport Management, 18*(2), 158–198.

Anapol, A. (2018, May 23). NFL Players Association criticizes new league policy on kneeling during national anthem. Retrieved from http://thehill.com/blogs/blog-briefing-room/389018-nfl-players-association-criticizes-new-league-policy-on-kneeling

Andrew, D. P. S., Kim, S., Stoll, J. A., & Todd, S. Y. (2011). To what extent does transformational leadership affect employees? An exploratory analysis of a collegiate athletic department. *Applied Research in Coaching and Athletics Annual, 26*, 178–207.

Antonakis, J. (2012). Transformational and charismatic leadership. In D. V. Day & J. Antonakis (Eds.), *The nature of leadership* (2nd ed., pp. 256–288). Thousand Oaks, CA: Sage.

Avolio, B. J., & Bass, B. M. (1991). *Full-range leadership development*. Binghamton, NY: Bass, Avolio & Associates.

Avolio, B. J., Gardner, W. L., Walumbwa, F. O., Luthans, F., & May, D. R. (2004). Unlocking the mask: A look at the process by which authentic leaders impact follower attitudes and behaviors. *Leadership Quarterly, 15*(6), 801–823.

Bass, B. M. (1985). *Leadership and performance beyond expectations*. New York: Free Press.

Bass, B. M. (1990). *Bass and Stogdill's handbook of leadership: Theory, research and management applications* (3rd ed.). New York: Free Press.

Bass, B. M. (2008). Development and identification of leaders and leadership. In B. M. Bass & R. Bass (Eds.), *The Bass handbook of leadership: Theory, research and managerial applications* (4th ed., pp. 1051–1158). New York: Free Press.

Bass, B. M., & Riggio, R. E. (2006). *Transformational leadership (2ⁿᵈ ed.)*. Mahwah, NJ: Lawrence Erlbaum Associates.

Bass, B. M., & Steidlmeier, P. (1999). Ethics, character, and authentic transformational leadership behavior. *Leadership Quarterly, 10*(2), 181–217.

Breevaart, K., Bakker, A., Hetland, J., Demerouti, E., Olsen, O. K., & Espevik, R. (2014). Daily transactional and transformational leadership and daily employee engagement. *Journal of Occupational and Organizational Psychology, 87*(1), 138–157.

Bryman, A. (1992). *Charisma and leadership in organizations.* London, UK: Sage.

Burns, J. M. (1978). *Leadership: Transformational leadership, transactional leadership.* New York: Harper & Row.

Burton, L., & Welty Peachey, J. (2009). Transactional or transformational? Leadership preferences of Division III athletic administrators. *Journal of Intercollegiate Sport, 2*(2), 245–259.

Burton, L. J., & Welty Peachey, J. (2013). The call for servant leadership in intercollegiate athletics. *Quest, 65*(3), 354–371.

Burton, L. J., & Welty Peachey, J. (2014). Organizational culture mediates the relationship between transformational leadership and work outcomes. *Journal of Intercollegiate Sport, 7*(2), 153–174.

Burton, L. J., Welty Peachey, J., & Wells, J. E. (2017). The role of servant leadership in developing an ethical climate in sport organizations. *Journal of Sport Management, 31*(3), 229–240.

Choi, J., Sagas, M., Park, S., & Cunningham, G. B. (2007). Transformational leadership in collegiate coaching: The effects of transformational leadership on job satisfaction, organizational commitment, and organizational citizenship behavior. *International Journal of Sport Management, 8*(4), 429–446.

Crippen, C. (2017). A case study of servant leadership in the NHL. *Interchange, 48*(2), 205–216.

Crippen, C. L., & Nagel, D. (2013). Exemplars of servant leadership in sport: Henrik & Daniel Sedin. *Revue PhénEPS/PHEnex Journal, 5*(2).

Cruickshank, A., & Collins, D. (2016). Advancing leadership in sport: Time to take off the blinkers? *Sports Medicine, 46*(9), 1199–1204.

D'Andrea, C. & Stites, A. (2018, May 24). NFL owners reach a 'compromise' about the national anthem. How bad is it? Retrieved from https://www.sbnation .com/2018/5/23/17368782/nfl-national-anthem -protests-rule-annual-spring-meeting

Dodd, R., Achen, R. M., & Lumpkin, A. (2018). Servant Leadership and Its Impact on Ethical Climate, *The Journal of Values-Based Leadership, 11*(1), 1–22.

Doherty, A. J. (1997). The effect of leader characteristics on the perceived transformational/transactional leadership and impact of interuniversity athletic administrators. *Journal of Sport Management, 11*(3), 275–285.

Doherty, A. J., & Danylchuk, K. E. (1996). Transformational and transactional leadership in interuniversity athletics management. *Journal of Sport Management, 10*(3), 292–309.

Eagly, A. H., & Carli, L. L. (2003). Finding gender advantage and disadvantage: Systematic research integration is the solution. *Leadership Quarterly, 14*(6), 851–859.

Eisenbach, R., Watson, K., & Pillai, R. (1999). Transformational leadership in the context of organizational change. *Journal of Organizational Change Management, 12*(2), 80–89.

Foels, R., Driskell, J. E., Mullen, B., & Salas, E. (2000). The effects of democratic leadership on group member satisfaction: An integration. *Small Group Research, 31*(6), 676–701.

Frontiera, J. (2010). Leadership and organizational culture transformation in professional sport. *Journal of Leadership and Organizational Studies, 17*(1), 71–86.

Graham, J. W. (1991). Servant-leadership in organizations: Inspirational and moral. *Leadership Quarterly, 2*(2), 105–119.

Greenleaf, R. K. (1977). *Servant leadership: A journey into the nature of legitimate power and greatness.* New York: Paulist Press.

Greenleaf, R. K. (1998). *The power of servant-leadership.* San Francisco: Berrett-Koehler.

Hammermeister, J., Burton, D., Pickering, M., Chase, M., Westre, K., & Baldwin, N. (2008). Servant-leadership in sports: A concept whose time has arrived. *International Journal of Servant-Leadership, 4,* 185–215.

Hannah, S. T., Sumanth, J. J., Lester, P., & Cavarretta, F. (2014). Debunking the false dichotomy of leadership idealism and pragmatism: Critical evaluation and support of newer genre leadership theories. *Journal of Organizational Behavior, 35*(5), 598–621.

Hesse, H. (1956). *Journey to the east.* London, UK: Owen.

Hind, P., Wilson, A., & Lenssen, G. (2009). Developing leaders for sustainable business. *Corporate Governance, 9*(1), 7–20.

House, R. J. (1977). A 1976 theory of charismatic leadership effectiveness. In J. G. Hunt & L. L. Larson (Eds.), *Leadership: The cutting edge* (pp. 189–207). Carbondale: Southern Illinois University.

Jaramillo, F., & Noboa, F. (2015). Impact of Servant Leadership on Ethical Climate, Supervisor Conflict, and Organizational Outcomes. In *Marketing Dynamism & Sustainability: Things Change, Things Stay the Same…* (pp. 5–5). Springer, Cham.

Judge, T. A., & Piccolo, R. F. (2004). Transformational and transactional leadership: A meta-analytic test of their relative validity. *Journal of Applied Psychology, 89*(5), 755–768.

Kent, A., & Chelladurai, P. (2001). Perceived transformational leadership, organizational commitment, and citizenship behavior: A case study in intercollegiate athletics. *Journal of Sport Management, 15*(2), 135–159.

Kim, H. (2009). Transformational and transactional leadership of athletic directors and their impact on organizational outcomes perceived by head coaches at NCAA Division II intercollegiate institutions (doctoral dissertation). Retrieved from ProQuest

Dissertations and Theses database. AAT 3393209. at https://etd.ohiolink.edu/!etd.send_file?accession =osu1258697980&disposition=inline

Kim, M, Kim, Y, & Wells, J. W. (2017) Being a servant-leader in sport: Servant leadership as the key to the coach-athlete relationship, *International Journal of Sport Management, 18*(1), 19–43.

Kim, S., Magnusen, M., Andrew, D., & Stoll, J. (2012). Are transformational leaders a double-edged sword? Impact of transformational leadership on sport employee commitment and job satisfaction. *International journal of sports science & coaching, 7*(4), 661–676.

Klimoski, R. J., & Koles, K. L. K. (2001). The chief executive officer and top management team interface. In S. J. Zaccaro & R. J. Klimoski (Eds.), *The nature of organizational leadership: Understanding the performance imperatives confronting today's leaders* (pp. 219–269). San Francisco, CA: Jossey-Bass.

Kouzes, J. M., & Posner, B. Z. (1993). *Credibility: How leaders gain and lose it, why people demand it.* San Francisco, CA: Jossey-Bass.

Krishnan, V. R. (2005). Leader-member exchange, transformational leadership, and value system congruence. *Electronic Journal of Business Ethics and Organization Studies, 10*(1), 14–21.

Kuhnert, K. W., & Lewis, P. (1987). Transactional and transformational leadership: A constructive/developmental analysis. *Academy of Management Review, 12*(4), 117–130.

Lee, J. (2005). Effects of leadership and leader-member exchange on commitment. *Leadership and Organization Development Journal, 26*(8), 655–672.

Lin, C. S., Huang, P. C., Chen, S. J., & Huang, L. C. (2017). Pseudo-transformational leadership is in the eyes of the subordinates. *Journal of Business Ethics, 141*(1), 179–190.

Martin, R., & Epitropaki, O. (2001). Role of organizational identification on implicit leadership theories (ILTs), transformational leadership and work attitudes. *Group Processes and Intergroup Relations, 4*(3), 247–262.

May, D. R., Chan, A. Y. L., Hodges, T. D., & Avolio, B. J. (2003). Developing the moral component of authentic leadership. *Organizational Dynamics, 32*(3), 247–260.

Men, L. R. (2014). Why leadership matters to internal communication: Linking transformational leadership, symmetrical communication, and employee outcomes. *Journal of Public Relations Research, 26*(3), 256–279.

Michel, R. (2018, May 23). Timeline of NFL protests during the national anthem. Retrieved from https://www.kiro7.com/news/local/timeline-of-nfl-protests-during-the-national-anthem/614679920

Murray, M., & Mann, B. (2006). Leadership effectiveness. In J. Williams (Ed.), *Applied sport psychology: Personal growth to peak performance,* (pp. 109–139). New York: McGraw-Hill.

Northouse, P. G. (2016). *Leadership: Theory and practice.* Thousand Oaks, CA: Sage.

Ott, J. (1996). *Classic readings in OB* (2nd ed.). Belmont, CA: Wadsworth.

Parris, D. L., & Welty Peachey, J. (2012). Building a legacy of volunteers through servant leadership: A case study of a cause-related sporting event. *Nonprofit Management and Leadership, 23*(2), 259–276.

Parris, D. L., & Welty Peachey, J. (2013). A systematic literature review of servant leadership theory in organizational contexts. *Journal of Business Ethics, 113*(3), 377–393.

Phelan, M. (2005). Cultural revitalization movements in organizational change management. *Journal of Change Management, 5*(1), 47–56.

Powell, G. N., Butterfield, D. A., & Bartol, K. M. (2008). Leader evaluations: A new female advantage? *Gender in Management: An International Journal, 23*(3), 156–174.

Rieke, M., Hammermeister, J., & Chase, M. (2008). Servant leadership in sport: A new paradigm for effective coach behavior. *International Journal of Sports Science and Coaching, 3*(2), 227–239.

Robbins, S. P., & Judge, T. A. (2003). *Organizational behavior.* Upper Saddle River, NJ: Pearson Education.

Robinson, G. M., Neubert, M. J., & Miller, G. (2018). Servant leadership in sport: A review, synthesis, and applications for sport management classrooms. *Sport Management Education Journal, 12*(1), 39–56.

Shamir, B., & Eilam, G. (2005). "What's your story?" A life-stories approach to authentic leadership development. *Leadership Quarterly, 16*(3), 395–417.

Schary, D. P. (2017). Servants in the Weight Room: Coaches Using Servant Leadership to Improve Student-Athlete Well-being. *Strength & Conditioning Journal.*

Schroeder, P. J. (2010). Changing team culture: The perspectives of ten successful head coaches. *Journal of Sport Behavior, 32*(4), 63–88.

Sendjaya, S., Sarros, J. C., & Santora, J. C. (2008). Defining and measuring servant leadership behaviour in organizations. *Journal of Management Studies, 45*(2), 402–424.

Slack, T., & Hinings, C. R. (1992). Understanding change in national sport organizations: An integration of theoretical perspectives. *Journal of Sport Management, 6*(2), 114–132.

Spears, L. C. (2002). Tracing the past, present, and future of servant leadership. In L. C. Spears, M. Lawrence, & K. Blanchard (Eds.), *Focus on leadership: Servant-leadership for the twenty-first century* (pp. 1–10). New York: John Wiley and Sons.

Sprecher, S., & Fehr, B. (2005). Compassionate love for close others and humanity. *Journal of Social and Personal Relationships, 22*(5), 629–651.

Stewart, G. L. (2006). A meta-analytic review of relationships between team design features and team performance. *Journal of Management, 32*(1), 29–55.

Stone, A. G., Russell, R. F., & Patterson, K. (2004). Transformational versus servant leadership: A difference in leader focus. *Leadership and Organization Development Journal, 25*(4), 349–361.

Strang, K. D. (2005). Examining effective and ineffective transformational project leadership. *Journal of Team Performance Management, 11*(3/4), 68–103.

Trail, G., Hanold, M., & Cuevas, K. (2012, June). *Servant leadership in sport.* Paper presented at the North American Society for Sport Management Annual Conference, Seattle, WA.

Trotter, J., & Reid, J. (2017, November 29). Players debating NFL's proposed donation to social justice organizations. Retrieved from http://www.espn.com/nfl/story/_/id/21606390/nfl-offers-100-million-plan-social-justice-organizations-partnership-players

Tse, H. H. (2008, August). Transformational leadership and turnover: The roles of LMX and organizational commitment. In *Academy of Management Proceedings, (2008*(1), (pp. 1–6). Briarcliff Manor, NY 10510: Academy of Management.

van Dierendonck, D. (2011). Servant leadership: A review and syntheses. *Journal of Management, 37*(4), 1228–1261.

van Dierendonck, D., & Patterson, K. (2015). Compassionate love as a cornerstone of servant leadership: An integration of previous theorizing and research. *Journal of Business Ethics, 128*(1), 119–131.

van Dierendonck, D., Stam, D., Boersma, P., De Windt, N., & Alkema, J. (2014). Same difference? Exploring the differential mechanisms linking servant leadership and transformational leadership to follower outcomes. *The Leadership Quarterly, 25*(3), 544–562.

Vinkenburg, C. J., van Engen, M. L., Eagly, A. H., & Johannesen-Schmidt, M. C. (2011). An exploration of stereotypical beliefs about leadership styles: Is transformational leadership a route to women's promotion? *The Leadership Quarterly, 22*(1), 10–21.

Wallace, M., & Weese, J. W. (1995). Leadership, organizational culture and job satisfaction in Canadian YMCA organizations. *Journal of Sport Management, 9*(2), 182–193.

Wang, Y. S., & Huang, T. C. (2009). The relationship of transformational leadership with group cohesiveness and emotional intelligence. *Social Behavior and Personality: An International Journal, 37*(3), 379–392.

Weese, W. J. (1995). Leadership and organizational culture: An investigation of Big Ten and Mid-American Conference campus recreation administrations. *Journal of Sport Management, 9*(2), 119–134.

Wells, J. E., & Welty Peachey, J. (2011). Turnover intentions: Do leadership behaviors and satisfaction with the leader matter? *Team Performance Management, 17*(1/2), 23–40.

Wells, J. E., Welty Peachey, J. (2016). Called to serve: Exploring servant leadership in the context of sport-for-development. *Journal of Sport for Development, 4*(7), 12–24.

Welty Peachey, J., Burton, L., Wells, J., & Chung, M. R. (2018). Exploring servant leadership and needs satisfaction in the sport for development and peace context. *Journal of Sport Management, 32*(2), 96–108.

Welty Peachey, J., Bruening, J., & Burton, L. (2011). Transformational leadership of change: Success through valuing relationships. *Journal of Contemporary Athletics, 5*(2), 127–152.

Welty Peachey, J., & Burton, L. J. (2011). Male or female athletic director? Exploring perceptions of leader effectiveness and a (potential) female leadership advantage with intercollegiate athletic directors. *Sex Roles, 64*(5/6), 416–425.

Welty Peachey, J., & Burton, L. J. (2012). Transactional or transformational leaders in intercollegiate athletics? Examining the influence of leader gender and subordinate gender on evaluation of leaders during organizational culture change. *International Journal of Sport Management, 13*(2), 115–142.

Welty Peachey, J., & Burton, L. (2017). Servant leadership in sport for development and peace: A way forward. *Quest, 69*(1), 125–139.

Welty Peachey, J., Zhou, Y., Damon, Z. J., & Burton, L. J. (2015). Forty years of leadership research in sport management: A review, synthesis, and conceptual framework. *Journal of Sport Management, 29*(5), 570–587.

Wyche, S. (2016, August 27). Colin Kaepernick explains why he sat during national anthem. Retrieved from http://www.nfl.com/news/story/0ap3000000691077/article/colin-kaepernick-explains-why-he-sat-during-national-anthem

Yusof, A., & Mohd Shah, P. (2008). Transformational leadership and leadership substitutes in sports: Implications on coaches' job satisfaction. *International Bulletin of Business Administration, 3*, 17–29.

CHAPTER 3

Understanding the Difference between Leadership and Management

Maylon Hanold

CHAPTER OBJECTIVES

- Understand the origins and conceptual evolution of management and leadership.
- Understand the perceived similarities between leadership and management.
- Differentiate between leadership and management.
- Identify tools important to both managers and leaders in sport.
- Develop a working definition of leadership.

CASE STUDY

Basketball Event Teaches Management and Leadership

The Naismith Memorial Basketball Hall of Fame in Springfield, Massachusetts, stages two large-scale, high school basketball events every year, the Hoophall West and the Spalding Hoophall Classic. Each tournament is a showcase of the best high school basketball players and teams in the country. Of the two, the Spalding Hoophall Classic is the longer event, spanning five days in January on the campus of Springfield College, where graduate student James Naismith invented basketball in 1891 ("Where Basketball Was Invented," n.d.).

Planning the five-day event is a logistical maze with stakeholders from teams all over the country, key personnel from the Hall of Fame, and many planning groups from Springfield College all working together to stage a successful event. The event requires both excellent management and leadership and

(continues)

CASE STUDY   (continued)

serves as a springboard to begin our discussion of the differences between leadership and management in this chapter.

Two groups of beneficiaries of the Spalding Hoophall Classic are Springfield College's sport management and sport communication students, who work at the event. "It's a great partnership with the Hall of Fame," noted sport management department Chairperson Kevin McAllister. "The students are doing everything from security to event management to media relations and some are working with the teams that come in" (Springfield College, 2015). In this way, the Hall of Fame and Springfield College's Office of Conferences and Special Events are able to utilize people—in this case, students—to coordinate many of the Hoophall's work activities. Personnel from the Hall of Fame, the director of the Office of Conferences and Special Events, and McAllister all help oversee these students. Overseeing or monitoring these activities is closely associated with the function of management. Implementation of the during-event activities mentioned by McAllister—security, media relations, and team liaison work—represent management functions as well.

Planning is also a prominent management function. The Hall of Fame and Springfield College special events office are charged with a multitude of planning functions, such as making accommodations for the many teams, credentialing media, scheduling student workers and security personnel, ordering enough food for teams and spectators, setting up VIP areas, and coordinating the event schedule with several stakeholders. These are all pre-event activities. The sport management students and McAllister begin planning in September—four months ahead of time—who will serve as supervisors and team liaisons. Roughly 14 supervisors (usually sophomores and juniors) oversee about 65 first-year event management students, who do the lion's share of the groundwork—seating customers, keeping pathways clear, providing customer service by answering questions, and making sure that teams know where they need to be at certain times. The two head supervisors organize the first-year students by putting them through training sessions in December and January. These two head supervisors also create a schedule of work shifts for the first-year students. Student leader Jordan Elkary, who was one of two head supervisors for the 2018 event, said, "As a supervisor, we need to make sure everyone knows their role and knows what to do." This was one of Elkary's first experiences in a leadership role and he noted that what was most important was to help the younger students understand what a successful event needs to look like. He had worked the event the past two years and knew how the event should run. In this way, he took on a role of influence among the student workers. He was entrusted by the sport management department to impart the values expected of our first-year students, such as professionalism, social intelligence, emotional intelligence, and a mature work ethic.

The Hoophall Classic is the cement in the partnership between Springfield College and the Hall of Fame. Both entities need to be involved in basketball events to market themselves. The Hall of Fame needs to attract consumers through its turnstiles and the college needs to attract anybody and everybody to campus who will speak kindly about the college after they leave. That kind of promotion helps attract future students. On Martin Luther King, Jr., Day, which is the Monday of the event, prospective Springfield College students who are still in high school and considering the sport management major, gather at the President's on-campus home where they are greeted by the college's president, sport management faculty and sport management students who are working at the Hoophall event. This is the President's way of rolling out the red carpet for these potential students and perhaps influencing them to grace the campus after graduating from high school. As a leader, the college's president understands the importance of brand-building and sharing the college's values with parents and students who are looking to make an important decision about where to attend college.

The leadership role of the Hall of Fame should not be underestimated in this case. Greg Procino, the director of events and awards for the museum and a Springfield College graduate, meets with the sport management students before the event to share his expectations for the event and for the students' behavior. This discussion with students is the Hall's way of building shared values and meaning about what the event means and how it should be managed successfully.

Questions for Discussion

1. Using an event staged in professional sport, can you identify organizational activities that would differentiate between management and leadership based on what you learned from this case?
2. The case touches on the importance of event planning. List five important planning aspects that would need to take place before a five-day, national high school basketball showcase.
3. Communicating shared values is something leaders attempt to do. Using the NCAA men's basketball tournament as an example, what values do the National Collegiate Athletic Association and President Mark Emmert communicate during that event?
4. Think of a successful leader in sport (someone other than a coach or team manager). What personal characteristics makes this leader successful?

▶ Introduction

Because the focus of this book is leadership within the sport management field, it is crucial to distinguish between the two concepts of leadership and management to understand perceived differences and similarities. Since Zaleznik's classic article, "Managers and Leaders: Are They Different?" in the *Harvard Business Review* in 1977, the debate about whether management and leadership are distinct activities continues. Research exploring the differences between management and leadership has grown considerably (see Kotter, 1990a; Bennis, 2009; Weathersby, 1999; Yukl, 1989; Macoby, 2000, Zimmerman, 2001; Perloff, 2007, Toor, 2011). While the debate is far from over, there tend to be three major assumptions present in current research. First, management and leadership are essentially the same because attempts to distinguish the two remain vague and confusing, and thus, impractical (Mangham & Pye, 1991). The second view of management and leadership acknowledges that the two concepts are intertwined, but distinct on some levels. Scholars have described the relationship such that (1) leadership is a form of management in that it is good or excellent management and (2) leadership is a function of management. The final approach considers management and leadership distinct with respect to what they are, how they are conceptualized, and the functions they serve.

Despite the different views, this textbook takes the position that **management** and **leadership** are different. Before moving on to why we consider management and leadership discrete activities, it is instructive to review the development of leadership studies. To this end, we begin the chapter with the two prominent ways that management and leadership have historically been associated with each other. Then, we consider how management and leadership are distinct activities and why it is important to see them this way. Finally, we examine the differences in detail and offer examples from the sport management literature and recent research to show the differences.

▶ Historical Perspective: Management versus Leadership

Manager and management have a history grounded in the industrial revolution when factory owners were interested in maximizing profits by making sure that work processes in place were streamlined, rational, and consistent. Efficiency and control were paramount. Management theory grew out of these concerns. While defined in many different ways, management has consistently been about organizing people to achieve organizational goals using limited resources (Chelladurai, 2009). Three distinct phases characterize the meanings of management and the function of managers.

The first phase was called the **scientific management movement**. Essentially codified in 1911 with the publication of *The Principles of Scientific Management* by Frederick Taylor, management in this context was about motivating employees through extrinsic rewards to perform prescribed, efficient movements. It was entirely focused on the work of organizations with little regard for either psychological or sociological concerns of employees. A reaction to this work-centered approach marked the second phase. This phase, called the **human relations movement**, took place during the late 1920s and early 1930s. In this movement, management became more concerned with motivating workers intrinsically. Finally, the last phase, organizational behavior, considers efficiency and human relations aspects to examine organizational success.

Unlike management, leadership study has not been defined by movements, or defined much at all. Although the word leadership appeared in English dictionaries in the early 17th century (Rost, 1993), it was not until Webster's *An American Dictionary of the English Language* from 1828 that a definition of leadership appears in this country. Webster omitted any definition of leadership from its dictionaries until 1965 when several definitions are listed in the third edition of the *New International Dictionary of the English Language*. Further, formal studies of leadership appeared only sparingly in the 19th century but more prominently in the latter half of the 20th century.

Leadership and Management as Synonymous

The strong presence of management as a concept early in the 20th century coupled with the absence of the word leadership from dictionaries may simply reflect the lack of perceived need to distinguish the two concepts. Rost (1993) explains this lack of clear distinction as a natural and logical result of the historical context:

> They [scholars and practitioners] were reflecting the reality as they saw it. Their perception of leadership as management was the reality they perceived in the industrial era in which they lived and worked. They did not distinguish between leadership and management because in their minds there was no need to do so. They were one phenomenon. (p. 92-93)

Indeed, the 1925 *Thesaurus Dictionary* by March and March listed synonyms for "take the lead" as "leading-following, management" and a synonym for "leader" as "manager."

With the onset of the human relations phase of management, more scholars became interested in identifying what was lacking in scientific management and needed in order to attend to the human side of organizations. As a result, the concept of leadership, while simply defined in dictionaries, began to be framed as a more human-oriented skill. Notably, there was a shift from the idea of a leader as someone who controls and directs as opposed to one who influences. Schenk (1928), a prominent voice in this shift, says, "Leadership is the management of men by persuasion and inspiration rather than the direct or implied threat of coercion" (p. 111). Although leadership appears to take on a form of its own, it is clear from this definition that leadership is never clearly disassociated from management.

As the concept of leadership developed during the second half of the 20th century, leadership studies, articles, and books abounded. However, what is more remarkable is that despite clearly writing about leadership, scholars often failed to provide specific definitions of leadership (Rost, 1993). Furthermore, two trends indicate the extent to which leadership and management were thought of as indistinguishable. First, throughout the 1980s, leadership was defined as achieving organizational goals, which resulted in confusion between management and leadership. Many scholars from fields such as education, military, business, feminist research, and political science included the idea of achieving organizational goals within either their definitions or notions of leadership (see Hersey & Blanchard, 1988; Hollander, 1985; Jago, 1982; Segal, 1981; Sergiovanni, 1984). Dating back to the 19th century, management scholars and practitioners pervasively agree that management is the process of achieving organizational goals. Thus, leadership scholars, who insist on organizational goals being accomplished as an indication of leadership, create confusion because two distinct words have the same characteristics. Second, several scholars during the 1980s overtly conceded to the indistinguishable qualities of leadership and management. For example, Kuhn and Beam (1982) concede, "The term leadership is already applied so widely to formal executives, officers, squad leaders, and the like that we may simply accept it and say that leadership is the performance of the sponsor, or managerial, function…" (p. 381). Also, in Yukl's (1989) widely used textbook, he states, "The terms leader and manager are used interchangeably in this book" (p. 5). To reflect this perspective, Yukl employs the phrase "managerial leadership." Today, there is a significant number of scholars who remain unsure as to whether the debate is useful because the distinctions between leader and manager remain obscure in practice and research

(Mangham & Pye, 1991). Furthermore, current debates often demonstrate that "a common confusion remains that leadership and management are similar and that leaders and managers play similar roles [such that] sometimes leaders manage and sometimes managers lead" (Toor, 2011, p. 311). Northouse (2010) says that it makes sense for researchers to "treat the role of managers and leaders similarly and do not emphasize the differences between them" (p. 11).

Leadership and Management Overlap

The idea that leadership and management are distinct but still overlap is the most prominent idea in leadership research today. Two distinct views about how leadership and management overlap are common in the literature. The first view imagines leadership as a higher form of management; that is, leadership is management done well. The second view comes from the stance that management is what goes on in organizations. Leadership is simply an essential skill of managers. The logic that management subsumes leadership makes sense given the historic dominance of management study, the lack of a coherent leadership theory, and the ultimate concern that the majority of people occupy management positions by title or collective understanding. This way of thinking has experienced resurgence since the exponential growth of organizations (Kotterman, 2006).

Leadership as Excellent Management

Concurrent to the idea that management and leadership were synonymous, leadership as good management became increasingly prominent during the explosion of the leadership literature. Rost (1993) coined the term, "the industrial paradigm of leadership"

(p. 94) to identify this development, which he considers the most important unifying factor among leadership literature through the 1980s. Upon review of hundreds of leadership articles, Rost noted that management and leadership were often described as being different in degree. What emerged during this time was an underlying sense that leadership could not possibly be just any kind of management. As a result, scholars and practitioners began to frame leadership as not simply management but rather good or excellent management.

With the introduction of Burns' (1978) seminal work, *Leadership*, the idea of excellence became much more highly correlated to leadership compared with management. Excellence was still tied to goal achievement, but goals could be achieved through transactional or transformational leadership, two terms that Burns used to describe two styles of leadership. Burns' concept of transformational leadership is discussed in more detail in Chapter 2 (Positive Leadership Theory: Transformational, Transactional, and Servant Leadership). What is important here is that **transformational leadership** sparks an interest in excellence beyond focusing on work processes. Burns essentially introduces the idea that leadership should not only help organizations realize purposes but also achieve excellence by bringing employees to a much higher state of being and, subsequently, performance. Katz and Kahn (1978) capture a similar sentiment with their articulation of leadership versus management. They say, "we consider the essence of organizational leadership to be the influential increment over and above mechanical compliance [management] with routine directives of the organization" (p. 302-303). This expanded view of excellence or something "over and above" as tied to leadership solidifies the idea that "leadership is that which is done by excellent managers and management is that which is done by average managers" (Rost, 1993, p. 116).

In his famous book, *The Managerial Mystique: Restoring Leadership in Business,* Zaleznik (1989) gives considerable attention to leadership as people-oriented. He argues that leadership is different from management. He proposes, "the distinction is simply between a manager's attention to how things get done and a leader's to what the events and decisions mean to participants" (Zaleznik, 1978, p. 12). Zaleznik describes this quality as being more related to humans. He says, "managers relate to people according to the role they play . . . while leaders, who are concerned with ideas, relate in more intuitive and empathetic ways" (Zaleznik, 1978, p. 11). Despite his attempt to distinguish leadership and management, Zaleznik ultimately frames a leader as a great manager. He talks about the actions of an "effective manager," defining this person as a leader. He contrasts this with "ineffective managers," who remain simply managers. Despite his efforts to distinguish leadership from management, Zaleznik's language choices reflect the view that leadership is excellent management.

Leadership as a Function of Management

Another position that grew out of the "leadership as good management" perspective during the 1970s and 1980s was that leadership was an essential management skill. While leadership was beginning to be distinguished from management, it could not entirely disassociate itself from management. Thus, when leadership began to be framed as distinct, it naturally developed as a function of management. Mintzberg (1973), a prominent scholar on business management, developed a list of 10 managerial roles from his study of executives. Being a leader is listed as one of those roles, which reflects the dominant thinking at the time. Yukl (2002) sums up this major assumption of several decades by saying, "Most scholars seem to agree that success as a manager or administrator in modern organizations necessarily involves leading" (p. 6).

Leadership as a unique management skill came about because of a growing sense that leadership as simply good or excellent management was not capturing the qualitative differences between leadership and management. Of this particular period of time, Bryman (1992) notes,

> There was considerable disillusionment with leadership theory and research in the early 1980s. Part of the disillusionment was attributed to the fact that most models of leadership and measurement accounted for a relatively small percentage of variance in performance outcomes such as productivity and effectiveness. (p. 21)

These measures were focused on goal setting, providing direction and support, leader-follower exchange relationships, and behaviors based on "cost-benefit assumptions" (Bass, 1985, p. 5). In other words, trying to measure leadership as some excellent version of management was not necessarily accounting for differences in performances. The resultant conclusion was that leadership must be a separate skill of management.

This special skill became associated with Burns' (1978) transformational leadership. As noted earlier, these skills were more human focused, were based in values, and relied on interpersonal skills. As Burns frames it, transformational leadership is more focused on vision, inspiration, higher purposes, and charisma. Despite being discussed as distinct and being concerned with people versus work processes, leadership was seen as a complementary skill, or rather, a skill to be developed as a manager to be effective.

Such thinking is evidenced in the various ways that scholars and practitioners have talked about these skills. Gomez-Mejia, Balkin & Cardy (2005) note that leadership is "a management function in which motivating

people to achieve higher purposes, perform to the best of their ability, and work with other people to do so" (p. 11) are key aspects. While exploring the notion of charisma, Conger & Kanungo (1994) use language that maintains the idea that leadership is a management function. They say, "managers in a charismatic leadership role are also seen to be deploying innovative and unconventional means for achieving their visions" (p. 443), and that they are attempting to "operationalize the charismatic leadership role of managers in organizations" (p. 443). This particular relationship between management and leadership also appears often in practitioner articles. One such example comes from the domain of human resources. McLean (2005) remarks that despite the differences between leadership and management, "there is the argument that leadership is a facet of management and, therefore, cannot be separated" (p. 16). In these instances, the inclination to keep management and leadership closely bound together is readily apparent.

▶ The Case for Differentiating Management and Leadership

Without the distinction between the activities of management and leadership, organizations could be set up for failure. Without differentiation, management tends to be denigrated and leadership exalted. Several scholars (Kotter, 1990a; Kotter, 1990b; Rost, 1993) warn that this confusion leads people to think of leadership as the remedy for all organizational dilemmas. Kotter (1990a) maintains that this is a dangerous view because both management and leadership are needed. If there is strong leadership but weak management in a complex world, the result is "a) emphasis on long-term but no short-term plans, b) strong group culture without much specialization, structure, or rules, c) inspired people who are not inclined to use control systems or problem-solving disciplines" (p. 17). The converse is also true. Organizations with strong management but weak leadership have trouble moving in new directions when the environment necessitates a change. In other words, efficient systems of organization operations are not enough when those systems need to be reconsidered altogether. Furthermore, without clear articulation of the differences, the myth that people want to be led and not managed gains ground. Yet, this myth does not match reality (Rost, 1993). People do like to be managed. They like order, clear expectations, and having a strong sense of how their work fits into accomplishing organizational goals. The act of ordering chaos is management. Organizations cannot thrive without this kind of order. In short, organizations need both leaders and managers.

Czarniawska-Joerges & Wolff (1991) believe that the distinction serves important cultural purposes. They argue that the terms leadership and management embody certain archetypes that have distinct meanings for cultures at specific points in time. Given that people operate based on shared understandings, clarity about the roles of managers and leaders is important. If an employee understands what is commonly accepted as typical activities of managers as opposed to leaders, they can more accurately discern their own feelings about their boss' relative strengths and weaknesses. These shared understandings allow for the culture to create itself in consistent ways. By eliminating confusion over the activities of management and leadership, organizational culture develops positively with fewer misunderstandings.

Furthermore, by clearly distinguishing management and leadership, it is possible to talk about good, bad, effective, ineffective, or mediocre management and leadership. In other words, distinguishing the two allows

scholars and practitioners to recognize various levels of competency. When one views leadership as an excellent form of management, this distinction is impossible to make. In contrast, by distinguishing the two, different skill sets can be identified for each, and the competency with which each is done can be evaluated. If those differences are not clearly articulated, confusion over the terms only brings about difficulties in performance assessments, hiring practices, and professional development. Simply put, misunderstandings about the differences as culturally defined ultimately hinder organizational practices. Distinction allows us to focus our efforts more clearly into developing people (Kotter, 1990b; Zacko-Smith, 2007). Organizations can more precisely assess relative strengths and weaknesses of people, focusing attention on developing the necessary skills or simply matching people to positions in which their strengths serve them well. As Kotter (1990b) puts it, "Once companies understand the fundamental difference between leadership and management, they can begin to groom their top people to provide both" (p. 104).

We stand in agreement with those who feel it is necessary to distinguish leadership and management in order to study, test, and develop the two skills within the sport industry. As such, we explore the conceptual, definitional and functional differences between management and leadership in more detail.

▶ Conceptual Differences between Management and Leadership

Many scholars view management and leadership as distinct but complementary activities, and both are necessary for organizations to succeed. Reviewing the historic development of this idea, three aspects about management versus leadership surface. First, management deals with tangibles such as how to do work. In contrast, leadership operates on the level of intangibles such as establishing values and creating social worlds in which mutual purposes are co-created. Second, management works in the present while leadership is focused on the future. Third, management focuses on making complex systems run smoothly. Leadership involves moving an organization through change. Scholars who support the view that management and leadership are different activities argue that both functions are needed for an organization to succeed.

One trend that has surfaced over the past 60 years regarding management and leadership is that management is a mechanistic process while leadership is a social process. Long before Zaleznik's (1977) classic article regarding the differences between management and leadership, various scholars have explored the idea that leadership is relational. Coming from an institutional leadership perspective, Selznick (1957) writes, "the task of building special values and a distinctive competence into the organization is a prime function of leadership" (p. 27). In this early account, Selznick points out a qualitative difference between management and leadership. Namely, leadership is essentially a social phenomenon because establishing values is a social activity. Continuing along this line of thinking, Hosking and Morley (1988) propose that leadership entails structuring not what people do but what events and actions mean to people. Scholars who see leadership as clearly different from management assert that leadership is about constructing shared values and meanings (Drath, 2001) based on trust (Bennis & Nanus, 1985) and is entirely relational (Rost, 1993). Leadership is about how communities "construct one another and become such things as leaders and followers" (Drath, 2001, p. xvi) while management is about the exercise of power and authority in accomplishing tasks (Rost, 1993).

A second theme that emerges in a review of the leadership literature is that management focuses on doing activities efficiently in the present moment, whereas leadership is future oriented and based on the notion of vision. Bennis (1977) assumed that "leading is different from management; the difference between the two is crucial. I know many institutions that are very well managed and very poorly led" (p. 3). Further study of leadership prompted Bennis and Nanus (1985) to observe many organizations as overmanaged and under led. They conclude that many people in organizations excel in the ability to handle the daily routine yet never question whether the routine should be done at all. [....] Managers are people who do things right and leaders are people who do the right thing.

The final theme that permeates the literature framing management and leadership as distinct has its roots in Burns' descriptions of transactional and transformational leadership. Burns' definition of transformational leadership marked an important step toward viewing management and leadership as fundamentally different. While his definition of transformational leadership is lengthy, the distinction between transactional and transformational leadership remains simple. Transactional leadership is effective for maintaining the *status quo* while transformational leadership moves organizations through change while focusing on the growth and development of people. Kotter (1990a, 1990b) takes this difference seriously. Kotter puts forth the most cogent argument for distinguishing management and leadership in his famous book, *Force for Change: How Leadership Differs from Management* (1990a). Kotter succinctly frames the difference. He says that management is about coping with complexity and leadership is about coping with change. Kotter aligns transactional activities with management and transformational actions with leadership. Kotter (1990b) maintains that "leadership and management are two distinctive and complementary systems of action. Each has its own function and characteristic activities" (p. 103). In other words,

Kotter assumes that management (transactional) and leadership (transformational) are essential for organizational success. **TABLE 3.1** summarizes these major trends between management and leadership as described in the literature.

TABLE 3.1 Summary of Trending Differences between Management and Leadership

Management	Leadership	Source
Status Quo versus Change		
Regulates existing systems	Seeks opportunities for change	Zaleznik (1978)
Accepts the *status quo*	Challenges the *status quo*	Bennis and Goldsmith (1997)
Works within current paradigms	Creates new paradigms	Covey, Merrill & Merrill (1994)
Mechanistic versus Social		
Focuses on how things get done	Focuses on what things mean to people	Zaleznik (1978)
Making complex systems work efficiently	Helping people accept and move through change	Kotter (1990)
Involves telling others what to do	Involves energizing people to take action	Bennis and Goldsmith (1997)
Relies on control	Relies on trust	Bennis & Nanus (1985)
Monitors results through methodical means to bridge performance gaps and solve problems	Inspires people to surmount obstacles through satisfying basic human needs	DuBrin (1995)
Efficiency versus Vision		
Achieves efficiency and effectiveness within mission of organization	Creates vision, sells vision, and evaluates progress and determines next steps	Perloff (2007)
Is a function consisting of planning, budgeting, evaluating, and facilitating	Is a relationship that is composed of identifying and selecting talent, motivating, coaching, and building trust	Macoby (2000)

Management	Leadership	Source
Present versus Future		
Consists of routine, structure that deals with the present	Is oriented toward the future	Perloff (2007)
Focuses on short-range goals, keeping an eye on the bottom line	Focuses on long-range goals, keeping an eye on the horizon	Bennis and Goldsmith (1997)

▶ # Defining Management and Leadership

Despite some clear trends regarding the differences between management and leadership, defining the two concepts has always been difficult. Scholars and practitioners shape various definitions based on the nuances they observe in real situations. Attempts to capture the essences of each are many. The following definitions of management exemplify some of the major characteristics associated with this concept:

> Management consists of the rational assessment of a situation and the systematic selection of goals and purposes (what is to be done?); the systematic development of strategies to achieve these goals; the marshaling of the required resources; the rational design, organization, direction and control of the activities required to attain the selected purposes; and, finally, the motivating and rewarding of people to do the work. (Levitt, 1976, p. 73)

Management is coordinating work activities so that they are completed efficiently and effectively with and through other people. (Robins, Coulter, and Langton, 2006, p. 9)

Leadership definitions are surprisingly harder to find. Historically, scholars and practitioners tended to explain traits, behaviors, and characteristics of managers and leaders without offering a clear succinct definition (Rost, 1993). Billsberry and colleagues (2018) hold that there can be no true definition of leadership since it is a socially constructed concept and thus, conceived differently by different people. Leadership is assessed internally and should be focused on the people observing others and is not about leaders per se (Toosi & Ambady, 2011). Despite the different perspectives, several scholars have tried to define leadership. Below are two that illustrate the most common qualities of leadership expressed in the literature.

> A shift in paradigm is in order. (Bass, 1985, p. xiii) . . . . To sum it up, we see the transformational leader as one who motivates us to do more than we originally expected. (p. 20)

Leadership is much more adequately seen as a *process of interaction*. This process includes everything that goes on in the group that contributes to its effectiveness. Leadership exists when group members deal with one another in ways that meet their needs and contribute to their goals. (Whitehead & Whitehead, 1986, p. 74-75)

▶ Definitional Differences between Management and Leadership

Despite some similarities between the concepts, important differences are evident. According to Rost (1993), there are four perceptible differences between the definitions of management and leadership. These differences extend from the idea that language matters (Lakoff, 2000). A review of these definitional differences illustrates how management and leadership are conceptually different. Furthermore, it establishes a clear picture of why both management and leadership are important to organizational success.

© AP Images

Authority versus Influence Relationship

Management is a relationship between managers and those they guide based on positional authority. Organizational structures, job descriptions, and contractual agreements determine this positional authority. When people use authority to get others to do things, management is happening. Certainly, directives given by a manager may be either coercive or non-coercive. Coercive means telling people what to do. This type of management is efficient and practical. These types of directives are usually very task oriented and to the point. For instance, the manager of game-day operations for a minor league baseball team will likely train employees by giving them specific procedures to follow. A non-coercive form of authority may involve some kind of democratic decision-making about how to improve procedures on game day or decide different promotions from season to season. Managers who ask for feedback and seek ideas for improvements about game day procedures before making changes are operating in a non-coercive way. In

either instance, everyone involved accepts the nature of this authority, and the fundamental arrangement is top-down.

Leaders are also involved in a relationship, but they guide people based on influence. Influence is perhaps the most widely articulated characteristic of leadership, and it involves the idea of persuasion. Leaders influence others by wielding all different kinds of power sources other than authority (Rost, 1993). They use sources such as charisma, rational arguments, expression of vision and ideals, perceptions, and symbols to move people to action. Influence never involves coercion and often leads to intrinsic motivation on the part of the followers. For example, John Wooden not only focused on the details of playing basketball but also used vision and ideals through his Pyramid of Success to inspire his players to excel.

Manager/Subordinate versus Leader/Follower Relationship

Understanding who plays what role in management and leadership is needed to identify when one or the other is occurring. When managers use their authority to guide work, it is helpful to frame this as a manager/subordinate relationship. **Subordinate** is by no means a derogatory term but rather an indicator that an authority/compliance act is occurring. Similarly, when the relationship changes to one involving influence, it is useful to describe the people involved in that relationship as leaders and **followers**. Such distinctions are necessary to determine what prompted people to do work in both relationships. More importantly, it is essential to recognize that both management and leadership do not occur simply because a manager directs and a leader articulates a vision. Without subordinates complying and followers taking action, neither management nor leadership exists. This language, which includes both subordinates and followers, ensures that management and leadership are recognized as relationships.

Given that sometimes managers lead and leaders manage, this framework also allows us to distinguish when each is happening. It also allows each to happen within the same person, simultaneously or at different times depending on the organizational context or goals to be achieved at the moment. As such, this language provides a roadmap to understanding complex behavior. These distinctions in language also inform ways managers and leaders make sure they are doing the right thing at the right time. Finally, identifying areas for professional development becomes an easier task.

Many sport organizations are understaffed. As a result, people frequently take on various tasks that require different skills. For instance, a university recreation department director needs to make sure that procedures are followed for safety reasons, resources are used judiciously, and students benefit from the programs. When discussing safety procedures and resource allocation with their staff, recreation directors would most likely be in a manager/subordinate relationship. Alternately, inspiring the staff to make sure that every student experience is positive and informed by current thinking would entail few routine

directives and more likely the use of power sources to inspire staff toward action.

Produce and Sell Goods/Services versus Intend Real Changes

Managers and subordinates accomplish specific tasks and goals. This work is required for the organization to meet its most immediate goals. When people work together in the direct production or selling of goods or services, this work is management. Much of the work in sport event operations falls into this category and involves managers and subordinates. The work of creating operational plans, securing sponsorships, and confirming facility needs are guided by managers and performed by subordinates.

In contrast, work directed toward intended change requires leadership. Organizations need to change in order to stay competitive and thrive with shifting demands, demographics and cultural contexts. The intention of creating change is sufficient to identify whether leadership is happening. Otherwise, leadership could only be identified after the fact, which is not ideal for recognizing what needs to happen in real time. In sport event management, working toward improving an event from one year to the next would best be accomplished by leadership with leaders articulating a compelling vision such that followers become excited about potential improvements that they are intrinsically motivated to act.

Coordinate Activities versus Establish Mutual Purposes

One of the most important defining aspects of management is that it is about coordinating activities of the organization so that differentiation and integration happen smoothly. Coordination emerges out of rational thought processes aimed at knowing what work is to be done, how it should be divided and how it comes together to accomplish the goals of the organization. In larger organizations, people are typically focused on their immediate tasks and hold individual goals specific to their tasks. It is the coordination of these disparate goals that is the work of the manager. Negotiated agreements, routine exchanges, meetings to share information, and compromises are characteristic of when coordination takes place. When a university athletics department goes through the process of restructuring and creating a new organizational chart, the actual negotiation of job responsibilities and authority is management at work.

The work of leadership is defined as establishing mutual purposes. Establishing mutual purposes is different from coordinating activities in that it entails bringing a community together around shared understandings about why the organization exists. This work is intangible in some ways because it does not involve direct negotiation over actions. Leadership happens when leaders and followers work together to generate and clarify the essential purpose of the organization, not the work that will be required to carry out that purpose. For this kind of work to be considered leadership, the three other criteria must also be met. In the case of a university athletics department, stepping back and setting the specific purposes of athletics within the larger university's mission is a leadership activity as long as the leader is relying on influence, followers are involved, and some sort of changes are mutually agreed upon.

▸ Functional Differences between Management and Leadership

Despite definitional differences, it is evident that management and leadership are both involved with carrying out an organization's mission, attending to human relationships, making sure that people take actions toward the mission and assuming responsibility for

the success of the organization. What differs is how management and leadership function differently within an organization. As Kotter (1990a) and Kotterman (2006) remind us, both functions are needed for an organization to fulfill its mission, goals, and objectives. Management is tactical and leadership is strategic (Kotterman, 2006). Kotter (1990a) noted that managers work at making the organizational systems work "efficiently and effectively hour after hour, day after day" (Kotter, 2012, para. 5). In contrast, leadership imagines and creates the systems and constantly looks toward the future (Kotter, 1990a). We now turn to the different functions in detail by looking at mission, human relationships, organizational processes, and key tasks.

Realizing the Mission

Management Plans and Budgets

In order to realize the mission—or the organization's purpose—an organization must have plans in place about how to do so as well as allocate resources to the key activities outlined in those plans. Planning is a deductive process in which people decide what to do to get from A to B. This work entails setting specific goals and establishing measures to reach those goals. These types of goals are often called operational or **tactical goals** (Chelladurai, 2009) and are often found in strategic plans. As part of the realistic achievement of the mission, resources need to be allocated to accomplish these specific goals. Keeping track of the budget and making sure that resources are used in ways that carry out the operational and tactical plans is the responsibility of management since this activity is part of the day-to-day agenda of an organization.

Leadership Creates Vision and Strategy

Ultimately, plans cannot be put in place or resources appropriately allocated without a clear vision and overall strategy about how an organization will fulfill its purpose. Understanding where an organization currently stands is part of the work of leadership. This is equivalent to knowing where A is when going from A to B. Establishing B is setting this overall direction of an organization. This is an inductive process that involves looking at industry patterns and relationships by asking questions such as who are our direct competitors, who is doing well, what kinds of things are they doing, and what are our strengths and weaknesses compared with them? This step involves many people at different levels in order to acquire accurate data. The next step involves establishing a **vision** in terms of what the company should be like. This includes ideas about organizational culture, business activity that is unique, desirable, and realistic. As Kotter (1990a) notes, a vision should be specific enough to provide something from which to plan but vague enough to remain relevant through changes and that would "encourage initiative" (p. 36). Whether or not a vision is desirable depends on the answer to the question, does it serve the needs of key constituents? Finally, leadership is responsible for determining a strategy based on all relevant data. This final step entails determining a sound strategy. In other words, what general implementation direction will the organization take that is realistic for achieving goals but not necessarily guaranteed. The vision and strategy concern moving toward something different, something never done before, but energizing and realistic. While the leader is ultimately responsible for the vision and strategy, he or she seldom establishes these alone.

Human Relationships
Management Implements Plans

Management is concerned with creating "human systems that can implement plans as precisely and efficiently as possible" (Kotter,

1990a, p. 49). Once plans and budgets are in place, management is responsible for many of the human resource concerns such as creating organizational charts, establishing job descriptions, hiring the right people for the job, and assuring progress toward goals. Organizational charts are about differentiation and integration. In other words, how will the work be divided and how will it be coordinated so that the mission is achieved? Specific job descriptions determine the details about the work assigned to specific people. At this level, management establishes what people do and delegates responsibility. Then, managers hire the right people to fulfill those needs. Ultimately, managers are responsible for telling people what to do. As noted earlier, telling is not always a negative thing. In fact, telling is necessary in many instances, but there are other more democratic methods that a manager can employ to establish the specific means to carry out plans. In short, management connects and integrates people so that work gets done efficiently and effectively.

Leadership Aligns People

Leadership connects and integrates people in different ways from management. One important function of leadership is to align people within and beyond the organization in order to achieve the mission. Kotter (1990a) defines alignment as "a condition in which a relevant group of people share a common understanding of a vision and a set of strategies, accept the validity of that direction, and are willing to work toward making it a reality" (p. 60). While management is concerned with the orderly division and coordination of work, alignment involves connecting people in ways that are much less routine. Kotter explains that leaders establish informal networks, creating "spider-like" webs of relationships depending on needs and timing. Alignment also results from communicating the vision frequently and consistently. Although such a task seems simple; Jack Welch, former CEO of General Electric, admits that, "communicating the vision and the atmosphere around the vision has been and is continuing to be, by far, the toughest job we face" (Welch, as cited in Kotter, p. 510). The goal of alignment is to link various visions so that people feel compelled to work together rather than compete with each other as they work to achieve their specific goals. The unity created through alignment is a powerful force that influences the creation of teams, coalitions, and partnerships made of people who believe in the mission (Kotterman, 2006). Often, organizations decide to decentralize and democratize so that people have more control over how to implement that vision. Again, exactly, how this happens is the work of management, but alignment of people allows management to happen in less coercive and more democratic ways. Finally, alignment results in an organizational culture that is self-sustaining and directed toward achieving the mission.

Processes

Management Oversees

Another important function of management is to control the process and problem-solve to make work more efficient, but still effective (Kotter, 1990a). It is about keeping things working smoothly, on time, on budget, and with quality. As Kotter reminds us, managers help people "complete routine jobs successfully, day after day" (p. 62). Controlling involves measuring processes such as ROI, systems analyses, and satisfaction of those who are primarily served by the organization. Management is responsible for sustaining those processes, reducing variation, and anticipating short-term needs. Managers are responsible for making sure benchmarks and goals are in place so that people can see real progress toward goals and adjust when necessary. While they can approach their work in a wide variety

of ways, "managers take responsibility for those processes and are constantly seeking to improve them" (Kotterman, 2006, p. 15).

Leadership Motivates

Leadership appeals to shared values, involves people, supports efforts, and recognizes successes in order to motivate people to do work. One way to describe leadership's role in getting work done is that unlike management, which is about getting people to do work based on control, leadership motivates people by "satisfying very basic human needs for achievement, belonging, recognition, self-esteem, sense of control over one's life, and living up to one's ideals" (Kotter, 1990a, p. 63). This type of motivation includes articulating a vision that aligns with people's values, involving people in creating the control processes; offering support in the form of development, training and feedback; and recognizing efforts of others in some public fashion (Kotter, 1990). **TABLE 3.2** summarizes the key tasks of leadership and management.

▶ A Working Definition of Leadership

Clearly, the complex world needs both managers and leaders, but it is leadership that is essential to meeting the demands of a rapidly changing world. As sport organizations grow and adapt to external forces, and technology improves—something sport observers have seen a lot of over the past decade—processes become so complex that management alone will not serve the organization well (Kotter, 1990a). Incremental improvements no longer lead to a competitive advantage. Kotter's research shows that for organizations to gain a competitive advantage in the 21st century, leadership is required alongside good management. Searching for new directions, innovations, and services become even more important in the current environment.

TABLE 3.2 Summary of Functions of Management and Leadership

Organizational Aspects	Management	Leadership
Realization of Mission	Plans and Budgets (Kotter, 1990a)	Creates vision and strategy (Kotter, 1990a) Establishes organizational culture (Kotter, 1990a)
Human Relationships	Implements Structure ■ Organizes and staffs (Kotter, 1990a) ■ Delegates responsibility and authority (Kotterman, 2006)	Aligns People ■ Communicates vision ■ Influences creation of teams, coalitions, and partnerships made of people who believe in mission and vision (Kotterman, 2006) ■ Uses informal networks (Kotter, 1990a) ■ Creates and sustains organizational culture
Processes	Oversees ■ Controls & problem solves (Kotter, 1990a) ■ Monitors results (Kotterman, 2006)	Motivates (Kotter, 1990a) ■ Appeals to shared values ■ Involves people ■ Supports efforts ■ Recognizes successes

Given the conceptual, definitional, and functional differences between management and leadership and the fact that this book takes the view that leadership is distinct from management, we offer the following definition of leadership:

Leadership is an influence relationship aimed at moving organizations or groups of people towards an imagined future that depends upon alignment of values and establishment of mutual purposes.

At its core, leadership is an influence relationship and dynamic process (Hosking & Morley, 1988; Rost, 1993). Leaders influence people such that they are inspired to do work, feel as though their values align with the organization, and become co-creators of organizational culture. Leaders know that their work is dynamic because it is based on the notion of possibility. They stay focused on the future and often take the view from 30,000 feet. From this vantage point, they are able to see a future that might be difficult to accomplish, but possible and realistic. They envision what the organizational culture might look like or which purposes will become important for long-term success. Leadership is about moving organizations or groups of people toward this imagined future. They rely more on personal power, such as friendship, loyalty, expertise, charisma, and dedication instead of only use of positional power such as formal authority, rewards, punishments, and control of information. In doing so, leaders understand that their work consists of establishing meanings for organizations and is extremely relational in nature. Good leaders embody the values of the organization and work hard to establish mutual purposes by appealing to shared values and being authentic in doing so.

▶ Summary

The concepts regarding management and leadership have evolved over many years. The industrial revolution marked a significant move toward organizing on a large scale. During this time, efficiency was paramount, facilitating the definitional and functional overlap of management and leadership. Since that time, the work of organizations has diversified, bringing more attention to the concept of leadership. We maintain that new complexities in organizations and rapid environmental change require people in organizations to make the distinction between management and leadership. Articulating conceptual differences regarding the purposes of management and leadership provides an important way of thinking about how each contributes to the success of organizations. Specific definitional differences help people identify the distinct roles of managers and leaders while functional differences clarify overall tasks. Once distinctions are made, assessment of leadership and leadership development are more easily achieved.

LEADERSHIP PERSPECTIVE

Kristin "Kiki" Jacobs

Kristin "Kiki" Jacobs was named the Director of Athletics, Intramurals and Recreation at Roger Williams University in Bristol, RI, in August of 2017. Before that, Jacobs was an associate athletics director at Springfield College in Massachusetts for seven years. She came to New England after working as an associate athletics director at Oberlin College from 2006 to 2010.

Q: What are some skills and attributes that a good manager should possess?

Some skills of a good manager, to me, are good organization; acquaintanceship with technical aspects of the position and those he/she supervises; someone who knows how to get things done and can "check the box" at the end of the day/month/year; someone who can give direction and hold people accountable; and someone who can follow direction and understands his/her position in the organization.

Q: What are some skills and attributes a good leader should possess?

A good leader is a good listener and communicator; someone who is willing to learn about the organization and the team; someone who has a vision and/or strategic plan to move the department forward; someone who "can show the way, teach the way, and then get out of the way"; someone who builds relationships within the team and outside the team; someone who brings new and creative ideas to the table; and someone who realizes others have areas of expertise to bring to the team. Leaders allow them to do this. Leaders value teamwork and motivate others to perform. A good leader needs to learn what makes their team tick. Each person has different needs. It is important for the leader to learn what makes each of them want to come to work each day. What motivates them? When I first got to Roger Williams University, I met with each member in the department and asked him or her the following questions: 1. Tell me about yourself. This question helped me learn how to communicate better with each of them. Is he or she a person who needs a heavy hand when things are not going well or does he or she need a softer approach? 2. What are your specific job responsibilities? 3. What do you like the most? 4. What do you like the least? 5. What is working? 6. What is not working? At Division III, coaches and administrators do many different jobs. By learning what they like and do not like to do, I was able to make some small changes to make each of their positions more fulfilling. 7. What do you want to be doing 5 to 10 years from now? 8. How can I help you to get there? I think this question is important because not everyone wants to be in the same position or at the same school forever. I believe that as an AD and/or leader, it is important to help them achieve their professional goals.

Q: In your experience, what are some of the pitfalls to avoid as a leader?
If you are new to a position, a common pitfall is moving too quickly and not listening. When a change in leadership occurs, it is very unsettling to most people, even if the change is for the best or by choice. A new leader needs to learn about the culture and the people before making too many changes. As a leader, you need to develop trust in your team, determine who is on-board and who is not. As Jim Collins says in his book *Good to Great*, you need to get the right people on the bus, put them in the right seats, and then get the wrong people off the bus. A common pitfall for a leader is to get bogged down in daily operations. If you have someone who can do the job, let them do it and do not do it for them. I have seen a lot of ADs get so caught up in the day-to-day operations of the department (compliance, event management, scheduling), that they could not do any planning to move the department forward. Having time to imagine, plan, and implement a long-term plan in areas of fundraising, personnel, branding, etc., all take time. Another pitfall for leaders is communication. Many do not communicate and keep everything "secret." Communication helps build trust in the department. I have specifically seen this with budgets. Currently with budget cuts and other financial pressures, I have found it helpful to let the coaches know about their own budgets. Instead of just hearing "yes, you can do this or no, you can't do that," this knowledge helps them understand where the answers are coming from. This also helps to build trust with your team. Honesty and trust are important to success.

Q: How would you describe the relationship between management and leadership?
In my eyes, most people can be a manager, but not all can be a leader. A manager is usually technically strong in a particular area, while the leader is more a "big picture" person. In a career, many go through an evolution moving from a manager to a leader. Personally, I believe leadership can be learned and you can be a great leader at any level. Sports teams are a great example of leadership versus management. There are athletes who may not be the most talented, but they are the ones who can "rally" the team to do things that were never thought possible (leaders). You then have the others who are great athletes, know the game, but just cannot muster the support of the rest of the team (managers). Some leaders have charisma. Other leaders are quiet leaders who lead by example. In any leader, there is an "it" factor that managers do not have.

Q: What does it take to move an athletic department through change?
It takes listening, learning, relationship building and time. As a leader (especially new to an institution), you have to be willing to learn about the culture and listen to what has worked and has not worked. After taking some time to listen and learn, you need to be able to bring your ideas and implement them slowly. One person whom I found very valuable on campus is the Faculty Athletic Representative (FAR). She gives me a faculty perspective on athletics as well as a "somewhat insider view" of the department. I would suggest any new AD at the college level to build a strong relationship with the FAR.

(continues)

LEADERSHIP PERSPECTIVE (*continued*)

Q: How do you move people through change?
You need to bring the department through the process of change. There are a number of different theories on change, but it boils down to five steps: 1. Create an awareness that change needs to happen; 2. Create a desire for change; 3. Get the department to understand the change (give them knowledge about the change); 4. Give them the tools and coaching so they have the ability to make the change; 5. Reinforce the change. It takes time to make these changes a habit (just think of it like a new diet when trying to lose weight). Change can happen SLOWLY in many cases! Build relationships to support you on the change. At the end of my first semester on campus, I formed some department committees (strategic planning and branding were the primary ones). Before asking for volunteers, I went to a couple of people to ask for their help and support. I knew before asking them they would be on board with the committees and some of the new ideas I was bringing to the table. They have been able to help "influence" others to participate and be committed to moving forward.

▶ Key Terms

Followers	Management	Tactical goals
Human relations movement	Scientific management	Transformational leadership
Leadership	movement	Vision
Manager	Subordinates	

▶ Discussion Questions

1. Is it possible for a manager to be a good leader and a leader to also be a good manager? Explain your answer.
2. If an organization has strong leadership and weak management, what problems can this cause? If an organization has weak leadership and capable management, what issues can arise?
3. Now that you know the definitions of management and leadership, give some thought to a former or current work situation. How would you describe the quality of leadership and management? Do you see aspects of both? Neither? One or the other? Give examples.
4. Researchers Bennis and Nanus wrote, "Managers are people who do things right, and leaders are people who do the right thing." How do you interpret this statement?
5. What characteristics of the sport business environment are likely to change in the future, thus requiring effective leadership of sport organizations?

▶ References

Bass, B. M. (1985). *Leadership and performance beyond expectations.* New York: The Free Press.

Bennis, W. (1977, March-April). Where have all the leaders gone. *Technological Review,* 3–12.

Bennis, W. (2009). *On becoming a leader* (4th ed.). Philadelphia, PA: Basic Books.

Bennis, W., & Goldsmith, J. (1997). *Learning to lead: A workbook on becoming a leader.* Reading, MA: Addison-Wesley.

Bennis, W., & Nanus, B. (1985). *Leaders: Their strategies for taking charge.* New York, NY: Harper & Row.

Billsberry, J., Mueller, J., Skinner, J., Swanson, S., Corbett, B., & Ferkins, L. (2018). Reimagining leadership in sport management: Lessons from the social construction of leadership. *Journal of Sport Management, 32*(2), 170–182.

Bryman, A. (1992). *Charisma and leadership in organizations.* London: Sage.

Burns, J. M. (1978). *Leadership.* New York, NY: Harper & Row.

Chelladurai, P. (2009). *Managing organizations for sport and physical activity: A systems perspective.* Scottsdale, AZ: Holcomb Hathaway.

Conger, J. A., & Kanungo, R. N. (1994). Charismatic leadership in organizations: Perceived behavioral attributes and their measurement. *Journal of Organizational Behavior, 15*(5), 439–452.

Covey, S. R., Merrill, A. R., Merrill, R. R. (1994). *First things first.* New York, NY: Free Press.

Czarniawska-Joerges, B., & Wolff, R. (1991). Leaders, managers, entrepreneurs on and off the organizational stage. *Organization Studies, 12*(4), 529–546.

Drath, W. (2001). *The deep blue sea: Rethinking the source of leadership.* San Francisco, CA: Jossey-Bass.

DuBrin, A. J. (1995). *Leadership: Research, findings, practice, and skills.* Boston, MA: Houghton-Mifflin.

Gomez-Mejia, L. R., Balkin, D. B., & Cardy, R. L. (2005). *Management: People, performance, change.* Boston, MA: McGraw-Hill Irwin.

Hersey, P., & Blanchard, K. (1988). *Management of organizational behavior: Utilizing human resources* (5th ed.). Englewood Cliffs, NJ: Prentice-Hall.

Hollander, E. P. (1985). Leadership and power. In G. Lindzey & E. Aronson (Eds.), *Handbook of Social Psychology* (3rd ed., Vol. 2, pp. 485–537). New York, NY: Random House.

Hosking, D. M., & Morley, I. E. (1988). The skills of leadership. In J. G. Hunt, B. R. Baliga, H. P. Dachler & C. A. Schriesheim (Eds.), *Emerging leadership vistas* (pp. 89–106). Lexington, MA: Lexington Books.

Jago, A. G. (1982). Leadership: Perspectives in theory and research. *Management Science, 28*, 315–336.

Katz, D., & Kahn, R. L. (1978). *The social psychology of organizations* (2nd ed.). New York, NY: Wiley.

Kotter, J. P. (1990a). *A force for change: How leadership differs from management.* New York, NY: Free Press.

Kotter, J. P. (1990b). What leaders really do. *Harvard Business Review, 68*(3), 103–111.

Kotter, J. P. (2012, December 4). Change leadership [website]. Retrieved from http://www.kotterinternational.com/our-principles/change-leadership.

Kotterman, J. (2006). Leadership versus management: What's the difference? *Journal for Quality & Participation, 29*(2), 13–17.

Kuhn, A., & Beam, R. D. (1982). *The logic of organizations.* San Francisco, CA: Jossey-Bass.

Lakoff, R. (2000). *The language war.* Berkeley, CA: University of California Press.

Levitt, T. (1976). Management and the postindustrial society. *The Public Interest 44*(Summer), 69–103.

Macoby, M. (2000). The human side: Understanding the difference between management and leadership. *Research-Technology Management, 43*(1), 57–59.

Mangham, I., & Pye, A. (1991). *The doing of managing.* Oxford, UK: Blackwell.

McLean, J. (2005). Management and leadership. *Manager: British Journal of Administrative Management, 49*(Oct./Nov.), 16–16.

Mintzberg, H. (1973). *The nature of managerial work.* New York, NY: Harper & Row.

Northouse, P. G. (2010). *Leadership: Theory and practice.* Thousand Oaks, CA: Sage Publications.

Perloff, R. (2007). *Managing and leading: The universal importance of, and differentiation between, two essential functions.* Presented at Oxford University, July 14–15.

Robbins, S. P., Coulter, M., & Langton, N. (2006). *Management.* Toronto: Pearson-Prentice Hall.

Rost, J. C. (1993). *Leadership for the 21st century.* New York, NY: Praeger.

Schenk, C. (1928). Leadership. *Infantry Journal, 33*, 111–122.

Segal, D. R. (1981). Leadership and management: Organizational theory. In R. H. Ruch & L. J. Korb (Eds.), *Military leadership* (pp. 41–69). Beverly Hills, CA: Sage.

Selznick, P. (1957). *Leadership in administration: A sociological interpretation.* Evanston, IL: Row, Peterson.

Sergiovanni, T. J. (1984). Leadership as cultural expression. In T. J. Sergiovanni & J. E. Corbally (Eds.), *Leadership and organizational culture* (pp. 105–114). Urbana, IL: University of Illinois Press.

Springfield College (2015, January 15). Kevin McAllister on ABC 40 promoting sport management students and Hoophall. Retrieved from https://www.youtube.com/watch?v=XODI06IdyUw

Taylor, F. W. (1967). *The principles of scientific management.* New York, NY: Norton.

Toor, S.-u.-R. (2011). Differentiating leadership from management: An empirical investigation of leaders and managers. *Leadership & Management in Engineering, 11*(4), 310–320.

Toosi, N. R., & Ambady, N. (2011). Ratings of essentialism for eight religious identities. *International Journal for the Psychology of Religion, 21*(1), 17–29.

Weathersby, G. (1999). Leadership vs. management. *Management Review, 88*(3), 5.

Where basketball was invented: The history of basketball (n.d.). Retrieved from https://springfield.edu/where-basketball-was-invented-the-birthplace-of-basketball

Whitehead, J. D., & Whitehead, M. A. (1986). *The emerging laity: Returning leadership to the faith community.* Garden City, NY: Doubleday.

Yukl, G. A. (1989). Managerial leadership: A review of theory and research. *Journal of Management, 15*(2), 251.

Yukl, G. A. (2002). *Leadership in organizations* (5th ed.). Upper Saddle River, NJ: Pearson/Prentice Hall.

Zacko-Smith, D. (2007). The leader label: Influencing perceptions, reality and practice, Kravis Leadership Institute. *Leadership Review, 7*, 75–88.

Zaleznik, A. (1977). Managers and leaders: Are they different? *Harvard Business Review, 55*(3), 67–78.

Zaleznik, A. (1978). Managers and leaders: Are they different? *McKinsey Quarterly* (1), 2–22.

Zaleznik, A. (1989). *The managerial mystique: Restoring leadership in business.* New York: Harper Row.

Zimmerman, E. L. (2001). What's under the hood? The mechanics of leadership versus management. *Supervision, 62*(8), 10.

CHAPTER 4

Leadership and Motivation

John Borland

CHAPTER OBJECTIVES

- Understand how motivation and leadership interact to affect workplaces.
- Differentiate intrinsic rewards and motivation with extrinsic rewards and motivation.
- Explain the importance of master, purpose, and autonomy as it relates to motivation.
- Develop a psychographic picture of millennials and Generation Z and understand what motivates them in the workplace.

CASE STUDY

New Leadership Motivates Sales Staff

The chapter to follow on motivation focuses largely on work environment and how leaders, through their own styles, can influence these work environments to enhance motivation in each employee, understanding that not every employee can be motivated in the same way. The chapter does not examine how organizational change can affect motivation, but that variable is explored briefly here. The Springfield Thunderbirds, the American Hockey League franchise in Springfield, Massachusetts, has played their home games at the MassMutual Center since October of 2016. The Thunderbirds are an affiliate of the Florida Panthers and used to be based in Portland, Maine. Essentially, the Springfield Thunderbirds replaced the Springfield Falcons, which were sold to the Arizona Coyotes in April of 2016, moved to the southwest, and became the Tucson Roadrunners. Charlie Pompea, the owner of the Falcons, decried the lack of fans coming to games in explaining the reason for the sale of the team. In Pompea's five-plus seasons as owner, the Falcons never averaged 4,000 fans per game. They flirted with that figure during back-to-back division titles in 2013 and 2014, when the Columbus Blue Jackets provided the players. "I really wanted this to work. We needed, at the very least, an average of 4,000 fans per game. We didn't come close" (Chimelis, 2016, para. 4).

(continues)

CASE STUDY (continued)

In the first two seasons since the new franchise, the Thunderbirds, has come to town, the team has averaged 4,664 and 4,985, far exceeding Pompea's goal. This still puts them at 20th out of 30 teams in the league so the franchise has nowhere else to go but up. The San Diego Gulls led the league in attendance for the 2017–2018 season at 9,305, 53% higher than what the Thunderbirds drew (American Hockey League, 2018). A closer look at the front office staffs for each team reveals a large discrepancy between personnel dedicated to selling tickets. The Gulls have 12 people dedicated to sales; the Thunderbirds have seven. Obviously, the Gulls can afford to hire more account executives with the extra revenue that they make from selling tickets. So how does a team like the Thunderbirds go after the "big boys" when they have fewer personnel selling? Motivation. It doesn't hurt, either, to have a leader who knows how to stoke that motivational fire.

Nathan Costa was promoted to team president after the Thunderbirds' successful 2016–2017 season at the box office. Even though the Falcons and Thunderbirds are different franchises, it is still the same market. Costa knew that his front office staff would have to change their approach to attracting fans or the Thunderbirds would suffer the same fate as the Falcons. Costa's "get out in the community" hustle approach has rubbed off on his sales staff and created a work environment that has elicited employee motivation and also shines a light on the many opportunities that Falcons' leadership left on the table.

"The community involvement has been huge," Costa said. "It's been a focus for our organization from Day 1. There has been a lot of support in the marketplace the last number of years. We want to provide an experience that the fans feel good about, and I hope we are doing that. As you can see, with a lot of the stuff that we have been working on—our promotions, our themes—we are trying to give back as much as possible and provide an experience that fans love." (MassLive, 2016).

Matt McRobbie has seen the Springfield hockey organizational landscape change since he has worked for both the Falcons and Thunderbirds. "From my experience being part of a hockey team that underwent a change of ownership, the leader of the organization is the one who dictates the culture and structure of the office. The team has thrived under the new management as our team president holds each employee responsible for their department, while also giving each employee a "longer leash" to do their job. At the end of the day, it's a results-driven business, and our president trusts the employees to get the job done. The president is also more visible in the office. Being present and involved sounds simple, but it goes a long way in setting that example for employees on the level of commitment we should have" (M. McRobbie, personal communication, June 27, 2018).

McRobbie, a senior account executive for the Thunderbirds, recently received recognition for his efforts in pushing up the Thunderbirds' sales ticker. He received the Eastern Conference's award for Top New Season Ticket Sales Executive (based on full season equivalents, which track the combined sales of all ticket packages) ("T-Birds Take Home," 2018) "Matt's award and all our sales award recognition is a testament to the strength of the Thunderbirds organization and the hard work the team undertakes to make Thunderbirds games a must-see event for Springfield and the surrounding community," said Costa ("T-Birds Take Home," 2018, para. 6). For a second consecutive season, the Thunderbirds were also recognized on a team level in business growth, in three different categories. First, the franchise attained award recognition for a > 15% increase in per game full Season equivalents. The Thunderbirds also received honors with a > 15% increase in per-game group ticket revenue, as well as a > 15% growth in corporate cash sponsorships ("T-Birds Take Home," 2018).

More telling than the arithmetic, though, is the perception. No longer is declining attendance the franchise's daily headline story. A capacity crowd is no longer breaking news. No longer can fans assume that if they walk up to buy a ticket on game night, they will get a choice seat in a mostly empty building. On some nights, they may not get a seat at all (Chimelis, 2018). "We hate turning people away, but we had nine legitimate sellouts this season. Our goal had been six. In our first year (2016–2017), we had three," Costa said ("T-Birds Take Home," 2018, para. 10).

With a new MGM casino (within short walking distance to the MassMutual Center) serving as an entertainment hub to bring more people to downtown Springfield, it is likely that the Thunderbirds' attendance will go up. But if it doesn't, it won't be for lack of leadership or lack of motivation by the team's sales staff.

Questions for Discussion

1. Now that the Thunderbirds have stabilized attendance in the Springfield market, what growth strategies can the team pursue to push its attendance over 5,000 per game?
2. What kind of cross-promotion opportunities can the MGM casino and the Thunderbirds create to help one another draw customers?
3. McRobbie mentioned the importance of leader presence in an organization's culture. How else can leaders motivate employees—particularly sales staff—to be productive?
4. Minor league teams often interact with the community as a public relations move to show that it is truly part of the community. How can interacting with the community translate into higher attendance?

▶ Introduction

College students entering their senior year can see the light at the end of the tunnel. Graduation. Freedom. No more exams. No more irritating comments from professors to read on their written work. Having logged more than 1,600 hours in the classroom over their first three and a half years of college (roughly 105 academic credits) and spending another approximately 4,800 hours (assuming three hours per hour of class time) doing schoolwork and studying takes its toll. This toll can manifest itself into a mysterious disease known as "senioritis," which afflicts many final-semester students. This affliction is unfortunate because students often need to muster their greatest motivation at the end of their college career since they need to spend considerable time either applying for internships or getting that first job. But students can struggle to find the motivation to do quality work up until that final hour of that last exam. Somehow, they get through it and look forward to the next chapter of their lives. They may not be aware that motivation will play an even bigger part of their everyday satisfaction as

their real-world employment supplants their classwork, and their job consumes up to 60% or more of their waking hours. The phenomenon of wavering motivation that they experienced as students also exists in the workplace, but it can be more volatile, and there is much more at stake. The following chapter has been included in this textbook to help members of Generation Z studying sport management to understand how leadership in the workplace can impact employees' motivation to perform their jobs at a high quality consistently. The chapter begins by defining motivation and then moves on to discuss how workplace rewards affect the motivation of employees. Next, a discussion of the importance of autonomy, mastery, and purpose and their link to intrinsic motivation is included. The influence of leadership style and how it affects the motivation of employees then follows. Any chapter on leadership and motivation would be remiss in not addressing what personal characteristics motivate individuals to pursue leadership positions. The chapter then takes a close look at the psychographics of both millennials and Generation Z and what organizational leaders should do to motivate them in the workplace. This is not to say that Generation X and Baby Boomers are not important to motivate, but the focus of 21st century work is squarely on millennials and Generation Z. The newest millennials are now in the workforce and the oldest millennials are taking on leadership roles. Members of Generation Z are poised to enter the workplace. The chapter is sprinkled with comments from millennials who now work for sport organizations; they explain what motivates them and how leadership influences motivation. Although opinions vary as to when each generation starts and ends, it is generally accepted that millennials were born between 1978 and 1994 and Generation Z began in 1996 (Montana & Petit, 2008). Because college-graduated members of Generation Z have just started entering the professional workplace, there is little research yet to share on what motivates them. The chapter includes discussion of how to motivate volunteers since sport organizations can be heavily reliant on them. Volunteering is a good place for Generation Z to focus their efforts while in school in order to build their resumes.

▶ Motivation

Motivation is a collection of factors internal and external to oneself that determines the direction and sustainability of a person's behavior, a person's level of effort, and the level of persistence (Nguyen, Mujtaba, & Ruijs 2014). Motivation is considered to be one of the strongest psychographic variables affecting behavior as it is a personal inner state that directly satisfies a felt need and triggers a behavioral intention (Park & Yoon, 2009). In the workplace, motivation directly affects the quality of the experience an employee/follower has within an organization and with its leadership. Job satisfaction, perceived equity, task visibility, and organizational commitment are key factors to make followers' experiences positive (Gilley, Dixon & Gilley, 2008) and, thus, motivate them. Because sport leaders can influence

these factors, they are in a position to persuade and influence others to work in a common direction. Although an organization's leader can affect an employee's motivation—and we will explain how later in the chapter— research has also looked inward, at the individual, to tap into why employees are motivated or not.

But what motivates individuals? Herein lies the difficulty for leaders: It is different for everyone, says Gary Nevolis, the director of corporate partnerships for the Jacksonville Jumbo Shrimp:

> "The tricky part is finding out what motivates each and every employee. Some will be much easier to figure out than others. Most employees will be a mix of growth, time off and money. And some employees, well, they may not know what motivates themselves. I have found communication, openness and a judgment-free environment leads to motivated employees." (G. Nevolis, personal communication, June 20, 2018)

Despite the psychographics of the different generations, people are still going to be motivated by different things. Nevolis helps us to begin to think about motivation by focusing on three factors that motivate individuals. He is also sharing that one leadership style may not work with every individual since different generations are living at different points of the life cycle. There are considerations internal to each person, which may be difficult to determine, as Nevolis attests. He mentions growth, which is important given its connection to the research about **self-actualization**. According to prominent psychologists Carl Rogers, Erich Fromm, Abraham Maslow, and Gordon Allport, striving for self-actualization and personal growth can be a central motivator in a person's life (Jahoda, 1958). Self-actualization refers to a feeling of continuous personal development and realizing one's potential. Maslow thought this feeling could be carried over to work and an organization could fill a need in an individual's life and not just the other way around. An organization that simply sets goals "with the company in mind" fails to see the opportunity to develop human beings. Personal goals for employees must be conceptualized as well. People with a high need for goal internalization likely focus on their personal value system, which would lead to persistence in achieving goals. Self-actualization sits atop Maslow's Hierarchy of Needs, above physiological needs (air, water, sleep); safety needs (personal security, employment); love and belonging (friendship, family, intimacy); and esteem (respect, self-esteem, status). In layman's terms, self-actualization means "to be all that one can be" (Maslow, 1954). For example, if a sport management graduate has a goal of running her own indoor sport facility for training youth in sports such as lacrosse and soccer, she has to be persistent and realize self-actualization is a long process and will not happen overnight. In addition to persistence, an important active work concept is "personal initiative." Frese, Kring, Soose, and Zempel (1996) defined **personal initiative** as a collection of behaviors with the following attributes: Consistent with the organization's mission, a long-term focus, goal-directed and action-oriented, persistent in the face of barriers and setbacks, and self-starting and proactive. Successful employees are motivated to behave proactively or "make things happen." Job advertisements sometimes use the phrase 'looking for a self-starter.' Organizations look for workers who do not have to be given detailed instructions about how to complete work; they seek employees who recognize problems early on and work to solve them with little guidance. They want employees who can set goals for themselves to make the supervisory evaluation process substantive and employee-focused. Finally, organizations covet employees who welcome challenges. In other words, workers who are motivated are most desired. There has been a growing recognition of the role that employees play in actively shaping and influencing their work environment. Employees can set goals for themselves and create their own rewards

(Crant, 2000; Frese & Fay, 2001; Grant & Ashford, 2008). Many entry-level jobs in the sport industry focus on selling tickets. Account executives are expected to make a certain number of calls per day and spend a certain number of hours per week meeting with sales targets. If a new sales executive does the minimum expectation of calls and contact hours, it cannot be said that he is acting proactively, showing much personal initiative, or creating his own rewards. But going beyond the minimum expectation shows a concerted effort to set challenging goals. James Warner, who works as sales manager for the Hartford Wolf Pack of the American Hockey League, says that motivation can wane in the offseason, and that is when an employee's personal initiative and proactivity can take a beating (J. Warner, personal communication, June 14, 2018). This illustrates a uniqueness to working for a professional sports team: There is often an off-season period and an in-season period. Employees, particularly account executives, can log so many hours during the season that it is only natural for them to perceive the off-season as more of a time to use vacation time and recharge one's batteries.

Rewards Expectancy

Rewards are the fruits of labor that individuals receive for doing the work of the organization (Taylor, Doherty, & McGraw, 2015). Many organizations function as meritocracies where employees receive rewards for hard work that produces results. In the sport industry, many of these results are quantifiable and can be measured through things such as tickets sold, sponsorships signed, social media followers collected, and new revenue earned from effective PR and marketing campaigns. Porter and Lawler (1968) conceived of a motivation model— **FIGURE 4.1**—that ties effort and performance to the expectancy of receiving a reward. Their model shows the complexities of motivation. Chelladurai (2006) provides an interpretation of the model: 1. A person's motivational state can be discerned by the amount of effort put forth. 2. The amount of effort put forth is related to

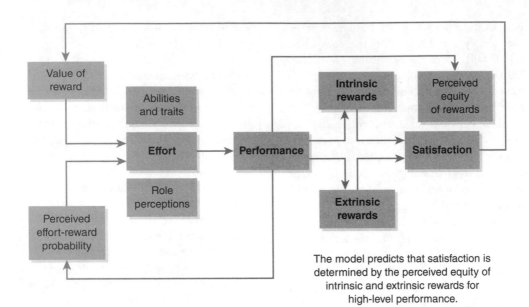

The model predicts that satisfaction is determined by the perceived equity of intrinsic and extrinsic rewards for high-level performance.

FIGURE 4.1 Porter and Lawler's model of motivation.

the expectancy that a reward will be received. This expectancy variable is the crux of motivation. Porter and Lawler's model refers to this as perceived effort-reward probability. Chelladurai (2006) sums it up: "Effort or motivation is maximized when an individual places high value on the rewards available through participation in the organization and activities, and when that person also believes that his or her efforts will lead to the desired rewards" (p. 103).

Porter and Lawler's model also highlights abilities, traits, and role perceptions. The researchers realized that effort was not enough to ensure a good performance. Employees need to possess the necessary skills to perform the work. If a person is hired to sell group tickets, he or she has to understand that selling for groups is very different from selling for season-ticket holders. A different set of skills is needed to be successful. In addition, employees must have a complete understanding of what activities are necessary to perform the job and how they should do them (Chelladurai, 2006). This is role perception. If a person does not fully understand his or her role or is constantly put into a position in which his or her skillsets do not match

what they are being asked to do, their motivation can be adversely affected. An organization's available rewards impact motivation as well. A glimpse of these rewards starts in the interview process when a prospective employee finds out how an organization values its employees. Bonuses, vacation time, and health benefits are all things that might be discussed, but that is only a small sample. **Extrinsic rewards** can be both financial and non-financial and are geared more toward materialism than are **intrinsic rewards**, which encompass recognition and self-achievement. Taylor et al. (2015) list extrinsic rewards as salary, bonuses, cost-of-living raises, health benefits, life insurance, paid vacation, complimentary tickets to sporting events, complimentary sports merchandise, a company car, and travel reimbursement. Warner of the Wolfpack says leadership uses extrinsic rewards to encourage account executives to stay motivated in the off-season:

"A few things I have seen here is giving them (account executives) revenue for call- and email activity incentives to achieve in order to get out early during the off-season. This is primarily because the hockey business does slow down at the end of the season and employees tend to lose their motivation or focus heading into the upcoming season. These incentives are typically given out monthly or weekly as well. From my experience with this structure, it truly has motivated me to achieve the numbers that are given by our director so I can be rewarded for my motivation and hard work." (J. Warner, personal communication, June 14, 2018)

Intrinsic rewards include a sense of achievement, a feeling of competency, or an internal observation of personal growth. People who gravitate toward intrinsic rewards are said to have **intrinsic motivation** while others who would rather be rewarded materially are said to have **extrinsic motivation**. It is likely that most people possess both types of motivation to varying degrees. Intrinsic motivation refers to a desire to perform a work task for its own sake rather than for extrinsic rewards (Alge, Ballinger, Tangirala, & Oakley, 2006). Intrinsic motivation is one of the most important factors affecting employee creativity (Amabile, Schatzel, Moneta, & Kramer, 2004). Employees with a high level of intrinsic motivation are more likely to be creative at work because they are fascinated with the task itself (Zhang & Bartol, 2010). In contrast, employees with a low level of intrinsic motivation are less likely to expend effort based on their interest in work. They may not become actively involved in creative work. Another component of Porter and Lawler's model that is crucial, particularly given the current focus on gender equity in the workplace, is perceived equitable rewards. If an employee perceives that he or she is being rewarded or treated differently for doing the same work, it can affect motivation. Furthermore, if an employee thinks he is doing more work or better work than some of his other colleagues and not reaping more rewards, this can affect motivation and, ultimately, satisfaction, the final stop on Porter and Lawler's model.

Returning to the earlier point about how everyone is motivated differently, it is important for leaders to realize that external rewards such as pay, vacation, and job promotions are not going to motivate and satisfy everyone. The carrot-and-stick approach to leadership has been discussed earlier in the text. Carrot-and-stick leadership is based on extrinsic motivation—if the follower does what the leader wants, he or she reaps an external benefit such as higher pay, more vacation, or a job promotion. This is the "carrot" that is dangled in front of him or her. If the follower does not fulfill a leader's request, he or she gets the "stick" in the form of some sort of punishment, whether it is lower pay, being fired, or a "chewing out" session. Daniel Pink's *Drive* (2011) refers to this leadership as Type X behavior, based on McGregor's work (McGregor, 1985). But, as Ryan and Deci (2000) learned, human beings have an inner drive to be autonomous, self-determined, and connected to one another. This is Type I behavior. Type I, in contrast to Type X, suggests that followers are less concerned with external rewards that a work activity can provide than with the inherent satisfaction of the activity itself (Pink, 2011). Furthermore, Pink (2011) reported that leaders who wanted to tap into intrinsic motivation should provide conditions that allow for autonomy, mastery, and purpose in their organizations.

Autonomy, Mastery, and Purpose

It is hard to believe that any employee would avoid **autonomy**—the ability to act with choice—in the workplace. The opportunity to work in an environment that is trusting and supportive, where new ideas are encouraged, criticisms are accepted positively, and information flows transparently sounds like a motivational dream come true. Unfortunately, that is not always the reality as workplaces are both autonomous and controlling and several shades between.

Self-determination theory (SDT) (Deci & Ryan, 2000) provides a comprehensive framework to understand the relationship between perceived job characteristics—autonomy being one of them—and employee motivation. An important distinction is made concerning the nature of motivation: Not only do people invest in an activity to varied degrees—a quantifiable aspect—but they also do so for various reasons—a qualitative aspect. Specifically, two broad forms of motivation—autonomous and controlled—capture the underlying reasons (motives) for performing a job (see Deci & Ryan, 2000; Gagné & Deci, 2005, for reviews). Ultimately, self-determination theory reveals the distinction between autonomous motivation and nonautonomous motivation (Gagne & Deci, 2005). **Autonomous motivation** occurs when people engage in an activity because they find it interesting, enjoyable, or rewarding, as well as when they perform the activity voluntarily. Autonomous motivation refers to acting with volition, as when employees engage in their job for the inherent pleasure and satisfaction (intrinsic motivation) and/or because they personally endorse the importance or value of a task. **Nonautonomous motivation** or **controlled motivation** involves acting under a sense of pressure, with a sense of having to engage in an activity in spite of one's desires, or performing an activity for instrumental reasons, such as pay and recognition. SDT-based research underscores the importance of considering the different forms of motivation as they are differentially associated with affective, attitudinal, and behavioral outcomes (Gagné & Deci, 2005). Autonomous motivation has been positively associated with psychological well-being, job satisfaction, work engagement, and occupational commitment, whereas controlled motivation has been positively associated with negative consequences for employees, including workaholism, burnout, and turnover intention (Fernet, 2013).

Pink (2011) notes in *Drive* that while complying (controlled environment) can be an effective strategy for physical survival, it is a poor one for personal fulfillment. It could be argued that young people, through the educational system they were raised in, are taught to adhere to a certain standard and then a reward will be given in the form of a grade. Sometimes, the classroom emphasizes performance goals over learning goals. It is hard to dispute this given the emphasis on standardized testing and GPAs. The college classroom is meant to be less compliant, providing a safe space for learners to think through their burgeoning ideas. Pink concluded that we enter the world ready to be active and self-engaged. He expresses his worry that work environments are not giving employees a long enough leash to be curious and engaged. He has a message for leaders of 21st century organizations:

> "… economic accomplishment, not to mention personal fulfillment, more often swings on a different hinge. It depends not on keeping our nature submerged but on allowing it to surface. It requires resisting the temptation to control people—and instead doing everything we can to reawaken their deep-seated sense of autonomy." (2011, p. 89)

Mastery is the second component to Pink's engagement equation. Mastery is the opportunity to become better at something that matters. That opportunity needs to be afforded by organizational leaders through an organization's governance structure and overall culture, but it also needs to be understood and grasped by employees. According to Pink, there are three tenets of mastery: Mastery is a mindset; mastery is a pain; and mastery is an asymptote. Mastery as a mindset assumes that our intelligence can grow, much like building a muscle. In other words, we can continue to learn more and more about how to do our jobs better as long as we work in a supportive environment and, personally, we have the mindset to actually seek out new knowledge and "perform" the learning. But not everyone is in a supportive work environment or they might possess what is called a **fixed mindset** rather than a **growth mindset**. These phrases were coined by Carol Dweck (2007), a psychology professor at Stanford University. Employees with a growth mindset consistently demonstrate a motivation to learn more. Employees with fixed mindsets are motivated to simply get the job done and give little thought to how they can get better at a certain task or job. There is no hunting for new knowledge; there is no challenging oneself. Professional athletes often reinvent themselves after struggles or a slump or having to change their approach following an injury. Often, this "reinvention" takes place after coming across a bit of newfound knowledge from a coach, mentor, fellow athlete, or even a physician. The newfound knowledge is not the key finding here; it is the fact that the athlete sought out new knowledge to continue trying to master their sport. In sport organizations large and small, the best employees are the ones who continue to learn by growing their intelligence, which improves the organization's goal achievement and helps employees move toward self-actualization. The second law of mastery—mastery is a pain—argues that if employees want to achieve something substantial, they need to put in the work. Staying motivated to master something that matters or reach a personal work goal is **grit**, a relatively new concept on the research landscape. Grit is finding the consistent motivation to keep pursuing a long-term goal in the face of all of the peaks and valleys (Duckworth, Peterson, Matthews, & Kelly, 2007). Angela Duckworth, who has pioneered research on grit, says, "I'd bet that there isn't a single highly successful person who hasn't depended on grit. Nobody is talented enough to not have to work hard, and that's what grit allows you to do" (Lehrer, 2009, para. 7). Duckworth has also used the word "passion" as an ingredient of grit. For someone to be "gritty," he or she has to find something that he or she truly cares about

achieving. Once he or she finds that, it is much easier to stay motivated. The final law about mastery is mastery is an asymptote. An asymptote is a combination of a curve and a line on a graph that never quite come together; the curve comes closer and closer to the line but never quite gets there. That is how mastery is. You will never quite master anything. You can *always* strive to get better, and that hunger to get better drives motivation.

Pink's third building block of intrinsic motivation, **purpose**, involves people working in the service of something larger than themselves. PeacePlayers International, a conflict resolution nonprofit that uses basketball to bring groups of youth together in Northern Ireland, Cyprus, the Middle East, and South Africa, is an example of an organization pursuing and achieving a great purpose. Brothers Brendan and Sean Tuohey started the organization in 2001, motivated to use basketball to bring together diverse groups as they had seen done in their own diverse, Washington D.C.-area neighborhood. The Tuoheys' story was built on motivation. In their early 20s, they wrote letters to everyone they knew looking for contributions, raising about $7,000, which Sean used to start an effort in South Africa. "I don't know that anybody could have done what he did in terms of his ability to go to a country and build this—knock on doors, hire coaches, build trust," Brendan said. "He didn't fear much. He lived there for three years. Sean was great being the face and inspiration, while I helped build the organization" (Madkour, 2018, para. 7). But the organization struggled financially—as many nonprofits do—until it received a $100,000 grant in 2004. The organization now has a $5 million operating budget and a partnership with Nike that aims to use sport to improve relations between youth and police in some inner cities (2018).

Only a small percentage of sport industry employees work for nonprofits with a great purpose like PeacePlayers International. So, can employees who work at for-profit organizations work with the same great purpose?

Gallup published its *State of the American Workplace* report in 2017, and it had this to say about purpose:

> Most workers, many of whom are millennials, approach a role and a company with a highly defined set of expectations. They want their work to have meaning and purpose. They want to use their talents and strengths to do what they do best every day. They want to learn and develop. They want their job to fit their life. (p. 5)

In sport organizations, many employees work with the greater purpose of making experiences memorable for customers. Many employees in sales and marketing are dedicated to making sure customers who come to their arenas, stadia, or events have the best possible experience. Part of this is about retaining that customer for future business, but many employees truly want customers to enjoy themselves. Creating this memorable experience motivates a salesperson to go into the stands and shake hands with a particular customer and see if she and her family are enjoying the game. It takes leaders to create the type of organizational culture needed for employees to care deeply about the customer experience.

▶ Leadership That Motivates

As you learned in Chapter 3, leadership involves an influence relationship between leader and follower. This influence can be both positive and negative. Leadership effectiveness is critically contingent on, and often defined in terms of, leaders' ability to motivate followers toward collective goals or a collective mission or vision (Shamir, Zakay, Breinin, & Popper, 1998). Relationships between the leader and the followers are important because these have perceptual, motivational, attitudinal, and behavioral consequences for each party. The leader-follower relationship reveals itself through a worker's social interactions with his or her supervisor and is commonly expressed as **leader-member exchange** (LMX) quality. LMX quality refers to the worth of a relationship between leader and follower. Research has shown that high-level LMX exchanges result in elevated levels of mutual trust, respect, loyalty, and obligation among the two parties (Gerstner & Day, 1997; Graen & Uhl-Bien, 1995; Ilies, Nahrgang, & Morgeson, 2007; Sias, 2005).

Several millennials were contacted for this chapter and asked specifically about leadership in their organizations and how it connects with their motivation. Eric Podbielski, an account executive at Madison Square Garden, confirms the importance of trust in the LMX exchange:

> So far in my career, I've found a few qualities in great leaders that have stuck with me and inspired me to work hard for them. Leaders who empower me to do my work and trust that I can do it correctly, rather than micromanage and tell me my every move, are my favorite. It is better to have a leader who is open to having you make mistakes and learn from it rather than tell you what to do every second of the day so you don't make a mistake. (E. Podbielski, personal communication, June 13, 2018)

Empirical evidence has consistently supported positive results emanating from high-quality LMX relationships: Leaders show influence and support beyond that specified in formal job descriptions, and the followers are given more autonomy and responsibility, thereby shaping employees' work attitudes and behaviors such as overall job satisfaction, organization commitment, well-being, task performance, organizational citizen behavior, role conflict, role clarity, and turnover intention (Gerstner & Day, 1997; Ilies, et al., 2007; Wayne, Shore, Bommer, & Tetrick, 2002). Podbielski's comments provide support for millennials who prefer autonomy and responsibility. Matt Delmonte, who works for the event and facilities staff in athletics at the University of Massachusetts-Lowell, endorsed the importance of trust and how it can lead to more responsibility: "When I get handed more responsibilities, it makes me feel like they appreciate the work that I have currently put in and they trust me to complete more difficult tasks and in an ideal work world, it eventually leads to a promotion" (M. Delmonte, personal communication, June 26, 2018).

Leadership style impacts interpersonal relations, rewards, and punishments, which shape employee behavior, motivation, and attitude; this can impact an organization's performance (Puni, Ofei, & Okoe, 2014). It can either lead to inspiration or disenchantment among employees resulting in increased or decreased productivity (Kahn & Katz, 1952). The style of leadership impacts LMX quality as some of the millennials interviewed for this topic confirmed. Ryan Coburn, director of partnership services at Spartan Race, Inc., says that it is important to see leaders sweating right along with their followers:

> Simply put, a leader's display of effort and attitude are the reason their employees are driven to keep pace. The level of effort and the type of attitude ultimately dictate what that pace is. It's certainly not the most leisurely or easily sustainable tactic to execute from a leadership position, but in my experience, it is my motivation for quality output from the top down, and what I anticipate is the reason for quality output among my employees. (R. Coburn, personal communication, June 22, 2018).

Delmonte of UMass-Lowell also highlighted the importance of a leader's work ethic: "When I see my boss coming in early or staying late just to complete a task, it motivates me to work even harder and assist in any way possible" (M. Delmonte, personal communication, June 26, 2018).

But leaders need to know when to keep the mood light as well. Nate Weissman, who works as an assistant director of stadium operations for the Midland (TX) Rock Hounds (AA affiliate of the Oakland Athletics), said the work culture of minor league baseball dictates a more upbeat, fun environment:

> Leaders can best motivate employees by keeping the mood light yet making sure everybody involved is working towards the same goal as well as making sure everybody is valued. Our GM does a great job motivating us because he jokes around with us yet we are constantly reminded what we are working towards and it genuinely seems like he values everybody's work because he talks with people regularly …. (N. Weissman, personal communication, June 14, 2018).

When supervisors are supportive, they show concern for employees' feelings, provide nonjudgmental, informational feedback about their work, and encourage them to voice their own concerns (Deci, Connell & Ryan, 1989). By contrast, controlling supervisors closely monitor employee behavior, make decisions without involving employees, and generally demand that employees follow strict rules and guidelines (Deci et al., 1989). Looking at supportive versus controlling styles of leadership, it should not be hard to discern which is more motivating for the 21st century employee. Many of the millennials queried for this chapter confirmed the importance of supportive leadership styles as a source of empowerment.

Empowerment Motivates

This text has dedicated a lot of space already to breaking down different leadership styles.

The word that comes up often in the research literature on leadership styles that best motivate is "**empowerment**." Empowering leadership, whether it is termed transformational, servant, or authentic, motivates employees to achieve organizational goals that exceed their individual interests (Bass, 1985).

Empowering leadership is also a leadership style that aims to transform followers into their own self-leaders (Pearce & Sims, 2002). It emphasizes the development of follower self-management skills (Pearce & Sims, 2002) by prompting followers to develop self-control and act on their own (Vecchio, Justin & Pearce, 2010). This style is concerned with leaders' actions in sharing power or giving more responsibility and autonomy to subordinates (Srivastava, Bartol & Locke, 2006). Some representative behaviors of empowering leadership include encouraging independent action, opportunity thinking instead of performance thinking, thinking of obstacles as opportunities to challenge oneself, self-development, and the use of participative goal-setting (Pearce & Sims, 2002). As such, the roles of empowering leaders are to assist subordinates to become their own self-leaders, roles which are different from those in more traditional organizational designs. Further, empowering leadership involves providing decision-making autonomy, expressing confidence in employees' abilities, and removing constraints to performance (Ahearne, Mathieu, & Rapp, 2005). These factors are vital conditions for creative outcomes (Amabile, Schatzel, Moneta, & Kramer, 2004); thus, leaders' empowering behavior can encourage employees to think beyond their comfort zone and to explore new and creative alternatives.

Feelings of confidence from leaders, mentioned above, can be empowering as Elise Brogan, Global Social Media Community Manager at Reebok, notes:

> Leaders in sports organizations can structure their leadership to motivate employees by establishing a foundation of trust, communication, and empowerment. The more confidence you feel generated from the top down, the more you are willing to take risks

and complete quality work within your role. Also, by feeling trusted and empowered, employees will be happier in the workplace and, therefore, will want to be a better employee for their manager and company as a whole (E. Brogan, personal communication, June 14, 2018).

Employees also feel empowered when leaders notice their efforts. Jason Mlodzianowski, an associate director of events, facilities and operations at Carnegie Mellon University in Pittsburgh, says that it is important for leaders to keep track of the progress employees are making in accomplishing both the organization's goals and their personal goals and *then* acknowledge that this goal-accomplishment has taken place:

> Checking in and tracking on these goals periodically to evaluate performance and provide feedback keeps employees engaged and connected in a way that rah-rah/inspiring speeches cannot. If you are not plugged into the motivations behind your direct reports' work, a disconnect develops, which can lead to inconsistent work during periods of increased workload and stress (J. Mlodzianowski, personal communication, June 14, 2018).

Mlodzianowski is referring to the importance of task visibility in his advice to leaders. Task visibility is employees' belief that what they do at work is noticed by others such as their leaders (Liden, Wayne, Jaworski, & Bennett, 2004). Low task visibility means employees' tasks are not noticeably observed by their leaders; this is likely to result in employees being less motivated to put in extra effort. Conversely, when employees' perception of task visibility is high, they believe leaders notice their work and are motivated to exert high effort (Vroom, 1964). Thus, employees may respond more to empowering leadership when task visibility is high. Individuals' motivation is likely to increase as their perceptions of the relationship between performance and outcomes becomes more positive.

The importance of empowering leadership cannot be understated. Not only does it garner intrinsic motivation among followers, it teaches those followers how to become leaders by modeling leadership's best practices. Shannon Lahiff, a customer support specialist at ISlide, has found someone to model in Peter Roby, featured in Chapter 6 of this textbook. Lahiff heard Roby speak as part of a speaker series and, "he said something that really stuck with me. He said it is important for leaders to *live their values* .... I want to work for someone who respects me and what I bring to the company while also working just as hard as I am" (S. Lahiff, personal communication, June 20, 2018). This is what motivates Lahiff: When she sees someone working just as hard despite having the leadership title, it compels her to want to achieve for that person.

Motivating Millennials

The birth years defining the millennial generation are not precise but correspond to the end of the 1970s through the middle of the 1990s (Levenson, 2010). This means that **millennials** have already entered the workplace in droves—and they are becoming leaders, too. This generation entered the professional workplace starting in the early 2000s. Although it is a danger to make sweeping generalizations about a group of people conceivably born almost 18 years apart, Gallup's *State of the American Workplace* study provides insight into millennials' work motivations. The research organization concluded that millennials want their work to have meaning and purpose and approach a role and organization with their expectations highly defined (Gallup, 2017). And if they cannot find an organization that fits their values, millennials have no problem looking elsewhere for work.

Another Gallup report, *How Millennials Want to Work and Live*, represented a wide-reaching research effort. Gallup gathered data from a variety of sources, including the Gallup Panel, Gallup Daily tracker, Gallup-Healthways Well-Being Index, and Gallup's employee and customer engagement databases. The report presents many key findings with implications for motivation. Millennials have the highest rates of unemployment and underemployment in the U.S., and only 29% of employed millennials are engaged at work. The report notes that this lack of engagement is concerning because if people are not engaged at work, companies' profitability, productivity, and innovation will suffer. The Gallup report also reveals that 21% of millennials report changing jobs within the last year, which is more than three times the number of non-millennials who report the same. Gallup estimates that millennial turnover costs the U.S. economy $30.5 billion annually. Forty-four percent of millennials who report that their manager holds regular meetings with them are engaged, while only 20% of millennials who do not meet regularly with their manager are engaged at work (Gallup, 2016). Millennials crave close relationships with their supervisors. Millennials have been encouraged to have, and continue to maintain, similarly close relationships with parents, teachers, mentors, and advisors. As a result, they are much more likely than Gen Xers to want their supervisors to take an interest in them (2016).

This chapter has shared the thoughts of millennials who work in sport organizations regarding motivation and leadership. They speak to the importance of leaders rowing the boat right along with the lower-level employees. This shows millennials' penchant for flatter organizational structures with more frequent communication with an organization's leaders. It is, therefore, not surprising that organizational tensions may occur when new hires circumvent the system and go immediately to the top to vent their frustration, vet their ideas, and build relationships. On the other hand, organizational structures not only provide accountability but also protection for more senior managers so that they are free to focus on higher-level issues.

One proactive approach is to build occasional opportunities for hierarchy-skipping interactions into the system. In doing so, it is possible to emphasize the chain of command, proper protocol, and the process for bringing ideas forward, while providing an approved forum for millennials to reach up through less formal interactions like town hall meetings. Another means of creating an appropriate vehicle for millennials to interact with higher levels of the organization is through mentoring programs. These relationships have been proven effective at socializing employees, enhancing career paths, and building institutional networks for every generation, but millennials are the first population to have been fully immersed in mentoring programs throughout their lives, starting with "big buddy" programs in elementary school.

As the youngest generation fully in the workplace, millennials are more invested in development than are employees who are perhaps closer to retirement or who may have already obtained their career goals. Organizations should ensure that their attraction and retention strategies highlight and deliver on learning opportunities, career pathing, and performance management standards. (Gallup, 2017). In *How Millennials Want to Work and Live*, Gallup (2016) reported that 87% of this generation rate "professional or career growth and development opportunities" are important to them in a job. However, only 39% strongly agree that they have learned something new in the past 30 days that they can use to do their job better.

Some portrayals of millennials have been less than flattering. The generation has been described as "needy" or "high maintenance." Managers of all generations may find the millennials' need for structure and reassurance draining. As "trophy kids" who spent their childhood receiving gold stars and shiny medals just for showing up, millennials were indoctrinated from their earliest moment to seek approval and affirmation. In the workplace, this has led to a sometimes excessive propensity to continually seek guidance and direction. Managers, therefore, often find themselves in the unenviable position of having to spend a disproportionate amount of time managing people who were presumably hired to help them (Hershatter & Epstein, 2010).

Generation Z

There is little research on Gen Z—born between the mid-1990s and early-2000s: 1996 to 2010—in the workplace since many of its members are just entering the workplace or are still in high school or college. However, it is not too early to discuss what might motivate this group. It is something leaders should already be considering. The norms of Gen Z are different from that of millennials. Since Gen Z was born into the world of technology, it is primarily important for them to be a part of a technology-rich environment. They are always online on any number of technical devices. Other forms of socialization are difficult for them. Compared with millennials, Gen Z is more impatient and more agile than their predecessors, and they look for new challenges and impulses continually. To solve problems, they try to find the solutions on the Internet (Tari, 2011).

Employers must learn that Gen Z wants to choose a career of their own interest, not because they want to meet someone else's demands. The result of this behavior is an intrinsic motivation; they have a tough enterprising spirit and they want to influence the world. So, these characteristics speak to both autonomy and purpose. At the same time, their most important career goals are work-life balance and workplace stability. Gen Z is not as optimistic as their predecessors were from the viewpoint of the workplace. They worry about unemployment, or if they will get stuck in their careers and cannot develop their talent (Bencsik, Horváth-Csikós, & Timea, 2016). This idea of not being able to "develop their talent" shows a similarity to millennials and a need for development.

Universum, a global employer branding company, surveys over 1.5 million students each year to gather insights meant to help employers understand how to identify, gather, and retain a young, talented workforce. In its 2015 report, *Generation Z Grows Up*, 50,000 high-school graduates in 46 countries were asked about their future careers, the necessity of higher education, and their attitudes about work and life (Universum, 2015). Since members of Gen Z are digital natives, they will be in demand for organizations that use digital means to innovate.

The survey asked students whether they would consider joining the workforce before attending college. While only 15 percent accepted the idea outright, 47 percent said that they would consider it. Sixty percent said they welcome information about how companies offer education to those with no university degree. What drives these attitudes? In some countries—including the United States—Gen Z is spooked by massive student loan debts saddling millennials. Other key findings from the Universum research: 1. Fifty-five percent of those polled said that they are interested in starting their own businesses since it gives them more control over their financial destiny but also there is a greater potential for them to make an impact on society; 2. Gen Z, despite being digital natives, want to be contacted about jobs through more personal forms of communication and not through seeing job advertisements on social media; and 3. About 37 percent of those polled worry that they will not find a job that fits their personality (Universum, 2015).

Sparks and Honey, a New York advertising agency that spots trends to help companies target groups of consumers, surveyed 1,000 13- to 17-year-olds in the U.S. about the future of work, money, technology, and education (Peterson, 2014). Hayley Peterson, reporting for *Business Insider*, highlighted some key findings, which include Gen Z's desire to change the world, a drop in affection for advanced college degrees from how millennials feel, their entrepreneurial spirit, their desire to work on multiple screens at once (digital over-connectedness), and their preference for working independently rather than in groups. The entrepreneurial spirit has much to do with The Great Recession and a distrust for large companies. Ultimately, Universum and Sparks & Honey had similar findings. What do these characteristics mean for leaders? If leaders are to connect with Gen Z, they need to communicate more frequently and in shorter bursts since Gen Z members have short attention spans; they need to tap into their entrepreneurial spirit; understand their need to fight for social causes; help them master something since they want to become experts; and feed their curiosity (Sparks and Honey, 2015). The onus is not just on the leaders, however. Members of Gen Z have to exhibit grit by working hard to gain professional experience before they enter the workplace. Furthermore, they need to learn how to critically think through problems and not simply turn to the Internet to find answers. Finally, Gen Zers must work on their ability to concentrate and not succumb to the short, fragmented attention spans that the digital age has imprinted on them.

▶ Motivation to Become a Leader

What motivates someone to emerge as a leader? Researchers have found a variety of factors, such as certain personality traits, self-efficacy, early leadership opportunities, a feeling of collectivism, and a duty to serve, just to name a few. According to Chan and Drasgow (2001), a potential leader with a **motivation to lead (MTL)** falls under three categories: affective-identity, noncalculative, and social-normative. Affective-identity simply means that a person likes to lead others. It feels like a natural action for them. These people are typically extraverted, display vertical individualism (the acceptance that inequality exists among individuals), possess leadership self-efficacy, and have past leadership experiences. A noncalculative MTL is characterized by agreeableness, emotional stability, and collectivist values. If someone possesses collectivist values, it means that they seek out collective harmony and equality in the workplace and are willing to subordinate their goals to those of the majority. Finally, a social-normative MTL perspective consists of individuals who feel a sense of social duty and obligation to lead. These individuals also tend to have past leadership experience and are confident in their leadership abilities. Also, personality, sociocultural values, leadership self-efficacy, and past leadership experiences are predictors of MTL (2001).

The Big Five personality traits of **neuroticism, extraversion, openness to experience, agreeableness**, and **conscientiousness** have been used to predict emergent leaders (Judge, Bono, Ilies, & Gerhardt, 2002). Neuroticism represents the tendency to exhibit poor emotional adjustment, which leads to feelings of anxiety, insecurity, and hostility. Extraversion describes people who are sociable, assertive, active, and energetic. Openness to experience is the disposition to be imaginative, nonconforming, unconventional, and autonomous. Agreeableness is the tendency to be trusting, compliant, caring, and gentle. Finally, conscientiousness is composed of two related facets: achievement and dependability (2002).

Bass (1990) indicated that almost all studies on the relationship of self-confidence—indicating low neuroticism—to leadership "were uniform in the positive direction of their findings" (p. 69). Evidence also indicates that neurotic individuals are less likely to be perceived as leaders (Hogan, Curphy, & Hogan, 1994). In light of this evidence, we would not expect neurotic individuals to emerge as leaders and if they did, they would not be effective. Extraversion provides a contrast to neuroticism. Hogan et al. (1994) noted that extraversion is related to being perceived as leader-like. Extraverts tend to be energetic, lively people. Adjectives used to describe individuals who emerged as leaders in leaderless

group discussions included active, assertive, energetic, and not silent or withdrawn (Gough, 1988). These are the characteristics of extraverts. Indeed, Gough (1990) found that both of the major facets of extraversion—dominance and sociability—were linked to self and peer ratings of leadership. Considering this evidence, extraverted individuals should have little difficulty motivating themselves to take on leadership roles when they see a void. Individuals who display openness to experience are strongly considered to have "the right stuff" of leaders. Openness correlates with divergent thinking (McCrae, 1987) and is strongly related to both personality-based and behavioral measures of creativity (McCrae & Costa, 1997). Creativity appears to be an important skill of effective leaders; it was one of the skills contained in Yukl's (1998) summary of the skills of leaders. Someone with an agreeable personality, or possessing agreeableness, is not necessarily motivated to emerge as a leader. On the one hand, cooperativeness tends to be related to leadership (Bass, 1990), and Zaccaro, Foti, & Kenny (1991) found that interpersonal sensitivity was related to leadership. That altruism, tact, and sensitivity are hallmarks of an agreeable personality, which would suggest that leaders should be more agreeable. On the other hand, agreeableness is associated with modesty (Goldberg, 1990) and leaders tend not to be excessively modest (Bass, 1990). A conscientiousness individual is one who achieves and one on which others can depend. Bass noted, "Task competence results in attempts to lead that are more likely to result in success for the leader, effectiveness for the group, and reinforcement of the tendencies" (p. 109). Furthermore, initiative and persistence are related to leadership. As Kirkpatrick and Locke (1991) noted, "leaders must be tirelessly persistent in their activities and follow through with their programs" (p. 51). Because conscientious individuals have more tenacity and persistence (Goldberg, 1990), we would expect conscientious individuals to emerge as effective leaders.

Narcissism and Humility

Because the Big Five personality traits are such a popular framework for research, the effects of "many more narrow, but also possibly more powerful" traits have been neglected (Judge, Piccolo, & Kosalka, 2009, p. 857). For example, **narcissism**, a dark trait that is characterized by arrogance, self-absorption, entitlement, self-esteem, and hostility (Kausel, Culbertson, Leiva, Slaughter, & Jackson, 2015); and **humility**, a bright trait that connotes a realistic and accurate self-view, a displayed appreciation of others' strengths and contributions, and teachability (Owens, Johnson, & Mitchell, 2013) have received increasing attention in leadership literature.

Because an individual's motivation to lead is largely determined by his or her personality, it is expected that both narcissism and humility would be positively related to affective-identity motivation to lead and social-normative motivation to lead. Narcissists have been condemned as having less integrality and showing more arrogance and high-handedness than other people, which may lead to negative consequences within organizational settings (Kausel et al., 2015). However, narcissism's positive components, such as confidence, self-esteem, entitlement, and self-sufficiency (Judge et al., 2009), may activate individuals' motivation to emerge as a leader. With a positive self-view, narcissists may show extreme self-confidence and self-esteem and are more likely than others to self-promote and self-nominate (Nevicka, De Hoogh, Van Vianen, Beersma, & McIlwain, 2011). Moreover, because of their unwavering desire to increase or maintain the positivity of the self (Nevicka et al., 2011), assuming leadership positions is a natural means for achieving narcissists' need for self-enhancement.

In contrast to narcissism, humility carries with it positive components such as a realistic self-concept, appreciation of others, and self-transcendent pursuits (Ou, Tsui, Kinicki, Waldman, Xiao, & Song, 2014), all of which can nurture individuals' motives to take leadership roles. First of all, an unexaggerated understanding of personal strengths and weaknesses helps humble people gain an accurate awareness of intrapersonal resources, allowing them to put their strengths in perspective and avoid arrogance or self-contempt (Ou et al., 2014). Furthermore, with a balanced self-view, humble people tend to be psychologically healthy and have high self-confidence and self-esteem (Owens et al., 2013), which drives them to embrace leadership roles with positive affective identification. Humble people are also more likely than others to be engaged in self-transcendent pursuits to embrace a collective organizational vision that is oriented toward the greater good, rather than a vision of personal glory (Ou et al., 2014). Therefore, humble people tend to view leadership as their responsibility (Ou, Waldman, & Peterson, 2015), which results in strong social-normative motivation to lead.

The desire for **dominance** has also received attention from researchers. Some empirical evidence indeed implicates dominance motivation, or the desire to hold a position of power and influence over others, in self-serving leadership behaviors. Because individuals high in dominance motivation strongly value power, they may do more to keep it—even to the point of harming others. In a series of studies, Maner and Mead (2010) investigated the implications of dominance motivation for leaders whose hold on power was tenuous, contingent on continued high performance. Under such circumstances, leaders high in dominance motivation were likely to see talented subordinates as threats to their own power, rather than as assets to the group, and tended to act against them in response. For instance, high-dominance-motivation leaders were especially likely to keep information necessary for problem-solving to themselves, exclude subordinates from the team, give subordinates poor evaluations, or banish them to lowly positions. Each of these behaviors had the effect of making the leader look good by boosting his or her comparative individual performance but hurting the group's performance by suppressing the contributions of talented team members.

Leadership **self-efficacy** refers to an individual's self-perceived capabilities for general leadership tasks (Murphy & Johnson, 2016). Korman (2001) stated that self-enhancement is the motivation to attain outcomes that signify personal growth. Having leadership self-efficacy enhances individuals' confidence in their leadership-related capabilities and competences, and motivates them to put in more effort on leadership tasks, thus leading to affective-identity motivation to lead (Chan & Drasgow, 2001). Compared with individuals low in leadership self-efficacy, those with a high level of leadership self-efficacy are encouraged to devote more effort to their work and to persist longer in the face of obstacles (Murphy & Johnson, 2016). Thus, people with strong leadership self-efficacy are more likely than others are to have a positive response to the responsibilities and duties associated with the leadership role, which results in a high level of social-normative motivation to lead. Thus, both narcissism and humility can help an individual to achieve greater motivation to lead through the enhancement of leadership self-efficacy.

▶ Motivating Volunteers

Sport organizations rely heavily on volunteers, particularly for event management. The 2018 Olympics in Pyeongchang used more than 16,000 volunteers. The New York City Marathon typically uses around 10,000 volunteers for the race and related events leading up to the race. The week-long Travelers Championship in Cromwell, Connecticut, relies on approximately 4,000 volunteers. Chelladurai (2006) concluded that nearly 20% of the volunteers in America were involved in some form of sport or recreation volunteering. These volunteers contributed about $50 billion in economic value.

In sport organizations, research has specifically noted the importance of volunteers, both for community sport (Edwards, 2015; Misener & Doherty, 2009) and sporting events, including mega-events such as the World Cup and the Olympics (Bang, Alexandris, & Ross, 2008; Bang & Chelladurai, 2009). In particular, it has been noted that sport managers struggle to retain long-term volunteers, due to a number of issues including a lack of personal growth and community involvement (Bang et al., 2008; Bang, Odio, & Reio, 2014; Giannoulakis, Wang, & Gray, 2007). Several studies have sought to identify factors that would increase volunteer satisfaction and experience at a single event, thereby encouraging these short-term volunteers to volunteer again in the future (Bang et al., 2014; Bang, Won, & Kim, 2009; Giannoulakis et al., 2007). These studies found, among others, that event image, congruity with personal values, development of personal contacts, community involvement, and personal growth were factors motivating sport volunteers.

Volunteers are essential for the sport industry as they enable event managers to maximize economic efficiency by minimizing staff costs and contribute innovative ideas in their area of expertise (Cuskelly, Auld, Harrington, & Coleman, 2004). Prior research has indicated the value of volunteers, noting the critical role that they play in the success of sport-related organizations and sporting events (Cuskelly, 1998; Green & Chalip, 1998; Shilbury & Moore, 2006). More specifically to the sport industry, volunteers are essential for the successful operation and overall management of sporting events (Berlonghi, 1994; Daly, 1991; Farrell, Johnston, & Twynam, 1998; Green & Chalip, 1998). This is particularly true for one-time events requiring many personnel for a limited amount of time.

It is not surprising that the research literature on volunteer motivation suggests a complex system of reasons for volunteering that differ, depending on the characteristics of the event or organization (Schlesinger & Gubler, 2016), but motivation is a central construct when attempting to understand an individual's decision to become a volunteer (Wang, 2004). To maintain volunteer services for community and society, it is of considerable practical interest for volunteering organizations to know how to retain their volunteers for long-term engagements, especially as volunteer turnover can be extremely costly and time-consuming in terms of decreased organizational morale, volunteer replacement costs (recruitment and training), and decreased ability to serve the public (McElroy, Morrow, & Rude, 2001; Musick & Wilson, 2008). This knowledge is likely to become even more pertinent because of the shift from traditional volunteering, with a lifelong commitment, to a new type of sporadic and episodic volunteering, with a decreased commitment to any particular organization (Vantilborgh et al., 2011). Therefore, it has become even more challenging to motivate volunteers to stay within an organization for continuing and long-term engagements. **TABLE 4.1** contains six areas likely to motivate volunteers.

Volunteer coordinators, as part of the organizational context, play a major role in

TABLE 4.1 Volunteer Functions Inventory: Six areas likely to motivate volunteers

Area	Explanation	Example
Values	Express concern for others through helping those who need assistance; volunteer is motivated by altruistic or humanitarian concerns.	Special Olympics is likely event where values are a motivation for volunteers.
Understanding	Gain learning experience while sharing one's knowledge, skills, and abilities.	A runner interested in understanding better how to manage running events might volunteer for a local 5K.
Social	Motivated by the opportunity to work with others and enhance social relationships.	Sport management students might be motivated to work at events in their field of interest to enhance their network of social relationships.
Career	Career-related benefits whereby people who volunteer can prepare for a new career or maintain career-relevant skills.	Someone who is a referee might volunteer at a state games (Nutmeg State Games) to maintain their officiating "edge."
Protective	Motivating the volunteer by reducing guilt related to being more fortunate than others.	Events that donate money to charity or donate money to fight a disease serve to help protect a volunteer's ego.
Enhancement	Centers on personal development and obtaining satisfaction related to individual growth and self-esteem.	Springfield College students volunteer at the Spalding Hoophall Classic to grow as event managers.

Reproduced from Clary, G. E., Snyder, M., Ridge, R. D., Copeland, J., Stukas, A. A. & Haugen, J. (1998). Understanding and assessing the motivations of volunteers: A functional approach. *Journal of Personality and Social Psychology, 74* (6), 1516-1530. doi: 10.1037/0022-3514.74.6.1516 inducing feelings of autonomy or control, as they are directly involved in activities to attract, orient, retain, and organize the volunteers in their charge (Studer & von Schnurbein, 2013). Volunteers stated that coordinators who enable them to act autonomously (e.g., offering opportunities for personal initiative) and who were not too controlling (e.g., establishing tight rules on work schedules) greatly increased their motivation to volunteer (Leonard, Onyx, & Hayward-Brown, 2004; Musick & Wilson, 2008; Vantilborgh et al., 2011). Research has shown initial evidence that inducing a feeling of acting autonomously through volunteer management has a positive effect on volunteering, whereas a feeling of being controlled or pressured by the volunteer coordinator (i.e., a feeling of being micromanaged) has the opposite effect, although further consideration on this topic is needed (Vantilborgh et al., 2011).

Due to the valuable contribution that volunteers make to sporting events, a better understanding of such distinct motivation-based profiles of sporting event volunteerism would greatly help event volunteer managers to develop more effective recruitment, selection, and retention strategies. **TABLE 4.2** contains four profiles of interest to organizational leaders that rely on volunteers. The researchers, Schlesinger & Gubler, used a sample of 1,169 volunteers working at the 2014 European Athletics Championships in Zurich to form their profiles. An inadequate handling of current trends in voluntary engagement and a lack of knowledge on the differences in motivation among volunteers could negatively impact their performance and behavioral intentions (Borzaga & Tortia, 2006) and have negative consequences for the events themselves.

By developing accurate knowledge about who sport event volunteers are and reasons for their engagement, sport event managers are better equipped to target the recruitment of volunteers.

TABLE 4.2 Types of Volunteers: Four profiles to help organizations' recruiting efforts

Cluster Name	Explanation
Community Supporters	They donate their time to support the event in order to be part of the local community and out of concern for others, the success of the event, and society.
Material Incentive Seekers	These volunteers expect to be recompensed materially in the form of getting free uniforms, food, accommodation, and admission.
Social Networkers	These volunteers were particularly motivated by developing interpersonal contacts. Through their voluntary activity, these individuals wanted to meet and interact with people, form friendships, and build up social networks. The motive of helping the event as part of the local community was obviously overlaid by helping in order to establish new social contacts.
Career and Personal Growth Orienteers	The main motives for these volunteers were career orientation and personal growth. People engaged voluntarily in order to gain both valuable career contacts and new perspectives or experiences that they considered to be important and necessary in other life areas.

Reproduced from Schlesinger, T., & Gubler, R. Rainer (2016). Motivational profiles of sporting event volunteers. *Sport in Society*, 19 (10), 1419-1439. doi:10.1080/17430437.2015.1133596

▶ Summary

Stuart Sokoloff, who recently graduated college and now works as an account executive in group sales for the Phoenix Suns, sums up well the important role that sport leaders play in motivating employees. But he is also careful to point out that the employee has to be self-aware and be able to ramp up his or her own motivation:

> It all starts with the leaders. The leaders need to be intrinsically motivated to help the organization move in a positive direction and be sure to hire employees who not only share the same values and vision, but employees who are intrinsically motivated as well. One can only be pushed to a certain limit and anything beyond that is on the employee. The leader's job is to find that limit and motivate the employee to go above that. There are too many people in sports who "get in" and have a job and take their foot off the pedal because they have "made it." Part of the leader's job is to make them appreciate the rare air they breathe by working in professional sports—who

has gotten them there, how they have gotten there, and the people who aren't there. (S. Sokoloff, personal communication, June 26, 2018)

Sokoloff highlights the important role that leaders have to play, but it is also important for employees themselves to look inward and seek out self-actualization. This self-actualization will require grit. There is something else that is going on in Sokoloff's comments. This idea that a young person has "made it" by getting into sport. It seems like that should be motivation enough, but once young people begin to work for sport organizations, they learn quickly that working for a sport organization takes motivation, even if it quenches your lifelong dream.

The chapter was meant to give leaders ideas about how to motivate their employees/followers, particularly all of the millennials who are flooding the job market. Quotes from sport industry employees brought "real life" to this discussion of motivation. Ideas about what might motivate our next generation of leaders were also included. A short section about motivating volunteers was also included given the importance of volunteer satisfaction and retention for sport organizations.

LEADERSHIP PERSPECTIVE

Dave McGillivray

Dave McGillivray has been the technical and race director for The Boston Marathon, the world's oldest marathon, for the past 30 years. The event, which draws about a half-million spectators each year, is one of the world's best known road-racing events. McGillivray created DMSE Sports in 1981, a firm that manages mass participatory road races. He has written two books: The Last Pick: The Boston Marathon Race Director's Road to Success and a children's book titled, Dream Big, released in 2018.

(continues)

LEADERSHIP PERSPECTIVE (*continued*)

Q: Author Daniel Pink notes that providing people with a purpose, autonomy, and an opportunity for mastery is the way to motivate people to do their best work. Do any of these concepts come into play with regard to leading people to create well-managed and memorable sporting events? If so, how?

I believe we first have to trust our help, whether staff, consultants, or volunteers. However, they also have to earn our trust. Once they have earned the right to handle a project or an area of the event, then we have to step back and allow them to do their job. Then it is up to them to prove themselves. Either they succeed or they fail. The key is to always subtly follow up as in the end, you are probably the one who is going to be held accountable for their actions.

Q: Because volunteers are not paid, it may be difficult to motivate them to perform at a high quality. What is your advice to event directors to incentivize work opportunities for volunteers?

First, you have to be selective and not just take anyone. They have to be responsible and accountable. Next, they need clear direction. Many times, if a volunteer does not perform, it could be that they were never clear on exactly what they were supposed to do. Immediately, we need to give them a sense of pride that what they are doing is very important and contributes to the overall success of the event. Constant communication is also important. They want to hear from you and be given regular updates on the event. That alone engages them even more. Lastly, acknowledge them for giving their time and energy to the event and thank them for playing a significant and important role.

Q: You have run across the United States from Oregon to Massachusetts, 3,452 miles in all. How did you stay motivated to keep on going?

I first made the commitment to MYSELF that this was something I both wanted to do and felt I had the ability to attempt. Once I felt at peace with that, I then tied it into a greater purpose and decided to run on behalf of the Jimmy Fund, the fundraising arm of the Dana-Farber Cancer Institute. I was told that this was one of the very first times someone has combined running with fundraising for cancer research. I also made the commitment to my family and friends. There was no turning back now. Additionally, I never looked at it as 3,452 miles, rather, I broke it up into 80 goals, to get through one day at a time. In fact, I broke it up even more by just focusing on it 10-miles at a time. These smaller pieces weren't as daunting as thinking about the entire effort while reaping the benefits of immediate gratification multiple times each day.

Q: In an interview with The *Boston Globe* earlier this year, it was noted that you have been giving motivational speeches for the past 38 years. Where did this ability to be a leader and motivate others come from?

Initially, it was not by design or choice. I was simply being asked to speak to various groups about my cross country run. I then realized that I might just be able to impact other people's lives and help motivate them to believe in themselves and to set goals, not limits. The more appearances I made, the better at it I became. It was all about sharing experiences with the goal of making the audience feel better about themselves on the way out the door than how they felt on the way in. For me, it is all about raising every person's level of self-confidence and self-esteem. If you feel good about yourself, you can achieve almost anything you want in life.

Q: This leadership book is designed to help upper-level sport management students understand leadership concepts. These students will eventually pursue entry-level jobs in the sport industry. What advice can you give new graduates to help them stay motivated as they start at the bottom and slowly work their way up the ladder?

I think it is critical to learn what it is like at the ground level to have a greater appreciation for how best to lead. So many who are thrust into leadership roles have never climbed the ladder and as such really don't know the challenges others are facing as they work their way up the ladder. I believe that true and affective leaders earn this position. One has to earn trust, not be handed it. This will give you the strength and confidence you will need once you are placed in a leadership position.

Q: On the flip side, how can organizations make entry-level workers feel like part of the team?
In many ways, no one is any more important than anyone else. Everyone has to understand this. The sum of the parts is greater than the whole. Every spoke on the wheel is important. We have to constantly remind everyone that their contribution is just as important as anyone else's. Constantly acknowledging people's efforts is the key.

▶ Key Terms

Agreeableness	Fixed mindset	Motivation to lead (MTL)
Autonomy	Grit	Narcissism
Autonomous motivation	Growth mindset	Neuroticism
Controlled motivation	Humility	Nonautonomous motivation
Conscientiousness	Intrinsic motivation	Openness to experience
Dominance	Intrinsic reward	Personal initiative
Empowerment	Leader-member exchange	Purpose
Extraversion	Mastery	Reward
Extrinsic motivation	Millennials	Self-actualization
Extrinsic reward	Motivation	Self-effiacy

▶ Discussion Questions

1. In looking at the section on intrinsic and extrinsic rewards, which type of rewards are most likely to motivate you? Why?

2. The chapter discusses what motivates event volunteers to volunteer. As a sport management student, which areas seem most appealing for someone who wants to work in sport?

3. Looking at the Big Five personality traits along with narcissism and humility, can you identify a leader or leaders who resemble the traits most closely associated with leader emergence?

4. There are many quotes from sport-industry employees. Which ones explain the type of work environment that most suits you and why?

5. Your sport management club or a group of upper-level sport management students have decided to organize and run a spring Spikeball tournament to help seniors blow off steam before finals. You want to get the lower-level sport management students involved in helping to market the tournament. What methods of motivation do you use to get them involved?

▶ References

Alge, B. J., Ballinger, G. A., Tangirala, S., & Oakley, J. L. (2006). Information privacy in organizations: Empowering creative and extrarole performance. *Journal of Applied Psychology, 91*(1), 221–232.

Ahearne, M., Mathieu, J., & Rapp, A. (2005). To empower or not to empower your sales force? An empirical examination of the influence of leadership empowerment behavior on customer satisfaction and performance. *Journal of Applied Psychology, 90*(5), 945–955.

Amabile, T. M., Schatzel, E. A., Moneta, G. B., & Kramer, S. J. (2004). Leader behaviors and the work environment for creativity: Perceived leader support. *The Leadership Quarterly, 15*(1), 5–32.

American Hockey League 2017–18 Attendance Graph (2018). Retrieved from http://www.hockeydb.com /nhl-attendance/att_graph_season.php?lid =AHL1941&sid=2018

Bang, H., Alexandris, K., & Ross, S. D. (2008). Validation of the revised volunteer motivations scale for international sporting events (VMS-ISE) at the Athens Olympic Games. *Event Management, 12*(3–4), 119–131.

Bang, H., & Chelladurai, P. (2009). Development and validation of the volunteer motivations scale for international sporting events (VMS-ISE). *International Journal of Sport Management and Marketing, 6*(4), 332–350.

Bang, H., Odio, M. A., & Reio, T. (2014). The moderating role of brand reputation and moral obligation: An application of the theory of planned behavior. *Journal of Management Development, 33*(4), 282–298.

Bang, H., Won, D., & Kim, Y. (2009). Motivations, commitment, and intentions to continue volunteering for sporting events. *Event Management, 13*(2), 69–81.

Bass, B. M. (1985). *Leadership and performance beyond expectations*. New York: Free Press.

Bass, B. M. (1990). *Bass and Stogdill's handbook of leadership*. New York: Free Press.

Bencsik, A., Horváth-Csikós, G., & Timea, J. (2016). Y and Z generations at workplaces. *Journal of Competitiveness, 8*(3), 90–106.

Berlonghi, A. (1994). The special event risk management manual (Rev. ed.). Dana Point, CA: Alexander Berlonghi.

Borzaga, C., and Tortia, E. (2006). Worker motivations, job satisfaction, and loyalty in public and nonprofit social services. *Nonprofit and Voluntary Sector Quarterly, 35*(2), 225–248.

Clary, G. E., Snyder, M., Ridge, R. D., Copeland, J., Stukas, A. A., Haugen, J., & Miene, P. (1998). Understanding and assessing the motivations of volunteers: A functional approach. *Journal of Personality and Social Psychology, 74*(6), 1516–1530.

Chan, K., & Drasgow, F. (2001). Toward a theory of individual differences and leadership: Understanding the motivation to lead. *Journal of Applied Psychology, 86*(3), 481–498.

Chelladurai, P. (2006). *Human resource management in sport and recreation*. Champaign, IL: Human Kinetics.

Chimelis, R. (2016, April 19). Springfield Falcons to be sold, AHL team expected to leave Western Massachusetts. Retrieved from https://www.masslive .com/news/index.ssf/2016/04/springfield_falcons _to_be_sold.html

Chimelis, R. (2018, April 22). Nine sellouts make Springfield Thunderbirds hanker for more. Retrieved from https://www.masslive.com/sports/2018/04/nine _sellouts_make_springfield.html

Crant, J. M. (2000). Proactive behavior in organizations. *Journal of Management, 26*(3), 435–462.

Cuskelly, G. (1998). Organizational commitment and committee turnover of volunteers in sport. *Australian Journal on Volunteering, 3*(2), 4–14.

Cuskelly, G., Auld, C., Harrington, M., & Coleman, D. (2004). Predicting the behavioral dependability of sport event volunteers. *Event Management, 9*, 73–89.

Daly, J. A. (1991). Volunteers in south Australian sport: A study. Canberra: Australian Sports Commission.

Deci, E. L., Connell, J. P., & Ryan, R. M. (1989). Self-determination in a work organization. *Journal of Applied Psychology, 74*(4): 580–590.

Deci, E. L., & Ryan, R. M. (1985). *Intrinsic motivation and self-determination in human behavior*. New York: Plenum Press.

Deci, E. L., & Ryan, R. M. (2000). The "what" and "why" of goal pursuits: Human needs and the self-determination of behavior. *Psychological Inquiry, 11*(4), 227–268.

Duckworth, A. L., Peterson, C., Matthews, M. D., & Kelly, D. R. (2007). Grit: perseverance and passion for long-term goals. *Journal of Personality and Social Psychology, 92*(6), 1087–1101.

Dweck, C. (2007). *Mindset: the new psychology of success*. New York: Ballantine Books.

Edwards, M. B. (2015). The role of sport in community capacity building: An examination of sport for development research and practice. *Sport Management Review, 18*(1), 6–19.

Elmore, T. (2014). How Generation Z Differs from Generation Y. Retrieved July 01, 2015, from http:// growingleaders.com/blog/generation-z-differs -generation-y/.

Epstein, M. (n.d.). Cross-generational perceptual survey of educational norms (Whitepaper).

Farrell, J., Johnston, M., & Twynam, G. (1998). Volunteer motivation, satisfaction, and management at an elite sporting competition. *Journal of Sport Management, 12*(4), 288–300.

Fernet, C. (2013). The role of work motivation in psychological health. *Canadian Psychology/ Psychologie canadienne, 54*(1), 72–74.

Frese, M., & Fay, D. (2001). Personal initiative (PI): An active performance concept for work in the 21st century. In B. M. Staw & R. M. Sutton (Eds.), *Research in organizational behavior* (Vol. 23): 133–187. Amsterdam: Elsevier Science.

Frese, M., Kring, W., Soose, A., & Zempel, J. (1996). Personal initiative at work: Differences between East and West Germany. *Academy of Management Journal, 39*(1), 37–63.

Gagné, M., & Deci, E. L. (2005). Self-determination theory and work motivation. *Journal of Organizational Behavior, 26*(4), 331–362.

Gallup (2016). How millennials want to work and live. Washington D.C. Retrieved from https://news.gallup.com/reports/189830/millennials-work-live.aspx

Gallup (2017). State of the American workplace. Washington, D.C. Retrieved from https://news.gallup.com/reports/199961/state-american-workplace-report-2017.aspx

Gerstner, C. R., & Day, D. V. (1997). Meta-analytic review of leader-member exchange theory: Correlates and construct issues. *Journal of Applied Psychology, 82*(6), 827–844.

Giannoulakis, C., Wang, C. H., & Gray, D. (2007). Measuring volunteer motivation in mega-sporting events. *Event Management, 11*(4), 191–200.

Gilley, A., Dixon, P. & Gilley, J. W. (2008). Characteristics of leadership effectiveness: Implementing change and driving innovation in organizations. *Human Resource Development Quarterly, 19*(2), 153–169.

Goldberg, L. R. (1990). An alternative "description of personality": The Big-Five factor structure. *Journal of Personality and Social Psychology, 59*(6), 1216–1229.

Gough, H. G. (1988). Manual for the California Psychological Inventory. Palo Alto, CA: Consulting Psychologists Press.

Gough, H. G. (1990). Testing for leadership with the California Psychological Inventory. In K. E. Clark & M. B. Clark (Eds.), *Measures of leadership* (pp. 355–379). West Orange, NJ: Leadership Library of America.

Graen, G. B., & Uhl-Bien, M. (1995). Relationship-based approach to leadership: Development of leader member exchange (LMX) theory of leadership over 25 years. *Leadership Quarterly, 6*(2), 219–247.

Grant, A. M., & Ashford, S. J. (2008). The dynamics of proactivity at work: Lessons from feedback-seeking and organizational citizenship behavior research. In B. M. Staw & R. M. Sutton (Eds.), *Research in organizational behavior* (Vol. 28): 3–34. Amsterdam: Elsevier.

Green, C., & Chalip, L. (1998). Sport tourism as the celebration of subculture. *Annals of Tourism Research, 25*, 275–292.

Hershatter, A., & Epstein, M. (2010). Millennials and the world of work: An organization and management perspective. *Journal of Business Psychology, 25*(2), 211–223.

Hogan, R., Curphy, G. J., & Hogan, J. (1994). What we know about leadership: Effectiveness and personality. *American Psychologist, 49*(6), 493–504.

Howe, N., & Strauss, W. (2000). Millennials rising: The next great generation. New York: Vintage Books.

Howe, N., & Strauss, W. (2007) The next 20 years: How customer and workforce attitudes will evolve. *Harvard Business Review, 85*(7–8), 41–52.

Ilies, R., Nahrgang, J. D., & Morgeson, F. P. (2007). Leader-member exchange and citizenship behaviors: A meta-analysis. *Journal of Applied Psychology, 92*(1), 269–277.

Jahoda, M. (1958). *Current concepts of positive mental health*. New York: Basic Books.

Judge, T. A., Bono, J. E., Ilies, R. G., & Gerhardt, M. W. (2002). Personality and leadership: a qualitative and quantitative review. *Journal of Applied Psychology, 87*(4), 765–780.

Judge, T. A., Piccolo, R. F., & Kosalka, T. (2009). The bright and dark sides of leader traits: A review and theoretical extension of the leader trait paradigm. *The Leadership Quarterly, 20*, 855–875.

Kahn, R. L., and Katz, D. (1952). Leadership practices in relation to productivity and morale. Institute for Social Research, University of Michigan.

Kausel, E. E., Culbertson, S. S., Leiva, P. I., Slaughter, J. E., & Jackson, A. T. (2015). Too arrogant for their own good? Why and when narcissists dismiss advice. *Organizational Behavior and Human Decision Processes, 131*, 33–50.

Kirkpatrick, S. A., & Locke, E. A. (1991). Leadership: Do traits matter? *Academy of Management Executive, 5*(2), 48–60.

Korman, A. K. (2001). Self-enhancement and self-protection: Toward a theory of work motivation. In M. Erez, U. Kleinbeck, & H. Thierry (Eds.), *Work motivation in the context of a globalizing economy* (pp. 121–130). Mahwah, NJ: Erlbaum

Lehrer, J. (2009). The truth about grit. Retrieved from http://jenni.uchicago.edu/press/Lehrer_2009_BostonGlobe_grit.pdf

Leonard, R., Onyx, J., & Hayward-Brown, H. (2004). Volunteer and coordinator perspectives on managing women volunteers. *Nonprofit Management and Leadership, 15*(2), 205–219.

Levenson, A.R. (2010). Millennials and the world of work. An economist's perspective. *Journal of Business and Psychology, 25*(2), 257–264.

Liden, R. C., Wayne, S. J., Jaworski, R. A., & Bennett, N. (2004). Social loafing: A field investigation. *Journal of Management, 30*(2), 285–304.

Madkour, A. (2018, May 21). PeacePlayers built on vision of 2 brothers. Retrieved from https://www .sportsbusinessdaily.com/Journal/Issues/2018/05/21 /Opinion/From-the-Executive-Editor.aspx

Maner, J. K., & Mead, N. L. (2010). The essential tension between leadership and power: When leaders sacrifice group goals for the sake of self-interest. *Journal of Personality and Social Psychology, 99*(3), 482–497.

Maslow, A.H. (1954) *Motivation and personality.* New York: Harper & Row.

MassLive. (2016, Oct. 6). Springfield Thunderbirds Executive VP Nathan Costa talks promotions, community engagement. Retrieved from https://www .youtube.com/watch?v=mupdJY1pqeU

McCrae, R. R. (1987). Creativity, divergent thinking, and openness to experience. *Journal of Personality and Social Psychology, 52*(6), 1258–1265.

McCrae, R. R., & Costa, P. T., Jr. (1997). Personality trait structure as a human universal. *American Psychologist, 52*(5), 509–516.

McElroy, J. C., Morrow, P. C., & Rude, S. N. (2001). Turnover and organizational performance: A comparative analysis of the effects of voluntary, involuntary, and reduction-in-force turnover. *Journal of Applied Psychology, 86*(6), 1294–1299.

McGregor, D. (1985). *The human side of enterprise: The 25th anniversary printing.* New York, NY: McGraw-Hill.

Misener, K., & Doherty, A. (2009). A case study of organizational capacity in nonprofit community sport. *Journal of Sport Management, 23*(4), 457–482.

Montana P.J., & Petit, F. (2008). Motivating Generation X and Y on the job and preparing Z. *Global Journal of Business Research, 2*(2), 139–148.

Murphy, S. E., & Johnson, S. K. (2016). Leadership and leader developmental self-efficacy: Their role in enhancing leader development efforts. *New Directions for Student Leadership, 2016*(149), 73–84.

Musick, M., & Wilson, J. (2008). Volunteers: A social profile. Bloomington, IN: Indiana University Press.

Nevicka, B., De Hoogh, A. H. B., Van Vianen, A. E. M., Beersma, B., & McIlwain, D. (2011). All I need is a stage to shine: Narcissists' leader emergence and performance. *The Leadership Quarterly, 22*(5), 910–925.

Nguyen, L. D., Mujtaba, B. G., & Ruijs, A. (2014). Stress, task, and relationship orientations of dutch: Do age, gender, education, and government work experience make a difference? *Public Organization Review, 14*(3), 305–324.

Ou, A. Y., Tsui, A. S., Kinicki, A. J., Waldman, D. A., Xiao, Z., & Song, L. J. (2014). Humble chief executive officers' connections to top management team integration and middle managers' responses. *Administrative Science Quarterly, 59*, 34–72.

Ou, A. Y., Waldman, D. A., & Peterson, S. J. (2015). Do humble CEOs matter? An examination of CEO humility and firm outcomes. *Journal of Management.* Advance online publication.

Owens, B. P., Johnson, M. D., & Mitchell, T. R. (2013). Expressed humility in organizations: Implications for performance, teams, and leadership. *Organization Science, 24*(5), 1517–1538.

Park, D.-B., & Yoon, Y.-S. (2009). Segmentation by motivation in rural tourism: A Korean case study. *Tourism Management, 30*(1), 99–108.

Patel, D. (2017). 8 ways Generation Z will differ from millennials in the workplace. Retrieved from https:// www.forbes.com/sites/deeppatel/2017/09/21/8-ways -generation-z-will-differ-from-millennials-in-the -workplace/#c1147c76e5e6

Pearce, C. L., & Sims, H. P., Jr. (2002). Vertical versus shared leadership as predictors of the effectiveness of change management teams: An examination of aversive, directive, transactional, transformational, and empowering leader behaviors. *Group Dynamics: Theory, Research, and Practice, 6*(2), 172–197.

Peterson, H. (2014, June 25). Here's what you need to know about Generation Z. Retrieved from https:// www.inc.com/hayley-peterson/heres-what-you-need -to-know-about-generation-z.html

Pink, D. H. (2011). *Drive: the surprising truth about what motivates us.* New York: Riverhead Trade.

Porter, L.W. & Lawler, E.E. (1968). *Managerial attitudes and performance.* Homewood, IL: Irwin.

Puni, A., Ofei, S. B. & Okoe, A. (2014). The effect of leadership styles on firm performance in Ghana. *International Journal of Marketing Studies, 6*(1), p. 177.

Ryan, R. M., & Deci, E. L. (2000). Self-determination theory and the facilitation of intrinsic motivation, social development, and well-being. *American Psychologist, 55*(1), 68–78.

Schlesinger, T., & Gubler, R. r (2016). Motivational profiles of sporting event volunteers. *Sport in Society, 19*(10), 1419–1439.

Shamir, B., Zakay, E., Breinin, E., & Popper, M. (1998). Correlates of charismatic leader behavior in military units: Subordinates attitudes, unit characteristics, and superiors' appraisals of leader performance. *Academy of Management Journal, 41*(4), 387–409.

Shilbury, D., & Moore, K. A. (2006). A study of organizational effectiveness for national Olympic sporting organizations. *Nonprofit and Voluntary Sector Quarterly, 35*(1), 5–38.

Sias, P. M. (2005). Workplace relationship quality and employee information experiences. *Communication Studies, 56*(4), 375–395.

Sparks & Honey (2015). Meet Generation Z: Forget everything you learned about millennials. New York. Retrieved from https://www.slideshare.net /sparksandhoney/generation-z-final-june-17

Srivastava, A., Bartol, K. M., & Locke, E. A. (2006). Empowering leadership in management teams: Effects on knowledge sharing, efficacy, and performance. *Academy of Management Journal, 49*(6), 1239–1251. Studer, S., & von Schnurbein, G. (2013). Organizational factors affecting volunteers: A literature review on volunteer coordination. *Voluntas: International Journal of Voluntary and Nonprofit Organizations. 24*(2), 403–440.

Tari, A. (2011). Generation Z. Budapest: Tericum Kiadó Ltd.

Taylor, T., Doherty, A., & McGraw, P. (2015). *Managing people in sport organizations: A strategic human resource management perspective.* New York: Routledge.

T-Birds take home multiple awards at AHL marketing meetings (2018, June 21). Retrieved from http://www.springfieldthunderbirds.com/news/detail/t-birds-take-home-multiple-awards-at-ahl-marketing-meetings

Universum (2015). Generation Z grows up: A look at the next wave of digital natives headed for your organization. Stockholm, Sweden. Retrieved from https://universumglobal.com/wp-content/uploads/woocommerce_uploads/2017/10/Gen-Z-eBook_FINAL.pdf

Vantilborgh, T., Bidee, J., Pepermans, R., Willems, J., Huybrechts, G., & Jegers, M. (2011). A new deal for NPO governance and management: Implications for volunteers using psychological contract theory.

Voluntas: International Journal of Voluntary and Nonprofit Organizations, 22(4), 639–657.

Vecchio, R. P., Justin, J. E., & Pearce, C. L. (2010). Empowering leadership: An examination of mediating mechanisms within a hierarchical structure. *The Leadership Quarterly, 21*(3), 530–542.

Vroom, V. H. (1964). Work and motivation. Oxford, UK: Wiley.

Wang, P. Z. (2004). Assessing motivations for sports volunteerism. *Advances in Consumer Research, 31,* 420–425.

Wayne, S. J., Shore, L. M., Bommer, W. H., & Tetrick, L. E. (2002). The role of fair treatment and rewards in perceptions of organizational support and leader-member exchange. *Journal of Applied Psychology, 87*(3), 590–598.

Yukl, G. (1998). Leadership in organizations. Upper Saddle River, NJ: Prentice Hall.

Zaccaro, S. J., Foti, R. J., & Kenny, D. A. (1991). Self-monitoring and trait-based variance in leadership: An investigation of leader flexibility across multiple group situations. *Journal of Applied Psychology, 76*(2), 308–315.

Zhang, X., & Bartol, K. M. (2010). Linking empowering leadership and employee creativity: The influence of psychological empowerment, intrinsic motivation, and creative process engagement. *Academy of Management Journal, 53*(1), 107–128.

CHAPTER 5

Leadership Communication and Crisis Management

Michael Mudrick

CHAPTER OBJECTIVES

- Understand the differing flows of organizational communication and the role of leaders in message dispensation.
- Recognize the importance of communication skills for leaders in sport.
- Develop an understanding of the different types of leadership communication tactics that exist.
- Recognize the importance of crisis communication strategies in sport.
- Develop an understanding of the strategies and processes involved in dealing with and communicating during sport crises.

CASE STUDY

Active Listening and Anthem Protests

One of the objectives of this chapter is to understand the different types of leadership communication tactics. Active listening is one tactic that leaders can use to show their empathy to those in their organization, according to chapter author Michael Mudrick. When considering the National Anthem protests that took place during the National Football League's 2017-2018 season, it would be instructive to look at the reactions of two NFL owners to these protests lodged by the players. In mid-October 2017, speaking at a meeting attended by NFL team owners and NFL Commissioner Roger Goodell, Houston Texans owner Bob McNair reportedly said, "We can't have the inmates running the prison," in response to NFL players taking a knee during the Anthem (Daniels, 2017). Following the comments, Texans Coach Bill O'Brien, Assistant Coach Romeo Crennel, and General Manager Rick Smith met with players. Wide

(continues)

CASE STUDY   (continued)

receiver DeAndre Hopkins did not attend the meeting, having left the practice facility. Later in the locker room, tackle Duane Brown told reporters that McNair's remarks "sickened me. … I'm very upset" (Breer, 2017, para. 12). Acknowledging the backlash, McNair apologized: "I regret that I used that expression. I never meant to offend anyone, and I was not referring to our players. I used a figure of speech that was never intended to be taken literally. I would never characterize our players or our league that way, and I apologize to anyone who was offended by it" (Breer, 2017, para. 6).

There are degrees of active listening. Some leaders show more empathy than others. Enter Martha Ford, the owner of the Detroit Lions. After week 3 of the NFL's slate of games, she asked her players to no longer kneel during the Anthem. Although Ford had linked arms during the singing of the Anthem, she told players she thought that there were better ways to address social injustice. In exchange for not kneeling any longer, Ford told her players that she would be willing to lend her name and pocketbook to any community issues the players deem fit to support. Lions running back Ameer Abdullah and defensive end Cornelius Washington said the trade-off in honoring Ford's request has the potential to be worthwhile if she keeps her word and helps the players have a more direct impact on problems they see in their community (Birkett, 2017).

Looking at the two cases, one leader acknowledged the players' concerns and one did not. One leader took an empathetic approach and actively listened to the players to find a compromise. In the end, the players said that they felt satisfied with the outcome. Ford has been acting owner of the Lions since 2014 when her husband died and is clearly not part of the 'ol boys club of NFL owners. According to *Sports Illustrated* writer Albert Breer, McNair's comments reflect a long-held perception that owners have of the players. Former Dallas Cowboys president Tex Schramm once told players union head Gene Upshaw, "You guys are cattle and we're the ranchers, and ranchers can always get more cattle" (Breer, 2017, para. 8). This perception is not limited to the NFL. Donald Sterling, the disgraced former owner of the Los Angeles Clippers of the NBA, once remarked about his players: "I support them and give them food, and clothes, and cars, and houses. Who gives it to them? Does someone else give it to them?" (Levin, 2014, para. 2). Sterling's comments contained disturbing racial overtones, which led National Basketball Association Commissioner Adam Silver to ban him from the league. McNair's comments, though not as offensive, contained racial overtones. Although McNair claims to respect his players, it was clear that Sterling did not. Chapter author Mudrick writes below that leadership communication is "communication that influences others' actions and attitudes, thus resulting in the fulfillment of a shared purpose or need" (Billings, Butterworth, & Turman, 2015, p. 158). Ford of the Lions seemingly did her best to listen to players to fulfill their needs off of the field. In return, she convinced them to take more direct action against social injustice. McNair of the Texans engaged in communication that clearly did not have a positive influence on the players or result in any fulfillment of a shared purpose among the players. Finally, Sterling took full credit for controlling his players' fulfillment. Readers can judge for themselves which of the three exhibited true leadership through empathetic communication and active listening.

In May of 2018, the NFL owners instituted a new rule regarding standing for the National Anthem. The owners decided that players on the field are required to stand for the anthem. If they do not want to stand for the anthem, they can remain in the locker room.

Questions for Discussion

1. Based on this case and what you know about professional sports communication hierarchy, what direction of communication seems most prevalent? Explain.
2. What leadership style did Ford display in this National Anthem case? Please connect her actions to her style.

3. Which image repair strategies did McNair use following his "inmates" comment? Were these strategies successful in your opinion?
4. Are there other strategies that McNair could have employed to display leadership beyond an apology released by the Texans to the media?
5. Based on information provided in the chapter with regard to crises, does the McNair/inmates' communication rise to the level of a crisis? Why or why not?

▶ Introduction

Communication can define an organization, as the way it is used plays a salient role in explaining a group's culture and behaviors (Ashcraft, Kuhn, & Cooren, 2009). Communication not only helps shape an organization's norms, values, and beliefs but it also facilitates such philosophies. Organizational leaders can be seen as communication catalysts, as these individuals have the power to create and sustain the mechanisms in place. Hence, leadership communication strategies can have a moderating effect on the internal (e.g., job satisfaction, productivity) and external (e.g., public perception) successes of an organization. If readers consider the case that opened the chapter, Ford's actions and McNair's comments had an effect on the players' job satisfaction, as will the NFL's May 2018 ruling on standing for the anthem. The owners likely had the fans' perceptions in mind when they made the decision requiring players on the field to stand for the anthem. This moderating effect of communication is especially vital in sport, given the unique challenges associated with its operation (i.e., immense public focus and identification, atypical cost and revenue systems, seasonal oscillation, varying organizational structures). Therefore, it is worthwhile to understand the importance of strong sport leadership communication and also examine the challenges and best practices associated with it.

Leadership communication is also exemplified when dealing with crises, an intermittent occurrence in sport. Not only must a system be in place to manage the issue internally, external communication is crucial given the aforementioned notoriety of sport-related entities. In other words, not only may leaders have to prepare for and manage a crisis as it unfolds but they must also deal with the aftermath and effectively communicate any resolution strategies to satisfy the bevy of stakeholders associated with the product (i.e., employees, family members, fans, sponsors), making for a particularly intricate challenge (Billings, Butterworth, & Turman, 2015).

This chapter will begin with an overview of basic communication processes, with an emphasis on the sport setting and the importance of leadership communication. Within that, key communication competencies and conflict management styles will be discussed. The chapter will also highlight the types of crises related to sport, in addition to the communication strategies and tactics used before, during, and after an incident occurs.

▶ Communication Processes

Communication is an incessantly practiced method of interaction. Lee and Hatesohl (1993) claimed that individuals spend between 70 and 80 percent of their non-sleeping hours communicating, be it writing, reading, speaking, or listening. Still, communication has been one of the more difficult constructs to define, given its complexity and continual evolution. According to Giffin and Patton (1976), communication is displayed through the processing and interpretation of symbols in the environment. It can be defined as a process in which an entity interacts, formulates, and transfers meaning and attributes via messages (Billings et al., 2015; Giffin & Patton, 1976).

Beyond the basic definition of communication, it is essential to examine how it is employed by organizational leaders and the various settings and factors of influence with its use. A setting of particular practical importance is that of the sport industry, which was said to be worth $1.5 trillion worldwide in 2015 (Plunkett, 2015). According to Pedersen (2013), communication is a major factor in the success of sport because aspects of it impact an array of influential entities related to the overall product. These entities include sport participants, organizations (and their support units, such as public relations), and the mass media. Although the media production component of sport is prominent, the study of sport communications entails much more. To that extent, **sport communication** has been defined as "a process by which people in sport, in a sport setting, or through a sport endeavor, share symbols as they create meaning through interaction" (Pedersen, Laucella, Miloch, & Fielding, 2007, p. 196).

The Strategic Sport Communication Model (SSCM) was proposed to illustrate the role of communication in varying contexts, dynamics, and settings related to sport (Pedersen, Miloch, & Laucella, 2007). The model segments sport communication into three main components: personal and organizational communication, mediated communication, and communication services and support. Personal communication is composed of intrapersonal, interpersonal, and small group communication, while organizational communication can be conducted internally (intraorganizational) or externally (interorganizational). Sport mass media involves the different types of publishing that provide sport coverage and analysis (i.e., print, new media). Services and support focus on external branding (public relations) and internal assessment (research) of the sport product.

Given that this chapter seeks to emphasize leadership's role in communication, the majority of content will focus on organizational communication. However, because organizations consist of many different individuals, it is prudent to skim the surface of personal communication, while emphasizing organizational-specific contexts. Hence, the following section will address the types of personal communication, before giving way to organizational and leadership communication. **TABLE 5.1** summarizes the five key forms of communication.

▶ Personal Communication

Intrapersonal communication, considered to be the most prevalent form of dialogue (Pedersen et al., 2007), encompasses conversation with oneself, often used as a mechanism for reflection or examination (DeVito, 2009). A message is turned inward ("intra" is a prefix that means "within") as a form of internal dialogue (Pedersen et al., 2007). For instance, if an athletic director is about to speak to his or her staff and notices that the group looks disinterested, by reading their body language and using it to impact their upcoming message, he or she is engaging in intrapersonal communication.

Interpersonal communication involves communication between two or more individuals (DeVito, 2009). Messages can be dispersed through many different channels, be it email, texting, face-to-face, or over the phone. This type of communication is a two-way process, as each individual involved acts as both the sender and receiver of messages.

Small group communication involves dialogue between a limited number of individuals. The quantity for what defines a small group can be subjective. Some claim that it can be as little as three (Pedersen et al., 2007), whereas others have deemed a small group to be composed of 5 to 10 individuals (DeVito, 2009). If a sales team has an account executives-only meeting, the exchange of

TABLE 5.1 Differentiating Types of Communication

Personal Type	Defined	Source
Intrapersonal	This is considered to be the most prevalent form of dialogue; it encompasses conversation with oneself, often used as a mechanism for reflection or examination.	DeVito (2009); Pedersen, Miloch, & Laucella (2007).
Interpersonal	Communication between two or more individuals. Messages dispersed through many different channels, be it email, texting, face-to-face, or over the phone. This type of communication is a two-way process.	DeVito (2009).
Small Group	This involves dialogue among a limited number of individuals (3 and 10).	DeVito, 2009; Pedersen, Miloch, & Laucella (2007).
Organizational Type	**Defined**	**Source**
Intraorganizational	Dialogue within the boundary of an organization. It may also be referred to as employee communications. Its goal is to establish desirable relationships between an organization's management and its other employees.	Stoldt, Dittmore, and Branvold (2012).
Interorganizational	Represents dialogue outside of the boundary of the group and is targeted to external publics.	Pedersen, Miloch, & Laucella (2007).

Data from: DeVito, J.A. (2009). Human communication: The basic course (11th ed.). Pearson Higher Ed.; Pedersen, P.M., Miloch, K.S., & Laucella, P.C. (2007). Strategic sport communication. Champaign, IL: Human Kinetics.; Stoldt, G.C., Dittmore, S.W., & Branvold, S.E. (2012). Sport public relations: Managing organizational communication (2nd ed.). Human Kinetics.

messages would be considered small-group communication since sales teams are typically composed of small groups of individuals. Given that a typical group, regardless of field, sets goals and communicates with each other to achieve said aspirations, this form of dialogue can serve both "relationship" and "task" needs (DeVito, 2009, p. 5). To that extent, small group communication is used extensively in organizational settings, as an organization represents a group of individuals with similar ambitions. As a result, the ability to conduct small group communication effectively is of particular value in leadership roles.

▶ Organizational Communication

Organizational communication refers to the sharing, interpreting, and processing of messages among individuals within a social unit (Giffin & Patton, 1976). Regardless of the industry, an organization's success lies in its ability to influence the group to work collectively in an effort to achieve its goals (Shockley-Zalabak, 1999). Communication plays a pivotal role toward these tasks and aspirations, as the matters in which it is conveyed can help shape an organization's philosophies and goals and catalyze the achievement of each (Ashcraft et al., 2009).

To illustrate, organizational communication has been found to be related to desirable outcomes such as employee satisfaction and profitability (Koys, 2001; Long & Thean, 2011). On the surface, this is important for various reasons. Satisfied employees are more likely to remain in their jobs, causing less turnover (Koys, 2006). Employee turnover can be costly, as a lack of personnel involvement will naturally impede task productivity (Long & Thean, 2011). Replacing employees can also be expensive due to recruitment costs and training of new hires. In fact, Koys (2006) found that employee satisfaction and turnover (lack thereof) independently predicted company profitability, demonstrating a clear, direct effect of employee satisfaction, and, in essence, the indirect benefits of strong organizational communication.

Sport organizations must also be cognizant of how they communicate internally because they receive much more media attention than a traditional business. Regardless of notoriety, each member of an organization can be seen as a point of inquiry for the press (Mullin, Hardy, & Sutton, 2014). As a result, educating employees on organizational values and its activities can protect from dealing with unnecessary and potentially false rumors. Knowledge of an organization's vision, goals, policies, and procedures is also instrumental toward task execution. Simple methods can be used to improve employee expertise in these areas, including producing regular eNewsletters and making pertinent organizational information a focus in regular meetings and reviews (Foltz, 1985).

Likewise, employees would seem to benefit from hearing information first-hand, as opposed to learning about it through news from an external source. These points represent internal organizational communication or intraorganizational communication, which involves dialogue within the boundary of an organization. It may also be referred to as employee communications, which Stoldt, Dittmore, and Branvold (2012) defined as a

"function that has the goal of establishing desirable relationships between an organization's management and its other employees" (p. 258). Again referring to the chapter case study, Martha Ford of the Lions attempted to establish a good working relationship with her players regarding the National Anthem protests. On the other hand, external communication or interorganizational communication represents dialogue outside of the boundary of the group and is targeted to external publics.

Organizational communication also seeks to "meet audience needs" (Foltz, 1985, p. 4). Audience needs may represent a variety of requests. It could mean a healthy working environment with desirable relationships (Stoldt et al., 2012). Employees are less likely to feel isolated and will feel more valued if adequate communication exists. Communication can foster a sense of being and appreciation within a group. Moreover, since task execution is a pre-eminent form of organizational evaluation, a clear articulation of duties is vital for productivity and success. It is important to consider external stakeholders as part of the audience, as well. Within sport, this means using effective communication mechanisms with fans to keep them informed. The Boston Celtics are a model organization in this fashion, as the team has traditionally written letters to season-ticket holders explaining key personnel decisions, such as trades (Forsberg, 2016).

Organizational Structure and Communication

In order to understand leadership communication, it is crucial to examine the formal structures that typically exist in an organization. It is common for organizations to devise a formal conceptual structure of working relationships (Pedersen et al., 2007). This is conventionally displayed in an organizational chart that outlines divisions of labor and supervisor-subordinate relationships. Organizational charts are integral to communicating authority and formally displaying direct communication channels within a unit. A sport leader's goal is to ensure that employees adhere to the chain of command in an effort to collectively relay information between factions (Jordan, Kent, & Walker, 2015). In the case that opened the chapter, Texans owner Bob McNair may have relied on the chain of command because the team's head coach and assistant coaches met with the players following McNair's controversial comments. Another example involves almost any organization at its grassroots: If a ticket sales representative detects a glitch in the team's ticketing software, it would behoove that individual to follow the chain of command and notify the direct supervisor, as opposed to alerting the team's general manager or owner.

These concepts relate to tenets of *communication direction*, which can be downward, upward, or horizontal (or lateral). **Downward communication** involves the stream of communication down an organizational chart, from supervisors to subordinates. It normally involves directions, guidelines, or news updates from those elevated on the chain of command. The supervisor-subordinate relationship is considered to be the "primary interpersonal relationship structured by the organization" (Shockley-Zalabak, 1999, p. 160). In fact, supervisors are said to spend between one-third and two-thirds of their overall work time engaged in some form of dialogue with subordinates (Shockey-Zalabak, 1999).

On the contrary, **upward communication** involves messages from subordinates to superiors. This is usually exemplified through asking questions, completing directed tasks, or providing assessment. **Horizontal communication** occurs when individuals or groups on the same level of authority transfer messages with each other. In sport, horizontal communication is pervasive due to the abundance of group collaboration among staff members. For instance, a game day promotion may require coordination from staff members in marketing, communication, and ticketing, among others. Because horizontal communication may involve

collaboration among different departments, it is important for each side to have a basic understanding of what the other does and of their respective cultures. Such exchanges can be promoted by way of including segments such as "for the good of the order" at meetings, in which each group provides an update on their area.

▶ Leadership Communication

Top-down and bottom-up communication success puts the onus on leaders to be strong communicators (Billings et al., 2015). While organizational communication is predicated on devising plans to achieve a group's ambitions (tasks that are fulfilled by leaders), communicating said goals is equally important. To that extent, Pedersen et al., (2007) defined **leadership communication** as "communication that influences others' actions and attitudes, thus resulting in the fulfillment of a shared purpose or need" (p. 158). The concept of influencing others is quite crucial to leadership duties, as subordinates need to be persuaded to buy in to the goals proposed. This is particularly evident in sport. Billings et al., (2015) noted that, if you are a skilled tactician in a certain sport, it does not necessarily translate into being a successful leader. There remains a need to communicate pertinent information and motivate others to complete their assigned tasks. In fact, the authors mentioned how great players have struggled as coaches (e.g., Isiah Thomas, Wayne Gretzky), showing the limitations of physical and experiential acumen.

The ability to motivate and connect with an audience is indicative of a concept known as interpersonal communication competence, as the style in which one dispenses messages can impact the receiver's attitudes and behaviors (DeVito, 2009). Successful leaders must showcase these behaviors when engaging in all directions of organizational communication, particularly downward with subordinates. Several key communication competencies that are said to resonate with and motivate subordinates include knowledge of communication context, trust, active listening, information accuracy, and cultural sensitivity (Giffin & Patton, 1976; Pettit Jr., Goris, & Vaught, 1997; Shockey-Zalabak, 1999; Spitzberg, 1988) (see **TABLE 5.2**).

Knowledge of communication context involves an understanding of appropriate dialogue in certain situations (Spitzberg, 1988). Leaders must know when it is appropriate to use certain motivational tactics, such as criticism or encouragement. This type of communication is situational-based and also involves a strong understanding of personnel characteristics.

Trust is one of the most important components of a leader-subordinate relationship. According to Giffin and Patton (1976), trust is needed when individuals are immersed in any of the following scenarios: One relies upon another, the relationship can result in loss/gain in terms of goal achievement, and the desired goal may be uncertain. All of these undoubtedly apply to sport. Trust with staff members has been cited as a foundation for the success had by college football coach P.J. Fleck, who led the Western Michigan University Broncos (a non-Power Five conference team) to a 13-0 record in 2016 and a trip to the Cotton Bowl. The synergy among Fleck's staff was

TABLE 5.2 Communication Competencies

Competency	Definition	Source
Knowledge of communication context	This involves an understanding of appropriate dialogue in certain situations.	Spitzberg, 1988
Trust	This is needed when individuals are immersed in any of the following scenarios: One relies upon another, the relationship can result in loss/gain in terms of goal achievement, and the desired goal may be uncertain.	Giffin and Patton, 1976
Active Listening	This competency substantiates the precision in which a message is received (as opposed to merely hearing and not listening); it also displays a degree of empathy to the message sender.	Giffin and Patton, 1976
Information Accuracy	When employees receive factual information, they are put in a better position to execute their tasks.	Pettit Jr., J.D., Goris, J.R., & Vaught, B.C., 1997
Cultural Sensitivity	The recognition of diversity without passing judgment on the benefits or disadvantages of similarities and differences in a group.	Dabbah, 2014

Data from: Spitzberg, B.H. (1988). Communication competence: Measures of perceived effectiveness. A handbook for the study of human communication: Methods and instruments for observing, measuring, and assessing communication processes, 67–105.; Giffin, K. & Patton, B.R. (1976). Fundamentals of interpersonal communication (2nd ed.). New York, NY: Harper and Row Publishers; Pettit Jr., J.D., Goris, J.R., & Vaught, B.C. (1997). An examination of organizational communication as a moderator of the relationship between job performance and job satisfaction. The Journal of Business Communication, 34(1), 81–98; Dabbah, M. (2014, October 31). What is cultural sensitivity? Retrieved from http://redshoemovement.com/what-is-cultural-sensitivity/

instrumental to the team's success. Offensive coordinator Kirk Ciarrocca noted that, as an assistant, it can be difficult working with a head coach who seeks to have too much influence on offense or defense, especially considering that coordinators spend more time watching film and studying in their specific areas (Olsen, 2016). Fleck, however, gives his coordinators the freedom to coach their units without micromanaging. Such trust has been seen as a vote of confidence in Fleck's subordinates, making him a desirable leader to work with.

Active listening is vital to message reception. Not only does it substantiate the precision in which a message is received (as opposed to merely hearing and not listening) but it also displays a degree of empathy to the message sender (Giffin & Patton, 1976). This can enhance the likeability of the message receiver, while also boosting the self-efficacy of the speaker. In support of this, Johnson and Bechler (1998) found a positive relationship between perceived leadership and listening abilities and suggested that an effective listener is more likely to be able to determine the desires of the group, thus making them viable leaders.

Information accuracy is also an important facet of leadership dialogue. Pettit Jr. and colleagues (1997) found that the reception of factual information serves as a link between job performance and satisfaction. By this, we infer that when one receives accurate information, they are put in a better position to execute their tasks. As a result of task success, they feel more positive about their performance.

Cultural sensitivity is practiced through the recognition of diversity without passing judgment on the benefits or disadvantages of similarities and differences in a group (Dabbah, 2014). Sport is a field that has seen a need for cultural understanding, as demographic diversity has been on display from both a participant and organizational support staff perspective (Doherty & Chelladurai, 1999). The practice of being culturally sensitive can proliferate interpersonal communication effectiveness (Giffin &

Patton, 1976). In particular, leaders must be mindful of existing stereotypes. By putting aside preconceived notions of certain qualities and behaviors associated with cultural groups, those impacted by such stereotypes will likely develop a greater level of identification with their leaders, which, in turn, can lead to positive production.

There are a bevy of skills and practices that foster leadership communication. It is also useful to examine common communication tactics that are often a product of a leader's persona, which will be an area of focus in the following section.

▶ Leadership Communication Styles

Leaders' preferred style of management is likely to impact how they communicate to subordinates. For instance, a task-oriented individual will provide intimate supervision and be direct in telling a subordinate of their duties, whereas one who is relationship-oriented will not closely supervise performance because they feel the distance helps to provide a trusting work environment (Pedersen et al., 2007). Leadership research has offered four supervisory philosophies: Autocratic, participative, consultative, and laissez-faire—all of which relate to one's preferred styles (Chelladurai & Saleh, 1980; Pedersen et al., 2007; Shockey-Zalabak, 1999; Turman & Schrodt, 2004).

Autocratic leaders tend to dominate decision-making and take pleasure in directing assignment responsibilities (Chelladurai & Saleh, 1980; Cruz, Henningsen, & Smith, 1999). These leaders are not known to consult others in the decision-making process. Part of this may be the product of an assumption that the audience has limited information on optimal task production strategies (Pedersen et al., 2007). This can be detrimental to subordinates, as it may induce a perception of mistrust. In fact, for such reasons, athletes have been found to lack preference for this style (Turman, 2001). Other work has found that this style has a negative impact on subordinate learning (Turman & Schrodt, 2004). Coaches who have enacted this style at the professional ranks have had their share of conflicts with players, likely due to the aforementioned reasons. In his lone, last-place season with the Boston Red Sox, manager Bobby Valentine was seen as an autocratic leader, to which his style caused turmoil with veteran players like David Ortiz, Dustin Pedroia, and Kevin Youkilis (Shaughnessy, 2013).

On the contrary, **participative** leaders seek perspectives from all stakeholders in a display of democratic behavior (Chelladurai & Saleh, 1980). In this environment, subordinates are encouraged to dispute ideas for the sake of providing feedback and quality assurance. Per Pedersen and colleagues (2017), this style is well suited when working with highly capable subordinates. **Consultative** leaders blend both autocratic and participative styles. They can be very directive but also relationship-oriented. These individuals may be demanding of their subordinates, but they are very involved in helping them meet expectations (Pedersen et al., 2007).

Laissez-faire leaders show zero blending of any of the aforementioned styles (Pedersen et al., 2007). These leaders are low in task-orientation and provide little direction toward assisting subordinates. While these all represent overarching styles, it is important to understand that specific leadership characteristics may also be employed in certain situations. These characteristics may be tangential to overall style but are often based on situational context. They include: Avoidance, vision-setting management, goal-setting meaning management, trust generating, and positive regard (Chelladurai & Saleh, 1980; Shockey-Zalabak, 1999; Turman & Schrodt, 2004).

Avoidance is a characteristic used by a leader who tends to agree with something, even though he or she may not support it, simply for the sake of not being involved in

discord. In an effort to quell discontent, an avoidant leader may also turn a blind eye to obvious issues within a group.

Vision setters prefer to use symbols to illustrate goals or ideas. Their communication is quite direct, as they seek to offer clear, measurable outcomes for tasks. Similarly, goal-setters use individual communication as a means of setting achievable outcomes. Basketball coaching great Pat Summitt was known as a staunch goal-setter and credited this strategy as a staple for her success. She claimed that it expressed a message to her players that she cared about, but also believed in, them (Wrisberg, 1990).

Meaning-management leaders seek to use others' feedback to ensure that a message was appropriately received. The intent is to confirm that the message was interpreted appropriately. Trust-generating leaders establish an environment ripe with open communication. They engage in specific activities to enhance the perception that others have legitimate access to communicate with them. Leaders with open door policies would fall in this category.

Leaders who use positive regard frequently offer praise. There tends to be less focus on blame, and more on how problems or shortcomings can be rectified in the future. This leader prefers to take a negative and turn it into an opportunity for positive task completion in the future.

▶ Conflict Communication

The style in which one communicates will resonate with some and irritate others. This can lead to organizational conflict. Shockley-Zalabak (1999) defined conflict as "a process that occurs when individuals, small groups, or organizations perceive or experience frustration in attaining goals" (p. 227). All organizations deal with conflict regularly, as people are bound to differ in thoughts and opinions. How individuals communicate to solve dilemmas, though, plays a large role in conflict resolution, as varying tactics, much of which stem from a leader's communication style, can be used. Shockley-Zalabak (1999) claimed that leaders exhibit the following conflict resolution tactics: Avoidance, competition, compromise, accommodation, and collaboration.

Avoidance, previously mentioned as a leadership characteristic, is also a conflict strategy. It can occur when individuals are distressed at the potential for conflict, and, as a result, seek to elude situations in which conflict is present. This can be problematic, as leaders are decision makers, and to avoid issues for this sake means that key figures are not being fully involved in the process. Leaders who embrace *competition* tend to see outcomes as dichotomous—either a right or wrong way (Shockley-Zalabak, 1999). Often, though, competitive leaders feel that their way is always correct, which can be problematic when dealing with issues. However, Shockley-Zalabak (1999) claimed that such tactics can be beneficial if the group is split and the lack of indecisiveness can push the group forward with a decision.

Compromise occurs when people communicate through exchanges. In conflict, they seek to "minimize losses while establishing some gains" (Shockley-Zalabak, 1999, p. 328). Because such give-and-take shows a willingness to listen, subordinates may prefer this type of conflict management. *Accommodation* transpires when individuals sacrifice aspects that benefit themselves for the sake of appeasing others and preserving enduring relationships. These are the people who have issues with saying "no," as they crave to be liked. While it is natural to seek positive perception, it can be problematic to practice this mindset at the expense of organizational benefit.

Those who seek to work with both sides to thoroughly examine the situation and seek to come to a conclusion to the best decision for all involved endorse a *collaboration* style. In essence, this combines a tactician and consultative approach. This conflict style, however, may only be efficient if the group is willing to work together to productively problem-solve. Thus, a leader must communicate to the group to get them to buy into a collaboration mindset (Shockley-Zalabak, 1999).

▶ Crisis Communication

A conflict that has drawn considerable attention in public relations work is that of crisis communication. As previously noted, public relations is a segment of the services and support component of the Strategic Sport Communication Model (SSCM). Crisis communication, an activity ripe with leadership involvement, is an integral topic in top-down communication.

A **crisis** can be defined as "the perception of an unpredictable event that threatens important expectancies of stakeholders related to the health, safety, environmental, and economic issues and can seriously impact an organization's performance and generate negative outcomes" (Coombs, 2014, p. 3). There are several key takeaways from this definition. First, the unpredictability of a crisis is what makes it unique from expected and foreseeable issues. Leaders can meticulously plan to deal with crises, but their time of arrival often cannot be foreseen. Because of this, Stoldt et al. (2012) said, "even the most comprehensive risk management plans cannot protect against all potential crises" (p. 196). Furthermore, the impact of a crisis can significantly affect an organization tangibly (e.g., monetarily) and intangibly (e.g., perception).

Using college athletics as an example, work by Goff (2000) demonstrated the substantial impact that sport crises can have on a university. For instance, not only did an NCAA football probation sentence at Mississippi State University carry perceptual damages to athletics and the school but alumni donations also decreased by $1.6 million in the aftermath.

Likewise, when Southern Methodist University received the NCAA "death penalty" in 1987—meaning its football operations were shut down for multiple years after repeated violations of paying players—the school saw a $31 million decrease in alumni contributions, along with a drop in student applications (Goff, 2010).

Sport is not immune to crises. A scan of ESPN.com headlines on a given day is likely to reveal multiple unpredictable incidents that have negative ramifications for stakeholders involved in the organization. In fact, Stoldt, Miller, and Comfort (2001) illuminated the pervasive nature of crises in sport, as a sample of college athletic directors across all three divisions of the NCAA reported having used crisis communication plans an average of 1.15 times per year. Seventy-one percent used them once per year, while approximately one-third indicated using them at least twice a year.

The consequences of these transgressions have altered the landscape of crisis management. Organizations used to have at least one day to publicly react to a crisis. It has now become a matter of minutes, mainly due to social media (Elfman, 2017). Given the compacted amount of time allotted toward dealing with crises nowadays, planning for an incident is paramount now more than ever. Crisis planning can be done to project the likelihood of a crisis and offer best practices on the subsequent organizational response.

Crisis Planning

Crisis communication plans are designed to provide a structure for an organization's response to an incident (Stoldt et al., 2012). By no means are they absolute, as the uniqueness of the crisis dictates the level of employee involvement. Nonetheless, since the public is quick to shape its perception soon after news of a crisis breaks, the speed and quality of a response is critical. Organizations must concoct plans to deal with these matters both *internally* and *externally*.

Dealing with potential crises can be forecasted by conducting research that examines prior incidents that have impacted other organizations (Stoldt et al., 2012). In the event that history may repeat itself, an assessment of what happened, the ensuing response, and the successes and failures of the plan can serve as a worthwhile comparable analysis. Organizations can also conduct internal audits to project the likelihood of a crisis occurrence, based on past behavior. Specifically, prior incidents can serve as predictors for a future situation. For example, if there are frequent reports of unruly behavior in a precise section of a venue, the area is at a high risk for an incident. Teams can use that information to adopt a plan to mitigate issues moving forward. One issue becoming more prevalent at Major League Baseball games is patrons being hit by batted balls and broken bats. Teams in the league extended the nets behind home plate to protect customers sitting behind the dugouts and not just those sitting behind home plate.

Crisis planning can also protect an organization from potential liabilities related to an incident. It is not uncommon for organizations to be accused of culpability for mishandling a crisis. To illustrate, Elfman (2017) noted that Baylor University was implicated for not having an appropriate plan in place when its football program was enmeshed in an extensive sexual assault crisis. A concrete plan can thus serve as a reference to demonstrate that the organization had formal guidelines to handle the situation properly.

Internal plans involve establishing a crisis communication pipeline within the organization. Stoldt et al. (2012) proposed a multi-step internal management plan: First, senior management support should be solidified. These are key individuals who will be involved in carrying out the plan, if activated. Without their endorsement, the plan risks failing. Second, key personnel must be involved in the planning process. Similar to the need for senior management unification, it is imperative to make sure that all necessary parties are involved in the planning process. This could include senior leadership employees, public relations, and legal staff members. In college athletics, it may be composed of the school president, dean of students, chief of police, athletic director, and sports information director (Elfman, 2017). Third, employees must be made aware of the plan. They do not need to know what each unit's specific role is in a crisis, but they should be cognizant of their own duties and communication directives if something were to occur. Fourth, organizations should test the plan as a crisis simulation. This can be done through rehearsed drills or through employee assessment.

Externally, league offices or national governing bodies may be worthwhile lines of communication (Favorito, 2007). There may be times when trusted contacts outside of the organization can provide an unbiased view to a response, along with a wealth of experience dealing with crises. Most external communication, though, involves working with the media on an initial crisis response and a plan for future dialogue. There are several steps to consider for media interaction, including identifying an appropriate spokesperson, using effective interaction strategies, and the crafting of key messages.

Spokesperson Identification

It is important for organizational leaders to decide who would be most suited to making public statements. The identification of a singular speaker, one ripe with perceived credibility, can deflect the potential for mixed messages being sent to the public (Favorito, 2007). In a college setting, it would likely be the school president or athletic director. Similarly, professional teams tend to assign those duties to an owner, president, or general manager. While some may suggest that coaches would be viable choices to speak on team related issues—and in some cases, they may be—the presence of superiority, meaning a coach's supervisor, can enhance the credibility

of the message dispensed. It also articulates that the organization acknowledges the severity of the situation by having its senior-most leaders speaking on the issue.

Media Interaction Strategies

Considering that sport leaders must interact with the media during a crisis, it is important to be cognizant of best practices in these settings. Such situations of this nature are atypical to traditional media interactions, thus effective communication strategies are essential. Stoldt et al., (2012) recommended the following rules:

- Honesty: Clearly, issues will be exacerbated if an organization is caught in a lie; hence, perceived trustworthiness is crucial in a time of crisis. Audiences are less likely to be persuaded if they do not genuinely believe the source (Hovland & Weiss, 1951).
- Anticipate difficult questions: Given the nature of the situation, media inquiries may not necessarily be amicable. Since they serve as the conduit to the public, it is the media's job to ask pertinent questions, regardless of who is at fault. Leaders must be cognizant of that prior to the interview.
- Be mindful of the use of "no comment": There may be times when a non-answer is warranted, especially if a situation is still in flux. Nonetheless, leaders must be mindful that the audience may perceive "no comment" to be an admission of guilt.
- Assess the public's stance prior: Be cognizant of what has been published and study the general consensus of how the public appears to perceive what happened. This will aid in the preparation for the types of questions anticipated.

Key Messages

The first form of media interaction involves providing a statement. Typically, this message is sent directly to the media in the form of a press release. However, since social media allows fans to have a direct link to the team, it is not out of the ordinary for the team to post a message on social media. Since the details of a crisis may take time to come to fruition, organizations are advised to acknowledge that the situation has occurred and to promise additional communication as more information is received (Stoldt et al., 2012). Depending on the crisis, there may be impending legal issues, to which it is recommended to keep initial details to a minimum, especially if dealing with student-athletes (Elfman, 2017).

As communication technologies continue to evolve, crisis communicators must incorporate online techniques into their crisis communication plans. Social media platforms have allowed online communities to form, increasing pressure among organizations to better manage crises (Coombs, 2012). Audiences are no longer passive receivers of information that traditional media, like television and newspapers, wish to disseminate. Instead, the Internet has transformed people into active information-seekers who wish to receive information instantly (Stephens & Malone, 2009). Brown and Billings (2013) studied the reputation-repair strategies used by University of Miami athletics fans in response to alleged NCAA violations involving Miami's athletics department. The researchers learned that fans active on Twitter tried to help the university's athletics department to be seen in a positive light. This illustrates the power of social media as these Twitter users attempted to get their followers to see University of Miami athletics the way they did. But there are others who can shape the narrative negatively. This can make it difficult for the organization—in this case, the University of Miami—to control the message.

Extended interactions with the media at a later point allow an organization to craft a takeaway message for the audience. One way to garner public support is for the speaker to communicate that he or she sincerely cares for those affected by the crisis. Without that, the source will be perceived to lack authenticity.

During the 2005 season, NFL star Terrell Owens struggled to garner public sympathy during a dispute with the Philadelphia Eagles (Brazeal, 2008). Owens had been instructed by the team to make a public apology after making disparaging remarks about the team and quarterback Donovan McNabb. He entered a press conference; read a message to the press, which was curt; and appeared to lack genuine remorse. He did not take questions from reporters and abruptly left (Brazeal, 2008). Consequentially, the apology did not appear to sway public opinion in Owens' favor.

Message retention is a difficult task for any audience. Grippo (2009) claimed that, even in an optimal environment, audiences only absorb 25 percent of the information given to them. The same concept can be applied to interviews. Thus, core messages are necessary. One way to ensure the receipt of a message is to emphasize it several times in a conversation. Such repetition, although redundant, increases the likelihood that the audience will retain the message.

Speakers can also use a technique called **flagging**, which, according to Stoldt et al. (2012), means to "emphasize to reporters what you want them to highlight—what one piece of information you want them to print or broadcast" (p. 175). To do this, specific phrases can be used to stress the importance of certain messages. Such expressions can include, "the fact of the matter is…" or "the bottom line is…" (Stoldt et al., 2012). The speaker is blatantly highlighting the importance of the statement, thus increasing the likelihood that the audience will recall the message. In the case of a crisis, an organization needs to maintain an appearance of stability, while also stressing its core values. Using these techniques in conjunction with key messages can be an advantageous strategy.

Types of Crises

Crises vary in type and severity. For planning purposes, it is advantageous to know the different types of crises in sport, which can help leaders to craft an appropriate corresponding message to the public. According to Favorito (2007), in sport, there are five frequent crisis situations: physical plant, on-field, public tragedy, corporate/internal, and player personnel (see **TABLE 5.3**). The following section will define each crisis, provide examples, and offer recommendations for how leaders can effectively communicate as a result of the incident.

TABLE 5.3 Crisis Types and Suggested Responses

Crisis Type	Example	Suggested Response
Physical Plant	During the second half of Super Bowl XLVII, the electricity went out for over a half-hour at the Superdome in New Orleans.	Sport leaders should communicate the issue to the public when information is available in an effort to lessen confusion and speculation.
On-Field	Late in the fourth quarter of a professional basketball game between the Indiana Pacers and the Detroit Pistons in 2004, a Pistons fan threw a drink at Pacers player Ron Artest, sparking a brawl between players and fans.	Sport leaders, in this case, league officials need to work with event management and law enforcement officials to rectify the situation and take steps to mitigate further incidents like these.
Public Tragedy	In September of 2016, Miami Marlins pitcher Jose Fernandez, just 24, died in a boating accident off the coast of Miami Beach.	Sport leaders must first determine the accuracy of the initial report. Next, that information needs to be connected to the appropriate crisis team members. Further emotional support will likely be needed by those affected by the tragedy.
Corporate/Internal	In 2013, Florida Atlantic University contemplated selling the naming rights to its football stadium to GEO Group, a private-prison corporation. Amid allegations that GEO allowed abuses at some of its prisons, followed by student protests, GEO withdrew the $6 million offer.	Leaders must communicate—and even apologize—the issues down to all staff in an organization to stem an internal tide of negativity.
Player Personnel	During the 2017 NBA offseason, the Boston Celtics traded popular point guard Isaiah Thomas to the Cleveland Cavaliers, the Celtics' Eastern Conference rival.	Sport leaders should accept outside criticism, whether right or wrong, but also make a concerted effort to support and communicate with the incoming player who is supplanting the popular figure.

Favorito, J. (2007). *Sports publicity: A practical approach*. Elsevier Science & Technology.

A physical plant crisis involves an issue specifically impacting the sport venue. It could be instigated externally (e.g., terrorism, inclement weather) or a result of an internal malfunction (e.g., power issue). Super Bowl XLVII experienced a physical plant crisis when the electricity went out for over a half-hour in the second half at the Superdome in New Orleans. During this time of uncertainty, sport leaders should communicate the issue to the public when pertinent information is available in an effort to mitigate confusion and speculation. Depending on the physical plant crisis, although, in an age of heightened security due to recent terrorist attacks at sporting events (e.g., 2013 Boston Marathon, 2015 France-Germany soccer match), organizations must have concrete communication plans to limit the catastrophic effects. Favorito (2007) recommended using a key word via the public address system to alert personnel of the crisis. In doing so, staff members could act accordingly and by not explicitly stating the issue to the crowd, this lessens the potential for widespread panic.

An on-field crisis is rather tangential to the physical plant and deals with incidents during a game/contest. Examples could be injuries to team personnel or fans or unruly fan behavior. In the 2016 NHL playoffs, a game between the Philadelphia Flyers and Washington Capitals was delayed when disorderly Flyers fans tossed bracelets, which had been a giveaway for the game, onto the ice to express their frustration with the team's lackluster performance (Mather, 2016). In cases like these, sport leaders must work with event management and law enforcement officials to rectify the situation, while understanding the desire for increased media inquiries and accommodating them.

A public tragedy involves a hardship or misfortune related to a public figure associated with the team. The degree of tragedy may vary, as it could be an unexpected death, a crime, or other legal issue in connection with organizational personnel. There is also a strong likelihood that these crises occur after hours. In 2009, University of Connecticut football player Jasper Howard was stabbed to death shortly after midnight during an on-campus event at the school's student union. This makes the response difficult for organizations in terms of controlling the message, as the media, or even general public, may find out beforehand due to social media reports. Basically, the story at that point is out of the team's control. Coach Randy Edsall delivered the news of Howard's death to the team some five hours later at a team meeting. This tragic incident, which occurred 10 years ago, would now likely have much more social media activity in the five hours between Howard's tragic death and Edsall's statement to the team. Favorito (2007) proposed several important rules for dealing with these types of crises, given the sensitive nature of the topic. First, the accuracy of the initial report must be confirmed. Next, that information needs to be connected to the appropriate crisis team members. Dealing with this type of crisis, which may be a "larger than sport issue," also lends a need to providing support to those affected, even if an individual appears guilty.

A corporate/internal crisis involves receiving negative publicity from an incident involving an associated corporate entity (e.g., Houston Astros and Enron Corporation, which owned stadium naming rights) or an internal change within the organization (e.g., sale of a team, firing of a general manager). Favorito (2007) noted that, if the crisis involves the firing of team personnel who may have strong relationships with remaining staff members, "it is very important to make sure the higher ups communicate the reasons and the issues down to the remaining staff...to stem the internal tide of negativity." (p. 248).

A player personnel crisis is commonly experienced in professional sport, given the transient nature of players. This occurs when a team cuts ties with a well-liked player and has to deal with the public fallout. It would be unprofessional for teams to openly critique the player with whom they have opted to part ways, so this makes honest communication with the fan base, at times, difficult. Favorito (2007) advised leaders to accept outside criticism, whether right or wrong, but also to make a concerted effort to support and communicate with the incoming player who is supplanting the popular figure. Taking over for a fan favorite can add pressure to that individual. A statement of appreciation for the exiting player may also garner goodwill with both the athlete and fan base. A similar situation occurred late in the 2017 NFL season when the New York Giants experienced much backlash after Head Coach Ben McAdoo decided to bench quarterback Eli Manning. It looked as if the Giants were bidding farewell to their two-time Super Bowl-winning quarterback. Instead, McAdoo was shown the door just days after Manning was benched (Wilson, 2017).

Crisis Response Strategies

Considering the amount of media attention given to sport, responses, can, at times, garner just as much attention as the actual crisis. For instance, in 2011, the Ohio State University football program was investigated when players were caught selling memorabilia. In a follow-up press conference related to the incident, the president of the university, E. Gordon Gee, was asked if he would consider firing Head Coach Jim Tressel for failing to communicate the transgressions to the appropriate superiors. Gee responded by saying, "Are you kidding me? I hope he doesn't fire me" (Wiedmer, 2011). Gee's comments sent a message to the public that football possessed superiority at the institution, and that a head coach, who was culpable in the debacle, held more power than the president. Perceptually, this response exacerbated the crisis.

When dealing with a crisis, whether or not the organization is truly at fault, an image repair strategy is recommended because of the branding implications of being associated with the incident. Scholars (e.g., Benoit, 1997; Billings et al., 2015; Brazeal, 2008; Favorito, 2007;

Stoldt et al., 2012) have thus recommended a variety of response strategies to employ for image restoration. They include: denial, evasion of responsibility, reducing offensiveness of event, compensation, corrective action, and mortification.

A **denial** stance could be conducted in two ways: through simply denying involvement (e.g., "I didn't do it.") or to shift the blame and claim that another party is culpable. Simple denial postures are usually employed when facing inaccurate claims or unjustified threats (Stoldt et al., 2012). With this posture, the accused may also challenge the accuser by threatening him or her with a lawsuit over false allegations. Such action can signal to the public a strong level of confidence that the accused is innocent.

Former MLB pitcher Roger Clemens used a denial posture when he was accused of using performance-enhancing drugs. Clemens strongly denied the allegations and went so far as to file a defamation lawsuit against the team's trainer, Brian McNamee, claiming that McNamee deliberately fabricated Clemens' involvement. In a series of lawsuits between the two, Clemens was eventually charged with perjury, but was acquitted (Schrieber, 2015). In the end, Clemens' representatives monetarily settled McNamee's counter-defamation suit. Clemens' case provides evidence that the use of a denial posture can be risky if the accusations are not entirely false.

Fuoli, van de Weijer, and Paradis (2017) conducted an experiment to examine the effectiveness of both denial and apology strategies to determine which approach was more suitable in certain situations. As expected, a simple denial was perceived to be more practical than an apology if there was minimal evidence of accused guilt. To the authors' surprise, the effectiveness of denial decreased with strong evidence but was still perceived as a stronger crisis management stance than an apology. The authors speculated that if people trust an organization, they are willing to give them the benefit of the doubt, even in the face of mounting evidence. This also speaks to the importance of perceived trustworthiness in organizational spokespeople.

When blame is shifted to others, it can also be known as **scapegoating**. In this behavior, an organization may not necessarily admit fault, rather it shifts attention to an external party and points to them as an instigator. For example, in light of a far-reaching sexual abuse scandal involving Dr. Larry Nassar, the former physician for Michigan State University and USA Gymnastics, MSU President Lou Anna K. Simon said to a university board trustee at a meeting, "I have been told it is virtually impossible to stop a determined sexual predator" (Meyers, 2017, para. 5).

According to Benoit (1997), **evasion of responsibility** can be displayed through several different behaviors. One would be *provocation*, in which one claims that others' offensive acts influenced an individual to act as a response. If a team were involved in a corporate crisis because it was relocating, it could employ a provocation strategy by citing a municipality's inability to provide sufficient funding as grounds for an exit. Another type would be *defeasibility*, in which one pleads ignorance. This appeared to be exhibited in 2010 when the University of Connecticut men's basketball program was implicated by the NCAA for recruiting violations. Head Coach Jim Calhoun claimed not to have known what was going on, and, as a result, sought the resignation of two assistant coaches who were said to be involved in the impropriety (Borges, 2010). A third form of evasion of responsibility is to claim that the crisis that occurred was not intentional. When a student assistant for the Notre Dame football team was killed while filming practice from a hydraulic lift, the administration called the incident an accident and cited an unexpectedly fierce gust of wind (Associated Press, 2010).

Per Benoit (1997), leaders can also employ a concept called **reducing the offensiveness of the event**. This can be done in a variety of ways, be it bolstering, differentiating, transcending, compensating, mortifying, or offering corrective action. A **bolstering** posture serves as a complement to other postures. It could be in the form of reminding the public of past positives, praising stakeholders for their support during the crisis, or playing the role of victim. When the New England Patriots were being investigated for illegally deflating footballs in 2015, the team's owner, Robert Kraft, made a point to rally his fan base around the team amidst the allegations (Young, 2015). The team also frequented the notion that the NFL was deliberately targeting their organization because of their on-field dominance over the previous decade and would not have done such to an unsuccessful team.

Differentiation is defined as seeking to "disconnect the event from the larger context" (Billings et al., 2015, p. 296). Billings and colleagues (2015) cited how the Cincinnati Reds handled the crisis of former manager Pete Rose, claiming that his betting on baseball had to do with his desire to gamble, as opposed to an abuse of managerial duties. On the other hand, **transcendence** occurs when an organization seeks to posit the act from a more positive perspective. A team may use this strategy to allay fan concerns over increased ticket prices by claiming that the additional revenue will be allocated toward investments into the team.

Compensation involves offering some sort of payment to make up for a fault. In an effort to restore his image after serving prison time for his involvement in a dog fighting operation, former NFL quarterback Michael Vick offered to donate time and money to PETA, an organization dedicated to the proper treatment of animals. A **mortification** approach calls for admitting fault, offering a confession, and asking for forgiveness. After reports revealed that Tiger Woods engaged in an extramarital affair, the golfer admitted his wrongdoings in a press conference and sought the public's clemency. Last, **corrective action** involves offering a plan to fix a problem and prevent it from happening in the future. The two steps to performing corrective action are to admit fault and outline the changes that have been made to rectify the issue. If a college athletics program produces consistently low APR ratings, to the point where it gets penalized, the school may use corrective action by not only bringing in a coach who emphasizes academic development but also by investing more resources into academic advising for the team.

▶ Summary

In general, sport organization communication can be quite challenging due to the unique aspect of the field, such as the size of the operation, augmented media coverage, and oscillating product. During times of crisis, these issues can pose a daunting test. Leadership communication can moderate the success of an organization through informing and motivating both internal and external publics.

It is thus crucial that leaders fulfill their obligations of articulating an organization's vision and goals and satisfying audience needs to effectively assist in task execution. Furthermore, leaders must be knowledgeable about and practice appropriate communication competencies such as demonstration of trust, active listening, providing accurate information, and exhibiting cultural sensitivity, all of which are related to employee satisfaction. Leaders should also be cognizant of their own supervisory styles, and how such communication may be received (positively or negatively) by subordinates.

Finally, a sport organization's ability to manage crises can have a substantial amount of tangible and intangible effects. As a result, sufficient planning must be done on the front end, given that the time to react to crises has diminished to a matter of minutes. For similar reasons, whether or not the organization is at fault, the adoption of certain repair strategies is important, as the time it takes for the public to form an opinion has likewise faded. All of the aforementioned strategies are a product of leadership communication. The more an organization can identify leaders who can effectively communicate, while managing conflict and crises, the stronger it will be in the short and long term.

LEADERSHIP PERSPECTIVE

Larry Dougherty

Larry Dougherty is the Senior Associate Athletic Director for Communications at Temple University. He has been at the school since 2002, after a 15-year stint in media relations at St. Joseph's University. Dougherty currently supervises athletic communications for all 19 sports at Temple, including sport related television and radio operations. Dougherty was the president of the College Sports Information Directors of America (CoSIDA) for the 2010-11 academic year, and in 2015, was inducted into the CoSIDA Hall of Fame.

(continues)

LEADERSHIP PERSPECTIVE (*continued*)

Q: How much has sport organizational communication evolved since you started in this industry?

It's like the prehistoric age to the Industrial Revolution. When I started as a student in 1978, everything was typewriters. The Internet wasn't even a thought at that point. Everything in the world has changed since the inception of the Internet because everything now is instantaneous. The news now is 24/7. You've got to get your message out and get it right the first time.

Q: Does that also impact how upper management in a sport organization communicates internally as well?

Everyone is aware of everything now because of the World Wide Web. We will also react to things that are happening at other institutions, possibly with opponents or what media might be saying about it.

Q: Why are crisis management plans in sport more important now than ever?

Right now, things can spiral by social media and the Internet quickly. The best example in a negative way is United Airlines. With United and that video, everyone in that organization has to realize what they're doing, and it has to be customer service. We're doing customer service in athletics. If something happened in a negative way, especially at a high-level, you're in an immediate crisis. Then, how quickly can you respond to it? That's the thing where you need to have your team in place to make decisions sometimes instantaneously to quell that crisis. United got it "sort of" right on the third try. They let that thing get worse and worse with every time they came out and spoke about it. They weren't ready to handle that kind of crisis. At the end of the day, it didn't matter if the passenger was right or wrong to resist being removed from the plane, what mattered was the billions of dollars of damage that United took by letting themselves be hung out there for a couple of days and not being ready to control the situation.

Q: Given the amount of focus that sport gets nowadays, how much does that magnify crises even more?

We have to be ready for something. You never know what could happen. You could have a crisis that's out of your control in the stands. A crisis isn't necessarily bad for your brand, but overall, you are still dealing with how you react over something you had no control over. In all aspects of sport, we're saying, "We have this coming. We have this information. How do we react to it?" Then, if it hits, what's our crisis plan? At the end of the day, many people are worried about wins and losses. I worry about the crises that are out of our control. We had the women's gymnastics team stuck on a bus a year ago on the Pennsylvania Turnpike for 36 hours. It was a blizzard. They were fine and were among many vehicles stuck in that snowstorm. But, what are we saying to the parents? How are we handling this and working with the authorities to make sure safety is taken care of? You never know when things can happen. We all want to win, but it's how you handle adversity and crises that matters the most.

Q: From your experiences, what are the most effective ways to communicate to the public and to the media during a crisis?

It depends how quickly you need a message out. Say, for instance, if a school had a shooter on campus, we would have a communications plan that we would have text alerts saying that something is going on. We would be on social media quickly with that. We wouldn't have a media conference until everything is settled. That form of communication has to be instantaneous. You'd have to use traditional electronic messages to all students and an email. However, in a crisis, if it's non-life threatening, quickly responding on social media might demean what we're trying to do. You would want to have a more professional response that maybe you post to your website and push on social media secondary. Of course, sometimes in a crisis, organizations and athletic departments, our hands are tied because we can't say anything. I think PR professionals, in this day and age, deal more and more with lawyers to find out what kind of language is usable even though we need to effectively communicate.

Q: Where do you see crisis communication strategic planning heading over the next 5 to 10 years?
The thing is, 10 years ago, you probably wouldn't have thought of using social media for this type of communication. I think we may not know that until the next form of technology evolves. I don't think we'll stop evolving how we communicate with people. Communication, no matter the technology, is critical. Everyone talks about brand and how you build it and sustain it. Having strong communications and great messaging helps create a grand brand. To me, that's not going to change. The only thing that changes is what tool you use for it. What's going to be the next resource? We'll have to learn how to use it. That, to me, is the next evolution of communication.

▶ Key Terms

Autocratic leadership
Bolstering
Compensation
Consultative leadership
Corrective action
Crisis
Denial
Differentiation
Downward communication
Evasion of responsibility

Flagging
Horizontal communication
Interpersonal communication
Intrapersonal communication
Laissez-faire leadership
Leadership communication
Mortification
Organizational
   communication
Participative leadership

Reducing the offensiveness
   of the event
Scapegoating
Small group communication
Sport communication
Transcendence
Upward communication

▶ Discussion Questions

1. Examine the organizational structure of your school's athletic department. From your perspective, does it appear to be structured in an efficient way for communication to flow accordingly?

2. Find several examples of sport leaders in either the amateur, collegiate, or professional ranks that are perceived to demonstrate the different types of communication/leadership styles. What variables may play a role in explaining their success?

3. Think of any head coaches who have led in both college and professional sports. How do you think their communication/leadership style impacted their successes or failures?

4. Think of a recent sport crisis; then find a news story detailing the organization's response. Based on crisis communication best practices, was the right approach taken?

5. What are the advantages and disadvantages to using social media as a primary crisis response channel?

▶ **References**

Ashcraft, K. L., Kuhn, T. R., & Cooren, F. (2009). Constitutional Amendments: Materializing organizational communication. *The Academy of Management Annals, 3*(1), 1–64. Associated Press (2011, March 16). Notre Dame at fault in Sullivan's death. Retrieved from http://www.espn.com/college-football/news/story?id=6219373

Benoit, W. L. (1997). Image repair discourse and crisis communication. *Public Relations Review, 23*(2), 177–186.

Billings, A. C., Butterworth, M. L., & Turman, P. D. (2015). *Communication and sport: Surveying the field*. Sage Publications.

Birkett, D. (2017, October 1). Martha Ford asked Lions not to kneel, promised to back players' agenda. Retrieved from https://www.freep.com/story/sports/nfl/lions/2017/10/01/martha-ford-asked-lions-not-kneel-promised-back-players-agenda/721571001/

Borges, D. (2010, July 2). UConn men's basketball replaces assistant coaches after NCAA probe. *The Middletown Press*. Retrieved from http://www.middletownpress.com/article/MI/20100702/NEWS/307029967

Brazeal, L. M. (2008). The image repair strategies of Terrell Owens. *Public Relations Review, 34*(2), 145–150.

Breer, A. (2017, Oct. 27). Bob McNair's comments show the fragility of relations between NFL players and owners. Retrieved from https://www.si.com/nfl/2017/10/27/bob-mcnair-houston-texans-owners-inmate-comments

Brown, N. A. & Billings, A. C. (2013). Sports fans as crisis communicators on social media websites. *Public Relations Review, 39*(1), 74–81.

Chelladurai, P. & Saleh, S. D. (1980). Dimensions of leader behavior in sports: Development of a leadership scale. *Journal of Sport Psychology, 2*(1), 34–45.

Coombs, W. T. (2012). *Ongoing crisis communication: Planning, managing, and Responding (2nd ed.)*. Thousand Oaks, CA: Sage Publications.

Coombs, W. T. (2014). *Ongoing crisis communication: Planning, managing, and Responding (4th ed.)*. Thousand Oaks, CA: Sage Publications.

Cruz, M. G., Henningsen, D. D., & Smith, B. A. (1999). The impact of directive leadership on group information sampling, decisions, and perceptions of the leader. *Communication Research, 26*(3), 349–369.

Dabbah, M. (2014, October 31). What is cultural sensitivity? Retrieved from http://redshoemovement.com/what-is-cultural-sensitivity/

Daniels, T. (2017, October 27). Texans owner Bob McNair on protests: 'We can't have inmates running the prison.' Retrieved from http://bleacherreport.com/articles/2741008-texans-owner-bob-mcnair-on-protests-we-cant-have-inmates-running-the-prison

DeVito, J. A. (2009). *Human communication: The basic course* (11th ed.). Pearson Higher Ed.

Doherty, A. J. & Chelladurai, P. (1999). Managing cultural diversity in sport organizations: A theoretical perspective. *Journal of Sport Management, 13*(4), 280–297.

Elfman, L. (2017, January 24). Experts: Game plan key to managing campus sports crisis. Retrieved from http://diverseeducation.com/article/91633/

Favorito, J. (2007). *Sports publicity: A practical approach*. Elsevier Science & Technology.

Foltz, R. G. (1985). Communication in contemporary organizations. In C. Reuss & D. Silvis (Eds.), *Inside organizational communication* (pp. 3–14). New York, NY: Longman Inc.

Forsberg, C. (2016, July 1). Celtics give extensions to Danny Ainge, Brad Stevens. Retrieved from http://www.espn.com/nba/story/_/id/15876998/boston-celtics-give-extensions-president-danny-ainge-coach-brad-stevens

Fuoli, M., van de Weijer, J., & Paradis, C. (2017). Denial outperforms apology in repairing organizational trust despite strong evidence of guilt. *Public Relations Review, 43*(4), 645–660.

Giffin, K. & Patton, B. R. (1976). *Fundamentals of interpersonal communication* (2nd ed.). New York, NY: Harper and Row Publishers.

Goff, B. (2000). Effects of university athletics on the university: A review and extension of empirical assessment. *Journal of Sport Management, 14*(2), 85–104.

Grippo, J. A. (2009). *A complete guide to public speaking*. Outskirts Press: Denver, CO.

Hovland, C. I., & Weiss, W. (1951). The influence of source credibility on communication effectiveness. *Public Opinion Quarterly, 15*(4), 635–650.

Johnson, S. D. & Bechler, C. (1998). Examining the relationship between listening effectiveness and leadership emergence: Perceptions, behaviors, and recall. *Small Group Research, 29*(4), 452–471.

Jordan, J. S., Kent, A., & Walker, M. (2015). Management and leadership in the sport industry. In A. Gillentine & R. B. Crow (Eds.), *Foundations of sport management* (pp. 49–72). Morgantown, WV: FiT Publishing.

Koys, D. J. (2006). The effects of employee satisfaction, organizational citizenship behavior, and turnover on organizational effectiveness: A unitlevel, longitudinal study. *Personnel Psychology, 54*(1), 101–114.

Lee, D. & Hatesohl, D. (1993). Listening: Our most used communications skill. *University of Missouri Extension*.

Levin, J. (2014, April 29). Yes, Donald Sterling sees his basketball team as a plantation. Retrieved from http://www.slate.com/articles/sports/sports_nut/2014/04

/donald_sterling_racism_yes_the_clippers_owner
_sees_his_basketball_team_as.html

Long, C. S., & Thean, L. Y. (2011). Relationship between leadership style, job satisfaction and employees' turnover intention: A literature review. *Research Journal of Business Management, 5*(3), 91–100.

Mather, V. (2016, April 19). On verge of sweep, Capitals have the Flyers and their fans frustrated. *The New York Times.* Retrieved from https://www.nytimes.com/2016/04/20/sports/hockey/capitals-in-command-as-series-with-flyers-turns-ugly.html

Meyers, D. (2017). Michigan State can't bury its role in the largest sex abuse scandal in sports history. *Deadspin.* Retrieved from https://deadspin.com/michigan-state-cant-bury-its-role-in-the-largest-sex-ab-1821129797

Mullin, B. J., Hardy, S., & Sutton, W. A. (2014). *Sport Marketing 4th Edition.* Champaign, IL: Human Kinetics.

Olsen, C. (2016, December 13). P. J. Fleck leaves X's and O's to coordinators, and that's how they like it. Retrieved from http://www.mlive.com/broncos/index.ssf/2016/12/western_michigan_offensivedefe.html

Pedersen, P. (2013). *Routledge handbook of sport communication.* New York, NY: Routledge.

Pedersen, P. M., Laucella, P. C., Kian, E. T. M., & Geurin, A. N. (2016). *Strategic sport communication* (2nd ed.). Champaign, IL: Human Kinetics.

Pedersen, P. M., Laucella, P. C., Miloch, K. S., & Fielding, L. W. (2007). The juxtaposition of sport and communication: Defining the field of sport communication. *International Journal of Sport Management and Marketing, 2*(3), 193–207.

Pedersen, P. M., Miloch, K. S., & Laucella, P. C. (2007). *Strategic sport communication.* Champaign, IL: Human Kinetics.

Pettit Jr., J. D., Goris, J. R., & Vaught, B. C. (1997). An examination of organizational communication as a moderator of the relationship between job performance and job satisfaction. *The Journal of Business Communication, 34*(1), 81–98.

Plunkett Research, Ltd. (2015). *Sports & recreation Business statistics analysis, business and industry statistics.* Retrieved from https://www.plunkettresearch.com/statistics/sports-industry/

Schrieber, J. (2015, March 19). Defamation lawsuit by Roger Clemens's ex-trainer is settled after 7 years. *The New York Times.* Retrieved from https://www.nytimes.com/2015/03/19/sports/baseball/defamation-lawsuit-by-roger-clemenss-ex-trainer-is-settled-after-7-years.html

Shaughnessy, D. (2013, February 19). Red sox blame a lot of their problems on Bobby Valentine. *The Boston Globe.* Retrieved from https://www.bostonglobe.com/sports/2013/02/19/red-sox-blame-lot-their-problems-bobby-valentine/iM2us1UeBXWevfB8NXoqgM/story.html

Shockley-Zalabak, P. (1999). *Fundamentals of Organizational Communication: Knowledge Sensitivity, Skills, Values* (4th ed.). Longman.

Spitzberg, B. H. (1988). Communication competence: Measures of perceived effectiveness. *A handbook for the study of human communication: Methods and instruments for observing, measuring, and assessing communication processes,* 67–105.

Stephens, K. K., & Malone, P. C. (2009). If the organizations won't give us information. . .: The use of multiple new media for crisis technical translation and dialogue. *Journal of Public Relations Research, 21*(2), 229–239.

Stoldt, G. C., Dittmore, S. W., & Branvold, S. E. (2012). *Sport public relations: Managing stakeholder communication* (2nd ed.). Human Kinetics.

Stoldt, G. C., Miller, L. K., & Comfort, P. G. (2001). Through the eyes of athletic directors: Perceptions of sports information directors, and other public relations issues. *Sport Marketing Quarterly, 10*(3), 164–172.

Turman, P. D. (2001). Situational coaching styles: The impact of success and athlete maturity level on coaches' leadership styles over time. *Small Group Research, 32*(5), 576–594.

Turman, P. D. & Schrodt, P. (2004). New avenues for instructional communication research: Relationships among coaches' leadership behaviors and athletes' affective learning. *Communication Research Reports, 21*(2), 130–143.

Wiedmer, M. (2011, July 12). Wiedmer: Ohio State still asking for trouble. Retrieved from http://www.timesfreepress.com/news/sports/columns/story/2011/jul/12/wiedmer-ohio-state-still-asking-trouble/53785/

Wilson, R. (2017, Dec. 4). Giants fire Ben McAdoo, Jerry Reese days after Eli Manning is benched. Retrieved from https://www.cbssports.com/nfl/news/giants-reportedly-fire-ben-mcadoo-days-after-he-benches-eli-manning/

Wrisberg, C. A. (1990). An interview with Pat Head Summitt. *The Sport Psychologist, 4*(2), 180–191.

Young, S. M. (2015, July 30). Robert Kraft defends Tom Brady, attacks NFL's suspension. *The Boston Globe.* Retrieved from https://www.bostonglobe.com/sports/2015/07/29/patriots-owner-robert-kraft-blasts-nfl-over-deflategate-penalty/18IqKehM9nAbE51OOQzOAK/story.html

CHAPTER 6

Applying a Principled and Ethical Approach to Sport Leadership

Meg G. Hancock

Mary A. Hums

CHAPTER OBJECTIVES

- Demonstrate an understanding of a historic grounding of ethics in the sport industry.
- Discuss ethics and ethical decision making within the context of sport and sport organizations.
- Recognize chronic and emerging ethical issues in sport at various levels.
- Establish a framework for becoming an ethical leader.

CASE STUDY

Legalizing Discrimination and Sport

On March 26, 2016, the North Carolina legislature passed the "Public Facilities Privacy & Security Act" most commonly known as House Bill 2 (HB2) or the "Bathroom Bill." HB2, signed into law by then-governor Pat McCrory, effectively "nullified local ordinances around the state that would have expanded protections for the LGBT community" (Gordon, Price, & Peralta, 2016). Under the new law, sexual orientation and gender identity expression were not considered "protected classes" (i.e., race, religion, color, national origin, age, disability, or biological sex) against discrimination. Furthermore, and perhaps the most controversial aspect of this law, is that it required transgender people to use public restrooms based on their birth sex rather than their gender identity.

(continues)

CASE STUDY   (continued)

Backlash to HB2 was immediate. Major corporations, national, and international corporations, including PayPal, Deutsche Bank, and Time Warner, halted expansion efforts that would have added thousands of jobs and millions of dollars to the North Carolina economy. By December 2016, seven states and over two dozen cities and counties issued travel bans prohibiting government employees from non-essential travel to North Carolina. Trade shows and professional associations canceled events and conferences in cities around the state, resulting in the loss of several million dollars. Bruce Springsteen, Ringo Starr, Pearl Jam, Demi Lovato, Nick Jonas, and Maroon 5 canceled shows in cities around the state in protest of the anti-LGBT legislation (Bort, 2016).

Sport organizations also expressed their opposition to HB2. The National Basketball Association (NBA) relocated the 2017 NBA All-Star game from Charlotte to New Orleans, Louisiana. The National Collegiate Athletic Association (NCAA) stripped North Carolina of hosting rights for seven NCAA-sanctioned tournaments and championships. The Atlantic Coast Conference (ACC) moved all neutral-site sport championships, including the ACC football championship, out of North Carolina. Leaders of state colleges and universities in Minnesota deemed sport travel non-essential, thereby banning travel to North Carolina (Shipley, 2016). This move also prevented some student athletes from participating in national championships. The University of Vermont women's basketball team also canceled their game at the University of North Carolina (UNC) in protest of HB2. Because Vermont canceled the game, they also forfeited $17,500 of guaranteed money from UNC (Carter, 2016).

HB2 has since been partially repealed and many companies and organizations, including the NCAA, have reinstated events and travel to North Carolina. However, given the potential for discriminatory legislation in other states, leaders in sport must follow ethical decision-making principles when considering their organization's position on discriminatory practices and practices that might harm the health and well-being of their athletes. In addition, sport leaders must also recognize the potential ethical issues (e.g., athletes lose opportunities to participate) that may arise when banning or boycotting activities.

Questions for Discussion

1. An important part of the ethical decision-making process is to first recognize an ethical dilemma. Considering the examples provided in this section, should sport organizations boycott participation in states with discriminatory laws?
2. What situational factors in sport can provide leaders with the tools to successfully navigate an ethical dilemma? Read through the chapter to help answer this question.
3. Explain how you could use the ethical decision-making model described in the chapter to determine whether you would allow your team to participate in a state with discriminatory laws.

▶ Introduction

A recent study of professional sport teams, leagues, and federations valued the global sport industry at $1.3 trillion (Plunkett Research, 2016). The size of the sport industry in the United States alone is estimated to be $496 billion. Even more astonishingly, the sport industry is growing faster than global

gross domestic products (GDP) for several countries including Brazil, China, France, the United Kingdom, and the United States (A.T. Kearney, 2015). In the United States, the "Big Four" professional sport leagues combined—Major League Baseball, the National Basketball Association, the National Football League, and the National Hockey League—accrue $23 billion in gate, media, and sponsorship revenues annually. Of the 32 NFL teams, 27 are valued at over $2 billion (Badenhausen, 2017). At the collegiate level, the National Collegiate Athletic Association (NCAA) generated over $900 million in annual revenue in 2016 (Statista, 2017). Conferences continue to negotiate astronomical media rights. For example, negotiations between the Atlantic Coast Conference (ACC) and ESPN resulted in a deal that equates to $20 million per school per year through 2026–2027 (Fowler, 2013). The International Olympic Committee (IOC) surpassed $4 billion in global broadcast revenues for the 2014 and 2016 Olympic Games contracts (IOC, 2018).

We are all keenly aware of the monetary magnitude of the sport industry. This industry is not alone in piling up billions of dollars or euros in revenues annually. However, we must also be keenly aware that with financial success come opportunities for pitfalls, missteps, and temptations along the way.

The National Business Ethics Survey (NBES) found that ethical misconduct in the workplace is at an all-time low. However, employees surveyed said that their supervisors did not model ethical behavior; in fact, managers were responsible for 60 percent of workplace misconduct (Ethics Resource Center, 2014). The survey also indicated an increase in the percentage of employees who perceived pressure to compromise personal and professional standards, experienced retaliation after reporting misconduct (whistle-blowing), and perceived a weak organizational culture of ethics.

Although the NBES was not specific to the sport industry, it is important to consider that as sport continues to grow on a national and global scale, many youth, intercollegiate, professional, and international sport organizations may face similar ethical challenges. In 2010, Ohio State was given the moniker "Tattoo U" when football players were found to have exchanged team memorabilia for free tattoos. The University of Miami football team (Robinson, 2011) and the University of Louisville men's basketball team (Cogan, 2017) were implicated in separate scandals that alleged players were provided with, among other things, cash and prostitutes. Events at Miami and Louisville were perceived to be two of the most egregious scandals in college sport since Southern Methodist University received the "death penalty" from the NCAA for providing football student-athletes with impermissible benefits. In 2011, however; Penn State defensive coordinator Jerry Sandusky was indicted and charged with the sexual abuse of eight boys that took place over 15 years. Athletic Director Tim Curley resigned when allegations of abuse surfaced. Head football coach Joe Paterno and university president Graham Spanier were subsequently fired.

Lest we forget, NFL scandals have also made headlines in recent years, including "SpyGate" and "Deflategate" (New England Patriots), "Bounty-gate" (New Orleans Saints), and "Bullygate" (Jonathan Martin, Richie Incognito, and the Miami Dolphins). Baltimore Ravens running back Ray Rice received a two-game suspension for the assault of his fiancé. When a video of the assault was released, Rice was suspended indefinitely and the NFL overhauled the league's domestic violence policy. Major League Baseball is rife with allegations of performance-enhancing drug use (see Barry Bonds, Mark McGwire, Manny Ramirez, and Melky Cabrera). Scandals even arise in youth leagues. In 2001, Danny Almonte and the Rolando Paulino All-Stars were stripped of their Little League World Series wins because Almonte was found to be 2 years older than Little League rules permitted (Malley, 2011). In 2016, Laura Zellerbach, a volunteer treasurer for the Fullerton Rangers youth soccer club, pled guilty to embezzling nearly $200,000 from the club (Froh, 2017). Incidents of violence involving parents at youth sporting events also persist. Then there was the seemingly infallible Tiger Woods and allegations of rampant adultery. In 2012, the U.S. Anti-Doping Agency and the International Cycling Union both stripped Lance

Armstrong of seven Tour de France victories and instituted a lifetime ban amid allegations of performance-enhancing drug use. In 2016, the International Paralympic Committee (IPC) banned the entire Russian delegation from competing in the Rio de Janeiro Summer Paralympic Games due to involvement with state-supported drug test tampering.

In short, the domain of sport has suffered from questionable ethical practices if not downright unethical behavior. Although many of the aforementioned examples focus on athletes, this chapter will focus on the sport leader. We begin with a historical grounding of ethics in the sport industry, followed by a section on ethics and ethical decision making within the context of sport and sport organizations. We offer information regarding chronic and emerging ethical issues in sport at various levels. The chapter concludes with a framework for becoming an ethical leader.

Eight Chicago White Sox players conspired with gamblers to throw the World Series in 1919. The players were banned from Major League Baseball in 1921.

Courtesy of *The Sporting News*.

▶ Historical Background

The modern sport industry evolved around 150 years ago in England. Since then, nearly every segment of the sport industry has encountered and addressed the unsavory and questionable behavior of players, coaches, and administrators. Money, or a bottom-line approach, has significantly influenced the decision-making process in sport. Consider the development of the club system to better manage the growing complexities of gambling in the thoroughbred racing industry to ensure fair and honest racing (Crosset & Hums, 2015b). Then came the Black Sox Scandal of 1919, after which, in 1921, Major League Baseball (MLB) banned eight players for intentionally throwing World Series games.

Social issues have also contributed to the complexities of ethical decision making. In 1947, Jackie Robinson was the first modern baseball player to break Major League Baseball's color barrier. To put this into perspective, it would be another seven years before the U.S.

Supreme Court declared segregation unconstitutional. Pierre de Coubertin, the founder of the modern Olympic Games, claimed: "An Olympiad with females would be impractical, uninteresting, unaesthetic, and improper" (Boulongne, 2000, p. 23). Although de Coubertin felt the inclusion of female athletes was "uninteresting," a number of scientists and medical doctors felt women's participation in sport was downright unhealthy, positing that physical activity could inhibit a woman's reproductive capability. Today, more women participate in sport than ever before. However, gender fraud, medical conditions such as hyperandrogeny, and the participation of transgender athletes have served as catalysts for policy (re)formation, such as sex testing by national and international sport governing bodies.

Historically, violence and the health and safety of athletes have led to intense ethical debate. Recently, the inclusion of athletes with disabilities has taken center stage in the United States and in countries around the world. Regardless of level or industry segment, you, as a sport management professional, will encounter situations requiring you to consider your personal values and the values of others. In these moments, you may begin to consider which behaviors or decisions are ethical versus those that are not. This chapter is designed to help you gain a better understanding of your own ethics and the ethics of others, ethical dilemmas, and ethical decision-making models.

▸ Ethics and Ethical Dilemmas

In our experience, few questions in a classroom cause students to shrink into their seats more than a discussion on ethics. A class that has been responsive and talkative all semester suddenly becomes eerily quiet. After a few seconds of silence, we pose the question again, "What is ethics?" More silence, then a muffled voice comes from the corner of the room, "The difference between right and wrong." The greatest consternation among students occurs in the debate around what or who determines right and wrong, as well as the context in which those determinations are made. **Ethics** is, in essence, the difference between right and wrong, but the difference is rarely so black and white. Perhaps the response, or lack thereof, reflects the "grey zone where clear-cut right versus wrong answers may not always exist" (Sims, 1992, p. 506).

Ethics and sport are perfect examples of the "grey zone"; they seem inherently contradictory (Volkwein, 1995). In one breath, we espouse the value of sport in teaching character, good sporting conduct, healthy lifestyles, and the importance of teamwork. In the next breath, we may cheer for a team whose players' coaching staff and owner have been accused of orchestrating a bounty system in which players receive rewards for injuring opposing players. In one of the most recent and well-publicized

scandals in college sport, University of Louisville men's basketball coach Rick Pitino was implicated in two separate scandals designed to lure elite high school prospects to the university. Think about it: When you learned about the New Orleans Saints' bounty system or recruiting scandals at Louisville, what were your initial reactions? Some of you may have reacted with outrage, whereas others may have taken the stance of "every other team does it, they just got caught."

DeSensi and Rosenberg (1996) suggested that the contradiction between sport and ethical behavior stems from a capitalistic, "win at all costs" mentality, which has, "misguided or misdirected individual thoughts and actions" (p. 5). Perhaps another reason many students become uneasy when discussing ethics is because the word seems to elicit the perception of judgment grounded in personal values. Ethics are, in fact, the "systematic study of **values** guiding our decision making" (Crosset & Hums, 2015a, p. 132). More simply, ethics are moral principles that govern decisions and behavior. **Morals**, then, are the enactment of ethical principles. It is important to understand the foundation of ethical philosophies (Malloy & Zakus, 1995) so that you, as a sport professional, can (1) identify your personal biases and (2) identify the personal biases of employees and stakeholders. Each tradition is briefly explained in the following sections.

Philosophical Traditions

Two dominant philosophies are perceived to govern ethical decision making and behavior—**teleology** and **deontology**. Teleology suggests that decisions can be judged good or bad, right or wrong based on the consequences of those decisions (DeSensi & Rosenberg, 1996). In other words, the fundamental principle of teleology is for the outcome of a decision to result in the greatest good for the most people (Volkwein, 1995). In 1972, the U.S. federal government passed Title IX, which outlawed sex discrimination in educational institutions receiving federal financial assistance. The intention of Title IX was to provide women equal opportunity, equal access, and fair treatment in educational settings. Increased athletic participation was a by-product of Title IX. Less than 300,000 women participated in interscholastic sport in 1972 compared with 3.6 million men (National Federation of State High School Associations [NFHS], 2017). Today, over 3.4 million women participate compared with 4.5 million men (NFHS, 2012). From a teleologist's perspective, Title IX passage was a "good" decision because it positively impacted the lives of millions of young women and men.

A second philosophical approach, deontology, contends that the right decisions are those that are in accordance with conduct, duties, or rules agreed upon by a community or society (DeSensi & Rosenberg, 1996). Repercussions of decisions are of no consequence because the decision was grounded in principle (Malloy & Zakus, 1995). Consider the case of Elijah Earnhart, the 6-foot, 300-pound 12-year-old who wanted to play Pee Wee football. During a preseason weigh-in, Earnhart was deemed "too big to play" because he exceeded the 135-pound weight limit set by the Pee Wee Football Association (PWFA). Ultimately, Earnhart was denied the opportunity to play. The PWFA president explained, "Rules are rules" (Ray, 2012). Rules are the principles that guide the governance of the PWFA. In another example, Max Beggs, a 17-year-old transgender boy (female-to-male), won the Texas girls' wrestling championship. Beggs was barred from wrestling against boys in his weight class, despite using testosterone as part of his treatment, because Texas wrestling rules dictate that wrestlers "must compete as the gender marked on their birth certificate" (Domonoske, 2017, para. 7). Similar to Earnhart's case, Texas league officials suggested that wrestling rules are unlikely to change any time soon as 95% of Texas high school superintendents voted for the rule as proposed (Domonoske, 2017).

As a sport manager, rarely will you find yourself or your staff members declaring allegiance to teleology or deontology. You may discover some of your staff making decisions for the "greater good" whereas others will make decisions based on principle. Although ethical traditions may help us understand the philosophies that guide decision-making behavior, they do little to help us identify and respond to ethical dilemmas.

Ethical Dilemmas

According to Volkwein (1995, p. 311), an **ethical dilemma** or moral dilemma exists "whenever an action is involved." More specifically, a dilemma exists when the action has the potential to harm or benefit others (Jones, 1991). The action must also be considered within the context of a community and the social norms to which that community subscribes. Social context is important because it defines what is legal and morally acceptable in a given community.

Sport managers encounter ethical dilemmas from youth to professional levels regarding issues pertaining to equity, diversity, competitive fairness, legal matters, personnel, and, more recently, technology and the use of social media (DeSensi & Rosenberg, 1996; Hutchens, 2011). On a daily basis, sport managers encounter myriad ethical dilemmas, some more unusual than others. The following section addresses current and emerging ethical issues in youth and interscholastic sport, intercollegiate athletics, professional sport, and international sport. As you read through each section, consider some of the ethical dilemmas that you think leaders in sport might encounter.

Youth Sport

For the purpose of this section, youth sport includes young men and women participating in recreational and interscholastic athletics. In a 2004 report compiled by Hedstrom and

Gould, the Institute for the Study of Youth Sports (ISYS) documented critical issues influencing youth participation in sport, which included participation and retention, health and safety concerns, and equity. In addition to these current issues, the sport leader would be remiss if he or she failed to acknowledge the emerging presence of youth with disabilities. The participation and retention of youth in recreational sport has been identified as a concern because recent data confirm that the number of youth participating in sport is on the decline. Consider this: Over 35 million youth participate in sport each year. That number drops to 7.5 million by the time students reach high school (National Center for Sports Safety [NCSS], 2012). The decline has been attributed to cost of participation, lack of interest, poor experiences with peers, poor experiences with coaches, and lack of opportunity (for girls) (Lee, 2015; NCSS, 2012).

Although health and safety issues (e.g., nutrition, training errors, lack of qualified coaching) have long been a concern of youth sport managers, several recent, highly publicized events have brought attention to hazardous playing conditions and the growing rate of injuries due to overuse or inadequate equipment. Heat-related illnesses and lightning strikes, in particular, have claimed the lives of youth athletes and spectators. A study by the National Center for Sports Safety (NCSS, 2012) found that nearly 3.5 million children age 14 or under receive medical treatment for sport injuries each year. Additionally, the NCSS reported, "injuries associated with sports and recreational activities account for 21 percent of all traumatic brain injuries among children in the United States" (para. 4). Between 1982 and 2002, 256 athletes died while participating in high school sport (NCSS, 2012).

One of the challenges youth sport leaders routinely face is hiring knowledgeable coaches who can also exercise sound judgment about playing conditions. Hedstrom and Gould (2004) contend that finding quality coaches is critical to enhancing the youth experience

while also ensuring health and safety. Unfortunately, the pool of qualified youth sport coaches is relatively shallow (Hedstrom & Gould, 2004), and most recreational and interscholastic programs offer little training. Training may also require financial commitment from the coach, prohibiting some people from being involved.

Some ethical dilemmas are more complicated than others. Regardless of the dilemma, the decision has consequences—positive and negative—for those involved. Let's go back to the example of Elijah Earnhart, the boy deemed "too big" to play Pee Wee football. The president of the PWFA was faced with an ethical dilemma—to let Earnhart play despite his size or to ban him because of his size. The president's statement, "Rules are rules," seems simplistic and may reflect the PWFA president's ethical philosophy; however, it is important to recognize that this ethical dilemma has repercussions for a number of individuals—players, coaches, and parents. Imagine, for a moment, that you are Elijah. How do you feel about being banned from Pee Wee football? Imagine that you are the parent of a child on a team opposing Elijah's. How do you feel about his ban? As the president of the PWFA, how would you go about making the decision? Would you consider what benefits the greater good? Do you stick to the rules? What factors would play into the decision-making process? Not sure where to begin? The following sections offer suggestions on ethical decision making.

Intercollegiate Athletics

Intercollegiate athletics has a history dating back to the 1800s and has been marred by the questionable behavior and decisions of players, coaches, fans, and administrators. The National Collegiate Athletic Association (NCAA) was founded in 1906 to "protect young people from the dangerous and exploitive athletics practices of the time" (NCAA, 2012b, para. 1). A report by the Carnegie Foundation issued in 1929 condemned colleges and universities for "academic abuses, recruiting abuses, payments to student athletes, and the commercialization of athletics" (Barr, 2015, p. 176). Not surprisingly, many issues that sport managers working in organized intercollegiate sport faced over 150 years ago persist today. Intercollegiate athletic departments, conferences, and the NCAA continue to wrestle with topics such as student-athlete health and safety, "pay for play" and extra benefits, the commercialization of sport, and equity (racial, gender, and disability).

Student-athlete health and safety have been identified as an area of concern for the NCAA and intercollegiate athletic programs. The recent deaths of current and retired NFL football players Tyler Sash, Junior Seau, Ray Easterling, and Dave Duerson brought to light the profound effects of repetitive head injuries also known as chronic traumatic encephalopathy (CTE). Aaron Hernandez, former tight end for the New England Patriots and convicted murderer, was found to "have the most severe case of CTE ever discovered in a person his age, damage that would have significantly affected his decision-making, judgment and cognition" (Kilgore, 2017, para. 1). Additionally, a study on young athletes ages 15 to 24 found the majority of concussions occurred in football, women's soccer, wrestling, and women's basketball; the concussion rate of girls was nearly twice as high as that of boys (Marar, McIlvain, Fields, & Comstock, 2012). Subsequently, the NCAA developed a partnership with the Centers for Disease Control and Prevention (CDC) to ensure student-athletes are "properly protected from and treated for concussions" (NCAA, 2012a, para. 1). Although the NCAA and CDC have taken steps to educate administrators, student-athletes, and coaches, we all know examples of student-athletes competing with concussions or other injuries. Many student-athletes feel pressured to compete regardless of injury, so how can intercollegiate athletic administrators monitor injuries? Should administrators intervene if it may mean the team loses a star athlete or a game? What if the star athlete in question has a potential professional career in sport? Should he or she be required to sit out a contest where scouts are present?

Perhaps the issue of student-athlete health and safety is a product of the "win-at-all-costs" mentality of a multi-million-dollar sport industry. In 2011, the NCAA reported revenues in excess of $838 million, which included an initial $617 million payout from a 14-year, $10.8 billion contract with Turner Broadcasting and CBS Sports (NCAA, 2012c). Although NCAA revenues are still shy of professional sport organizations and leagues, the amount of revenue generated has created concern about the commercialization of college sport as well as the benefits—or lack thereof—afforded to student-athletes. Other companies, like EA Sports, have profited to the sum of millions from using the likenesses of NCAA student-athletes.

Nike, Adidas, and Under Armour brands profit heavily through sponsorships with marquee athletic programs at colleges and universities around the United States. In 2016, UCLA signed the largest deal in NCAA history with Under Armour worth $280 million, which includes at least $18.67 million per year in apparel and equipment, facility upgrades, and cash (Wharton, 2016). The most infamous deal, however, may be the $160 million extension between Adidas and the University of Louisville. In August of 2017, Louisville celebrated its new place at the top of Adidas' college portfolio, which ranked the University's apparel deal fourth behind UCLA ($280 million; Under Armour), Ohio State ($252 million; Nike), and Texas ($250 million; Nike) (Greer, 2017). One month later, Louisville men's basketball coach Rick Pitino was alleged to be "Coach 2" in an FBI "pay for play" investigation of bribery in college basketball. In June of 2017, Pitino, along with Adidas executive Jim Gatto, was alleged to have funneled $100,000 from Adidas to the family of a top-ranked high school recruit. The recruit subsequently and unexpectedly committed to the University of Louisville. While the case is still under investigation, Pitino was fired as was athletic director Tom Jurich. The student athlete involved has yet to be reinstated to the team as of this writing.

As top-tier college programs such as Louisville, Miami, and North Carolina continue to recover from "extra benefit" scandals, coaches and administrators debate whether such benefits would be eliminated if student-athletes were paid for their performance. Given the profitability of college sport, administrators must grapple with questions, including: Should student-athletes be paid? If so, which student-athletes and how much? Does paying some student-athletes and not others create issues of equity among all student-athletes?

The ethical dilemmas in college athletics are plentiful and plague intercollegiate administrators, coaches, student-athletes, and fans. Thus, it is important for leaders in sport to consider the scope of their decisions. Who is involved? Who is affected? And, at what cost to the person(s) and organization? How can you make the best decision? Finally, it is important to consider that your decision might have repercussions for industry segments other than your own.

Professional Sport

The world of professional sport is also littered with ethical dilemmas, whether on the field or in the front office. In North American professional sport, the "Deflategate" scandal in New England, where Patriots personnel were found to have deliberately deflated footballs during the AFC championship game, resulted in the suspension of quarterback Tom Brady, a $1 million team fine, and the loss of two first-round draft picks (ESPN, 2016). Were the sanctions too harsh? Too lenient? The debate continues. One question was how involved and informed the coaching staff was of this questionable player behavior.

A completely different ethical dilemma facing people in the front offices of professional

sport franchises deals with the current state of the economy. It has become evident that the sport industry is not recession-proof. As money gets tight, owners and general managers must make decisions about laying off front-office employees. Workforce questions in a tight economy become even more complicated in the face of labor disputes. The 2012 NHL lockout resulted in actions like those taken by the St. Louis Blues, which laid off employees and forced other employees to work fewer hours (Logan, 2012). The ethical dilemma here is: Which employees are deemed expendable and which can remain? What happens to employee benefits during this time? One more ethical issue deals with the front office controlling players' ability to express their opinions. Major League Baseball's Miami Marlins Manager Ozzie Guillen created a firestorm of controversy by making public comments praising Cuba's Fidel Castro. The team responded by suspending him for five games (Thompson & Macur, 2012).

In other cases, Brendon Ayanbadejo of the NFL's Baltimore Ravens was publicly criticized by a Maryland state legislator after the player publicly supported same-sex marriage. The legislator called on the Ravens ownership to silence Ayanbadejo; ownership refused (Klemko, 2012). Super Bowl quarterback Colin Kaepernick refused to stand for the national anthem before an NFL game. Kaepernick explained his decision, "I am not going to stand up to show pride in a flag for a country that oppresses black people and people of color" (Wyche, 2016). Despite his efforts to bring awareness to racism and racial oppression in the United States, and even garnering support from players across the league and nation, Kaepernick's actions brought a firestorm of negative backlash to the NFL. Kaepernick remains a free agent and has not been signed by another NFL team.

These are very different examples of team management weighing in on the ethical dilemma of what opinions an employee should be able to express publicly. Similar dilemmas exist in intercollegiate athletics with regard to student-athletes' use of Twitter.

International Sport

There may be no industry more global than sport, and that scope brings with it some interesting situations. First of all, sport managers working in an international environment will work with people from different cultures, and different cultures may deal with ethical issues differently. For example, Sholtens and Dam (2007) found that there were significant differences in ethical policies among firms that were headquartered in different countries. This means that sport managers working in a diverse workplace will need to be cognizant of this and also respectful of it. For example, although some people may feel that not allowing women the opportunity to compete in the Olympic Games is discriminatory, others may feel just the opposite (Al Nafjan, 2012). These are two dichotomous views, and sport managers need to be aware of them. Issues will vary in importance depending on where one lives and works.

Some of the most discussed ethical issues internationally revolve around the world's most popular sport—football (soccer). The president of the international federation governing football, Sepp Blatter of FIFA, has been a lightning rod for the organization's allegations of corruption and a lax approach to racism on the pitch (Associated Press, 2012; Murphy, 2011). Match fixing by players and referees seems commonplace and sometimes part of the culture of the sport. Officials are finally starting to step up and take concerted actions to try and rein in this blot on the sport's character (Bang, 2012). Another issue clouded with ethical questions is the awarding of the location of the World Cup, the sport's flagship event. The awarding of the 2022 World Cup to Qatar sparked controversy over a voting scandal (Sale, 2012). In September 2015, Swedish officials began investigating Blatter on suspicion of criminal mismanagement and misappropriation,

including financial misappropriation and corruption. By October, Blatter was suspended by the FIFA ethics committee; he was barred from soccer after being found guilty of ethics violations in December of 2015 (New York Times, 2015).

The Olympic and Paralympic Games are not without their own ethical dilemmas. Every time the Olympic and Paralympic Games—or almost any other major international multisport event for that matter—are staged, a host city will need to build new sport facilities. Often, this results in the displacement of people living where the new construction takes place. In Beijing, nearly 1.5 million people were to be displaced during preparations for the 2008 Summer Olympic and Paralympic Games (Bulman, 2007). The Games in Seoul, Barcelona, Athens, and Rio de Janeiro also resulted in displacements (Zirin, 2012).

▶ Ethical Decision Making

Every day, leaders and managers in sport are faced with ethical dilemmas that require decision making. As a student still learning about the sport industry, you are likely to be less familiar with certain ethical dilemmas than senior-level administrators are. The purpose of this chapter is not to make you aware of every ethical dilemma in sport, but rather to prepare you to identify and address ethical dilemmas in a manner that is congruent with the law and values in a sport organization and the larger sport community. Many **ethical decision-making models** are out there for your consideration, but the critical factor in each is the initial recognition that an ethical dilemma exists. Once the dilemma is identified, the decision-making process can commence. Ethical decision making is complex and includes the consideration of multiple factors (Beu, Buckley, & Harvey, 2003). When engaging in ethical decision making, Cooke (1991) offers five cautionary points (pp. 250-251):

- Decision making is a process of reasoning through an actual or potential dilemma.
- Reasonable people may disagree about which ethical course of action is appropriate.
- Not all ethical situations are clear cut.
- There are seldom "quick fixes" to an ethical dilemma.
- Sound management practice requires the assessment of all relevant information.

When resolving ethical dilemmas, a number of variables have the potential to impact the decision maker and, thus, the decision itself. As Cooke (1991) points out, decision making is a process of reasoning. Reasoning is the process of making a fair decision (Crosset & Hums, 2015a). Furthermore, people you perceive to be reasonable (i.e., of sound judgment) may disagree. This disagreement is, in part, due to their personal values and experiences, ethical foundations, and moral principles. It is important for you, the sport manager, to identify and understand variables so as to reduce bias as you try to reach a final decision (Cooke, 1991). Variables influencing the decision-making process happen at two levels: individual and situational (Sims, 1992; Sinha & Mishra, 2011).

Individual

Individual factors include demographics, personality, and cognitive moral development. As sport becomes more global, populations of athletes, coaches, and administrators become more diverse. Gender, age, race, cultural variables (e.g., birth nation, religion, political and religious affiliations), and sexual orientation are but a few demographic factors that influence our ethical philosophies, moral actions, and ethical decision making (Beu et al., 2003; Kuntz, Kuntz, Elenkov, & Nabirukhina, 2012). For example, studies have shown that women and people of color are underrepresented in

all levels of coaching and sport management (Acosta & Carpenter, 2014; Lapchick, 2016). The underrepresentation of these groups has been attributed to discriminatory hiring practices; white, male-dominated organizational structures; and stereotypes about women and people of color. When it comes to hiring practices, women and people of color may be more sensitive to ethical issues and dilemmas due to the personal relevance of their experience (Kuntz et al., 2012).

As another variable, everyone brings his or her own individual personality to the workplace. Over the years, psychologists have defined personality in various ways. For the purpose of understanding personality as it applies to ethical behavior, personality is defined as "a pattern of relatively permanent traits, dispositions, or characteristics that give some consistency to people's behavior" (Lefton, Brandon, Boyes, & Ogden, 2005, p. 14). Personality is shaped by heredity as well as environmental influences such as family and social groups, culture, and behavior in specific situations (Chelladurai, 2006).

Cognitive moral development (CMD) also has been identified as an individual factor that has the potential to affect ethical decision making. CMD is an active process in which people learn that a behavior is right or wrong. Although multiple theories of CMD exist, the most important component to CMD is acknowledging that social, cultural, and demographic variables aid in the formation of which behaviors people perceive to be "right" and "wrong." Thus, when presented with an ethical dilemma, reasonable people may use different cognitive processes to resolve it (Beu et al., 2003).

In sum, the way people perceive a situation may be determined by their experience as a member of a particular demographic group, their cognitive development, and/or their personality. Thus, it is important for a sport manager to recognize how these variables affect the ethical decision-making process.

Situational Factors

Situational factors are, perhaps, the most important and difficult factors to navigate because they account for the interaction among organizations, the law, and the social norms of a community. Organization factors include the structure, culture, and socialization practices of a given company, business, or team (Jones, 1991). Thus, organization factors play a critical role in ethical decision making and behavior. In other words, these factors may influence otherwise reasonable people to make poor ethical decisions and engage in unethical conduct.

Structure represents the division of labor in an organization. Additionally, structure establishes the formal and informal flow of communication through the organization. The manner in which information about the organization is communicated is critical to establishing an organizational culture. An **organizational culture** is established by communicating an organization's mission, goals, values, employee attitudes, and policies. Many organizations establish a code of ethics or an **ethical code of conduct**. These codes are sets of rules in an organization that guide behavior. As suggested by Helin and Sanström (2007), the mere existence of an ethical code of conduct does not ensure ethical behavior. Furthermore, "not everyone in an organization has a moral orientation or is willing to do the right thing" (Komives, Lucas, & McMahon, 2007, p. 181). To be effective, a code of conduct should be a part of organizational culture and, ideally, the behavior of the people at all levels of an organization should reflect this code.

Socialization is the process of integrating a person into a particular environment. It requires introducing employees to organizational rules and expectations, culture, and behavior. The socialization process is a critical organizational factor to consider. As a leader of a sport organization, it is important to consider how information about organizational goals, codes of conduct, and expectations are communicated, as well as who is engaged in communicating such information.

Other situational factors beyond the sport organization itself include external forces that have the potential to significantly impact your sport organization. External forces may include the economy, government and law, the use of technology, social and media perception, competition, and fan behaviors. When external forces affect your organization, they also affect how you make decisions within and about your organization and employees. Although external forces affect the decision-making process in terms of what and how information is considered, it is up to the sport manager to ensure that decisions remain ethical.

To illustrate, in the late 1990s, Nike was the most profitable sporting goods organization in the world. Associated with top-name athletes like Michael Jordan, Bo Jackson, Deion Sanders, and Tiger Woods, Nike soon found itself embroiled in controversy over child labor issues, toxic work environments, and substandard working wages in factories overseas. Its labor practices with regard to workers in developing countries were put under the microscope. Nike's image was tarnished in the media, which affected consumers' perception of the organization.

The Ethics Resource Center (2014) found that companies behave differently during economic difficulties in that managers and employees tend to make ethical decisions that involve a higher level of ethical reasoning. It is not clear why decisions are more ethical in nature at this time. It could be assumed, however, that people make more ethical decisions in a time of uncertainty because they perceive that ethical behavior is important for retaining their jobs. Conversely, the Center also found that ethical behavior declines during periods of economic growth. So what does that mean for a growing and profitable industry like sport? Does it mean that in times of economic growth, people in organizations are less ethical? No, but it does illustrate the importance of understanding how an external force, like the economy, has the potential to affect ethical decision making.

Individual and situational variables can potentially affect the ethical decision-making process. Given the myriad of factors, how can one person make sense of it all? First, it is important to understand that one person cannot make sense of it all. If anything, that is where ethical decision making goes wrong. Remember the discussion on how individual factors like race, gender, culture, age, and experience affect how we perceive issues? Ethical decision making requires social interactions with other people (Cottone & Claus, 2000). More importantly, it should include interaction with people who share perspectives, experiences, knowledge bases, and backgrounds different from your own. Once you have those people in the room and the ethical issue has been identified, the decision-making process can begin.

Ethical Decision-Making Models

Now that you have an understanding of factors to consider when making an ethical decision,

let's turn our attention to applying what you know. Please note, ethical decision-making models do not make ethical decisions; instead, they describe a process for examining a situation (Cottone & Claus, 2000). There are hundreds of ethical decision-making models that cannot possibly be addressed in this chapter. Instead, we will focus on two types of decision-making models: Issue-contingent (Jones, 1991) and practice-based (Hums & MacLean, 2013).

Issue-Contingent

The issue-contingent model (Jones, 1991) shown in **FIGURE 6.1** is different from practice-based models. Issue-contingent, ethical, decision making places more emphasis on identifying the characteristics of an ethical dilemma. The foundation of the issue-contingent model is the concept of moral intensity. Moral intensity is a multidimensional construct composed of five components: Magnitude of consequences, social consensus, probability of effect, temporal immediacy, and proximity. Intensity varies from issue to issue; therefore, it is contingent on a situation.

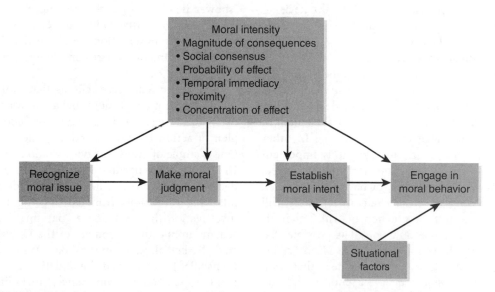

FIGURE 6.1 Ethical decision making by individuals in organizations: An issue-contingent model.

Reproduced from Jones, T. M. (1991). Ethical decision making by individuals in organizations: An issue-contingent model. *Academy of Management Review, 16*(2), 366–395.

Think back to the discussion on ethical philosophies. Remember teleology—a decision should benefit the most people? **Magnitude of consequences** is just that—how many people will benefit from or be harmed by the decision. For some ethical dilemmas, the magnitude of consequences of the corresponding decision may be minimal; for others, the consequences could be extensive. **Social consensus** is the amount of agreement in an organization or community that the proposed decision is "good" or "bad." **Probability of effect** is the likelihood that the decision will result in the benefit or harm to a group or individual, as predicted. The time that elapses between the point at which an ethical decision is made and when the consequences resulting from the decision surface is **temporal immediacy**. Depending on the situation, some decisions must be made and executed in a short period of time, whereas other decisions occur over a span of weeks, months, or even years. Similarly, some decisions will result in immediately observable consequences; other consequences may unfold over time. **Proximity** is the "feeling of nearness (social, cultural, psychological, or physical)" (Jones, 1991, p. 376) the decision maker(s) has for individuals who could be affected by the decision.

Moral intensity is the manner in which a decision maker considers an ethical dilemma. A key factor in understanding moral intensity, however, is the decision maker's ability to recognize the moral element of his or her decision (Jones, 1991). In other words, as a sport manager, it is important to recognize how your decision will affect other people and that you have a choice when addressing an ethical dilemma. Rarely will you encounter a situation in which there is only one course of action. It is possible that you may feel as though there is no "right" or "good" decision. If you feel that way, remember that you have a choice, and you are responsible for the consequences of that choice. This is known as a **moral judgment**.

When you make a moral judgment, all of the factors (i.e., individual, organizational, industry) influencing the decision-making process are in play. The moral judgment is your understanding of what is "right" and "wrong" within a given context.

Finally, moral intent is a person's intention to act on a particular decision. A sport manager may choose a "right" judgment about how to handle an ethical dilemma. However, several factors such as pressure from a supervisor, career advancement, or negative media perception may prevent the decision maker from implementing the "right" decision. For example, many unethical decisions were made during the Penn State sex abuse scandal. According to reports, Joe Paterno, Tim Curley (then athletic director), and university president Graham Spanier settled on a plan of action to address sex abuse allegations against Jerry Sandusky. That plan included reporting the offense to an outside law enforcement agency. Curley then contacted Spanier via email and indicated that, following a discussion with Paterno, the two decided it would be best to handle the matter internally. The three men agreed not to report the "shower incident" to authorities despite the acknowledgment that failure to report such an egregious observation would leave the Penn State athletic department "vulnerable" (Balingit, 2012).

The Penn State case tells us that moral intent does not equal moral behavior. Moral behavior is engaging in a "right" or "good" plan of action to solve an ethical dilemma. One example of moral behavior would be the University of Louisville's Board of Trustees' decision to fire athletic director Tom Jurich following revelations from an ongoing FBI investigation that included a "pay for play" scheme implicating members of the University's basketball staff and Adidas. While at Louisville, Jurich moved the athletic department to national prominence, including gaining membership to the Atlantic Coast Conference, a national championship in men's basketball, and a Heisman Trophy winner (Lamar Jackson). However, Jurich also endured multiple scandals resulting in local, state, and federal investigations and sanctions from the NCAA. The University Board of Trustees relieved Jurich of his role as Vice President and Director of Athletics, citing ineffective management, divisive leadership, unprofessional conduct, bullying, and a pattern of willful misconduct harmful to the University (Sayers, 2017).

The components of moral intensity, when combined with moral judgment, moral intent, and moral behavior, are effective guides for identifying an ethical dilemma. Now that you understand how to identify a dilemma, the following section provides a simple, practice-based model for addressing the issue.

Practice-Based

We make personal and business decisions every day when we gather and analyze information and then act upon that information. These decisions can be as simple as where to park at work or as complicated as which employees a sport organization chooses to lay off in hard times. To an extent, all business decisions are ethical decisions to a greater or lesser degree. A critical element of ethical decision making is having a framework to guide you through ethical dilemmas. One such model suggested by Zinn (1993) has been modified for use in the sport industry (Hancock & Hums, 2011; Hums & McLean, 2013) and includes the following steps:

1. Identify the correct problem to solve.
2. Gather all pertinent information.
3. Explore codes of conduct relevant to one's profession or to this particular dilemma.
4. Examine one's own personal values and beliefs.
5. Consult with peers or other individuals in the industry who may have experienced similar situations.
6. List decision options.
7. Look for a win–win situation if at all possible.
8. Ask the question, "How would my family feel if my decision, and how and why I arrived at my decision, were posted on the Internet tomorrow?"
9. Sleep on it.
10. Make the best decision possible, knowing that it may not be perfect.
11. Evaluate the decision over time.

Let's step through this model with an example. You are the athletic director at an NCAA Division II school. Your men's basketball coach is well known among Division II circles and has done a good job carrying out the mission of Division II athletics. The coach has an excellent win/loss record, but, more importantly, he has been skillful at developing young men and helping them to understand that getting an education is more important than success on the basketball court. He has often spoken with his players about the evils of alcohol and drugs. The coach has asked to meet privately with you in your office. Because you are a strong supporter of the basketball team, the coach knows you well and trusts you. But what he has to say comes as a surprise. He tells you, "I have been going to Alcoholics Anonymous meetings secretly for the past 2 months because I'm pretty sure I have a drinking problem." Becoming visibly emotional, he pleads with you, "I needed to tell someone so I came to you . . . but please don't tell the president [of the university]. I could lose my job and be disgraced. Everything I worked for would be gone." You are definitely on the horns of an ethical dilemma.

Let's identify the problem first, which, in this case, is what to do with the information that the coach has just shared. Next, you need to gather as much information as possible about how the coach came to believe he had a drinking problem, the school's culture, and the culture of the athletic department, who may know or not know already, and laws about confidentiality. Codes of conduct that may be of help would include clauses dealing with confidentiality or treatment of people with alcoholism.

Next, you need to examine your personal values and beliefs. Perhaps you harbor certain feelings about people with alcohol addiction, perhaps you know and trust the president of the college much more than the coach does, or perhaps you know someone who also has an alcohol addiction. All those factors may enter your mind when making your decision. Although you can know and name those values and beliefs, you may need to step back from them to examine the whole picture. After looking into your own values and beliefs, you need to reach out and consult others whose judgment you trust and respect such as other athletic directors or even friends. Sit down and make a list of decision options, including who needs to know about his condition, not telling the president, or telling the president.

This decision is complex and involves some heavy issues and personal information. It must be made rationally and fairly. You may think your decision will never see the light of day, but in this world of social media, your decision and what went into it may show up anywhere with no prior notice. How would your family feel about how you decided on a course of action? When possible, sleep on your decision. What this really means is take as much time as you possibly can to make your decision. Ethical decisions must not be made too hastily, yet the reality of an athletic director's life is that the decision must be made in a timely fashion. After that, make what you perceive to be the best decision possible. Finally, you will need to evaluate the decision. This will take time, but you will need to look back and see how your decision played out in the long run.

An ethical decision-making model like this can help a sport manager make some sense from the chaos that often surrounds an ethical dilemma. Situations requiring ethical decision making are never simple or straightforward. Having a structure to follow helps one map out the best decision possible.

▶ Becoming an Ethical Leader

You have no doubt heard the adage, "What is popular is not always right. What is right is not always popular." Managing ethical issues effectively requires that sport administrators and employees know how to recognize and deal with ethical dilemmas in their everyday work lives (Sims, 1992). As we have discussed, you will have to identify ethical dilemmas and engage in ethical decision-making processes that require an awareness of personal and professional values, situational contexts, and consequences. For those decisions, you will be either reviled or revered. Thus, it is important that, as an ethical leader, you are fair, honest, and trustworthy.

Sport practitioners and scholars have recently called for "servant leadership" in sport organizations at all levels (Burton & Welty Peachey, 2014; DeSensi, 2014; Wells & Welty Peachey, 2016; Welty Peachey, Zhou, Damon, & Burton, 2015). Servant leaders focus on the well-being of followers (Greenleaf, 1977). They embody humility and authenticity; they are adept at developing and empowering, interpersonal acceptance (understanding the experiences and feelings of others), providing direction (i.e., setting expectations), and stewardship (van Dierendonk, 2011). Leaders and managers who identify as servant leaders may make better and more informed ethical and moral decisions, which may be particularly helpful for sport leaders and the myriad ethical dilemmas they face (DeSensi, 2014).

Whether you supervise yourself or a staff of 100, it is up to you to construct the ethics and morals that will guide your conduct and, hopefully, the conduct of others. As previously discussed, a code of ethics is one way to establish a culture of ethics in an organization. Additionally, the ethical leader must empower employees to identify and report unethical behavior. For example, in 2006, Anucha Browne Sanders said she was fired from her job with the New York

Knicks after she filed a sexual harassment lawsuit against the president of basketball operations and NBA legend, Isiah Thomas. In college athletics, administrators and coaches have lost their jobs after reporting episodes of discrimination, harassment, or other questionable behaviors by school officials. A code of ethics and a well-defined reporting structure can help mitigate unethical behavior.

Unethical behavior erodes the **integrity** of organizational culture and has the potential to negatively impact how people perceive the organization. One need look no farther than the public criticism Nike has had to handle over the years because of its labor practices around the world. Those who contend that in 2012 the NFL was attempting "union busting" with regard to the officials lock-out certainly saw the league take a public hit when 70,000 calls flooded NFL headquarters on the day after a non-union replacement referee crew made a game-altering call.

As an ethical leader, it is important to understand why unethical behavior occurs in sport organizations. Sims (1992) attributes unethical behavior to four factors. First, people engage in unethical behavior because it is rewarded. Second, the values of top-level management are not congruent with organizational values. The ethical climate of an organization is "the shared set of understandings about what is correct behavior and how ethical issues will be handled" (Sims, 1992, p. 510). Third, an organization appears ethical, but moral actions suggest otherwise. Finally, an ethical climate cannot exist in an organization where unethical behavior is justified. One way that unethical behavior is justified is when it goes unreported. The Ethics Resource Center (2014) offered several reasons why employees may not report misconduct: (1) the belief that no corrective action would take place; (2) reporting was not confidential; (3) fear of retaliation from co-workers, supervisors, or upper management; and (4) not knowing who to contact.

As an ethical leader, it is your responsibility to ensure your employees are comfortable reporting unethical behavior, while also encouraging ethical conduct. Ethical leadership is important because it increases employees' satisfaction with their supervisors, job attitudes, and optimism about the future of the organization (Piccolo, Greenbaum, & Eissa, 2012). It is also positively related to higher levels of trust in management and co-workers (Piccolo et al., 2012). Piccolo et al. (2012) offer five suggestions for an ethical approach to leadership:

1. Broaden employee's evaluation criteria.
2. Craft policies, processes, and stories that highlight ethical commitment and foster an ethical culture.
3. Model ethical behavior.
4. Publicly celebrate wins that are not exclusively financial in nature.
5. Provide employees with more autonomy in the workplace and the opportunity to see their work as significant beyond the bottom line.

As the economic growth of sport continues, ethical dilemmas and decision-making processes will become more complex. As an ethical sport leader in the 21st century, you must not only address current ethical issues but also anticipate potential dilemmas and decisions within the sport industry and respective organizations. It is important to promote an ethical climate and organizational culture. Set ethical standards for yourself, your employees, and your organization. Model those standards and expect your employees to model them for each other. Your decisions will not be easy, and they will not always be popular.

▶ Summary

The sport industry is rife with ethical dilemmas. As a sport manager, it is up to you to recognize and address ethical issues that affect you, your employees, and your organization. To be an ethical leader, you must first be able to identify ethical dilemmas, and then employ an ethical decision-making strategy. Regardless of the scope, your decision will impact multiple stakeholders—employees, fans, sponsors, donors, parents, athletes, and community members. When appropriate, engage your stakeholders to help you determine the best course of action for your organization. You will be held responsible and accountable for the consequences—positive and negative—of your decisions and ethical actions. Finally, it is important to consider that the ethical decisions you make as a sport manager not only have immediate consequences for those involved but may also play a key role in the future of your organization and the sport industry.

LEADERSHIP PERSPECTIVE

Courtesy of Peter Roby.

Peter Roby

Peter Roby was the Athletic Director for Northeastern University in Boston, Massachusetts, since 2007 and retired in June of 2018. Prior to his time as the leader of the athletic department, Peter served as the Director of Northeastern's Center for Sport and Society. He will continue to support ethical leadership in college athletics while serving on the Knight Commission on Intercollegiate Athletics.

Q: What skills are required of leaders of sport organizations to best address ethical issues?

Whether you are a leader in business, a leader in sports, or most simply, a person in your community, you have to be committed to leading a life of integrity. As a leader, you have to follow your values, abide by those values, and try to live by those values. You have to stay focused on the reasons why you are making those decisions be sure those decisions are consistent with those values.

Consider all of the scandals that we have seen in intercollegiate athletics that have failed to protect the basic safety and health of students (both athletes and non-athletes), how can that be? If fundamentally, as a leader, you have a set of values, one of those should be the health and safety of your students, but instead we see leaders in college athletics and university leaders prioritize the success of athletic programs and the ability to generate revenue. This is repeated again and again at many different universities. There is a pattern; it is about missed prioritization and a lack of adherence to an espoused set of values.

Leaders cannot be responsible for every employees' behavior, but you establish a culture for your organization and a guiding set of values and you hold people in your organization accountable to that culture and those values. When people do not adhere to that culture or violate that set of values, you hold them accountable. If leaders do this, you do not have to be fearful of a backlash. You can say, "we espouse these values; we told everyone that they would be accountable to these values and now that we found that people are not doing what they are supposed to be doing, these are the consequences. And whatever backlash we take from the media or from the public, we take it because we acted on unethical behavior as soon as we knew about it." We see in the recent ethical scandals (e.g., Penn State, Michigan State, USC) that the leaders did not prioritize their values; they abdicated their leadership responsibilities and it has come back to haunt them.

Q: How can leaders of sport organizations develop and improve their ethical decision-making skills?

Leaders have to lead by example. You have to call out the transgressions when they arise and to celebrate those who are doing things the correct way. You have to keep advocating for ethical leadership and support others who come to you to learn how to lead ethically. You have to keep promoting to the idea that it can be done the right way and you can still have success.

You must concentrate on critical-thinking skills and not only responding to stimuli and information without being thoughtful. Students face those decisions in their college life—they have to think about how they want to be perceived by others on campus—the decisions they make around going out at night, how you represent yourself, and if you're a student-athlete, how are you representing yourself and your college/university.

Students have to make decisions based on their goals; they have to make choices in support of those goals. If you want to be respected, you can't make bad decisions. If you want to be a leader, you have to make decisions that put you in a positive light with your peers. Leaders must be respectful, truthful, consistent, and empathetic. Leaders must live those things every day. If you live that way on a consistent basis, you can improve your ethical decision making.

Q: In your opinion, what are the most significant ethical issues facing leaders in intercollegiate sport?

We must continue to focus on the fact that in college athletics we are in the education business and we are not in the revenue-generating business. If we keep chasing that brass ring of more money we lose focus on treating the students whom we serve with respect. We have to lead our students in a fair manner, be sure they are treated fairly, and that they are given a voice and treated like an adult and held accountable for their behaviors. As leaders, we do everything in our power to provide students with an education and be sure they know that first and foremost we are there to provide them with an education. That is what we, as leaders in college sports, need to get back to doing. We need to remind ourselves of those things and stay consistent to that commitment. We have to hire people into college athletics who share those values. We have to make sure we are consistent and fire people for violating those values. If we continue to fire coaches after two to three years, we are going to continue to have controversy. If coaches pressure to take shortcuts toward success and are not able to focus on building a winning program, they are going to be focused only on a winning season.

Q: Do you believe that leaders in intercollegiate sport are facing more significant ethical issues today than leaders of previous generations of intercollegiate sport?

I believe ethical issues are more significant now than they were for previous generations of leaders in intercollegiate sport. As the cost of higher education increases, so do the demands on colleges to satisfy multiple competing priorities. Leaders of colleges have looked to intercollegiate sport as a place to generate revenue to help meet those increasing costs.

As a result of the exposure that colleges receive and the potential for revenue generation from athletics, the recognition of sport as an important co-curricular activity is being lost. Intercollegiate sport has now become a place where everything is magnified. There is intense pressure. People are quick to lose their jobs if teams are not successful. People are quick to jump from job to job without any sense of loyalty.

▶ Key Terms

Cognitive moral
  development (CMD)
Deontology
Ethical code of conduct
Ethical decision-making
  models
Ethical dilemma

Ethics
Integrity
Magnitude of consequences
Moral intensity
Moral judgment
Morals
Organizational culture

Probability of effect
Proximity
Situational factors
Social consensus
Teleology
Temporal immediacy
Values

▶ Discussion Questions

1. Aside from the examples provided in the chapter, discuss two or three current ethical scandals (youth, intercollegiate, professional, or international) that need to be addressed by leaders in the field.

2. Can you provide examples (other than the example provided in the chapter) within sport that followed the philosophy of teleology in ethical decision making? Can you provide examples that followed the philosophy of deontology in ethical decision making?

3. Ethical decision-making models take into account both individual-level factors and situational factors to help explain how an individual moves through the process of making a decision regarding an ethical dilemma. Consider your individual-level factors and describe how these factors can influence how you make a decision regarding an ethical dilemma.

4. Describe some of the similarities and differences you note when reviewing the two models of ethical decision making included in the chapter (i.e., issue-contingent model and practice-based model).

5. What can you do to improve your skills as a leader to best support ethical decision making? Use information from the chapter to support your answer.

▶ References

Acosta, R. V., & Carpenter, L. J. (2014). Women in intercollegiate sport: A longitudinal study: Thirty-seven year update, 1977-2014. Retrieved from http://www.acostacarpenter.org

Al Nafjan, E. (2012). The Olympic triumph of Saudi Arabian women. Retrieved from http://www.guardian.co.uk/commentisfree/2012/jul/31/olympic-triumph-saudi-arabian-women

Associated Press. (2012). FIFA meets to appoint prosecutor to examine World Cup winning bids. Retrieved from http://www.guardian.co.uk/football/2012/jul/16/fifa-prosecutor-world-cup-bids

A.T. Kearney (2015). Winning in the business of sports. Retrieved from https://www.atkearney.com/communications-media-technology/article?a/winning-in-the-business-of-sports

Badenhausen, K. (2017, Setpember 18). The Dallas Cowboys head the NFL's most valuable teams at $4.8 billion. *Forbes*. Retrieved from https://www.forbes.com/sites/kurtbadenhausen/2017/09/18/the-dallas-cowboys-head-the-nfls-most-valuable-teams-at-4-8-billion/#3caaf1e243f8

Balingit, M. (2012, June 12). Ex-PSU president Spanier's emails on Sandusky surface. Retrieved from http://www.post-gazette.com/state/2012/06/12/Ex-PSU-president-Spanier-s-emails-on-Sandusky-surface/stories/201206120204

Bang, S. (2012). Report recommends European cooperation against match-fixing. Retrieved from http://www.playthegame.org/news/detailed/report-recommends-european-cooperation-against-match-fixing-5377.html

Barker, J. (2011). Under Armour's Kevin Plank an important source of funds for Maryland. Retrieved from http://articles.baltimoresun.com/2011-04-09/sports/bs-sp-terps-kevin-plank-0410-20110409_1_maryland-athletics-maryland-special-teams-ralph-friedgen

Barr, C. A. (2015). Collegiate sport. In L. P. Masteralexis, C. A. Barr, & M. A. Hums (Eds.), *Principles and practice of sport management* (5th ed., 173–197). Burlington, MA: Jones & Bartlett Learning.

Beu, D. S., Buckley, M. R., & Harvey, M. G. (2003). Ethical decision-making: A multidimensional construct. *Business Ethics: A European Review, 12*(1), 88–107.

Bort, R. (2016, September 14). A comprehensive timeline of public figures boycotting North Carolina over the HB2 'Bathroom Bill.' *Newsweek.* Retrieved from http://www.newsweek.com/north-carolina-hb2-bathroom-bill-timeline-498052

Boulongne, Y. (2000). Pierre de Coubertin and women's sport. *Olympic Review, 26*(31), 21–26.

Bulman, E. (2007, June 5). Rights group: 1.5 million people displaced by preparations for 2008 Beijing Games. Retrieved from http://www.usatoday.com/sports/olympics/2007-06-05-3431055449_x.htm

Burton, L. & Welty Peachey, J. (2014). Ethical leadership in intercollegiate sport: Challenges, opportunities, future directions. *Journal of Intercollegiate Sport, 7*, 1–10.

Carter, A. (2016, August 25). Vermont cancels women's basketball game at UNC due to HB2. *The News and Observer.* Retrieved from http://www.newsobserver.com/sports/college/acc/unc/article97859247.html

Chelladurai, P. (2006). *Human resource management in sport and recreation* (2nd ed.). Champaign, IL: Human Kinetics.

Cogan, S. (2017, June 30). Katina Powell details how she planned 22 parties with Andre McGee. Retrieved from http://www.wave3.com/story/35729068/katina-powell-details-how-she-planned-22-parties-with-andre-mcgee

Cooke, R. A. (1991). Danger signs of unethical behavior: How to determine if your firm is at ethical risk. *Journal of Business Ethics, 10*(4), 249–253.

Cottone, R. R., & Claus, R. E. (2000). Ethical decision-making models: A review of the literature. *Journal of Counseling and Development, 78*(3), 275–283.

Crosset, T. W., & Hums, M. A. (2015a). Ethical principles applied to sport management. In L. P. Masteralexis, C. A. Barr, & M. A. Hums (Eds.), (2015). *Principles and practice of sport management* (5th ed., pp. 131–148). Burlington, MA: Jones & Bartlett Learning.

Crosset, T. W., & Hums, M. A. (2015b). History of sport management. In L. P. Masteralexis, C. A. Barr, & M. A. Hums (Eds.), *Principles and practice of sport management* (5th ed., pp. 3–26). Burlington, MA: Jones & Bartlett Learning.

DeSensi, J. T. (2014). Sport: An ethos based on values and servant leadership. *Journal of Intercollegiate Sport, 7*, 58–63.

DeSensi, J. T., & Rosenberg, D. (1996). *Ethics in sport management.* Morgantown, WV: Fitness Information Technology.

Domonoske, C. (2017, February 27). 17-year-old transgender boy wins Texas girls' wrestling championship. Retrieved from https://www.npr.org/sections/thetwo-way/2017/02/27/517491492/17-year-old-transgender-boy-wins-texas-girls-wrestling-championship

ESPN. (2016, July 15). Deflategate timeline: After 544 days, Tom Brady gives in. Retrieved from http://www.espn.com/blog/new-england-patriots/post/_/id/4782561/timeline-of-events-for-deflategate-tom-brady

Ethics Resource Center. (2014). National business ethics survey of the workforce: Key findings. Retrieved from http://ethics.org/research/nbes/nbes-reports/nbes-2013

Fowler, J. (2013, April 22). ACC approves grant of rights deal. Retrieved from https://www.cbssports.com/college-football/news/acc-approves-grant-of-rights-deal/

Froh, T. (2017, July 7). 'They're stealing from children': US youth soccer's embezzlement scourge. Retrieved from https://www.theguardian.com/football/blog/2017/jul/07/usa-youth-soccer-embezzlement-scandal from http://www.charlotteobserver.com/news/politics-government/article68401147.html

Gordon, M., Price, M. S., & Peralta, K. (2016, March 26). Understanding HB2: North Carolina's newest law. Retrieved from https://www.charlotteobserver.com/news/politics-government/article68401147.html

Greenleaf, R. K. (1977). *Servant-leadership: A journey into the nature of legitimate power and greatness.* New York, NY: Paulist Press.

Greer, J. (2017). Where does Louisville's new Adidas deal rank among college program sponsorships? *Courier Journal.* Retrieved from http://www.courier-journal.com/story/sports/college/louisville/2017/08/25/where-does-louisville-new-adidas-rank-among-college-program-sponsorships/600528001/

Hancock, M., & Hums, M. A. (2011). Participation by transsexual and transgendered athletes: Ethical dilemmas needing ethical decision making skills. *ICSSPE Bulletin, 68.* Retrieved from http://www.icsspe.org

Hedstrom, R., & Gould, D. (2004). *Research in youth sports: Critical issues status.* East Lansing, MI: Institute for the Study of Youth Sports.

Helin, S., & Sandström, J. (2007). An inquiry into the study of corporate codes of ethics. *Journal of Business Ethics, 75*(3), 253–271.

Hums, M. A., & MacLean, J. C. (2013). *Governance and policy in sport organizations* (3d ed.). Scottsdale, AZ: Holcomb Hathaway.

Hutchens, B. (2011). The acceleration of media sport culture. *Information Communication & Society, 14*(2), 237–257.

IOC. (2018). Olympic marketing fact file 2018 edition. Retrieved from https://stillmed.olympic.org/media/Document%20Library/OlympicOrg/Documents/IOC-Marketing-and-Broadcasting-General-Files/Olympic-Marketing-Fact-File-2018.pdf

Jones, T. M. (1991). Ethical decision making by individuals in organizations: An issue-contingent model. *Academy of Management Review, 16*(2), 366–395.

Kilgore, A. (2017, November 9). Aaron Hernandez suffered from most severe CTE ever found in a person his age. *Washington Post*. Retrieved from https://www.washingtonpost.com/sports/aaron-hernandez-suffered-from-most-severe-cte-ever-found-in-a-person-his-age/2017/11/09/fa7cd204-c57b-11e7-afe9-4f60b5a6c4a0_story.html?utm_term=.207e01323157

Klemko, R. (2012, September 7). Brendon Ayanbadejo responds to delegate on gay marriage. *USA Today*. Retrieved from http://usatoday30.usatoday.com/sports/football/nfl/ravens/story/2012-09-07/brendan-ayanbadejo-gay-marriage/57680822/1

Knight Commission on Intercollegiate Athletics. (2010). Restoring the balance: Dollars, values, and the future of college sports. Retrieved from http://www.knightcommission.org/restoringthebalance

Komives, S. R., Lucas, N., & McMahon, T. R. (2007). *Exploring leadership: For college students who want to make a difference* (2nd ed.). San Francisco, CA: Jossey-Bass.

Kuntz, J. C., Kuntz, J. R., Elenkov, D., & Nabirukhina, A. (2012). Characterizing ethical cases: A cross-cultural investigation of individual differences, organisational climate, and leadership in ethical decision-making. *Journal of Business Ethics, 113*(2), 317–331.

Lapchick, R. (2016). 2016 racial and gender report card: College sport. Retrieved from http://nebula.wsimg.com/38d2d0480373afd027ca38308220711f?AccessKeyId=DAC3A56D8FB782449D2A&disposition=0&alloworigin=1

Lee, A. (2015). 7 charts that show the state of youth sports in the US and why it matters. Retrieved from https://www.aspeninstitute.org/blog-posts/7-charts-that-show-the-state-of-youth-sports-in-the-us-and-why-it-matters/

Lefton, L. A., Brandon, L., Boyes, M. C., & Ogden, N. A. (2005). *Psychology* (2nd ed.). Toronto, ON: Pearson, Allyn and Bacon.

Logan, T. (2012, September 25). St. Louis Blues lay off 20 employees as NHL lock-out drags on. Retrieved from http://www.stltoday.com/sports/hockey/professional/st-louis-blues-lay-off-employees-as-nhl-lockout-drags/article_4e156e8c-0743-11e2-be33-0019bb30f31a.html

Malley, B. (2011, September 27). The 20 biggest scandals in sports history. Retrieved from http://bleacherreport.com/articles/854416-the-20-biggest-scandals-in-sports-history

Malloy, D. C., & Zakus, D. H. (1995). Ethical decision making in sport administration: A theoretical inquiry into substance and form. *Journal of Sport Management, 9*(1), 36–58. *Management, 37*, 1228–1261.

Marar, M., McIlvain, N. M., Fields, S. K., & Comstock, D. R. D. (2012). Epidemiology of concussions among United States high school athletes in 20 sports. *American Journal of Sports Medicine, 40*(4), 747–755.

Murphy, C. (2011, November 18). FIFA chief Blatter: There is no on-field racism in football. Retrieved from http://edition.cnn.com/2011/11/16/sport/football/football-blatter-fifa-racism/index.html

Myerberg, P. (2013, February 20). FAU sells stadium naming rights to for-profit prison operator. *USA Today*. Retrieved from http://www.usatoday.com/story/gameon/2013/02/20/florida-atlantic-geo-group-stadium-naming-rights/1933013/

National Center for Sports Safety. (2012). Sports injury facts. Retrieved from http://www.sportssafety.org/content/ResourcesNews/SportsSafetyInformation.aspx

National Collegiate Athletic Association. (2012a). Concussion. Retrieved from http://www.ncaa.org/sport-science-institute/concussion

National Collegiate Athletic Association. (2012b). History. Retrieved from http://www.ncaa.org/about/resources/media-center/ncaa-101/what-ncaa

National Collegiate Athletic Association. (2012c). National Collegiate Athletic Association and subsidiaries consolidated financial statement. Retrieved from http://www.ncaa.org/about/resources/finances

National Federation of State High School Associations. (2017). 2016-17 high school athletics participation survey. Retrieved from http://www.nfhs.org/ParticipationStatistics/PDF/2016-17_Participation_Survey_Results.pdf

New York Times. (2015, December 21). The rise and fall of Sepp Blatter. Retrieved from https://www.nytimes.com/interactive/2015/05/27/sports/soccer/sepp-blatter-fifa-timeline.html#/#time376_11002

Ostrowski, J. (2012, August 25). Dogged by complaints, prison operator GEO Group keeps growing. *Palm Beach Post*. Retrieved from http://www.palmbeachpost.com/news/news/dogged-by-complaints-prison-operator-geo-group-kee/nRHZ8/

Piccolo, R. F., Greenbaum, R., & Eissa, G. (2012). Ethical leadership and core job characteristics: Designing jobs for well-being. In N. Reilly, M. J. Sirgy, & C. A. Gorman (Eds.), *Work and quality of life: Ethical practices in organizations*. New York: Springer.

Plunkett Research. (2016). Sports industry statistic and market size overview, business and industry statistics. Retrieved from https://www.plunkettresearch.com/statistics/Industry-Statistics-Sports-Industry-Statistic-and-Market-Size-Overview/

Ray, R. (2012, August 13). Boy, 12, ruled too big to play football. Retrieved from http://www.foxnews.com /us/2012/08/14/texas-seventh-grader-nearly-300 -pounds-told-too-big-to-play-pee-wee-football.html

Robinson, C. (2011, August 16). Renegade Miami football booster spells out illicit benefits to players. Retrieved from http://sports.yahoo.com/news/renegade-miami -football-booster-spells-213700753—spt.html

Rosenberg, M. (2011, January 7). Nike's Phil Knight has branded Oregon into national power. Retrieved from https://www.si.com/more-sports/2011/01/07/oregon -knight

Sale, C. (2012, March 27). FIFA urged to look at World Cup vote. Retrieved from http://www.dailymail.co.uk /sport/article-2121334/Charles-Sale-FIFA-urged -look-World-Cup-vote.html

Sayers, J. (2017, October 24). Jurich was fired from Louisville with a scathing letter about his 'ineffective' leadership. *Courier Journal.* Retrieved from http:// www.courier-journal.com/story/sports/college /louisville/2017/10/24/postel-jurich-failed-promote -zero-tolerance-scandals/795596001/

Sharp, A. (2011, November 22). Is Nike's influence on the University of Oregon football team bordering on interference? Retrieved from http://www .businessinsider.com/nike-influence-university-of -oregon-football-interference-2011-11

Shipley, J. (2016, May 3). North Carolina travel ban means colleges can't compete for championship. Retrieved from http://www.twincities.com/2016/05/03/mnscu -bans-sports-teams-from-north-carolina/

Sholtens, B., & Dam, L. (2007). Cultural values and international differences in business ethics. *Journal of Business Ethics. 75*(3), 273–284.

Sims, R. R. (1992). The challenge of ethical behavior in organizations. *Journal of Business Ethics, 11*(7), 505–513.

Sinha, A. K., & Mishra, S. K. (2011). Factors affecting ethical decision making in a corporate setting. *Purushartha, 4*(1), 135–154.

Statista. (2017). NCAA revenue returned to Division I conferences and member institutions from 2010/11 to 2017/18. Retrieved from https://www.statista.com /statistics/219586/revenue-returned-to-its-members -by-the-ncaa/

Thompson, E., & Macur, J. (2012, April 10). In Miami, winning clearly isn't the only thing. Retrieved from http://www.nytimes.com/2012/04/11/sports/baseball /marlins-suspend-manager-for-5-games-over -comments-on-castro.html?_r=0

van Dierendonck, D. (2011). Servant leadership: A review and synthesis. *Journal of Management, 37*(4), 1228–1261.

Vasquez, M. (2013, April 1). Prison firm withdraws gift to name FAU football stadium. Retrieved from https:// www.miamiherald.com/latest-news/article1948737 .html

Volkwein, K. A. (1995). Ethics and top-level sport: A paradox? *International Review for the Sociology of Sport, 30*, 311–320.

Wells, J. E., & Welty Peachey, J. (2016). Called to serve: Exploring servant leadership in the context of sport-for-development. *Journal of Sport for Development, 4*(7), 12–24.

Welty Peachy, J., Zhou, T., Damon, Z. J., & Burton, L. J. (2015). Forty years of leadership research in sport management: A review, synthesis, and conceptual framework. *Journal of Sport Management, 29*, 570–587.

Wharton, D. (2016, May 24). UCLA's Under Armour deal for $280 million is the biggest in NCAA history. *Los Angeles Times.* Retrieved from http://www.latimes .com/sports/ucla/la-sp-0525-ucla-under-armour -20160525-snap-story.html

Wyche, S. (2016, August 27). Colin Kaepernick explains why he sat during national anthem. Retrieved from http://www.nfl.com/news/story/0ap3000000691077 /article/colin-kaepernick-explains-why-he-sat -during-national-anthem

Zinn, L. M. (1993). Do the right thing: Ethical decision-making in professional & business practice. *Adult Learning, 5*(7-8), 27.

Zirin, D. (2012, September 17). Letter from Rio: Save Armando's house from the Olympics. *The Nation.* Retrieved from http://www.thenation.com/blog /169975/letter-rio-save-armandos-house-olympics

CHAPTER 7

Strategic Leadership

Kathryn Shea

CHAPTER OBJECTIVES

- Understand the main characteristics that strategic leaders possess.
- Understand and differentiate mission and vision within the context of leadership.
- Recognize instances when organizations need strategic leadership.
- Explicate the connection that organizational values have to strategic vision.
- Differentiate the four levels of strategy.

CASE STUDY

Setting Suns: Jumbo Shrimp Rebranding Took Strategic Vision

When one first meets Ken Babby, the owner of the Jacksonville Jumbo Shrimp and Akron RubberDucks minor league baseball teams, it is hard to believe his level of success at the tender age of 39. Moreover, he is as humble as he is young. He won the prestigious Ernst and Young Entrepreneur of the Year Award in 2017. In accepting the award, he deflected praise to anyone but himself: "This is an incredible honor, but it reflects the dedication and passion our amazing team has contributed throughout the last five seasons. Everyone on our team plays an essential role in our growth and success" ("RubberDucks Owner/ CEO," 2017, para. 3). Although his remarks refer to the success of the RubberDucks in Ohio, he has been able to duplicate his recipe for fun at the franchise he purchased in 2015 in northeast Florida.

The minor-league baseball team in Jacksonville, Florida, was called the Jacksonville Suns between 1962 and 2016. In November 2016, the team became the Jacksonville Jumbo Shrimp. Some minor-league baseball teams are known for their quirky names. After all, there are the Rumble Ponies of Binghamton (NY), the Flying Squirrels of Richmond (VA), the Shuckers of Biloxi (MS), and the IronPigs of Lehigh Valley (PA), to name a few. A sport industry observer might argue that the Jacksonville team changed its name as a quick public relations and merchandise grab or for a short-term attendance boost.

(continues)

CASE STUDY   (continued)

So, why was the name ultimately changed? Well, for fun, of course. "There's something fun and quirky about minor-league team names," Babby said. "In our league alone, you have the [Pensacola] Wahoos and [Montgomery] Biscuits. When people see this logo and hear the name for the first time, they'll see this experience is all about fun" (Frenette, 2016). However, Babby had more than just fun in mind for the Double A affiliate of the Miami Marlins. The name change was also about forging a new identity for the team—one seamlessly interwoven into the community.

Predictably, not everyone in Jacksonville was happy about the name change as comments both positive and negative blew up the Twitter-sphere. Babby expected some backlash so he made sure that he did his homework beforehand. As the owner of the club, he was ultimately behind the bold move to change the name and identity of the team. As a leader, the buck stops with him. However, he took an inclusive approach to considering the name change by talking to the team's most important stakeholder: the fans. "The ownership has been in constant conversation with the community and fans," remarked Marco LaNave, the team's media and public relations manager, after the name change was announced (Gelman, 2016, para 8). Consulting Jacksonville residents before making the decision showed Babby's recognition of how important it is for leaders to understand their customers, an important external environment for any sport franchise. The team went through a process of thinking strategically before taking the plunge. Babby's understanding of minor-league baseball's values—the ability to see MLB's future stars at an affordable price with a community feel to boot—combined with the values of Jacksonville formed his strategic plan for the Jacksonville franchise. In speaking with people throughout northeast Florida, the team's leaders learned that although the "Suns'" moniker held a soft spot in the hearts of Jacksonville residents, many people had not been to a game in two years or more ("One of Us: Ken Babby," 2018). One of the characteristics of any leader, strategic or otherwise, is a focus on the bottom line. Any baseball team owner wants more butts in the seats. Attendance had declined in recent years at the Baseball Grounds, where the team plays its games ("Southern League: Attendance," 2018). Since the team changed the name, attendance has increased by about 900 people per game on average. Babby and his staff have breathed new life into the franchise.

Coming up with a new name, logo, and color scheme for the Jacksonville team was an exercise in understanding the organization's external environments, a staple of strategic thinking. "We started a process of really exploring what northeast Florida stood for," Babby said ("One of Us: Ken Babby," 2018, para. 6). He learned four important things about Jacksonville: 1. Jacksonville is known for its military presence; there are six military installations with nearly 109,000 jobs associated with them ("Office of Economic Development," n.d.); 2. The coastal city where the St. John's River meets the Atlantic Ocean has a strong affinity to water; 3. Jacksonville is the largest city in the lower 48 United States by land area at 840 square miles; and 4. Although large, the city operates in a lot of ways like a small community. When you add up these four things, you get the Jacksonville Jumbo Shrimp. The logo's red, white, and blue color scheme is a salute to the city's military presence. "Jumbo" refers to the city's large land area while "shrimp" brings in the affinity for water and Jacksonville's small-town feel.

Part of strategic planning is understanding the external environment in which an organization operates. Babby is no novice to understanding the draw and community feel of minor league baseball. He has owned the Akron franchise since 2012. He understands the philosophy of affordable family fun as it relates to minor league baseball. A Double-A baseball franchise is not necessarily going to be known for its players more than its ability to provide a family night out that won't break the bank, but Babby does not overlook the opportunity to see tomorrow's baseball stars. "The idea that you can come into a ballpark … for $5, have a $2 hot dog every single game, great promotions, great fireworks, and, on top of that, be able to see the next cut of talent in Major League Baseball, is a pretty rich value proposition" ("One of Us: Ken Babby," 2018, para. 4).

As you read about strategic leadership on the pages that follow, it is likely that you will connect concepts such as entrepreneurship, problem-solving, differentiation, and values with the actions of Ken Babby, who, with the help of residents, made a jumbo decision to help Jacksonville's minor league team re-instill pride in its community for years to come.

Questions for Discussion

1. The Jacksonville Jumbo Shrimp went through a strategic rebranding. Can you think of other professional sports teams that have changed their nickname and team logo? Which strategic steps would these teams have to take to achieve the same success that the Jumbo Shrimp has?
2. In 2016, Babby was named to *Sports Business Journal's* "40 Under 40" list. The sport industry is seeing younger leaders make their mark. Doing some quick research on Babby, what experiences do you think helped him hone his leadership skills?
3. Using the content toward the end of the chapter that lists characteristics of strategic leaders, which characteristics—both situational and personal—do you think impacted Babby's decision to rebrand the Jacksonville team?
4. Minor-league baseball games stage creative promotions. Based on what you now know about Jacksonville and the city's minor-league team, can you suggest two promotions that would resonate with the community?

▶ Introduction

The commissioner of the National Football League (NFL), Roger Goodell, stands at the helm of the organization, which is composed of 32 organizations. Furthermore, every employee of those 32 organizations is also a league employee. Given the league's structure, any NFL strategy or changes in the league will largely depend on Goodell's ability to build consensus, or coalitions, among the owners of those 32 organizations. Even when Goodell successfully builds consensus among NFL team owners for changes in the league, these changes may lead to public scrutiny and backlash. It is not an easy job, especially when situations arise that place the NFL in unfamiliar landscape. In 2017, the National Anthem-related player protests and President Donald Trump's criticism of the league for allowing players to kneel during the Anthem put the NFL in the political spotlight. Additionally, the NFL's television ratings in 2017 were down for a second straight season and sales of NFL-licensed merchandise have been weak

(Lefton, 2017). Some believe that the NFL should avoid political discussions and focus on football. "Politicizing the game is damaging and takes the focus off the greatness of the game itself and those who play it," Carolina Panthers owner Jerry Richardson expressed (Kaplan, 2017a, p. 32). Others believe that the NFL is responsible for using its platform to advocate for social causes and believe that the league should endorse an aggressive social justice campaign. It is a contentious issue and, given the delicate balance between Goodell and his relationship with owners, it is not surprising that it took a while for the owners and commissioner to reach a consensus on how to move forward. In May of 2018, the NFL owners approved a new policy that requires players to stand for the Anthem if they are on the field but gives them the option to remain in the locker room if they prefer not to stand.

It is difficult to determine causality as there are many other incontrovertible factors to consider when trying to understand why the NFL, once the king of professional sports, appears to be in a vulnerable position. These factors include changes in media consumption, over-saturation of the market, the growing awareness of head trauma injuries, changes to the rules of the game, and the amount of attention on officiating. Regardless of the cause, the NFL's future success will depend on Goodell and the NFL team owners' ability to adapt strategically to the tumult over its current environment.

This chapter focuses on the importance of understanding strategy and how leaders like Goodell use it to move their organizations forward in a sea of competitors, technological changes, and unforeseen circumstances. The different levels of strategy, strategic planning, achieving strategic focus, implementation of strategy, and execution and evaluation of strategies are explicated with numerous companion examples to help students understand the importance of leaders getting all organizational members to row the same way to differentiate their organization in a crowded marketplace. Further, the chapter offers a particular focus on developing a strategic vision and how organizational values relate to strategy. The chapter ends with a discussion of the characteristics of strategic leaders. Exploring these characteristics is crucial for millennials and 21st century employees working for sport organizations who will need to develop these traits to lead organizations in an entrepreneurial, innovative, and democratic manner.

▶ Strategy and Strategic Planning

The challenges of leading a successful sport organization are staggering. The responsibility of developing an effective **strategy**, a plan of action to achieve a major aspiration, is daunting. It requires addressing how an organization will grow itself, satisfy customers, outcompete rivals, respond to changes in market conditions, manage each functional component of the business, develop required competencies and capabilities, and achieve business objectives (Thompson, Strickland, & Gamble, 2010). The development of strategy is carried out across four different levels of the organization's hierarchy (2010). **Corporate strategy** is characterized by the efforts of senior corporate executives to boost combined performance across all businesses and programs and devising ways to innovate new approaches to take advantage of cross-business synergies that can be leveraged to gain a competitive advantage. Adidas' corporate strategy reads: "Adidas strives to be the global leader in the sporting goods industry with brands built upon a passion for sports and a sporting lifestyle" ("Corporate strategy," n.d.). **Business strategy** refers to the approaches, actions, and steps that are devised to produce intended results and achieve goals in one specific line of business or in one particular program. Using Adidas as an example again, one area in which it may look to achieve goals is targeting female CrossFit enthusiasts with its products. Corporate strategy offers an overarching, macro approach for the entire company whereas business strategy is more focused on a certain area of production. **Functional strategy** involves the practices and behaviors used in operating specific business processes and activities. Functional strategic leaders are charged with adding important details and specifics to operationalize and support the overall business-level strategy. So, if Adidas is looking to reach more female CrossFitters, it may look to boost functional areas such as marketing and research and development to help achieve the business-level strategy of gaining more market share with female CrossFit athletes. Finally, operating strategies are the specific and concrete actions taken to manage key operating units (distribution centers, plants) and to support strategic initiatives (marketing campaigns, online distribution). Operating strategies are narrower in scope and focus on specific strategic steps that must be taken to manage the operations of the business. So, if Adidas needs to revamp its marketing to reach more female CrossFitters, a possible **operating strategy** could be to create advertisements on social media and traditional media using the slogan, "Women First" (Green, 2018).

These different strategies are only as effective as the strategic plan that supports them, and developing a strategic plan requires a strong understanding of both the business and the external environment in which an organization resides. **Strategic planning** refers to setting the mission and vision; developing policies, programs and strategies; evaluating performance; and focusing on the forces driving change in the external environment and their likely influence on the organization's competitive position in the market (Ferkins, Shilbury, & McDonald, 2005). Youth participation in sport represents a key external environment that professional sport leagues monitor regularly. Lack of involvement from youth can spell trouble for the future of an Olympic national governing body or a professional sports league. The National Basketball Association sponsors a Jr. NBA World Championship that features both boys' and girls' divisions; Major League Baseball holds a Pitch, Hit, and Run youth skills competition; the NFL has the Let's Play Football Initiative; and every U.S. Olympic sport has youth programs developed by their respective national governing bodies. These programs are strategic in nature and are intended to keep youth interested in future participation in the sport in any way possible as spectator, customer, or possible player.

Once a strategic plan is in place, to be successful, it must be implemented across all organizational units and functions and embraced by all individuals in the organization. It must also be continually reevaluated and adapted to changes in the external environment and the competitive landscape. A strategic plan as described here is all-encompassing and requires jumping in the water with both feet. For example, the U.S. men's national soccer team has reached a make-or-break moment in need of a strategy going forward. The team

failed to qualify for the 2018 World Cup in Russia. Poor leadership and an inability to develop players from the youth levels are common reasons for the team's recent failure. Executing a successful strategic plan to achieve a sport organization's mission depends on the ability of those at the top to lead and direct organizational change, create or reinvent business processes, manage and motivate people, and achieve performance goals. Carlos Cordeiro, elected the new president of the U.S. Soccer Federation in February of 2018, has his work cut out for him. It will be Cordeiro who is on the hot seat to implement a strategy to help the men's national team make it to Qatar in 2022 and reignite enthusiasm among U.S. soccer fans about the men's national team.

▶ Strategic Leadership

Strategic leadership focuses on those who have overall responsibility for the organization, as Cordeiro does for U.S. soccer. These leaders steer and direct the organization and oversee the top management team (Cyert & March, 1963). Strategic leadership refers to the capacity of individuals to articulate a **strategic vision**—to "see" that organization's future and think about how to achieve it and to motivate and influence others to achieve that vision. Strategic leadership centers on the ability to use strategy in the management of employees to accomplish the mission. There has long been interest in what differentiates successful strategic leaders from others, and strategic leadership research examines these individuals at the strategic center of the organization (Mintzberg, 1979) to learn about what it is that they do and how they go about doing it (Hambrick, 1989).

Development of Strategic Leadership

The study of strategic leadership has evolved in the past 30 years. In the 1970s and 1980s, scholarship in the field of leadership dwindled and its future was unclear. Researchers questioned the direction of the field and they even questioned whether leadership mattered. Earlier strategic leadership research examined small group leadership and applied it to middle and lower managerial levels (Bass, 1990; Yukl, 1994). However, the description of the relationship between executives and their followers did not offer a realistic view of the influence of top management on organizational success (Vera & Crossan, 2003). Beyond the notable research efforts on charismatic leadership (House, 1977) and implicit leadership theories (Lord, 1977), there were few new theories developed in the field of strategic leadership. A shift in the mid-1980s centered on the Upper echelon theory (Hambrick & Mason, 1984), the antecedent of the strategic leadership theory. This directed attention away from supervisory leadership theories toward the study of strategic leadership and "new" theories of leadership: Charismatic leadership (Conger & Kanungo, 1987; House, 1977; Shamir, House, & Arthur, 1993), transformational and transactional leadership (Bass, 1985), and visionary leadership theories (Bennis & Nanus, 1985; Kouzes & Posner, 1987). Bass's framework of transactional/transformational leadership has proven to be useful for studying top-level executives (Lowe, Kroeck, & Sivasubramaniam, 1996), and this is primarily because it was developed within larger organizational contexts. Therefore, transformational and transactional leadership theories are important to understanding strategic leadership. This textbook has a chapter dedicated to these theories, but it is instructive to include their link to strategic leadership here.

Transformational and transactional leadership styles are distinct. Transactional leadership focuses on motivating individuals through carrots and sticks, or contingent-reward exchanges (Bass, 1985, 1990). Transformational leadership is characterized by individual consideration, charisma,

inspiration, and intellectual stimulation (Avolio et al., 1999). The behavior of the strategic leader has a significant impact on the culture of an organization. Strategic leaders who tend towards transactional behaviors will work within the existing culture, norms, rules, and procedures (Hurley & Hult, 1998; Schein, 1992). By doing so, these leaders reinforce the existing culture, norms, and rules that have been established (Nahavandi, 1993). Transformational leaders will challenge the existing culture, norms, and rules and make changes to realign these with a new vision. Transformational leaders challenge the existing order and inspire employees to explore new ways of doing things. The transactional or transformational tendencies of strategic leaders will lead to distinct elements within the organization being emphasized over others, which results in the creation of different cultures and organizational structures. The most effective leaders are those who are able to adopt transactional or transformational behaviors, depending on which behavior fits best given the situation (Tushman & O'Reilly, 1996).

Widely debated at one time, the current conventional thinking is that strategic leadership does matter. Strategic leadership involves the creation of meaning and purpose for the organization (House & Aditya, 1997). Commissioners, presidents, corporate administrators, top executives, and boards of directors for non-profit organizations are strategic leaders who are responsible for steering organizations toward success in the high-paced and dynamic sport industry.

▶ What Strategic Leaders Do

The sport industry has experienced tremendous growth in the past decade. *Forbes* reports that the North American sports market will grow to $75.7 billion by 2020 from \$63.9 billion in 2015 (Heitner, 2016). The gains in revenues are largely attributed to revenues generated from media rights and sponsorship, and these revenues are expected to exceed gate revenues, which have been the sport industry's largest segment. The dynamic environment and the fast pace of change in the sport industry make it one of the most complex and challenging industries for achieving strategic objectives. While the costs of doing business continue to rise, the globalization of the marketplace has increased the number of competitors, both foreign and domestic, who seek to gain a competitive advantage and a larger share of the market. Sport scholars have found that the most successful strategic leaders in sport focus their attention on the factors over which they have some control to lead strategy, implement change, foster innovation, and build their business (Rein, Shields, & Grossman, 2015). Because of increased competition and an expectation for innovation from fans and sponsors, some sport-organization leaders have participated in the "disruption" of traditional revenue models. The Atlanta Falcons of the NFL have introduced cheaper food options at the Falcons' new Mercedes-Benz Stadium. At the beginning of the MLB season, the Baltimore Orioles said it would offer free admission to its home ballpark to any child age 9 and younger for the 2018 season with the purchase of a full-price adult ticket. The aggressive marketing and sales strategies are believed to be unprecedented in professional sports (Fisher, 2018). These examples illustrate **disruption**. Professional firms can no longer rely on tried-and-true business models—not in a digital age where consumers get information quicker and in myriad different ways. "The basic rules of the game for creating and capturing economic value were once fixed in place for years, even decades, as companies tried to execute the same business models better than their competitors did. But now, business models are subject to rapid displacement, disruption, and, in extreme cases,

outright destruction" (de Jong & van Dijk, 2015, para. 1). This is true in sport organizations as professional sports teams ponder innovative strategies to get fans' attention and persuade them to continue attending games in their stadiums and arenas.

Wendell Brooks, investment chief at Intel, confirmed this strategic focus on innovation when he noted that a large influx of venture capital has been invested in the disruption of sports in the past five years. This has put the sports industry into a period of flux and upheaval (Smith & Ourand, 2018). Michael Rubin, a co-owner of the Philadelphia 76ers of the National Basketball Association and the New Jersey Devils of the National Hockey League, expects the disruption of traditional business models to be just as prevalent over the next five years. He said it is important for sports franchises to figure out how to make both the outside-the-stadium experience and the inside-the-stadium experience better for the fans. He said franchises need to move quickly in this fans-expect-more world or their businesses will become antiquated (Smith & Ourand, 2018).

Managing a sport organization centers on the performance of top-level managers and their leadership in the development and execution of a strategy. Strategic leaders are responsible for setting the vision for the organization, charting the strategic plan, which involves setting targets for performance, crafting competitive maneuvers that will lead the organization to achieve its goals, evaluating performance, and making adjustments to ensure that the organization is on course. The decision to use one weapon in their business arsenal over another requires careful research and the consideration of a number of organizational and environmental factors. Any conclusion about changes in the organization's focus and long-term direction must be drawn carefully. Ultimately, organizations are a reflection of leaders' decisions about where the organization is going and how it will get there.

▶ Developing a Strategic Vision

Strategic leadership begins with the development of a **strategic vision** of where the organization aims to be in the future. Developing a strategic vision involves wrestling with questions about which direction the organization should take. Would changes in the organization's delivery of products or services to customers improve the organization's competitive position? A strategic vision expresses the aspirations for the organization and provides a bird's-eye view of where the organization is going. To be effective, leaders must develop a vision that clarifies the organization's direction and path. Secondly, it must provide a reference point for all strategic decisions involved in preparing the organization for the future. Good strategic visions are distinct and unique to the organization. They should stretch beyond an organization's immediate reach to initiate action and motivate employees to move toward the directional path of achieving the vision. The absence of a strategic vision leaves the organization without a sense of direction. And as the Cheshire Cat said to Alice in Lewis Carroll's *Alice in Wonderland* (2013), "If you don't know where you are going, any road will take you there."

Dave Andrews, the commissioner of the American Hockey League (AHL), has carved out a specific road for the National Hockey League's main developmental league. According to Andrews, strategic leadership is the requisite leadership type necessary to envision, plan, direct, motivate, and execute a successful governance strategy (McAllister, 2015). In 1994, when Andrews took over as commissioner, the league launched a strategic plan based on a thorough analysis of its external environment. The strategy included making the AHL brand more vibrant, pursuing expansion into new markets with stronger ownership, and refocusing the AHL's on-ice product on a new commitment to develop players for the NHL. In 2001, the International Hockey League ceased operations after 56 years, and the AHL absorbed its top six markets and ownership groups. Since then, the AHL has increased its membership to 31 teams, all with NHL affiliations (2015).

Strategic Vision Differs from Mission

As one can see from the AHL example, an effective strategic vision centers on an organization's future strategic direction—the course that the organization takes and what the organization's future product or service will be. Andrews of the AHL possesses such a vision. A **mission statement** captures an organization's present business and purpose. While a vision and mission statement can be expressed in ways that capture similar meaning, the mission statement clarifies the organization's scope and purpose. The strategic vision is forward looking, whereas the mission statement focuses on "who we are, what we do, and why we are here." An organization's mission statement should be unique from its competitors and should identify the organization's products and services, who the organization serves, and how it delivers value to meet the needs and wants of its customers. Consider the mission statement of Nike Inc. (2017):

> "Bring inspiration and innovation to every athlete* in the world
> *If you have a body, you are an athlete."

Nike's mission statement has been recreated over time to ensure that it reflects the company's current business situation. Nike's mission statement does a good job of expressing "who we are, what we do, and why we are here." There are three primary components of Nike's mission statement: inspiration, innovation, and every athlete in the world. Inspiration represents Nike's intention as a leading sporting goods and manufacturing company to inspire people to embrace a winning attitude to succeed. By emphasizing innovation, Nike prioritizes continual improvement through the use of new technologies across the entire company. The final component, "every athlete in the world," indicates that Nike aims to target every consumer around the world in the future. This provides an important strategic reference point for decision-makers who must ensure that Nike designs products that will attract and satisfy a broad and diverse global consumer market. Nike's mission statement goes beyond focusing on the present business situation by integrating a sense of "where we are headed" because it includes Nike's future strategic goal of its continued expansion into the global market, which is a forward-looking quality that is usually associated with a vision statement. This may help to explain why Nike has not published an official company vision statement.

Nike's **vision statement** for its corporate social responsibility (CSR) serves as a strong indication of the business' future strategic path. Nike's CSR vision statement is "to help NIKE, Inc. and our consumers thrive in a sustainable economy where people, profit and planet are in balance" (Sustainable Innovation, n.d.). The core components of Nike's CSR vision highlight the company's strategic direction toward a sustainable economy in which people, profit, and planet are in balance. It conveys that the company and its consumers are the primary participants in Nike achieving sustainability in the future. Nike's CSR vision statement's "sustainable economy" principle implies the corresponding strategic objectives and this provides a reference point for managers to make strategic decisions and prepare the company for the future. The third principle of Nike's CSR vision statement, "people, profit and planet are in balance," emphasizes sustainability and reinforces the priority of achieving balance that will allow all to benefit from Nike's business (Smithson, 2017). Nike's CSR vision statement offers a strong indication about what the company aims to become in the future. However, Nike would benefit from developing a formal corporate vision statement to clearly convey the strategic course that executives have charted for the company and to provide managers with a tool that gives the organization a sense of direction.

Communicating the Vision

Strategic leaders must not only create a long-term strategic direction that provides the organization with meaning and purpose to win the support of personnel but they must also effectively communicate the strategic vision down the line to mid- and lower-level managers and employees. Employees must be provided with a clear and convincing strategic vision that is supported by a compelling and engaging case for the direction in which the organization is going. To move this forward, employees must understand the underlying reasons for the strategic direction that management has charted for the organization. Without this understanding, it will be difficult to hold employees accountable for uniting behind management's efforts to achieve the vision. An executive's ability to illuminate a clear and inspiring view of the organization's path and destination has an important impact on the extent to which members of the organization commit, and rally behind, managerial efforts to move personnel in a common direction. Expressing the sentiment of the company's vision is often made easier when the vision is captured in a slogan that is both intriguing and memorable. Nike's slogan "Just do it" captures the essence of Nike's vision, and it is easily imprinted in one's mind. Articulating a vision that resonates with employees and makes people passionate underlies the art of strategic leadership.

▶ Values

What an organization truly **values** should underlie and inform its strategic vision. Nike's CSR vision illustrated its values, people, and sustainability as much as profit. Organizational leaders hold positions that provide them with the unique power to change or reinforce existing patterns within their organization (Sitkin, 1992). Top administrators are responsible for grounding the operations of the business on core values to sustain an effective organizational culture. Developing and maintaining a strong organizational culture and ethical value system is a cornerstone of good strategic leadership. Many organizations develop a statement of values to guide the organization's pursuit of its vision. These core values are the beliefs, traits, norms, and behaviors expected of organizational members as they conduct business and undertake activities in the pursuit of achieving the organization's vision. Values often relate to notions of integrity, ethical behavior, fair treatment, innovation, teamwork, superior quality, exceptional customer service, social responsibility, and civic responsibility. Typically, statements of values center on four to eight beliefs about the traits that organizational members should embrace. Top management must carefully select values, traits, and behaviors that will help move the organization strategically forward. Nike's "11 Maxims" represent the set of principles to guide employees in their work and their representation of the global brand and include (Nike, n.d.):

> It is our nature to innovate.
> Nike is a company.
> Nike is a brand.
> Simplify and go.
> The consumer decides.
> Be a sponge.
> Evolve immediately.
> Do the right thing.
> Master the fundamentals.
> We are on the offensive—always.
> Remember the man.

To be effective, it is a priority for strategic leaders in the sport industry to bolster energy, excitement, and enthusiasm about the organization's core values and purpose. Nike developed a core set of management values in its "Manager Manifesto" to guide the leadership of the company. The core principles of Nike's Manager Manifesto are (in order): Lead, coach, manage, inspire (Nike, n.d.). While Nike's 11 Maxims and its Manager Manifesto are abstract, to Nike executives, they reflect everything that the brand represents and provides room for the development of one's own interpretation.

The degree to which an organization's value statement translates to reality varies widely. Strategic leaders must hold organizational personnel accountable for displaying stated values to successfully infuse an ethical value system into the cultural fabric of an organization. It is critical that standards and values be supported with a monitoring and information distribution system to create transparency and, therefore, ensure compliance. Sport organizations that fail to monitor compliance are less likely to detect violations of standards and codes of conduct. Nisen (2013) provides a descriptive narrative of Nike's experience in overseeing the values that guide business activities in the company. In 1992, activist Jeff Ballinger published an exposé of Nike in which he documented exploitation and abuse at the hands of Nike. For example, he reported that a Nike subcontractor employed an Indonesian worker for 14 cents an hour, less than the minimum wage required in Indonesia. The poor working conditions at Nike's factories gained mainstream media attention during protests at the Barcelona Olympics in 1992 and a 1993 CBS interview of Nike factory workers. During the 1990s, Nike's sales declined as the company received criticism for its labor practices. By the end of the 1990s, the Nike swoosh had become the global face of abusive labor practices. In the face of declining demand and constant criticism, Nike recognized the need to change. During a May 1998 speech, then-CEO Phil Knight expressed this sentiment. "The Nike product has become synonymous with slave wages, forced overtime, and arbitrary abuse. I truly believe the American consumer doesn't want to buy products made under abusive conditions" (2013, para 18). During this speech, Knight also announced that Nike would raise the minimum age of its workers, increase monitoring, and comply with United States clean air standards in all factories. To this end, Nike created the Fair Labor Association, a non-profit organization in which representatives from companies, human rights, and labor agencies collaborate to establish independent monitoring and a code of conduct, including a minimum age and a 60-hour work week. Nike conducted an estimated 600 factory audits from 2002 to 2004, and revisited factories that were not in compliance. In 2004, human rights activists reported that Nike's increased monitoring efforts had helped to address the most glaring and worst issues, like employees' exposure to unsafe chemicals. In 2005, Nike made strides toward increasing transparency by becoming the first in the industry to publish a complete list of the factories it contracts with and a detailed 108-page report on the conditions and pay in its factories—in which Nike acknowledged the existence of widespread problems. Nike was able to reverse its downward spiral in the 1990s by acknowledging problematic practices and taking responsibility for making improvements. Nike has continued to fulfill its commitment to publishing the results of audits conducted, and the company has embraced corporate social responsibility as a strategic priority.

There are several ways in which strategic leaders in sport can develop a strong organizational culture. One primary tactic for developing a strong organizational culture is highly abstract and involves setting an inspiring and meaningful vision (Peters & Waterman, 1982). In sport, values can be expressed in many forms. Traditions such as pregame rituals, signage at the stadium, fight songs, band formations, and mascots are just a few examples of how an organization conveys its values

and vision to inspire purpose and meaning for stakeholders. Top executives should seek every opportunity to instill the strategic vision and the organization's values through deeds rather than words. The second way that a strategic leader in sport can develop a strong organizational culture is to pay attention to details in their development of the organization's culture (1982). For example, consider the NBA's efforts to expand into Asian markets. The potential for the NBA to succeed in China was unclear when NBA China launched in 2004. When the NBA set up its office for NBA Asia in Hong Kong, they originally had three people trying to run China, Japan, and everywhere else in Asia. Since then, the NBA has been wise to continue to dedicate resources to China, which has become the league's largest international fan base. Commissioner Adam Silver believes that the NBA has more staying power in China than they had previously thought was possible. As Silver explained, "... some people predicted that when Yao retired that we would lose popularity, in fact post Yao Ming, we're even more popular than when he was playing. We've been embraced by the Chinese government, and the people – I believe – in large part because of the values of our game. Those values, like respect and teamwork and hard work, (mean) the game itself resonates with the people of China" (Amick, 2017, p.1). It is clear that the long-term success of an organization is influenced when strategic leaders instill a set of values that resonate with internal and external stakeholders.

▶ Setting Objectives

For strategic visions to become a reality, they must be translated into concrete objectives and tactics that embody the organization's values. Managers convert the strategic vision into reality by setting objectives, or the actual steps taken to achieve desired results. **Strategic objectives** refer to performance targets that measure the strength and competitiveness of the organization in the marketplace and its future business prospects. Creating specific performance targets involves developing quantifiable, or measurable, hard objectives that must be achieved by a certain deadline. For example, the NFL has a goal of $25 billion in revenue by 2027. With the Supreme Court paving the way for sports wagering, that goal seems ever closer for one of the most popular leagues in the world. Objectives serve as yardsticks for measuring the success of the organization in achieving its mission and moving toward fulfilling its vision. Clarifying measurable concrete objectives is of utmost value to keep track of the organization's performance and progress. Well-stated objectives spell out exactly *how much* of *what kind* of performance is expected and *when* (Thompson et al, 2010, p. 37). When they are concrete and measurable, objectives are an invaluable tool for managers to communicate to employees the level of performance that is expected. Vague objectives that do not specify how much, what kind, or when leads to inconsistencies in performance that inhibit the organization's progress.

Strategic leadership is responsible for steering the organization to perform at its full potential and to deliver the best outcomes. To fulfill this responsibility, "stretch" objectives challenge personnel to perform at their highest level by setting objectives that motivate employees to push past their current performance targets to improve efficiencies and foster innovation. For example, a senior account executive might challenge him- or herself to surpass his or her number of group tickets sold from the previous year. Organizational leaders express their values and priorities to personnel in the form of incentive structures. By consistently linking extrinsic and intrinsic rewards for desirable behavior and using punishments to deter undesirable behavior, strategic leaders can strengthen the expectations and norms to support a culture that fosters the success of employees. However, leaders should be wary of a carrot-and-stick approach to achieve strategic objectives as different motivations appeal to different people.

▶ Developing a Sound Strategy

A company's strategic intent is exhibited in its relentless pursuit and commitment to achieving an ambitious strategic goal. Organizations pursue a strategic objective by rallying around efforts to achieve higher performance targets, analyzing the competitive landscape, crafting offensive and defensive strategies to beat out the competition, and by carefully using the resources and organizational capabilities in ways to maximize progress toward achieving the strategic vision.

The development of a competitive strategy involves examining how to best grow the business, provide value to customers, gain a competitive advantage, respond to changes in the market, manage business operations and functions, develop needed competencies, and achieve objectives and the strategic vision. The most successful strategies involve the differences in the ways the organization does things in comparison to its rivals. According to Porter (2008), "competitive strategy is about being different. It means deliberately choosing a different set of activities to deliver a unique mix of value." The more fierce the competition, the stronger the organization's commitment to differentiation should be (Moon, 2010). In order to break away from the competitive herd, it is necessary for sport organizations to examine the external environment, including all of the relevant factors and influences beyond the borders of the organization, to identify any changes or potential developments that may have an impact and influence on competitive conditions in their market. The most important strategy-shifting impacts will relate to the organization's immediate competitive environment and the forces that drive competition: The actions of rivals, consumer behavior, supplier-related conditions, and the potential of new organizations entering into the market.

How does an organization start achieving a needed strategic focus? Birshan and Kar (2012) outline three tips. First, an organization should contextualize strategy relative to its distinct industry. In 2017, the pace of sneaker sales plunged, leaving sneaker brands and footwear retailers reeling (Liu, 2017). However, Adidas was able to escape unscathed from the downward sales trend and steal market share from their big rivals in the United States. How? Adidas' competitive maneuvers to outwit Nike and Under Armour reflect a strong understanding of the dominant economic factors driving the industry and the competitive landscape. According to Bair analyst Jonathan Komp, Adidas realized it was crucial "to embrace non-athlete social influencers who have resonated well within current consumer trends" (2017). Building on the company's association with Jay Z and Kanye West, Adidas developed a strong following among those who wear sneakers as part of their casual wardrobe. Adidas figured out a game-changing factor to buck the downward sales trend: Sneakers are not only athletic gear; they are fashion statements. This factor became a major component to Adidas' competitive strategy, leading Adidas to revive some of its classic products to cater to the retro chic footwear trend. Adidas' Superstar, a popular shell-toe shoe from the 1960s, bumped Nike out of the top position and became the top-selling shoe in 2017. Adidas' U.S. market share increased by 11.3% and overall footwear sales increased by around 30% in 2017. Nike was slow to pick up on the fashion statement trend and, historically, the Nike brand is associated with athletes, such as Michael Jordan, and is centered on helping athletes perform better through cutting-edge technology. Nike's sneakers that tap into the retro and fashion trends are selling well; however, these sales did not offset the decline in performance brands. The trends demonstrate that the competitive landscape is changing. Sneaker brands do not have the long-term traction in the market that they once had due to the shorter attention spans of customers. This makes it more difficult to predict the shelf life of a style when it is released to the market. Organizations seek to gain a competitive advantage by doing things differently in ways that count. From developing innovative products and new styles to providing superior customer service, organizations aim to deliver unrivaled value to customers.

Second, effective strategists also address or identify future industry related changes or disruptions (Birshan & Kar, 2012). A common concern is what will be the next generation of smartphone technology because teams that do not make effective use of social media will fail to capture markets of new generation consumers who demand instant information and access to the experience. Traditional sport business success depended on putting fans in the stands or getting them to watch through the traditional media of television. If consumers are not in the stands or in front of a screen, how can sport businesses attract future consumers from different demographics who access information differently? (McAllister, 2015). To address future industry changes, organizations should consider performing **SWOT analyses** of their industries. A sport organization should make itself aware of threats (e.g., poor economy) and opportunities (e.g., increased use of social media) that may negatively or positively impact their ability to deliver value. Threats and opportunities represent the external analysis of the SWOT. The "S" and "W" in the acronym refer to strengths and weaknesses. An organization must consider an internal analysis of things that it does well and areas in which it needs to improve. For example, now that many fans use social media to communicate with their favorite teams, they want quick feedback. If an organization has not set aside money for human resources to nimbly handle social media communication, this could be a weakness.

Birshan and Kar's final suggestion notes that communication among those in the strategic process is paramount (2012) in maintaining strategic focus. Usually, there is no dearth of information or data available to the strategy team, but it is important that they communicate effectively about interpreting the data to fully understand the issues facing the business. For a team, knowing which of the following: group sales, walk-up sales, season ticket sales, or corporate sponsor sales is important. More and more, sport organizations are hiring employees for the sole purpose of sifting through these data of key performance indicators, looking for ebbs and flows and reasons for valleys and peaks in sales and overall revenue production. The business must also coordinate consistent efforts among the various sales points in a way that reinforces the most important contributor (i.e., group sales) while improving the lowest performing (i.e., walk-up sales) [McAllister, 2015].

On the court or on the field, many believe that the best way for organizations to maximize their success is to win at all costs. However, it is risky for organizations to focus their competitive strategy on fielding a winning team. As highlighted by Rein, Shields, and Grossman (2015), over the long term, a winning team does not necessarily translate into a winning business and there are many examples that illustrate this point: The University of Connecticut women's basketball team has won eleven National Collegiate Athletic Association (NCAA) titles under Coach Geno Auriemma. However, even after winning the NCAA championship and having a 90-game winning streak from 2009 to 2011, the team reported financial losses every year. The U.S. Department of Education reports that the Huskies' financial losses were up to $1.2 million after the 2012-2013 season (2015, p. 5). On the flip side, teams with losing records on the field may still be able to win in sports business. Rein, Shields, and Grossman

point to the Chicago Cubs, or the "lovable losers," and a brand identity associated with the inability to win. Even before the Cubs captured the World Series in 2016, fans continued to attend Cubs games to enjoy a Chicago-style hot dog with an Old Style beer, or to celebrate Harry Caray's tradition of singing "Take Me Out to the Ballgame" during the seventh inning. Cub fans continued to pay high ticket prices and, when the team was losing, revenue from gate receipts actually increased. Since the Cubs started to win after 2008, Cubs attendance rates declined consistently from 2009 to 2014 and television ratings decreased by over 64% (2015, p. 6).

It is clear that sport organizations can be successful without relying on a strategy that is centered on winning and relying on winning is a risky proposition in the sport industry. The key to long-term stability and success is to devise strategies that center on delivering value to customers using the factors that strategic leaders and organizations have some control. Researchers have identified reasons why people attend sports games and found that the quality of the stadium and the opportunity to socialize and the excitement associated with the games are often much more important than whether a team wins.

Implementing and Executing the Strategy

Implementing and executing strategy is the most challenging and time-consuming step for top executives. Translating strategic plans into real action and results requires leaders to oversee organizational changes; motivate people; invest in the development of company strengths, key competencies, and competitive capabilities; and to support a work environment that fosters strategy and learning. To be successful, strategic leaders must determine what has to be done in their area to execute the strategic plan and must develop the organizational structures, processes, and controls that are needed to efficiently and effectively execute the strategic plan.

Strategy execution involves staffing the organization with individuals who have the appropriate skills and expertise, and strategic allocation of resources. We must rely on best industry practices to perform business activities, motivate people, sustain a strong organizational culture and work climate conducive to executing strategy and, most importantly, strategic leadership must exist to drive implementation forward and to overcome any hurdles encountered along the way. Researchers have discovered strategic leaders' capacity to learn is crucial in their ability to develop and execute a sound strategic direction that reflects environmental forces and changes in the competitive landscape. The capacity to learn requires a willingness to tolerate small failures (Sitkin, 1992) and an organizational context and culture that fosters learning. Cooperation, discipline, trust, and support are important elements that influence the context of an organization and its capacity to foster learning (Ghoshal & Bartlett, 1994) in the process of executing strategy.

Although this is a book about leadership, the importance of managers in implementing strategy cannot be underestimated. Smaller organizations are often characterized by a CEO-centered strategy, but strategy making and the implementation of strategy should be a collective effort that involves every manager and sometimes key employees throughout the entire organizational hierarchy. The collaborative approach to developing an organization's strategic plan ensures that the individuals who will be held responsible for implementing strategy are also involved in developing the strategy. A collaborative approach to developing and implementing strategy often leads to more success in winning the support of personnel across the organizational hierarchy and rallying members of the organization behind the strategic vision. So, frontline managers

need to be in on the strategic-planning process, particularly when it involves functional and operational strategies, which were touched on at the beginning of this chapter.

Evaluating Performance

Strategic leaders must constantly monitor the environment and external changes, evaluate the progress of the organization, and make corrective adjustments to ensure that the company's direction, performance, and progress are in line with the implemented strategy, as long as the strategy continues to be well-matched to the industry and the competitive landscape. Strategic leaders can reinforce and change the culture of a sport organization by directing their attention to the important aspects of the organization, from existing norms, patterns, roles and beliefs to what is measured, controlled, rewarded, or systematically addressed (Schein, 1992). Shifts in competitive conditions often serve as triggers for decisions about whether to continue or change the organization's strategic direction, objectives, strategy, and the steps used to execute strategy. Changes that are disruptive to competitive conditions raise questions about the relevance and strength of the strategic direction of the organization. Therefore, the strategic vision, objectives, strategy, and the steps used to execute the strategy are never final; strategic leaders must be engaged in an ongoing process of revisiting the strategic plan and keeping an eye on internal and external conditions.

Good business entrepreneurship underlies the ability to craft a good strategy. The chief executive officer (CEO) of the organization serves as the captain of the organizational ship. The CEO carries the torch when it comes to being the chief direction setter, objective setter, strategy maker, and implementer of strategy since they are ultimately held responsible for the results that the entire enterprise achieves and the progress that is made toward the strategic vision.

▶ Situational and Personal Characteristics of Strategic Leaders

The building blocks of strategy making are straight-forward: Develop a strategic plan, implement it, and execute it to the fullest extent possible, while making adjustments and corrective actions as necessary to succeed. However, the leadership challenges throughout this process are complex. Researchers have found many factors that influence the effectiveness of strategic leaders, such as discretion, strategic flexibility, and managerial wisdom.

The extent to which leaders found themselves in a situation where they had discretion determined the relationship between their strategic choices and organizational performance and outcomes (Hambrick & Finkelstein, 1987). Discretion reflects the ability to take actions and the extent to which these actions are met with resistance or accepted in light of environmental constraints, demographic and personality characteristics, and organizational factors. When a leader has more discretion, the greater the impact their choices will have on the organization's success. Additionally, past research suggests that demands, expectations, and constraints on leadership have a significant impact on the choices made by leaders (Selznick, 1984; Stewart, 1982). Interestingly, the degree to which strategic leaders believe that they have discretion has an impact on their success. When leaders enjoy large degrees of discretion but they do not perceive this, they are unlikely to take action. Whereas, when leaders mistakenly believe that they enjoy a large degree of discretion, their actions will usually be met with fierce resistance and lead to failure. In sport, the discretion that strategic leaders use may be met with public scrutiny and there are numerous examples of this, from NFL Commissioner Roger Goodell's discretion in determining the degree of severity for sanctions against players for domestic violence to NCAA President Mark Emmert's decision to impose harsh sanctions against Penn State following the Jerry Sandusky case. It is clear that strategic leaders must carefully assess the degree of discretion used in decision-making.

Strategic leadership occurs in an ambiguous, complex, and increasingly turbulent environment in which leaders are overloaded with information (Hambrick, 1989; Eisenhardt, 1989). In an increasingly competitive landscape, organizational success is dependent on the ability to change and demonstrate strategic flexibility (Hitt, Keats, & DeMarie, 1998). **Strategic flexibility** refers to the ability of an organization to quickly act and respond to changes in competitive conditions and the environment. Again, this is situational. The organization's capacity to change allows the organization to perform and take advantage of future opportunities (Sanchez, Heene, & Thomas, 1996). Leaders at the top of the organization largely determine the extent of an organization's ability to change and respond to environmental changes and market dynamics. The capacity of senior executives to recognize new information, process it, and be able to apply it to achieving organizational objectives is important to enhancing the fit between an organization and its environment. Therefore, it is important for CEOs to exhibit cognitive and behavioral complexity in decision-making, strategic flexibility, and be open to and accepting of change (Black & Boal, 1996).

The success of strategic leaders often depends on their approach to completing tasks and their ability to effectively manage the most important resource of an organization: People. Managerial wisdom (Malan & Kriger, 1998) refers to the capacity to recognize patterns and changes in the environment, along with the understanding of people and their relationships, or social intelligence. The ability to recognize changes in the environment (Osborn, Hunt & Jauch, 1980) and to understand others and their relationships is interwoven in the fabric of managerial wisdom. Social awareness (for example, showing empathy) and social skills (for instance, managing conflict) are two important components of social intelligence and managerial wisdom. The third component of managerial wisdom is the ability to take the correct approach at the critical moment or right time (Bartunek & Necochea, 2000).

TABLE 7.1 captures the key characteristics of strategic leaders. Readers will note that the characteristics are either termed "situational" or "personal" in the table, meaning that the characteristic is either personal to the leader or emanates from the external and internal environments the organization operates in (situational).

TABLE 7.1 Situational and Personal Characteristics that Impact Strategic Leaders

Characteristic	Explanation	Example
Discretion (Situational)	Reflects the ability to take actions and the extent to which these actions are met with resistance or accepted in light of environmental constraints, demographic and personality characteristics, and organizational factors.	When MLB players were questioned by members of Congress about PED use in a 2005 hearing, the nation's lawmakers had little discretion to change baseball. However, the commissioner of MLB at the time, Bud Selig, and MLB players' union lawyer Donald Fehr had more discretion to take action to solve MLB's PED issue.
Flexibility (Situational)	The ability of an organization to quickly act and respond to changes in competitive conditions and the environment.	Despite the regular occurrence of spectators being struck by foul balls, it was not until 2018 that MLB teams extended netting to the end of each dugout. This delayed action illustrates a lack of flexibility for MLB to make changes quickly.
Managerial Wisdom (Personal)	The capacity to recognize patterns and changes in the environment, along with the understanding of people and their relationships, or social intelligence.	In 2014, defensive end Devon Still was cut by the Cincinnati Bengals but then re-signed to the team's practice squad so he could continue to get health benefits to cover his daughter's cancer treatment. The move showed managerial wisdom by Bengals leadership and illustrated the importance of relationships over revenues.
Interdisciplinary View (Personal)	Recognize the impact of department decisions on other departments and units in the business.	When the Baltimore Orioles made the decision to allow youngsters 9 and under to get into games for free, this directive clearly took an interdisciplinary approach as the unprecedented move would clearly also impact the team's marketing and community outreach departments.

(continues)

TABLE 7.1 Situational and Personal Characteristics that Impact Strategic Leaders *(continued)*

Characteristic	Explanation	Example
Problem-oriented (Personal)	Understand the source of the problem they are trying to resolve and search for methods and information that may contribute to the solution.	The Atlanta Falcons recognized the inability of families to afford coming to games due to high concession prices. Falcons' ownership showed it is problem-oriented by offering less expensive food options as a solution.
Committed to differentiation (Personal)	Constantly examine what they can do differently from others to offer unique value.	Newly built sport venues seek differentiation, particularly in addressing a memorable fan experience. Little Caesars Arena, which houses the Detroit Red Wings and Detroit Pistons, offers innovation not seen in other venues. The venue has a 12-laser projection system that allows the teams to animate the entire arena, projecting full motion video and images.
Students of technology (Personal)	Interested in learning about innovations in technology and recognize ways these can be leveraged into new opportunities for their organizations.	Bowling industry executives have had to become students of technology in order to reach new customers. HD video walls, massive sound systems, and food-ordering kiosks are some of the innovations that Bowlero Corp. is using to attract young bowlers.
Bottom-line focus (Situational/ Personal)	Understanding the important role of generating revenue for the organization and keeping costs under control.	The phenomenon of "cord-cutting" has hurt media organizations like ESPN. Fewer people are subscribing to cable TV, which has cut into the network's bottom line. This has caused leaders to enact layoffs to cut costs.

Data from: Hambrick, D. C., & Finkelstein, S. (1987). Managerial discretion: A bridge between polar views of organizations. In L. L. Cummings & B.M. Straw (Eds.), *Research in organizational behavior* (vol. 9; pp. 396–406). Greenwich, CT: JAI Press; Hitt, M. A., Keats, B. W., & DeMarie, S. M. (1998). Navigating in the new competitive landscape: Building strategic flexibility and competitive advantage in the 21st century. *Academy of Management Executive, 12,* 22-41; Malan, L.C., & Kriger, M.P. (1998). Making sense of managerial wisdom. *Journal of Management Inquiry, 7,* 242-251; Rein, I., Shields, B., & Grossman, A. (2015). *The sports strategist: developing leaders for a high-performance industry.* Oxford, UK: Oxford University Press.

Five Key Characteristics of Strategic Leaders

Rein, Shields, and Grossman (2015) examined the traits of strategists in the sport industry and identified five key characteristics exhibited among successful strategic leaders: Interdisciplinary view, problem-oriented, committed to differentiation, students of technology, and focus on the bottom line.

First, strategic leaders maintain an interdisciplinary, holistic view of their organizations and recognize the impact of department decisions on other departments and units in the business. Secondly, they are issue-oriented because they begin with the source of the problem that they are trying to resolve and search for methods and information that may contribute to the solution. Packers President Mark Murphy's investment of hundreds of millions of dollars in a mixed-use development next to the Lambeau Field was a solution to a potential future issue: Whether the team would be able to stay in Green Bay. With the Packers ranked ninth in revenue during the 2017 NFL season and a 131,000-person waiting list for Packers season tickets, it may seem unlikely for the team to move. However, the recent decisions by the NFL to allow three teams to leave their long-time markets is cause for concern. According to Murphy (Kaplan, 2017b), "Maybe we get a collective bargaining agreement with no salary cap, or revenue-sharing changes," when the current CBA expires in four years (para. 2). The purpose of this investment in Titletown is to help secure the team's future in the smallest market of the NFL, Green Bay. By dedicating the acres next to the stadium to offer the community a recreational area with a snow tubing hill, a football field, a playground, an NHL-size skating rink, and a plaza featuring restaurants, cafes, and other stores, Murphy believes that, "this will allow the Green Bay economic base to become strong enough to support an NFL team at a high level" (para. 41). Murphy analyzed his environment, identified a potential future issue in the long-term economic feasibility of maintaining the Packers in Green Bay, and developed a strategic solution.

The third key characteristic of strategic leaders is their commitment to differentiation. They constantly examine what they can do differently from others to offer unique value. President Jonathan Ressler of Like a Pro, an athletic equipment and memorabilia company, demonstrated this commitment to differentiation when he came up with the idea to launch a digital division to offer fans the chance to buy social media posts on Facebook, Instagram, and Twitter from their favorite athlete (Mullins, 2017). The company's main line of business focused on selling shoes, apparel, and equipment worn and used by professional athletes, and memorabilia. However, autographed photos and trading cards were items that did not resonate with today's social currency. More than 230 current and retired professional athletes have signed on with Like a Pro. Each athlete is given an equity stake in the company and Like a Pro splits the profits with them 50-50. Fans will send in a request for a social media post and the athlete will have the choice to accept or reject it. Posts will start out at the price of $50 each and will most likely increase once the market has been tested with this new line of business. While $50 a post may seem like a small payoff, Ressler envisions that the business has the potential to grow.

The fourth characteristic of successful strategic leaders in sport is their commitment to learning about technology. As students of technology, they learn about innovations in technology and recognize ways that these can be leveraged into new opportunities for their organizations. For example, the National Hockey League (NHL) has invested in research and analysis of the application of in-game tracking system technologies for the past few years. During a test conducted in 2016, infrared cameras were installed in the rafters of Toronto's Air Canada Centre to track RFID chips in both the puck and the back of jerseys. This new technology provides data on the location and speed of the puck and players, the relative distance between players, the relative distance between players and the puck, and the players' time on the ice. David Lehanski, NHL senior vice president of business development and global partnerships, believes that new technology provides, "an opportunity to take some of the "oohs and aahs" you hear in an arena . . . and bring that to people on their couches and help them feel it" (Thomas, 2017, p.7). Finally, the fifth critical characteristic of effective strategic leaders is their focus on the bottom line and the important role that they play in generating revenue for the organization. After all, many sport organizations are profit-driven. Effective strategy helps these organizations achieve higher profits to satisfy key stakeholders.

▶ Summary

It is clear that there is considerable money to be made in sports. Success requires a disciplined and strategic approach to managing any sport business. A sport organization's long-term growth and sustainability depends on the ability of strategic leaders to navigate the increasingly complex, dynamic, and fast-paced sport industry. Unprecedented challenges, from managing political and social issues, to rising costs of doing business, to increased competition—both domestic and foreign—have made it more difficult for sport organizations to meet their objectives. A brilliant strategy can put a business on the competitive map, but only solid execution can keep you there and this requires strategic leaders who are competent and capable of navigating the organization in an increasingly complex, competitive landscape.

LEADERSHIP PERSPECTIVE

Mary Kay Wydra

Mary Kay Wydra is president of the Greater Springfield Visitors and Convention Bureau, which includes the Western Mass Sports Commission. Her mission as president is to lead the organization in promoting the Massachusetts' Pioneer Valley as a year-round destination for sporting events, conventions, meetings, group tours, and leisure travel. Wydra has worked for the organization for 30 years.

Q: This book is largely academic. But it is equally important to have the view of the practitioner. So, to start, how do you view or characterize vision, strategy, and leadership? What is the connection?

In this context, I tend to think of "vision" as having an ideal for an organization. Strategy is determining how you're going to constantly move toward that ideal. Leadership is the process of inspiring one's team to get the work done that points us toward that ideal. So they are definitely connected.

I think it's important to state that I work for a non-profit destination marketing organization with a small staff, and resources are always a challenge for us. So I have the double-duty of trying to achieve many things simultaneously and also keep my hand in fundraising at the same time.

I always tell my team that for the lucky few marketers who are working with large budgets, well, the world's their oyster. Then, you can do whatever promotions you want. But I've long believed that really good, savvy marketers can still produce solid efforts, essentially on a shoestring, which is typically more our reality. We are always very mindful of the finite resources we have.

So given that background, I think of strategic leadership as my working to influence various groups of people to come together and get a tough job done.

Q: Can you describe a situation in which you had to articulate a strategy for the Convention and Visitors Bureau (CVB) to your board and other key stakeholders?

Definitely. Here in mid-2018, we are working on a wholly new funding model for our organization; it's a major strategic initiative. I've been here 30 years and we do a familiar and sometimes difficult dance year after year in terms of securing our funding sources. We have been very careful to be realistic at all times, and because of that, we've been able to weather the storm during periods when funding sources have been curtailed or nearly dried up.

Currently, we are putting a lot of resources toward one particular initiative that should change and strengthen our funding model for the long term. The strategy I'm referring to involves bringing together a vital segment of our industry—primarily the hoteliers. It's innovative, and the effort to date is something I'm really proud of.

The GSCVB, my organization, is taking the lead, and if we're successful, every Regional Tourist Council in the Commonwealth can take advantage of what we're trying to create. This will represent a huge change in the status quo and will require enabling legislation to come to fruition. So, we're educating our lawmakers statewide on this new initiative, and not just our own regional delegation.

In order for a law to pass in Massachusetts, it has to have statewide support. This means that I spend a lot of time in Boston at the State House. I have gotten to know many key people in our legislative leadership.

Our strategy is to articulate the value of our various Bureaus and show the legislators how the Commonwealth benefits from our collective work—meaning the Regional Tourism Councils together with our member investors. If we can message that effectively, we will be able to get the legislature to join us in making this new funding process a reality. And as part of this, we also have to influence our local city governments.

The good news in all this is that I'm not going it alone. The Bureau has a very good legislative committee, and my job in terms of strategic leadership is to keep them all on task. Every two weeks, we hold a conference call; my job is to develop an agenda for each call. I pretty much lead the group's conversation while ensuring that everyone participates. I think it's important that when you're leading people that they know they can be heard.

I never claim to have all the answers. And after all these years, I'm always so impressed by how often—when you put talented, collective minds together at the table—that great things will bubble up.

Q: You haven't always been president of the CVB. What things/steps did you take to become a leader and put yourself in a position to do this job?

I started working at the Bureau in 1988. I have been at the Bureau for 30 years now. I prefer a small working environment and I really like marketing this destination because I live here, and I truly believe in how much it offers to visitors.

When I graduated from Springfield College in 1987, I had no strong idea what I wanted to do career-wise. I'd really liked Professor Doyle in the Business Department and that became my best subject. But I never felt a true "calling" to business. I got a job working in accounting in a hotel in Connecticut and I found an instant attraction to hospitality, so when the opportunity came along at the GSCVB, I jumped at the chance to get into the promotions side of the industry. I think I had an advantage in starting at the Bureau as a 22-year-old and working with a group of four savvy, older people. I took something from each of these four individuals. The woman who headed the Bureau at the time was incredibly smart and a very solid administrator. I learned good basic management skills from her.

The salesperson at the time was very outgoing and I learned tremendous people skills from her. I always say that colleges need to offer a prep course in how to launch students out into the real world,

(continues)

LEADERSHIP PERSPECTIVE (*continued*)

look at somebody and maintain eye contact. Introduce yourself and be proud of your background and strike up a conversation. This woman took me to every social event we could go to and it was at a time in the 80s and early 90s when there were a lot of social networking events. So, I developed a love for people and in talking to people. My minor is in psychology, and I think that has helped me a lot there. We're all in people businesses. I hate the wave of the future with technology. I still prefer a phone call. I want to talk to somebody. I want to be at a table with someone and get to know them.

I worked with a gentleman who is an excellent communicator and I think that what I learned from him is really at the heart of what I do today. My ability to speak and write are hugely important. I think back to when I was 22; I used to chew my gum and it seemed as if "like" was every other word out of my mouth. He really polished me up and showed me the importance of good writing and speaking skills.

The last person I worked for was just tough as nails. Initially, I was intimidated by her. I spent enough time working with her that I got to know her as a person. She showed me how to be tough when I needed to be tough and it's served me many times through the years. I give each of those four people tremendous credit.

When I joined on as the administrative assistant at the Bureau, they said I was overqualified. I said, "Yes, but I need to start somewhere." So, I went in and opened every piece of mail I could get my hands on. I took phone calls, I learned the players and scheduled the meetings. I was a sponge for information and just learned all I could, as fast as I could.

Honestly, I was very fortunate to have many good role models in my life. I really believe in finding mentors, and learning from what they can offer. When people demonstrate professionalism and good work skills, you can model yourself after that same behavior, and successes can grow from that foundation.

Q: How would you describe your relationship with your board, employees, and the various communities with which you come into contact?
I think of them as distinct audiences and they are all different, but I also think there is a similarity to my fundamental approach in dealing with each of them. At the end of the day, people are people, and being respectful and understanding is vital. A big part of my job is to make sure each group has the key information and situational understanding they need in order to address the issues and further the Bureau's main goals. Keeping the peace while bringing people together is at the center of my professional livelihood.

Q: How does the CVB approach and conduct the strategic planning process? Is there a formal, planned meeting or process?
Yes, there is, and we take strategic planning seriously. The GSCVB has engaged an expert consultant on three occasions during my tenure, a gentleman nationally-respected in our industry. He works with a wide variety of destination marketing organizations. So we have had three different three-year plans.

The consultant is from Madison, Wisconsin, and he would typically come in for three days of meetings and discussions. I would spend a day and a half with him and then we would do a separate session with the whole staff. We then moved to an informational retreat with the board, and based on all of that input, the consultant would write the plan. The shape of the plan(s) depended to some degree on who was chairing the board at the time, because the priorities shifted over time.

It's my job to be the keeper of the plan. Ideally, at any point, I can tell you those plans, and how effective or how closely we operated within the plan and hit our goals. Then I would create what I would call my report card, a progress report of where we were in the steps of the plan. Where are we in the process? Have we completed it? Are we still working on it? Do we have to amend the goal? What I've learned is that long-term planning is important, but you still have to be able to be nimble and shift when circumstances change.

Q: Do you have objectives that you try to reach that are written down? How do you come up with those?

Yes, we do, and that arises, again, from board involvement and the various long-term strategic plan(s). We set a written series of goals each fiscal year, drawn from a consensus of the board. They establish the priorities and that helps guide us within the year. Though I should repeat that what we want to do and what we can actually accomplish are not always in synch, due to the funding challenges we typically face each year. At the beginning of our conversation I referred to finite resources, and with that as the background, I say to my staff all the time: what happens in "Bureau-land" can't always happen at the pace people want it to. It all goes back to the availability and timing of resources plus many unpredictable outside influences. So, being resilient and able to deal with change is not only an asset in this industry, it's pretty much a requirement. But that said, I still love hospitality and I'm excited to come to work each day—not everyone can say that after 30 years!

▶ Key Terms

Business strategy	Operating strategy	Strategic vision
Corporate strategy	Strategic flexibility	Strategy
Disruption	Strategic leadership	SWOT
Functional strategy	Strategic objectives	Values
Mission statement	Strategic planning	Vision statement

▶ Discussion Questions

1. Now that you have a firm grasp on strategic leadership, can you think of 2 to 3 leaders in professional or college sport that fit many of the characteristics of a strategic leader?

2. Looking again the characteristics of a strategic leader, which ones do you think are most important in the sport industry in the 21st century and why?

3. The chapter opens with a discussion of the NFL's vulnerability. Put yourself in the position of Roger Goodell. What strategies should the league implement over the next several years to regain its credibility with fans?

4. In groups of four to five, select a sport organization, assume roles in its leadership structure, and suggest some strategic objectives the organization should pursue in the future to differentiate itself from its competitors.

5. The author writes about the four levels of strategy and provides an example regarding Adidas. Using *Sports Business Journal* as a primary form of research, locate an organization that is in the midst of employing corporate strategy and make suggestions for the final three levels of strategy.

6. Carlos Cordeiro was elected the new president of the U.S. Soccer Federation in 2018. What strategic moves should he engineer to make the U.S. national men's soccer team a global power and a favorite to win the 2026 World Cup, which will be staged in North America?

▶ References

Amick, S. (2017, October 4). NBA's massive growth in China 'beyond what anybody could have anticipated.' *USA Today.* Retrieved from https://www.usatoday.com/story/sports/nba/2017/10/04/nba-massive-growth-china-beyond-what-anybody-could-have-anticipated/732025001/

Avolio, B. J., Bass, B. M., & Jung, D. I. (1999). Re-examining the components of transformational and transactional leadership using the multifactor leadership questionnaire. *Journal of Occupational and Organizational Psychology, 72*, 441–462.

Ballinger, J. (1992, August). The new free-trade heel: Nike's profits jump on the backs of Asian workers. *Harper's Magazine.* Retrieved from https://harpers.org/archive/1992/08/the-new-free-trade-heel/

Bartunek, J. M., & Necochea, R. (2000). Old Insights and New Times: Kairos, Inca Cosmology and their Contributions to Contemporary Management Inquiry. *Journal of Management Inquiry, 9*(2), 103–113.

Bass, B. (1990). *Bass and Stogdill's handbook of leadership: Theory, research and managerial applications.* New York: Free Press.

Bass, B. (1985). *Leadership and performance beyond expectations.* New York: Free Press.

Bennis, W., & Nanus, B. (1985). *Leaders: The strategies for taking charge.* New York: Harper & Row.

Birshan, M., & Kar, J. (2012). Becoming more strategic: Three tips for any executive. *McKinsey Quarterly.* Retrieved from http://www.mckinseyquarterly.com/Becoming_more_strategic_Three_tips_for_any_executive_2992

Black, J. A., & Boal, K. B. (1996). Assessing the organizational capacity to change. In A. Heene & R. Sanchez (Eds.), *Competence-based strategic management* (pp. 151–18). Chichester, UK: John Wiley & Sons.

Carroll, L. (2013). *Alice in wonderland.* London: Penguin Classics. (Original work published in 1865).

Conger, J. & Kanungo, R. (1987). Toward a behavioral theory of charismatic leadership in organizational settings. *Academy of Management Review, 12,* 637–647.

Corporate strategy – Adidas (n.d.). Retrieved from https://www.adidas-group.com/en/investors/group-strategy/

Cyert, R., & March, J. (1963). *A behavioral theory of the firm.* Englewood Cliffs, NJ: Prentice Hall.

de Jong, M. & van Dijk, M. (2015, July). Disrupting beliefs: A new approach to business-model innovation. Retrieved from https://www.mckinsey.com/business-functions/strategy-and-corporate-finance/our-insights/disrupting-beliefs-a-new-approach-to-business-model-innovation

Eisenhardt, K. (1989). Making fast strategic decisions in high-velocity environments. *Academy of Management Journal, 32*(3): 543–576.

Ferkins, L., Shilbury, D., & McDonald, G. (2005). The role of the board in building strategic capability: Towards an integrated model of sport governance research. *Sport Management Review, 8,* 195–225.

Fisher, E. (2018, March 12). Orioles' bold bet offers youth free admission. Retrieved from https://www.sportsbusinessdaily.com/Journal/Issues/2018/03/12/Franchises/Orioles.aspx

Frenette, G. (2016). Jacksonville Suns changing name to Jumbo Shrimp. Retrieved from http://www.jacksonville.com/metro/2016-11-01/jacksonville-suns-changing-name-jumbo-shrimp

Gelman, S. (2016). Two Marlins minor league affiliates have new names. Here's why. Retrieved from https://www.fishstripes.com/2016/11/23/13734046/marlins-minor-league-name-change-jumbo-shrimp-baby-cakes

Ghoshal, S. & Bartlett C. (1994). Linking organizational context and managerial action: The dimensions of quality of management. *Strategic Management Journal 15*(S2), 91–112.

Green, D. (2018, March 24). One of the hottest '80s fitness brands is banking on female CrossFitters and a swanky new office to be its saving grace. Retrieved from https://www.businessinsider.de/reebok-new-office-photos-comeback-plan-2018-5?r=US&IR=T

Hambrick, D. (1989). Putting top managers back in the strategy picture. *Strategic Management Journal, 10,* 5–15.

Hambrick, D. C., & Finkelstein, S. (1987). Managerial discretion: A bridge between polar views of organizations. In L. L. Cummings & B.M. Straw (Eds.), *Research in organizational behavior* (vol. 9; pp. 396–406). Greenwich, CT: JAI Press.

Hambrick, D. & Mason, P. (1984). Upper echelons: The organization as a reflection of its top managers. *Academy of Management Review, 9,* 193–206.

Heitner, D. (2016, October 16). North American sports market at $75.7 billion by 2020, led by media rights. *Forbes.* Retrieved from https://www.forbes.com/sites/darrenheitner/2016/10/10/north-american-sports-market-to-reach-75-7-billion-by-2020/#84ca4cc217bc

Hitt, M. A., Keats, B. W., & DeMarie, S. M. (1998). Navigating in the new competitive landscape: Building strategic flexibility and competitive advantage in the 21st century. *Academy of Management Executive, 12,* 22–41.

House, R. (1977). A 1976 theory of charismatic leadership. In J. G. Hunt & L. L. Larson (Eds.), *Leadership: The cutting edge* (pp. 189–207). Carbondale, IL: Southern Illinois University Press.

House, R. J., & Aditya, R. (1997). The social scientific study of leadership: Quo vadis? *Journal of Management, 23,* 409–474.

Hurley, R., & Hult, T. (1998). Innovation, market orientation, and organizational learning: An integration and empirical examination. *Journal of Marketing, 62*, 42–54.

Kaplan, D. (2017a, November 6). NFL sponsors cite impact of anthem protests. *Street & Smith's Sports Business Journal, 20*(29), 32.

Kaplan, D. (2017b, September 4). The promise of Titletown: How the Packers are working to reshape Green Bay and why. *Street & Smith's Sports Business Journal, 20*(20), 1.

Kouzes, J. M., & Posner, B. Z. (1987). *The leadership challenge: How to get extraordinary things done in organizations.* San Francisco: Jossey-Bass.

Lefton, T. (2017, December 4). How big a part are protests playing? It's hard to say, but… *Street & Smith's Sports Business Journal, 20*(33), 14.

Liu, E. (2017, August 29). How Adidas blew past NIKE and Under Armour. *Barron's.* Retrieved from https://www.barrons.com/articles/how-adidas-blew-past-nike-and-under-armour-1504037913

Lord, R. (1977). Functional leadership behavior: Measurement and relation to social power and leadership perceptions. *Administrative Science Quarterly, 22*, 114–133.

Lowe, K. B., Kroeck, K. G., & Sivasubramaniam, N. (1996). Effectiveness correlates of transformational and transactional leadership: A meta-analytic review of the MLQ literature. *Leadership Quarterly, 7*, 385–425.

Malan, L.C., & Kriger, M.P. (1998). Making sense of managerial wisdom. *Journal of Management Inquiry, 7*, 242–251.

McAllister, K. (2015). Strategy and leadership. In J. F. Borland, G.M. Kane, & L.J. Burton (Eds.), *Sport Leadership in the 21st Century.* (pp. 127–147). Boston: Jones & Bartlett Learning.

Mintzberg, H. (1979). *The structuring of organizations.* Englewood Cliffs, NJ: Prentice Hall.

Moon, Y. (2010). *Different: Escaping the competitive herd.* New York: Crown Publishing Group.

Mullins, L. (2017, October 9). NHL aims for player-tracking system this year. *Street & Smith's Sports Business Journal, 20*(25), 14.

Nahavandi, A. (1993). Integrating leadership and strategic management in organizational theory. *Canadian Journal of Administrative Science, 10*, 297–307.

NIKE, Inc. (2017). Mission statement. Retrieved from: https://nike.com

Nisen, Mike (2013, May 9). How Nike solved its sweatshop problem. *Business Insider.* Retrieved from http://www.businessinsider.com/how-nike-solved-its-sweatshop-problem-2013-5.

Office of Economic Development – Military Presence (n.d.) Retrieved from http://www.coj.net/departments/office-of-economic-development/about-jacksonville/jacksonville%E2%80%99s-military-presence

One of Us: Ken Babby (2018, April 12). Retrieved from http://pontevedrarecorder.com/stories/one-of-us-ken-babby,6106?

Osborn, R.N., Hunt, J.G., & Jauch, L.R. (1980). *Organization theory: An integrated approach.* New York: Wiley.

Peters, T., & Waterman, R. (1982). *In Search of Excellence: Lessons from America's Best-Run Companies.* New York: Harper & Row, Publishers.

Porter, M. (2008, January). The five competitive forces that shape strategy. *Harvard Business Review*, 78–93.

Rein, I., Shields, B., & Grossman, A. (2015). *The sports strategist: developing leaders for a high-performance industry.* Oxford, UK: Oxford University Press.

RubberDucks owner/CEO Ken Babby named EY Entrepreneur of the Year Award (2017, June 23). Retrieved from https://www.milb.com/akron/news/rubberducks-ownerceo-ken-babby-named-ey-entrepreneur-of-the-year-award174 2017-winner/c-238308316

Sanchez, R., Heene, A., & Thomas, H. (1996). Introduction: Towards the theory of practice of competence-based competition. In R. Sanchez, A. Heene, & H. Thomas (Eds.), *Dynamics of Competence-Based Competition* (pp. 1–37). Oxford, UK: Elsevier.

Schein, E. H. (1992). *Organizational culture and leadership.* San Francisco: Jossey-Bass.

Selznick, P. (1984). *Leadership in administration: A sociological interpretation.* Berkeley: University of California Press [originally published in 1957].

Shamir, B., House, R. J., & Arthur, M. B. (1993). The motivational effects of charismatic leadership: A self-concept theory. *Organization Science, 4*, 1–17.

Sitkin, S. (1992). Learning through failure: The strategy of small losses. In B. M. Staw & L. L. Cummings, *Research in organizational behavior* (vol. 14; pp. 231–266). Greenwich, CT: JAI Press.

Smithson, N. (2017, February 7). Nike, Inc. Vision Statement & Mission Statement. Retrieved from http://panmore.com/nike-inc-vision-statement-mission-statement

Smith, M. & Ourand, J. (2018, April 23). World Congress 2018: Dissecting the disruption. Retrieved from https://www.sportsbusinessdaily.com/Journal/Issues/2018/04/23/World-Congress-of-Sports/Disruption.aspx

Southern League: Attendance (2018). Retrieved from http://www.milb.com/milb/stats/stats.jsp?y=2018&t=l_att&lid=111&sid=t564

Stewart, R. (1982). *Choices for the manager: A guide to understanding managerial work.* Englewood Cliffs, NJ: Prentice-Hall.

Sustainable Innovation. (n.d.). Retrieved January 2, 2018 from https://about.nike.com/pages/sustainable-innovation

Thomas, I. (2017, October 9). NHL aims for player-tracking system this year. *Street & Smith's Sports Business Journal, 20*(25), 7.

Thompson, A., Strickland, A., & Gamble, J. (2010). *Crafting and executing strategy* (17th ed). NY: McGraw-Hill Irwin.

Tushman, M. L., & O'Reilly, C. A., III. (1996). Ambidextrous organizations: Managing evolutionary and revolutionary change. *California Management Review, 38*(4), 8–30.

Vera, D., & Crossan, M. (2003). Organizational learning and knowledge management: Toward an integrative frame work. In M. Easterby-Smith & M. Lyles (Eds.), *Handbook of organizational learning.* (pp. 122–141). Oxford, UK: Blackwell.

Yukl, G. (1994). *Leadership in organizations.* Englewood Cliffs, NJ: Prentice-Hall.

CHAPTER 8

Forging Significant Change

Jon Welty Peachey

Janelle E. Wells

CHAPTER OBJECTIVES

- Define the concept of organizational change.
- Describe the factors that may contribute to resistance to and acceptance of organizational change.
- Describe how organizational change is realized differently at the individual, group, and organizational levels.
- Differentiate the types of leadership styles and their relationship with transformational change.
- Identify the steps in organizational change.

CASE STUDY

Penn State

The intercollegiate football world was rocked in 2012 when long-time Penn State University football defensive coordinator, Jerry Sandusky, was convicted of molesting 10 boys (Orso, 2014). In the wake of this scandal, legendary late coach of 46 seasons, Joe Paterno, was fired, along with athletic director Tim Curley, while the president of the university, Graham Spanier, was forced to resign. Many thought that the Penn State football program, and the university more broadly, would never recover due to crippling National Collegiate Athletic Association (NCAA) sanctions and negative publicity, and because of the Freeh report, which implicated three administrators as well as Paterno in a cover-up of Sandusky's acts (Orso, 2014; Tolley, 2014).

However, not only have the university and football program recovered from this horrific scandal but they are thriving. The university had its largest endowment ever at around $2 billion in 2013, and it set a record in 2013–2014 season for freshman class applications. Funding for research grants has grown, and the university retained some of its top donors throughout the aftermath of the scandal (Orso, 2014). In 2014, President Eric J. Barron, Athletic Director Sandy Barbour, and Head Football Coach James Franklin were all hired to revitalize the institution.

(continues)

CASE STUDY (continued)

Penn State football is again recruiting the best caliber players from around the nation, a class ranked number three nationally headed into the 2017 season. Franklin won a Big 10 Championship and led Penn State to its first 10-win season (11–3) since 2009 in 2016, in addition to being named Big 10 coach of the year (Simmons, 2017). As of this writing, the 2017 football team is 6-0 and ranked number 4 nationally. Thus, the trajectory appears to be positive both from an institutional and program perspective.

How did this transformational change happen? Which factors were involved? At the institutional level, widespread changes in leadership and governance policies were instituted, as described by Terry Hartle, senior vice president of the American Council on Education:

> Penn State had to replace its leadership team, and it had a lot of people stabilize the institution and continue to move it forward. The other thing Penn State had going for it is that it took hard steps to improve governance, ethics, and compliance (Orso, 2014, para. 12)

Responding to this catalytic event and crisis, Penn State implemented institution-wide leadership and policy changes recommended in the Freeh report, and it has become a leader in studying child abuse prevention and treatment. The Center for Child Protection was launched in 2011, and it spearheaded the formation of The Network on Child Protection and Well Being. It also implemented employee training to recognize and report child abuse (Orso, 2014).

For the football program, Coach Franklin focused his efforts on changing the culture in order to improve results. His predecessor, Bill O'Brien, had more of an NFL style culture, according to players, where everything was about the business of winning. O'Brien treated the players as if they were professionals and already playing in the NFL, and they were expected to buy into this philosophy. Coach Franklin, on the other hand, came in and implemented a family-style culture much more focused on building a team, on the players and their needs, and on creating support structures and solid relationships between the players and the coaching staff (Simmons, 2017). Franklin expended great effort to build this positive, family-oriented culture and create a new vision for the program, and then enact that vision and communicate it effectively to internal and external stakeholders. Clear and consistent communication with stakeholders was and is a priority for Franklin, as is designing a change plan and being sure that there is buy-in for the plan throughout the program (Moses, 2016). All of these strategies have helped to turn around a program that many thought would never recover.

However, leading change was not a smooth process, and there were challenges to overcome. One of the biggest hurdles to change was overcoming resistance of stakeholders due to the long and storied tradition associated with Penn State football. Many did not want to lose sight of these traditions, even in the wake of the scandal. This created a challenge and tension for Franklin:

> I think that is the ultimate challenge here. How do you balance the history, the traditions, all the wonderful things that are deep rooted here and have been here forever, (while) also making moves that you need to be progressive and to be moving towards a healthy present and a healthy future (Russo, 2016, para. 4).

University and athletic department officials also have the complex task of trying to convey to some stakeholders, for whom Paterno will never be redeemed, that the values of Penn State are not tied directly to one individual (Russo, 2016). In addition, there are many notable, distinguished alumni, such as Hall of Fame running back Franco Harris, who are trying to redeem the coach (Russo, 2016). This presents many challenges for new university and athletic department leadership as they navigate through how best to honor and recognize both the past and the successes of the football program, with the changes needed to move the program forward.

Administrators and athletic officials at Penn State recognize that changing the culture and redeeming the program will take time, and that it will not be a quick fix. They realize that garnering full support and buy-in from constituents will not come quickly, for according to new Athletic Director Sandy Barbour, "I think we are still going through a healing process" (Russo, 2016, para. 20). Recent events have been a learning process for the institution, and it remains committed to being better than it was, according to Executive Vice President and Provost Nick Jones: "We learned a great deal about ourselves, and I think moving forward, we are absolutely committed to being better than we were" (Orso, 2014, para. 72). The revitalization of Penn State is an example of successful transformational change, but while positive steps have been taken, only time will tell if the university and football program truly move beyond the taint of the Sandusky events.

Questions for Discussion

1. What forms of resistance do you think Penn State leaders encountered when trying to lead transformational change? Which strategies are they using to try and mitigate resistance from stakeholder groups? Would you recommend any additional strategies? Support your answer by connecting the details from the chapter to the details in the case study.

2. Reading ahead in the chapter, the authors talk about four environmental constraints for change agents. Which constraints can be applied to the Penn State case study?

3. Which type of leader — transformational, transactional, or servant—is best suited to initiate the change discussed in the case study? Support your answer by connecting the details from the chapter to the details in the case study.

▶ Introduction

Organizations in many industry sectors, including sport, are recognizing that it is no longer feasible to conduct business as usual in the 21st century. The pace of organizational change is increasing exponentially in today's turbulent, challenging, and unpredictable economic climate. For sport organizations to survive and grow, they must adapt quickly and nimbly to changes in strategy, size, environment, and technology (Slack & Parent, 2006). The organization must be ready to change, and then develop the organizational capacity to sustain the change over time (Legg, Snelgrove, & Wood, 2016; Millar & Doherty, 2016). Large-scale organizational change initiatives, or transformational change, have become commonplace in the sport industry, with continual change models being more the rule than the exception. Sport organizations are constantly reorganizing, restructuring, and repositioning the organization's culture, revising strategy,

revamping policies and procedures, or replacing key leaders and other personnel as a result of various external and internal pressures. In the opening case study, administrators at Penn State evaluated the catalytic crisis and environment—internal and external—before implementing institution-wide leadership and policy changes, similar to many other schools.

Successful organizational change is difficult to accomplish because stakeholders typically resist change efforts (O'Toole, 1996) or are ambivalent or unsure about the changes (Legg et al., 2016; Welty Peachey & Bruening, 2012b). Research has identified three key barriers to effective change in organizations: Lack of management visibility and support, inadequate skills of management, and employee resistance (Jick & Peiperl, 2003). Lack of organizational capacity for change can also hinder change efforts (Legg et al., 2016; Millar & Doherty, 2016). Initiating change can be a competitive, hostile activity, benefiting some while injuring others. Many organizational change efforts fail and end up generating recalcitrance, building resentment, and fostering dissatisfaction. To many stakeholders, change suggests loss of control and increased uncertainty, posing a threat to traditional procedures, values, and status levels (Turnley & Feldman, 1998).

To overcome resistance, the leadership style and behavior of change agents, or those leading and guiding change, become vitally important. The leadership demonstrated by the change agent, how he or she works with different stakeholder groups inside and outside of the sport organization, and the change processes undertaken by the change agent all play an important role in gaining widespread acceptance of transformational change. In fact, certain types of leadership behavior are critical for fostering change acceptance, mitigating resistance, and securing the success of transformational change over time (Wells & Walker, 2016; Welty Peachey, Bruening, & Burton, 2011). When Peter Roby took over as athletic director at Northeastern University in Boston, he was faced with the difficult reality of needing to discontinue the football program in order to better serve student-athletes and achieve financial objectives for the athletic department. Of course, the thought of dropping football sparked widespread resistance from various stakeholders, including student-athletes, football alumni, athletic department coaches and staff, students, donors, and other community stakeholders. Three years after taking the helm, Roby decided to discontinue football. Although resistance to this transformational change was high in the beginning, over time, Roby's transformational leadership style, open and honest communication, and strategic thinking about how to best implement this change garnered more and more support, to the point where a year after the program was dropped, the voices of dissatisfaction with the decision were minimal. Roby's transformational leadership was a key factor leading to change success.

In this chapter, we begin by providing historical context for organizational change, where we define organizational change, introduce the different types and driving forces of organizational change, and give examples of transformational change in the sport industry. Next, we provide an overview of potential responses to organizational change. In this section, we examine the individual, group, organizational, and process factors that can lead to resistance or acceptance of change, and discuss the environmental constraints that can make leading change challenging. We then elaborate on ambivalence as a first response to organizational change. Following, we address leadership and organizational change, where we review various leadership styles and their association with change implementation success. The final section covers the change implementation process and examines leadership strategies that can be employed for overcoming resistance or ambivalence and marshaling support for organizational change.

▶ Nature of Organizational Change

No matter the size of the organization, change can have a ripple effect (Miles, 2001). Organizational change may be a foreseen or unforeseen response to an internal or external force and perceived as either continuous or episodic (Weick & Quinn, 1999). Continuous change emerges incrementally without end, whereas episodic change is infrequent and possibly radical (Weick & Quinn, 1999). Whether the organizational change is broad or narrow in scope, continuous or episodic, scholars agree that the rate of change is increasing (Quinn, 2004). To survive, organizations may be required to exchange tradition for uncharted territory in order to move into the future. As they progress down this unfamiliar path, sport organizations may experience three types of change: Developmental, transitional, or transformational (Appelbaum et al., 2008).

An organizational change in which natural growth occurs is referred to as **developmental change** (Appelbaum et al., 2008); this includes simple modifications to a sport organization's policy and procedures manual. As an organization slowly evolves, it moves through the most common change, **transitional change**, to improve the current state gradually (Want, 2003). An example of transitional change is when a sport organization reallocates office space among employees or allows more employees to work from home. Unfortunately, if several challenges occur simultaneously, transitional change may not suffice quickly enough for organizations. Thus, organizations are forced to make possibly unknown, radical alterations, which are defined as transformational change (Schneider, 1987). **Transformational change** efforts, the focus of this chapter, question the current assumptions and reject the current paradigm (Kuhn, 1970). Ending the football program at Northeastern was a transformational change. Although transformational change can be disruptive in nature, when executed successfully it is competitive and differentiating (Denning, 2005). When a leader-driven transformational change occurs, drastically different strategies are formulated and modifications of the organization's structure and culture may occur.

Whether broad or narrow in scope, change can be prompted by internal or external pressures, which are responded to proactively or reactively by organizations. Specifically, external environmental forces including, but not limited to, reduced revenue, enhanced competition, and unsatisfied customers have increased the pace of organizational change (Attaran, 2004). Pressure for change can also be political, functional, or social, all of which comprise deinstitutionalization, or the action of abandoning legitimate practices (Danylchuk, Snelgrove, & Wood, 2015; Oliver, 1992). Political pressure for change revolves around the legitimacy of organizational practices, such as when an

organization is not meeting objectives, and in response, its stakeholders (external and internal) push the organization to make a change (Cunningham, 2002). Functional pressure for change occurs when questions arise about the technical aspects (functions) of how a sport organization is delivering its products and services (Danylchuk et al., 2015; Oliver, 1992). Finally, social pressures for change are external to the sport organization and necessitate that the organization changes in order to survive, whether or not it desires such change (Danylchuck et al., 2015; Legg et al., 2016). Examples here include changes in cultural practices, laws and regulations, and to the industry as a whole (Danylchuck et al., 2015).

Danylchuck and colleagues (2015) found that a golf course changed the format of its women's golf leagues due to political pressure to maintain membership numbers and functional pressures to consolidate into a single league as running multiple leagues was too unwieldy. In another study with youth soccer organizations in Canada examining structural and policy-level changes, it was found that political, functional, and social pressures combined to initiate the modification of practices and policy (Legg et al., 2016). External political pressures (from the media, government, researchers, and other groups) also shaped the National Football League's (NFL) evolving policy regarding concussions, although internal stakeholders did foster inertia and resistance to these league-wide policy changes (Heinze & Lu, 2017).

When a change is employed to avoid a crisis, it is known as a **proactive change**; when the change is in response to a situation, it is referred to as a **reactive change**. Change triggered by a crisis, such as downsizing for financial reasons, may require a transformational change that could result in resistance due to the unknown future state of the organization. In sport, organizational change may be experienced in performance or management domains. A highly visible performance change can occur on a sport team when the coach's strategy shifts to gain competitive advantage. However, this chapter is concerned with change in the management domain, which Slack and Parent (2006) categorize into four functional areas for sport organizations: People, productivity, structure/system, and technology.

▶ Responses to Organizational Change

Sport organizations will have a range of responses to external and internal forces driving change. In addition, individual stakeholders will have varied responses to change due to a number of individual, group, organizational, process, and environmental factors. By far, most of the research in this area has centered on resistance and how to overcome resistance in order to enable change success. Recently, researchers have suggested that ambivalence may be the initial response to organizational change by many stakeholders. Of course, some stakeholders will accept transformational change from its inception, whereas others will grow to accept change, or parts of the change over time. In this section, we review these common responses to organizational change—**resistance**, **acceptance**, and **ambivalence**. Skilled leaders must understand the nature of these responses, when and why they come about, and employ strategic leadership strategies in order to react to these responses and enable successful change.

Organizational Responses to Pressures for Change

Sport organizations can adopt various strategies when faced with the need for change, primarily centering on dismissing, decoupling, co-opting, and acquiescence (Heinze & Lu, 2017). Dismissing is a reaction that considers the change as non-consequential and thus not important for the sport organization to enact and can often be an initial response to pressure for change (Oliver, 1991). This type of response was initially rendered by the NFL when faced with pressure to change/modify its concussion protocols (Heinze & Lu, 2017). Decoupling is a form of change avoidance where the sport organization only symbolically adopts structures and practices deemed to be necessary by the broader field, rather than fully supporting the need for change and implementing changes to a substantive degree (Heinze & Lu, 2017; Washington & Patterson, 2011). Co-opting occurs when a sport organization compromises with, or manipulates, external stakeholders by embracing the source of pressure for change to neutralize the opposition and enhance legitimacy (Heinze & Lu, 2017; Oliver, 1991). Again, the NFL is a classic example of employing a co-opting strategy, initially dismissing the need to change concussion protocols. The league later changed protocols and appeared to be an advocate for safety to make allegations disappear and gain control of the situation (Heinze & Lu, 2017). Finally, sport organizations may acquiesce to the institutional pressures for change, as the NFL finally did with regards to its concussion protocols when faced with continued pressure from external stakeholder groups (Heinze & Lu, 2017).

Resistance and Acceptance

At the individual stakeholder level, resistance is a three-dimensional negative attitude toward change that includes affective, behavioral, and cognitive components (Oreg, 2006). Some sources of resistance may have the strongest impact on stakeholders' emotions, others may more directly influence behaviors or thoughts about the change. Many organizational change efforts fail, which can foster resentment toward leaders, result in stakeholder resistance to future change, and provoke discontent toward leaders and the organization.

In fact, when confronted with organizational change, stakeholders are less concerned with what the change actually is instead of focusing on how they will personally adapt to it. They do not see this as resistance, but as survival. In essence, stakeholders resist change that exceeds their coping capabilities (Jick & Peiperl, 2003). In addition, managers often try to avoid resistance because it can have negative consequences for the organization (Oreg, 2006), such as lower levels of job satisfaction and organizational commitment among employees, as well as greater intentions to leave the organization (Rush, Schoel, & Barnard, 1995; Wanberg & Banas, 2000).

Individual Level

There are many reasons why individuals resist change, including personality dispositions. For example, individuals high in agreeableness who are trusting, forgiving, caring, altruistic, and have cooperative values (Costa & McCrae, 1992) will be more accepting of change than individuals who are manipulative, self-centered, suspicious, and ruthless (Vakola, Tsausk, & Nikolaou, 2004). Individuals high in neuroticism experience negative emotions such as anxiety, hostility, depression, self-consciousness, impulsiveness, and vulnerability. Not surprisingly, individuals lower in neuroticism have been found to be more accepting of organizational change (Oreg, 2003). Individuals open to new experiences will be creative, innovative, imaginative, reflective, and untraditional, whereas individuals low in openness will be conventional, unanalytical, and have narrow interests (Costa & McCrae, 1992). Individuals more open to new experiences also tend to be more accepting of change. Sport management students looking to succeed in the sport industry would do well to adopt this adventurous spirit of possibility because change is necessary for organizational success. Neuroticism represents individual differences in adjustment and emotional stability (Costa & McCrae, 1992).

Outside of personality dispositions, stakeholders will resist change due to the perceived impact that change may have on them, both professionally and personally. Stakeholders' views of change often depend on how they believe their own work and home situations will be impacted and to what degree the change program aligns with what they value most in their working lives. Consequently, there will be less resistance if stakeholders' interests are met and they see ways in which they will benefit from the change. For instance, in a major restructuring of the Canadian Intercollegiate Athletics Conferences, researchers found that different perceptions of the impact of this organizational change on personal goals, interests, and values led to disagreements, conflict, and resistance to the implementation of the change process (Hill & Kikulis, 1999). Within the sport industry, it has been suggested that if goals relating to power, money, prestige, convenience, job security, or professional competence are threatened as a result of a proposed organizational change, the change will be resisted, even in situations where the change is good for the organization as a whole (Slack & Parent, 2006).

In addition, if a stakeholder had prior negative experiences with organizational change, he or she may resist change more than if prior experiences were positive (Jick & Peiperl, 2003). For example, a study conducted with two organizations competing in the English Premier Football (Soccer) League revealed that there were deteriorating employee attitudes toward change and higher levels of resistance as employees went through repeated change events and had negative experiences during the change process (Wagstaff, Gilmore, & Thelwell, 2016). Finally, there are also indications that stakeholders will resist change if they believe that the values being espoused through the organizational change conflict with their personal values or beliefs. At a Division I institution going through major transformational change, some coaches did not believe that the student-centered philosophy being promoted by the new athletic director aligned with their old-school attitudes about coaching, and thus the new philosophy change was highly resisted (Welty Peachey & Bruening, 2012a).

Group Level

In a sport organization pursuing transformational change, existing subunits (e.g., departments or divisions) may gain or lose power and autonomy, be restructured, or disbanded entirely. Other subunits may have their roles in the organization reconfigured, with employees either gaining or losing responsibility. Additionally, work routines and tasks will likely be influenced either positively or negatively by change. The subsequent reallocation of resources will lead to resistance among group members of subunits, depending on how much group/team roles and functioning are negatively impacted by change. If subunits stand to gain power/prestige, increased intrinsic job satisfaction, and rewards as a result of the change, they will likely offer support more readily than if a subunit stands to lose power/ prestige and other resources that affect the job satisfaction of its members. Also, if a subunit perceives a threat to its continued existence as a result of the proposed change, resistance from members of that subunit is expected. Conversely, if a subunit does not perceive a threat to its existence, that subunit may embrace change to a greater degree (Oreg, 2006). For example, if a sport organization is considering outsourcing its marketing activities, this transformational change will be resisted by the organization's marketing department, because group members will likely lose their jobs due to the change.

Organizational Level

One organizational-level variable that can have an influence on resistance or acceptance of transformational change is the leadership displayed by the change agent. The organizational change phenomenon is complex and requires skillful leadership to mitigate resistance and showcase the organizational benefits related to the change. The importance of leadership to the change management process is underscored by the fact that change, by definition, requires creating a new system and then institutionalizing these new approaches (Kotter, 1995). Good leaders have a vision for the organization and know how to achieve that vision (Banutu-Gomez & Banutu-Gomez, 2007).

Managerial support for change and employee trust in managers' actions are essential. For example, lack of managerial support for organizational change initiatives can lead to increased levels of resistance among stakeholders. However, if stakeholders believe that managers support the change initiatives and are transparent about the change process, this will build trust and establish credibility, lessening resistance (Meyer, Srinivas, Lal, & Topolnytsky, 2007; Wells & Walker, 2016). If trust is broken during the change process, stakeholders will be more resistant to change efforts. This was found to be the case during the previously mentioned repeated organizational change that occurred in the English Premier League where trust in management deteriorated and resistance increased (Wagstaff et al., 2016). Thus, leadership displayed by change agents and other managers is critical to the success of transformational change. In fact, some leadership styles, such as transformational leadership, are better suited to guiding transformational change and mitigating resistance than other leadership styles. The relationship among leadership styles, resistance, and organizational change success is discussed in more detail in the Leadership and Organizational Change section, which follows our discussion on ambivalence.

In addition to leadership, another organizational-level variable that can influence responses to change is organizational culture. **Organizational culture**, as defined by Schein (1996) is "the set of shared, taken-for-granted implicit assumptions that a group holds and that determines how it perceives, thinks about, and reacts to its various environments" (p. 236). In layperson's terms, organizational culture is "the way we do things around here." From 2008 to 2012, Scott O'Neil, president of Madison Square Garden Sports, changed the way the popular entertainment facility did things. He instituted a more aggressive sales culture predicated on improvements in service and creativity. He instilled a greater emphasis on revenue development, raising ticket prices for the Knicks and Rangers and creating two job positions/titles directly concerned with revenue development—executive vice president of revenue performance and executive vice president of business development and operations (Lombardo, 2012).

Scholars have noted the connection between leadership and organizational culture, and whether organizational culture is a source of resistance to or acceptance of change (Rashid, Sambasivan, & Rahman, 2004). It is suggested that organizational culture is created by leaders, and that "the only thing of real importance that leaders do is to create and manage culture" (Schein, 1988, p. 2). To this end, scholars have examined types of organizational cultures that best support organizational change and mitigate resistance. Generally, organizational cultures with flexible structures and supportive climates are more conducive to change acceptance than mechanistic structures characterized by many hierarchal levels, inflexibility, and high formality and rules (Harper & Utley, 2001; Welty Peachey et al., 2011).

Change Process

Leaders must also pay attention to the change process factors of active participation, communication, and pace of change in order to mitigate resistance and facilitate acceptance of transformational change. With regard to participation, even in the midst of a crisis, employee involvement in decision making and problem solving will generate support for change (Carroll & Hatakenaka, 2001).

Participation by stakeholders from all levels of the organization in the change process is critical to implementation success and mitigating resistance. Employees who are active participants in the change process will resist change less than employees who do not actively engage and participate in the process (Lines, 2004; Wells & Walker, 2016; Welty Peachey et al., 2011). In a study with youth soccer associations in Canada, board members, coaches, and parents were all involved in the change process of league reformatting, thus heightening their acceptance of, and commitment to, the change (Legg et al., 2016). This is instructive for leaders in that they should encourage active participation from followers.

In addition to participation, effective communication strategies will lessen stakeholder resistance to change (Danylchuk et al., 2016; Elving, 2005; Legg et al., 2016; Wells & Walker, 2016; Welty Peachey et al., 2011); stakeholders who are informed about the reasons for change and provided with consistent communication on change efforts will resist change less than stakeholders who have change thrust upon them in a top-down manner with little communication. The stakeholders mentioned above in the youth soccer associations were provided with accurate, consistent, and timely communication from leaders, which again fostered greater change acceptance (Legg et al., 2016). Furthermore, if employees do not receive adequate and timely information about changes taking place in the organization, they will engage in sensemaking on their own, which will lead to cynicism and, ultimately, to resistance (Reichers, Wanous, & Austin, 1997).

Finally, change agents must pay attention to the pace at which change is introduced into the organization. Some research has shown that the most effective transformational changes are initiated rapidly throughout the organization (Nadler & Tushman, 1988). If transformational change is implemented more gradually, it runs the risk of being sabotaged by internal politics, structures, culture, organizational history, and status quo. However, others have argued that rapidly implementing widespread, revolutionary change across an organization is not the most effective method for engaging in transformational change, nor an accurate depiction of how it occurs (Child & Smith, 1987). Additionally, there is ambiguity in terms of the order in which different parts of an organization should be transformed. Some scholars suggest that change should be initiated rapidly throughout the entire organization to overcome initial inertia and prevent resistance from building up among organizational members (Romanelli & Tushman, 1994). Others have argued that change should take place first in an organization's most central, functional elements (Hinings & Greenwood, 1988), whereas alternate views suggest that transformational change is more successful when peripheral elements of an organization are changed first (Beer, Eisenstat, & Spector, 1990).

Environmental Constraints

Leaders who are change agents may face a number of environmental constraints when attempting to lead transformational change, which may hinder the change process and spark resistance on the part of stakeholders. First, change agents must pay attention to the resources and facilities that are available to support the transformational change. Physical, financial, and human resources must be sufficient enough to support the change initiatives, or the change program runs the risk of failing and generating stakeholder resistance. In essence, the sport organization must have the capacity for change and the ability to sustain the change over time (Legg et al., 2016; Millar & Doherty, 2016). For example, in the Division I intercollegiate athletic program going through transformational change to a more student-athlete–centered philosophy, stakeholders resisted change if they did not perceive the resources of the department or university to be sufficient to support the change initiative (Welty Peachey & Bruening, 2011).

Second, the internal politics of the organization can undermine change initiatives

and foster resistance. Sport organizations have many different stakeholders, from players to employees to coaches to management to fans to boosters, donors, and community leaders. Different stakeholders will have different agendas and interests and may not support changes that are deemed to go against their own agendas. For instance, at the Division I athletic department mentioned previously, the success of athletics brought about by the organizational changes sparked jealousy on the part of other institutional stakeholders who were not happy that athletics was receiving more attention and university support. These were political constraints that the athletic director had to navigate daily as he charted a new course for the department (Welty Peachey & Bruening, 2011).

A third constraint faced by change agents in sport organizations is organizational history and tradition. Sport organizations will have traditions, histories, policies, and procedures in place that create expected ways to operate on the part of various stakeholders. When changes go against these rich traditions and histories, they can be resisted by stakeholders who do not wish to deviate from how things have always been done. For instance, at the intercollegiate athletic department described previously, some of the longer tenured staff resisted because the changes were forcing these individuals to do things differently, moving them out of their comfortable routines (Welty Peachey & Bruening, 2011). Finally, stakeholder concerns for legitimacy of the sport organization are another constraint that change agents face as they lead transformational change. Recently, there have been instances of Division I intercollegiate athletic programs discontinuing football (e.g., Hofstra, Northeastern University, University of the Pacific), and this transformational change was resisted vehemently by many stakeholder groups who believed dropping the football program would undermine the foundation of what they likely believe makes a Division I athletic department legitimate—having a competitive and visible football program (Welty Peachey & Bruening, 2011).

Ambivalence

Although most of the focus on responses to transformational change has centered on resistance and acceptance, recent research has suggested that ambivalence may actually be the most prevalent initial type of response among stakeholders (Piderit, 2000; Welty Peachey & Bruening, 2012b). Ambivalence connotes the mixed evaluations or motives that individuals experience with respect to attitude objects (i.e., the idea, issue, or object about which an employee has a feeling or belief) in their social environments (Sparks, Harris, & Lockwood, 2004). In this vein, it might be difficult for an individual to form an immediate opinion about transformational change. Instead, he or she may take some time to decide whether to welcome or reject change. For instance, a sport organization employee might not know immediately how he or she feels, or what he or she believes about new changes being implemented in the organization. Full judgment might be reserved until the employee can ascertain how the changes will impact him or her personally, his or her subunit, work routines and roles, and the organization as a whole. In fact, in one Division I intercollegiate athletic department going through transformational change, ambivalence was the typical response among many stakeholders (Welty Peachey & Bruening, 2012b). The new athletic director enacted major changes to the department's philosophy, strategy, resource allocations, and coaches' treatment of student-athletes, but many stakeholders, particularly longer-tenured individuals who had seen changes come and go before, adopted a wait-and-see attitude. They wanted to observe how they would be personally affected and how the changes would impact organizational performance before giving full support. Ambivalence was also found to be an initial

Major League Baseball and its owners' refusal to banish the color line until 1947 deeply illustrates the reluctance of a sport organization to go against tradition.

© Everett Collection Inc./Alamy Stock Photo.

response to organizational structural change among some stakeholders in the example of youth soccer leagues in Canada (Legg et al., 2016).

▶ Leadership and Organizational Change

Leaders are critical to the success of transformational change and to overcoming stakeholder resistance and ambivalence. Next, we review different types of leadership styles and their relationship with transformational change.

Transformational and Transactional Leadership

By now, transformational and transactional leadership styles should be well known to you. Organizational change and leadership research has shown that certain leadership qualities are more appropriate for specific types of change. For instance, transformational leaders are better suited for non-routine situations where adaptation is the goal (Pawar & Eastman, 1997). Conversely, when an organization is centered on maintaining progress, transactional leaders who emphasize a reward-based system for task completion may be a better fit (Bass, 1995). As such, in relatively stable work environments, transactional leadership is used when both the leader and group members are satisfied with their purpose and process (Chelladurai, 1999). Group members have a set of needs and desires, and the leader distributes rewards or punishments in exchange for followers' compliance or resistance.

A transactional ticket office manager initiating new ticket sales procedures may reward employees in the form of bonuses for the amount of sales each employee brings to the organization. The ticket manager may exercise his or her influence by setting challenging goals, assisting goal achievement by enhancing group members' abilities, and supporting the group members' efforts (House, 1971). Specifically, the ticket manager may guide employees on how to obtain new business, set challenging goals, and provide support. In contrast, a transformational ticket office manager faced with a financial hardship and reduced employee benefits, such as the loss of complimentary athletic tickets, may need to influence major change in organization members' attitudes and assumptions while building commitment to the organization's new mission and strategies (Yukl & Van Fleet, 1992).

Transformational leadership (Bass, 1985) has been portrayed as one of the most effective leadership styles when change is prominent (Burke et al., 2006; Mumford, Scott, Gaddis, & Strange, 2002). According to Tichy and Devanna (1990), transformational leaders follow a process whereby they recognize the need for change, create a new vision, and then institutionalize the change. During the initial phase of organizational change under transformational leadership, developing a vision and inspiring employees toward the vision are major facets used to set the direction and assemble resources for the change (Kotter, 1995).

Transformational leaders explicitly engage employees' attention to the vision and instill confidence to achieve expectations (Bass, 1985; Bono & Judge, 2003). By articulating a clear vision and demonstrating enthusiasm, transformational leaders inspire and motivate their employees to work hard (Bass, 1985). Also, when the leader models the expected behavior required to institutionalize the change, he or she emulates what Kotter (1996) argues is "the way things are done around here." In addition, through the use of charisma, transformational leaders are able to generate employee buy-in for their vision (Bass, 1998; Podsakoff, MacKenzie, Moorman, & Fetter, 1990). Specifically, research on transformational leaders has revealed how influential they are on followers' affective experiences (e.g., Bono & Ilies, 2006). First, by being enthusiastic and optimistic about change and confident in themselves and their employees, transformational leaders affect the feelings of their employees. Second, the individualized consideration provided by transformational leaders (Bass, 1990; Bono & Judge, 2003) has helped alleviate their employees' fear or resentment of organizational change (Kiefer, 2005).

Leadership begins with an executive officer of an organization and filters to lower levels through empowerment. In the context of sport, the status, image, and profitability of the National Basketball Association (NBA) has been largely attributed to a transformational leader, Former Commissioner David Stern. Owners bought into his vision, and the image of the NBA was transformed. Similarly,

Billie Jean King, the founder of the Women's Sports Foundation in 1974, transformed the perception of women in sport. However, transformational leaders may not be confined to large organizations with hierarchical organizational structures. An example is the hiring of a new coach for an athletic team. This new hire may transform the values, aspirations, and beliefs of the team.

Not only are transactional and transformational leadership important for managing change, depending on the timeframe of change, so are servant, participative, and authoritative leaders. Thus, it is important to understand that different leadership styles need to be used in different situations.

Servant Leadership

Due to the ethical component and people-centered focus of servant leadership, it may contribute to the success of transformational change. Introduced by Greenleaf (1977), servant leadership is as an "altruistic-based form of leadership in which leaders emphasize the needs and development of others, primarily their followers" (Barbuto, Gottfredson, & Searle, 2014, p. 2). Emphasizing integrity, authenticity, and trustworthiness (van Dierendonck, 2011), servant leaders foster trust in the leader and the organization by doing what is promised, being visible within the organization, and leading with vulnerability and honesty. Although Wells and Walker (2016) did not specifically measure servant leadership, they did reveal ethics, which is at the core of being of a servant leader, garnered employee buy in, and acceptance of organizational change during a merger of an intercollegiate athletic department. While servant leadership research in sport has grown over the past decade (Welty Peachey, Damon, Zhou, & Burton, 2015), only limited components of servant leadership have been studied during an organizational change, thus further research is warranted.

Participative Leadership

Similar to transformational and servant leadership, participative leadership is referred to as a change-oriented style and is linked to stimulating positive outcomes in employees (de Poel, Stoker, & van der Zee, 2012; Kahai, Sosik, & Avolio, 2004; Spreitzer, 2007). If time and resources are allotted, participative leaders are able to actively engage their workgroup followers to share in the decision-making process (Somech, 2003). Numerous studies have revealed positive associations between participative leadership and employee outcomes, such as increased effectiveness, increased job satisfaction, and lower conflict (Burke et al., 2006; Kotlyar & Karakowsky, 2006; Lovelace, Shapiro, & Weingart, 2001; Williams, 1998), which may contribute to the success of participative leadership during transformational change.

Autocratic Leadership

Finally, when time is limited, the use of an autocratic leadership style is appropriate during change. Dictated by the leader's information, an autocratic leader personally makes a decision with little input from followers (Chelladurai, 1999). Because the leader and the group are unable to take the time to engage in participative decision making, the leader must make the decision. In order for the decision to be effectively executed by the group, the members must understand and accept the leader's autocratic decision (Chelladurai, 1999). For example, if a sport leader is facing a crisis-ridden predicament, such as immediate dissolution of the organization due to financial loss, a directive stance may be necessary to implement a transformational change. This way, the leader communicates the urgency of the situation, as well as engages and motivates stakeholders accordingly (Pascale, Millemann, & Gioja, 2000).

▶ Change Implementation

Regardless of the leadership style of the change agent, many sport organizations are insufficiently prepared for implementing change and mistakenly view implementation as a step-by-step, linear process. In reality, implementing change is a messy proposition. Before beginning a change implementation process, it is important for change agents to consider the nature of resistance and ambivalence, and how these responses can be used to gain widespread stakeholder support over time. The sport organization must also be ready for change and have the organizational capacity to implement and carry it forward. If not, the change program runs the risk of failure or not being sustainable over the long term (Millar & Doherty, 2016).

Encouraging Resistance and Ambivalence

Resistance is often viewed by management as dysfunctional to the organization. This one-sided story neglects the fact that resistance can be a resource during change, and leaders acting as change agents often contribute to resistance through their own actions and inactions, most notably through breach of agreements and failure to restore trust. Breaches in trust can occur when there are changes to the allocation and distribution of resources, the processes and procedures through which these reallocations are made, or the ways in which individuals in power relate to those with less power or authority. This often takes place in transformational change, and change agents will ultimately be more successful in leading change if they repair damaged relationships first (Reichers et al., 1997). It is crucial for change agents to realize that stakeholder resistance is often based on valid concerns and should be used by the organization to improve itself.

Contrary to popular belief, resistance can actually be an asset to the organization during change rather than an indicator of dysfunction. A continued challenge for change agents is to ensure that new conversations are heard and spoken about often enough that they take root and grow. This is where resistance can be of value, because it keeps the topic in play and at the forefront of conversations, giving stakeholders from all levels in the organization an opportunity to participate in the conversation and offer feedback (Caruth, Middlebrook, & Rachel, 1985). This feedback gives change agents data to improve the change process and adjust the pace, scope, and sequencing of the change (Ford, Ford, & D'Amelio, 2008). Thus, paradoxically, resistance could be a factor in the ultimate success of change. Furthermore, change agents may wish to acknowledge and even encourage ambivalent attitudes toward change rather than discourage them. Ambivalence may provide a basis for motivating new action, rather than the continuation of old, stale routines (Piderit, 2000).

Change Implementation Steps

After change agents acknowledge that resistance and ambivalence can be assets to guiding successful transformational change, careful thought must be given to the change implementation process in order to gain widespread support from stakeholders throughout the sport organization. One helpful guide for change implementation has been developed by Jick and Pieperl (2003). These steps for implementing transformational change and gaining widespread stakeholder support are outlined in **TABLE 8.1**.

First, change agents in sport organizations must analyze the organization and determine the forces driving the change and the organization's need for change. A study of the organization's history of change should take place, and traditional barriers to change

TABLE 8.1 Change Implementation Steps
Analyze the organization and determine the need for change.
Create a shared vision.
Examine organizational history and tradition, and separate from the past, if needed.
Create a sense of urgency for change.
Exhibit strong leadership.
Line up informal leaders in the organization who can work as advocates for change.
Design an implementation plan.
Develop enabling structures.
Pay attention to communication and participation.
Reinforce and institutionalize change.

Data from Jick, T., & Peiperl, M. (2003). *Managing change: Cases and concepts* (2nd ed.). New York: McGraw-Hill.

must be identified. If these barriers are not addressed, patterns of resistance are likely to reoccur. The organization should also determine that it has the organizational capacity to implement and sustain the changes (Millar & Doherty, 2016).

Second, a shared vision among all stakeholders in the sport organization should be created so that stakeholders understand the need for change and the implications that this will have on their roles. The formulation of vision needs to begin at the top of the organization and then be translated and disseminated effectively throughout the organization through good communication and information-sharing strategies. As mentioned previously, a transformational leader is well-suited to create this shared vision for change and gain acceptance for the vision throughout the sport organization.

Third, change agents must address past organizational history and traditions, and make a concerted effort to separate from them if warranted. However, traditions in sport organizations do provide stability and a frame of reference amidst the chaos of change, so change agents must recognize the value of heritage as an anchor in change, reinforcing the positive aspects of this heritage while disengaging from elements of the organizational history that will impede effective change.

Fourth, change agents should create a sense of urgency and need for action, without appearing to fabricate a crisis. This sense of urgency is essential for aligning stakeholders at all levels of the organization. Also, it is critical that middle managers understand the need for change, because they will likely be the ones communicating and reinforcing changes to front-line staff. Thus, frequent and consistent communication is needed between change agents and implementers of change.

Fifth, a strong leader is needed to envision and guide change. Leadership plays a critical role in creating an organization's vision, motivating employees to embrace the vision for change, and designing organizational structure, policies, and procedures that reinforce the desired change and discourage old, stale practices. It must also be noted that the leadership of change can be distributed to teams of leaders initiating change (change leader teams), which offers the advantage of combining the multiple skill sets of various leaders.

Sixth, change agents should obtain broad-based support for transformational change throughout the sport organization. This support must come not only from managers and change agents but also from recipients of change who will carry out the vision. Change agents should first focus on lining up support from informal leaders in an organization who will be receptive to change and can then work as advocates for change in their respective areas.

Seventh, an actual implementation plan needs to be created to map out the change effort, listing timelines and dates by which the organization hopes to achieve its goals. The change process is not something that is done without careful thought and must be guided by a detailed and thorough map of how to get to the end result. It is also important that the plan maintains a level of flexibility to environmental contingencies that may develop and be broken into steps so as not to overburden stakeholders with multiple demands, which could lead to overload and burnout.

This leads to the eighth recommendation, which is that enabling structures must be developed to facilitate and support the changes. These structures can encompass workshops for stakeholders and training as to how to function within a new environment, and also include creative reward systems for stakeholders who embrace the changes. Also, small accomplishments along the way should be celebrated when working toward achievement of hard and specific goals to foster motivation and adherence to the implementation plan.

Ninth, as mentioned previously, change agents must pay attention to communication and participation processes when guiding change. They should communicate early and often about the change process, and be as transparent and honest as possible about the ramifications and benefits for the organization as a whole, and for stakeholders individually. It is recommended that stakeholders at all levels of an organization being affected by change

have involvement in the planning and implementation process.

Finally, it is important to reinforce and evaluate the change program continually throughout the process.

▶ Summary

In this chapter, we have focused on forging transformational change in sport organizations. We began by providing an overview of the nature of change and forces driving change in the sport industry, which was followed by a discussion of factors influencing and constraining the three most common responses to transformational change: resistance, acceptance, and ambivalence. We then reviewed various leadership styles and their association with change outcomes, primarily looking at transactional, transformational, servant, participative, and autocratic leadership. Because transformational change is dynamic and situational, the most appropriate leadership style must match the type of change and its context. We concluded by presenting a specific 10-point plan for change implementation to guide change agents who are leading transformational change.

Transformational change is a continual process in the 21st-century sport industry. Sport leaders will need to recognize how their leadership contributes to or hinders the success of transformational change, develop implementation strategies that take into account the varied interests of stakeholders, and garner support from these stakeholders in order for change to be successful. We hope that this chapter was illustrative and informative as to the importance of leadership in forging significant change.

LEADERSHIP PERSPECTIVE

Andy Hawk
Andy Hawk is the Managing Director of Active Interest Media's Mountain Group. In this role, Hawk is responsible for SKI Magazine, Warren Miller Entertainment, and the SIA Snow Show Daily, among other properties. Under Hawk's leadership and vision, Warren Miller Entertainment has grown to be a prominent brand due to innovative ideas and strategic partnerships.

Q: Describe some of the biggest organizational changes you have encountered with your organization over the past 5 years?
The nature of work, or rather the time for work, has shifted dramatically in the last five years. In the ever-connected world, there is increased pressure from clients and from the organization to always be available. The instant delivery of information, goods, or services outside of work has translated to a perception that this velocity of workflow can and should be available at any organization. What has not yet translated is the cultural acceptance to dismiss the rigid structure of the 9 to 5 attendance requirement. This creates challenge for employees and management, as the demand for real-time response seems to be here to stay, but the relief to a more flexible work schedule has not followed as quickly.

From an engagement perspective, the notion that the millennial workforce requires significant meaning or purpose in their work certainly holds true. For this cohort, job satisfaction is linked to their ability to feel like they are contributing to something great, which is rarely evaluated on the basis of profitability. We see employees who are more interested in moving from project to project than committing to what would traditionally be accepted as a defined path for career growth.

Q: Of those changes that you just mentioned, let's focus on one to analyze. Were there any major obstacles or challenges that the organization had to overcome to implement the change?
The shift of the nature of work and the cohort of employees that is positioned to propel that work forward are certainly linked. For better or worse, our organization is right in the middle of this shift. While sports and active lifestyle media likely draw a bit of a younger workforce overall, there is nothing that we are seeing that varies significantly from what seems to be the evolution of work at many companies in a variety of industries.

The critical obstacle that exists today is that we have a broad cross section of age and experience across the workforce, including on the senior management team. What would have traditionally been dismissed as an expected divide between the way management expects employees to engage in their work and the shifting nature with which the employees desire to complete that work is becoming

(continues)

LEADERSHIP PERSPECTIVE (*continued*)

increasingly more challenging to navigate as millennial workers move into senior management roles. Those (younger) senior managers are now in the difficult position of joining the leadership structure that operates with a more traditional expectation of employees, while having been members of the cohort that has come into the corporate world with a different view on the nature of work.

Q: How did employees respond to the organizational change? Why do you think they responded this way?

A divide certainly exists between the two styles of work at all levels of the organizational chart, which is a source of tension that, at times, leads to more significant conflict. When employees exit the company, it seems less frequently about money than one would assume these days. Moving to a more flexible culture or just a simple change in opportunity appears to be as much of a motivation as anything else. We've seen a surprising number of employees exit their roles with the organization to move to self-employment or contract work situations, which they feel offer the flexibility that they are seeking.

Q: What strategies were employed by leadership to guide the organization through the change?

At the heart of the matter, the leadership team is consistently working hard to cultivate the engagement of the best employees. "Best employees" does not necessarily mean the ones who are putting in the most hours at their desk, but rather, those who are consistently pushing to bring new ideas to the forefront, evolve the work and the image of the company, and engage with their peers and with the leadership team to explore new possibilities. As these rising stars aren't necessarily motivated by the 9 to -5 engagement, "put in the time, get a promotion" mentality, it requires more trust from the leadership team that the cultivation of talented employees will lead to positive results.

Q: Do you have any advice for the next generation of sport management leaders?

Good ideas and a commitment to business evolution are just as important, if not more important, than the willingness to work hard. This requires asking tough questions about why the organization does what it does, and the ability to recognize that doing things the same way they were done in the past is sometimes very important, yet sometimes very detrimental. There is this saying that goes something like, "50% of what we are doing is working great, the problem is I don't know which 50%." In my experience, that is the crux of organizational leadership. It always seems a bit out of control, even during periods of tremendous achievement.

▶ Key Terms

Acceptance	Organizational culture	Resistance
Ambivalence	Proactive change	Transformational change
Developmental change	Reactive change	Transitional change

▶ Discussion Questions

1. Some of the chapter examples focused on the elimination of a college football program. List stakeholders who might resist this change. What potential reasons would they have for resisting such a move?

2. Referring to Question 1, put yourself in the position of an athletic director. What arguments can you make that will counter some of the resistance you expect to receive?

3. Under the leadership of Roger Goodell, the National Football League (NFL) has undergone much change with regard to rules and safety. What changes have you seen, and has there been any resistance to these changes? Finally, why has the NFL undergone such extensive organizational change?

4. Suppose a Triple A minor league baseball team is moving from one city to another and has only 6 months to complete the move. Which leadership style or styles should the team's president employ to hasten acceptance of this change and get employees moving in the same direction? Is quelling all resistance a good idea? Why or why not?

5. Using the change implementation process, which steps seem most important for the commissioner of the American Hockey League if he wanted to outlaw fighting in league games?

▶ References

Appelbaum, S. H., Mitraud, A., Gailleur, J., Iacovella, M., Gerbasi, R., & Ivanova, V. (2011). The impact of organizational change, structure and leadership on employee turnover: A case study. *Journal of Business Case Studies, 4*(1), 21–38.

Attaran, M. (2004). Exploring the relationship between informational technology and business process reengineering. *Information and Management, 41*(5), 585–596.

Banutu-Gomez, M. B., & Banutu-Gomez, S. M. T. (2007). Leadership and organizational change in a competitive environment. *Business Renaissance Quarterly, 2*(2), 69–91.

Barbuto, J. E., Gottfredson, R. K., & Searle, T. P. (2014). An examination of emotional intelligence as an antecedent of servant leadership. *Journal of Leadership & Organizational Studies, 21*(3), 315–323.

Bass, B. M. (1985). *Leadership and performance beyond expectations.* New York: Free Press.

Bass, B. M. (1990). *Bass and Stogdill's handbook of leadership* (3rd ed.). New York: Free Press.

Bass, B. M. (1995). Transformational leadership redux. *Leadership Quarterly, 6*, 463–478.

Bass, B. M. (1998). *Transformational leadership: Industry, military, and educational impact.* Mahwah, NJ: Erlbaum.

Beer, M., Eisenstat, R. A., & Spector, B. (1990). *The critical path to corporate renewal.* Boston, Massachusetts: Harvard Business School Press.

Bono, J. E., & Ilies, R. (2006). Charisma, positive emotions and mood contagion. *The Leadership Quarterly, 17*(4), 317–334.

Bono, J. E., & Judge, T. A. (2003). Self-concordance at work: Toward understanding the motivational effects of transformational leaders. *Academy of Management Journal, 46*(5), 554–571.

Burke, C. S., Stagl, K. C., Klein, C., Goodwin, G. F., Salas, E., & Halpin, S. M. (2006). What type of leadership behaviors are functional in teams? A meta-analysis. *The Leadership Quarterly, 17*, 288–307.

Carroll, J. S., & Hatakenaka, S. (2001). Driving organizational change in the midst of crisis. *MIT Sloan Management Review, 42*(3), 70–79.

Caruth, D., Middlebrook, B., & Rachel, F. (1985). Overcoming resistance to change. *S.A.M. Advanced Management Journal, 50*(3), 23–27.

Chelladurai, P. (1999). *Human resource management in sport and recreation.* Champaign, IL: Human Kinetics.

Child, J., & Smith, C. (1987). The context and process of organizational transformation: Cadbury Ltd. in its sector. *Journal of Management Studies, 24*(6), 565–593.

Costa, P. T., Jr., & McCrae, R. R. (1992). *Revised NEO personality inventory (NEO-PI-R) and NEO five factor inventory (NEO-FFI) professional manual.* Odessa, FL: PAR.

Cunningham, G. B. (2002). Removing the blinders: Toward an integrative model of organizational change in sport and physical activity. *Quest, 54*(4), 276–291.

Danylchuck, K., Snelgrove, R., & Wood, L. (2015). Managing women's participation in golf: A case study of organizational change. *Leisure/Loisir, 39*(1), 61–80.

Denning, S. (2005). Transformational innovation: A journey by narrative. *Strategy and Leadership, 33*(3), 11–16.

de Poel, F. M., Stoker, J. I., & van der Zee, K. I. (2012). Climate control? The relationship between leadership, climate for change, and work outcomes. *International Journal of Human Resource Management, 23*(4), 694–713.

Elving, J. L. W. (2005). The role of communication in organisational change. *Corporate Communications, 10*(2), 129–139.

Ford, J. D., Ford, L. W., & D'Amelio, A. (2008). Resistance to change: The rest of the story. *Academy of Management Review, 33*(2), 363–377.

Greenleaf, R. K. (1977). *Servant leadership: A journey into the nature of legitimate power and greatness*. New York: Paulist Press.

Harper, G., & Utley, D. (2001). Organizational culture and successful information technology implementation. *Engineering Management Journal, 13*(2), 11–15.

Heinze, K., & Lu, D. (2017). Shifting responses to institutional change: The National Football League and player concussions. *Journal of Sport Management, 31*(5), 497–513.

Hill, L., & Kikulis, L. M. (1999). Contemplating restructuring: A case study of strategic decision-making in interuniversity athletic conferences. *Journal of Sport Management, 13*(1), 18–44.

Hinings, C. R., & Greenwood, R. (1988). *The dynamics of strategic change*. Oxford, England: Basil Blackwood.

House, R. J. (1971). A path goal theory of leader effectiveness. *Administrative Science Quarterly, 16*(3), 321–339.

Jick, T., & Peiperl, M. (2003). *Managing change: Cases and concepts* (2nd ed.). New York: McGraw-Hill.

Kahai, S. S., Sosik, J. J., & Avolio, B. J. (2004). Effects of participative and directive leadership in electronic groups. *Group and Organization Management, 29,* 67–105.

Kiefer, T. (2005). Feeling bad: Antecedents and consequences of negative emotions in ongoing change. *Journal of Organizational Behavior, 26*(8), 875–897.

Kotlyar, I., & Karakowsky, L. (2006). Leading conflict? Linkages between leader behaviors and group conflict. *Small Group Research, 37*(4), 377–403.

Kotter, J. P. (1995). Leading change: Why transformational efforts fail. *Harvard Business Review, 73*(2), 59–67.

Kotter, J. P. (1996). *Leading change*. Boston, MA: Harvard Business School Press.

Kuhn, T. S. (1970). *The structure of scientific revolutions* (2nd ed.). Chicago, IL: University of Chicago Press.

Legg, J., Snelgrove, R., & Wood, L. (2016). Modifying tradition: Examining organizational change in youth sport. *Journal of Sport Management, 30*(4), 369–381.

Lines, R. (2004). Influence of participation in strategic change: Resistance, organizational commitment and change goal achievement. *Journal of Organizational Change Management, 4*(3), 193–215.

Lombardo, J. (2012, September 10). Unexpected exit for MSG's change agent. *Street and Smith's SportsBusiness Journal*. Retrieved from http://www.sportsbusinessdaily.com/Journal/Issues/2012/09/10/Franchises/ONeil.aspx?hl=Organizational%20change&sc=0

Lovelace, K., Shapiro, D. L., & Weingart, L. R. (2001). Maximizing cross-functional new product teams' innovativeness and constraint adherence: A conflict communications perspective. *Academy of Management Journal, 44*(4), 779–793.

Meyer, J. P., Srinivas, E. S., Lal, J. B., & Topolnytsky, L. (2007). Employee commitment and support for organizational change: Test of the three-component model in two cultures. *Journal of Occupational and Organizational Psychology, 80*(2), 185–211.

Millar, P., & Doherty, A. (2016). Capacity building in nonprofit sport organizations: Development of a process model. *Sport Management Review, 19*(4), 365–377.

Miles, R. M. (2001). Accelerating corporate transformations by rapidly engaging all employees. *Organizational Dynamics, 29,* 313–321.

Moses, A. (2016, December 1). How James Franklin and Bill O'Brien revived Penn State football. *Huffpost*. Retrieved from: https://www.huffingtonpost.com/andrew-moses/how-james-franklin-and-bi_b_13352732.html

Mumford, M. D., Scott, G. M., Gaddis, B., & Strange, J. M. (2002). Leading creative people: Orchestrating expertise and relationships. *Leadership Quarterly, 13*(6), 705–750.

Nadler, D. A., & Tushman, M. L. (1988). *Competing by design*. New York: Oxford University Press.

Oliver, C. (1991). Strategic responses to institutional processes. *Academy of Management Review, 16*(1), 145–179.

Oliver, C. (1992). The antecedents of deinstitutionalization. *Organization Studies, 13*(4), 563–588.

Oreg, S. (2003). Resistance to change: Developing an individual difference measure. *Journal of Applied Psychology, 88*(4), 587–604.

Oreg, S. (2006). Personality, context and resistance to organizational change. *European Journal of Work and Organizational Psychology, 15*(1), 73–101.

Orso, A. (2014, July 3). Has Penn State shed the Sandusky slump? Academic, financial indicators point to 'yes.' *Penn Live*. Retrieved from http://www.pennlive.com/midstate/index.ssf/2014/07/too_big_to_fail_penn_states_im.html

O'Toole, J. (1996). *Leading change: The argument for values-based leadership*. New York: Ballantine.

Pascale, R., Millemann, M., & Gioja, L. (2000). *Surfing the edge of chaos*. New York: Crown Business.

Pawar, B. S., & Eastman, K. K. (1997). The nature and implications of contextual influences on transformational leadership: A conceptual examination. *Academy of Management Review, 22,* 80–109.

Piderit, S. K. (2000). Rethinking resistance and recognizing ambivalence: A multidimensional view of attitudes toward organizational change. *Academy of Management Review, 25*(4), 783–794.

Podsakoff, P. M., MacKenzie, S. B., Moorman, R. H., & Fetter, R. (1990). Transformational leader behaviors, and their effects on followers' trust in leader, satisfaction, and organizational citizenship behaviors. *Leadership Quarterly, 1,* 107–142.

Quinn, R. E. (2004). *Building the bridge as you walk on it*. San Francisco, CA: Jossey-Bass.

Rashid, Z., Sambasivan, M., & Rahman, A. (2004). The influence of organizational culture on attitudes towards organizational change. *Leadership and Organization Development Journal, 25*, 161–179.

Reichers, A. E., Wanous, J. P., & Austin, J. T. (1997). Understanding and managing cynicism about organizational change. *Academy of Management Executive, 11*(1), 48–59.

Romanelli, E., & Tushman, M. (1994). Organizational transformation as punctuated equilibrium: An empirical test. *Academy of Management Journal, 37*, 1141–1166.

Rush, M. C., Schoel, W. A., & Barnard, S. M. (1995). Psychological resiliency in the public sector: "Hardiness" and pressure for change. *Journal of Vocational Behavior, 46*, 17–39.

Russo, R. (2016, August 30). College football: Penn State tries to move forward without abandoning Paterno. *Daily Times Sports*. Retrieved from: http://www.delcotimes.com/article/DC/20160830/NEWS/160839992

Schein, E. H. (1988). *Organizational culture and leadership.* San Francisco, CA: Jossey-Bass.

Schein, E. H. (1996). Culture: The missing concept in organization studies. *Administrative Science Quarterly, 41*, 229–240.

Schneider, B. (1987). The people make the place. *Personal Psychology, 40*, 437–453.

Simmons, B. (2017, May 25). James Franklin proving change is possible at Penn State. *Lions 247*. Retrieved from: https://pennstate.247sports.com/Article/James-Franklin-proving-change-is-possible-at-Penn-State-52899485

Slack, T., & Parent, M. (2006). *Understanding sport organizations: The application of organization theory* (2nd ed.). Champaign, IL: Human Kinetics.

Somech, A. (2003). Relationships of participative leadership with relational demography variables: A multi-level perspective. *Journal of Organizational Behavior, 24*, 1003–1018.

Sparks, P., Harris, P. R., & Lockwood, N. (2004). Predictors and predictive effects of ambivalence. *British Journal of Social Psychology, 43*, 371–383.

Spreitzer, G. M. (2007). Giving peace a chance: Organizational leadership, empowerment, and peace. *Journal of Organizational Behavior, 28*, 1077–1095.

Tichy, N. M., & Devanna, M. A. (1990). *The transformational leader.* New York: John Wiley.

Tolley, T. (2014, January 21). Penn State football: Replacing leaders won't be a problem for Nittany Lions. *Bleacher Report*. Retrieved from: http://bleacherreport.com/articles/1930271-penn-state-football-replacing-leaders-wont-be-a-problem-for-nittany-lions

Turnley, W. H., & Feldman, D. C. (1998). Psychological contract violations during corporate restructuring. *Human Resource Management, 37*(1), 71–83.

van Dierendonck, D. (2011). Servant leadership: A review and syntheses. *Journal of Management, 27*, 1228–1261.

Vakola, M., Tsausk, I., & Nikolaou, I. (2004). The role of emotional intelligence and personality variance on attitudes toward organizational change. *Journal of Managerial Psychology, 19*, 88–111.

Wagstaff, C., Gilmore, S., & Thelwell, R. (2016). When the show must go on: Investigating repeated organizational change in elite sport. *Journal of Change Management, 16*(1), 38–54.

Wanberg, C. R., & Banas, J. T. (2000). Predictors and outcomes of openness to changes in a reorganizing workplace. *Journal of Applied Psychology, 85*(1), 132–142.

Want, J. (2003). When worlds collide: Corporate culture—Illuminating the black hole. *Journal of Business Strategy, 24*, 14–22.

Washington, M., & Patterson, K. D. (2011). Hostile takeover or joint venture: Connections between institutional theory and sport management research. *Sport Management Review, 14*(1), 1–12.

Weick, K. E., & Quinn, R. E. (1999). Organizational change and development. *Annual Review of Psychology, 50*, 361–386.

Wells, J. E., & Walker, N. A. (2016). Organizational change and justice: The impact of transparent and ethical leaders. *Journal of Intercollegiate Sport, 9*(2), 179–199.

Welty Peachey, J., & Bruening, J. (2011). An examination of environmental forces driving and constraining organizational change in a Football Championship Subdivision intercollegiate athletic department. *Sport Management Review, 14*(2), 202–219.

Welty Peachey, J., & Bruening, J. (2012a). Are your values mine? Exploring the influence of value congruence on responses to change in a Division I intercollegiate athletics department. *Journal of Intercollegiate Sport, 5*(2), 127–152.

Welty Peachey, J., & Bruening, J. (2012b). Investigating ambivalence towards organizational change in a Football Championship Subdivision intercollegiate athletic department. *Sport Management Review, 15*, 171–186.

Welty Peachey, J., Bruening, J., & Burton, L. (2011). Transformational leadership of change: Success through valuing relationships. *Journal of Contemporary Athletics, 5*(2), 127–152.

Welty Peachey, J., Damon, Z. J., Zhou, Y., & Burton, L. J. (2015). Forty years of leadership research in sport management: A review, synthesis, and conceptual framework. *Journal of Sport Management, 29*(5), 570–587.

Williams, T. (1998). Job satisfaction in teams. *International Journal of Human Resource Management, 9*, 782–799.

Yukl, G. A., & Van Fleet, D. D. (1992). Theory and research on leadership in organization. In M. D. Dunnette & L. M. Hough (Eds.), *Handbook of industrial and organizational psychology* (2nd ed., pp. 147–197). Chicago, IL: Rand McNally.

CHAPTER 9

Fostering Innovation

Larena Hoeber
Orland Hoeber

CHAPTER OBJECTIVES

- Define the concept of innovation in the context of sport organizations.
- Describe the relationship between leadership and innovation.
- Describe how leadership supports innovation from managerial, organizational, and environmental perspectives.
- Identify managerial determinants necessary to foster innovation in sport organizations.
- Demonstrate an understanding for how organizational structure, culture, size, and complexity provide support for the innovation process in sport organizations.
- Identify elements from the environment that impact innovation in organizations.

CASE STUDY

Innovation Saves the Data for CSO

During her time as executive director of a nonprofit, community-based soccer facility in a mid-sized city, Sarah recognized potential liability issues with her senior soccer league. This league allows older adults to play recreational soccer to maintain an active, post-retirement lifestyle. While the league has been well-received by seniors in the community, a recent issue with a player having a heart attack during a game has caused concern for Sarah.

In the first board meeting after this event, Sarah fielded a series of questions from board members about the league itself, liability issues for the facility, and whether the facility should cancel the league. Sarah was prepared for these questions and had already prepared an updated liability waiver to use for the senior league. After the meeting, she received a phone call from a senior league player and

(continues)

CASE STUDY   (continued)

retired health care professional who suggested that the players wear heart rate monitors. While Sarah appreciated that this was a good idea, the heart rate monitors did not address the issue of liability. After discussing this problem with another member who runs a local software development company, they came up with an innovative solution.

A specific manufacturer of heart rate monitors was identified that makes a WiFi-enabled product. Using the existing WiFi network in the facility and custom software developed by the local company, each player's heart rate data could be measured in real time and linked to their identity through the facility's membership database. Consulting with the retired healthcare professional who initiated the idea about using heart rate monitors, Sarah and the software development company identified a set of conditions that would indicate levels of risk for heart attacks. The software development company leveraged existing smartphone and smartwatch technology to push alerts to the referees, including the name, jersey number, and team of the at-risk player, as well as the player photo and an assessment of the risk level. This enabled the referees to quickly glance at their watches to determine if there was a potential problem, identify the player, and even stop the game if the risk was critical.

During the pilot testing of this innovation, Sarah worked closely with her staff, key team contacts in the senior league, and referees to be sure everyone was comfortable with the system. A retired lawyer in the league identified possible issues with data privacy and consent. Sarah worked with the software development company to install a private WiFi network on which the heart rate monitoring and alert system would run. She also developed a data privacy policy for the staff and consent form for players using the heart rate monitoring and alert system. She coordinated between the software development company and the facility staff to hand over the final roll-out and maintenance of the system to the staff. This transfer empowered the staff members to take ownership of the heart rate monitoring and alert system and to ensure that it was addressing the needs of the players and facility.

Staff members and referees working for the facility noted that Sarah's strategic leadership skills were instrumental in adopting this innovation. Sarah noted that it was important to have a big-picture approach to using technology in the organization and also be willing to take risks on new and unproven systems. She envisioned using the new heart rate monitoring and alert system to not only address the risk and liability issue of running the senior league but also as a training tool for more competitive leagues. Sarah demonstrated a proactive, visionary style of leadership. The board of directors also showed leadership skills in allowing Sarah to pursue this new innovation as a solution to the problem. Board members saw the benefits of using technology in the facility and were supportive of Sarah's willingness to pursue the use of new technology to improve the safety of the senior soccer league and address the risk and liability issues for the facility.

Questions for Discussion

1. Which leadership skills were necessary for Sarah to successfully lobby for adoption of the heart rate monitoring and alert system?
2. What challenges might Sarah have had to overcome to be sure that the heart rate monitoring and alert system was implemented successfully?
3. Why is it important for leaders to recognize innovation in organizational operations?
4. Identify an innovation in sport that was successfully implemented by the leader of that organization.

▶ Introduction

Innovation has been, and continues to be, of interest to many organizations because of its connection to competitiveness, effectiveness, growth, and survival (Damanpour & Schneider, 2006; Hage, 1999; Rattan, 2010; Tidd, 2001; Wolfe, 1994; Zahra & Covin, 1994). Despite the wealth of research and interest in this topic (see Crossan & Apaydin, 2010; Hage, 1999; Wolfe, 1994), there is still some ambiguity with respect to the definition of innovation.

One commonly accepted definition of innovation is "any idea, practice, or material artifact perceived as new by the relevant unit of adoption" (Zaltman, Duncan, & Holbek, 1973, p. 10). This definition recognizes that newness is defined by the context in which the innovation is occurring. Innovations can be identified as new based on their frame of reference at the group, organizational, industry, and global levels (Crossan & Apaydin, 2010; Johannessen, Olsen, & Lumpkin, 2001). The group level refers to units, divisions, or departments within an organization. Using a professional sport team as an example, the marketing department could be the first one to use a new internal communication platform. If a sport club is using something new relative to other sport clubs in a community, this would be considered an innovation at the organizational level. For example, a rock climbing club might be the first in its community to have a partnership with the private sector to build a new sport facility. Innovations at the industry level are ones that distinguish one industry from another. An example of this is when one sport league is the first to use high speed cameras to enable precise tracking of players and movement, which is later adopted by other sport leagues. Innovations at the global level are new to the world. For example, 3D filming and 24/7 specialty channel broadcasting were first introduced to society in the sport sector.

There is some debate if every new idea is an innovation. Some argue that the term innovation is overused (Kwon, 2012). If everyone is claiming to be innovative, how do innovative organizations or leaders stand out? People generally agree about newness (or improvement) at the global level—that is, something that has never been seen before in the world and results in improvements in performance or experience. There is much to be learned from these innovations, which can also be referred to as inventions, as they challenge traditional ideas and practices. However, global-level innovations are relatively rare. It is more common to see innovations at the group, organizational, or industry levels. These innovations can represent a minor or incremental change from the status quo, such as the redevelopment of an existing program for a new target market or demographic (see for example Hoeber, Doherty, Hoeber, & Wolfe, 2015). If a swim club offered a learn-to-swim program to new immigrants, they might make minor changes to the program to address different cultural norms or translate marketing campaigns and communications into other languages. Innovations can also reflect fundamental or radical shifts from the status quo. The introduction of instant replay in televised sports radically changed how viewers experienced the game, as well as how these games were officiated and coached.

Another area of confusion with respect to innovation is that there are different forms of innovation. Products or goods are the more visible forms of innovation; however, innovations can also be in the form of services, processes, structures, or systems (Damanpour, 1996; Hoeber et al., 2015; Winand, Vos, Zintz, & Scheerder, 2013; Wolfe, 1994). For example, a local, nonprofit sport club could introduce babysitting as a new service for members (service innovation), smartphone-based membership renewals (process innovation), or hire professional staff (structural innovation).

TABLE 9.1 lists some service and process innovations identified by presidents of Canadian community sport organizations (Hoeber et al., 2015).

TABLE 9.1 Service and Process Innovations in Community Sport Organizations

Sport	Service Innovations	Process Innovations
Curling	New game format (e.g., "pick-up" curling) Online newsletters New membership payment options	Target new potential members (e.g., new immigrants, students) Establish a succession plan for board members
Soccer	New leagues for women, different age groups Creation of websites	Establish partnerships for constructing facilities Create new board positions Adopt an electronic database program
Swimming	Programs for persons with disabilities, First Nations youth Live Internet streaming of meets	Create paid staff positions Establish sponsorship packages
Ultimate Frisbee	New tournaments Support charities	Pay volunteers "Carbon flip" to start the game

Data from Hoeber, L., Doherty, A., Hoeber, O., & Wolfe, R. (2015). The nature of innovation in community sport organizations. *European Sport Management Quarterly, 15*(5), 518–534.

For the purpose of this chapter, we highlight innovations at the local, regional, national, and international levels of sport, recognizing that some organizations strive to be cutting edge and ahead of the pack, and others innovate to survive within their community. We examine both the role of leaders in innovative organizations (e.g., how leaders encourage innovation within their organizations) and leading organizations within the sport field. Conceptualization is a key skill for leaders. Conceptualization is the process by which leaders evaluate the sport industry's environment, trends, dynamics, and shifts in perceived value or expectations, and attempt to set a future direction for the organization (vision). If leaders are truly examining their organizations' external environments, innovation can play an important role in making operations run more efficiently and improving both the spectator and participant experience in sport.

▶ Historical Grounding

The sport industry offers an interesting arena for examining innovation. Sport organizations are characterized by passion and commitment to the product (Babiak & Wolfe, 2009; Santomier, Hogan, & Kunz, 2016). This passion can be a deterrent to innovation if leaders are resistant to change because of nostalgia, tradition, and history (Smith & Shilbury, 2004; Thiel & Mayer, 2009; Wolfe, Wright, & Smart, 2006). However, passion can also result in key stakeholders becoming deeply committed to organizational innovations, especially if they improve performances on the field or contribute to more marketable products (Cruickshank & Collins, 2012). Golf is an interesting example of both a commitment to tradition and openness to change. On the one hand, some golf clubs have remained loyal to their traditional approaches to restricted membership and course maintenance, which may contribute to negative public image, at the expense of including a wider range of members or adopting more environmentally-friendly maintenance procedures. On the other hand, professional and recreational golfers demand cutting-edge innovations with their golf equipment to improve performance in areas like accuracy and swing speed.

It is also interesting to examine innovations in the sport industry because it includes sectors that produce tangible goods and those that provide services. Within the sporting goods sector, improvements in manufacturing and production processes, materials, and the integration of new technology such as sensors result in tangible differences in products that can be experienced by customers and clients. These improvements can result in improved athletic performance, analytics, and experiences, which translates into competitive advantages. Thus, innovation is key for success in the sporting goods sector. As **TABLE 9.2** indicates, there are numerous examples of such innovations to sporting goods in a range of sports. Such technological innovations are changing fast, and in some cases are having transformational effects on sport at all levels.

A large sector of the sport industry, including sport media, focuses on the delivery of services. Sport media are reliant on innovations in technology and communications to reach a wider or more specific audience and to provide a better viewing and/or listening experience for spectators. Broadcasting of sporting events has been the catalyst for innovations in televised media. For example, 3D sport broadcasting was introduced at the 2010 FIFA World Cup (Host Broadcast Services, n.d.). Other broadcasting innovations include using dynamic banners and graphics over live televised coverage, virtual images such as the yellow first-down line in football, and the Hawk-Eye ball-tracking system used in tennis (shown in **FIGURE 9.1**). Television media companies have been investing heavily in new technology to enhance the delivery of the sport

TABLE 9.2 Sample of Sporting Goods Innovations

Sport	Product Innovation	Purpose
Running	Self-lacing shoes (e.g., Nike HyperAdapt 1.0)	Dynamically adaptable fit
Golf	Sensors in golf clubs (e.g., Zepp Golf 4.0)	Training and analytics
Soccer	Sensors in soccer balls (e.g., Adidas miCoach Smart Ball)	Training and analytics
Cycling and football	Cooling vests (e.g., Arctic Heat Body cooling vest)	Reduce overheating while training
Surfing	Aerospace-inspired surfboard materials (e.g., Varial)	Lighter and stronger surfboards
Soccer, lacrosse, ice hockey, football, rugby	Neck collar (e.g., Q-collar)	Reduce injury to the brain as a result of head impact

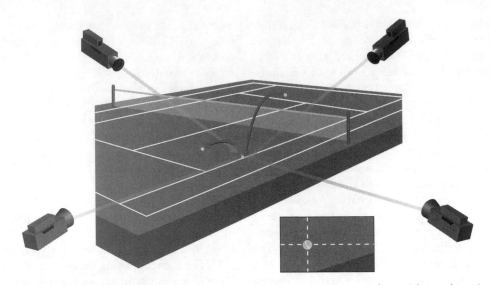

FIGURE 9.1 Hawk-Eye is a computer tracking system used in numerous sports, such as cricket and tennis, to visually track the trajectory of the ball.

© Dorling Kindersley/Getty Images.

product for fans. ESPN has been developing innovative ways to integrate the interactive aspects of smartphone and tablet use with real-time sport event content (McCracken, 2016). For example, they created software that is able to extract video clips from live sport events and make these available for posting to a variety of social media platforms in a matter of seconds. (See **TABLE 9.3** for more examples of technological innovations in sport broadcasting.)

Training is another area of the sport service sector in which innovations are important and visible. Here, coaches, athletes, and sport organizations use innovations in various areas, including technology, data analytics, nutrition, exercise physiology, and sport psychology to gain competitive advantages. Companies like Zepp are making wireless sensors that synchronize with smartphones to measure and analyze the movement associated with a range of sports (e.g., baseball, softball, golf, tennis, soccer). The underlying motion sensor technology is essentially the same across these sports; how the data are processed and presented to support analysis and training differs depending on where the motion sensor

is positioned and the movement in the sport (e.g., end of a bat or tennis racket grip, top of a golf glove, back of a soccer sock). Integrating the analytics of the data with smartphone technology enables athletes to have easy access to personalized coaching and feedback. With the help of a software company, the U.S. Ski and Snowboard Association (USSA) created an athlete-management system that allows athletes to record everything from the number of hours they sleep to the number of sets they do in the weight room. The information is recorded in a smartphone app and shared with USSA coaches and the organization's high-performance teams. In addition, the software system assigns athletes a training regimen from 6,500 available exercises (Mickle, 2013).

It is more difficult to identify service innovations in some sport sectors, such as professional sport leagues or sport governing bodies, because there may be internal processes and structures that are less obvious to the general public (see for example Winand et al., 2013) or they may be intentionally protected as trade secrets. However, Wolfe and colleagues' (2006) discussion of the use of sabermetrics

TABLE 9.3 Technological Innovations in Sport Broadcasting

Sport / Event	Area of Innovation	Examples
Summer Olympics	Timing	Official automatic timing provided by Omega, the lone manufacturer of stopwatches—Los Angeles (1932) Electronic automated timing—Tokyo (1964)
	Televised broadcasts	First televised broadcasts—Berlin (1936) First televised home broadcasts—London (1948)
	Virtual imaging	Virtual lines on swimming lanes to indicate record times—Sydney (2000)
Baseball	Cameras	Center field cameras—Chicago (1951) Slow motion cameras—ABC and NBC (1984) High speed HD cameras in all MLB facilities (2015)
	Graphics	Electronic character graphics (1970s) Pictorial graphics—Fox (1990s)
	Digital television	High-definition transmission (1997)
Football	Instant replay	CBS (1963)
	Virtual imaging	1st and ten line—ESPN (1998)
Motor sports	Graphics	Highlight lead car (2000s) Virtual dashboard (2000s)
Basketball	Virtual imaging	Live broadcast in virtual reality (2015)

Data from CNBC. (2015). NBA to broadcast first live pro sports event in virtual reality. Retrieved from https://www.cnbc.com/2015/10/26/nba-to-broadcast-first-live-pro-sports-event-in-virtual-reality.html; IEEE Global History Network. (n.d.a). Technological innovations and the Summer Olympic Games. Retrieved from http://www.ieeeghn.org/wiki/index.php/Technological_Innovations_and_the_Summer_Olympic_Games; IEEE Global History Network. (n.d.b). Technological innovations in sports broadcasting. Retrieved from http://www.ieeeghn.org/wiki/index.php/Technological_Innovations_in_Sports_Broadcasting; National Public Radio. (2015). MLB to debut 'statcast' tracking technology tonight. Retrieved from http://www.npr.org/2015/04/21/401319039/mlb-to-debut-statcast-tracking-technology-tonight

to assess human resources in Major League Baseball and Sheridan's (2007) assessment of Wimbledon's revised seeding system serve as examples of such innovations. Some professional sport teams have also started to explore innovative business-to-business sponsorship partnerships, with a focus on the co-creation of value for both the sponsor and the team (Buser, Woratschek, & Schönberner, 2017). Here, sport is viewed as a platform, rather than an event, with skills and technology shared between the organizations. For example, SAP sponsorship of sailing goes beyond simply placing a logo on a sailboat. It also includes the development of analytics tools for athletes, fans, and media (Buser et al., 2017).

▶ Determinants of Innovation

Organizational innovativeness is one of the main streams of research in innovation studies (Wolfe, 1994). In this stream, researchers are interested in identifying the determinants, or any activity, process, or condition, which either supports or hinders the ability of an organization to innovate (see for example Winand & Hoeber, 2017). These determinants can be grouped into three levels of analysis: managerial, organizational, and environmental (Damanpour & Schneider, 2006). **Managerial determinants** relate to top managers' and leaders' support of and attitude toward innovation. **Organizational determinants** refer to elements of the internal environment, including the structure, culture, size, and complexity of the organization, which impact innovation. **Environmental determinants** exist in the social, political, economic, cultural, and technological contexts outside of the organization that facilitate innovation or act as a barrier to it. For the purpose of this chapter, we highlight how leadership supports innovation from these three levels of determinants (managerial, organizational, and environmental). First, we examine managerial characteristics and actions that support innovation. Second, we consider how leaders can foster innovation within the organization. Third, we examine how leaders embrace environmental determinants when they work in support of innovation or manage them when they work against innovation.

Managerial Determinants

Leadership is a critical element in fostering organizational innovation because leaders and managers have the opportunity and the authority to offer support and guidance when innovations are developed or proposed and to create an environment that is conducive to implementing innovations (Crossan & Apaydin, 2010). Damanpour and Schneider (2006) suggest that "top managers heavily influence organizational capabilities by establishing organizational culture, motivating and enabling managers and employees, and building capacity for change and innovation" (p. 220). Management can develop and maintain an environment that fosters innovation and provides the necessary resources to implement it. In their overview of the literature on innovation in the sport and recreation industries, Boutroy, Vignal, and Soule (2015) argue that the critical managerial determinant is not the characteristics and attitudes of leaders but rather whether they direct resources to the innovation process.

We often think of leadership support for innovation happening in a top-down approach (Daft, 1978). What distinguishes top managers who support innovation from those who do not? Some of the individual factors that contribute to innovation include favorable attitudes toward innovation such as acceptance of risk, tolerance of ambiguity, openness to change, originality, proactiveness, entrepreneurship, and independence (Crossan & Apaydin, 2010; Damanpour & Schneider, 2006, 2009; Ratten, 2010, 2017; Winand & Anagnostopoulos, 2017). Leaders are instrumental in getting buy-in for change from skeptical employees, volunteers, clients, participants, and other stakeholders. Winand and Anagnostopoulos (2017) found that because leaders in sport federations communicated the idea that change was needed to be successful, sport federation staff were receptive to service innovations.

Leaders' failure to communicate and involve members or their lack of awareness of different views on innovation can hinder the innovation process. In a case study of a proposed technological change in judging the half pipe of snowboarding, the innovation was met with negative reactions because members were not included or consulted (Harding, Lock, & Toohey, 2016). Harding et al., (2016, p. 229) argued that "When constituents are empowered as members of the initiation stages of technological innovation processes they can provide crucial insight into the potential harm and benefits of an innovation." Nite and Washington's (2017) historical study of the impact of television broadcasting (a technological innovation) on the NCAA provides insight into how leaders can mismanage members' disparate perceptions of innovations. NCAA leadership were aware that some members, especially small universities, saw television as a threat to the institution. In response, the NCAA instituted regulations to address television broadcasting, in particular, the revenue-generating potential from it. However, their approach failed to address the rapid growth and development of the television industry, and it "became a key source of tension as the NCAA's regulations became stifling to the interests of powerful members" (p. 584). Nite and Washington (2017) suggest that "sports managers remain adaptive with their management of innovation so that rules and policies are current with advancements in the field."

In contrast to the assertion by Boutroy et al. (2015), others argue that managerial demographics are key determinants of innovation (Crossan & Apaydin, 2010; Damanpour & Schneider, 2006). Demographics such as age, level, and amount of education (more education), tenure in the organization and position (less tenure; newer to the organization), and variety of background and experience have been connected with innovation. Age has been a particular focal point for some innovation research as it is expected that younger managers will support and develop more innovations because they are receptive to new ideas, and for technological innovations, they are familiar and comfortable with technology (Berry, Berry, & Foster, 1998; Damanpour & Schneider, 2006). Tjønndel (2017) suggested that the young age of the coaches and board members (between 16 and 35 years of age) of a Norwegian skateboard club contributed to their receptivity to innovative approaches to include more women and girls. Similarly, in a case study of the adoption and implementation of a technological innovation in a community sport organization, the board's openness to technology and willingness to try something new were attributed to the young age of many of the board members (Hoeber & Hoeber, 2012). In contrast, older managers may be less willing to pursue innovations because they are committed to the status quo (Damanpour & Schneider, 2006).

Sometimes, leadership for innovation rests with one individual, referred to as an **innovation champion** (Damanpour & Schneider, 2006; Wolfe, 1994; Wolfe et al., 2006). These are individuals, at any level in the organization, who propose, develop, advocate for, and in some cases, implement, innovations. A high-profile example of an innovation champion in professional sport is Billy Beane, the general manager of the Oakland Athletics, a Major League Baseball team. His adoption of sabermetrics, a system to assess baseball players' skills that emphasized past performances and unconventional statistics (Wolfe et al., 2006), challenged the conventional system used by scouts. Beane turned to sabermetrics because he had limited financial resources to recruit expensive players who were highly rated on traditional skills, like hitting power or arm strength. Sabermetrics allowed Beane and the Athletics to scout players with undervalued talents, like on-base percentage. Although there was some hesitation by A's ownership to adopt this approach, Beane "had the necessary energy, commitment, and organizational power" (Wolfe et al., 2006, p. 117), characteristics associated with innovation champions, to ensure that sabermetrics was adopted by the team. His use of this human-resource management innovation provided him with a competitive advantage, because he recruited quality players at low salaries. This is an example of the need for sport leaders, even if they are questioned, to challenge the "old school" system or ways of thinking.

Organizational Determinants

Innovation is not always initiated or actively supported by top managers and leaders. Rather, innovation can arise from a bottom-up or shared approach (Daft, 1978). Leaders still play an important role in this approach, through the establishment of structures and cultures that promote and support innovation within the organization.

Large, complex organizations are seen as conducive to innovation because they have formal structures, resources, and systems in place to support the innovation process. One key structure is research and development departments (R&D), which are specifically tasked with creating innovations. Large sporting goods manufacturing companies, like Nike and Under Armour, rely on R&D to establish cutting-edge innovations that will translate into competitive advantages. Other research has found that smaller organizations with flexible and simple structures, such as regional sport federations, are also innovative (Winand et al., 2013).

Leaders are instrumental in establishing an organizational culture that supports risk taking, openness to change, and forward thinking by their staff, volunteers, members, and board members (Igira, 2008; Jaskyte, 2004; Tjønndal, 2017). Leaders can establish this culture through stated organizational values and discourses. Nike has a stated commitment to innovation. Their Innovation Kitchen provides a "safe space for failure," thus allowing employees to take risks through "ask[ing] ridiculous questions, and play[ing] with crazy materials" (Danford, 2015). In addition to those specifically tasked with research and development, Nike employees in all other areas of the organization are encouraged to suggest and develop innovation. Thus, Nike can reap the benefits of innovations in fabrics, materials, and design, as well as in the areas of supply chain management, marketing, and workplace environments.

In the sport industry, innovations are sometimes proposed, initiated, or supported by **boundary spanners** (Daft, 1978). They are involved in multiple domains (e.g., work in the private sector, volunteer for a nonprofit sport club) and bring ideas into an organization.

These boundary spanners can include athletes, coaches, customers, volunteers, board members, or other key stakeholders. Carey and Mason (2014) examined the strategic and innovative partnerships that were established to foster support for a tax increase to cover the costs of multiple sport, culture, and recreation facilities in one Canadian community. They identified community opinion leaders as instrumental in gaining citizens' support for the tax increases. These individuals came from community organizations, such as the local university, chambers of council, and sport clubs, who would benefit from the new facilities. Franke and Shah (2003) studied the development and diffusion of product innovations in amateur sport communities. They found a "community-based innovation system" (Franke & Shah, 2003, p. 169) in which the sport participants (i.e., users) developed product innovations, which were readily shared within the sport communities. These individuals are participants in the sport as well as members of other communities and industries, and thus brought ideas from a variety of sources to the sport. Boundary spanners are an important source of innovation in nonprofit sport organizations, which are governed by a volunteer board of directors. These individuals represent many different sectors in society (e.g., education, marketing, business, law, health, construction) and can use their knowledge and expertise from these other sectors as a source of new ideas for the sport organization. Hoeber and Hoeber (2012) found that such boundary spanners were present in the development of a technological innovation for a local soccer club, where some of the key developers of the innovation were members of the club and, therefore, had extensive tacit knowledge of the requirements.

Environmental Determinants

Innovations can develop as a result of environmental pressures and opportunities. Leaders play a vital role in recognizing and capitalizing on opportunities to do something different, to keep up with competitors, and to respond to demands from key stakeholders by turning to innovation (Cruickshank & Collins, 2012; Cruickshank, Collins, & Minten, 2014; Damanpour & Schneider, 2006). Additionally, they must also be cognizant of constraints to innovation, such as regulations from higher levels of sport governing bodies or government agencies (Winand & Hoeber, 2017).

Leaders can identify opportunities for innovation within their market or industry. These opportunities can arise from changing demands of their members or clients, innovations being adopted by competitors in their sector, or external stakeholders (e.g., suppliers, funders, sponsors) sharing ideas with them. Under Armour is known for its focus on innovation and entrepreneurship. The Idea House is a section in their website to encourage people outside of their organization to submit ideas, a practice referred to as "open sourcing." Under Armour is capitalizing on the creativity of others and their willingness to share their ideas. In doing so, they are expanding their options for sources of new ideas beyond their employees. The BC Lions, a team in the Canadian Football League, worked with multiple partners with expertise in telecommunications, virtual reality video, augmented reality, and app development to create 360° virtual reality videos for fans (Chartrand, 2017). Many of these partners were also headquartered in the same city (Vancouver) as the team, thus facilitating in-person discussions and collaborations.

Not all innovations need to be copied, but nevertheless, leaders must be aware of what their competitors are doing to gain competitive advantages. While the use of social media is now well established, we can consider the innovative aspects of its adoption in sport. When Facebook and Twitter were first established, social media was viewed as an innovation that sport teams adopted because they could see how other sport teams and other companies, outside of

the sport industry, were benefiting from it. It is difficult to know which professional team or which leader was the first to use Facebook or Twitter, but it is clear that teams recognized the value of these for marketing and communicating with fans, and for public and community relations. The subsequent use of Instagram and, more recently, Snapchat have followed a similar trajectory; we expect the next generation of social media platforms to follow suit.

Leaders must also monitor the social, political, economic, and cultural environments in which the organization operates, because changes and shifts in these environments may mitigate the need to be innovative. For example, Tjønndel's (2017) study of innovation in a skateboarding club found that in response to the social exclusion of women and girls, club leaders implemented policies and bylaws to ensure they were the "leading skateboard club for girls and women" (p. 53). Leaders of community sport organizations (CSOs) are addressing a range of social issues in their communities, such as poverty, environmental sustainability, and cultural integration, which in itself is innovative because they are meeting more than their members' demands for sport and recreation programming (Misener, 2016; Misener & Babiak, 2015a, 2015b). These initiatives allow CSOs to align themselves with social causes that their members, constituents, and other stakeholders find important. See **TABLE 9.4** for a list of initiatives that CSOs have implemented to address social innovation. Consumer demands for online interactions is a significant societal trend that leaders in all areas of the sport industry must attend to and respond with innovations in areas such as communications, purchasing, and broadcasting. Another major area of consideration for leaders is demographic changes in society, including an aging population, immigration, and reductions in family sizes, as well as shifts in societal attitudes about gender identity, sexuality, disability, environmentalism, and sustainability. Leaders can address these

TABLE 9.4 Innovative Approaches to Social Issues

Social Issue	Initiatives
Bullying	Cyber-bullying awareness campaign
Cultural integration	Free sport clinics in schools for newcomers Translation of club materials into multiple languages
Environmental sustainability	Equipment swap Wildlife preservation policy
Gender equity	Leadership clinics for women
Poverty	Clothing drive Toy drive Athletes volunteered for Habitat for Humanity
Youth-at-risk (crime)	Free sport clinic and access to facility for residents of youth detention center

Data from Misener, K., & Babiak, K. (2015a). A new 'arena': Social responsibility through community sport. North American Society for Sport Management Conference. June 2 - 6. Ottawa, ON.

environmental shifts through the adoption and implementation of innovative services and products. Toronto is recognized as the most multicultural city in Canada and one of the most multicultural in the world, with almost half of its population in 2006 being foreign-born (City of Toronto, n.d.). The South Asian and Chinese communities are two of the largest visible minorities in the city. In response to this shift in the population, the National Basketball Association's Toronto Raptors began broadcasting their games in Punjabi in 2009 and Mandarin in 2012 (National Basketball Association, 2009, 2012).

▶ Summary

The goal of this chapter has been to formalize the concept of innovation, and discuss it from the perspective of managerial, organizational, and environmental determinants in the context of sport organizations. Regardless of the driving force behind innovation, the leaders in a sport organization play a critical role in not only directly supporting the undertaking of an innovation but also fostering an environment that is supportive and open to both internal and external sources of innovative practices.

Although technological innovation within the sporting goods sector is easy to identify, innovation is also occurring within the service sector of sport, as well as in the internal operational processes, structures, and systems of many sport organizations. Such innovation spans the professional/recreational divide and may occur within both the product domain (sporting goods sector) and the process domain (sport organizations/teams). Supporting innovations in these contexts is a crucial role for sport leaders.

LEADERSHIP PERSPECTIVE

Kelly Krauskopf

Kelly Krauskopf joined Pacers Sports and Entertainment as the Chief Operating Officer of the newly formed WNBA franchise, the Indiana Fever. In 2004, she was named President and General Manager of the Fever. Beginning in 2017, Krauskopf took on a new role and now serves as President of both the Fever and Pacers Gaming as a part of the new NBA2K League.

Q: Tell us more about your role as Senior Vice President for Pacers Sports & Entertainment and your work with Pacers Gaming, of the NBA2K league.

I am in my 19th season at PS&E, and I originally came to Indiana to build and lead our WNBA franchise— the Indiana Fever. When our owner decided we would be one of the first 17 teams to join the NBA2K League, I was asked to set up the franchise operation, which involves hiring staff, creating a strategic business plan, and building an infrastructure that would enable us to compete at the highest level.

Our owner Herbert Simon provides leadership to the PS&E organization and has always been on the cutting edge and pushing the innovation. We were one of the first to get a WNBA team because he wanted to provide opportunities for women and girls; he saw the value of having a women's professional sport franchise in the community. And now, this new generation of digitally connected young men and women, their lifestyles and entertainment are very different compared with traditional sports fans. Simon wants to continue to innovate and stay relevant to fans and our community so he felt it was important to enter the space of NBA2K and build a franchise around competitive eSports gaming, which has grown exponentially worldwide.

Q: When you consider innovation with regard to sport, what are you paying attention to in your role as SVP for PS&E organization?

We are in a very competitive environment, so we are always looking ahead for innovative solutions to better market and sell our teams to reach a changing fan base. We also look at innovative opportunities that would give us a competitive advantage for our teams, whether it is scouting, game play, or individual player performance.

NBA2K is a videogame that has been around since 1999, and now that we are a league, everything from scouting software to performance analysis is being used to help our team. We actually hired students who recently graduated from Southern Indiana University who started a business called NBA2K Lab. Their company provides our team with analysis; just like you would

(continues)

LEADERSHIP PERSPECTIVE (*continued*)

with conventional basketball, scouting opponents, they provide us with software to help provide an advantage to our players.

Q: What advice would you give to students to help develop skills to be a leader who recognizes and pursues innovation?

Stay open and up to date on the business sector that you are most interested in. Spend time reading and educating yourself on your own time, not just because it is an assignment. Innovation happens because someone saw a market opportunity and stayed diligent in his or her pursuit.

Students should read the industry trade publications, including Street and Smith Sports Business Journal and Sports Business Daily. You can read about what other leagues or teams are doing and learn new innovative ways to meet your fans' needs. And there are so many niche publications regarding eSports, the ESports Observer is one where students can find more information about the industry. Also, reading in more traditional publications like the Wall Street Journal and Forbes can be beneficial to students.

Q: What are some challenges leaders face when implementing new innovations?

Staying true to the process. Many times, people give up on the process just prior to breaking through. I would say staying on course and not getting discouraged with the many setbacks that can happen when you are the "first" of any kind. Any new business comes with risk and comes with a set of challenges. I have had the opportunity to work with two different sports properties; one is with women. The challenges of having to build a sports property that is credible and that is a challenge because there are a lot of men who are covering sports that don't see women's sports as viable sports properties. But that is more of a larger social issue or challenge. In the NBA2K, there are a lot of ways to try to build the business in a streaming environment, so you try to develop a plan that you think in 3 to 5 years will hit your goals while also hitting yearly goals. Sometimes, you won't meet those yearly goals but you have to stay focused on your long-term goals. You also have to remember that your overall goal is to enhance the lives of your fans and remain an important part of the larger community you serve.

▶ Key Terms

Boundary spanners
Environmental determinants
Innovation

Innovation champion
Managerial
   determinants

Organizational determinants
Organizational
   innovativeness

▶ Discussion Questions

1. Explain the concept of innovation within a sport organization. Aside from those listed in the chapter, what other examples of innovation have had an impact on the success of a sport organization or sport league?

2. Organizational innovativeness is contingent on three levels of determinants. What are these determinants and how do they relate to organizational innovation?

3. Why are the demographic characteristics of a manager important determinants of organizational innovativeness?

4. Innovation can be a top-down, bottom-up, or shared approach. Describe each of these approaches to innovation and describe how leaders can support each approach.

5. If you were the marketing manager for a minor-league baseball team, what steps

would you take as a leader to be sure that your organization fosters innovation with regard to in-game promotions?

What would be your most significant challenges as you attempted to foster innovation in your organization?

▸ References

Babiak, K., & Wolfe, R. (2009). Determinants of corporate social responsibility in professional sport: Internal and external factors. *Journal of Sport Management, 23*(6), 717–742.

Berry, F. S., Berry, W. D., & Foster, S. K. (1998). The determinants of success in implementing an expert system in state government. *Public Administration Review, 58*(4), 295–305.

Boutroy, E., Vignal, B., & Soule, B. (2015). Innovation theories applied to the outdoor sports sector: Panorama and perspectives. *Loisir et Société/Society and Leisure, 38*(3), 383–398.

Buser, M., Woratschek, H., & Schönberner, J. (2017). Sport events as a platform for sponsoring engagement: A conceptual framework based on empirical insights. *European Association for Sport Management Conference.* September 5-7, Bern, Switzerland.

Carey, M., & Mason, D.S. (2014). Building consent: Funding recreation, cultural, and sports amenities in a Canadian city. *Managing Leisure, 19*(2), 105–120.

Chartrand, S. (2017, October 6). How the BC Lions are using AR and 360° video to drive fan engagement. Front Office Sports. https://frntofficesport.com/how-the-bc-lions-are-using-ar-and-360%C2%BA-video-to-drive-fan-engagement-d62b4f7c68b1

City of Toronto. (n.d.). Toronto's racial diversity. Retrieved from http://www.toronto.ca/toronto_facts/diversity.htm

CNBC. (2015). NBA to broadcast first live pro sports event in virtual reality. Retrieved from https://www.cnbc.com/2015/10/26/nba-to-broadcast-first-live-pro-sports-event-in-virtual-reality.html

Crossan, M. M, & Apaydin, M. (2010). A multi-dimensional framework of organizational innovation: A systematic review of the literature. *Journal of Management Studies, 47*(6), 1154–1191.

Cruickshank, A., & Collins, D. (2012). Change management: The case of the elite sport performance team. *Journal of Change Management, 12*(2), 209–229.

Cruickshank, A., Collins, D., & Minten, S. (2014). Driving and sustaining culture change in Olympic sport performance teams: A first exploration and grounded theory. *Journal of Sport & Exercise Psychology, 36*(1), 107–120.

Daft, R. L. (1978). A dual-core of organizational innovation. *Academy Management Journal, 21*(2), 193–210.

Damanpour, F. (1996). Organizational complexity and innovation: Developing and testing multiple contingency models. *Management Science, 42*(5), 693–716.

Damanpour, F., & Schneider, M. (2006). Phases of the adoption of innovation in organizations: Effects of environment, organization and top managers. *British Journal of Management, 17*(3), 215–236.

Damanpour, F., & Schneider, M. (2009). Characteristics of innovation and innovation adoption in public organizations: Assessing the role of managers. *Journal of Public Administration Research and Theory, 19*(3), 495–522.

Danford, G. (2015, September 17). The Innovation 'Kitchen' at Nike. LinkedIn. https://www.linkedin.com/pulse/innovation-kitchen-nike-dr-gerard-danford/

Franke, N., & Shah, S. (2003). How communities support innovative activities: An exploration of assistance and sharing among end-users. *Research Policy, 32*(1), 157–178.

Hage, J. T. (1999). Organizational innovation and organizational change. *Annual Review of Sociology, 25*, 597–622.

Harding, J., Lock, D., & Toohey, K. (2016). A social identity analysis of technological innovation in an action sport: Judging elite half-pipe snowboarding. *European Sport Management Quarterly, 16*(2), 214–232.

Hoeber, L., Doherty, A., Hoeber, O., & Wolfe, R. (2015). The nature of innovation in community sport organizations. *European Sport Management Quarterly, 15*(5), 518–534.

Hoeber, L., & Hoeber, O. (2012). Determinants of an innovation process: A case study of technological innovation in a community sport organization. *Journal of Sport Management, 26*(3), 213–223.

Host Broadcast Services. (n.d.). 2010 FIFA World Cup South Africa™. Retrieved from http://www.hbs.tv/past-hbs-missions/2010-fifa-world-cup-south-africatm.html

IEEE Global History Network. (n.d.a). Technological innovations and the Summer Olympic Games. Retrieved from http://www.ieeeghn.org/wiki/index.php/Technological_Innovations_and_the_Summer_Olympic_Games

IEEE Global History Network. (n.d.b). Technological innovations in sports broadcasting. Retrieved from http://www.ieeeghn.org/wiki/index.php/Technological_Innovations_in_Sports_Broadcasting

Igira, F. T. (2008). The situatedness of work practices and organizational culture: Implications for information systems innovation uptake. *Journal of Information Technology, 23,* 79–88.

Jaskyte, K. (2004). Transformational leadership, organizational culture, and innovativeness in non-profit organizations. *Nonprofit Management and Leadership, 15*(2), 153–168.

Johannessen, J. A., Olsen, B., & Lumpkin, G. T. (2001). Innovation as newness: What is new, how new, and new to whom? *European Journal of Innovation Management, 4*(1), 20–31.

Kwon, L. (2012, May 23). You call that innovation? Wall Street Journal, B1.

McCracken, H. (2016, June 13). The technology behind ESPN's digital transformation. Fact Company. Retrieved from https://www.fastcompany.com/3060717/the-technology-behind-espns-digital-transformation

Mickle, T. (2013, July 22). Idea innovators: Troy Flanagan, high performance director, U.S. Ski and Snowboard Association. Retrieved from http://www.sportsbusinessdaily *Street & Smith's SportsBusiness Journal*.com/Journal/Issues/2013/07/22/Idea-Innovators/Troy-Flanagan.aspx

Misener, K., & Babiak, K. (2015a). A new 'arena': Social responsibility through community sport. North American Society for Sport Management Conference. June 2-6. Ottawa, Ontario.

Misener, K., & Babiak, K. (2015b). Exploring the link between social responsibility and strategy in community sport. European Association for Sport Management Conference. September 9-12. Dublin, Ireland.

Misener, K. (2016). Understanding community sport as a school of generosity. Sport Management Association of Australia and New Zealand Conference. November 23-25. Auckland, New Zealand.

National Basketball Association. (2009, November 20). Raptors to broadcast CBC games in Punjabi. Retrieved from http://www.nba.com/raptors/news/raptors_punjabi_112009.html

National Basketball Association. (2012). Raptors to broadcast game in Mandarin. Retrieved from http://www.nba.com/raptors/news/raptors-broadcast-game-mandarin

National Public Radio. (2015, April 15). MLB to debut 'statcast' tracking technology tonight. Retrieved from http://www.npr.org/2015/04/21/401319039/mlb-to-debut-statcast-tracking-technology-tonight

Nite, C., & Washington, M. (2017). Institutional adaptation to technological innovation: Lessons from the NCAA's regulation of football television broadcasts (1938–1984). *Journal of Sport Management, 31*(6), 575–590.

Ratten, V. (2010). Developing a theory of sport-based entrepreneurship. *Journal of Management & Organization, 16*(4), 557–565.

Ratten, V. (2017). Sport leadership, psychology and innovation. In V. Ratten & J.J. Ferreira (Eds.) Sport entrepreneurship and innovation (pp. 75–87), New York: Routledge.

Santomier, J. P., Hogan, P. I., & Kunz, R. (2016). The 2012 London Olympics: Innovations in ICT and social media marketing. *Innovation: Organization & Management, 18*(3), 251–269.

Sheridan, H. (2007). Evaluating technical and technological innovations in sport: Why fair play isn't enough. *Journal of Sport and Social Issues, 31*(2), 179–194.

Smith, A. C., & Shilbury, D. (2004). Mapping cultural dimensions in Australian sporting organisations. *Sport Management Review, 7*(2), 133–165.

Thiel, A., & Mayer, J. (2009). Characteristics of voluntary sports clubs management: A sociological perspective. *European Sport Management Quarterly, 9*(1), 81–98.

Tidd, J. (2001). Innovation management in context: Environment, organization and performance. *International Journal of Management Reviews, 3*(3), 169–183.

Tjønndal, A. (2017). Innovation for social inclusion in sport. In V. Ratten & J. J. Ferreira (Eds.) Sport entrepreneurship and innovation (pp. 42–58). New York: Routledge.

Winand, M., & Anagnostopoulos, C. (2017): Get ready to innovate! Staff's disposition to implement service innovation in non-profit sport organisations. *International Journal of Sport Policy and Politics, 9*(4), 579–595.

Winand, M., & Hoeber, L. (2017). Innovation capability of non-profit sport organisations. In V. Ratten & J. J. Ferreira (Eds.) Sport entrepreneurship and innovation (pp. 13–30), New York: Routledge.

Winand, M., Vos, S. B., Zintz, T., & Scheerder, J. (2013). Determinants of service innovation: A typology of sports federations. *International Journal of Sport Management and Marketing, 13*(1/2), 55–73.

Wolfe, R. A. (1994). Organizational innovation: Review, critique, and suggested research directions. *Journal of Management Studies, 31*(26), 405–431.

Wolfe, R., Wright, P. M., & Smart, D. L. (2006). Radical HRM innovation and competitive advantage: The *Moneyball* story. *Human Resource Management, 45*(1), 111–145.

Zahra, S. A., & Covin, J. C. (1994). The financial implications of fit between competitive strategy and innovation types and sources. *Journal of High Technology Management Research, 5*(2), 183–211.

Zaltman, G., Duncan, R., & Holbeck, J. (1973). Innovations and organizations (pp. 45–68). New York: Wiley.

©Gorilla Images/Shutterstock

CHAPTER 10

Team Leadership and Group Dynamics

Peter Bachiochi
Wendi Everton

CHAPTER OBJECTIVES

- Develop an understanding of team leadership and group dynamics.
- Identify problems when working in a group.
- Describe the conditions in which teams operate successfully in sport organizations.
- Discuss current sport management examples of team leadership.

CASE STUDY

Team Leadership within ESports

Special thanks to Tyler Hernandez for major contributions to this case study.

The world of online gaming has experienced exponential growth over the last several decades to the point where there are now professional teams, international competitions, and universities that offer scholarships to players who compete on school teams. Recruiting, managing, and coaching these teams pose some unique challenges in terms of team dynamics, motivation, and leadership. Team Liquid illustrates some of these challenges.

Since 2015, Team Liquid—an eSports franchise—has been experiencing an internal struggle between players and management for their League of Legends team. This internal struggle among players and management stems from the nature of profit earning for an eSports organization but can also be attributed to management's response to concerns as they arise.

(continues)

CASE STUDY (continued)

DoubleLift, whose real name is Peng Yiliang, is a top player in eSports for League of Legends and has made public remarks against Team Liquid (Erzberger, 2017). DoubleLift has voiced three concerns with management and its players: Poor communication, a lack of in-game/on-field awareness, and a lack of team sportsmanship. At the start of his first season, he was openly positive about playing with Team Liquid, having said that, "It feels good to be back in LCS [League Championship Series], competing and playing" (p. 1). By the end of the season, he expressed concerns with leadership on the team saying, that its members do not consider each other a resource during gameplay, making it a struggle to compete. He also cited mismanaged communication practices that were not being addressed by management, practices considered by others to be a historical norm for the franchise.

The co-CEO of the organization exacerbated the poor communication by micromanaging all 11 teams under the franchise. The co-CEOs' hands-on approach (e.g., frequent coaching and roster changes) has impacted team cohesiveness, communication, and continuity. This approach has been questioned by coaches and players who don't think someone at his level should need to hold people individually accountable in order for them to perform better (Buffee, 2017).

During the 2017 North America LCS Summer Split (one of the most competitive times of the year for eSports), a former member of Team Liquid known as Dardoch (Joshua Hartnett), stated this regarding Team Liquid:

> They're just hot garbage like always, bro. They're just real bad, I think. They have a lot of issues, and none of them are getting fixed it seems. I don't have a lot of respect for Liquid, as an organization, or players, or a team (Lilly, 2017, p. 3).

Dardoch left the team during 2016, when tensions were at their highest between pro-gamers on the team and their head coach at the time. Although minor staffing changes were made to the organization since then, Dardoch recognizes that the culture of the team has not changed. The players have changed, and the coaches have changed, but the organization and its management staff have not. In fact, what is most notable is that despite the players on the team changing, the new players are almost exactly like the prior members. And it has a performance record indicating that the status quo does not work. Since 2016, Team Liquid has not placed in the top 3 spots for any premier or major tournament for League of Legends. In 2016, they placed 4th for both the spring and Intel series, and by 2017, they placed 9th and 10th in the spring and summer series, respectively.

Although pro-gamers may seem to have a simple job: Play a video game and preferably win; sponsorship work is another divisive issue. Work weeks over 60 hours are the industry norm and many of these hours are spent doing sponsorship work. Professional gaming teams and franchises, such as Team Liquid, cannot depend on ticket sales for their matches and tournaments, nor on broadcasting rights, to earn money. Sponsors such as Red Bull, LogiTech, Razor, and others are their primary sources of earnings. These sponsorships in turn require players not only to represent their sponsors on their uniforms but also to participate in events and other advertising activities that the sponsors request. A pro-gamer can spend over 8 hours a day practicing with his or her team and an additional 6 or more hours doing sponsorship work. A work schedule like this inevitably has a negative impact on team performance. This schedule is an industry norm of which management for any eSports team is well aware. Rather than taking precautions to reduce performance declines, team cohesiveness declines, burnout, distress, and other concerns, management turned a blind eye to these problems.

Given the relatively flat structure of eSports organizations, the responsibility to address these issues is in the hands of the co-CEO. Instead, the co-CEOs' micro-management tended to increase the problems and it is not fair to expect the players to handle these issues on their own. As a result, Team Liquid's League of Legends performance declined with current and former players expressing concerns regarding team communication and management's approaches and little to no change resulting from conflicts and concerns.

Questions for Discussion

1. Using Hill's team leadership model, explained in the chapter, which internal team leadership actions played a role in the performance decline for Team Liquid?
2. Which external team leadership actions played a role in the performance decline for Team Liquid?
3. How did the various leadership decisions impact the performance of the team?
4. What could team leaders have done differently to amend the decline in performance?

▶ Introduction

As someone who follows sport, when you think of team leadership in sport, the first people who probably come to mind are team captains, coaches, and star players. However, team leadership happens both during the game and away from the field and court. At game time, players and coaches are the key leaders, but away from the game, athletic directors, event directors, general managers, and team owners take action and make decisions that have a lasting impact. The focus of this chapter will largely be on the leadership that happens away from the game, on the business side of the operations.

Several developments in the world of business and the world at large have raised the profile of teams in many organizations. Decades of downsizing have created greater spans of control, which have, in turn, created a greater reliance on teams to get work done. Constantly evolving technological advances (e.g., file sharing, online conferencing) have made it possible for teams to be more efficient and to work together from nearly anywhere. Similarly, the environment in which teams must work is growing more complex with "multiple stakeholders who have clashing agendas sometimes, high

information load, dynamic situational contingencies, and increased tempo of change" (Zaccaro, Rittman, & Marks, 2001, p. 452). In the world of professional sport, travel schedules, changing rosters, and constant press coverage introduce daily challenges to teams. These developments have also fundamentally changed the role of leaders in organizations, thus requiring a new combination of old skills as well as the acquisition of some new skills.

To maximize the effectiveness of teams, organizations must understand that sometimes teams do not use the correct approach for the task at hand. The failure of teams is often a function of using them at inappropriate times or for inappropriate tasks. Sometimes, a situation calls for a decision to be made by an individual without consultation. This chapter will begin with some models about how groups develop over time, followed by some of the key group dynamics that could undermine or facilitate the effectiveness of teams, followed by a typology of tasks that addresses when teams are most (or least) appropriate. Then, we will outline and close with coverage of models of team leadership that illustrate the delicate balance of the broad range of skills that team leaders must incorporate in both face-to-face team settings and virtual teams.

▶ Group Development

One of the first models to describe the formation and development of groups is the Tuckman (1965) model, as revised by Tuckman and Jensen (1977). According to this model, groups go through the following stages in order: Forming, storming, norming, performing, and adjourning. In the forming stage, group members initially get together and get to know each other and may begin to lay guidelines for the task at hand. The storming phase is marked by expected conflict between group members as the rules for the group's work are detailed. In the norming phase, such rules are agreed upon. In the performing stage, the group accomplishes the task at hand. During the adjourning stage, members say their goodbyes as the group parts

ways. This model describing how groups form has received decades of attention (Bonebright, 2010) and has withstood the test of time. Subsequent models have emerged that describe the evolution of groups in terms of the types of functions they must perform (such as McGrath's 1990 project model) or describing how groups use and mark the time they have to complete their task (Gersick, 1988), but Tuckman's model is the "most predominantly referred to and most widely recognized" (Miller, 2003, p. 122).

▶ Group Decision Making

TABLE 10.1 shows that there are a variety of paths that groups can use to make decisions, and each path will have an impact on the

TABLE 10.1 Decision-Making Pathways

How Is the Decision Made?	Level of Influence that Group Members Feel	Potential for Conflict Within the Group	Time It Takes to Make a Decision
Group leader alone makes the decision	None	Low (but may yield resentment later)	Fast
Group leader assigns an expert from the group to make the decision	Limited	Low (but may yield resentment later)	Fast
Group leader consults with the group to receive input, and then makes the decision	Moderate	Low	Not as fast
Mathematical computations (such as an average)	Moderate	Low	Fast
Voting	Somewhat	Low (but can alienate minority)	Fast
Consensus	Full	High	Slow

Data from Johnson, D. W., & Johnson, F. P. (2017). *Joining together: Group theory and group skills* (12th ed.). New York: Pearson.

potential for conflict within the group, the time that it takes to make the decision, and how "included" group members feel. These decision styles can be placed on a continuum of group member input (Johnson & Johnson, 2017), from no group input at all (the leader makes the decision) to full and complete group input (group consensus).

The leader decides which process the group will use, but that decision must be thoughtful—leaders must weigh the amount of time the decision can take with the level of influence and conflict desired within the group. If the decision will have a large impact on the group, or if it must have the buy-in of the group for its implementation to be successful, the decision should include group input (Kerr & Tindale, 2004; Murnighan, 1981). For example, captains of sport teams typically are not chosen by the coach, but by team members. A captain chosen by the coach may or may not have the endorsement of the team, but if the team is allowed input (such as by using a voting technique), the members are more likely to accept the outcome. Other decisions can be made by the group leader alone and will be accepted by the group, such as how practice sessions will be designed.

More inclusive decision-making strategies tend to increase group member interdependence and, therefore, group cohesion, while also increasing the social skills of individual members and individual accountability toward the end product (Wagner, 1994). If these outcomes are desired, leaders ought to include group members in decisions. In fact, most research indicates that groups produce output that is higher in quality than that produced by individuals (Kerr & Tindale, 2011; Larson, 2010). On the other hand, if the group members do not have enough knowledge about the topic, or if members lack maturity, the decisions will not be of high quality and there may be few benefits for the group (Johnson & Johnson, 2017).

▶ Groupthink

It does not take much for a cohesive team with strong leadership to stray from the path of effective decision making. In 2003, when the Detroit Pistons took Serbian player Darko Milicic with the No. 2 pick in the National Basketball Association (NBA) Draft, it was not considered a surprise. Many scouts had lined up behind the drafting of Milicic, citing his versatility and potential. Milicic played three seasons in Detroit, averaging less than 2 points per game. Although it is likely that Milicic would have played much more on a less-talented team (the Pistons won the NBA championship in 2004) and would potentially have developed into a better player, he never became the superstar that many scouts predicted he would become. Why was Milicic so highly touted? Slate writer Jack Hamilton noted, "Darko was the dubious beneficiary of a hazy mixture of groupthinking and magical thinking, a pre-YouTube moment made of wishful scouting reports from distant lands . . ." (Hamilton, 2013, para. 3). Pistons General Manager Joe Dumars admitted later that the team did not have much predraft information on Milicic. It appears that Dumars was swept away by the groupthink of professional basketball scouts hoping for an infusion of European big men into the league. Media reports print what NBA scouts say and think, which can create a consensus that may affect a decision when little information is available. Groupthink can infect teams and negatively affect team leadership decision making.

Groupthink was coined and identified by Irving Janis (1972) during his research on a variety of poor decisions made by groups. For example, during World War II, there were several warning signs that the Japanese were planning an attack on the United States (increased radio traffic, the presence of a Japanese submarine in Pearl Harbor the night before the attack), but these signs were ignored by commanders. If commanders had allowed reconnaissance flights, the Japanese fleet would have been spotted and the attack on Pearl Harbor would not have been a surprise. The decision to not send reconnaissance flights had baffled historians for some time. Janis explained that the failure was because of groupthink.

Groupthink happens within cohesive groups with strong leaders, both of which are desirable characteristics for a group to have. Usually, decisions made by such groups are high-quality decisions, but sometimes the group feels pressure to maintain cohesion and allegiance to the leader at the cost of good decision-making practices, which can result in bad decisions. Janis explains that groups operating with groupthink share similar characteristics. In addition to being highly cohesive and having strong, directive leadership, they tend to be isolated from outside group influences and experiencing a high-stress situation. Under these conditions, Janis says that a group is likely to have most or all of the eight features of groupthink.

1. *Illusion of invulnerability* occurs when there is a collective agreement that the group is strong and invincible, so decisions tend to be risky. For instance, successful teams may acquire a player or coach known to be a lightning rod for controversy, assuming that the team cannot be hurt by the turbulence that accompanies such a player or coach.

2. *Collective rationalization* happens as the decision is being finalized, whereby group members create reasons for why the decision will work and do not seek out problems with the decision. Team members may focus exclusively on that same lightning rod player's talent and ignore the controversy that he or she creates.

3. *Stereotypes of outgroups* begin to occur that paint all within the group as having desirable and superior qualities and those outside the group (particularly those

perceived as oppositional to the group) as having undesirable qualities.

4. Such stereotypes feed into the *belief in the inherent morality of the group*, wherein the group and its members are morally correct. For instance, the Dallas Cowboys are often called "America's Team," and this moniker may bring with it beliefs in the inherent superiority of the team and its management.

5. If people in the group disagree with the decision, a process begins to *place direct pressure on dissenters* so that comments that are perceived as critical are suppressed. There are likely people on a team who have reservations about acquiring a lightning rod–type player, but their thoughts are suppressed directly or indirectly.

6. This pressure will cause other group members to engage in *self-censorship* and not voice their own misgivings about the emerging decision.

7. Because multiple members are engaging in self-censorship, an *illusion of unanimity* emerges, and it appears that nobody in the group has misgivings about the decision (although multiple members do).

8. Finally, groups operating under groupthink have *self-appointed mind guards* who shield group members from controversial information coming from outside the group and who also suppress dissent within the group.

Given that bad decisions can occur under desirable circumstances (such as cohesion and strong leadership) as a result of groupthink, it is Robert Zajonc (1965) with his discovery that being in the presence of others will cause performance to increase only if the task being performed is either easy or well-learned (what he called a dominant response) (Weber & Hertel, 2007). If the task is not easy and/or is unfamiliar, being in the presence of others will impair performance compared with if one is working alone.

In an interesting test of this hypothesis, researchers surreptitiously watched bar patrons playing billiards. They watched long enough to detect whether players were skilled (they made at least two-thirds of their shots) or not skilled (they missed at least two-thirds of their shots). After making this determination, one of the researchers moved closer to the billiard table and made it obvious that they were watching the player. A second researcher then recorded what percentage of shots the player made. Those who had been initially identified as skilled increased their shot percentage on average from 71 percent to 80 percent; those who were unskilled decreased their shot percentage on average from 36 percent to 25 percent (Michaels, Blommel, Brocato, Linkous, & Rowe, 1982).

Social Loafing

Latané, Williams, and Harkins (1979) coined the phrase **social loafing** to describe circumstances in which people perform some group tasks with less effort than when they were performing the same task alone. The researchers had participants, as individuals, clap their hands and shout as loud as they could and measured the loudness of the noise using a decibel reader. These individuals were then put into differently sized groups and were asked to, within their group, clap their hands and shout as loud as they could. The amount of noise produced per person shrank more and more as group sizes increased. Social loafing is more possible in a group, however, when that group is performing particular tasks (such as additive tasks, described in Steiner's Typology of Tasks later in this chapter), which is important for group leaders to take active steps to help prevent groupthink. Such steps are relatively easy to enact. For example, group cohesion differs from group conformity, so steps can be taken to reduce conformity without having an impact on cohesion. A cohesive group can set up systems to allow and foster dissent,

worries, and doubts among members. The strong leader can intentionally not state his or her personal opinion on the topic. The leader can go further by creating a norm that would require formalizing pros and cons of every option, including the appointment of a "devil's advocate."

▸ Group Productivity

As a sport management student, you have likely been involved in group projects in some of your courses. Faculty members hypothesize that you will likely work in teams in a professional environment, so it is a good idea to get experience in the classroom doing similar work. As you have probably learned, being in a group environment sometimes causes individuals to work more, but sometimes they work less. The social aspect of group work can be both a deterrent and a boon to productivity.

Social Facilitation

Being in a group can lead people to work harder. With **social facilitation** present, groups can provide support and encouragement to members who enable productivity. A long history of research has found that, compared with working alone, people perform a number of tasks better when in the presence of others. Triplett (1898) found that people will ride a bicycle faster when they are racing others than when they are timed. Other early studies confirmed this finding, but contradictory findings began to emerge as well. Under some circumstances, being in the presence of others would impair performance (e.g., Allport, 1920; Burwitz & Newell, 1972). These contradictions were resolved by Robert Zajonc (1965) with his discovery that being in the presence of others will cause performance to increase only if the task that is being done is either easy or well-learned (what he called a dominant response) (Weber & Hertel, 2007).

If the task is not easy and/or is unfamiliar, being in the presence of others will impair performance compared with if one is working alone.

In an interesting test of this hypothesis, researchers surreptitiously watched bar patrons playing billiards. They watched long enough to detect if players were skilled (they made at least 2/3 of their shots) or not skilled (they missed at least 2/3 of their shots). After making this determination, one of the researchers moved closer to the billiard table and made it obvious that they were watching the player. A second researcher then recorded what percent of shots the player made. Those who had been initially identified as skilled increased their shot percentage on average from 71% to 80% and those who were unskilled decreased their shot percentage on average from 36% to 25% (Michaels, Blommel, Brocato, Linkous, & Rowe, 1982).

Group Size

There are other critical group dynamics that a leader must manage to maximize the productivity of the team once the decision to use teams has been made, such as the size of the group. Generally, smaller groups perform better compared to larger groups (Liden, Wayne, Jaworski, & Bennett, 2004), though more recent research shows these performance differences might be related to the amount of perceived social support, which, ironically, dissipates with larger groups (Mueller, 2012). Being in a group adds complexity to all things people do, and those leading groups must take these dynamics into consideration. The leader of a group sets the tone and structure of how a group will operate. The decisions he or she makes can either help the group to be successful or hamper its functioning and performance, particularly in terms of group decision making and group productivity.

Working in a group adds complexity to all things people do, and those leading groups must consider these dynamics.

© Action Sports Photography/Shutterstock

Given that several of these well-established (and very preventable) group dynamics can completely derail the effectiveness of a group, team leaders need to pay particular attention to each of them. It is also important to keep in mind that the terms *team* and *group* are often used interchangeably (incorrectly). Although every team is a group, not every group is a team. Teams have a level of interdependence (Salas, Dickinson, Converse, & Tannenbaum, 1992) that is not a quality of every group. Therefore, the group dynamics discussed apply to teams, but there are a number of factors unique to teams and to team leadership in particular.

▶ Are Teams Always Better?

How tasks are structured can have a big impact on how well (or poorly) the group functions. One of the most useful ways of looking at the impact of the nature of tasks on productivity is with Steiner's Typology of Tasks (Steiner, 1972). In his typology, Steiner outlines the tasks that are better suited for groups and those better suited for individuals. The first way to think about tasks is to determine whether they are divisible (i.e., the task can be broken up into distinct parts) or unitary (i.e., there is no way to break the task into parts). Generally, Steiner says, groups tend to do better with divisible tasks. Whether groups are superior to individuals with unitary tasks depends on a secondary **task typology**.

- *Additive tasks* are those in which the group performance is summed, as in a tug-of-war rope-pulling competition. Additive tasks are more subject to shirking of duties (see social loafing), particularly if individual efforts are not tracked.
- *Disjunctive tasks* are those in which the end product is a function of the best score of an individual member. In this type of task, for example, a group might be given a word puzzle to solve and the group would choose to present the answer proposed by their best problem solver. In sport, whoever comes up with the best promotion idea for a theme night would represent the group's "best score."
- *Conjunctive tasks* are those in which the end product is a function of the worst performer in the group (the weakest link). For example, a mountain-climbing team roped together is limited in its speed by its slowest member.
- *Compensatory tasks* are those tasks that use a mathematical averaging of all group members in order to produce the group's end product. For instance, team members may participate in the interviews and ratings of new applicants to the team. The ratings of all team members would be averaged to determine the new team member.
- *Discretionary tasks* are those in which it is up to the group to decide how individual efforts are combined to create a final product. The group has full autonomy to design the task any way they wish.

Therefore, discretionary tasks are a natural fit for teams, but a leader needs to consider the appropriateness of teams for other types of tasks.

▶ Historical Grounding of Team Leadership

Although teams have been used within organizations for as long as there have been organizations, a more concerted focus on team leadership has only emerged in the last several decades. In one of the earliest treatments of team leadership, McGrath (1962) laid out a core that has become a central element of most current models of team leadership: There is a boundary-spanning balance between internal team functions and external environmental monitoring/action. More specifically, team leaders engage in internal diagnostic functions as well as external monitoring functions. Team leaders not only compare team performance with accepted standards but also engage in forecasting to assess the potential effects of external conditions on the team. Based on this monitoring, team leaders must also make decisions about whether taking action is necessary. For instance, team leaders may need to make changes to team composition if the team is not performing at acceptable levels or may need to steer the team in a different direction to avert the negative effects of a volatile external environment.

These functions can be seen clearly in all professional sport leagues nearly every year as teams retool in response to trades, retirements, injuries, and other changes that are foreseen and unforeseen. The Miami Heat is a perfect example of a team that has gone through several roster changes, building around the centerpiece of Dwyane Wade in the hope of bringing a championship to Miami. However, it was not until it became clear that LeBron James was looking to leave Cleveland that the owners of the Heat pulled together the block-buster deal that brought James and Chris Bosh to South Beach. They followed the approach that had worked so well for the Boston Celtics when the Celtics acquired Ray Allen (who later also went to the Heat) and Kevin Garnett to create the first Big Three, including Paul Pierce. In both cases, the owners of the teams saw internal weaknesses and external opportunities and built truly high- performing teams.

In a similar vein, Hackman and Walton (1986) described team leaders as monitors of and actors within a larger social system. They outlined the knowledge and skills needed by team leaders to manage teams most effectively. Specifically, team leaders must have basic knowledge of team processes, data-gathering skills, and diagnostic skills. Team leaders also need to have knowledge of change processes, negotiation skills, decision-making skills, and creativity to take appropriate action within the team.

Komaki, Desselles, and Bowman (1989) used a behavioral approach to study sailing team leaders. The researchers outlined the monitoring, feedback, and team coordination behaviors necessary to maintain team performance. In a related approach, Zenger, Musselwhite, Hurson, and Perrin (1994) found that team leaders must engage in internal team-building functions such as building trust, inspiring teamwork, making the most of team differences, and creating a team identity. If you read the case study for the chapter, it is easy to see that the Boston Red Sox had little team identity or inspiration to work with one another. This is a far cry from the Francona-led 2004 team that was flush with camaraderie and dubbed itself the "Idiots." Team leaders also need to support team decisions, expand team capabilities, and foresee and influence change.

Consistent with early leadership studies, Kozlowski, Gully, McHugh, Salas, and Cannon-Bowers (1996) found that decision-making team leaders serve two primary roles: Developmental and task-contingent. The developmental role consists of behaviors such as defining social structure, coaching, and creating a cohesive whole. Head coaches serve these functions

when they select their assistant coaches and team captains. If all those people are not on the same page, the team will not gel. The task-contingent role consists of behaviors such as goal setting, monitoring, providing feedback, and taking action to get the team back on track. Again, the assistant coaches are the network that the head coach manages to achieve the task of winning games. A meta-analysis by Burke et al. (2006) demonstrated that person-oriented team leader behaviors, especially empowerment, were the best predictors of perceived team effectiveness and actual team productivity. Boundary-spanning behaviors, a key function that team leaders serve to keep the team connected to and aware of the rest of the organization, were strongly connected to team effectiveness perceptions. Given that team leadership is an inherently social process, the conditions for team effectiveness need to be understood.

▶ Conditions for Team Effectiveness

Team leaders are particularly instrumental in establishing certain conditions for **team effectiveness** (Hackman & Walton, 1986). Hackman (2002) elaborated on these, emphasizing they are really necessary preconditions for teams to thrive and that team leaders play an integral role in developing and maintaining them. The five conditions also emphasize the complexity of team leadership as well as the balance among internal functions, external functions, and the boundary spanning necessary for the team to flourish. The sport organizations that foster these conditions create the context for management, as well as their teams, to thrive. These conditions could very well be the difference between good leadership and great leadership. These five conditions are being a real team, rather than a team in name only; having a compelling direction; having an enabling structure; maintaining a supportive organizational context; and having expert coaching.

A Real Team

All too often a group of people working on a task is called a team when they really are just a group of people working on a task. In order to be a real team, they first need to have a team task. The task must require a level of interdependence that can allow members to capitalize on the varied skills that the team provides. Hackman (2002) identified co-acting groups, individuals who, although they work together, do not rely upon one another. In creating interest in a new season, members of the ticket and sales staff of a minor league hockey team will perform different mini-tasks that work toward the main task: Selling tickets for the upcoming season. One employee might concentrate on acquiring group sales, one member might concentrate on selling season tickets, and yet another member might concentrate on the sale of luxury suites. The team must also be bounded, in that the membership of the team is clear. Given that team members often have other responsibilities, it is critical for a team leader to clarify roles and membership within the team. The team must also have clearly delimited authority. Teams can be manager-led, self-managing, self-designing, or self-governing, and each type has varying levels of authority. The level of team authority must be specified at its inception. Finally, a real team is stable over time. Dealing with the ongoing arrivals and departures of members can undermine the performance of the team (Hackman, 2002). This can be difficult in minor league sports because many ticketing and sales jobs are entry-level positions and employees are eager to leave for greener pastures.

This can also happen in collegiate sport. As assistant coaches move on to become head coaches, the internal task and relationship-management skills of the team leader are truly tested. Effective team leaders like Nick Saban at the University of Alabama expect their protégés to develop and move on. The head coaches who win on a consistent basis and build dynasties are effective at "reloading" and

carrying on. They have a "system" that makes it easier for new coaches to join the team and to immediately contribute.

Compelling Direction

Decades of research on goal setting have established the importance of specific goals that motivate action (Locke & Latham, 2006). The benefits of a compelling direction are that it energizes, orients, and engages the team. Clear direction also serves as a compass, moral or otherwise, to orient the team members for the task at hand. This direction also engages every member of the team to play the role for which they were chosen. It helps to orchestrate the players who need to take the lead at certain points and those who need to wait for their turn in the process. Phil Jackson, called the "Zen Master," brought this clarity of focus to both the Chicago Bulls and the Los Angeles Lakers, resulting in multiple NBA championships for both teams.

Enabling Structure

Managers or leaders composing teams can make three big mistaken assumptions: Assuming bigger is better, that similarity facilitates team process, and that everyone knows how to work as a team member (Hackman, 2002). Although the size of the team is a function of the complexity of the task, Steiner (1972) demonstrated that productivity does not improve in a linear fashion as group size increases, but rather levels off in predictable ways. For instance, as group size grows, social loafing becomes more likely. Similarly, as group size increases, process losses (coordination challenges, individual motivational decrements) increase. There is no optimal size for groups, but Hackman's research suggests that four- to six-member teams are sufficient for many tasks.

When managers compose teams with the first priority that members get along well together, the homogeneity that often results can doom those teams to mediocrity. Task-focused conflict can actually lead to more creative and improved decisions compared with homogeneous (similar characteristics) groups. Team composition needs to be a balance between too many similarities and too many differences (Hackman, 2002). The third element of an enabling structure involves interpersonal skills, because some people lack the basic skills to be effective team members. There are times to challenge others and times to cooperate, and team members who do too much of either bring down the team. High-profile athletes (e.g., Terrell Owens) can bring their talents to a team, but they often bring a level of dysfunction along with them. When the team cannot manage the dysfunction, the team ultimately fails.

Supportive Organizational Context

The environment in which teams operate can support or undermine the work of the team, and this all starts with reward systems. Most organizations have established human resources systems that typically reward individual performance. To optimize team performance, the reward system needs to provide *reinforcement* (not just rewards) that is contingent upon effective *team* performance. Rewards are viewed as valuable by the provider but not necessarily by the receiver, whereas reinforcement is something that will increase the likelihood of the desired behavior. Reinforcement, therefore, is contingent upon engaging in the behavior that makes the team more successful, and is provided in a timely manner. In other words, it is usually not a weekly paycheck. Player contracts with bonuses for postseason performance can achieve the right level of reinforcement.

Information systems must provide the information needed to the people who need it when they need it. Information is power, and restricting it can hinder the performance of teams. Furthermore, an education system must provide the technical and group-process training that is necessary for teams to thrive. The constantly evolving context in which

teams operate makes the timeliness of training absolutely essential as well. Although leaders develop the skills of their employees, leaders need regular training to stay sharp, too.

Expert Coaching

Team leaders also play a critical role in coaching team members. Although similar to coaching a team, expert coaching in this context is separate from what has been discussed previously. The focus is on developing the skill set of the team as well as the resources available to them. One key role of a team coach is to minimize process losses, those "inefficiencies or internal breakdowns" (Hackman, 2002, p. 169) that inhibit the team's performance given its resources and members. Although coaching may be thought of as focusing on interpersonal dynamics, great coaches attend to task performance as well. Coaches motivate effort levels, facilitate appropriate performance strategies, and ensure the sharing of member knowledge and development of their skills. Effective team leaders are also not intimidated by high-performing contributors and embrace their role as the developer of their members.

The team leader is instrumental in establishing and/or maintaining these enabling conditions. Many of the team leader actions that are summarized in the model that follows illustrate the means by which leaders foster an environment within the team, as well as how they manage the external context in which the team must operate.

▶ Hill's Model for Team Leadership

Hill (2012) presents **Hill's model for team leadership**, which integrates many of the components of existing models and research. The model in **FIGURE 10.1** begins with the leadership decisions that must be made, consistent with the work of McGrath (1962). Team leaders

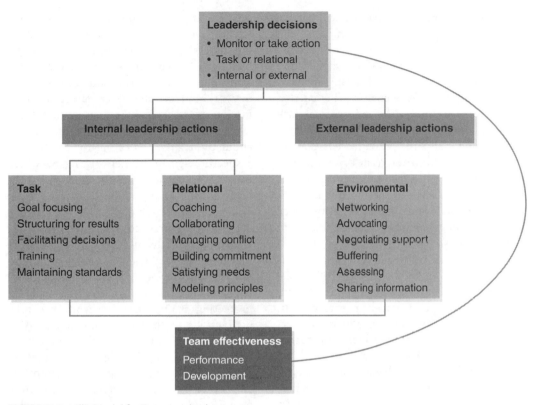

FIGURE 10.1 Hill's Model for Team Leadership.

Reproduced from Hill, S. E. K. (2012). Team leadership. In P.G. Northouse, *Leadership: Theory and Practice* (6th ed., pp. 287-318). Los Angeles: Sage Publications.

must decide whether events within or outside of the team simply need to be monitored or if they require action. If action is required, does the situation call for a task-related or relational intervention? Finally, if action is required, is the focus internal or external? For instance, if team members are not cooperating, the team leader must first decide whether the situation is merely temporary and requires monitoring only or if the team members appear to be embroiled in a long-term debate. If action is required, Hill's model provides several avenues to pinpoint the correct action to take.

Internal Leadership Actions

Hill (2012) broke down internal actions into two categories: Task and relational. The internal task actions include goal focusing, structuring for results, facilitating decisions, training, and maintaining standards. As Hackman and Walton (1986) mentioned, goals must be clear and motivating. A lack of cooperation among team members could be a sign that individual goals rather than team goals have taken precedence and the team leader may need to step in to refocus team members. Sometimes, a reminder of the team's mission may be all that is required. Structuring the team for results is not only a function of having the right number of team members but also of having the right balance of skills for the task(s) at hand. Particularly in sport organizations, an employee's success in some individual area of sport business may not be a clear indication of their potential for team performance. Individual achievers may not have the right skills to put the needs of the team first and for some, no amount of training will change that. Facilitating decisions is another essential task. Training for teams must be seen as ongoing and not simply a means of compensating for deficiencies. Given the changing environment in which teams operate, staying current depends on training. The last internal task action (although this list is not exhaustive) is maintaining standards. Team leaders play an essential role within the team of monitoring and maintaining performance levels. In this sense, the team leader plays the role of manager as well as evaluating team performance and addressing inadequate contributions by team members.

The internal relational leadership actions in Hill's model include coaching, collaborating, managing conflict, building commitment, satisfying needs, and modeling principles. In this model, coaching team members in interpersonal skills is the primary focus, but coaching could involve any number of team-related skills. Collaborating addresses the actions of the leader to involve members in the activities of the team. Managing conflict and power issues include actions to address the conflict that is nearly inevitable in team settings. Building commitment and esprit de corps can be accomplished through a wide variety of tactics, including formal recognition events or simple get-togethers. Satisfying individual member needs is something that often is forgotten in a team setting. Although the team and its goals are the primary focus, an effective team leader does not forget that the team is a collective of individuals who need differing levels of support. Modeling ethical and principled practices is also important to maintain perceptions of fairness.

External Leadership Actions

Hill's model also addresses the external leadership actions that are at the heart of the boundary-spanning nature of team leadership and the monitoring function described by McGrath (1962) and others. Networking, advocating, negotiating support, buffering, assessing, and sharing information are included. Networking serves several functions for the team; the alliances built via networking facilitate the gathering of information necessary for the team's functioning as well as the dissemination of information about the team. Advocating for the team is a specific element of networking by which the team leader serves as the defender of the team as well as its public relations officer. Online newsletters, blogs, and other publicity activities (e.g., press conferences) inform key stakeholders of team successes and ensure that the necessary team resources are maintained. Buffering not only entails "taking a hit for the team" on occasion but also includes protecting team members from potential distractions in the environment. Assessing environmental indicators of the team's effectiveness is essential to gauging the success of the team in the eyes of customers, suppliers, and other key stakeholders. For instance, owners and coaches pay attention to ticket sales and luxury box attendance, among other things. Lastly, sharing relevant environmental information involves a filtering process related to buffering. The team leader conveys mission-relevant information while protecting the team from the inevitable noise in the environment. Many a post-event press conference has been conducted by owners or coaches to defuse volatile situations created by internal and external controversies.

Team Effectiveness

The last element of Hill's model is related to the outcomes of the team. In particular, Hill focuses on both performance and development of the team itself. The reason a team exists is to accomplish the task at hand and to improve the "quality of decision making, the ability to implement decisions," (p. 24), with the outcome of teamwork measured by the work completed and the problems solved (Nadler, 1998), Development focuses on the relational side of team outcomes. Ideally, team members should be satisfied with their individual contributions to the team while keeping team goals at the forefront. Feelings of cohesiveness and effectiveness are the focus of the development outcomes of teams.

As we have mentioned before, the environment in which teams operate is constantly evolving and growing increasingly complex. This complexity has been affected by technological advances. Specifically, technology has facilitated the development of geographically dispersed teams that are able to function in a virtual world. Virtual teams, though, create new challenges for team leaders.

▶ Leading Virtual Teams

Managing sport organizations in today's business world will inevitably require connecting team members in multiple regions of the country, if not from multiple countries. Therefore, virtual contact via computers, smartphones, and other technology is simply the way that business gets done. The fact that "**virtual teams** differ from face-to-face teams in terms of coordination, communication, and collaboration" (Malhotra, Majchrzak, & Rosen, 2007, p. 61) has been supported by an extensive body of research (e.g., Bachiochi, Rogelberg, O'Connor, & Elder, 2000; Fiol & O'Connor, 2005; Kirkman, Rosen, Gibson, Tesluk, & McPherson, 2002; Saunders, Van Slyke, & Vogel, 2004). The reliance on communication technology to conduct the team's business changes nearly all of the team leader actions summarized previously in this chapter, some in minor ways and others rather fundamentally. Establishing team norms, managing work, networking, and more team functions are affected by moving the team to a virtual setting. Malhotra et al. (2007) outline six practices of effective virtual team leaders.

Effective virtual team leaders "establish and maintain trust through the use of communication technology" (Malhotra et al., 2007, p. 62). This is accomplished by setting norms for information sharing, having virtual get-togethers to reinforce those norms, and communicating progress via the virtual workspace. Effective team leaders also ensure that the suffering (early starts for videoconferences, late calls with clients) of the geographically dispersed is evenly distributed across the team. Effective team leaders also "ensure diversity in the team is understood, appreciated, and leveraged" (p. 62). This requires the maintenance of an online directory of the prominent team expertise and skills, rotation of team members, and the use of online discussion threads to promote expression of diverse opinions.

Effective virtual team leaders also manage the virtual work cycle and meetings. Brainstorming and disagreements can happen *among* meetings via asynchronous discussion threads, but idea convergence and conflict resolution occur *during* virtual meetings. The virtual nature of meetings also affects some basic meeting processes. The start of virtual meetings should be used for relationship building, and during the meetings, the leader should check in with everyone to ensure that they are engaged in the discussion. At the end of the meeting, the minutes and future plans need to be posted at a common accessible online site. The virtual team leader should also monitor team progress through the use of technology. This involves scrutiny of electronic discussion threads and the use of balanced scorecard measures posted in the team's virtual workspace.

The effective team leader must also "enhance external visibility of the team and its members" (Malhotra et al., 2007, p. 62) by reporting to a virtual steering committee of the bosses of team members. Finally, team leaders need to "ensure individuals benefit from participating in virtual teams" (p. 62) by holding virtual reward ceremonies, providing individual recognition at the start of virtual meetings, and ensuring that team members' bosses are aware of these achievements as well.

▶ Summary

Work in teams continues to evolve and, as such, the work of team leaders also continues to evolve. Effective team leaders need to optimize a combination of task-management and people-management skills because there is no one-size-fits-all approach to leading teams to their potential. The type of organization, the type of task(s), and the people involved all have an impact on the approach

taken by a leader. Leaders must be wary of the tenets of groupthink, social loafing, and the size of groups. Steiner's Typology of Tasks serves as an important reference to decide whether a team is needed to perform a task or an individual working on a task would suffice. Once a team has been formed, Hackman's five preconditions for team success can help leaders start the team process with a good chance at achieving the desired results. Finally, Hill's model for team leadership equips the leader with a roadmap to know which internal and external actions to take to enhance team effectiveness. Taken together, Steiner's, Hackman's, and Hill's suggestions can help teams achieve success, whether it is in the ticket office for a minor league hockey team or in the classroom of your sport finance class.

LEADERSHIP PERSPECTIVE

Mark "Garvey" Candella

Mark "Garvey" Candella is the director of strategic partnerships in the world's biggest streaming platform, Twitch. He started in the eSports industry in 1993 as a professional Magic: The Gathering player. Garvey leads the Twitch student program and has dedicated himself to creating gaming and eSports opportunities for students and universities around the world.

Q: What is your role/responsibilities and how long have you been with Twitch?
My role at Twitch is Director of Strategic Partnerships and I have worked there since February of 2014. My main responsibility is to know the industry I serve in a holistic fashion. With a deep knowledge of the mechanics of the industry, I strive to put long-term projects together that serve the industry as a whole. It's very much "the rising tide raises all ships" mindset that resonates deeply with me.

Q: Do members of your team ever work in small/large groups to accomplish tasks? Do you ever encounter problems with groups not getting along or not working together?

My team works in both small and large groups as appropriate to accomplish project goals. There have not been any problems as I ensure that everyone understands the vision of the project and understands what part they play in it and how it fits into the bigger picture. By ensuring buy-in for the vision and combining it with the understanding of how each individual contributes to the expected result, everyone then works together happily in accomplishing the end goal. At Twitch, one of our core values is shared vision over coordination. To quote our CEO, Emmett Shear:

The enemy of speed is coordination. Waiting to coordinate with even one person or group results in a significant slowdown. Waiting to coordinate with multiple others can make even the most productive person or team grind to a halt. Be ruthless in pruning coordination. Every dependency you eliminate will improve your life indefinitely thereafter.

On the flip side, the enemy of good decision making is ignorance. Making a decision in ignorance of the knowledge of others in the company is a good way to make the same mistakes over and over and a good way to miss opportunities.

Instead of coordinating to fix that problem, establish a shared vision of the future. For your team, you establish a shared vision by communicating clearly where you're going and how you're getting there. For other teams, if you don't understand where they're going, let them know that.

Q: How do you encourage the involvement of your team in decision making that affects the organization?

To begin with, it is very important to me that the team understands every aspect of a program or project. Active discussions based on a team member's subject matter expertise is then encouraged to iterate on certain aspects in which he or she would be engaged. It is also important to empower each individual by slowly expanding his or her comfort zone until he or she is confident in running his or her part fully. My job should then be to mentor, remove barriers and blockers, identify synergy, and reduce overlap to build efficiency and accelerate momentum. I avoid alienation by ensuring that everyone knows how his or her contribution fits into the larger picture of the program and stress that each contribution, whether large or small, is equally important. The way that I verbalize this is to liken a program to a fine Swiss timepiece—no matter how small or large a cog seems, if you remove one cog, the timepiece as a whole will not work. I will close with asking if any cog is not as important as another no matter the perceived size.

Another method that I use is to have my people listen in on my external meetings. I then schedule time to ask if they understood why I presented the vision and information as I did and why I used certain examples. I then ask them to present to me as they might have using their own examples and close with their explaining how they might have approached it differently. Active listening is the surest way to build confidence that their voice is being heard and their contributions being respected.

Q: Sport management students are often asked to work in groups to complete assignments. Why do you think the ability to work in groups is such an important skill for the professional workplace in sport?

Working in groups is an important skill for any endeavor. A well put-together group will have the ability to minimize weaknesses and maximize strengths while having access to different skillsets and mindsets. Working in groups is also important as it grows the soft skills needed to work with others. Good communication, identification of both individual strengths and weaknesses to complement one another, active listening, and a host of other skills are honed in this way and allow them to show by example the value of these skills to the team or individual athlete with whom they work.

It is important for there to be a leader who structures discussions, coordinates efforts, and owns the project and vision though. Too many chefs spoil the broth is real and can cause undue stress and inefficiency and having a team lead solves this issue.

(continues)

LEADERSHIP PERSPECTIVE (*continued*)

Q: How do you encourage group members to be honest and suggest ideas that might put them at odds with other people they work with and organization leaders?

I encourage honest and direct feedback from my team to me and only ask that they object with a well thought-out argument and an example of how something could potentially be done differently. Being ok with constructive criticism is essential to being a leader and by working in this fashion, I lead by example and set the tone for team discussions. Part of being a leader involves mediating as well to come to a resolution of disagreements. It is important to explain why something is decided upon when mediating, again, to have buy-in from all parties in the vision of each execution.

Q: Have you ever seen a situation in which individual goals of group members take precedence over the group's collective goal or power dynamics derailed a group project? If so, what happened?

The core value of shared vision over collaboration creates a culture in which everyone is working toward the same goal and each contribution is acknowledged as valuable. By wholeheartedly believing in this philosophy it becomes easy to set the bar in which the group's goals inherently come first. It is not bad to have individual goals but when people have buy-in, they are all working together toward something they believe in. Working in this fashion has eliminated the power dynamics that is found elsewhere and has led to more and more people leading in this fashion.

▶ Key Terms

Groupthink

Hill's model for team
   leadership

Social facilitation

Social loafing

Task typology

Team effectiveness

Virtual teams

▶ Discussion Questions

1. How would you describe team effectiveness for the front office staff of a Major League baseball team? Which conditions are necessary to achieve team effectiveness?

2. Have you seen evidence of groupthink in group projects you have worked on in a class? Cite a specific example. Using the tenets of groupthink mentioned in the chapter, which characteristics of groupthink were most prevalent in the example you cited?

3. Using Hackman's five conditions for team effectiveness, suggest which conditions are crucial for a "street team" of marketers that has been organized to come up with a marketing campaign for a new WNBA team moving to Austin, Texas.

4. The authors suggest the growing prominence of virtual teams. What methods, in general, can a leader use to make virtual teams succeed when half of the team works in New York and the other half works in Hong Kong?

5. Looking at Hill's model and internal leadership actions, specifically, which task or relational actions seem most important when a general manager has six employees working in his or her box office and three of them are fresh out of college?

▶ References

Abraham, P. (2012, October 3). Bobby Valentine says Red Sox coaches were disloyal. Retrieved from http://www.boston.com/sports/2012/10/03/bobby-valentine-says-red-sox-coaches-were-disloyal/s4Fbb3ETulUojnKlqA7QMP/story.html

Allport, F. H. (1920). The influence of the group upon association and thought. *Journal of Experimental Psychology, 3*, 159–182.

Associated Press. (2012, August 26). Adrian Gonzalez 'excited' for Dodgers. Retrieved from http://espn.go.com/mlb/story/_/id/8302934/josh-beckett-adrian-gonzalez-packed-gone-boston-red-sox-dodgers-blockbuster-trade-looms

Bachiochi, P. D., Rogelberg, S. G., O'Connor, M. S., & Elder, A. E. (2000). The qualities of an effective team leader. *Organizational Development Journal, 18*(1), 11–27.

Bonebright, D.A. (2010). 40 years of storming: A historical review of Tuckman's model of small group development. *Human Resource Development International, 13*(1), 111–120.

Buffee, N. (2017, March 28). What's wrong with Team Liquid? Retrieved from https://www.youtube.com/watch?v=Wkfh388qoBM.

Burke, C. S., Stagl, K. C., Klein, C., Goodwin, G. F., Salas, E., & Halpin, S. M. (2006). What type of leadership behaviors are functional in teams? A meta-analysis. *Leadership Quarterly, 17*(3), 288–307.

Burwitz, L., & Newell, K. M. (1972). The effects of the mere presence of cofactors on learning a motor skill. *Journal of Motor Behavior, 4*, 99–102.

Edes, G. (2012, July 16). Bobby V puts onus on Kevin Youkilis. Retrieved from http://espn.go.com/boston/mlb/story/_/id/8168192/boston-red-sox-bobby-valentine-blames-kevin-youkilis-poor-relationship

Erzberger, T. (2017, March 16). DoubleLift: "There are three pretty big problems [for Team Liquid]." Retrieved from http://www.cspn.com/csports/story/_/id/18929039/there-three-pretty-big-problems-[for-team-liquid].

Fiol, C. M., & O'Connor, E. J. (2005). Identification to face-to-face, hybrid, and pure virtual teams: Untangling the contradictions. *Organization Science, 16*(1), 19–32.

Fraser, C. (1971). Group risk-taking and group polarization. *European Journal of Social Psychology, 1*, 493–510.

Gersick, C. (1988). Time and transition in work teams: Toward a new model of group development. *Academy of Management Journal, 31*, 9–41.

Hackman, J. R. (2002). *Leading teams: Setting the stage for great performances*. Boston, MA: Harvard Business School.

Hackman, J. R., & Walton, R. E. (1986). Leading groups in organizations. In P. S. Goodman (Ed.), *Designing effective work groups* (pp. 72–119). San Francisco, CA: Jossey-Bass.

Hamilton, J. (2013, June). The Darko ages: How magical thinking and racism produced the NBA's most notorious draft bust. *Slate.com.* Retrieved from http://www.slate.com/articles/sports/sports_nut/2013/06/darko_milicic_draft_how_magical_thinking_and_racism_produced_the_nba_s_most.html

Harrison, I. (2012, September 15). Bobby V: Weakest roster in September. Retrieved from http://espn.go.com/boston/mlb/story/_/id/8379248/weakest-roster-red-sox-history-bobby-valentine

Hill, S. E. K. (2012). Team leadership. In P. G. Northouse (Ed.), *Leadership: Theory and practice* (6th ed., pp. 287–318). Thousand Oaks, CA: Sage.

Janis, I. I. (1972). *Victims of groupthink.* Boston, MA: Houghton-Mifflin.

Johnson, D. W., & Johnson, F. P. (2017). *Joining together: Group theory and group skills* (12th ed.). New York: Pearson.

Kerr, N. L., & Tindale, R. S. (2004). Group performance and decision making. *Annual Review of Psychology, 55*, 623–655.

Kerr, N. L., & Tindale, R. S. (2011). Group-based forecasting: A social psychological analysis. *International Journal of Forecasting, 27*, 14–40.

Kirkman, B. L., Rosen, B., Gibson, C. B., Tesluk, P. E., & McPherson, S. O. (2002). Five challenges to virtual team success. *Academy of Management Executive, 16*(3), 67–79.

Komaki, J. L., Desselles, M. L., & Bowman, E. D. (1989). Definitely not a breeze: Extending an operant model of effective supervision to teams. *Journal of Applied Psychology, 74*, 522–529.

Kozlowski, S. W., Gully, S. M., McHugh, P. P., Salas, E., & Cannon-Bowers, J. A. (1996). A dynamic theory of leadership and team effectiveness: Developmental and task contingent leader roles. In G. R. Ferris (Ed.), *Research in personnel and human resources management* (Vol. 14, pp. 253–305). Greenwich, CT: JAI Press.

Larson, J. R. (2010). *In search of synergy in small group performance*. New York: Psychology Press.

Latané, B., Williams, K., & Harkins, S. (1979). Many hands make light the work: The causes and consequences of social loafing. *Journal of Personality and Social Psychology, 37*, 822–832.

Liden, R. C., Wayne, S. J., Jaworski, R. A., & Bennett, N. (2004). Social loafing: A field investigation. *Journal of Management, 30*(2), 285–304.

Lilly, D.J. (2017, July 26). What the hell is Team Liquid Doing? Retrieved from https://mmoexaminer.com/hell-team-liquid/.

Locke, E. A., & Latham, G. P. (2006). New directions in goal-setting theory. *Current Directions in Psychological Science, 15*(5), 265–268.

Malhotra, A., Majchrzak, A., & Rosen, B. (2007). Leading virtual teams. *Academy of Management Perspectives, 21*, 60–70.

McDonald, J. (2012, June 22). David Ortiz tired of negative reports. Retrieved from http://espn.go.com/boston/mlb/story/_/id/8082136/david-ortiz-fed-reports-turmoil-boston-red-sox-clubhouse

McGrath, J. E. (1962). *Leadership behavior: Some requirements for leadership training.* Washington, DC: U.S. Civil Service Commission, Office of Career Development.

Michaels, J. W., Blommel, J. M., Brocato, R. M., Linkous, R. A., & Rowe, J. S. (1982). Social facilitation and inhibition in a natural setting. *Replications in Social Psychology, 2*, 21–24.

Miller, D. (2003). The stages of group development: A retrospective study of dynamic team processes. *Canadian Journal of Administrative Sciences, 20*, 121–143.

Mueller, J. S. (2012). Why individuals in larger teams perform worse. *Organizational Behavior and Human Decision Processes, 117*, 111–124.

Murnighan, J. (1981). Group decision making: What strategies should you use? *Management Review, 25*, 56–62.

Nadler, D. A. (1998). Executive team effectiveness: Teamwork at the top. In D. A. Nadler & J. L. Spencer (Eds.), *Executive teams* (pp. 21–39). San Francisco, CA: Jossey-Bass.

Salas, E., Dickinson, T. L., Converse, S. A., & Tannenbaum, S. I. (1992). Toward an understanding of team performance and training. In R. W. Sweeney & E. Salas (Eds.), *Teams: Their training and performance* (pp. 3–29). Norwood, NJ: ABLEX.

Saunders, C., Van Slyke, C., & Vogel, D. (2004). My time or yours? Managing time visions in global virtual teams. *Academy of Management Executive, 18*(1), 19–31.

Silvia, S., & Neslin, L. (2012, September 11). How the 2012 Red Sox unraveled. Retrieved from http://www.bostonglobe.com/sports/2012/09/11/how-red-sox-unraveled/sX2wPnh3Pt4uB0pKuTesoN/story.html

Steiner, I. (1972). *Group process and productivity.* New York: Academic Press.

Triplett, N. (1898). The dynamogenic factors in pace-making and competition. *American Journal of Psychology, 9*, 507–533.

Tuckman, B. (1965). Developmental sequence in small groups. *Psychological Bulletin, 63*(6), 384–399.

Tuckman, B. & Jensen, M (1977). Stages of small group development revisited. *Group and Organizational Studies, 2*(4), 419–427.

Wagner, J. A. (1994). Participation effects on performance and satisfaction: A reconsideration of research evidence. *Academy of Management Review, 19*, 312–330.

Weber, B., & Hertel, G. (2007). Motivational gains of inferior group members: A meta-analytic review. *Journal of Personality and Social Psychology, 93*, 973–993.

Zaccaro, S. J., Rittman, A. L., & Marks, M. A. (2001). Team leadership. *Leadership Quarterly, 12*, 451–483.

Zajonc, R. B. (1965). Social facilitation. *Science, 149*, 269–274.

Zenger, J., Musselwhite, E., Hurson, K., & Perrin, C. (1994). *Leading teams: Mastering the new role.* Homewood, IL: Business One Irwin.

CHAPTER 11

Shepherding Sport for Development Organizations

Jennifer (Bruening) McGarry
Nadia Moreno
Brooke Page Rosenbauer

CHAPTER OBJECTIVES

- Recognize how Sport for Development and Peace (SDP) programs can use sport to bring people together across gender, ethnicity, religion, ability, and/or political system.
- Demonstrate understanding of using a critical lens to examine the leadership and evaluation of SDP organizations.
- Describe the various classifications of SDP programs.
- Demonstrate an understanding of SDP programs based on category, acknowledging possible overlapping goals.
- Describe the key skills for leaders of SDP programs.
- Demonstrate an understanding of the importance of program quality, monitoring, and evaluation of SDP programs.

CASE STUDY

When a Grassroots Revolution and the Private Sector Unite: Reebok's BOKS Initiative

After 17 years in the corporate real estate world, Kathleen Tullie experienced a shocking cancer scare and a rude awakening that she needed to change her life. She quit her job and decided to be a stay-at-home mom, determined to spend more time with her two young children. Within weeks, Tullie felt restless. She tried to start a number of small businesses, including selling gluten-free banana bread, with little success.

(continues)

CASE STUDY (continued)

After reading the book *Spark*, by Harvard psychiatry professor Dr. John Ratey, she felt a deep sense of purpose to do something great for her kids—and the world. Dr. Ratey's work focuses on the impact that exercise has on the brain and how it can mitigate or even prevent the burden of conditions such as depression, anxiety, and attention deficit hyperactivity disorder (ADHD). Exercise is even more important for the developing brains of children. For a growing mind and body, movement is a powerful medicine. One thing about today's society is crystal clear and unmistakably tragic: Children are sitting more and moving less. Along with rising trends in obesity, children are experiencing more anxiety, depression, and mental illness than ever and sedentary behavior is to blame.

With her *Spark* book in hand, Tullie could not sit still. Wielding a whistle, she started playing games and running soccer drills with her own kids at the bus stop in her suburban Massachusetts town. Friends and other children started to join. The demand for this exercise outlet grew quickly and, before she knew it, she was running a before-school physical activity program at her school, With the help of two other moms, she created a curriculum, formed a non-profit called Fit Kidz Get Up and Go, raised some local funding, and launched the program in all five elementary schools in the district. "Word of mom" started to spread through the surrounding towns and a fitness revolution was born.

The program, which includes 45 minutes of running, games, and functional fitness (such as squats, push-ups, and burpees) is simple in concept: Let kids get the wiggles out before school so that they are more ready to learn. The power of this model, however, lies in the universal appeal and adaptability. Anybody can pick up the curriculum and run the program. Any kid can participate. The "trainers" need zero sports coaching background, just a positive attitude and enthusiasm for getting kids moving, and the kids need zero sports skills or experience. In fact, children who despise organized sports actually love BOKS because it is simply about getting exercise and movement through fun games. Through these games, the program has a proven and significant impact on a child's mind and body, measured by BMI, body fat percentage, cardiovascular fitness, school engagement, positive affect, and energy/vitality (Whooten 2018; Westcott, et al., 2015).

Tullie's grassroots fitness revolution turned a sharp corner on one fateful Friday afternoon when she showed up at the Reebok International Headquarters in Massachusetts. With a simple PowerPoint and a Flip Video camera full of rough videos of the program, she was given 10 minutes to speak to Reebok's President and ask for some T-shirts. Hours later, after an intense discussion of two visionaries sharing their dreams for a better, healthier world, Tullie walked away with an offer to take her program "in-house," with substantial funding and corporate backing.

At first contemplation, she was inclined to politely refuse the offer, afraid of selling out and losing the grassroots momentum. Upon further consideration, Tullie decided to go for it and see what they could accomplish together.

From five Massachusetts schools in 2010 to now 3,000 schools across the globe, the program was renamed Build Our Kids' Success (BOKS) and has now become the flagship initiative of the Reebok Foundation, whose mission is to close the "fitness gap" and bring more fitness access and inspiration to disadvantaged women and children. Any parent or community volunteer can download the free materials to run the BOKS program and complete online or in-person training modules. In addition to these strong powerful networks of passionate individuals, Reebok was joined by other companies and Foundations such as Toyota, Blue Cross Blue Shield, and The Boston Foundation, which have pitched in to support the growth of BOKS in urban school districts through funding for trainers and equipment.

As obesity and mental illness continue to seep through the corners of the globe, the demand for BOKS is limitless. Some similar programs exist, but many are exclusive based on gender or income level. The challenge now for BOKS is rallying competing companies and organizations behind the greater mission of getting kids to be active and fall in love with movement so they continue healthy habits into adulthood.

Questions for Discussion

1. What are the benefits and drawbacks of promoting fitness as a "sport" rather than an organized sport?
2. How could the trajectory of BOKS have been different if Kathleen Tullie hadn't accepted the offer from Reebok?
3. What are some other potential challenges that Tullie will face by being part of a corporate foundation versus being independent?
4. How could partnerships help the BOKS program expand more quickly to reach all of the children and schools in need?
5. If Reebok funding were to be at risk, how could you measure the impact of the BOKS program to prove its value to Reebok?

▶ Introduction

Sport can play a role in improving the lives of individuals, not only individuals, I might add, but whole communities. I am convinced that the time is right to build on that understanding, to encourage governments, develop agencies and communities to think how sport can be included more systematically in the plans to help children, particularly those living in the midst of poverty, disease and conflict.

—**Kofi Annan** (United Nations, 2002, para. 6)

The statement by the late Kofi Annan, former secretary-general of the United Nations (UN), speaks to the potential of sport to function as a tool for positive social change for individuals and communities. It is critical to note that Annan's use of the word "can" and continue to recognize the possibility of sport, not the inherent nature of sport, to "address a wide range of needs related to: Education, health, social inclusion, youth development, gender equality, peace-building, and sustainable development" (IOC in Schulenkorf, 2017, p. 245). In this chapter, we will highlight **sport for development and peace (SDP)** organizations from around the world to demonstrate how they use sport to bring people together across gender, ethnicity, religion, ability, and/or political system "based

upon opportunities to foster trust, obligations, redistribution and respect for sport" (Jarvie, 2007, p. 422). Ideally, SDP organizations provide deliberate programming in response to the social needs of both individuals and communities. When delivered in this fashion, sport has the capacity to impact individuals through physical, emotional, psychological, and social development while simultaneously playing a role in community development.

The United Nations and its partners, such as national governments, the International Olympic and Paralympic Committees, nongovernmental organizations, and corporations have recognized the value of sport and have come together to think critically and strategically about sport for development and peace. Recently, scholarship on and about sport for development and sport for development organizations has grown significantly, (Sherry, Schulenkorf, & Rowe, 2016) and scholars have urged the global sporting community "to be reflective, proactive and engaged on the topic of social change and human rights as a central area of concern for all stakeholders." (Wolff & Hums, 2017, para 4). As such, we will also highlight the critiques of SDP as exclusionary (Spaaij, Magee, & Jeanes, 2014) and the role of leadership in the current state of SDP (Schulenkorf, 2017; Sherry, Schulenkorf, & Chalip, 2015) as well in its future, in this chapter.

We will focus on the continued emergence of sport for development organizations and the different skills needed by leaders to facilitate the realization of organizational missions (Holmes, Banda, & Chawansky, 2015; Svensson, 2017). As the potential of sport as a developmental tool continues to be understood by a larger audience, we see SDP organizations as possible destinations for graduates of sport management programs. In order to provide more information for these future managers and leaders, we provide a history of sport for development and peace, speak to the power dynamics at work in SDP organizations, and then move on to examine the types of sport for development and peace programs and the roles of leaders in these programs. We conclude by highlighting the elements of quality programs and the role of monitoring and evaluation.

History

The concept of sport for development and peace can trace its origins to the spirit of **Olympism**, which can be defined as:

> . . . [the] philosophy of life, exalting and combing in a balanced whole the qualities of body, will and mind. Blending sport with culture and education, Olympism seeks to create a way of life based on the joy found in effort, the educational value of good example and respect for universal fundamental ethical principles. (International Olympic Committee, 1994, p. 10)

SDP has strong roots in European culture as well. Victorians led the way in understanding that sport was a means by which to learn discipline and develop strong character. Originally, sport was viewed as a luxury or escape from work, but soon it became more organized, institutionalized, and competitive (Coakley & Pike, 2009; Guttman, 1978). Then, as the 1900s

began, working-class citizens around the globe began to ask for safe spaces for recreation as they recognized that sport and physical activity offered positive outcomes for both adults and children beyond what had been thought by previous generations (Ingham & Hardy, 1984). Expanding one's ability to function within a team and exhibit tolerance of others was seen as a desired impact (Darnell, 2012). In contemporary times, sport has grown to be seen as a means to build human agency and social equity, and, as a result, foster a strong and civil society (Harris, 1998).

One prime example of using sport to build human agency and social equity was the work of Sir Ludwig Guttman, a German neurologist, who practiced at Stoke Mandeville Hospital in England. In 1948, while the Olympics took place in London, Guttman hosted the precursor to the Paralympics. The Stoke Mandeville Games provided the opportunity for wheelchair-bound athletes to build strength and self-respect (O'Hare, 2012). The next major addition to SDP occurred when youth development and education, a focus of many SDP programs today, was formalized by the United Nations Educational, Scientific and Cultural Organization (UNESCO) in 1952 (UNESCO, 1952). Soon thereafter, the UN Declaration of the Rights of the Child (United Nations, 1959) stated: ". . . the child shall have full opportunity for play and recreation" (para. 14) and reinforced that society as a whole should support this fundamental right.

More recently, many organizations and policy makers have paved the way for a sport for development and peace approach and, as a result, programs have emerged. Leaders of physical education and sport organizations and government offices worldwide have emphasized the importance of access to sport for all, in particular, women and children. Other stakeholders in SDP who have established a presence in recent years are mega sport organizations. England's Football Association (FA), the National Basketball Association (NBA), and the Fédération Internationale de Football

Association (FIFA) are three prime examples with programs like Just Play, Basketball without Borders, and Football for Hope (Darnell, 2012; Millington, 2010). In addition, transnational organizations such as the International Olympic Committee (IOC) reinforce the spirit of Olympism mentioned earlier in its most current charter, which states that Olympism in action serves to "build a better world" through the development of programs "that provide concrete responses to social inequity" (Darnell, 2012, p. 6).

It is important to note the growth in state and national governments' involvement in SDP policy and programming. Huish (2011) examined the role of the Cuban government in supporting the training of professional coaches across the southern hemisphere as a form of sport-based solidarity. Canada's Ministry of Heritage and its Youth Employment Strategies support the SDP internship program organized by Commonwealth Games Canada (Darnell, 2012). However, the UN has remained the main force behind international SDP efforts. The General Assembly created and passed the World Fit for Children resolution, calling for all (i.e., public and private sectors) to recognize sport and recreational opportunities as a fundamental human right, as well as developing critical thinking skills and increasing overall benefits for participants. Many SDP programs provide open opportunities, thus increasing participation by those often excluded; when leaders facilitate social inclusion with a critical social consciousness, meaning that they are aware of the experiences of marginalized groups and can include individuals from these groups in a positive way, sport for development program cultures have the capacity to build emotional safety and promote personal development (Spaaij, Magee, & Jeanes, 2014). SDP can bring people together to watch, play, learn, and compete through sport or sport-based activities in order to promote interaction and inclusion of individuals. "[S]port is well-positioned to play a role in fostering the inclusion of newcomers by breaking down barriers and encouraging cross-cultural understanding" (Winnipeg Community Sport Policy, 2012, p. 3). While it is true that the explicit social exclusion is less prevalent in sport currently, the ways in which individuals and groups come to sport, or not, have been institutionalized over time (Lake, 2013). In fact, the evolving expectation that sport has in fact become more accessible and equitable in recent years remains "in direct variance with reality" (Spaaij, Magee, & Jeanes, 2014, p. 3). At once, SDP can represent the intentional "use of sport to exert a positive influence on public health, the socialization of children, youths and adults, the social inclusion of the disadvantaged, the economic development of regions and states, and on fostering intercultural exchange and conflict resolution" (Lyras & Welty Peachey, 2011, p. 311). It can extend to larger developmental outcomes beyond those that are simply sport-related (Schulenkorf et al., 2016). However, as a result, SDP leaders need to continue to critically examine the history of the field and how power has become entrenched in practice (Darnell, Chawansky, Marchesseault, Holmes, & Hayhurst, 2016; Harris & Adams, 2016).

Power Dynamics of SDP

Issues of development give cause for further examination. Darnell (2012) states that sport is not a "benign social institution;" rather, sport reflects the power dynamics of the larger society. Some scholars have positioned sport as providing a "level playing field" (Lapchick, 1996) devoid of the inequalities found in other social institutions. However, an understanding of the potentially hegemonic nature of sport is critical in leading SDP organizations and efforts. As such, leaders who develop and advocate for a commitment to analyzing the ways in which power operates within sport demonstrate that the conferring of positive social change implies a power dynamic. The professed need for development, also known as benevolence or stewardship, can, if not intentionally addressed, foster a power relationship. A dynamic can be established in which the providers of the sport program perceive themselves as the helpers and those receiving the program as needing help (Harris & Adams, 2016; Welty Peachey, Musser, Shin, & Cohen, 2017). This provider/receiver relationship can cause more harm than good, if not checked, because providers and receivers do not engage in shared decision-making in which the opinions of both groups are taken into account (Darnell, 2012). With knowledge of the inherent power structure of sport at hand, leaders can better examine SDP scholarship and evaluation. Simultaneously, we must understand that a considerable number of questions focus on outcomes that "reinforce the evangelical claims made by many [SDP programs]" (Adams & Harris, 2014, p. 141), and that evidence exists to indicate that SDP programs have had positive outcomes.

▶ Sport for Development and Peace Programs

At last count, there were more than 800 registered SDP organizations throughout the world (https://www.sportanddev.org/). Although sport for development initiatives vary in size, scope, and focus, all attempt to use sport to promote social change (Darnell, 2012; Welty Peachey & Cohen, 2012). Several authors have attempted to classify SDP programs due to this variance. The United Nations (2003) identified three broad areas of focus for SDP programs: social issues, health and education, and economic development. Then, Levermore (2008) devised seven categories that centered on the developmental outcomes desired by a program: Conflict resolution, cultural understanding, infrastructure development, educational awareness, empowerment of marginalized groups, encouragement of physical activity and health, and driving economic

development. More recently, Richards, et al. (2013) adapted Levermore's seven areas into the following: Sport and Peace, Sport and Social Cohesion, Sport and Livelihoods, Sport and Education, Sport and Disability, Sport and Gender, and Sport and Health. We have attempted to blend these categories, i.e., 1.) conflict resolution/sport and peace, 2.) cultural understanding/ sport and social cohesion, 3.) educational awareness/sport and education, 4.) empowerment marginalized groups/sport and disability/ sport and gender, 5.) encourage sport and physical activity/sport and health, and 6.) drive economic development/ infrastructure development/sport and livelihoods) and provide examples of programs that focus on these approaches. It is challenging to categorize programs, as so many SDP organizations have goals that cut across categories. As such, we categorized the programs according to their main goals or focus.

Conflict Resolution/Sport and Peace

In **conflict resolution** or sport and peace programs, sport is used as a replacement for deviant behaviors or to bring together individuals or groups who typically do not come together. Programs are typically located, as Football 4 Peace, in "areas suffering from high levels of cross-community conflict and various forms of political disorder and social disintegration" (http://www.football4peace.eu/about-us/). Since sport participation is a more socially desirable behavior than conflict (Green, 2008), programs attempt to provide youth with positive activities so as to distract them from delinquency and crime, and/or from spending time with peers who might encourage that type of behavior (Burrows, 2003). Programs also focus on exposure to protective factors such as promoting wellness, social bonding, working with adult mentors, opportunities to be involved and to lead, building social skills, and the use of recognition and positive reinforcement.

(Burrows, 2003; Henley, Schweizer, de Gara, & Vetter, 2007). By encouraging more socially acceptable values and behaviors, programs can address and even prevent youth delinquency and crime (Ewing, et. al., 2002; Green, 2008).

True conflict resolution or sport and peace programs do not have sport skill development as the primary goal. Rather, it is the combination of social and emotional interactions with peers and mentors, as well as the sport experience that characterizes these programs. In designing and managing conflict resolution or sport and peace programs, leaders must understand the context and be sensitive to the experiences and needs of the participants. Van Standifer, the founder and director of Midnight Basketball, studied police reports to find clues as to what would assist in crime reduction during the hours when most crimes occurred—10 p.m. to 2 a.m. and committed almost exclusively by young men ages 17 to 22. He decided, again through his understanding of the youth involved, that basketball would be the most effective tool. He partnered with law enforcement officers for support, local businesses for sponsorship, and political leaders to help provide positive media coverage (http://amblp.com/basketball/history/) to develop educational and employment workshops. Today, there are at least 20 active chapters of Midnight Basketball across the country. And even more cities have borrowed from the general concept of Midnight Basketball. Police calls reporting juvenile crime drop during the summer when basketball courts and other recreation facilities are kept open until 2 a.m. in cities like Norfolk, Virginia; Phoenix, Arizona; and Cincinnati, Ohio (Hartmann & Depro, 2006; Mendel, 2000).

Cultural Understanding/Sport and Social Cohesion

Perhaps the most famous example of cultural understanding or sport and social cohesion and sport is the image of Black Olympians Tommie Smith and John Carlos raising their gloved fists from the medals podium at the 1968 Mexico City Olympics as a symbol of protest against the racial discrimination in the United States. The Olympics have also been a platform to call attention to other social injustices in an effort to promote cultural understanding. Dating back to World War I, boycotts of and suspensions from Olympic Games have provided countries with opportunities to protest wars, military conflicts and invasions, and apartheid (Hums, Wolff, & Mahoney, 2008; Masteralexis, Barr, & Hums, 2011). But beyond individual actors and countries, SDP organizations have also harnessed the power of sport to achieve their objectives. The US State Department sponsors the Global Sport Mentoring Program (GSMP), operated by a team from The Center for Sport, Peace, and Society at the University of Tennessee-Knoxville (https://eca.state.gov/programs-initiatives/sports-diplomacy/global-sports-mentoring-program). The program has used, and continues to use, sport as a platform for cultural understanding and social cohesion across the world. GSMP pairs emerging female leaders from around the world with female sport leaders in the United States. Emerging leaders create action plans alongside their mentors to be put into practice in their home countries to enhance sport opportunities for girls and women.

Educational Awareness/Sport and Education

The Guerreiras Project (GP), a Brazil-based multimedia initiative that uses soccer as a platform to stimulate gender dialogue, which educates both participants and those who observe the organization at work (http://www.guerreirasproject.org/). The project is composed of four parts: First, *GP Multimedia* uses stories, still photos, sound, and film from women's soccer to prompt reflection about gender norms. Next, the *GP Community*

Campaign involves professional female soccer players in Brazil in community workshops where they share their own sport experiences in an effort to encourage women and girls to participate in sport, and by doing so, challenge prejudice and gender and racial stereotypes. Then, *GP Gender Research* uses ethnographic and experiential approaches to shed a feminist perspective on gender and sport, particularly in light of the growing economic benefits to those who "feminize" the women's game. And lastly, *GP Gender Dialogues* is a partnership with a London-based organization, The People Speak, using soccer as a tool to bring about discussion on gender norms in sport and society. Not unlike Midnight Basketball, the Guerreiras Project is the creation of an individual leader. Caitlin Davis Fisher moved to Brazil from the United States to play professional soccer. She quickly realized that women's soccer and women's soccer athletes were not treated the same way as their male counterparts. In talking to her teammates about the stereotypes and prejudice they faced, Fisher decided to conduct research of women's soccer for the Fédération Internationale de Football Association (FIFA) while she continued to play professionally in Sweden and the United States. With her former teammates, Fisher developed the Guerreiras Project. Through the use of educational opportunities, both formal academic programs and life experiences, as well as the understanding of the life experiences of others, she recognized an opportunity to share her knowledge with others. Fisher's organization challenges gender norms in both sport and society as a whole through the lens of soccer. Like Van Standifer, Fisher recognized that sport as a context could be used to develop individuals in some manner. In her case, it is the development of educational awareness, although the organization certainly empowers the girls and women who participate, which is the goal of the next category of programs.

Empower Marginalized Groups/Sport and Disability/Sport and Gender

SDP leaders believe in social inclusion, providing opportunities for all to participate in sport, acknowledging historical exclusion due to culture, gender, race, nationality, religion, ability, or class. Typically, SDP leaders facilitate sport programs and work with local leaders to build capacity for sport to marginalized societies (Kidd, 2008) and with underserved populations (Green, 2008). Two groups that tend to be the focus of many SDP efforts are young girls and women. Girls, particularly those from low-income communities, face more barriers to sport participation than boys because they often have responsibilities in the home and tend to be subject to restrictive gender conventions (Lee & Macdonald, 2009). Mathare Youth Sports Association (MYSA) (www.mysakenya.org) was founded in 1987 by UN advisor Bob Munro. From its simple beginnings with Bob refereeing pickup youth soccer games in the slums of Mathare, just outside of Nairobi, Kenya, in exchange for the children picking up trash around the area where they played, MYSA has grown to 25,000 members. The organization, now run entirely by adults who grew up as participants in the program, operates a program that uses soccer as a method of inclusion in an attempt to create safe spaces for girls and young women and to assist with school retention (Brady, 2005).

Encourage Physical Activity/Health or Sport and Health

Dating back to Perkins and Noam (2007), it has been understood that in SDP programs "the sport skill was a secondary goal to the life lessons being learned . . . but sports are the hook that entice[s] young people to participate . . ." (p. 76). Sport is the vehicle through which youth learn larger life lessons and skills.

The Mathare Youth Sports Association (MYSA) in the slums of Nairobi, Kenya pioneered the now global sport for development movement since 1987 and has grown to over 1,800 boys and girls teams with over 30,000 members and relies on past participants to lead the organization.

© MYSA SHOOTRACK

In many cases, sport is what attracts participants to a program or a location where they can receive other services. The most successful programs are those where sport is not the intervention, although the physical activity and lessons learned through sport are of benefit, but in which sport becomes integrated into the intervention (Green, 2008). Founder and director of GOALS Haiti, Kona Shen, spent many years studying, visiting, and working in Haiti before starting the organization in 2010. It was through playing soccer that she made friends, learned Creole, and was hosted by multiple families during her trips to Haiti. Participants in GOALS Haiti engage in soccer, education, community service, and local capacity development. GOALS uses soccer as a fun and exciting hook for children who are also involved in community work to address environmental issues in Haiti and provides educational seminars to assist them in achieving academically (Can Soccer Save the World, 2012).

Drive Economic Development/ Infrastructure Development/ Sport and Livelihoods

Sport can also be used to encourage an active lifestyle for adults, and more. Street Soccer USA (SSUSA), founded in 2005 by Lawrence Cann (interviewed in Chapter 2), forms partnerships with other community social service providers to help affect positive life changes among its homeless participants in 20 U.S. cities (http://www.streetsoccerusa.org/). Sport serves as a hook to engage homeless individuals in taking positive steps toward regaining their livelihoods. Homeless individuals play on soccer teams coached by volunteers and participate in local soccer leagues in each city. SSUSA has three goals: (1) build community and trust through sports, transforming the context within which homeless individuals live from one of isolation, abuse, and marginalization to one of community, purpose, and achievement; (2) require participants to set 3-, 6-, and 12-month life goals; and (3) empower individuals by marrying clinical services to sport programming and providing access to educational and employment opportunities. Each summer, SSUSA stages the SSUSA Cup, a national tournament that brings teams together from its 20 U.S. locations. The tournament, which began in 2006, serves as an incentive for participants to keep striving to achieve their life goals. A team from the SSUSA Cup is selected every summer to compete in the Homeless World Cup.

We would also like to highlight a new organization, Station Soccer (http://www.soccerstreets.org/station-soccer-play), which is focusing on infrastructure development where sport is introduced in an everyday setting in order to encourage and promote physical activity (so another overlapping category of program). Station Soccer uses spaces accessible by public transportation (i.e., near train stations) to engage adults and youth in soccer. Every dollar that adults pay to participate funds social impact soccer programs run by Soccer in the Streets.

▶ Skills Needed by Field Leaders

The next several sections of the chapter rely both on the observations and experiences of the three practitioners who have written this chapter as well as current research. Shepherding effective SDP organizations requires leaders to have the following strengths: Caring deeply about people, possessing a deep commitment to **equity** and understanding of the systemic barriers to equity, and being able to operate with few resources while also being adept at developing multiple sources of funding. Leaders in the SDP field must be like soccer midfielders: They need to have a good vision of the entire field, know when to get back on defense, and know how to thread together

passes to move the team forward. In order to orchestrate a successful play, they must know the strengths, weaknesses, and preferences of the individual players as well as the collective chemistry of the team on the field. When necessary, they must be willing to step up and take a strike. Lastly, they must be well-conditioned to have the endurance necessary for the entire game. They have to be prepared to be in it for the duration.

In order to achieve success in the SDP world, leaders must be able to mobilize their own strengths, as listed in the paragraph above, in order to build capacity through facilitating stakeholder relationships, including creating and sustaining a winning team (Edwards, 2015). Leaders must also be able to create and leverage impacts (immediate) and outcomes (long-term) (Schulenkorf, 2017). The leveraging of impacts and outcomes is often accomplished through intentionally designed programs. Finally, leaders need to pay attention to advances in both the theories and practices of SDP (Bruening, et. al., 2015; Scheulenkorf, 2017; Svensson, 2017). If one overarching skill were to be gleaned out of the three key leadership qualities highlighted here, it would be communication. Effective communication— listening and speaking—is the primary tool used to keep the different stakeholders within the SDP arena and improve and expand programs. No one player's skill set can ever float an entire team; a true leader can mobilize people diverse in ideas, experiences, and backgrounds toward common goals.

We believe that we have demonstrated in the chapter that SDP is a complex environment. The increased attention on SDP programs has led to an influx of stakeholders, including but not limited to multilateral organizations such as the World Bank; international development agencies such as the U.S. Agency for International Development (USAID); major and small donors and foundations; local governments; nongovernmental organizations (NGOs) and community-based organizations (CBOs); sport organizations, leagues, and federations; and individual scholars, coaches, athletes, philanthropists, students, and citizens across the world. Managing these stakeholders in successful partnerships is a difficult juggling act. As such, the ability to build through facilitating stakeholder relationships is key for SDP leaders (Edwards, 2015; Svensson, 2017). Stakeholder relationships are built and sustained through communication and balancing the expectations and objectives of the internal and external players involved in an initiative. It is important to garner support from different types of stakeholders, but they often come to the table with different—even conflicting—objectives or expectations, as well as cultural understandings of program participants and host communities (Adams & Harris, 2014; Darnell, 2012). In the increasingly competitive horizon of SDP, where programs battle for funds and credibility on the international stage, the leaders of SDP organizations must be able to optimize "organizational structures, processes, and inter-organizational linkages" (Svensson, 2018, p. 445). They must combine short-term thinking and long-term vision to manage successful programs and be prepared to adapt as needed (Bruening, et. al., 2015; Svensson & Levine, 2017).

SDP leaders must also regularly demonstrate excellent communication skills with their internal team. Communicating respectfully, by listening to the concerns and opinions of one's staff, is the only way to successfully navigate the complex environment of SDP. A leader must see themselves as a member of the team and, through trust, empathy, and good listening, draw from the knowledge and experiences of everyone touched by the program. Similarly, SDP leaders must be able to identify the right facilitators, coordinators, coaches, and administrators who bring the creativity, motivation, and flexibility necessary to operate in an environment characterized by low resources and limited training opportunities. Considering that SDP programs often work with under-resourced youth populations, positive mentors are one of the most important

determinants of success through providing emotional support and encouragement. A perfectly designed program can quickly go off track if the facilitation and daily interaction with youth is not positive. Youth model the behaviors of adults around them, and coaches or facilitators in a sporting environment have an even greater ability to influence (Gould & Voelker, 2010).

In order to leverage immediate impacts and long-term outcomes, SDP leaders must strike the careful balance between understanding the coaching or sporting side of SDP and understanding the programmatic side. Sometimes, program leaders, and members of their teams, are too focused on sport or, an opposite extreme, too focused on the educational or social outcomes. Everyone on the team has to buy into the concept of SDP and have an unwavering dedication to balancing both the sport and developmental sides. A successful SDP leader has the ability to use sport as a *tool* for development with the understanding that sport is a means to the end, not the end in itself. An excellent leader knows the difference between using sport for sport's sake and using sport for something greater. The leader can effectively communicate that vision to others and mobilize a community coalition around the use of sport for a development-related objective.

Finally, SDP leaders must seek out and work to understand how **strategic decision making** influences SDP practice. They need to look to their colleagues' best practices and to scholars who have outlined conceptual frameworks and theories to facilitate design, implementation, and evaluation decisions (Hayhurst, Kay, & Chawansky, 2015; Schulenkorf, 2017; Schulenkorf, et. al. 2016). In the earlier days of SDP, programs rarely included research outcomes as part of their operational goals, let alone the regular consulting of research or practical applications in other settings (Schulenkorf, 2017). As a result, the academic world was critical of SDP programs touting impacts on the health, education, and life paths of participants (Adams & Harris, 2014). Currently, the movement of SDP organizations to build upon as well as using theory to evaluate outcomes (Bowers, & Green, 2016; Bruening, et. al, 2014) is shifting the critical perspectives of scholars.

▶ Program Quality: Monitoring and Evaluation

Some (e.g., Levermore, 2008) have sought to include participatory approaches within theory-driven approaches and have begun to advocate interviews, focus groups and informal discussions as useful tools to M&E. During the past decade, the heightened attention on SDP has increased not only the flow of donor funding but also accountability and expectations for demonstrated impact and results. How does a leader demonstrate the impact of a program to his or her stakeholders? How does a leader gauge program progress? How does a leader determine if the program is achieving expectations? This is possible through **monitoring and evaluation (M&E)**, which consists of collecting information as the program progresses (monitoring) and assessing the information (evaluation). The central purpose of an M&E system is to determine the quality of a program's implementation—does it reach its objectives, to what extent is it successful, and why—and to apply these lessons internally, to improve the program, or externally, to replicate the results in other programs.

Program Quality

Like most nonprofit organizations, SDP programs involve a painstaking process to become established and effective. It takes far more than simply tossing a ball onto a field or throwing money at a group of disadvantaged children to achieve positive impact. There is a significant amount of work that goes into creating an organization that can have an impact and be sustainable over time. In the SDP field, there needs to be constant innovation and research to assess what is successful and what needs improvement.

Monitoring and Evaluation

Why is monitoring and evaluation important? Although some major, multilateral donors such as the World Bank have been slow to jump onto the SDP bandwagon, other entities such as USAID and its Australian counterpart, AUSAID, have become some of the biggest supporters of SDP programs throughout the world. These entities, like many other major agencies and foundations, require a high level of accountability to justify their investment. Many require in-depth logistical frameworks, extensive indicators, frequent reports on results, and, sometimes, expensive impact evaluations. Although some of the pressure for M&E comes from international funding organizations, the importance of M&E is universal. In addition to accountability, M&E can also provide the information that programs need to make adjustments and improvements. A well-oiled M&E system can alert a program when something is not working because it has a strong learning component, or feedback loop. If too much time elapses between implementation and evaluation, a program will not have the chance to review strengths and weaknesses. If the feedback loop is effective, however, a program will review data throughout implementation and respond to the preliminary results. In the case of Grassroot Soccer, which integrated an online database called Salesforce, an upgraded M&E system led to operational and cultural program improvements. According to Tommy Clark, CEO and founder of Grassroot Soccer, he noted that using Salesforce has helped his organization to become a world leader in SDP and has helped to create a culture of transparency and accountability. Clark also noted that use of Salesforce has also helped Grassroot Soccer make more data-driven decisions that have lent credibility to the organization.

M&E is not just about collecting and reporting data. It is about using data effectively to improve program delivery and build a better path to pursuing an organization's mission.

Speaking of an organization's mission, the first step in successful M&E of SDP programs is to determine the ultimate objective. It is helpful to classify the program first as either "Sport Plus" or "Plus Sport" (Lyras & Welty Peachey, 2011; Whitehead, Lambert, & Telfer, 2013). Sport Plus programs are focused more on the sporting component than development and often work toward removing barriers to sport participation, training coaches, developing basic sporting skills, or advocating for the right to recreational activities. Plus Sport programs focus more on development objectives such as reducing HIV/AIDS, increasing educational outcomes, or providing employment opportunities. It is important to note that sometimes the boundary between these distinctions is blurry, but it is a helpful starting point to developing an M&E system.

Once the objective of a program is identified, it is important to develop the logical framework that outlines the outcomes that a program strives to reach and the steps that will be taken to get there. These steps are called *indicators* and will form the basis of the monitoring component of M&E. During the course of the program, it is important to collect information related to the indicators in order to measure achievement. Indicators are *measurable* benchmarks and should be clearly defined. Examples could include participant attendance, school retention rates, or number of mentors trained. It is important to measure these indicators against a baseline or existing data in order to measure change. Although the compilation of information can often be tedious, time consuming, and difficult with limited access to human resources, it creates an important feedback loop that allows an organization to improve implementation.

After a program's objective and the indicators to measure are defined, the third step is to create tools to collect the information. There are endless ways to collect information during the M&E process. Generally, information is split into two groups: quantitative and qualitative. It is a good idea to have a balanced mix of both types of data. *Quantitative* information is composed of numerical data that answer the questions of how many and how much: numbers, percentages, and rates. Quantitative data can be measured through various tools such as questionnaires and surveys. However, we know that numbers do not tell the whole story. *Qualitative* data can provide a deeper perspective on how or why a program works or doesn't work. Qualitative data can be collected through interviews, testimonials, focus groups, or a tool called Most Significant Change, which focuses on an individual's personal transformation during a program.

The *evaluation* component of M&E is often more difficult, especially for organizations with less experience or capacity (Collison, Giulianotti, Howe, & Darnell, 2016). The gold standard of impact evaluation is the experimental design, which involves a control group and a longitudinal design. Few SDPs can afford to undergo such an evaluation, which is why little research exists to provide a credible argument for the strength of SDP programs versus traditional development programs. Although many can attest to the "magic" of sport and the value that sport brings to development programs, it is difficult to articulate and measure the impact in academic terminology. In addition to *summative* evaluations, which are done at the end of a program, it is important to conduct *formative* evaluations, or ongoing assessments that can help a program determine if it is on track to achieve its goals.

One of the foremost researchers on M&E of SDP programs, Fred Coalter, argues that although *outcome-led* M&E is important, such a focus on evaluation and final results does not tell the whole story and does not necessarily assist in building the capacity needed to help the SDP reach maturity and credibility. Coalter (2008) argues that *process-led* or *formative* M&E can lead to improvements of organizations because it focuses on learning from a program's experience rather than just reporting on it. The reality is that many of the organizations have turned to SDP as a cost-effective way to reach "unreachable" youth and do not have the capacity, training, or resources to meet the M&E expectations of donors. With limited training, resources, and capacity, smaller organizations struggle with M&E requirements and run the risk of losing funding or not being able to obtain it in the first place.

Even with limited budgets, a number of SDP organizations have integrated M&E into their programming to satisfy donor requirements and improve their own capacity. Grassroot Soccer "uses the power of sport to educate, inspire, and mobilize communities to stop the spread of HIV" (www.grassrootsoccer.org). Its M&E focuses on the pre- and post-program knowledge tests of its youth participants, program attendance, and coach and participant demographics. The coaches who work directly with the youth are involved not only in implementing the program, but also in monitoring results. Because they are aware of the results of the tests, they are able to adjust the way the curriculum is facilitated to improve youth learning and retention. As mentioned by Clark of Grassroot Soccer, the use of technology in the M&E system has increased the organization's capacity to provide essential information to donors and make better decisions about the curriculum and program implementation.

The Caribbean Sport and Development Agency (www.ttaspe.org), one of the most prolific Caribbean SDP organizations, coaches its local implementing partners in a variety of data collection tools including questionnaires, interviews, surveys, Most Significant Change stories, case studies, and impact assessments. As an umbrella organization, its goal is not only to be accountable to donors and improve capacity but also to engage in advocacy for the SDP field to better inform practitioners, policy makers, and donors. With an extensive and diversified armory of qualitative and quantitative data about the impact of its programs, the Caribbean Sport and Development Agency (formerly the Trinidad and Tobago Alliance for Sport and Physical Education, or TTASPE) has paved the way for future SDP organizations. It is continuing to address gaps in research and capacity to ensure that SDP organizations have the tools, resources, and knowledge to maximize their impact.

▶ Summary

This chapter outlined the purpose and history of global Sport for Development and Peace (SDP) organizations to demonstrate how they use sport to bring together different genders, ethnicities, religions, abilities, or political systems. Additionally, we defined and gave examples of SDP programs that use sport to accomplish their goals of conflict resolution/sport and peace, cultural understanding/sport and social cohesion, educational awareness/sport and education, empowering marginalized groups/sport and disability/sport and gender, encouraging sport and physical activity/sport and health, and driving economic development/infrastructure development/sport and livelihoods. Finally, we outlined issues in SDP for leaders to be aware of as well as the skills necessary for leaders to operate quality SDP programs. We firmly believe that SDP is strongest with deliberate programming aligned with the social needs of both individuals and communities. Sport has the capacity to transform individuals through physical, emotional, psychological, and social development while simultaneously playing an integral role in community development.

LEADERSHIP PERSPECTIVE

Mark Mungal

Mark Mungal is a co-founder of the Caribbean Sport and Development Agency (formerly known as the Trinidad and Tobago Alliance for Sport and Physical Education) and has led the organization since 2003. He has also served as a Teacher Educator in the Physical Education Department at Corinth Teachers' College in South Trinidad. Mark has also been a lecturer at the Sport and Physical Education Department of the University of the West Indies and played a lead role in the development of degree programs in sport and physical education at both the University of Trinidad and Tobago and at the University of the West Indies.

Q: Within this chapter, communication is identified as one of the most important skills necessary for effective leadership of Sport for Development and Peace (SDP) programs. Can you provide insights into or examples of effective communication you have used within your program?

From my personal experiences of working in the SDP field, there are three broad dimensions of communication that we need to consider. First, when we think about communication in the context of leadership of SDP programs, we may want to consider the idea of how we use communication to build relationships with the stakeholders involved in the planning, coordination, and implementation of the program. For example, before we start an SDP program in a community, we meet with the community gate-keepers (elders/leaders) - it's an approach that lets them (the gate-keepers) know that we respect and value their role in the community and that we acknowledge their importance and their leadership positions. The communication in that context is less about the program and more about building a relationship with the gate-keepers and showing them that we value/respect them.

Depending on the context, we sometimes recommend that we spend the first three months of the 'program' focused on building relationships with the community. This lays the foundation and provides a basis for working with the community based on trust and respect. It is critical that during this relationship-building period, we use communication that reflects respect for the value that each member of the community brings to the table.

The second dimension of communication in the context of SDP leadership is the operational communication—this is about ensuring that we communicate accurately, effectively, and efficiently, etc. When people involved in programs are unaware of what is expected, things begin to fall apart. Early on we must establish the best ways to communicate—sometimes it's a community notice board, sometimes a public address system hitched on a vehicle that drives through the community. Sometimes, it's flyers being distributed at the market and sometimes it's phone, text, messaging, etc. The key principle is to ensure that the message gets out and that all parties are aware.

(continues)

Within the operational context of communication, it's also important to ensure that there is clarity. Whether it's at meetings or via emails, etc., leaders must ensure that there is clarity by following up with the stakeholders. This is essential for good stakeholder management. For example, when you send out tasks, you can follow up by giving the individual some tips for completing the task and asking if they need any further guidelines and/or if they need any help to complete the task. Leading up to completion of the task, you should be following up to get a sense of where they are with the task and if they need additional support, etc. In the case of the operational dimension of communication, your priority is ensuring that communication supports the success of the program.

The third important context for communication addresses the issue of perceptions—and the reality that when we communicate, our messages may sometimes be skewed by perceptions. Sadly, if these perceptions are not addressed, they can erode the entire fabric of an organization and negatively impact the success of programs. In this regard, it's important that as leaders we maintain a high level of awareness and that any misperceptions that may arise should be addressed. The basis for addressing perceptions is honest, open conversation—creating a safe, non-judgmental environment where all parties are comfortable sharing thoughts in the "pool of shared understanding." When everything is placed in that pool of shared understanding, we can now clarify misperceptions and begin the process of rebuilding trust.

Q: What skills do you look for when seeking partners and/or volunteers to with your sessions? Why are these skills important for the CSDA methodology?
The number one criteria for selecting volunteers/partners is commitment. We believe that anyone can acquire and develop the necessary skills needed, but I can't as easily teach commitment. And we have witnessed the unfortunate and frustrating challenge of engaging "qualified/certified" persons who come with the skills, but lack the commitment.

In the context of communication, we do look out for behaviors that match the three dimensions mentioned above—that respectful/valuing disposition—recognition of the value of building relationships; the sense of willingness to do what it takes to get the correct info shared and to ensure that the way we communicate leads to success; the sense of sincerity and honesty that facilitates open sharing that avoids misperceptions.

Q: How do you handle issues of power (with those developing the programs and those participants in the programs) when developing and implementing the CSDA program activities?
We believe that the most significant dimension of power is decision-making… we cannot say that we promote an individual to a leadership position, but we are not allowing opportunities for her to make meaningful decisions. This is the same for both the facilitators and the participants. Our role as SDP leaders is to provide the necessary skills, knowledge, support, etc., to allow persons (both program leaders and participants) to make informed decisions… and then to create as many opportunities for them to practice and apply their decision-making skills.

The challenge for leaders is to be able to accept the decisions of others…, which, in a sense, is like giving up power. Good leaders must manage this context.

Q: Can you discuss the importance of measuring and evaluating the impact of the CSDA programs? How have you used these findings to help enhance or develop new programs?
Measuring impact has been one of the more challenging areas of work, mainly because of the point of intervention that CSDA is engaged. To a large extent, we focus on building capacity of teachers, coaches, and volunteers who support the implementation of SDP programs across several of the Caribbean islands. The challenge is that we can measure the success of training workshops, but we have not been as successful at measuring the impact that those workshops (trained teachers, coaches, etc.) have on children and young people in the schools and communities where they work. And the reason that we do the workshops is so that we can impact the lives of children and young people in

the Caribbean…. We have worked with other partners (e.g., Brunel University, University of Western Cape) to improve our monitoring and evaluation—still a work in progress.

The good news is that the data that we have been collecting continues to inform the policy work that we do up and down the islands. It has also helped us to improve our practice (the workshops) and materials that we use.

Q: Going forward, can you highlight one or two of the most significant challenges you will face as one of the leaders of CSDA. How do you anticipate addressing these challenges?

One of the great successes in the SDP field is that we now have more persons aware of and interested in pursuing careers in SDP—and we do have more programs being offered at universities to prepare persons to work in the field. There's also more research happening in the field—and an expected improvement in SDP practice.

The challenge is that the SDP field still remains, to a large extent, a volunteer field, with many SDP agencies depending on volunteers for the delivery of programs. And in the case of organizations like CSDA, we depend heavily on development agencies for funding. Organizations that rely heavily on development funding are often vulnerable to the geopolitical forces that shift the priorities of development agencies. In the past five years or so, we have seen a significant reduction in the global development funding for SDP programs from some of the long-standing agencies, including the ASC (funded by AusAID), UKSport, NIF, and CGC.

The stronger SDP organizations have been able to stay alive, but we are yet to address the gap in the global funding for SDP despite significant evidence of the value added and savings to governments—particularly in the area of health (which is one area that is well documented).

Addressing the funding deficit requires greater collaboration among all SDP stakeholders and an outreach to the non-sport sectors (health, education, crime prevention, etc.) at all levels. Some of these efforts have already begun.

▶ Key Terms

Conflict resolution
Equity
Monitoring & Evaluation (M&E)

Olympism
Sport for development and peace (SDP)

Strategic decision making

▶ Discussion Questions

1. Why is it important for leaders of SDP programs to develop inclusive programs using a critical social consciousness?

2. Which challenges do leaders face by developing and implementing SDP programs?

3. Which important skills are necessary to successfully lead an SDP program? Provide an example of a leader from an SDP who demonstrates these skills.

4. If you are leading an SDP program, describe why it is of the utmost importance to maintain program quality and monitor the performance of the program. Finally, explain how you would evaluate an SDP program and why this is also of significant importance when leading an SDP program.

▶ References

Adams, A., & Harris, K. (2014). Making sense of the lack of evidence discourse, power and knowledge in the field of sport for development. *International journal of public sector management, 27*(2), 140–151.

Association of Midnight Basketball League Programs. (2013). History. Retrieved from http://amblp.com/basketball/historyBowers, M. T., & Green, B. C. (2016). The theory of development of and through sport. *Managing Sport Development: An International Approach,* 12–28.

Brady, M. (2005). Creating safe spaces and building social assets for young women in the developing world: A new role for sports. *Women's Studies Quarterly, 33*(1/2), 35–49.

Bruening, J.E., Welty Peachey, J., Evanovich, J.M., Fuller, R.D., Murty, C. J., Percy, V.E., Silverstein, L.A., & Chung, M. (2015). Managing sport for social change: The effects of intentional design and structure in a sport-based service learning initiative. *Sport Management Review, 18*(1), 69–85.

Burrows, M. (2003). *Evaluation of the youth inclusion programme: End of phase one report.* London: Youth Justice Board.

Can Soccer Save the World. (2012). Goals Haiti named best new project at Beyond Sport Summit. Retrieved from http://cansoccersavetheworld.com/2012/news-goals-haiti-named-best-new-project-at-beyond-sport-summit/

Coakley, J., & Pike, E. (2009). *Sports in society: Issues and controversies.* Columbus, OH: McGraw-Hill Higher Education.

Coalter, F. (2008). *Sport-in-development. A monitoring and evaluation manual.* London: UK Sport.

Coalter, F. (2013) *Sport for Development: What Game are We Playing?* Routledge, London, UK.

Collison, H., Giulianotti, R., Howe, P. D., & Darnell, S. (2016). The methodological dance: critical reflections on conducting a cross-cultural comparative research project on 'Sport for Development and Peace'. *Qualitative Research in Sport, Exercise and Health, 8*(5), 413–423.

Darnell, S. (2012). *Sport for development and peace: A critical sociology.* London: Bloomsbury.

Darnell, S. C., Chawansky, M., Marchesseault, D., Holmes, M., & Hayhurst, L. (2016). The state of play: Critical sociological insights into recent 'Sport for Development and Peace' research. *International Review for the Sociology of Sport. 53*(2), 133–151.

Darnell, S. C., Whitley, M. A., & Massey, W. V. (2016). Changing methods and methods of change: Reflections on qualitative research in Sport for Development and Peace. *Qualitative Research in Sport, Exercise and Health, 8*(5), 571–577.

Edwards, M. B. (2015). The role of sport in community capacity building: An examination of sport for development research and practice. *Sport Management Review, 18*(1), 6–19.

Ewing, M. E., Gano-Overway, L. A., Branta, C. F., & Seefeldt, V. D. (2002). The role of sports in youth development. In M. Gatz, M. Messner, & S. Ball-Rokeach (Eds.), *Paradoxes of youth and sport* (pp. 31–47). Albany: State University of New York Press.

Gould, D., & Voelker, D.K. (2010), Youth sport leadership development: Leveraging the sports captaincy experience. *Journal of Sport Psychology in Action, 1* (1), 1–14.

Grassroot Soccer. Mission and vision. Retrieved from http://www.grassrootsoccer.org/what-we-do/mission-and-vision

Green, B. C. (2008). Management of sports development. In V. Girginov (Ed.), *Sport as an agent for social and personal change* (pp. 129–147). Oxford, England: Elsevier.

Guerreiras Project. Retrieved from http://guerreirasproject.org

Guttmann, A. (1978). *From ritual to record: The nature of modern sports.* New York: Columbia University Press. (pp. viii, 198).

Harris, J.C. (1998). Civil society, physical activity, and the involvement of sport sociologists in the preparation of physical activity professionals. *Sociology of Sport Journal, 15*(2), 138–153.

Harris, K., & Adams, A. (2016). Power and discourse in the politics of evidence in sport for development. *Sport Management Review, 19*(2), 97–106.

Hartmann, D., & Depro, B. (2006). Rethinking sports-based community crime prevention: A preliminary analysis of the relationship between Midnight Basketball and urban crime rates. *Journal of Sport & Social Issues, 30*(2), 180–196.

Hayhurst, L. M., Kay, T., & Chawansky, M (2016). *Beyond Sport for Development and Peace: Transnational Perspectives on Theory, Policy, and Practice. Volume 53 of Routledge Research in Sport, Culture, and Society.* Routledge, London, UK.

Henley, R., Schweizer, I. C., de Gara, F., & Vetter, S. (2007). How psychosocial sport and play programs help youth manage adversity: A review of what we know and what we should research. *International Journal of Psychosocial Rehabilitation, 12*(1), 51–58.

Holmes, M., Banda, D., & Chawansky, M. (2015). Towards sustainable programme design? An examination of CSR initiatives within a Zambian SfD NGO. *International Journal of Sport Management and Marketing, 16*(1–2), 36–51.

Huish, R. (2011). Punching above its weight Cuba's use of sport for south–south co-operation. *Third World Quarterly, 32*(3), 417–433.

Hums, M. A., Wolff, E. A., & Mahoney, M. (2008). Sport and human rights. In J. Borms (Ed.), *Directory of sport science* (5th ed., pp. 469–480). Champaign, IL: Human Kinetics.

Ingham, A., & Hardy, S. (1984). Sport, structuration and hegemony. *Theory, Culture & Society, 2*(2), 85–103.

International Committee. (1994). Olympic charter. Retrieved from http://www.olympic.org/Documents /olympic_charter_en.pdf

International Platform on Sport and Development. (2011). All organisations. Retrieved from http:// www.sportanddev.org/en/connect/organisations /organisations list/

Jarvie, G. (2007). Sport and national identity in the post-war world by Adrian Smith and Dilwyn Poerter (eds.). *Nations and Nationalism, 13*(1), 159–161.

Kidd, B. (2008). A new social movement: Sport for development and peace. *Sport in Society, 11*(4), 370–380.

Lake, R.J. (2013). 'They treat me like I'm scum': Social exclusion and established-outsider relations in British tennis club. *International Review for the Sociology of Sport, 48*(1), 112–128.

Lapchick, R. (1996). Race and college sports: A long way to go. In R. E. Lapchick (Ed.), *Sport in Society* (pp. 5–18). Thousand Oaks, CA: Sage.

Lee, J., & Macdonald, D. (2009). Rural young people and physical activity: Understanding participation through social theory. *Sociology of Health & Illness, 31*(3), 360–374.

Levermore, R. (2008). Sport: A new engine of development? *Progress in Development Studies, 8*(2), 183–190.

Lyras, A., & Welty Peachey, J. (2011). Integrating sport-for-development theory and praxis. *Sport Management Review, 14*(4), 311–326.

Masteralexis, L. P., Barr, C. A., & Hums, M. A. (2011). *Principles and practice of sport management* (4th ed.). Sudbury, MA: Jones & Bartlett Learning.

Mendel, R. (2000). What works in the prevention of youth crime? Retrieved from http://www.cyc-net.org/cyc -online/cycol 0500 mendel.html

Millington, R. S. (2010). *Basketball with(out) borders: Interrogating the intersections of sport, development, and capitalism* (Master's thesis). Queen's University, Kingston, Ontario, Canada.

O'Hare, M. (2012, August). The history of the Paralympic games. Retrieved from http://sport.uk.msn.com /paralympics2012/the-history-of-the-paralympic -games-53?page=5#image=1

Perkins, D. F., & Noam, G. G. (2007). Characteristics of sports-based youth development programs. *New Directions for Youth Development, 115*, 75–84.

Richards, J., Kaufman, Z., Schulenkorf, N., Wolff, E., Gannett, K., Siefken, K., & Rodriguez, G. (2013). Advancing the evidence base of sport for development: A new open-access, peer-reviewed journal. *Journal of Sport for Development, 1*(1), 1–3.

Schulenkorf, N. (2017). Managing sport-for-development: Reflections and outlook. *Sport Management Review. 20*(3), 243–251.

Schulenkorf, N., & Adair, D. (2013). Sport-for-Development: The emergence and growth of a new genre. In *Global Sport-for-Development* (pp. 3–11). Palgrave Macmillan UK.

Schulenkorf, N., Sherry, E., & Rowe, K. (2016). Sport for development: An integrated literature review. *Journal of Sport Management, 30*(1), 22–39.

Sherry, E., Schulenkorf, N., & Chalip, L. (2015). Managing sport for social change: The state of play. *Sport Management Review. 18*(1), 1–5.

Spaaij, R. (2011). *Sport and social mobility: Crossing boundaries.* New York: Routledge.

Sport for children and youth: Fostering development and strengthening education. (n.d.). Retrieved from http:// www.righttoplay.com/International/our-impact /Documents/Final_Report_Chapter_3.pdf

Spaaij, R., Magee, J., & Jeanes, R. (2014). *Sport and Social Exclusion in Global Society.* Routledge, London, UK.

Street Soccer USA. Retrieved from http://www .streetsoccerusa.org/

Svensson, P.G. (2017). Organizational hybridity: A conceptualization of how sport for development and peace organizations respond to divergent institutional demands. *Sport Management Review. 20*(5), 443–454.

Svensson, P. G., & Levine, J. (2017). Rethinking sport for development and peace: The capability approach. *Sport in Society, 20*(7), 905–923.

United Nations. (1959). Declaration on the rights of the child. Adopted by UN general assembly resolution 1386 (XIV) of 10 December 1959. Retrieved from https://www.unicef.org/malaysia/1959-Declaration -of-the-Rights-of-the-Child.pdf

United Nations. (2002). "Right to play belongs to everyone," secretary-general tells Olympic aid forum [Press release]. Retrieved from http://www.un.org /News/Press/docs/2002/sgsm8119.doc.htm

United Nations. (2003). *Sport for development and peace: Towards achieving the millennium development goals.* Report from the United Nations Inter-Agency Task Force on Sport for Development and Peace. Geneva, Switzerland: United Nations.

United Nations Development Programme. (2000). The millennium development goals: Eight goals for 2015. Retrieved from http://www.undp.org/content/undp /en/home/mdgoverview.html

United Nations Educational, Scientific and Cultural Organization. (1952). Records of the general conference, seventh session, Paris 1952, resolutions. Retrieved from http://unesdoc.unesco.org/images/0011 /001145/114587E.pdf

United Nations Inter-Agency Task Force on Sport for Development and Peace. (2005). Sport as a tool for development and peace: Towards achieving the United

Nations millennium development goals. Retrieved from http://www.un.org/sport2005/resources/task_force.pdf

Welty Peachey, J., & Cohen, A. (2012). Sport for social change and development. In G. B. Cunningham & J. N. Singer (Eds.), *Sociology of sport and physical activity* (2nd ed., pp. 191–211). College Station, TX: Center for Sport Management Research and Education.

Welty Peachey, J., Cohen, A., Shin, N., & Fusaro, B. (2016). Challenges and strategies of building and sustaining inter-organizational partnerships in sport for development and peace. *Sport Management Review. 21*(2), 160–175.

Welty Peachey, J., Musser, A., Shin, N. R., & Cohen, A. (2017). Interrogating the motivations of sport for development and peace practitioners. *International Review for the Sociology of Sport.*

Westcott, W. L., Puhala, K., Colligan, A., Loud, R. L., Cobbett, R. (2015). Physiological effects of the BOKS before-school physical activity program for preadolescent youth. *Journal of Exercise, Sports, and Orthopedics. 2*(2): 1–7.

Wolff, E., & Hums, M. (2017). Examining the purpose of sport and why it matters. https://www.huffingtonpost.com/entry/examining-the-purpose-of-sport-and-why-it-matters_us_5a0c779ce4b006523921857c

Whitehead, J., Lambert, J., & Telfer, H. (2013). Introduction: Exploring youth sport values. In *Values in Youth Sport and Physical Education* (pp. 21–32). Routledge.

Whooten, R. C. Perkins, M. E., Gerber, M. W., & Taveras, E. M. (2018). Effects of before-school physical activity on obesity prevention and wellness. *American Journal of Preventive Medicine, 54*(4), 510–518.

Winnipeg Community Sport Policy. (2012). Retrieved from http://sportforlife.ca/wp-content/uploads/2016/12/WPG-COMMUNITY-SPORT-POLICY-Jan-6-2012.pdf

CHAPTER 12

Addressing the Gender Gap in Sport Leadership

Heidi Grappendorf

CHAPTER OBJECTIVES

- Demonstrate an understanding of the historical overview of women's leadership in sport.
- Recognize the significant influence of Title IX legislation on women and leadership in sport in the United States.
- Demonstrate an understanding of the reasons for the continued underrepresentation of women in leadership in sport.
- Describe strategies to address the persistent gender gap in sport leadership positions.

CASE STUDY

Few Women Leaders in Olympic Leadership

The 2012 London Summer Olympics were dubbed the "Year of the Women" by several media outlets, including *The New York Times*, because, for the first time ever, Saudi Arabia, Qatar, and Brunei sent female athletes to the Olympic Games (Longman, 2012). However, despite these claims, not every country participating in the Summer Olympics sent female athletes to the Games. What is increasingly evident is that wealthy countries (e.g., the United States) are able to send a large delegation of male and female athletes, but developing nations continue to struggle to field an entire team and will only bring a small contingent of athletes. With the 2016 Rio Olympics having 45 percent participation of female athletes, women have failed to exceed 45 percent of participants at any Olympic Games (International Olympic Committee, 2016).

When considering leadership in the Olympic movement, women continue to be underrepresented at all levels. The International Olympic Committee (IOC) requested that by 2005, women be provided

(continues)

CASE STUDY (continued)

with at least 20 percent of the leadership opportunities in international sport organizations. However, even the IOC failed to meet its own threshold until 2012. By 2016, twenty-two of the 99 members of the IOC were women, allowing the organization to meet the more than 20 percent threshold (24.4 percent) (Lapchick, 2016b). There are other firsts for women within leadership at the IOC—there are now three female members on the 15-member IOC Executive Committee (20 percent) and one female vice president of the IOC Executive Committee (25 percent) (Lapchick, 2016b). This is progress for women in leadership positions within international sport; however, there is much work to be done. At the national level, men continue to dominate leadership positions for National Olympic Committees. All-male leadership teams constitute the majority (85.3 percent) of National Olympic Committees. Only 14.1 percent of countries have male/female leadership teams, and only one country (Zambia) has an all-female leadership team. The International Paralympic Committee (IPC) has set a threshold of 30 percent for gender equity in its leadership structures (Smith & Wrynn, 2013). However, it has not met that threshold, because only 4 of the 15 members of the IPC are female (26.7 percent). Only 26 of 174 National Paralympic Committees have female presidents (14.9 percent).

Despite the increase in the number of U.S. women competing in the Olympics, the National Governing Bodies (NGBs) of U.S. Olympic teams continue to be dominated by men. There are only five women in leadership positions out of a total of 39 U.S. NGBs. Of the 39 U.S. NGBs, there is only one all-female leadership team. The underrepresentation of women in leadership within the Olympic movement is a problem that will not be addressed by merely setting quotas for leadership, as evidenced by the IOC's inability to meet its own quota until 7 years after the deadline. In the United States, where the passage of Title IX has led to significant increases in sport participation opportunities for girls and women, women are not gaining access to leadership positions within sport, including within the Olympic movement.

As you will read in the chapter to follow, there are a myriad of reasons for the underrepresentation of women in sport leadership. As a leader for the next generation of sport organizations, you will be faced with the challenge of ensuring gender equity in leadership positions at all levels of sport. If women are competing in greater numbers in sports, in particular in the United States, why are there so few women leading the organizations for which these female athletes are representing the United States on the international stage of competition?

Questions for Discussion

1. The IOC has set requirements for a minimum number of women to hold leadership positions on the committee but failed to meet its own requirements for several years. What other ideas and solutions, in addition to setting a quota, should the IOC take to that ensure women are provided with leadership positions within the Olympics?
2. As you will read in this chapter, there are a myriad of reasons why women continue to be underrepresented in leadership positions in sport organizations. If you were a member of the IOC, how would you instruct the leaders of National Olympic Committees that have no female leadership (the majority) to begin to include women on their committees? Provide two potential options.
3. In the United States, the 2012 Summer Olympics team was composed of more female athletes than male athletes for the first time ever. Discuss why it is important for women to also be equally represented in leadership positions within the U.S. Olympic Committee (USOC) and within leadership positions for U.S. NGBs.
4. If you were a member of the USOC, what specific steps would you recommend to help increase the number of women in leadership positions for U.S. NGBs?

▶ Introduction

Despite the increasing numbers of girls and women participating in sport, women's representation in sport leadership positions has been limited. Like many other traditionally male-dominated fields, the farther up one looks into the higher administrative and leadership ranks, the fewer women there are. There is a long and storied history of women's efforts and struggles to gain a place in the decision-making and leadership positions in sport. Although women continue to make progress and obtain leadership positions in all realms of sport, there is still a vast underrepresentation of female sport leaders at the high school, college, and professional levels. Efforts by researchers examining the reasons for underrepresentation and suggestions to increase the number of women in sport leadership, as well as actions of female leaders and policy makers, has led to some progress by women moving into the upper echelons of sport leadership. However, increasing the number of women in sport leadership remains a work in progress, and a gap remains regarding the number of women in sport leadership jobs.

This chapter begins with a historical overview, followed by a section on the influence of Title IX. Furthermore, information on the reasons why this underrepresentation has persisted is offered. The chapter concludes with a discussion of some prominent female sport leaders and some suggested strategies to address the persistent gender gap in sport leadership positions.

▶ Historical Overview

Women in sport leadership have a storied past that has included conflict and debate regarding their roles and abilities to lead. Following the Civil War, there was great demand from women to participate in physical education and sport. Due to this demand, a need arose for women to oversee physical education and sporting opportunities for women. Thus, some of the first leadership ideals for women in sport developed during this time from those involved with sporting opportunities and later with competitions related to intercollegiate participation (Rintala, 2001; Swanson & Spears, 1995).

While male students were often in charge of competitions for male students, female physical educators were responsible for the organizing and oversight of sporting opportunities for women. This was true at both the interscholastic and collegiate levels (Swanson & Spears, 1995). These female physical educators had their own ideas as to how sport should be organized for women, and they worked tirelessly toward the values they held. Those women leading physical education and women's sport rejected the competitive and commercial male model of sport and emphasized cooperation, academics, and physical activity. Female physical activity leaders also had to be very sensitive to the ongoing evolvement of women's roles and the societal expectations of women (Rhode & Walker, 2007). These activities were organized for fun, enjoyment, social interaction with other women, and health (Boutilier & SanGiovanni, 1983). It is important to note that female physical educators organized opportunities for women to participate, but—unlike men's sports—they did not receive any financial backing. In 1892, the first women's intercollegiate athletic competition took place when Sandra Berenson, a physical education teacher at Smith College, organized and adapted the rules of basketball for women. As the opportunities expanded for women to participate in sport throughout the late 1800s, the philosophical divide between men's and women's sports and those leading each widened (Rintala, 2001).

The Intercollegiate Athletic Association was created in 1905 to 1906 to oversee men's sports only. This organization changed its name to the National Collegiate Athletic Association (NCAA) in 1910 (Chepko & Couturier, 2001). Regarding women's participation in sport, female physical educators recognized a need to organize and develop a governing body for women's participation in sport as well. During the early 1900s, as female physical educators were trying to figure out and support a governing body, the American Physical Education Association (APEA) created a Standing Committee on Women's Athletics. The APEA has gone through many changes over the years, and is currently known as the American Alliance for Health, Physical Education, Recreation and Dance (AAHPERD) (Hult, 1991). In 1928, the APEA went through more reorganization, which led to the formation of the National Section on Women's Athletics (NSWA). This organization merged with the Women's Division of the National Amateur Athletic Federation (NAAF) and became the National Section on Girls' and Women's Sports (NSGWS). In 1958, NSGWS became part of AAHPERD and was known as the Division for Girls' and Women's Sports (DGWS). In 1974, when AAHPERD restructured, DGWS became the National Association for Girls and Women in Sport (NAGWS) (Hult, 1991).

At the college level, as women's sports continued to grow, there was a recognized need to organize and structure as well. Further, women in sport expressed a desire to compete, both against other teams and at advanced levels (Acosta & Carpenter, 2007; Hums, 2010). In 1967, the Commission for Intercollegiate Athletics for Women (CIAW) was founded as a volunteer organization to encourage development of sport programs for all (Hult, 1980). In 1971, due to the continued growth of intercollegiate sports for women, female physical educators established the **Association for Intercollegiate Athletics for Women (AIAW)** (Hultstrand, 1993; Swanson & Spears, 1995), an outgrowth of the CIAW. Women created the AIAW because they believed women had been deprived of the sporting learning experience, and they believed there were better approaches than the men's model in the NCAA (Uhlir, 1987). The AIAW accomplished many things for women's athletics, but one of the greatest contributions that the AIAW made was related to its role in helping get Title IX passed.

▶ Title IX

Female leaders, and particularly the AIAW, played a significant role in getting Title IX passed in 1972. **Title IX** states: "No person in the United States shall, on the basis of sex, be excluded from participation in, be denied the benefits of, or be subjected to discrimination under any educational programs or activities receiving federal financial assistance" (Office for Civil Rights, 1979, para. 3). Title IX was and is a piece of landmark legislation mandating equality for girls and women in sport. Despite the fact that girls and women were playing sport, and women were involved in the oversight of women's participation in sport, Title IX is a significant piece of legislation to note because it was an indicator of how far women's sport had grown and evolved. With that growth, Title IX was passed to ensure that girls and women in sport were provided with opportunities, financial support, and other necessary areas that were equitable with what boys and men in sport received. However, despite the fact that it contributed to more girls and women participating in sport and it required that administrators and leaders in sport treat women's sport equitably, no one predicted the decline of women in sport leadership to come.

▶ Status of Women in Sport Leadership

To gain a broad understanding of the situation for women in sport leadership, it is important to examine past data as well as current available data. In other words, it is necessary to look at the number of women currently holding leadership positions within sport, as well as the history of representation of women in these positions.

High School

If there has traditionally been an overlooked area of study of women in leadership, it has occurred at the interscholastic level. Unlike intercollegiate athletics, where Acosta and Carpenter (2014) have longitudinally provided status updates and data on the numbers of women in leadership, there is no similar study that tracks this information at the interscholastic level.

Research by the National Federation of State High School Associations (2017) does indicate that there are more females participating at the high school level than ever before. However, as noted by the Women's Sports Foundation (n.d.), 80 percent of all coaches at the high school level are male. Regarding athletic directors, Whisenant (2003) noted in data from 22 of 50 state high school athletic associations that of the 7,041 athletic directors, only 899, or 13 percent, were female. Five years later, there was little improvement as only 15 percent of athletic directors (a 2 percent increase) were female (Whisenant, 2008). In coaching, the Tucker Center for Research on Girls & Women in Sport (2014) reported that only 21 percent of high school head coaches were women. Ultimately, although more females may be playing sports, they are likely to be participating in programs led by men.

In one of the limited studies conducted regarding females and high school athletics, Whisenant, Miller, and Pedersen (2005) found that job descriptions and job qualifications relating to football may prevent women from applying for jobs. If a qualification for athletic director includes having been a football coach, women would almost certainly be excluded from being considered for an athletic director position. Whisenant et al. (2005) found this in 17 percent of job descriptions for athletic director in Texas.

Opportunity for women in sport has increased since the time of this Smith College basketball game in 1903; equitable treatment for men's and women's sport was mandated in 1972 by the passage of Title IX legislation.
© Katherine Elizabeth McClellan/Smith College Archives.

College

In their 2014 longitudinal study that has tracked participation since 1972, researchers R. Vivian Acosta and Linda Carpenter found the highest-ever participation on intercollegiate teams by women. Despite the tremendous participation opportunities, there has unfortunately been a downside to Title IX. One of the unintended consequences or backlash effects of Title IX has been a decline in the number of women in leadership positions, particularly in coaching and administration at the intercollegiate level. Prior to Title IX being passed, women coached more than 90 percent of female teams and more than 90 percent of women's athletic programs had a female athletic director. As **TABLE 12.1** indicates, Acosta and Carpenter (2014)

TABLE 12.1 Percentage of Female Head Coaches for All Divisions, in All Women's Sports	
Year	**Percentage of Head Coaches**
1972	90+
1978	58.2
1988	48.3
1998	47.4
2008	42.8
2010	42.6
2012	42.9
2014	43.4

Data from Acosta, R. V., & Carpenter, L. J. (2012). Women in intercollegiate sport: A longitudinal, national study thirty-five year update, 1977–2012. Retrieved August 29, 2012 from: http://acostacarpenter.org/AcostaCarpenter2012.pdf

TABLE 12.2 Percentage of Female College Athletic Directors	
Year	**Percentage of All Divisions**
1972	90.0+
1980	20.0
1988	16.1
1998	19.4
2008	21.3
2010	19.3
2012	20.3
2014	22.3

Data from Acosta, R. V., & Carpenter, L. J. (2012). Women in intercollegiate sport: A longitudinal, national study thirty-five year update, 1977–2012. Retrieved August 29, 2012 from: http://acostacarpenter.org/AcostaCarpenter2012.pdf

found only 43.4 percent of female teams being coached by females. Additionally, as **TABLE 12.2** indicates, only 22.3 percent of athletic directors are women, compared with over 90 percent of the administrators who headed women's programs in 1972 (Acosta & Carpenter, 2014).

Professional Sport

Like interscholastic and intercollegiate sport, women are underrepresented in the leadership ranks of professional sport. Although there are growing opportunities for women in women's professional sports with the expansion of leagues such as the Women's National Basketball Association (WNBA), the Women's United Soccer Association (WUSA), and Women's Professional Soccer (WPS), there is still a lack of women in sport leadership because few women's leagues have survived and most professional sports are traditional male sports in which men have dominated the leadership ranks.

The University of Central Florida's Devos Sports Business Management Program and the Institute for Diversity and Ethics in Sport publishes the Racial and Gender Report Card. The report card examines the racial and gender hiring practices of Major League Baseball (MLB), Major League Soccer (MLS), the National Basketball Association (NBA), the National Football League (NFL), and the

Women's National Basketball Association (WNBA) as well as college athletic departments. To receive an A for gender, 45 percent of positions need to be held by women (Lapchick, 2017a). Notorious for lower grades, the NFL in 2016 received a C+ for its hiring practices related to gender. On the other hand, the WNBA has regularly been the leader for all professional sports when it comes to diversity and gender hiring. The NBA received a B for 2017 whereas MLB received a C+. Similar to what Acosta and Carpenter do with their studies of intercollegiate athletics, the University of Central Florida publishes its report card to indicate areas of improvement, stagnation, and regression in the racial and gender composition of professional and college sport personnel and to contribute to the improvement of integration in front office and college athletics department positions (Lapchick, 2012).

▶ International Sport

Examining the international landscape for women in sport leadership is important so as to provide a complete picture of leadership throughout the global sports industry. The United States is not unique, many other countries including Germany, Denmark, Norway, and Canada, also face the problem of the underrepresentation of women in sport leadership (Skirstad, 2005). Furthermore, on the International Olympic Committee (IOC), there are only 22.6 percent female board members (IOC, 2016), which led Lapchick (2016b) to give the IOC a D+ for the lack of women in leadership roles. Additionally, on international sport federations, women comprise 14 percent of board of director positions and only 8 percent of president positions (Adriaanse, 2015), leading Lapchick to give them an F. At the international level, women are underrepresented, leaving them out of some of the most visible and influential positions in sport worldwide.

▶ Reasons for Underrepresentation of Women in Sport

Women in sport leadership have and continue to face barriers that have limited them in attaining positions in the upper echelons of sport organizations. A significant amount of research has been done to examine these reasons as well as reasons for the continued underrepresentation of women in sport leadership. Potential barriers examined include stereotypes, discrimination, *hegemony*, and societal views about women's capabilities to lead in a traditionally male-dominated area. However, as noted by Shaw and Hoeber (2003), the reasons for the lack of women seen in leadership positions are "overwhelming" (p. 348). It would be impossible to list all of the reasons noted in the research regarding the lack of women in sport leadership. Everything from social forces and phenomena to structural forces to psychological reasons are identified and noted next.

In early work by Acosta and Carpenter (1988), they note a variety of reasons that may lead to the underrepresentation of women in sport leadership: (1) lack of support systems for women, (2) failure of the "old girls' network," (3) female burnout, and (4) failure of women to apply for job openings. Although this was a study done over 25 years ago, the research related to these categories continues. It is noteworthy, however, that in this study Acosta and Carpenter pointed out the underrepresentation of women at the individual level, focusing on what women could do to alleviate the situation.

Shaw and Frisby (2006) proposed examining the underrepresentation of women in sport leadership in a way that was different from previous research. They noted the importance for researchers to challenge power structures within sport organizations and to go beyond three dominant frameworks that have been used to examine gender issues in organizations. The three frameworks they believed researchers need to move beyond were (1) fixing women, (2) valuing femininity, and (3) creating equal opportunity. Shaw and Frisby suggested examining practices about assumptions regarding men's and women's roles in organizations.

Burton (2015) suggested that the underrepresentation of women in sport leadership must be examined from a multi-level perspective (i.e., individual, organizational, societal levels), as there are multiple reasons from a variety of factors and levels that can impede women. Cunningham (2007) identified three categories to explain the underrepresentation of women in sport leadership: (1) stereotypes, (2) structural forces, and (3) personal characteristics. Stereotypes affect people's beliefs about women's abilities to lead and in which roles they are capable of being successful. Structural forces are those that constrain or prevent women from advancing in athletics and can include the lack of social networks, discrimination, or the hours and days associated with careers in sport. Finally, personal characteristics, although influenced by stereotypes and structural forces, include things such as attitudes and intention to move up, or the decision to leave one's career (Cunningham).

Stereotyping has been shown to impact women in leadership and in sport leadership. Stereotypes, prejudice, and discrimination based on stereotyping have been explored as one mechanism accounting for inequity in the workforce for women (Sigleman & Tuch, 1997; Steinbeck & Tomaskovic-Devey, 2007). Prejudice can arise from perceptions regarding the characteristics of members of a social group (e.g., emotional) and the requirements of the social roles that group members occupy (e.g., caretakers, leaders, subordinates) (Eagly & Karau, 2002; Garcia-Retamero & López-Zafra, 2006, 2009; Heilman, Wallen, Fuchs, & Tamkins, 2004). A high potential for prejudice exists when perceivers hold a stereotype about a social group that is incongruent with the attributes that are thought to be required for success in certain classes of social roles. As an example of this potential for prejudice, when compared with women, men are perceived to have the stereotypical characteristics of successful managers (Schein, 2001).

When examining **gender equity** in management, **role congruity theory** has been applied to explain the lack of women in leadership positions through examination of gender role stereotyping and lack of fit-for-leadership roles. Gender expectations (e.g., being aggressive, self-confident, and dominant for men; being nurturing, affectionate, and weak for women) impact whether women and men are perceived to successfully fulfill their stereotypical gender roles. When evaluators review the qualifications of women for management positions, they are often influenced by stereotypical gender role expectations (Eagly & Karau, 2002). Role congruity theory describes prejudice that exists for women in management and leadership because leadership ability is more generally ascribed to men (Eagly & Karau, 2002). Hence, women may be disadvantaged in obtaining management and leadership positions because of the perception that they do not possess the requisite skill set to lead effectively. Additionally, even if women are in leadership positions, they may not be evaluated as favorably as men if they are perceived as violating gender norms attributed to women (Eagly & Karau, 2002).

Burton, Grappendorf, Henderson, and Dennis (2008) applied this perception to sport and found that male athletes benefit most and have been evaluated as more competent for upper-level positions compared with male nonathletes, female athletes, and female nonathletes with identical educational backgrounds. Furthermore, additional research revealed that equally qualified candidates for the position of athletic director were perceived to be capable of success, but women were less likely to be hired for positons than men.

Ultimately, the findings from this research indicated that female candidates were evaluated as significantly less likely to be offered the position of athletic director compared with the male candidate (Burton, Grappendorf, & Henderson, 2011)

At the structural level, the concept of **homologous reproduction**, which is the tendency to hire those most like ourselves, has been cited as a reason for underrepresentation of women in sport leadership (Knoppers, 1994; Stangl & Kane, 1991). Homologous reproduction would suggest that typically, because White males are in the top leadership positions in sport at the high school, college, and professional levels, they would then tend to also hire other White males. The theory of homologous reproduction describes that people tend to feel comfortable and can identify with others most like themselves (Knoppers; Stangl & Kane), so when it comes to making a hiring decision they are often biased in whom they select. Whisenant (2008) found the presence of homologous reproduction at the interscholastic level in girls' basketball and softball. Acosta and Carpenter (2014) studies have indicated that intercollegiate athletic departments led by men have fewer women in other positions of leadership lending support to homologous reproduction.

Although a study done by Darvin and Sagas (2016) found that female head coaches coaching women's intercollegiate teams were more likely to hire other female assistants, male head coaches of women's intercollegiate teams were not as likely to hire male assistants. Although this study contradicts homologous reproduction, it is too early to indicate without further studies to eradicate all previous research indicating that homologous reproduction is still a factor impacting women in sport leadership.

Hegemony, which can be defined as the power and dominance of one group over another, has also been well documented in sport (Coakley, 2017; Sage, 1998; Whisenant

et al., 2005) and could also be identified as a structural barrier. Hegemonic masculinity occurs when masculinity and the preservation of power of men over women is evident. As applied to sport, men are in power positions in leadership and, thus, are in a position to exert control. Whisenant et al., (2002) noted that, "Although Title IX and its enforcement chipped away at male hegemony on the playing field, hegemonic masculinity became even more entrenched in upper management "(p. 486).

Stroh, Langlands, and Simpson (2004) examined the **glass ceiling effect**, which refers to an invisible, but real barrier that prevents women from moving upward in administration. The glass ceiling effect literally refers to women who may be able to see those above them but face barriers that prevent them from reaching and attaining higher-ranking positions. Another term, the **glass wall**, refers to the horizontal restrictions and barriers to women achieving leadership roles (Miller, Kerr, & Reid, 1999). Walker and Bopp (2010) applied the term glass wall to describe the lack of access that women have to working in men's sports. Walker and Sartore-Baldwin (2013) used the glass wall as a framework for their work where they found evidence of men's sports as being an exclusive domain of men, and one where masculinity was highly valued.

The aforementioned reasons for the underrepresentation of women in sport leadership are far from an extensive list. However, they may provide some insight into helping further the understanding of some of the complex and complicated issues that have impacted the lack of women in sport leadership.

Women of Color: Double Jeopardy

As noted in this chapter, women are underrepresented in sport leadership positions. Women of color are notably absent from leadership positions in sport as sport leadership is not merely a male domain, but a White male domain. Ultimately, women of color face additional challenges due to their status in two historically underrepresented groups in sport. **Double jeopardy** (Alexander, 1978; Beale, 1979) describes the challenges that women of color face when trying to access formal networks (e.g., educational training) and informal networks (e.g., social relationships) that can enhance career advancement (Abney, 2000; Knoppers, Meyer, Ewing, & Forrest, 1991).

Although there have been two recent notable women of color hires, including Carla Williams at the University of Virginia and Desiree Reed-Francois at the University of Nevada-Las Vegas (UNLV), there is still an underrepresentation of women of color in sport leadership (Brewer, 2017; Wang, 2017). According to Lapchick (2016b), in the key leadership positions at Football Bowl Subdivision (FBS) schools and conferences, 85.9 percent of athletics directors are White and 100 percent of conference commissioners are White. In those positions, 75.8, 78.9, 62.9 and 90 percent are White men. Caple, Lapchick and LaVoi (2017) report that 87.9 percent of head coaches of women's teams were White, 6.93 percent African-American, 2.83 percent Latino and Asian, and 2.2 percent Hawaiian/Pacific Islanders. Furthermore, only 43.1 percent are women. For NCAA Division I athletic director positions, White men are most likely to hold the position, followed by White women, Black men, and, finally, Black women (NCAA, 2016). Additionally, the position of Senior Woman Administrator (SWA) is only held by 9.4 percent of Black women (NCAA, 2016).

The data from professional sport indicates a similar situation as in the collegiate ranks. In the Major League Baseball (MLB), women comprise only 29.3 percent of total central office professional employees, and only 28.1 percent are people of color (Lapchick, 2017b). The NBA has 35.1 percent of professional positions held by people of color while 38.8 are held by women (Lapchick, 2017c). The WNBA

has been the exception when it comes to professional leagues, as they have consistently had the highest percentages of racial and gender diversity. Of professional staff level positions, 69.6 percent of women held positions and 26.1 percent were held by people of color (Lapchick 2016c). In professional sport, the overall picture is one where White men continue to dominate the management and leadership ranks.

▸ Notable Females in Sport Leadership

There have been women who have worked diligently, advocating for women in sport leadership and those who have broken into the ranks of sport leadership at all levels. These women have worked diligently in their own spheres to help women advance in the sport realm. Some have led as athletes, coaches, advocates, researchers, or administrators. What has been evident is their influence on and impact for females in sport leadership as well as interest in sport leadership in the future. To highlight a few:

Katrina Adams is the CEO and President of the United States Tennis Association (USTA), and the Chair for the US Open. A former player on the Women's Tennis Association (WTA) tour, she is the first African-American to hold the position of President of the WTA (USTA, 2017).

Billie Jean King was a professional women's tennis player who infamously beat Bobby Riggs in the "Battle of the Sexes," and, in doing so, helped break down stereotypes and perceptions of female athletes. King later started the Women's Sports Foundation (WSF), a leading advocacy and educational organization (Spencer, 2000).

Lisa Borders is the current President of the Women's National Basketball Association (WNBA). Before being named the President of the WNBA, Borders held several high-profile leadership positions as she chaired The Coca-Cola Foundation, was Vice Mayor of Atlanta, and President of the City Council (WNBA, 2016).

Linda Carpenter and **R. Vivian Acosta** are two professors and researchers who have been tracking the numbers of women in leadership positions, as well as participation numbers over the past 35 years. They have arguably provided the most comprehensive look at the status of women in sport leadership positions over the years. Their longitudinal tracking of the numbers of women in leadership has brought awareness and insight to the ongoing issue of the underrepresentation of women as leaders (Hums & Yiamouyiannis, 2007).

Anita DeFrantz is the senior member of the International Olympic Committee (IOC) for the United States. She was only the fifth woman ever named to hold a seat on the 93-member IOC. DeFrantz is both the first African-American and the first American woman to serve on the committee (Dwyre, 2012; Hums & Yiamouyiannis, 2007).

Donna Lopiano was the chief executive officer of the Women's Sports Foundation from 1992 to 2007. Lopiano is known as an advocate for and expert on women's sport and has been named to "Most Powerful Women in Sports" lists over the years. She also served as the women's athletic director at the University of Texas at Austin for 18 years. She is well-respected in the sport world and recently started Sports Management Resources, a consulting company (Hums & Yiamouyiannis, 2007).

Val Ackerman was founding president of the WNBA and is current commissioner of the Big East Conference. When she resigned as president, she was named the first female president of USA Basketball in 2005. Both men's and women's basketball have garnered gold medals in both Olympic games since she took the reins (NCAA, 2017; O'Connor McDonogh, 2010).

▶ Strategies to Increase Women in Sport Leadership

Although there are numerous barriers to overcome for women to achieve equitable representation in sport leadership, research has been done regarding strategies to overcome underrepresentation. Researchers have focused on various tools, strategies, and methods to assist women with moving into the ranks of sport leadership.

Grappendorf, Burton, and Lilienthal (2007) recommended that women (1) get an education in sport management or a business-related area, (2) get involved in networking activities, (3) build networks, (4) get involved with national organizations, (5) gain knowledge of career paths and key positions that lead to leadership positions, (6) be willing to self-promote, and (7) get a mentor. Grappendorf et al., also note that it is not just important for women to take steps to attain leadership positions in sport. They recommend that it is crucial to educate those involved in the hiring process. This education would include disseminating information to those hiring (often men) regarding recruitment, evaluation, supervisor support, discrimination, stereotypes, and biases that could occur. In other words, it is important to look at strategies not just at the individual level to increase the representation of women in sport leadership but also at the organizational and structural levels.

In a study funded by the NCAA, Drago, Hennighausen, Rogers, Vescio, and Stauffer (2005) studied why women were underrepresented in the leadership ranks of coaching and athletic administration. In the Coaching and Gender Equity (CAGE) Project report, they recommended: (1) increasing the number of women in the pipeline; (2) formalizing the hiring practices, decision-making processes, training and development, and career paths of women; (3) making the environment for coaches and administrators more welcoming and flexible in response to family commitments; and (4) providing a more inclusive environment for women.

Other approaches toward increasing the number of women in leadership have been advanced. Leberman (2017) noted ways in which to foster young women's interests toward sport leadership, highlighting the importance of programs, training, and participation in sport from an early age. Adriaanse (2017) examined the effectiveness of setting quotas by sport entities, finding some success when they were established. Wells and Hancock (2017) suggested the use of networks, mentors, and sponsorship. Although many are familiar with the importance of building networks and having mentors, not as much is known about sponsorship. Sponsorship goes beyond mentoring, as it is a person who advocates and promotes their mentee's career progression (Ibarra et al., 2010).

The reasons for the underrepresentation are numerous, and, therefore, require a variety of strategies to increase women in sport leadership. Furthermore, it is important to note that strategies to address the underrepresentation of women in sport leadership are not just women's issues. In other words, everyone involved with sport can be an advocate who adopts the aforementioned or other strategies in addressing the lack of women in sport leadership.

▶ Summary

One may have thought that Title IX would increase not only the number of women participating in sport, but also the numbers in leadership. However, clearly, this has not occurred, and the numbers of women in leadership at the high school, college, and even professional levels have not improved. More women participating in sport has not led to more women in leadership in sport. Women continue to be under-represented in the ranks of sport leadership. At all levels, including the high school, college, and professional ranks, women continue to struggle with issues and barriers that have limited their leadership opportunities. It is important not only to continue to track these numbers but also to continue to examine the reasons why the underrepresentation persists. Finally, it is essential that strategies and tools be developed for women, and that the education and training of those responsible for hiring or already in leadership positions continue.

LEADERSHIP PERSPECTIVE

Courtesy of Amy Huchthausen.

Amy Huchthausen

Amy Huchthausen has served as commissioner of the America East Conference since September 2011. She is the fourth commissioner and is the first woman to serve in that role. Has a result of her success at the AEC, Huchthausen was recognized by the Sports Business Journal as a "Game Changer" in September of 2015 and she was named a "2016 Forty Under 40" honoree in April of 2016.

Q: What are your perceptions regarding why there continue to be so few women in senior levels of leadership in sport organizations?

I believe one of the biggest reason why there are so few women in senior leadership positions in sport organizations is because the primary decision makers are still predominantly male. And we are still not through the generational let alone cultural change that would have those senior level people, those who are doing the hiring, move away from selecting people who they know or people who look like them (i.e., other men). Until we cycle through a portion of a generation of leaders, we won't see significant change.

It is also pipeline effect; these senior level positions require a certain amount of experience and that takes time. There haven't been as many women in deputy or associate level leadership positions on the college side or vice president or senior vice president on the professional side of sport leadership. You need women in those positions so that they can develop the necessary skills for senior leadership. You need to have that pipeline built that includes women ready to take on senior leadership positions.

Q: How do you improve the pipeline to help more women gain access to senior leadership positions?

I think it is doing the hard work at the entry level on recruitment of women into sport organizations and then it is retention of women in those positions. The sport industry is an attractive place to work, there is more demand for jobs than there is an available supply. It is incumbent upon those who are in senior leadership positions in sport organizations to recruit women into those entry-level positions. As there are more women working in sport organizations, it now becomes a retention issue. There are a lot of factors regarding why women leave the workforce, including in the sport industry, so we need to deal with the challenges women face working in any industry but also address the challenges that are unique to the sport industry, including late nights and weekend work. Education, good mentors, more contemporary workplace policies that allow women the flexibility necessary to make life decisions that help women to stay in their positions are all important trigger points to help support women and to help retain women who will be available for senior level positions moving forward. You must bring along and provide support for those women who are strong, have shown potential, and want to remain in and advance through to senior level positions.

Q: What are the challenges women face when working in leadership positions (senior level) in sport organizations?

Many of the challenges are related to family, whether it is children or taking care of elderly parents, women are still viewed as the primary caretakers of the family. Even when there are shared partnerships, women are taking on a large portion of those caretaking responsibilities. Also, women may still struggle or take longer to come to recognize our own skill level. Women are resistant to being brave and applying for jobs, moving across industry, or accepting a different position, yet men don't seem to hesitate about applying for those jobs. I think generally women are resistant to apply for those positions that will help lead to advancement. However, those are things that can be changed, those are coachable things. I think we can educate and inform women and men to create organizational policies that help reduce the burden of family constraints and family obligation. But it is also important to help women gain the confidence to develop the necessary skill sets for leadership and to apply for new positions. Providing that mentorship and support that women need, that is something that can be done to address the issue of lack of confidence.

Q: What strategies would you suggest for those in senior leadership positions to help women to advance to higher levels of leadership in the sport industry?

I think that having networking conferences and workshops, all of those educational types of programming, I don't think there can ever be enough of that. It needs to be focused and intentional. There is a lot of room for major conferences (500 to 1,000 people) where you can go listen to a keynote speaker and be informed and inspired, but that only resonates to a certain level. I think it needs to

(continues)

LEADERSHIP PERSPECTIVE (*continued*)

be done more at the grassroots level, with speakers and colleagues who are more relatable. If I'm a woman who has just started my career, is there someone I can reach out to and have a conversation with about my experiences as a woman in the field. That is where I think there is a big opportunity for women to help build confidence and an opportunity to support women. The second step is being able to express that confidence among men as well—you need to help support women to express confidence and demonstrate competence not only in female supportive spaces or around only female colleagues but also around male colleagues. There is value in women-only programming, but the next step is to display leadership characteristics around both men and women. It is also really important to have male champions and male advocates for women. Women developing in their careers must form strong networks of women at the senior level of support but also expand those networks to include both men and women.

▶ Key Terms

Association for
    Intercollegiate Athletics
    for Women (AIAW)
Double jeopardy

Gender equity
Glass ceiling effect
Glass walls
Hegemony

Homologous reproduction
Role congruity theory
Title IX

▶ Discussion Questions

1. If you were hiring for an open position for athletic director at the high school level, how would you avoid the perception that *homologous reproduction* may influence your selection of a candidate for that position?

2. Consider Cunningham's three categories to explain the underrepresentation of women in sport leadership: (1) stereotypes, (2) structural forces, and (3) personal characteristics. Research how one of the major professional sports leagues (NFL, NBA, NHL, MLB, or MLS) attempts to address the lack of women in leadership positions within its own league.

3. Describe the concepts of the glass ceiling and glass wall and how these concepts can help to explain why there are so few women in athletic director positions in Division I FBS and FCS universities.

4. Considering the challenges women face in obtaining leadership positions in sport organizations, how would you mentor young women graduating with sport management degrees regarding strategies to advance to leadership positions in sport organizations?

5. Research a woman serving in a leadership position for a major professional sport organization and provide details about her education and career path. How has her experience in the field of sport been influenced by *Title IX*?

▶ References

Abney, R. (1988). The effects of role models and mentors on career patterns of Black women coaches and athletic administrators in historically black and historically white institutions of higher education. *Dissertations Abstract International, 49*(11), 3210. (UMI No. 8903907).

Abney, R. (2000). The glass ceiling effect. In D. Brooks & R. Althouse (Eds.), *Racism in college athletics: The African-American athlete's experience* (2nd ed., pp. 119–130). Morgantown, WV: Fitness Information Technology.

Acosta, R. V., & Carpenter, L. J. (1988). *Perceived causes of the declining representation of women leaders in intercollegiate sports—1988 update* (unpublished manuscript). Brooklyn College, Brooklyn, NY.

Acosta, R., & Carpenter, L. (2014). Women in intercollegiate sport: A longitudinal national study, thirty-seven year update: 1977-2014. Retrieved from www.acostacarpenter.org

Acosta, R. V., & Carpenter, L. J. (2012). Women in intercollegiate sport: A longitudinal, national study thirty-five year update, 1977-2012. Retrieved from http://acostacarpenter.org/AcostaCarpenter2012.pdf

Acosta, R. V., & Carpenter, L. J. (2007). Intercollegiate sports. In M.A. Hums, G.G. Bower, & H. Grappendorf (Eds.), *Women leaders in sport: Impact and influence (pp. 45–62).* Oxon Hills, MD: National Association for Girls and Women in Sport.

Adriaanse, J. (2017). Quotas to accelerate *gender equity* in sport leadership: Do they work? In L. J. Burton & S. Leberman (Eds.), *Women in sport leadership: Research and practice for change.* London: Routledge.

Adriaanse, J. (2016). Gender diversity in the governance of sport associations: The Sydney Scoreboard Global Index of Participation. *Journal of Business Ethics, 137*(1), 149–160.

Alexander, A. (1978). *Status of minority women in the Association of Intercollegiate Athletics for Women* (unpublished master's thesis). Temple University, Philadelphia, PA.

Beale, F. (1979). Double jeopardy: To be Black and female. In T. Cade (Ed.), *The Black woman: An anthology* (pp. 90–100). New York: New American Library.

Boutilier, M. A., & SanGiovanni, L. (1983). *The sporting woman.* Champaign, IL: Human Kinetics.

Brewer, R. (2017). New UNLV athletic director brings great resume, great energy. Retrieved from https://lasvegassun.com/news/2017/apr/23/new-unlv-athletic-director-brings-great-energy/

Burton, L. (2015). Underrepresentation of women in sport leadership: A review of research. *Sport Management Review, 18*, 155–165.

Burton, L., Grappendorf, H., & Henderson, A. C. (2011). Perceptions of gender in athletic administration: Utilizing *role congruity theory* to examine potential prejudice against women. *Journal of Sport Management, 25*(1), 36–45.

Burton, L. J., Grappendorf, H., Henderson, A. C., Field, G. B., & Dennis, J. A. (2008). The relevance of intercollegiate athletic participation for men and women: Examination of hiring preferences to entry-level management positions based on role congruity theory. *International Journal of Sport Management, 9,* 175–192.

Caple, N., Lapchick, R., LaVoi, N. M. (2017, June). Gender, race, and LGBT inclusion of head coaches of women's collegiate teams: A special collaborative report on select NCAA Division I conferences for the 45th anniversary of Title IX. Retrieved from http://www.cehd.umn.edu/tuckercenter/library/docs/research/2017_Title_IX_at_45_Report.pdf

Chepko, S., & Couturier, L. (2001). From intersection to collision: Women's sports from 1920–1980. In G. Cohen (Ed.), *Women in sport: Issues and controversies* (pp. 79–110). Oxon Hill, MD: American Association of Health, Physical Education, Recreation and Dance.

Coakley, J. (2017). *Sport in society: Issues and controversies* (12th ed.). Boston, MA: McGraw-Hill.

Cunningham, G. B. (2007). *Diversity in sport organizations.* Scottsdale, AZ: Holcomb Hathaway.

Darvin, L., & Sagas, M. (2016). An examination of homologous reproduction in the representation of assistant coaches of women's teams: A 10-year update. *Gender Issues,* 1–15.

Drago, R., Hennighausen, L., Rogers, J., Vescio, T., & Stauffer, K. D. (2005). CAGE: The coaching and gender equity project. Retrieved from http://www.epi.soe.vt.edu/perspectives/policy_news/docs/CAGE.doc

Dwyre, B. (2012). Anita DeFrantz is still pulling an oar for the Olympic movement. Retrieved from http://articles.latimes.com/print/2012/aug/08/sports/la-sp-oly-dwyre-defrantz-20120809

Eagly, A. H., & Karau, S. J. (2002). Role congruity theory of prejudice toward female leaders. *Psychological Review, 109*(3), 573–598.

Garcia-Retamero, R., & López-Zafra, E. (2006). Prejudice against women in male-congenial environments: Perceptions of gender role congruity in leadership. *Sex Roles, 55*(1-2), 51–61.

Garcia-Retamero, R., & López-Zafra, E. (2009). Causal attributions about feminine and leadership roles. *Journal of Cross-Cultural Psychology, 40*(3), 492–509.

Grappendorf, H., Burton, L. J., & Lilienthal, S. (2007). *Strategies for improving opportunities for women in sport management positions.* In M. Hums, G. Bower, & H. Grappendorf (Eds.), *Women as leaders in sport: Impact and influence* (pp. 299–320). Oxon Hill, MD: American Association of Health, Physical Education, Recreation and Dance.

Heilman, M. E., Wallen, A. S., Fuchs, D., & Tamkins, M. M. (2004). Penalties for success: Reactions to women who succeed at male tasks. *Journal of Applied Psychology, 89*(3), 416–427.

Hooks, B. (1981). *Ain't I a woman: Black women and feminism* (Vol. 3). Boston: South End Press.

Hult, J. (1991). The governance of athletics for girls and women: Leadership by women physical educators, 1899-1949. In J. S. Hult & M. Trekell (Eds.), *A century of women's basketball: From frailty to final four,* (pp. 53–82). Reston, VA: American Association of Health, Physical Education, Recreation and Dance.

Hult, J. S. (1980). The philosophical conflicts in men's and women's collegiate athletics. *Quest, 32*(1), 77–94.

Hultstrand, B. J. (1993). The growth of collegiate women's sports: The 1960's. *Journal of Physical Education, Recreation, and Dance, 64*(3), 41–43.

Hums, M. A. (2010). The Conscience and commerce of sport management: One teacher's perspective. *Journal of Sport Management, 24,* 1–9.

Hums, M. A., & Yiamouyiannis, A. (2007). Women in sport careers and leadership positions. In M. A. Hums, G. G. Bower, and H. Grappendorf (Eds.), *Women as Leaders in Sport: Impact and Influence* (pp. 1–24). Oxon Hill, MD: American Association of Health, Physical Education, Recreation and Dance.

Ibarra, H., Carter, N. M., & Silva, C. (2010). Why men still get more promotions than women. *Harvard Business Review, 9,* 80–85.

International Olympic Committee (2016). *Women in the Olympic movement* [Fact sheet]. Retrieved from https://stillmed.olympic.org/Documents/Reference _documents_Factsheets/Women_in_Olympic _Movement.pdf

Knoppers, A. (1994). Gender and the coaching profession. In S. Birrell & C. L. Cole (Eds.), *Women, sport and culture* (pp. 119–133). Champaign, IL: Human Kinetics.

Knoppers, A., Meyer, B. B., Ewing, M., & Forrest, L. (1991). Opportunity and work behavior in college coaching. *Journal of Sport and Social Issues, 15*(1), 1–20.

Lapchick, R. (2017a). Important change as TIDES updated its grading scale for the racial and gender report cards. *The Institute for Diversity and Ethics in Sport.* Retrieved from http://www.tidesport.org/reports.html

Lapchick, R. (2017b). The 2017 racial and gender report card: Major League Baseball. *The Institute for Diversity and Ethics in Sport.* Retrieved from http://nebula.wsimg.com /d96daf1e011b077b2fd9ff4cfe4bf1bc?AccessKeyId= DAC3A56D8FB782449D2A&disposition=0&allow origin=1

Lapchick, R. (2017c). The 2017 racial and gender report card: National Basketball Association. *The Institute for Diversity and Ethics in Sport.* Retrieved from http://nebula.wsimg.com/74491b38503915f2f148062f f076e698? AccessKeyId=DAC3A56D8FB782449D2A &disposition=0&alloworigin=1

Lapchick, R. (2016a). Collegiate athletic leadership still dominated by white men: Assessing diversity among campus and conference leaders for Football Bowl Subdivision (FBS) schools in the 2016-17 academic year. *The Institute for Diversity and Ethics in Sport.* Retrieved from http://nebula.wsimg.com /d24d52ce0c3444baaa316c9a2dc58ad8?Access KeyId=DAC3A56D8FB782449D2A&disposition =0&alloworigin=1

Lapchick, R. (2016b). Gender report card: 2016 International sports report card on women in leadership roles. *The Institute for Diversity and Ethics in Sport.* Retrieved from https://nebula.wsimg.com/0e5c5c3e23367795e9ec9 e5ec49fc9b2?AccessKeyId=DAC3A56D8 FB782449D2A&disposition=0&alloworigin=1

Lapchick, R. (2016c). The 2016 Women's National Basketball Association racial and gender report card. *The Institute for Diversity and Ethics in Sport.* Retrieved from http://nebula.wsimg.com/75d5182d7b10f789a d38bc8e9f188ed4?AccessKeyId=DAC3A56D8 FB782449D2A&disposition=0&alloworigin=1

Lapchick, R. E. (2012). The 2012 Racial and gender report card: College sport. Retrieved from https://www.ncaa .org/sites/default/files/Final%2B2012%2BCollege %2BRGRC.pdf

Leberman, S. (2017). Future sport leaders: Developing young women to lead. In L. J. Burton & S. Leberman (Eds.), *Women in sport leadership: Research and practice for change.* London: Routledge.

Longman, J. (2012, July 13). Before games, wins for women. Retrieved from http://www.nytimes.com/2012/07/14 /sports/olympics/before-london-games-wins-for -women.html?_r=0

Lovett, D., & Lowry, C. (1994). "Good old boys" and "good old girls" clubs: Myth or reality? *Journal of Sport Management, 8,* 27–35.

Miller, W., Kerr, B., Reid, M. (1999). A national study of gender-based occupational segregation in municipal bureaucracies: Persistence of glass walls? *Public Administration Review, 59*(3), 218–230.

National Collegiate Athletic Association. (2017). Past experiences help Big East Commissioner Val Ackerman enhance conference growth. Retrieved from http://www.ncaa.com/news/ncaa/article/2017-08-17 /past-experiences-help-big-east-commissioner -val-ackerman-enhance

National Collegiate Athletic Association. (2016). Athletics administrative staff: 2015-2016.

Southwestern Athletic Conference figures search [Data file]. Retrieved from http://web1.ncaa.org/rgdSearch/exec/instSearch

National Federation of State High School Associations. (2017). 2016-2017 high school athletics participation survey. Retrieved from http://www.nfhs.org/ParticipationStatistics/PDF/2016-17_Participation_Survey_Results.pdf

O'Connor McDonogh, M. (2010). Women as leaders in professional sport. In K. O'Connor (Ed.), *Gender and women's leadership: A reference handbook* (pp. 869–875). Thousand Oaks, CA: Sage.

Office for Civil Rights. (1979). *A policy interpretation: Title IX and intercollegiate athletics.* Retrieved from http://www.ed.gov/about/offices/list/ocr/docs/t9interp.html

Rhode, D. L., & Walker, C. J. (2007). Gender equity in college athletics: Women coaches as a case study. Retrieved from http://law.bepress.com/cgi/viewcontent.cgi?article=9336&context=expresso

Rintala, J. (2001). Play as competition: An ideological dilemma. In G. L. Cohen (Ed.), *Women in sport: Issues and controversies* (pp. 37–56). Oxon Hill, MD: American Association of Health, Physical Education, Recreation and Dance.

Sage, G. H. (1998). *Power and ideology in American sport: A critical perspective* (2nd ed.). Champaign, IL: Human Kinetics.

Schein, V. E. (2001). A global look at psychological barriers to women's progress in management. *Journal of Social Issues, 57*(4), 675–688.

Shaw, S., & Frisby, W. (2006). Can gender equity be more equitable? Promoting an alternative frame for sport management research, education, and practice. *Journal of Sport Management, 20*(4), 483–509.

Shaw, S., & Hoeber, L. (2003). "A strong man is direct and a direct woman is a bitch": Gendered discourses and their influence on employment roles in sport organizations. *Journal of Sport Management, 17*(4), 347–375.

Sigleman, L., & Tuch, S. A. (1997). Metastereotypes: Blacks' perceptions of Whites' stereotypes of Blacks. *Public Opinion Quarterly, 61,* 87–101.

Skirstad, B. (2005) Women's influence in sport as internal and external stakeholders. In G. Doll-Tepper, G. Pfister, D. Scoretz, & C. Bilan (Eds), *Sport, women and leadership* (pp. 131–146). Koln, Germany: Sport und Buch StrauB GmbH.

Smith, M., & Wrynn, A. (2013). *Women in the 2012 Olympic and Paralympic Games: An analysis of participation and leadership opportunities.* Ann Arbor, MI: SHARP Center for Women and Girls.

Spencer, N. E. (2000). Reading between the lines: A discursive analysis of the Billie Jean King vs. Bobby Riggs "Battle of the Sexes." *Sociology of Sport Journal, 17*(4), 386–402.

Stangl, J. M., & Kane, M. J. (1991). Structural variables that offer explanatory power for the underrepresentation of women coaches since Title IX: The case of homologous reproduction. *Sociology of Sport Journal, 8*(1), 47–60.

Steinbeck, K., & Tomaskovic-Devey, D. D. (2007). Discrimination and desegregation: Equal opportunity progress in U.S. private sector workplaces since the Civil Rights Act. *Annals of the American Academy of Political and Social Science, 609*(1), 49–84.

Stroh, L. K., Langlands, C. L., & Simpson, P. A. (2004). Shattering the glass ceiling in the new millennium. In M. S. Stockdale & F. J. Crobsy (Eds.), *The psychology and management of workplace diversity* (pp. 147–167). Malden, MA: Blackwell.

Swanson, R., & Spears, B. (1995). *The history of sport and physical education in the United States.* Burr Ridge, IL: McGraw-Hill.

Tucker Center for Research on Girls and Women in Sport. (2014) Minnesota high school coaches report 2013-14. Retrieved from http://www.cehd.umn.edu/tuckercenter/library/docs/research/MSHSCA-2013-14-MN-High-School-Coaches-Report.pdf

Uhlir, G. A. (1987). Athletics and the university: The post-woman's era. *Academe, 73*(4), 25–29.

United States Tennis Association. (2017). USTA Chairman of the Board & President Katrina M. Adams. Retrieved from https://www.usta.com/en/home/about-usta/usta-leadership/national/katrina-adams.html

Walker, N. A., & Bopp, T. (2011). The underrepresentation of women in the male-dominated sport workplace: Perspectives of female coaches. *Journal of Workplace Rights, 15*(1), 47–64.

Walker, N. A., & Sartore-Baldwin, M. (2013). Hegemonic masculinity and the institutionalized bias toward women in men's collegiate basketball: What do men think? *Journal of Sport Management, 27*(4), 303–315.

Wang, G. (2017). Virginia set to be first power five schools with African American woman as athletic director. Retrieved https://www.washingtonpost.com/news/sports/wp/2017/10/21/virginia-set-to-announce-carla-williams-as-new-athletic-director/?utm_term=.24b1bd231df9

Wells, J. E., & Hancock, M. G. (2017). Networking, mentoring, sponsoring: strategies to support women in sport leadership. In L. J. Burton & S. Leberman (Eds.), *Women in sport leadership: Research and practice for change.* London: Routledge.

Whisenant, W. A. (2003). How women have fared as interscholastic athletic administrators since the passage of Title IX. *Sex Roles, 49*(3-4), 179–184.

Whisenant, W. A. (2008). Sustaining male dominance in interscholastic athletics: A case of homologous reproduction…or not? *Sex Roles, 58*(11/12), 768–775.

Whisenant, W. A., Miller, J., & Pedersen, P. M. (2005). Systematic barriers in athletic administration: An analysis of job descriptions for interscholastic athletic directors. *Sex Roles, 53*(11-12), 911–918.

Whisenant, W., Pedersen, P., & Obenour, B. (2002). Success and gender: Determining the rate of advancement for intercollegiate athletic directors. *Sex Roles, 47*(9-10), 485–491.

Women's National Basketball Association. (2016). Lisa Borders named WNBA President. Retrieved from http://www.wnba.com/news/lisa-borders-named-wnba-president/

Women's Sports Foundation. (n.d.). Coaching—Do female athletes prefer male coaches: The Foundation position. Retrieved from http://www.womenssportsfoundation.org/home/advocate/foundation-positions/equity-issues/do_female_athletes_prefer_male_coaches

CHAPTER 13

Lingering Issues in Race and Leadership

Jacqueline McDowell
Algerian Hart
Emmett Gill

CHAPTER OBJECTIVES

- Understand the historical implications of prejudicial attitudes and discrimination that have come to bear on sport leadership in the 21st century.
- Describe how stereotypes manifest themselves into prejudicial biases that can limit leadership avenues for minority groups in the United States.
- Recognize situations of race underrepresentation in leadership within sport organizations.
- Identify and understand the different leadership issues in collegiate sport and professional sport leagues.

CASE STUDY

Staley and Legette-Jack Offer Glimmers of Hope

"Thank you for that question."

It is rare that a college basketball coach thanks a member of the media for a question following a loss in the Sweet 16 of the NCAA Tournament, but that is how University of Buffalo head coach Felisha Legette-Jack responded after she was asked about a lack of diversity in college athletics (Mandell, 2018). Legette-Jack's Bulls had just lost to Dawn Staley's South Carolina team in the 2018 tournament. It was a matchup of two Black female coaches who are in the upper echelon of college basketball coaches—something to be celebrated. For Legette-Jack, getting a second chance following her firing at Indiana University in 2012 was not easy, but she persevered; Staley has avoided a lot of the normal barriers. Less than a year

(continues)

CASE STUDY   (continued)

earlier, Staley's Gamecocks topped Mississippi State University, 67 to 55, in the National Collegiate Athletic Association (NCAA) women's tournament basketball championship. The victory in 2017 was significant for many reasons, but three things stand out: It was the basketball program's first NCAA title; a team other than the University of Connecticut was left standing triumphant as the final buzzer sounded; and Staley became just the second Black female coach to win a title in Division I women's basketball, a sport in which rosters are largely composed of Black players. Carolyn Peck was the first Black woman to lead her team to a national title with Purdue in 1999. It took 18 years for another Black female coach to do it.

But what is most significant is how Staley's path has differed from most Black women who gain head coach positions. Staley's meteoric rise offers a glimmer of hope for Black women. Would-be coaches tend to start out as college players. Sometimes, they play professionally as well. Staley played at the University of Virginia from 1988-1992. After a stellar career, she played in the American Basketball League and then eight seasons in the Women's National Basketball Association (WNBA). She began her coaching career at Temple University in 2000 and coached there for eight seasons, compiling a 172-80 record. Staley began at the University of South Carolina in 2008 and has compiled a 221-80 record in her nine seasons (Gamecocks Women's Basketball, 2018). Staley sidestepped the long ladder that many have to climb to run their own program. Often, future coaches start off as a graduate assistant to a team, move on to roles in basketball team operations, possibly become an assistant coach and, if the program they are in is successful, they might get some head coach offers. But many women toil away as assistant head coaches for years and never get a chance to move up. Like other workplaces, athletic departments have glass ceilings. The problem with this glass ceiling is that it not only serves as a deterrent to gender but it blocks race too. The 2017 Racial and Gender Report Card noted that only 10.9 percent of women's basketball coaches were Black females. Yet, Black women made up 45.4 percent of the player rosters (Lapchick, Marfatia, Bloom, & Sylverain, 2017). This percentage difference led *Chicago Tribune* writer Shannon Ryan (2017) to declare, "Colleges are the worst employers for women and people of color in sports."

Consider the curious case of basketball legend Cheryl Miller. Carter-Francique and Olushola (2016) reported that when Miller attempted to return to college coaching, she found it difficult to break back in at a big school. "There were a lot of doors that were slammed" (Steckley 2014, para. 7). Ultimately, she was hired at Langston University in 2014. Langston is a National Association of Intercollegiate Athletics (NAIA) school. It could be argued that Miller's prowess as a player (she earned Basketball Hall of Fame honors for accomplishments at both the collegiate and Olympics levels) and as a coach (she was head coach at her alma mater, the University of Southern California and the WNBA's Phoenix Mercury) should have earned her a better head coaching job than at Langston. In 2016, she became head coach at California State-Los Angeles, a Division II school. Given Miller's knowledge of the game, it is a surprise that not more Division I athletic departments were clamoring to hire her. But people tend to hire those with whom they are comfortable and in sports, like society, Whites and Blacks still are not as comfortable with one another as they should be (Powell, 2008). Most athletic directors at major universities are White, likely did not grow up in a Black neighborhood, and may not have had many Black friends growing up. A White athletic director's (AD) circle of close friends is mostly all White (Powell, 2008) and "Whites in power tend to rely on a tired formula: Go with whom you know" (p. 214).

Legette-Jack acknowledges how difficult it can be for Black women to get noticed: "It took an African-American woman to notice me when I lost my job at Indiana. Had she not noticed me, Danny White (former AD at Buffalo) would never have known about me; and because she spoke to him and I was able to present myself to him, I was able to get this opportunity to bring this—from where it was to where it is now" (Mandell, 2018, para. 4).

Despite the barriers, Legette-Jack sounds undeterred: "The fight is for the next young lady who needs a person who looks like her to rise above and to be coached up and create a foundation so that she can become the COO, the CFO of something very big. It's important that they stay in the race and keep fighting. We see them. You're out there. Keep fighting. Go forward" (Mandell, 2018, para. 7).

Questions for Discussion:

1. What can athletic departments and hiring committees do to encourage diversity in coaching positions in Division I athletics?
2. Powell noted that White men, who hold many of the power positions in Division I sports, tend to only pay attention to other Whites since they most closely associate with that racial group. How can hiring committees be composed to avoid such favoritism?
3. According to Legette-Jack, a Black woman trying to become a head coach often needs some luck to get noticed. Knowing this, what can Black female assistant coaches who want to become head coaches do to get noticed by a mostly White establishment in Division I athletics?
4. Black women make up 45% of players in Division I basketball but only 10.9% of head coaches of the teams. Researchers point to this as an example of Black women not getting enough opportunities in leadership roles. Are there other possible explanations for these varying percentages?

▶ Introduction

In every organization, there is a person at the top who oversees and guides the organization in the best direction. These leaders are essentially individuals who have the ability to understand their own times, who express or articulate programs or policies that reflect the perceived interests and desires of particular groups, and who devise instruments or political vehicles that enhance the capacity to achieve effective change. In limited ways, leaders imprint their personal characteristics or individual stamp on a given moment in time. Leaders do make history, but never by themselves and never in ways that they fully recognize or anticipate[1].

In a commencement speech delivered to Knox College in 2005, a newly elected U.S. Senator Barack Hussein Obama said:

"The true test of the American ideal is whether we're able to recognize our failings and then rise together to meet the challenges of our time. Whether we allow ourselves to be shaped by events and history, or whether we act to shape them. Whether chance of birth or circumstance decides life's big winners and losers, or whether we build

a community where, at the very least, everyone has a chance to work hard, get ahead, and reach their dreams."

Commencement Address: Barack Obama. (2013, July 18). Retrieved from https://www.knox.edu/news/president -obama-to-visit-knox-college-speak -on-economy/2005-commencement -address.

In 2008, Obama became the 44th "Leader of the Free World"—becoming the first Black American[2] to hold the most prestigious leadership position in the nation. President Obama has an exceptional educational background and was admitted into Occidental College and Columbia University, and he earned his Juris Doctorate from Harvard University Law School. Moreover, he was the first Black-American to serve as president of the Harvard Law Review; and prior to his ascension into the U.S. presidency, he was elected to the Illinois State Senate and the United States Senate. With these great accomplishments and his historic achievement, many people see this as evidence that the U.S. is in a post-racial era in which all Americans, regardless of race, can attain

---

[1] Portions of the introductory paragraph were generated from ideas espoused by Dr. Jack Thomas, president of Western Illinois University in December 2012.

[2] President Obama would be considered bi-racial because he has a White mother and a Black Kenyan father, but in the racial understanding of U.S. society, many people consider a person with "one drop of Black blood" to be Black (Hickman, 1997; Ho, Sidanius, Levin, & Banji, 2011).

prestigious leadership positions if they take advantage of educational resources and work hard (Jimenez, 2011; Rachlinski & Parks, 2010).

A Black American may have held the most prestigious position in the nation, but are we in a post-racial era? As evidenced by a lot of the rhetoric surrounding President Obama's campaigns and elections (Hehman, Baertner & Dovidio, 2011; Rachlinski & Parks, 2010; Piston, 2010) and also rhetoric by American citizens two years into the Trump Presidency—particularly surrounding the protests in Charlottesville, VA—prejudicial attitudes and discrimination still persist in U.S. society (Pew Research Center, 2016). Progress has been made and many people of color[3] have made notable accomplishments, but there are still barriers and obstacles that prevent all Americans from getting ahead and reaching their dreams. In many organizations, people of color still struggle to obtain and retain leadership positions and are disproportionally concentrated in lower service positions.

The sports industry is no exception, as a "**black-bottomed pyramid**" exists with more people of color overrepresented as athletes at the bottom of the pyramid than in top leadership roles in sport organizations (Shropshire, 1996). Discussions about the low representation of people of color in leadership positions have lingered for years and have many people asking about when the conversations will cease and is progress being made? Defining progress is subjective and "we are not going to be able to paint, in advance, a statistical picture of success" (Shropshire, 2004, p. 194). Despite difficulty in objectively defining progress, in this chapter, we provide evidence that progress is being made, but equity and parity have not been reached and persistent discriminatory and non-discriminatory behaviors continue to affect opportunities for persons of color in sport leadership positions.

Accordingly, this chapter focuses on the underrepresentation of men and women of color in front office (e.g. manager/general managers, athletic directors, owners) and head coaching positions in college and professional sport organizations—with a particular focus on American football, baseball, and basketball. In sport organizations, **underrepresentation** has been determined by comparing the number of people of color in leadership positions to U.S. Census demographic percentages (e.g., Race and Gender Report Cards) or to their representation as student-athletes (e.g., BCA Reports). However, unlike most industries that use specific geographic locations to determine underutilization, we contend that a local or regional labor market is not appropriate when determining underrepresentation of people of color in sport leadership positions. Moreover, extant sports research suggests that players are the most plausible labor force for determining underutilization (Cunningham & Sagas, 2002; Everhart & Chelladurai, 1998). Hence, in this chapter, we define underrepresentation based on demographic comparisons between leadership and playing positions. We, however, challenge readers to assess critically the limitations and strengths of both methods for claiming underrepresentation.

Based on this working definition of underrepresentation, Hispanics/Latinos, Asians, and Native Americans would not be referred to as being underrepresented in sport leadership positions because the reference group—their representation as athletes at the college and professional levels—has traditionally been very low. As a result of not being deemed underrepresented in leadership positions, the experiences of these racial groups are often neglected in research, mass media, and **social justice** efforts. According

[3]The expression "persons/people of color" has recently emerged as a preference over using non-White and minority to refer to Native Americans, and Americans of African, Asian, or Hispanic descent. In this chapter, we have chosen to use this expression because it is more inclusive and the expression "non-White" defines people by what they are not; whereas the term minority can convey inferiority and subordination (Clark & Arboleda, 1999; Safire, 1988).

to Chideya (1999), "In the basest and most stereotypical terms, White Americans are considered "true" Americans; Black Americans are considered inferior Americans; Asians and Latinos are too often considered foreigners; and Native Americans are rarely thought of at all" (p. 7). These sentiments ring true as dominant discourses on race and sport focus primarily on "Americans"—White and Black—and the experiences of Asians, Latinos, and Native Americans are often neglected. This **binary** racial thinking has served to exclude and marginalize the experiences of these racial groups.

In this chapter, we center the experiences of Black Americans, Hispanics/Latinos, Asians, and Native Americans in sport leadership positions. In order to obtain a more accurate understanding of the experiences and opportunities for people of color in sport, a broader understanding of current and socio-historic leadership barriers is needed. Hence, we first present an overview of educational and socio-psychological barriers to leadership attainment, followed by a discussion of the current status of people of color in sport leadership positions. This chapter concludes with a review of current social justice efforts to increase the representation of people of color into sport leadership positions.

▶ Historic and Current Leadership Barriers

The United States has a remarkable history that has situated it as one of the most powerful nations in the world, but this history is tainted with the forced servitude of Africans, Native-American genocide, Chinese exploitation, segregation of Whites and "colored" individuals, and subordination of women. Historic events have influenced people of color's current experiences, opportunities, and access to power, and subsequently, have shaped the way

that they are evaluated as leaders. For example, an Ivy League education has been viewed as a key to President Obama's success (Dierenfield & White, 2012); however, compared with White Americans, people of color have higher school dropout rates and hold significantly fewer higher education degrees. These negative trends can be explained by numerous individual, community and societal factors and also by the lingering effects of historic race relations in the United States.

Prior to the Civil War, education of Black Americans was virtually nonexistent, and after the abolishment of slavery, segregation laws prevented many from attending public institutions (Harris, 1956; Thomas, 2005). It would not be until 1823, 181 years after the first White college graduates, when Alexander Lucius Twilight would become the first Black person to earn a bachelor's degree from a U.S. college (Middlebury College). He would later become the first Black American elected to public office as a state legislator. It would take another 39 years, however, before a Black woman, Mary Jane Patterson, would earn a similar degree.

Similar to Black Americans, Mexican Americans were exposed to inferior public schools with poorly trained teachers and segregated facilities or classrooms (San Miguel, 1987; Verdugo, 2006). School segregation was challenged in the 1940s in the *Mendez v. Westminister* and *Delgado v. Bastrop Independent School District* federal court cases rulings; it was determined that segregation of students of Mexican descent into separate schools and classrooms was unconstitutional (Vélez, 1994; Verdugo, 2006). Black Americans, however, did not receive the same benefits of the law until 1954 when the *Brown vs. Board of Education* Supreme Court case declared "separate educational facilities are inherently unequal" and unconstitutional for *all* Americans. Integration, however, did not necessarily mean equal opportunity as curriculum and educator deficiencies continued. Native Americans likewise faced many barriers to obtaining quality education. Children were forced to go to boarding schools—separating them from their reservation and family and forcing them to abandon tribal mores and their native languages (U.S. Senate, 1969). In the 1960s, Native Americans gained autonomy to make educational decisions and choices, but earlier coercive practices instilled in many a mentality that "school is the enemy" (U.S. Senate, 1969, p. 9).

Explicit structural barriers to education may have been removed, but as noted by former U.S. president Lyndon B. Johnson in a commencement address at Howard University in 1965:

> You do not wipe away the scar of centuries by saying: Now you are free to go where you want, and do as you desire, and choose the leaders you please. You do not take a person who, for years, has been hobbled by chains and liberate him, bring him up to the starting line of a race and then say you are free to compete with all others, and still justly believe that you have been completely fair. (Johnson, 1965)

Internal (controllable) and external (uncontrollable) barriers and constraints still persist today to limit people of color's attainment of quality education and, subsequently, their leadership opportunities.

In addition to the role that education plays in leadership attainment, implicit and explicit stereotypes, and discrimination limit leadership opportunities. **Stereotypes**, manifested into prejudicial thoughts, along with discriminatory behaviors coalesce in work environments, creating a figurative glass ceiling that inhibits increased **diversities** among leadership positions (Thomas, 2005). Black Americans, Hispanics, and Native Americans, for instance, are more likely than other racial groups to be perceived as lazy, incompetent, and having a lower work ethic and ambition than White Americans (Devine & Elliot, 1995; Dixon & Rosenbaum, 2004; Fiske, Cuddy,

Glick, & Xu, 2002; Smith, 1990)—all of which are characteristics deemed antithetical to leadership (Lord, Foti, & de Vader, 1984; Rudman & Glick, 1999). In contrast, Asians and Asian Americans are often deemed "model minorities" and are stereotyped as being smart and gifted in math and science. These stereotypes may appear to be positive; however, they result in Asians' leadership opportunities being limited because "those who are oriented toward the math and sciences are rarely presumed to have a comparably high level of people skills and leadership abilities" (Thomas, 2005, p. 79). Also, many Asians are stereotyped as having presumed language barriers so when hiring managers see names on résumés that allude to Asian national origin, biases can affect the hiring decision (Thomas, 2005).

Leadership then becomes defined by more than just qualifications and characteristics; it becomes defined by race and ethnicity. These views and stereotypes are implanted throughout society and organizations through various socializing agents (e.g., family, friends, and media) that consciously and subconsciously implant racialized thoughts into people's heads. Explicit verbalization and consciously applying racial stereotypes has lessened over the years; still, implicit stereotypes that function outside of a person's conscious awareness still linger, affecting decision-makers' attitudes and behaviors (Greenwald & Krieger, 2006).

▶ Historic and Current Barriers in Sport Leadership

Deep-Rooted Barriers in Baseball

Stereotypes and prejudices that exist in the larger society spill into organizations and interfere with people's ability to obtain and retain leadership positions. The infamous statement made by Al Campanis in 1987—40 years after Jackie Robinson broke the color line in a Brooklyn Dodgers uniform—clearly illustrates the pandemic nature of societal stereotypes. Specifically, in an interview with Ted Koppel, former Los Angeles Dodgers general manager Al Campanis stated that the low number of Black managers in baseball (or as pitchers, catchers, or football quarterbacks) was because they were thinking positions and Black people lacked the ability to adequately fill those positions. He emphatically stated, "No, I don't believe it's prejudice. I truly believe that [African-Americans] may not have some of the necessities to be a field manager or perhaps a general manager" (Hoose, 1989). In striving to discount the role of prejudice in hiring decisions, Campanis inadvertently reinforced that hidden prejudicial attitudes play a significant role. In response, Frank Robinson, MLB's first Black manager, acknowledged the hidden prejudicial view that Blacks are acceptable on the field, but not in the front office:

> Baseball has been hiding this ugly prejudice for years—that Blacks aren't smart enough to be managers or third-base coaches or part of the front office. There's a belief that they're fine when it comes to the physical part of the game, but if it involves brains, they just can't handle it. Al Campanis made people finally understand what goes on behind closed doors: that there is racism in baseball. (Wilhelm, 1987, p. 46)

Following the interview, Campanis was immediately fired with promises from the league regarding improved advancement opportunities for Black players. The fulfillment of those promises, however, has been sparse.

In the 21st century, there have been slight increases in the number of Black American players, coaches, and team vice-presidents in Major League Baseball, but the number of Black managers and general managers has been on the decline (Lapchick et al., 2017). In 2017, there were no Black owners and only one Black manager. Historically, only one Black owner and eleven Black managers and general managers have been hired since Campanis' statement and those hires were often short-lived (Lapchick et al., 2017). With the demise of the Negro Leagues and the shifting cultural significance of baseball to basketball in Black communities, a significant increase in the number of Black managers is uncertain, as the number of Black players and programs to encourage children to play baseball are disappearing.

Historically, Native-Americans and Latinos were allowed to play professional baseball so some Black-Americans would try to pass as these racial groups in order to play or manage the game (Shropshire, 1996). However, despite having an earlier entry into professional baseball, Native-American representation in MLB leadership positions is negligible (Lapchick et al., 2017). As of 2017, 49 verifiable full-blooded Native-Americans have played major league baseball (three active in 2017; Baseball-Almanac, 2018), but none has become a manager. In contrast, in 2017, Latinos represented the largest minority group (31.9%) of players, but the majority of these players have been recruited outside of the United States, which does not translate into increased leadership opportunities given that the majority of coaches/managers are U.S.-born (McGovern, 2017). As of 2017, only one Latino was a manager in MLB (Lapchick et al., 2017); and in 2003, Arturo Moreno, a Mexican-American, became the first Latino owner of *any* major sports league when he purchased the Anaheim Angels (Shaikin, 2003).

Are these statistics a byproduct of prejudicial attitudes and discrimination or people of color not having the "necessities" to lead professional baseball teams? The social closure theory of stacking—the discriminatory assigning of players of color to non-central outfield positions—has been a popular explanation for the "**glass ceiling**" in baseball (Sack, Singh, & Thiel, 2005) because the majority of MLB managers had infield playing experience. Evidence supporting or refuting the occurrence of this phenomenon, however, has been mixed. Multiple factors, working conjointly, such as the centrality hypothesis of stacking, social closure, personal choices, human capital differences (Sack, Singh & Thiel, 2005), and the uncertainty thesis of discrimination, which contends that "positional segregation is due to a form of racial discrimination that becomes effective when it is difficult to measure performance" (Lavoie & Leonard, 1994, p. 141) may provide a more holistic picture of what occurs in baseball. Furthermore, Rimer's (1996) investigation of MLB managers' qualifications suggests that the players of color are held to higher standards to obtain similar jobs as White managers. Specifically, Black-Americans and Latinos had more major league playing experience and a longer tenure in the league before they were given the opportunity to trade in the title of player for manager.

Implicit Biases in National Football League Leadership

In 1988, sentiments expressed about Blacks in baseball possessing inferior leadership skills would be repeated by late CBS sports commentator Jimmy "the Greek" Snyder when he espoused that Blacks were better athletes than Whites because they are offspring of slaves who were bred to be big and strong (Goodwin, 1988). He further expressed his concern with Black-Americans obtaining coaching positions: "If they take over coaching, like everybody wants them to, there is not going to be anything left for White people." These explicit sentiments about protecting prized coaching positions from Blacks and that they were more suited to be players and not managers, unfortunately, are not antiquated nor are they views held by only a few people.

A 2002 report released by lawyers Johnnie Cochran and Cyrus Mehri posited that Black coaches were being discriminated against in the hiring process, face increased criticisms and judgments for mistakes and "are the last hired and the first fired." In response to Cochran and Mehri's report, the NFL instituted the Rooney Rule, which required each NFL team to interview at least one racial minority candidate when interviewing for head coaching vacancies (see Social Justice section later in the chapter for more information), but this diversity hiring policy is constantly criticized and violated. Outcries about the inefficiencies of the Rooney Rule and discrimination prevail in the media. A recent report sanctioned by the NFL found that coaches of color are not getting second chances as head coaches, coordinators, or college head coaches (Harrison, 2013). It was recommended that efforts be made to increase coaches' social networks, and the NFL should increase transparency in the hiring process and institute an incentive and disincentive model for diversity efforts. Recent research also suggests that the Rooney Rule should be focused on hiring for positional (e.g., quarterback coach) and coordinator positions (e.g., offensive or defensive coordinator) [Madden & Ruther, 2011; Solow, Solow & Walker, 2011].

These diversity efforts will spur social change but do not necessarily change prejudicial attitudes and stereotypes. A recent analysis of more than 600 sport news articles, representing all National Collegiate Athletic Association (NCAA) Division I colleges, suggests that "goal-based stereotyping may systematically bias leader evaluations against Black leaders, in part explaining the glass ceiling faced by Black leaders in organizations" (Carton & Rosette, 2011, p. 1153). Mainly, their analyses revealed that if a Black quarterback had a good performance, that performance was attributed to athleticism (e.g., physical ability, strength, speed, and agility), but if the performance was poor, evaluators highlighted the Black quarterback's lack of competence (e.g., determination, analytical ability, intelligence, and decisiveness), not athleticism. These evaluations did not hold for White quarterbacks. This suggests that beliefs of Black-Americans' diminished leadership capabilities still prevail (Carton & Rosette, 2011).

These biases and stereotypes are manifested in more implicit ways and are evident in hiring trends in sport leadership positions. For instance, Fredrick "Fritz" Pollard was the first Black to be hired as a National Football League (NFL) head coach, but it took 68 years after his hiring before another Black American would gain the same opportunity. Between 1921 and 2017, only 21 Black Americans had been hired out of over 400 NFL head coaching openings (Lapchick & Marfatia, 2017); and as of 2017, there have only been three Latino and no Native-American or Asian head coaches in the NFL. History was made when Shahid Khan, a Pakistani American, became majority owner of the Jacksonville Jaguars in 2012, making him not only the first Asian owner of color but also the first owner of color of a NFL franchise (Lapchick & Marfatia, 2017). His historic accomplishment was followed in 2014 with the hiring of Kim Pegula (Asian-American), who became the first female of color to own a franchise. This positive trend continued in 2015 when Paraag Marathe (Indian) was named president of the San Francisco 49ers. He is recognized as the first person of color to become a president of an NFL team; but it is important to note that in 1920 Jim Thorpe of the Sac and Fox Nation was the first commissioner/president of the American Professional Football Association (later changed to National Football League). This historic achievement has essentially gone unmentioned in sport research, thus supporting Chideya's (1999) statement about the invisibility of Native Americans. This oversight could be due to the fact that in 1920, the NFL was originally named the American Professional Football Association. Regardless, Thorpe's accomplishment should not be overlooked in sports history.

Diversity in the National Basketball Association

The National Basketball Association (NBA) has been heralded as having the most racial diversity in leadership positions of any professional sports league, but the number of head coaches of color has declined. In 2012, there were more head coaches of color than White head coaches; but in 2017, White coaches held 70% of head coaching positions, whereas 74% of players were Black (Lapchick & Balasundaram, 2017). Black-Americans entered into leadership positions starting in 1966, 16 years after the NBA integrated, when Bill Russell was hired to coach the Boston Celtics. As of 2017, there have been 71 Black NBA head coaches (Gray, 2017), but African-Americans are grossly underrepresented as owners, general managers, and president/CEOs. In December 2002, a significant milestone was achieved when Robert Johnson become the principal owner of the Charlotte Bobcats (Rhoden, 2006). This historic moment was "heralded as one of the most significant milestones since Jackie Robinson desegregated MLB" (Rhoden, 2006, p. 247), as he was the first Black American majority owner of a professional sports franchise (Powell, 2008). Johnson's hiring opened the door for other Black owners, such as Shawn "Jay-Z" Carter, Fred Jones, Earl Stafford, and Dr. Sheila Johnson. Although Black Americans are not highly represented in non-coaching leadership positions, in contrast to other professional sport organizations, they are increasingly being provided with opportunities to shatter the glass ceiling and showcase their talents on and off of the court.

In the 21st century, progress for Black-Americans in sport leadership is becoming evident for other people of color—albeit on a smaller scale. As noted in **TABLE 13.1**, in the 21st century, Latino and Asian Americans have started making inroads into NBA head coaching positions (Lapchick & Balasundaram, 2017). Native-Americans' presence and power in

TABLE 13.1 "Firsts" in Sport Leadership Positions (non-exhaustive list)
20th Century
1920—Jim Thorpe: Native American NFL Commissioner
1921—Fritz Pollard: Black NFL football coach (Akron Pros)
1938—Miguel "Mike" Angel Gonzalez: Hispanic MLB Manager (St. Louis Cardinals)
1951—Al Lopez: Latino MLB manager (Cleveland Indians)
1962—John Jordan "Buck" O'Neil: Black MLB coach (Chicago Cubs)
1966—Bill Russell: Black NBA head coach (Boston Celtics)
1967—Tom Fears: Hispanic American NFL coach (New Orleans Saints)
1970—Will Robinson: Black NCAA Division I basketball coach (Illinois State University)
1972—Wayne Embry: Black NBA general manager (Milwaukee Bucks)
1975—Frank Robinson: Black MLB manager (Cleveland Indians)
1977—Bill Lucas: Black MLB general manager (Atlanta Braves)
1979—Willie Jeffries: Black NCAA Division I-A head football coach (Wichita State University)
1988—Dick Versace: Hispanic (Puerto Rican) NBA coach (Indiana Pacers)
1989—Art Shell: First Black NFL coach of the modern era (Los Angeles Raiders)
1989—Bertram Lee, Peter Bynoe, Arthur Ashe, Ron Brown: First Blacks to become managing general partners of a major sports franchise (Denver Nuggets)
1990—Barry Alvarez: Latino NCAA D-I football coach (University of Wisconsin–Madison)
1995—Ted Nolan: Native American NHL coach (Buffalo Sabres)
21st Century
2002—Robert L. Johnson: First Black to become majority owner of a U.S. major sports league team (Charlotte Bobcats, NBA)
2002—Ozzie Newsome: Black NFL general manager (Baltimore Ravens)
2002—Omar Minaya: Latino MLB general manager (Montreal Expos)
2003—Arturo "Arte" Moreno: Hispanic MLB team owner (Anaheim Angels)
2008—Erik Spoelstra: Asian-American NBA head coach (Miami Heat) and first Asian American head coach in any of the Big 4 professional sports
2008—Don Wakamatsu: Asian-American MLB manager (Seattle Mariners)
2010—Rich Cho: First Asian general manager in any major men's professional sports league (Portland Bobcats)

21st Century
2011—Norm Chow: Asian-American Division I football coach (University of Hawaii)
2011—OB Osceola, Jr.: Native-American (Seminole) NASCAR team owner (Germain-Osceola Racing)
2012—Shahid Khan (Pakistani-American): First owner of color of an NFL franchise (Jacksonville Jaguars)
2012—Earvin "Magic" Johnson: Black-American owner of an MLB franchise
2014—Kim Pegula (Asian-American) became the first female of color to own a NFL franchise (Buffalo Bills)
2015—Paraag Marathe (Indian) named president of the San Francisco 49ers
2016—Earl Watson: First NBA head coach of Hispanic descent (Phoenix Suns)
2017—Gift Ngoepe becomes first African-born Major League Baseball player

Source: Table was compiled by the author from multiple sources.

the NBA and other sports is also increasing. Native-Americans traditionally invest in the gaming industry but more recently have used money earned from gaming to promote boxers (e.g., Sycuan Ringside Promotions, Seminole Warriors Boxing), develop golf courses, sponsor NASCAR races, and buy basketball sport franchises (Boeck, 2007). For example, the Mohegan tribe purchased the WNBA Connecticut Sun in 2003 and has also used gaming dollars to sponsor Matt Kobyluck, a Busch East Series auto racer (Boeck, 2007). Also, in 2005, The Yakama Nation purchased the now-defunct Yakima Sun Kings, a minor-league basketball team in the Continental Basketball Association.

▶ NCAA College Sports

Racial occupational stratification would predict that minority groups would have higher representations in lower positions of a hierarchy, but college sports' brand equity is starting to surpass professional sports. This has resulted in people of color facing increased challenges and barriers to obtaining leadership positions. The "black-bottomed pyramid" (Shropshire, 1996) is evident for people of color whereas White-Americans are disproportionately represented

in more powerful leadership positions in intercollegiate athletics. As noted in Table 13.1, in 1979, Willie Jeffries was the first Black-American to be hired as a head coach of a NCAA Division I-A team, but since then, only 46 (of more than 200 vacancies) have been hired to coach at the highest level of collegiate football (Lapchick, Marfatia, Bloom, & Sylverain, 2017). During the 2016 football season, among the Football Bowl Subdivision (FBS)' 128 institutions, there were only 13 Black-Americans, one Latino, two Asian head football coaches, and no Native-Americans.

However, these dismal numbers represent progress. Between 1992 and 2002, 4 percent of vacant NCAA head coaching positions (181) were filled by coaches of color; whereas this percentage increased to 15 percent between 2003 and 2014 (of 141 vacancies; DuBois, 2016). Many speculate that this positive hiring trend is partially attributed to the success of two Black NFL football coaches, Lovie Smith and Tony Dungy, in leading their teams to the Super Bowl in 2007. Unlike the positive trajectory witnessed in the hiring of Black coaches, there have only been three Latino and two Polynesians hired as head coaches in FBS schools and one Native-American hired as head coach of a FCS (Football Championship Subdivision) school (Lapchick et al., 2017; Lapchick, Marfatia, Bloom, & Sylverain, 2017).

Public debate in the media and sports research suggests that racial stereotyping and discrimination are still prevalent in limiting coaching opportunities for people of color. In 2008, ex-professional basketball player Charles Barkley publicly opined that race was the "No. 1 factor" for Gene Chizik to get the head football coaching position at Auburn over Turner Gill (Schlabach, 2008). Informal and prejudicial hiring mechanisms, such as homologous reproduction, pressures from boards of trustees and athletic boosters, lack of formal interviews and search committees, and designations of successors for head coaching positions, have also been suggested as prominent factors contributing to limited opportunities in Division I football for coaches of color. Researchers have also suggested that the "black-bottomed pyramid" in collegiate football is a result of discriminatory stacking of Black athletes in running back or wide receiver positions, in contrast to quarterback and offensive-line positions, positions that are viewed as a pipeline to coordinator positions (Anderson, 1993; Finch, McDowell, & Sagas, 2010).

Men's and women's collegiate basketball also have a history of inequitable hiring practices for coaches of color. Following the integration of college teams, the representation of Black players quickly became the dominant demographic group on the court. Many of these players were recruited from Black high schools and college coaches at HBCUs, but the upward mobility of the Black coaches who trained these players did not transpire. In 1970, Will Robinson would become the first Black-American to lead a major college program as a coach instead of a player. Since Robinson's hiring, the number of Black coaches has steadily been on the rise, but similar to trends in the NBA, there has been a subtle decline in recent years. Hence, some Black-Americans have shattered the glass ceiling; but for many others, biases and discrimination in the hiring process prevent them from moving up.

In 2012, the inaugural Black Coaches and Administrators (BCA) Division I men's basketball hiring report card reported 20 open head coaching positions—of which seven Black-Americans were hired—bringing the number of Black coaches to 29 of 120 positions at the FBS schools (Laucella, 2012). The report indicated that the majority of the universities have good-to-excellent hiring practices, but in contrast to hiring trends in football, the number of coaches of color has gradually declined since 2008, despite a steady rise in players of color. This negative hiring trend is evident in women's Division I basketball as well. The access to athletics has been extended to Black female athletes but not too many Black women in coaching and administration (Lapchick et al., 2017; Lapchick, Marfatia, Bloom, & Sylverain, 2017).

Racial demographics in athletic director positions parallel that of head coaching positions. As recently as 2017, over 85 percent of NCAA Division I, II, and III athletic directors were White (National Collegiate Athletic Association, 2017). Black men and women hold approximately 10 percent of athletic director positions; whereas Hispanic/Latino men and women account for approximately 2 percent and Asian- and Native-Americans have less than 1 percent combined representation at all three division levels. Moreover, an analysis of leadership positions in FBS conferences—the most powerful and influential conferences in college sport—reveals a major disparity between the diversity of college leaders compared with students and student-athletes. As of 2017, approximately 90 percent of the presidents of FBS universities were White, 83 percent of athletics directors were White, 87 percent of faculty athletics representatives were White, and 100 percent of conference commissioners were White. Dr. Richard Lapchick, director of **The Institute for Diversity and Ethics in Sport (TIDES)**, noted that these percentages "reflect the stagnation of movement and the continued dominance of White men in the leadership roles affecting who is hired in college sport's top coaching jobs" (Lapchick et al., 2017, p. 2).

Research suggests that discrimination, perceived human capital deficiencies, and occupational segregation—or the disproportionate number of people of color working in academic support positions and not athletic director pipeline positions (e.g., donor relations, business operations, and marketing)—has a substantial effect on the number of people of color attaining athletic leadership positions (Cunningham, 2012; McDowell & Cunningham, 2007; McDowell, Cunningham & Singer, 2009; Wells & Kerwin, 2017). McDowell, Cunningham, and Singer (2009) concluded that career preferences, working in conjunction with structural limitations, such as discrimination, informal hiring practices, lack of career role models, and social networks, contributed to occupational segregation.

▶ Social Justice Efforts

As highlighted in this chapter, lingering issues of race and professional and collegiate sports persist, but the concerns are increasingly being addressed by advocacy groups and governing organizations, in particular, in sports where a large percentage of participants are racial minorities. Internal and external diversity efforts are resonating within sports and among states with prominent football teams.

The Rooney Rule

On September 30, 2002, Johnnie L. Cochran, Jr. and Cyrus Mehri issued a landmark report, *Black Coaches in the National Football League: Superior Performance, Inferior Opportunities*, revealing that National Football League's (NFL) Black head coaches are held to a higher standard compared with their White counterparts. *Superior Performance, Inferior Opportunities* supported the notion that Black-American males are denied opportunities for NFL head coaching positions. The report raised aware-

ness of the disparate NFL team hiring practices and as a result, the league formed a diversity committee headed by the Pittsburgh Steelers owner Dan Rooney. In 2003, the NFL Diversity Committee announced a plan including minority training and development programs, internships, and the implementation of the **Rooney Rule**, which requires that NFL teams interview at least one candidate of color for open head coaching positions (Holder, 2012; National Football League, 2002; Nichols, 2008; Thornton, 2007). In 2009, Rooney Rule requirements were strengthened to apply to all senior NFL football operations position searches, regardless of a team's title and racial/ethnic diversity (Brandt, 2011).

Black NFL coaches have successfully demonstrated their leadership capabilities and a Black head coach or general manager has participated in four of the last six Super Bowls (Holder, 2012; Wells, 2011). Still, some NFL owners and general managers continue to circumvent the Rooney Rule. In 2003, the NFL fined the Detroit Lions $200,000 for failure to interview a Black candidate for the team's vacant head coaching job. The Lions fired Marty Mornhinweg and immediately hired former San Francisco 49ers head coach Steve Mariucci. Detroit's leadership said they attempted to interview Black candidates, but the candidates withdrew, citing the inevitability of Mariucci's hiring (Associated Press, 2003). The granting of coaches of color "token" interviews is in direct opposition to the intent of the Rooney Rule. Other avoidance strategies include head coaches who name a successor to their imminent retirement and the lack of transparency in the hiring process.

Despite concerns that the Rooney Rule amounts to affirmative action, the NFL continues to form relationships with diversity advocates and the Fritz Pollard Alliance to help promote inclusion in NFL hiring. NFL teams must request permission to interview external candidates, positioning the commissioner to monitor the demography of team hiring processes. Still, one prevailing issue is the lack of diversity among offensive and defensive coordinators. Between 1992 and 2014, coaches of color were hired for only 91 offensive and defensive coordinator positions out of 541 vacancies (DuBois, 2016). This low representation of coordinators of color is noteworthy because serving as a coordinator typically leads to a head coaching opportunity (Johnson, 2012). Despite these lingering issues, an analysis of 1992 to 2014 hiring trends suggests that the Rooney Rule has been effective. Coaches of color are roughly 20 percent more likely to be hired in the post-Rooney era (after 2003) than the pre-Rooney era (DuBois, 2016).

The Robinson Rule

Prior to ceasing operations in 2016, Advocates for Athletic Equity (AAE), formerly the **Black Coaches and Administrators (BCA)**, made meaningful efforts to increase racial diversity in collegiate athletic administration and coaching positions. The BCA was formed in part to assist persons of color aspiring to have a career in sports through education and professional development. Over the BCA's 27-year history, one of its most meaningful contributions was the *BCA Football Hiring Report Card* developed in 2004 in conjunction with TIDES. The report card graded FBS schools based on who was on the search committee, who was interviewed, the length of the process, and whether the school sought assistance from the BCA in the hiring process (Singer, Harrison, & Bukstein, 2010). The BCA had also discussed pursuing Title VII under the 1964 Civil Rights Act as another remedy, and last resort, to diversity and inclusion (Duru, 2007; Gordon, 2008; Moye, 1998; Nichols, 2008). The Civil Rights Act of 1964 prohibits both intentional and unintentional employment discrimination practices that have the effect of discriminating on the basis of race, religion, sex, or national origin. Efforts of the AAE and BCA, such as the Hiring Report Cards and the Achieving Coaches Excellence programs, have resulted in positive strides toward racial equity; but in 2016, the AAE ceased operations due to limited funding.

In 2005, the NCAA created the Office of Diversity and Inclusion (ODI) to increase representation among women and people of color in collegiate sports. ODI, led by former DHL executive Charlotte Westerhaus, was charged with developing and implementing strategies, policies, and programs to promote empowerment, diversity, inclusion, and accountability. There were tangible outcomes of BCA, TIDES, and ODI efforts, such as the 27 ethnic minorities who were interviewed for 22 Division I head football coaching vacancies in 2008 (Carey, 2009). In a move to refocus diversity efforts, the Office of Diversity and Inclusion was renamed as The Office of Inclusion in 2010 (NCAA Inclusion Statement, n.d.). The new office "represents a shift from embracing diversity as a metric to encouraging inclusion as a value in leadership and decision-making processes" (NCAA Inclusion Statement, n.d, para. 4). The new diversity structure involves joint efforts with the Minority Opportunities and Interests Committee (MOIC) and the Committee on Women's Athletics (CWA) to implement inclusion-focused strategic initiatives. Despite a shift in focus, diversity remains on the NCAA's radar according to current association president Mark Emmert, who encourages NCAA university presidents and chancellors to, "identify, recruit and interview individuals from diverse backgrounds in an effort to increase their representation and retention as commissioners, athletic directors, coaches and other leaders in athletics" (Presidential Pledge, n.d.).

Recently, advocates and legal scholars have lobbied for extending the Rooney Rule to college football (Lapchick, 2009; Nichols, 2008). Lapchick has proposed "The Robinson Rule," named after legendary former Grambling University head football coach Eddie Robinson. Robinson, the winningest coach in Division I-AA football, was never offered a Division I-A (now FBS) head coaching position. The rule would require institutions to interview at least one minority candidate for head coaching and other athletic leadership positions

(Harrison, Lapchick, & Jansen, 2009). The National Association for Coaching Equity and Development and the Institute For Sport & Social Justice have recently advocated for NCAA schools to adopt the Robinson Rule, as the need for the Robinson Rule in college athletics is increasingly necessary to address gross racial inequities in football and men's and women's basketball.

The 2012 firing of football coach Jon Embree by the University of Colorado after only two seasons raised the issue of low ethnic minority retention and rehiring (Henderson, 2012). White head coaches are given more years than Black head coaches to lead their programs (Turick & Bopp, 2016); and only one Black coach fired from a FBS head coaching position has been rehired to lead an FBS program (Reid, 2015). This was Tyrone Willingham, who was fired from Notre Dame in 2004 and became head coach at the University of Washington. Former Colorado football head coach Bill McCarty said: "I believe Black men have less opportunity, shorter time if you will" (Henderson, 2012). The recent reversal in ethnic minority hiring and retention demographics has led state governments to explore Rooney-like requirements in collegiate football (Lapchick, 2009).

Oregon House Bill 3118

Change via advocacy groups and the NCAA are not the sole avenues for diversity and inclusion. Collegiate sports are a part of the social fabric of state-run colleges and universities; and thus, state government is increasingly involved in the industry. The state of Oregon has developed and implemented social policy that encourages diversity and inclusion in head coach hiring (Lapchick, 2009). Oregon House Bill (HB) 3118 requires each public institution under the jurisdiction of the Oregon State Board of Higher Education to "interview one or more qualified minority applicants when hiring a head coach or athletic director, unless the institution was unable to identify a qualified minority applicant who was willing to interview for the position."

(H.B. 3118, 2009) HB 3118 was enacted in September 2009 after Oregon state representative Mitch Greenlick (D-Portland) drafted HB 3118 at the request of Sam Sachs, a college football minority rights activist.

House Bill 3118 covers seven state universities, including Oregon, Oregon State, Portland State, Eastern Oregon, Western Oregon, Oregon Institute of Technology, and Southern Oregon (Bachman, 2009). The bill was received favorably and passed by 53 of 60 members of the House and unanimously by voting Senators (2009 Session: House Bill 3118). Still, H.B. 3118 also allows institutions to provide an affirmative defense to a claim of a violation if, in good faith, search committee members are "unable to identify a qualified candidate who was willing to interview for the position" (H.B. 3118, 2009). Hence, while H.B. 3118 accounts for one of the challenges of the Rooney Rule—reactions to token interviews—it does not provide a solution, only relief, to universities. In 2013, a hearing was held to discuss the effectiveness of HB 3118. It was concluded that universities are adhering to the letter of the law but not necessarily the spirit of the law (Fentress, 2013). Sam Sachs, the original requestor of the law, asserted that some universities limited opportunities for minority candidates to be hired by seeking hiring waivers or holding token interviews. Moreover, he criticized the law for lacking penalties for violators (Fentress, 2013).

▶ Women of Color in Sport

Few organizations have advocated for women of color in sports participation and administration like the Black Women in Sport Foundation (BWSF). Women of color in sport face two daunting issues—limited post-Title IX participation of female athletes of color in sports and the subsequent lack of women of color in sport administration and coaching. As such, the BWSF is focused in grassroots efforts to spur girls and women of color involvement in sports. In particular, the foundation emphasizes programming aimed at increasing participation of women of color in the female prep sports including soccer, volleyball, and lacrosse. The BWSF Next Step Forum has served as a space and a tool to discuss barriers and facilitators to the participation of women in sports as athletes, coaches and administrators (Black Women in Sport Foundation, 2018). One issue believed to restrict the hiring of female athletic directors is their ability to navigate the BCS football culture.

▸ Summary

Even in the dawn of a new era of access and proven success, there continue to be concerns about a lack of diversity in leadership positions across the sporting industry. This chapter highlighted some of the lingering issues related to race in professional and collegiate sport and asserts that progress toward equal opportunities has been made,

but racism still prevails in limiting persons of color opportunities in sport leadership positions. As noted by Rosellini (1987), "The new-fashioned racism is like a chill breeze that sneaks through the dugout late in the season, creeping among the stands, nosing into stadium offices, wandering, unexpected and unwanted, across the field. It is so subtle, yet systematized." These words were in references to the racism that persist in MLB but are also reflective of other sport organizations, associations, and departments.

We live in a global community that is becoming increasingly intertwined and interdependent. Demographic, cultural, technological, and economic changes are compelling us to live and work with a wide variety of people. To survive and thrive in this modern society means to understand that each of us is mutually connected to the other. Thus, it is in our best interest to embrace diversity, develop cultural competencies, increase leadership capacities, and create inclusive spaces as a means of fully using all human resource potential.

LEADERSHIP PERSPECTIVE

Brent Cahwee

Brent Cahwee is a Pawnee/Euchee Indian and co-founder of NDNSports.com. He has reported on and written about Native American athletes on his website since the fall of 2000. The site's purpose is to promote awareness of Native American athletes competing in college and professional sports.

Q: The NDNSports.com site has been around for the past 18 years, highlighting the success of Native athletes. It has a vision of promoting Native-American athletes to Native youth and to provide an outlet for inspirational reading. Do you believe you have achieved this vision?

I think when we started NDNSports that was one of our main objectives, to promote Native-American athletes to the youth of Indian Country, but looking back, we really should have developed a quantitative method to really measure if this was something we were achieving or not. In the beginning, we kind of just put our noses to the grindstone and were just trying to first figure out a method to disseminate the information on Native Athletes as well figure out how to find these athletes. But to answer the question, I do believe we have had an impact on Indigenous youth from the various tribal nations with the information we have provided over the years. In recent times, at different Native-American sporting events, people will introduce themselves to us as being a former athlete who we covered over the years and express gratitude for our coverage or we will have teachers or coaches from various tribal schools thank us for what we do and they will proceed to tell us that they have printed some of our graphics of athletes, that we have developed over the years, as posters, and hang them in the locker rooms. With the onslaught of technology and the development of social media, we have been able to have a greater reach directly to the Native-American youth. In the past, we just had the website available so we were only able to impact the people who would visit the website, but now, with social media and the ability of a friend "liking" a post, which really helps drive our information that we post to reach more and more people.

Q: You have chosen not to use your website as a platform to address the Native-American mascot issue. Do you believe athletic directors—both high school and college—the NCAA and commissioners and owners in professional sports leagues, have exhibited leadership on this issue?

This has always been an ongoing issue in the United States and with Native-American peoples for as long as I can remember and was a topic from day one that co-founder, John Harjo and I addressed with each other. We decided that it would be something that we weren't going to focus on with the website or other issues as such as cultural identity. The focus that we wanted to portray has always been about the on-the-field and in-the-classroom accomplishments. But with regard to the issue of it being addressed, yes, I do think you see a shift in approach to the issue. Whereas schools in the past who have been staunch supporters of keeping the mascot, now you see a shift in understanding the issue as it directly impacts its Native students. Also, the NCAA developed a policy to address the issue directly and provide sanctions to those who don't follow the policy. Colleges are being proactive to either change the name and mascot completely or to really develop a meaningful partnership with Native-American tribes to use the logo and mascot. For example, you see the University of Utah Utes, who have a website dedicated to providing a better understanding of the mascot name and meaning and information on the school's partnership with the tribe. It also has a list of rules of dos and don'ts for fans attending the games on campus.

Q: Much of the sport leadership literature that focuses on race and ethnicity calls attention to the high percentage of Whites in leadership positions in professional and college sport. Typically, leaders in sport are former athletes. You cover Native athletes with your website. What challenges do Native athletes face after their playing careers are over in moving into sport leadership positions?

I think that Native athletes face the same challenges and hurdles that exist for any athlete whose career is finished and who is looking to get into sports positions. For Native athletes, being a member of a tribe means growing up with the responsibility of continuing the language, traditions, and ceremonies. So, the first thing to do when your college career is over is to go home and become a part of that process; however, most reservation and indigenous communities are in areas in which there is very little

(continues)

LEADERSHIP PERSPECTIVE (*continued*)

opportunity to have professional sports careers other than working for the tribe directly or a subsidiary business that the tribe owns or operates. I see a lot of our college-graduated athletes either try to establish a professional career right away or will continue on to graduate school while others will try to continue a career in their homelands as a coach and then work their way into school administration as time moves on. But those sports positions on some reservation are few and far between, which will require some athletes to seek those type of positions on other reservations who have many more opportunities or enter the mainstream coaching market, which means competing with all races and backgrounds.

Q: Are there certain sports or certain areas of sport where you see future and continued involvement and success of Native people? Are there areas of sport that have begun that have untapped potential?

Within our Indigenous communities across the United States, basketball has been just as popular as the cultural games tribes participate in for social fun or ceremonies. After Naismith invented the game, a lot of it was participated in by Native-American boarding school students at Haskell Institute in Lawrence, Kansas, when Dr. Phog Allen was at Kansas University (only a mile from Haskell). In fact, the first known concept of a zone defense was identified at Haskell Institute when Coach Allen was a coach for Kansas and Haskell. The teams were scrimmaging and a Haskell player was guarding two players at once. In recent times, players like Shoni and Jude Schimmel, from the Umatilla Reservation in Oregon, reached the pinnacle of college basketball sports as they not only reached the women's Final Four but they also reached the championship game, which had never happened before for Native American women athletes. Then you follow that up with players like Bronson Koenig, from the Ho-Chunk Nation, a four-year starter with the University of Wisconsin and Derek Willis, from the Northern Arapaho tribe and University of Kentucky, whose teams both met in the men's Final Four championship. Both would become the first to reach the National Championship game as well for native men players. Ironically, one of the areas of untapped potential that is starting to grow, as well as the game itself, is the college game of Lacrosse. Invented by Iroquois tribes in the northeast and played by Indigenous youth for ceremony over hundreds of years, it is becoming more prevalent as a mainstream sport than an "alternative" sport. But even as long as it has been played at the college level for decades, only a few Indigenous players from these northeast reservations have had the opportunity to compete in college; however, when they have, they have always had success. As the sport continues to grow, teams such as Denver University and the University of Virginia are embracing the cultural roots of the game and they are reaching out to reservation Lacrosse programs to assist in any capacity they can.

▶ Key Terms

Binary	Diversity	Rooney Rule
"Black-bottomed pyramid"	Glass ceiling	Social justice
Black Coaches and Administrators (BCA)	The Institute for Diversity and Ethics in Sport (TIDES)	Stereotypes
		Underrepresentation

▶ Discussion Questions

1. Chideya states, "In the basest and most stereotypical terms, White-Americans are considered "true" Americans; Black-Americans are considered inferior Americans; Asians and Latinos are too often considered foreigners; and Native-Americans are rarely thought of at all." Do you agree with this statement when it comes to sport leadership? Why? Why not?

2. Other than the examples mentioned in the chapter, what other social justice initiatives should the NCAA and professional sport leagues undertake to ensure diversity in leadership positions?

3. What stereotypes in sport can be attached to Black-Americans? Latinos? Asians? Native-Americans? List some for each group. How do these charac-teristics affect these groups' ability to obtain leadership positions in sport?

4. Why do you think there has been more racial diversity seen in sport leadership positions in the NBA versus MLB and the NFL? Although not discussed in this chapter, why is there such a lack of diversity in player participation in the NHL and the PGA?

5. Given that there is a large percentage of Black players evident on the football fields and basketball courts of Division I schools—much higher than the percentage of Blacks in the U.S. population—why don't these high percentages translate into higher percentages of Blacks in leadership positions, such as coaches and athletic directors at Division I schools?

▶ References

Anderson, D. (1993). Cultural diversity on campus: A look at intercollegiate football coaches. *Journal of Sport and Social Issues, 17*(1), 61–66.

Associated Press. (2003, July 25). Lions Millen fined $200k for not interviewing minority candidates. Retrieved from http://wwwcbssports.com/nfl/story6498949

Associated Press. (2007, February 4). Dungy becomes first Black coach to win Super Bowl. Retrieved from http://sports.espn.go.com/nfl/playoffs06/news/story?id=2754521

Bachman, R. (2009). *Oregon set to enact landmark bill on minority hiring in athletic departments.* Retrieved from https://www.oregonlive.com/sports/index.ssf/2009/06/oregon_passes_landmark_bill_on.html

Baseball-Almanac (2018). American Indian baseball players. Retrieved from http://www.baseball-almanac.com/legendary/american_indian_baseball_players.shtml

Black Women in Sport Foundation (2018). Next step mini-forum. Retrieved from https://www.blackwomeninsport.org/next-step/

Boeck, G. (2007, February 23). Native American athletes face imposing hurdles. Retrieved from http://usatoday30.usatoday.com/sports/2007-02-21-native-american-cover_x.htm

Borland, J. & Bruening, J. E. (2010). Navigating barriers: A qualitative examination of the under-representation of Black females as head coaches in collegiate basketball. *Sport Management Review, 13*(4), 407–420.

Brandt, A. (2011, January 5). *The Rooney Rule: An analysis.* Retrieved from https://www.huffingtonpost.com/andrew-brandt/the-rooney-rule-an-analys_b_804691.html

Carey, J. (2009, July 24). New Oregon law requires minority interviews for coaching positions. Retrieved from http://www.usatoday30.usatoday.com/sports/college/football/2009-07-23-collegiate-rooney-rule

Carter-Francique, A. & Olushola, J. (2016). Women coaches of color: Examining the effects of intersectionality. In N. M. Lavoi (Ed.), *Women in Sports Coaching* (pp. 81–93).

Carton, A. M., & Rosette, A. S. (2011). Explaining bias against black leaders: Integrating theory on information processing and goal-based stereotyping. *Academy of Management Journal, 54*(6), 1141–1158.

Chideya, F. (1999). *Color of our future.* New York, NY: William Morrow and Company, Inc.

Clark, C., & Arboleda, T. (1999). *Teacher's guide for in the shadow of race: growing up as a multiethnic, multicultural, and "multiracial" American.* Mahwah, NJ: Lawrence Erlbaum Associates.

Cunningham, G. B. (2012). Occupational segregation of African-Americans in intercollegiate athletics administration. *Wake Forest Journal of Law & Policy, 2*(1), 165–178.

Cunningham, G. B., & Sagas, M. (2002). The differential effects of human capital for male and female Division I basketball coaches. *Research Quarterly for Exercise and Sport, 73,* 489–495.

Devine, P. G. & Elliot, A. J. (1995). Are racial stereotypes *really* fading? *Society for Personality and Social Psychology, 21*(11), 1139–1150.

Dierenfield, B. & White, J. (2012). *A history of African-American leadership.* Harlow, UK: Pearson Education Limited.

Dixon, J. C., & Rosenbaum, M. S. (2004). Nice to know you? Testing contact, cultural, and group threat theories of anti-Black and anti-Hispanic stereotypes. *Social Science Quarterly, 85,* 257–280.

DuBois, C. (2016). The impact of "soft" affirmative action policies on minority hiring in executive leadership: The case of the NFL's Rooney Rule. *American Law and Economics Review, 18*(1), 208–233.

Duru, N. J. (2007). Fritz Pollard Alliance, the Rooney Rule, and the quest to level the playing field in the National Football League. *The Virginia Sports & Entertainment Law Journal, 7,* 179–197.

Dungy, T., Caldwell, J., & Whittaker, N. (2011). *The mentor leader: Secrets to building people and teams that win consistently.* Carol Stream, IL: Tyndale Momentum.

Everhart, C. B. & Chelladurai, P. (1998). Gender differences in preferences for coaching as an occupation: The role of self-efficacy, valence, and perceived barriers. *Research Quarterly for Exercise and Sport, 69*(2), 188–200.

Fentress, A. (2013, March 20). State legislature holds hearing on how universities have progressed under minority interviewing law. *The Oregonian.* Retrieved from http://www.oregonlive.com/ducks/index.ssf/2013/03/state_legislature_holds_hearin.html

Finch, B., McDowell, J., & Sagas, M. (2010). An examination of racial diversity in collegiate football. *Journal for the Study of Sports & Athletes in Education, 4*(1), 47–58.

Fiske, S., Cuddy, A., Glick, P. & Xu, J. (2002). A model of (often mixed) stereotype content: Competence and warmth respectively follow from perceived status and competition. *Journal of Personality and Social Psychology, 82*(6), 878–902.

Gamecocks Women's Basketball (2018). Dawn Staley biography. Retrieved from http://www.gamecocksonline.com/sports/w-baskbl/mtt/dawn_staley_351574.html

Goodwin, M. (1988). *CBS dismisses Snyder.* Retrieved from http://www.nytimes.com/1988/01/17/sports/cbs-dismisses-snyder.html

Gordon, H. (2008). Robinson Rule: Models for addressing discrimination in the hiring of NCAA head football coaches. *Sports Lawyers Journal 15,* 1–19.

Gray, G. N. (2017). *The history of Black NBA head coaches.* BASN Newsroom. Retrieved from https://basnnewsroom.com/2017/10/17/the-history-of-black-nba-head-coaches/

Greenwald, A. G., & Krieger, L. H. (2006). Implicit bias: Scientific foundations. *California Law Review, 94*(4), 945–967.

Harris, R. (1956). The Constitution, education, and segregation. *Temple Law Quarterly, 29*(4), 409–433.

Harrison, K. (2013). Examining coaching mobility trends and occupational patterns: Head coaching access, opportunity and the social network in professional and college sport. *NFL Diversity and Inclusion, Coaching Mobility, Volume 1.* Retrieved from http://usatoday30.usatoday.com/sports/nfl/2013-05-28-nfl-diversity-report.pdf

Harrison, C. K., Lapchick, R. E. & Jansen, N. K. (2009). Decision making in hiring: Intercollegiate athletics coaches and staff. *New Directions for Institutional Research, 144,* 93–101.

Hattery, A. J. (2012). They play like girls: Gender and race (in)equity in NCAA Sports Symposium: "Losing to win: Discussions of race and intercollegiate sports. *Wake Forest Journal of Law & Policy, 2*(1), 247–266.

H. B. 3118. 75th Oregon Legislative Assembly. Reg. Sess. (Or. 2009)

Hehman, E., Baertner, S., & Dovidio, J. (2011). Evaluation of presidential performance: Race, prejudice, and perceptions of Americanism. *Journal of Experimental Social Psychology, 47,* 430–435.

Henderson, J. (2012, November 27). *Bill McCartney takes to airwaves to blast Colorado firing Jon Embree.* Retrieved from http://www.denverpost.com/cu/ci_22076669/bill-mccartney-blast-colorado-firing-jon-embree

Hickman, C. (1997). The devil and the one drop rule: Racial categories, African Americans, and the U.S. Census. *Michigan Law Review, 95,* 1161–1265.

Ho, A., Sidanius, J., Levin, D., & Banji, M. (2011). Evidence for hypodescent and racial hierarchy in the categorization and perceptions of biracial individuals. *Journal of Personality and Social Psychology, 100,* 492–506.

Holder, S. F. (2012, January 19). *NFL's Rooney Rule has boosted minority coaches and general managers.* Retrieved from http://www.tampabay.com/sports/football/bucs/nfls-rooney-rule-has-boosted-minority-coaches-and-general-managers/1211219

Hoose, P. (1989). *Necessities: Racial barriers in American sports.* New York, NY: Random House Publishing Group.

Jimenez, L. (2011). Are we in a post-racial America? *Profiles in Diversity Journal.* Retrieved from http://www.diversityjournal.com/4493-are-we-in-a-post-racial-america/

Johnson, L. B. (1965, June 4). "To fulfill these rights": Commencement address at Howard University. Washington, D.C.

Johnson, R. S. (2012, January 13). *Modify the Rooney Rule.* Retrieved from http://espn.go.com/espn/commentary /story/_/id/7450944/modify-rooney-rule-include-nfl -hires-offensive-defensive-coordinators

Lapchick, R. E. (2009, May 26). *Oregon hears the call to action.* Retrieved from http://today.ucf.edu/oregon -hears-the-call-to-action/

Lapchick, R., & Balasundaram, B. (2017). *The 2017 racial and gender report card: National Basketball Association.* Retrieved from http://nebula.wsimg.com /74491b38503915f2f148062ff076e698?AccessKeyId =DAC3A56D8FB782449D2A&disposition=0 &alloworigin=1

Lapchick, R., Boyd, A., Bredikhina, N., Brown, K., Cartwright, D., Costa, G., Feller, A., Gerhart, Z., Lee, C., New, C., Rainey, P., Shaw, I., Troutman, T., & Young, C. (2017). The 2017 DI FBS leadership college racial and gender report card: Collegiate athletic leadership gets a D+ as it is still dominated by white men. Retrieved from http://nebula.wsimg.com /ad2f35c9f4915087b67da2f08830d43a?AccessKeyId =DAC3A56D8FB782449D2A&disposition=0 &alloworigin=1

Lapchick, R., & Marfatia, S. (2017). *The 2017 racial and gender report card: National Football League.* Retrieved from http://nebula.wsimg.com /1a7f83c14af6a516176740244d8afc46? AccessKeyId=DAC3A56D8FB782449D2A&disposition =0&alloworigin=1

Lapchick, R., Marfatia, S., Bloom, A., & Sylverain, S. (2017). *The 2016 racial and gender report card: College sport.* Retrieved from http://nebula.wsimg .com/38d2d0480373afd027ca38308220711f?Access KeyId=DAC3A56D8FB782449D2A&disposition=0 &alloworigin=1

Lapchick, R., Mueller, M., Currie, T., & Orr, D. (2017). *The 2017 racial and gender report card: Major League Baseball.* Retrieved from http://nebula.wsimg.com /d96daf1e011b077b2fd9ff4cfe4bf1bc?AccessKeyId =DAC3A56D8FB782449D2A&disposition=0 &alloworigin=1

Laucella, P. (2012, November 15). *BCA hiring report card for NCAA Division I men's college basketball head coaching positions.* Retrieved from http://www .bcasports.org/images/pdf/finalbcapdf.pdf

Lavoie, M., & Leonard, W. (1994). In search of an alternative explanation of stacking in baseball: The uncertainty hypothesis. *Sociology of Sport Journal, 11,* 140–154.

Lord, R. G., Foti, R. J., & de Vader, C. L. (1984). A test of leadership categorization theory: Internal structure, information processing, and leadership perceptions. *Organizational Behavior and Human Performance, 34,* 343–378.

Madden, J., & Ruther, M. (2011). Has the NFL's Rooney Rule efforts "leveled the field" for African American head coach candidates. *Journal of Sports Economics, 12,* 127–142.

Mandell, N. (2018). See Buffalo's Felisha Legette-Jack's incredibly powerful statement about diversity. Retrieved from https://ftw.usatoday.com/2018/03 /felisha-legette-jack-buffalo-ncaa

McDowell, J., & Cunningham, G. B. (2007). The prevalence of occupational segregation in athletic administrative positions. *International Journal of Sport Management, 8,* 245–262.

McDowell, J., Cunningham, G. B., & Singer, J. N. (2009). The demand and supply side of occupational segregation: The case of an intercollegiate athletic department. *Journal of African American Studies, 13,* 431–454.

McGovern, J. (2017). The boundaries of Latino sport leadership: How skin tone, ethnicity, and nationality construct baseball's color line. *Sociological Inquiry, 87*(1), 49–74.

Moye, J. (1998). Punt or go for the touchdown: A Title VII analysis of the National Football league's hiring practices for head coaches. *UCLA Entertainment Law Review, 6,* 105.

National Collegiate Athletic Association. (2017). Sport sponsorship, participation and demographics search [Data file]. Retrieved from http://web1.ncaa.org /rgdSearch/exec/main

National Football League (2002). NFL clubs to implement comprehensive program to promote diversity in hiring. Retrieved from https://www.nfl.info/nflmedia /News/2002News/NFLDiversityProgram.htm

NCAA Inclusion Statement. (n.d.) Retrieved from http:// www.ncaa.org/about/resources/inclusion/ncaa -inclusion-statement

Nichols, M. J. (2008). Time for a Hail Mary? With bleak prospects of being aided by a college version of the NFL's Rooney Rule, should minority college football coaches turn their attention to Title VII litigation? *Virginia Sports & Entertainment Law Journal, 8,* 147.

Obama, Barack. (2013, July 18). Retrieved from https:// www.knox.edu/news/president-obama-to-visit-knox -college-speak-on-economy/2005-commencement -address

Pew Research Center. (2016, June 27). On Views of Race and Inequality, Blacks and Whites Are Worlds Apart. Retrieved from http://assets.pewresearch.org /wp-content/uploads/sites/3/2016/06/ST_2016 .06.27_Race-Inequality-Final.pdf

Piston, S. (2010). How explicit racial prejudice hurt Obama in the 2008 election. *Political Behavior, 32,* 431–451.

Powell, S. (2008). *Souled Out? How blacks are winning and losing in sports.* Champaign, IL: Human Kinetics.

Presidential Pledge (n.d.). Retrieved from http://www.ncaa .org/about/resources/inclusion/ncaa-presidential -pledge

Rachlinski, J. & Parks, G. (2010). Implicit bias, election '08, and the myth of a post-racial America. *Cornell Law Faculty Publications,* Paper 178.

Reid, A. (2015, August 26). Black head coaches don't get second chances. Retrieved from http://www.stlamerican.com/sports/sports_columnists/sports_eye/black-head-coaches-don-t-get-second-chances/article_00d64010-4c4b-11e5-9045-57588bb5b35c.html

Rhoden, W. (2006). *Forty million dollar slaves: The rise, fall, and redemption of the Black athlete*. New York, NY: Three Rivers Press.

Rimer, E. (1996). Discrimination in major league baseball: Hiring standards for major league managers, 1975-1994. *Journal of Sport & Social Issues, 22*, 118–133.

Rosellini, L. (1987). Strike one and you're out. *U.S. News & World Report, 103*, 52–58.

Rudman, L. A., & Glick, P. (1999). Feminized management and backlash toward agentic women: The hidden costs to women of a kinder, gentler image of middle managers. *Journal of Personality and Social Psychology, 77*(5), 1004–1010.

Ryan, S. (2017). College sports needs more women – and women of color – in coaching ranks. Retrieved from http://www.chicagotribune.com/sports/columnists/ct-womens-college-coaching-diversity-ryan-spt-0419-20170417-column.html

Sack, A., Singh, P., & Thiel, R. (2005). Occupational segregation on the playing field: The case of major league baseball. *Journal of Sport Management, 19*, 300–318.

Safire, W. (1988, Nov. 20). On language; people of color. *The New York Times*. Retrieved from http://www.nytimes.com/1988/11/20/magazine/on-language-people-of-color.html

San Miguel, G. (1987). *Let all of them take heed, Mexican Americans and the campaign for educational equality in Texas, 1910–1981*. Austin, TX: University of Texas Press.

Schlabach, M. (2008, December 16). Lobbying for Gill, alum Barkley says Auburn should have hired black coach. *ESPN.com*. Retrieved from http://sports.espn.go.com/ncf/news/story?id=3770769

Shaikin, B. (2003, May 16). Moreno dream comes true: He becomes the first Latino owner of any major sports after baseball approves his purchase of the Angels for $183.5 million. *Los Angeles Times*. Retrieved from http://articles.latimes.com/2003/may/16/sports/sp-angelsale16

Shropshire, K. (1996). *In Black and White: Race and sports in America*. London, UK: New York University Press.

Shropshire, K. (2004). Minority issues in contemporary sports. *Stanford Law & Policy Review, 15*, 189–215.

Singer, J. N., Harrison, C. K., & Bukstein, S. M. (2010). A critical race analysis of the hiring process for head coaches in NCAA college football. *Journal of Intercollegiate Sport, 3*, 270–296.

Smith, T. W. (1990). Ethnic images. *GSS Topical Report No. 19*. Chicago, IL: National Opinion Research Center.

Solow, B., Solow, J., & Walker, T. (2011). Moving on up: The Rooney Rule and minority hiring in the NFL. *Labour Economics, 18*, 332–337.

Steckley, K. (2014). Miller is new Langston coach. Retrieved from http://www.tulsaworld.com/miller-is-new-langston-coach/article_3283c461-466a-5d28-b99b-cf7ca112b115.html

Thomas, K. M. (2005). *Diversity dynamics in the workplace*. Belmont, CA: Thomson Wadsworth.

Thornton, P. K. (2007). The Legacy of Johnnie Cochran, Jr.: The National Football League's Rooney Rule. *Texas Southern University Law Review, 33*(1), 77–81.

Turick, R., & Bopp, T. (2016). A current analysis of black head football coaches and offensive coordinators at the NCAA DI-FBS level. *Journal of Intercollegiate Sport, 9*(2), 282–302.

U.S. Senate. (1969). Committee on Labor and Public Welfare. Indian Education: A National Tragedy—A National Challenge (Kennedy Report) (S.Rpt. 80). Washington, DC: Government Printing Office.

Vélez, W. (1994). Educational experiences of Hispanics in the United States: Historical notes. In F. Padilla (Ed.), *Handbook of Hispanic cultures in the United States: Sociology* (pp. 151–159). Houston, TX: Arte Publico Press.

Verdugo, R. (2006). A report on the status of Hispanics in education: Overcoming a history of neglect. Washington, DC: National Education Association of the United States.

Wells, B. (2011, February 6). Super Bowl 2011: Notice how no one made a big deal Steelers coach Mike Tomlin is Black. Retrieved from http://www.stampedeblue.com/2011/2/8/1981752/super-bowl-2011-notice-how-no-one-made-a-big-deal-steelers-coach-mike

Wells, J., & Kerwin, S. (2017). Intentions to be an athletic director: Racial and gender perspectives. *Journal of Career Development, 44*(2), 127–143.

Wilhelm, M. (1987, April 27). In America's national pastime, says Frank Robinson, White is the color of the game off the field. *People Weekly, 27*(17), 46.

CHAPTER 14

Leading Athletes with Disabilities

Mary A. Hums
Eli Wolff
David Legg

CHAPTER OBJECTIVES

- Demonstrate an understanding of the history of the development of disability sport.
- Understand the influence of leaders making key contributions to disability sport.
- Recognize and highlight current issues facing leaders in disability sport.
- Describe the necessary skill set for leaders in disability sport.

CASE STUDY

Providing Athletic Participation Opportunities for College Student-Athletes with Disabilities

Recently, the Department of Education (DOE) issued what is known as a Dear Colleague Letter related to sport participation for students with disabilities. The DOE's guidelines stress that students with disabilities must be treated equitably with regard to interscholastic sport participation opportunities (Hums & MacLean 2017). In summary, the Dear Colleague Letter clarified a school's obligations under the Rehabilitation Act of 1973 to provide extracurricular athletic opportunities for students with disabilities. It established a clear road for how schools can integrate students with disabilities into mainstream athletic programs and create adapted programs for students with disabilities.

(continues)

CASE STUDY (continued)

How are schools to offer these opportunities? Participation opportunities to allow students with disabilities to participate in athletics to the greatest extent possible can include:

- *Mainstream programs*—school-based activities that are developed and offered to all students.
- *Adapted physical education and athletic programs*—programs that are specifically developed for students with disabilities.
- *Allied or unified sports*—programs that are specifically designed to combine groups of students with and without disabilities together in physical activities. (Active Policy Solutions, 2013, p. 1)

An example of a mainstream program would be a swimmer with one arm who can swim fast enough to be a regular member of the varsity swim team. An example of an adapted athletic program would be establishing a school wheelchair basketball team. An example of a unified program would be establishing a wheelchair basketball team where team members include students both with and without disabilities.

While most of the discussion of the document has focused on high school sport, its information is equally applicable to college sport as well. It is foreseeable that more college students with disabilities will now have the opportunity to compete in high school and may want to continue to compete in college.

As a leader in this movement, in 2016, the Eastern College Athletic Conference (ECAC), in collaboration with U.S. Paralympics, a division of the United States Olympic Committee, hosted two men's and two women's Paralympic swimming demonstration events (100-meter freestyle and 100-meter backstroke). A similar demonstration was held at the 2016 ECAC/IC4A Division I Track & Field Championships in Princeton, New Jersey, with several Para-track & field events. Like swimming, it is expected that these track & field events will be added to these championships as new events, thus providing new and expanded opportunities for student-athletes with disabilities within intercollegiate varsity sports (ECAC, 2016).

Questions for Discussion

1. You have been hired as an Assistant Athletic Director at Big State University (BSU), a Division I school offering the typical 20 sports that any NCAA DI athletic department would sponsor. Recognizing the opportunity for your Athletic Department to be a leader in this area, the Athletic Director has tasked you with creating potential opportunities for student-athletes with disabilities to compete for BSU. How would you address the following?
   a. Which individual or team sports would you consider adding and why?
   b. Who on campus would you reach out to in order to help identify potential student-athletes?
   c. How would you locate potential high school athletes with disabilities to recruit?
   d. Which facility issues would you have to take into consideration in determining how to proceed?
2. One potential barrier that you would need to overcome in order to establish opportunities would be finances. What types of companies would you contact in attempting to secure sponsorships for these new sport opportunities?
3. Where would you find coaches and/or what information would you provide to the current coaching staff to get them on-board with your plans?

▶ Introduction

When people talk about diversity in sport, most often, the dialogue revolves around race and gender. Only since the mid-2000s has disability found a voice at the table. Now, with the rapid growth of the **Paralympic Games** and the recent ratification of the United Nations Convention on the Rights of Persons with Disabilities (CRPD), people with disabilities in sport are being better recognized and valued. This chapter will provide a brief history of the development of disability sport, including information about some outstanding leaders in disability sport. Then several timely and sometimes controversial issues facing people in leadership positions in sport for people with disabilities will be discussed.

Disability sport refers to sport in which people compete or participate, specifically by people with disabilities. Examples of major events in disability sport include the summer and winter Paralympic Games, the **Deaflympics**, and **Special Olympics**. Disability sport is not limited to events such as these; however, it also encompasses grassroots-level activities such as adaptive physical education, participation by people with disabilities in community or recreational sport, and physical activity for children with disabilities. This chapter, however, will focus mainly on major events such as the Paralympic Games, present information about some leaders in disability sport, and highlight current issues that these leaders face.

▶ History of the Paralympic Games

This section recounts some of the historic steps along the way in the founding of the Paralympic Games. Following World War II, hospitals around the world began using recreation to benefit injured war veterans. The most iconic example was Sir Ludwig Guttmann at Stoke Mandeville Hospital in England, who established what we now refer to as the Stoke Mandeville Games, which ultimately became the Paralympic Games. In the aftermath of World War II, the hospital served scores of veterans with disabilities. Guttmann believed strongly in the positive impact of sport in making people "whole" again. Yes, the people at the hospital needed physical and occupational therapy, but they were mainly young, physically active people, and sport and physical activity were important to them. The first competition in 1948 at Stoke involved 16 men and women who competed in archery. Interestingly,

today, we see sport used in the rehabilitation of injured war veterans in programs such as the Warrior Games, Invictus Games, and Wounded Warrior Project. Following the slow and deliberate growth of the Stoke Mandeville Games in the 1950s, Guttman contacted the International Olympic Committee (IOC) with hopes of organizing the Stoke Games in Rome to coincide with the IOC's hosting of the 1960 Summer Olympic Games. The IOC leadership agreed, and wheelchair events were held at different venues for 400 athletes from 23 countries. These events are now viewed as the founding Paralympic Games. At these Games, Pope John XXIII declared Guttmann ". . . the de Coubertin [the founder of the modern Olympic Games] of the paralyzed" (Steadward & Foster, 2003).

The second Summer Paralympic Games followed in Tokyo, coinciding with the Olympic Games. Also being held there in 1968, the Paralympic Games were held in Tel Aviv while the Olympic Games were held in Mexico City. In the 1970s, both Games were held in the same countries—Germany in 1972 with Munich hosting the Olympic Games and Heidelberg for the Paralympic Games. In Canada in 1976, Montreal hosted the Olympic Games and Toronto the Paralympic Games. In 1980, Olympic Games were held in Moscow while Paralympic Games were hosted in Arnhem, the Netherlands. A small profit was garnered at these Games, which then allowed the creation of a secretariat to help manage the burgeoning movement and Games (Steadward & Foster, 2003).

In 1981, four international sport organizations representing athletes with spinal injuries, cerebral palsy, amputations, and visual impairments determined that there was a need to coordinate Games and thus, in 1982, they created the International Coordinating Committee Sports for the Disabled (ICC). This came about, in part, because of IOC President Juan Antonio Samaranch's request to correspond and collaborate with only one umbrella organization representing disability sport as opposed to organizations representing wheelchair, blind, amputee, and cerebral palsy sport in addition to Deaf Sport and the Special Olympics (Robert Steadward, personal communication, 2012). In 1983, the new group met in Lausanne, Switzerland, and reaffirmed the need for one voice. In the fall of 1984, Dr. Robert Steadward, a university professor leading the growth of disability sport in Canada, circulated a proposal worldwide recommending a new organizational structure and democratically elected governance and asked that other nations and disability sport organizations consider submitting alternative proposals. The ICC secretariat helped plan and organize an event in March of 1987, where representatives discussed various proposals. Here, disability sport leaders spent a day presenting a variety of proposals in 15- to 20-minute sessions. After sifting through the various ideas, 23 resolutions stood out as most essential (Steadward & Foster, 2003), in particular:

- Change the structure of the existing organization,
- Include national representation as well as regional and athlete representation,
- Reduce the number of classifications,
- Implement a functional classification system,
- Develop a structure by sport and not by disability,
- Work toward integration with the International Olympic Committee and other international sport federations.

It is also important to note that demonstration status events for athletes with disabilities had been staged during the summer and winter Olympic Games in 1984. The demonstration events for the winter Games continued for only one more Games event in Calgary in 1988 while the two summer events continued until 2008 in Beijing (Legg, Fay, Hums, & Wolff, 2009).

The IOC had been asked to upgrade the events from demonstration status to full medal status several times but for unknown reasons, it was never granted. Where the IOC and IPC did agree, however, was the need for an official agreement that all bidding cities for Olympic Games also had to bid for Paralympic Games (Robert Steadward, personal communication, 2012). This practice began in 2001 and continues today with the 2024 Summer Olympic and Paralympic Games awarded to Paris and the 2028 Summer Olympic and Paralympic Games awarded to Los Angeles.

This practice, while not becoming official until 2001, actually began in 1988 in Seoul, where the Korean Host Organizing Committee decided to host both Games and this precedent was then followed in Barcelona in 1992, Atlanta in 1996, and Sydney in 2000. The Winter Paralympic Games, meanwhile began in 1976 with a similar pattern, with Games being held in the same city starting in 1992 in Albertville, France.

The pattern of hosting both Games together thus occurred perhaps organically since 1988 with some ebbs and flows of growth. Most, but not all, host cities during this time and after the 2001 agreement had one host organizing committee that staged both Games. Subtle changes have also occurred with each Games. For example, in Vancouver 2010, where "Paralympic" was included in the official name of the host organizing committee, a joint marketing agreement with the host National Paralympic Committee was created, and a member from the National Paralympic Committee was named to the organizing committee's board of directors (Coward & Legg, 2011). Other new initiatives in Vancouver that were echoed by London in 2012 included creating a separate countdown clock for the Paralympic Games and flying the Olympic and Paralympic flags side by side. In 2012 at the London Games, the logos for the Olympic and Paralympic Games were essentially the same, with the only difference being the five rings for the Olympic Games and the three *agitos* for the Paralympic Games. The agitos (Latin for "I move") are three asymmetrical crests used to symbolize movement.

The next three Games are being held in PyeongChang 2018, Tokyo 2020, and Beijing 2022 and will likely see even more changes with regard to the merger of the two Games.

Whether this results in greater cooperation or separation between the organization and movements, however, is yet to be seen (see **TABLE 14.1**).

TABLE 14.1	Sports of the 2018 Winter and 2020 Summer Paralympic Games
Pyeongchang 2018 Winter Paralympic Games Sports	
Para alpine skiing	Para ice hockey
Para biathlon	Para snowboard
Para cross-country skiing	Wheelchair curling
Tokyo 2020 Summer Paralympic Games Sports	
Archery	Para swimming
Badminton	Rowing
Boccia	Shooting para sport
Canoe	Sitting volleyball
Cycling	Table tennis
Equestrian	Taekwondo
Football (five a side)	Triathlon
Goalball	Wheelchair basketball
Judo	Wheelchair fencing
Para athletics	Wheelchair rugby
Para powerlifting	Wheelchair tennis

Data from The International Paralympic Committee, www.paralympic.org

▶ Influential Leaders in Disability Sport

It is important to highlight people who are leaders in the arena of disability sport. The odds are that most of you may not be aware of these names because they are not necessarily those names we read about in traditional sport management textbooks or see interviewed on ESPN or TSN. They are not nearly as visible in the media as leaders in the Olympic Movement. This section mentions some of the men and women who have helped move disability sport forward.

Robert Steadward, as mentioned earlier, served as founding president of the International Paralympic Committee (IPC), holding the office from 1981 to 2001. A Canadian, Dr. Steadward led the IPC through a series of organizational transitions and was pivotal in its growth as a major international multisport governing body. These transitions included the coming together of different disability groups to form a common umbrella organization; the founding of the **International Paralympic Committee**; the securing of a site for the IPC Headquarters in Bonn, Germany; and ongoing negotiations with international sponsors and the International Olympic Committee leading to the agreement whereby host cities would bid for both Games. The IPC grew to over 175 members during his term (Canadian Paralympic Committee, n.d.). He also served on the IOC's Commission on Ethics and Reform. He is a recipient of both the Olympic Order and the Paralympic Order in honor of his lifetime contributions to these organizations.

Sir Phil Craven, the second president of the IPC, represented Great Britain in wheelchair basketball in five consecutive Paralympic Games. He became the president of the IPC in 2001, following Steadward in that office (Dugan, 2012). He was also a member

Rio Paralympic Games.

© A. Ricardo/Shutterstock.

of the IOC and a board member of the London Organising Committee of the Olympic and Paralympic Games (LOCOG). Sir Craven was bestowed his title MBE (Member of the Most Excellent Order of the British Empire) in 2001 in honor of his service to wheelchair basketball, and he was knighted in 2005 for his service to Paralympic sport. During his tenure, the Paralympic Movement has grown to over 200 members, and the worldwide coverage of the Summer Paralympic Games has expanded, with close to 4 billion people watching the London 2012 Games (Davies, 2012). The IPC elected its third President in September of 2017, Andrew Parsons, a native of Brazil. Parsons has served as the President of the Brazilian Paralympic Committee.

Ann Cody is currently the Program Officer at the U.S. Department of State in Washington, DC. Formerly, she was the Director of Policy and Global Outreach for BlazeSports America, an organization devoted to promoting sport and physical activity for children with disabilities. Cody is a recognized leader in the fields of disability sport and human rights and was pivotal in the development of the IPC's Committee on Women (Sportanddev, n.d.). She served multiple terms on the IPC Governing Board. She is also a Paralympic Gold Medalist in Athletics and competed on three U.S. Paralympic teams (basketball, 1984; athletics 1988, 1992) (BlazeSports, 2012).

Muffy Davis, elected in 2017 as a member of the IPC Governing Board, was a skiing medalist in the 1998 and 2002 Winter Paralympic Games (Muffy Davis, 2013). She went on to win three gold medals in handcycling at the 2012 London Summer Paralympic Games. Davis has been a member of the IPC's Women in Sport Committee for a number of years and is a staunch advocate for increasing opportunities for girls and women with disabilities to participate in sport.

Cheri Blauwet, M.D., is the Chair of the IPC's Medical Commission. As an athlete in the sport of wheelchair racing, Blauwet competed for Team USA in the Sydney 2000, Athens 2004, and Beijing 2008 Summer Paralympic Games, earning seven Paralympic medals along the way. She is also a two-time winner of two Boston Marathons. She serves on the Board of Directors for the USOC and also the United States Anti-Doping Agency (USADA), promoting clean competition in sports (Brigham and Women's Hospital, 2017).

Kirk Bauer has been in the service of Disabled Sport USA since 1982, over half of those years as executive director. An amputee from an injury in the Vietnam War, he was awarded a Bronze Star and a Purple Heart during his time in the service. Perhaps first among Bauer's many accomplishments and contributions was the 2003 establishment of the Wounded Warrior Disabled Sport Program. This program offers instruction in over 20 sports for wounded servicemen and servicewomen in the U.S. military (Disabled Sports USA, 2011). A number of veterans who have gone through the program have represented the United States in the 2008 Beijing, 2010 Vancouver, 2012 London Paralympic Games, 2014 Sochi Paralympic Games, and the 2016 Rio Paralympic Games.

Another organization active in providing opportunities for people with disabilities to practice sport is the Special Olympics. Special Olympics would not have existed without the support and leadership of the Kennedy-Shriver family and Frank Hayden, a Canadian professor who had identified fitness gaps between people with disabilities and those without disabilities (Department of Kinesiology and Community Health, n.d.).

In the 1960s, Eunice Kennedy Shriver saw how unfairly people with intellectual disabilities were treated and decided to do something about it (Special Olympics, n.d.b). What started as a summer camp program rapidly grew, and with the support of the Shriver family, Special Olympics was born and gained momentum. Dr. Hayden was contacted and together they helped organize the first Special Olympics World Summer Games held in Chicago. The first Special Olympics World Winter Games followed in 1977 in Steamboat Springs. The 2011 Summer Games, which took place in Athens, Greece, drew over 7,000 participants from 170 countries. Special Olympics continues to be a global advocate for people with disabilities. Today, Special Olympics touches the lives of more than 4.9 million people with disabilities in 172 countries (Special Olympics, n.d.b).

Although arguably the most recognizable disability sport organizations are the International Paralympic Committee and Special Olympics, we would be remiss in not mentioning the world of Deaf Sport, whose showcase event is the Deaflympics. The international governing body for Deaf Sport is the Comité International des Sports des Sourds, CISS (International Committee of Sports for the Deaf, ICSD). The ICSD was the first international sport organization founded for people with disabilities. It was the brainchild of Eugène Rubens-Alcais of France and Antoine Dresse of Belgium, who saw the need for competition for the deaf (Ammons, 1990). The first Deaflympics, then called The Silent Games, were held in Paris in 1924, and the first Winter Deaflympics followed in 1949 in Seefeld, Austria. At the 2016 Deaflympics, over 3,000 athletes from 97 countries around the world competed (International Committee of Sports for the Deaf, 2016). Deaf athletes also compete at different levels, including intercollegiate sport in the United States. Gallaudet University, the world's only university specifically designed to meet the needs of deaf and hearing-impaired students, offers a 14-sport program plus cheerleading (Gallaudet University, 2017).

All of the people described in this chapter, and many more whose names are not mentioned here, are leaders in disability sport. Their vision and dedication created opportunities for people with disabilities around the world to be active. But it was not without struggles and challenges and many of these remain. The next section of this chapter thus highlights some of these issues.

▶ Current Issues Facing Sport Leaders Working in Disability Sport

Just as in any segment of the sport industry, sport managers in disability sport face numerous challenges. If these managers want to truly be leaders, they will need to step up and respond to these challenges using a global view for solutions. Although some of the following issues are unique to disability sport, others tie directly to other segments of the sport industry.

Technology

Although technology impacts many aspects of sport, from lighter racing bicycles to new materials in running shoes to swimsuits with less drag, one could argue that the industry segment in which technology has had the greatest impact is in disability sport. World records continue to be shattered at the Paralympic Games in events such as downhill skiing and track and field, often as the result of newer and increasingly high-tech equipment. Improved racing chairs, mono-skis, and competition-level prosthetics are being developed on a regular basis.

The person who perhaps brought the issue of technology to the forefront was double below-the-knee amputee sprinter Oscar Pistorius,

who represented South Africa at the 2012 London Olympic Games. The first amputee to compete in the Olympic Games, Pistorius raced in both the 400-meter individual race and the 4×100-meter relay team. His participation began the discussion about whether his prosthetic legs gave him an advantage over the other competitors.

Since then, advanced technology has now become an accepted part of Paralympic sport. Knowles (2016) pointed out nine examples of innovative technologies present at the 2016 Rio Summer Paralympic Games. These include:

- The running blade and sports knee
- High tech swim caps
- Carbon body kits
- BMW's wind tunnel bikes
- Indoor bike training
- Altitude chamber and anti-gravity treadmill
- 3D printed prosthetics
- Trick bike bits
- New improved boccia kits

A major question related to this technology, however, is the cost associated with it. Not all competitors would be able to afford the latest technological innovations. That reality results in athletes from less-developed countries being unable to acquire these improvements. Because of that, the gap between athletes from more highly developed countries and less-developed countries may widen. This would have the effect of enhancing the opportunities for athletes from more highly developed countries to win more medals.

Media Coverage

Media coverage of disability sport, in particular the Paralympic Games, is significantly less than what is found in the able-bodied sport system. That being said, it is improving and media coverage of the Paralympic Games has evolved. Since the 1992 Games, there has been a sharp increase in the number of accredited media covering the Games (Brittain, 2010), but the coverage is not uniform around the world. The 2012 London Paralympic Games delivered the largest television audience of any Paralympic Games (Mackay, 2012). In the United Kingdom, Channel 4's coverage proved to be a leader in this area. International viewers tuned in with the British Broadcasting Corporation (BBC) estimating the peak number of viewers for the Paralympic Games Opening Ceremonies at 11.2 million (British Broadcasting Corporation, 2012). Chanel 4 was also unique in that this was the first time that the contract for the Olympic and Paralympic Games was split. This allowed Channel 4 to put together a unique and extensive advertising campaign in the run-up to the Games. During the Games, Channel 4 then scheduled 400 hours of coverage, built up profiles of British Paralympic athletes, and highlighted disability transport problems in London. Channel 4 continued in its leadership role in Paralympic coverage in Rio in 2016, where viewers were told, "This will be the largest broadcast in both Channel Four and Paralympic history, so brace yourselves." (Tate, 2016, para. 5). The British broadcaster was then rewarded, winning a prestigious domestic award in recognition of its coverage of the Rio 2016 Paralympic Games beating the BBC's coverage of the Olympics and ITV's coverage of the Rugby World Cup." Channel 4 has also more recently entered into an agreement with the IPC to broadcast the 2018 Winter Games from PyeongChang and the 2020 Games from Tokyo. "Channel 4 has committed to building on its coverage of the Games in London, Sochi, and Rio for the PyeongChang 2018 Paralympic Winter Games and Tokyo 2020 Paralympic Games. The broadcasters will also be the showcase for other IPC major events such as the London 2017 Para Athletics World Championships with programming created, promoted, and scheduled to draw large audiences" (Channel 4, 2017, para. 12).

While Channel 4 was an exemplar of great coverage in the U.K., this was not the case in the United States, however, where events received minimal coverage and were not broadcast live on network television. NBC chose not to be the rights holder for the Paralympic Games in the United States (Associated Press, 2012a), and this angered some fans, particularly given that a number of the U.S. athletes are military veterans, and they see these Wounded Warriors as national heroes (DeWind, 2012). A positive change occurred, however, after 2012 where the Sochi 2014 and Rio 2016 Paralympic Games with NBC and NBCSN provided 50 hours of coverage from Sochi and 66 hours from Rio (International Paralympic Committee, n.d.a).

Social media has also become a prominent presence at the Paralympic Games with organizations such as Channel 4, Around the Rings, and the IPC, as well as numerous athletes such as the United States' Josh George who also blogged for the *New York Times*, tweeting about the Paralympic experience. The London Paralympic Games were an online success. Close to 9 million views of videos featuring London 2012 sporting action or ceremonies were uploaded to www.youtube.com/paralympicsporttv, a 130% growth of IPC's official Facebook group, and four-figure growth of athlete Facebook fan pages (IPC, 2012). Rachael Latham, an ex-Paralympian and current broadcaster, explained that Channel 4 also made social media a large part of Paralympic Games coverage (Stewart-Robinson, 2012). Here, sport managers showed great resourcefulness in using the most up-to-date methods of communicating information about the Paralympic Games. Social media then ramped up for the 2016 Rio Games, as "The IPC's digital media strategy for the Rio 2016 Paralympics engaged more than 1.3 billion people. Through a mixture of engaging and interactive content, fans were brought closer than ever before to one of the world's biggest sport events. The plan for Rio was simple—educate, engage, and entertain. Using 25 digital media channels, three-full staff and multiple dedicated volunteers implemented a campaign in six languages that raised the profile of each Paralympic sport and the awareness of leading international athletes" (International Paralympic Committee, 2016, paras 1-4).

Recognizing the challenges with television coverage noted earlier, and knowing that many countries did not have Paralympic Games live on local television, the IPC established an Internet-based broadcasting system called ParalympicSport TV, which provided full coverage of the games (British Library Board, n.d.). The video initially was available at the IPC web site and featured three channels in English (Williams, 2012). This coverage has expanded and includes live events as well as 24/7 on-demand replays of competitions as well. The platform provides coverage of not just the Paralympic Games but also world championships and other disability sport events.

Sponsorship

People around the world can name at least a few of the International Olympic Committee's worldwide partners—the corporations that are part of the TOP (The Olympic Partners) program. Examples include McDonald's, Visa, and Coca-Cola. But what about corporate sponsorship of the Paralympic Games?

The IPC currently has six Worldwide Partners—Visa, Atos, Samsung, Panasonic, Toyota, and Otto Bock—and two International Partners—Allianz and BP. DB Schenker has been a longtime IPC official supplier of logistics and recently renewed its partnership through 2020. The German Ministry of the Interior, the regional government of North Rhine-Westfalia, and the city of Bonn are government partners who provide the IPC with financial support because of the IPC headquarters being based in Bonn. Additionally, a number of companies, such as Proctor and Gamble, Coca-Cola, and McDonald's, have extended their Olympic sponsorship to also include the Paralympic Games. Some companies, such as J Sainsbury, a U.K. supermarket chain, have been able to negotiate Paralympic Games–only sponsorship deals, flying a bit under the strict IOC guidelines related to Olympic sponsorship (Gillis, 2011). Interestingly, one study showed that "On average, brands generated three times more likeability from the Paralympics than the Olympics, but only 55 percent of the visibility—although results varied substantially from partner to partner" (Smith, 2016, para. 3).

In a *Wall Street Journal* article, Gillis (2011, para. 3) stated, "Today, endorsement opportunities for elite disabled athletes like (Great Britain's) Baroness Grey-Thompson are no longer solely a matter of altruism. For reasons ranging from growing crowds to greater exposure, the Paralympic Games has turned into a full-fledged marketing opportunity."

Another major force in the disability sport arena is Special Olympics. A visit to the Special Olympics International web site indicates 31 sponsors, including well-known companies such as Hilton, ESPN, Coca-Cola, and Wal-Mart (Special Olympics, n.d.a). Here in the United States, Special Olympics has been named the nation's Most Credible Charity, and polls indicate that people would be likely to purchase products from companies that sponsor Special Olympics (Special Olympics Kentucky, 2012).

Universal Design

A fourth issue faced by sport managers in disability sport is the importance of universal design. In the United States, we are used to seeing how the Americans with Disabilities Act has opened up physical access to buildings, including sport facilities. Our neighbors to the north in Canada do not have a similar federal act, and only Ontario, the largest province, has a specific piece of legislation. The Accessibility for Ontarians with Disabilities

Act hopes to improve accessibility standards to all public establishments by 2025. But the "bricks and mortar" of a building are only part of the way leaders can think about making sport facilities truly accessible for all (Hums, Schmidt, Novak, & Wolff, 2016). The term **universal design** was coined by the architect Ronald L. Mace to describe the concept of designing all products and the built environment to be aesthetic and usable to the greatest extent possible by everyone, regardless of their age, ability, or status in life (Human Centered Design, n.d.). Universal design has not been extensively applied to the realm of disability sport, but we believe that the assessment elements of universal design, similar to the criteria for inclusion, offer a useful framework to consider inclusion in sport at the present as well as possibilities for the future. The Institute for Human Centered Design (2012), an international nonprofit based in Boston, Massachusetts, articulates the five dimensions for examining universal design as follows:

- Built environment (indoors and outdoors).
- Information environment (print materials, way-finding/navigation and signs).
- Communication environment (telephone, web, and multimedia).
- Policy environment (evidence of policies that impact equality of experience).
- Attitudinal environment (staff or administrative behaviors or beliefs).

In the next section, we will discuss an inclusion model that sport managers can use called the, "Criteria for Inclusion," which also considers the framework of universal design and its application to the realm of disability sport.

Inclusion

The fifth issue that certainly relates to Universal Design is **inclusion**, of which there are various definitions, interpretations, and perspectives about the inclusion of people with disabilities in sport. For example, Nixon (2007, p. 417) defines inclusion as, "the final stage of integration of people with disabilities in a sport competition or organization, in which they are involved, accepted, and respected at all levels of the competition or organization."

The authors of this chapter have focused their work over the years on looking at inclusion frameworks and models for individuals with disabilities in the sporting environment. The authors have also investigated inclusion from comparative, historical, social justice, and human rights perspectives to examine disability in sport in context with opportunities for women in sport and race and ethnic minorities in sport. The Centers for Disease Control and Prevention (CDC) has weighed in on its definition of disability inclusion, saying,

> Including people with disabilities in everyday activities and encouraging them to have roles similar to their peers who do not have a disability is *disability inclusion*. This involves more than simply encouraging people; it requires making sure that adequate policies and practices are in effect in a community or organization. Inclusion should lead to increased participation in socially expected life roles and activities—such as being a student, worker, friend, community member, patient, spouse, partner, or parent (2017, para. 1-2).
>
> CDC. (2017). Disability inclusion. Retrieved from https://www.cdc.gov /ncbddd/disabilityandhealth/disability -inclusion.html.

For the purposes of this chapter, we will examine how people in leadership positions in the sport industry can apply inclusion in a sport organization setting. One strategy to promote inclusion is to be able to establish an assessment for sport organizations to see how well sport managers provide service and deliver opportunities to individuals with disabilities. As one example, the Criteria for Inclusion

(Wolff, Hums, & Fay, 2012) provide a framework to be able to research and study all areas and aspects of a sport organization to determine where there is progress toward inclusion and where invisibility and exclusion are still evident. The Criteria for Inclusion outlines eight areas of assessment to consider for a full evaluation of a sport organization (Hums, Moorman, & Wolff, 2009; Wolff et al., 2012). Each area and examples for each area are included here:

1. Funding/sponsorship (budget distribution to athletes with disabilities in the organization; sponsorship money designated to people with disabilities).
2. Media/information distribution (use of images of athletes with disabilities; advertising events for people with disabilities).
3. Awards/recognition (awards such as ESPN's ESPY for Best Male and Best Female Athlete with a Disability).
4. Governance (people with disabilities in governance structure of the organization).
5. Philosophy (disability mentioned in mission statement).
6. Awareness/education (educating organizational members about disability).
7. Policy environment (evidence of policies that impact equality of experience).
8. Attitudinal environment (staff or administrative behavior or beliefs).

According to Wolff, Hums, and Fay (2012, p. 2):

> Through a review of sports organizations from the perspective of Universal Design, it is possible to gather information and data to be able to provide an in-depth review and assessment. The Universal Design review process allows "user-expert" consumers to be able to identify the gaps, barriers, and challenges as well as the strengths and models of success. The assessment is a way to further articulate and define inclusion in concrete

terms and to be able to help others understand what is and what is not working smoothly.

Using universal design allows sport managers to be ahead of the game in providing access for all people. When they do so, they take the role of leaders by being proactive in promoting inclusion in the sport industry through quality customer service and policy development.

▶ The Rights of Persons with Disabilities

A second means by which to assess inclusion is through the lens of human rights for persons with disabilities. From 2003 to 2006, the United Nations (UN), governments, and civil society drafted the United Nations Convention on the Rights of Persons with Disabilities (CRPD). The CRPD, the first UN human rights convention of the 21st century, is a legally binding document that articulates and defines the rights that people with disabilities have in all aspects of life, including in sport and recreation. The authors of this chapter contributed to the drafting process, serving as the coordinators and facilitators for drafting Article 30.5. This article, or section of the Convention, specifically addresses the right to sport, recreation, leisure, and play for individuals with disabilities. Through the process, the International Disability in Sport Working Group (IDSWG) was formed by international disability sport and disability rights organizations. These groups then worked together to finalize the text for Article 30.5, which offered a shared view on the significant elements defining inclusion and the right to sport for all persons with disabilities (International Disability in Sport Working Group, 2007).

Significantly, Article 30.5 articulates inclusion in both mainstream and disability-specific settings, representing the view that individuals with disabilities should be able to have access to be able to reach their potential in all sporting settings and environments. Furthermore, Article 30.5 specifically addresses venues, services, and also activities in the schools. Along the lines of universal design, Article 30.5 sets out an ideal standard for what inclusion can and should look like in sport, recreation, and play for people with disabilities around the world. Access to sport not only happens on the playing fields but it also takes place in all aspects of the sporting culture, such that we are working toward building an inclusive sporting environment.

The text of Article 30.5 states (United Nations, n.d., p. 23):

> 5. With a view to enabling persons with disabilities to participate on an equal basis with others in recreational, leisure, and sporting activities, States Parties shall take appropriate measures:
>
> (a) To encourage and promote the participation, to the fullest extent possible, of persons with disabilities in mainstream sporting activities at all levels;
>
> (b) To ensure that persons with disabilities have an opportunity to organize, develop and participate in disability-specific sporting and recreational activities and, to this end, encourage the provision, on an equal basis with others, of appropriate instruction, training, and resources;
>
> (c) To ensure that persons with disabilities have access to sporting, recreational, and tourism venues;
>
> (d) To ensure that children with disabilities have equal access with other children to participation in play, recreation and leisure, and sporting activities, including those activities in the school system;
>
> (e) To ensure that persons with disabilities have access to services from those involved in the organization of recreational, tourism, leisure, and sporting activities.

From Convention on the Rights of Persons with Disabilities, by (United Nations General Assembly_Sixty-first session - Item 67 (b)), © United Nations. Reprinted with the permission of the United Nations.

▶ Summary

As evidenced by this chapter, disability sport is alive and growing. Millions of spectators, viewers, and participants make this a vibrant segment of the sport industry. Sport is something that makes all of us more fully human, and sport, recreation, and play are essential for fully realizing the promise of human rights (Hubbard, 2004).

Sport managers working in disability sport need to put into action some basic leadership skills, including (1) being proactive versus reactive, (2) showing flexibility, (3) being resourceful, (4) being open to change, and (5) taking initiative (Holden Leadership Center, 2009). Using these skills to address specific issues will help move disability sport forward as a strong segment of the sport industry.

Why is it important for future sport managers and leaders in the sport industry to have an understanding of sport for people with disabilities within the sport? Well, that same question was likely asked "back in the day" when other underrepresented groups wanted access to sport. Just as women and men and women of racial/ethnic minority status have become a force in the sport industry, so, this too could happen with disability sport. Perhaps in years to come, you will look back on reading this chapter and realize that reading this put you "ahead of the game."

LEADERSHIP PERSPECTIVE

Amy Rauworth

Amy Rauworth is the Director of Policy and Public Affairs for Lakeshore Foundation in Birmingham, Alabama, and also the Associate Director of the National Center on Health, Physical Activity and Disability (NCHPAD). Amy has over 19 years of experience in health promotion development and implementation, focusing on the delivery of physical activity programming for people with disability across the lifespan. Lakeshore Foundation is an internationally renowned organization serving over 4,000 unique individuals annually through physical activity, sport, recreation, advocacy, policy, and research for athletes with disabilities at all levels. Lakeshore has produced over 50 Paralympic athletes, coaches, and staff, including athletes who have captured 30 Paralympic medals. Lakeshore carries the designation as an official United States Olympic Committee Olympic and Paralympic Training Site. According to James Rimmer, Ph.D., Director of the UAB/Lakeshore Research Collaborative and Lakeshore Foundation Endowed Chair in Health Promotion and Rehabilitation Sciences, "Amy has evolved into one of the most important and influential leaders in promoting the rights of people with disabilities in all areas of health and wellness."

Q: What can leaders in sport for people with disabilities do to help generate more media interest in and subsequent public interest in sports involving athletes with disabilities?

First, it is important for this question to be asked at the onset of any competition or event. Planning for promotion and dissemination is critical. It is important that the organization wanting to promote interest in a specific athlete or competition has a staff or volunteer who is knowledgeable about media relations and marketing. Understanding the use of social marketing is very important along with the ability to use web-based analytics to measure and improve future dissemination efforts. Whenever possible, use a multi-media approach including video, graphics, blogs, and photos to share your messages.

It is imperative that messaging involve the input and feedback of athletes with disabilities. The audience you wish to reach should be segmented as we know that one size messaging does not fit all. Messaging that relates to the target audience should identify who needs the information the most as well as who is motivated to use it and share with others. Promotion and dissemination efforts should also target influencers who are trusted by a specific target audience and can provide extended reach for your message. Organizations that serve people with disabilities, consumer advocacy organizations, faith-based organizations, and broad-based sport organizations should be used as dissemination channels. Communication efforts should also be strategic about timing and positioning. If there are trending topics that relate to your narrative, use them to amplify your reach. This means you must have material ready and available in advance to be able to respond quickly. Positioning your communication messages in multiple sites, sharing talking points with multiple influencers, and champions of the disability movement is important to drive visibility and awareness. Dissemination is an ongoing process needing a clear plan of action that identifies the strategies, frequencies, platforms, influencers, and evaluation plan the leader or leader's organization will engage in and implement around the communication efforts.

Q: Technology to improve performance seems to be a prevalent topic these days. What are your thoughts on the influence of technology on participation for athletes with disabilities?
Personally, I feel technology that advances participation and performance has the most value when it can be made available to all people with disabilities. If the technology advances the performance but cannot be directly translated to the widest audience due to cost or some other limitation, I feel its value is diminished. Sport science and technology is making great strides for people with and without disabilities and many of the advances would not be possible without the research that supports elite competition. Innovation should be supported in the field of sport performance and athletes with disabilities with consideration to the transferability of the technology to the community of people with disabilities.

Q: One of the questions posed by the authors of this chapter is: "Why is it that in sport, when people with disabilities become more gifted or talented than able-bodied people, there is an uproar?" How would you answer this question?
First, I would rephrase the question and state people without disabilities rather than utilizing the term "able bodied." That statement in and of itself speaks volumes about ableism in our society. How we frame our viewpoint or our unconscious attitudes around defining disability as lacking independence, as an impairment or in relation to the norm, leads to biased views regardless of our conscious attitudes that we openly present to others. Sport has the power to change attitudes. If leveraged correctly, it can move the understanding of disability far beyond impairment to understanding disability as simply a general difference or a form of human variation. The more people are exposed to athletes with disabilities not only in the media but also in life, the better this concept will be understood. The narrative should not be about being a superhero but rather about being an accomplished athlete who has demonstrated the level of commitment and determination it takes to become an elite athlete.

Q: How can the disability sport movement *continue* to be a movement? What does *full integration* mean to you? What would that look like?
Sport appeals to a large diverse group of people from many backgrounds—age, race, religion, and gender. The disability sport movement has the potential to bring together individuals and groups in a setting for socialization that, given the right supporting conditions, can lead to a broader understanding of our collective life experiences. Understating the power of sport and changing negative stigmas around disability is not something athletes with disabilities or other leaders in the field can take lightly. When given a platform, an athlete with a disability, or a leader, must make a conscious effort to address stigma and discrimination and not simply try to blend in to a very ableistic sporting culture. Athletes with disabilities who have influence in the field should be well versed and understand the disability rights movement. They have the opportunity to provide a voice for many who are often not heard. The best leaders I have seen in the field recognize the importance of bringing the disability community along with them or actively working as an ally to garner a seat at the decision-making table for the disability community. As the slogan states: *"Nothing about us without us!"* If this slogan is truly followed, the movement will continue to have momentum.

Full integration to me relates to having equal choice and opportunity. If all people have access to conditions and resources that ensure optimal health such as physical activity, sport, and recreation are provided an opportunity to have a lifetime of good health. Inclusion in physical activity and athletics is how children learn from each other, build social skills, and optimize their growth and development. Across the lifespan, sport participation provides the opportunity to learn teamwork, leadership, and communication skills in addition to the importance of increasing a sense of belonging and decreasing social isolation. I believe that this can occur in unified or adapted sports. The outcome of inclusive physical activity communities is a society that respects and values the rights of all to have equal access to physical activity. In this sense, sport and sport participation can serve as a way to better understand one another, support integration, and decrease negative stigmas.

(continues)

LEADERSHIP PERSPECTIVE (*continued*)

Q: What are the most significant challenges facing leaders in sport for people with disabilities as we look to the future?

Some would probably say monetary issues but I would counter that argument and state the importance of intentionally focusing efforts in and among partnerships and collaborations with other like-minded entities that prioritize work based on the importance of collective impact in the disability sport movement. If we continue to separate our organizations, we will negate the greater impact we could have if we were actively and intentionally working together.

In addition, as leaders we must look beyond the disability sport movement to ensure the sustainability of the program or organization. The importance of partnership diversity cannot be overstated. We must look to non-traditional partners to become allies. Inclusion of representatives of all members of the community is the only way to ensure that as many perspectives as possible are factored into outreach strategies to create sustainability and longevity.

▶ Key Terms

Deaflympics	International Paralympic	Special Olympics
Disability sport	Committee	Universal design
Inclusion	Paralympic Games	

▶ Discussion Questions

1. Several major challenges for leaders in disability sport were discussed in this chapter. Consider one of those challenges and discuss how you would address that challenge if you were working within disability sport.

2. Media coverage of disability sport is lacking in the United States compared with other countries. As a leader in this field, how would you try to generate greater media interest in disability sport?

3. Consider the Criteria for Inclusion as outlined by Wolff, Hums, and Fay (2000). How would a director of a YMCA adopt those criteria within the sports program supported by the department? How would the facility director for the NBA arena do the same? Discuss at least three of the nine Criteria for Inclusion in your answers.

4. Research the concept of universal design and how it has been applied to sports facilities. Using universal design principles, think about how a specific sport facility where you have attended a game or where you have worked could improve access for athletes, fans, or workers with disabilities. Use examples to support your answer.

5. Sport managers are finding more and more unique ways to use social media to promote their athletes and their products. As a leader within the sports industry, how would you suggest managers in the disability sport world use social media to their advantage?

▶ References

Ammons, D. (1990). Unique identity of the World Games for the Deaf. *Palaestra, 6*(2), 40–43.

Associated Press. (2012a, August 23). Full TV coverage for Paralympics, just not in US. Retrieved from http://sports.espn.go.com/espn/wire?section=oly&id=8295913

Associated Press. (2012b, August 27). Paralympics to be broadcast in more than 100 countries after the new deals following Olympics. Retrieved from http://summergames.ap.org/article/more-100-countries-broadcast-paralympics

BlazeSports. (2012). Ann Cody among 40 women honored for impact during 40 years of Title IX. Retrieved from http://www.blazesports.org/2012/05/ann-cody-among-40-women-honored-for-impact-during-40-years-of-title-ix

Brigham and Women's Hospital. (2017). Cheri A. Blawet, M.D. Retrieved from https://physiciandirectory.brighamandwomens.org/Details/12560

British Broadcasting Corporation. (2012). Paralympics opening ceremony attracts 11 million. Retrieved from http://www.bbc.co.uk/news/entertainment-arts-19408222

British Library Board. (n.d.). The media and the Paralympics. Retrieved from http://www.bl.uk/sportandsociety/exploresocsci/sportsoc/media/articles/paramedia.html

Brittain, I. (2010). *The Paralympic Games explained.* London, UK: Routledge.

Canadian Paralympic Committee. (n.d.). Former IPC President Robert Steadward to be inducted into Alberta Hall of Excellence. Retrieved from http://www.paralympic.ca/news-and-events/press-releases/former-ipc-president-dr-robert-steadward-be-inducted-alberta-order

Castagno, K. S. (2001). Special Olympics Unified Sports: Changes in male athletes during a basketball season. *Adapted Physical Activity Quarterly, 18*, 193–206.

Centers for Disease Control and Prevention (CDC). (2017). Disability inclusion. Retrieved from https://www.cdc.gov/ncbddd/disabilityandhealth/disability-inclusion.html

Channel 4. (2017). IPC and C4 agree to new partnership for 2018 and 2020 Paralympic Games. Retrieved from http://www.channel4.com/info/press/news/ipc-and-c4-agree-new-partnership-for-2018-and-2020-paralympic-games

Coward, D., & Legg, D. (2011). Vancouver 2010. In D. Legg & K. Gilbert (Eds.), *Paralympic legacies* (pp. 131–142). Champaign, IL: Common Ground.

Davies, G. A. (2012). Sir Philip Craven receives Lifetime Achievement Award at Sport Industry Awards. *The Telegraph.* Retrieved from http://www.telegraph.co.uk/sport/olympics/paralympic-sport/9242746/Sir-Philip-Craven-receives-Lifetime-Achivement-Award-at-Sport-Industry-Awards.html

Department of Kinesiology and Community Health. (n.d.). Frank J. Hayden, MS '58, PhD '62. Retrieved from http://kch.illinois.edu/Alumni/Hayden.aspx

DeWind, D. (2012). U.S. military finish proudly in the 2012 London Paralympics. Retrieved from http://themoderatevoice.com/159245/u-s-military-finish-proudly-in-the-2012-london-paralympics

Disabled Sports USA. (2011). Our staff. Retrieved from http://www.dsusa.org/about-staff.html

Dowling, S., McConkey, R., Hassan, D., & Menke, S. (2009). A model for social inclusion? An evaluation of Special Olympics Unified Sports Programme. Annual Special Olympics Symposium, Berlin, Germany.

Dugan, E. (2012, August 26). Sir Philip Craven: Meet a real straight-shooter. *The Independent.* Retrieved from http://www.independent.co.uk/news/people/profiles/sir-philip-craven-meet-a-real-straightshooter-8081245.html

ECAC (2016, February 23). ECAC Announces Forward Movement for Inclusive Sport Initiative. Retrieved from http://www.ecacsports.com/news/2016/2/23/2_23_2016_36.aspx?path=gen

Gallaudet University. (2017). Gallaudet athletics. Retrieved from http://www.gallaudetathletics.com/landing/index

Gillis, R. (2011, January 23). Paralympic gold lures sponsors. *Wall Street Journal.* Retrieved from http://online.wsj.com/article/SB10001424052748703398504576099680221267872.html

Holden Leadership Center. (2009). Leadership characteristics. Retrieved from http://leadership.uoregon.edu/resources/exercises_tips/skills/leadership_characteristics

Hubbard, A. (2004). The major life activity of belonging. *Wake Forest Law Review, 39*(1), 217–267.

Human Centered Design. (n.d.). Ron Mace. Retrieved from http://humancentereddesign.org/adp/profiles/1_mace.php

Hums, M. A., & MacLean, J. C. (2017). *Governance and policy in sport organizations.* Taylor & Francis.

Hums, M. A., Moorman, A. M., & Wolff, E. A. (2009). Emerging disability rights in sport: Sport as a human right for persons with disabilities and the 2006 UN Convention on the Rights of Persons with Disabilities. *Cambrian Law Review, 40*, 36–48.

Hums, M.A., Schimdt, S., Novak, A., & Wolff, E.A. (2016). Universal Design: Moving the Americans with Disabilities Act from access to inclusion. *Journal of Legal Aspects of Sport, 26*(1), 36–51.

Institute for Human Centered Design. (2012). Universal design. Retrieved from http://humancentereddesign.org/universal-design

International Committee on Sports for the Deaf. (2016). A month after the 2017 Deaflympics. Retrieved from http://www.ciss.org/news.asp?a-month-after-the-2017-deaflympics

International Disability in Sport Working Group. (2007). Sport in the Convention on the Rights of Persons with Disabilities. Retrieved from http://assets.sportanddev.org/downloads/34__sport_in_the_united_nations_convention_on_the_rights_of_persons_with_disabilities.pdf

International Paralympic Committee. (n.d.a). NBC TV deal monumental for Paralympic Movement – Tatyana McFadden, Alana Nichols, Angela Ruggiero. Retrieved from https://www.paralympic.org/video/nbc-tv-deal-monumental-paralympic-movement-tatyana-mcfadden-alana-nichols-angela-ruggiero

International Paralympic Committee. (n.d.b) The IPC—Who we are. Paralympic media awards. Retrieved from http://www.paralympic.org/TheIPC/HWA/AboutUs

International Paralympic Committee. (2017, Feb. 2). Channel 4 wins prestigious award for Paralympic coverage. Retrieved from https://www.paralympic.org/news/channel-4-wins-prestigious-award-paralympic-coverage

International Paralympic Committee. (2016). No. 10 Rio Paralympics capture world's imagination on social media. Retrieved from https://www.paralympic.org/feature/no-10-rio-paralympics-capture-world-s-imagination-social-media

International Paralympic Committee. (2012). London 2012 Paralympic Games prove to be online success [Press release]. Retrieved from http://www.paralympic.org/news/london-2012-paralympics-prove-be-online-success

Knowles, K. (2016). 9 awesome technologies at the 2016 Rio Paralympics. Retrieved from https://www.thememo.com/2016/09/05/rio-paralympics-2016-technology-rio-paralympics-tech-sports-2016/

Legg, D., Fay, T., Hums, M. A., & Wolff, E. A. (2009). Examining the inclusion of wheelchair exhibition events within the Olympic Games, 1984-2004. *European Sport Management Quarterly, 9*(3), 243–258.

Mackay, D. (2012, November 22). London 2012 Paralympics watched by billion more TV viewers than Bejing 2008. Retrieved from http://www.insidethegames.biz/paralympics/summer-paralympics/2012/1011836-london-2012-paralympics-watched-by-billion-more-tv-viewers-than-beijing-2008

Muffy Davis. (2013). Muffy's story. Retrieved from http://www.muffydavis.com/untitled

Nixon, H. L. (2007). Constructing diverse sports opportunities for people with disabilities. *Journal of Sport and Social Issues, 31*(4), 417–433.

Smith, R. (2016, September 22). Rio 2016 sponsorships: Olympics gives visibility, Paralympics boost likeability, study finds. *PR Week.* Retrieved from http://www.prweek.com/article/1409712/rio-2016-sponsorship-olympics-gives-visibility-paralympics-boosts-likeability-study-finds

Special Olympics. (n.d.a). Meet our sponsors. Retrieved from http://www.specialolympics.org/meet_our_partners.aspx

Special Olympics. (n.d.b). What we do. Retrieved from http://specialolympics.org/Sections/What_We_Do/What_We_Do.aspx?src=navwhat

Special Olympics. (2012). Special Olympics Unified Sports quick reference guide. Retrieved from http://resources.specialolympics.org/uploadedFiles/special-olympics-resources/Topics/Unified_Sports/Files/4.18-SO%20Unified%20Sports%20Qk%20Ref%20Guide_09%2020%2012.pdf

Special Olympics Kentucky. (2012). Corporate giving: Special Olympics is good business. Retrieved from http://www.soky.org/corporate.htm#.UEUHTkxHsmU

Sportanddev. (n.d.). Ann Cody. Retrieved from http://www.sportanddev.org/en/connect/userprofile.cfm?user=2988

Steadward, R., & Foster, S. (2003). History of disability sport: From rehabilitation to athletic excellence. In R. D. Steadward, G. D. Wheeler, & E. J. Watkinson (Eds.), *Adapted physical activity* (pp. 471–496). Edmonton, Alberta, Canada: University of Alberta Press.

Stewart-Robertson, T. (2012, August 14). Channel 4 gives blanket coverage to Paralympics, while NBC falls short. Retrieved from http://www.pbs.org/mediashift/2012/08/channel-4-gives-blanket-coverage-to-paralympics-while-nbc-falls-short227.html

Tate, G. (2016). Rio Paralympics 2016: How to watch on TV. Retrieved from http://www.telegraph.co.uk/tv/2016/09/07/rio-paralympics-2016-how-to-watch-on-tv/

United Nations. (n.d.). *Convention on the Rights of Persons with Disabilities.* Retrieved from https://www.un.org/development/desa/disabilities/convention-on-the-rights-of-persons-with-disabilities.html

Williams, A. (2012, September 5). Paralympics 2012: Wheelchair racing can take off with TV's help. Retrieved from https://www.theguardian.com/sport/blog/2012/sep/05/paralympics-2012-wheelchair-racing

Wilski, M., Nadolska, A., Dowling, S., McConkey, R., & Hassan, D. (2012). Personal development of participants in Special Olympics Unified Sports teams. *Human Movement, 13,* 271–279.

Wolff, E. A., Hums, M. A., & Fay, T. (2012). *Access and inclusion in sport for people with disabilities: Article 30.5, Universal Design and a call to action.* Boston, MA: Institute for Human Centered Design.

CHAPTER 15

Real World Applications and Career Paths

Tim Liptrap

CHAPTER OBJECTIVES

- Recognize the importance of taking on leadership roles, regardless of how small, while at school, work, home, or an internship site, or on sport teams.
- Identify leadership and experiential opportunities at school, work, home, or an internship site, or on the field of play.
- Discuss the ethics, professionalism, and maturity required at work and internship sites.
- Understand how to network with individual leaders to seek a mentorship or future opportunities.

CASE STUDY

The Internship Dilemma

It was the week prior to Spring Break in March of 2018, and junior sport management student Monique Jones was wrestling with a decision that could change the course of her career path for years to come. She explained to her advisor that she had two internship opportunities on the table and had to make a decision by April 1, which was less than 2 weeks away. It was apparent to her advisor that the decision was difficult because both internships offered excellent opportunities for her leadership development, but one internship site had a perceived stronger brand in the marketplace than the other.

Both internships would start June 1 and continue through the end of the fall semester of her senior year, at which time she would return to campus to complete her degree. Both internships would require her to move away from home and school; the money for rent, food, and living expenses were about the same and each internship site was willing to provide a small weekly stipend to help offset expenses.

(continues)

CASE STUDY

Monique was offered an internship opportunity outside of Boston, Massachusetts interning with a not-for-profit agency, Good Sports. Good Sports is a small organization that provides donated sports equipment to youth sport programs serving children living in underprivileged communities. Although the organization is small, its impact is not; as of 2018, Good Sports had donated over $26 million in sports equipment. In the internship, she would help organize events for both fund- and friend-raising. These events—fundraising galas and kick-off parties for kids—were particularly attractive to Monique because they involved event management, which was the type of work she wanted to become involved with for her career. In the position, she would have a leadership role in each event, travel throughout the area including New York City and New England, and work with a well-known event planner. Monique also had an emotional interest in the cause, as she had worked in a sport for development program, Husky Sport, in Hartford, Connecticut, and knew how difficult it was for children from underprivileged communities to get access to new sports equipment.

The second opportunity was to be a ride operator at a nationally known theme park (Disney World). The theme park was different from Good Sports in that it has a well-defined internship training program in place and works with thousands of students each year. Monique went through three interviews, which included a phone screen, a Skype interview, and a final phone call with a placement officer. She felt that she was competing with many other students for the same position, which gave her a sense of accomplishment when she was offered the internship. In this position, Monique would be trained in the particulars of the ride she would work on, visitor safety, extensive customer service, leadership, and, in addition, she would be exposed to other student interns from around the world. In her conversation with her advisor, Monique felt that being a ride operator was not for her, but she was willing to consider this unique opportunity because it was with Disney in Florida.

Prior to the meeting with her advisor, Monique developed a SWOT (strengths, weaknesses, opportunities, threats) analysis for both positions. The strengths of Disney were the brand name and the training program for customer service and leadership, along with the opportunity for growth at the end (potential employment). The strengths of Good Sports included the event management skills, being able to do a "little of everything," having a professional mentor in the field, traveling throughout New England and New York City, and the opportunity to develop her leadership skills.

The weakness of the Disney program was focused on the type of work she would be doing as a ride operator. She did not think that the title or the work were what she wanted to have on her resume, and she was afraid of being pigeonholed in one area and not being able to work in other parts of the business. The weaknesses of Good Sports were that the operation was small (fewer than 10 people), she was concerned she would not have adequate support from her supervisors because they would be busy with other projects, and there was little potential to be employed later on.

The opportunity for employment at Disney and its related companies (ABC, ESPN) seemed more extensive than that of Good Sports, but learning to run events in a nonprofit agency could open doors into the not-for-profit world. Not-for-profits employ 12 million people per year, or 9% of the workforce (University of Wisconsin-Madison, n.d.). Monique's parents were leaning toward Disney because the brand name and logo would be with her for the rest of her career. They felt that the Disney name would initiate a conversation with potential recruiters and employers.

Knowing Monique from her classroom experiences, her advisor thought Disney might be a better experience overall for her. The advisor believed going away for an internship would allow Monique to focus on the internship and not her family or social life. By doing so, Monique could focus more on the task at hand—her career. In comparison, Good Sports was located within a 2-hour drive of her family home in Connecticut, and she would have been encouraged by her family and friends to come home on a regular basis, including some nights and most weekends.

Questions for Discussion

1. What is the value of a brand name on your resume? Would you be willing to forego experiences in exchange for being associated with a larger brand name?
2. What differences in training could Monique receive in a larger organization versus a smaller one?
3. Do you agree with her advisor's suggestion to focus solely on her career during an internship experience?
4. If you were Monique, which internship would you have chosen, and why? Which internship seemed to give Monique the better chance to develop and display leadership skills?

▶ Introduction

This chapter seeks to help students develop leadership skills, both while they are in school and during their first years in the workplace. The chapter begins with thoughts and research on how to build leadership skills, differentiating some of the core leadership skills from the top-level competencies. The author then recommends several ways to take advantage of opportunities on campus or in nearby communities. He touches on the importance of itemization, which is the act of identifying the skills you are developing and then connecting them with your leadership development.

The importance of practical experience gained through internships cannot be understated, and the chapter spends a fair amount of time discussing how to search for internships, how to apply for them, and how to conduct yourself at an internship interview and at a site after you have received the position. Furthermore, the chapter makes it clear why internships are important for young people. For many students, internships and other practical experiences open up opportunities for networking and acquiring mentors, concepts that are also covered in the chapter. Finally, the author gives advice on how to initially build leadership skills after a graduate has landed that first job.

The information in this chapter is of great value to upper-level undergraduate students and graduate students who are getting ready to make their way into the workplace. It should get them thinking about which leadership skills they already possess and which ones they need to acquire to be a successful professional in the sport industry.

▶ Building Leadership Skills

Sport teams, sponsors, agencies, and other related businesses are looking for new and energized leaders. A study conducted by the National Association of Colleges and Employers (NACE) found that employers hiring a new employee are looking for leadership skills that include communication, teamwork, problem solving, decision making, and the ability to influence others. In the same study, it was found that 91% of employers believe that work experience should factor into a hiring decision (NACE, 2012).

The youth unemployment rate at the national level for the 16 to 24-year age group in August of 2017 was reported at 8.9% (Statista, 2017), which is a drop from 13.1% in 2013 (MyCommNet, 2013). Although this is good news for college graduates, employers, professors, and college students understand that college students need to develop their skills and experience to compete in the job market. Competition for jobs is not just with fellow classmates; it extends to the entire workforce. For instance, older adults have been found to be working longer into their retirement because they cannot afford to retire, thus limiting the open positions and promotions within companies. Since 2000, employment for those 65 and older has grown from 12.8% or about 4 million people, to 9 million workers, or 18.8% of the total workforce in 2016. Yet, the outlook for college graduates is positive, as there is an expected 17% increase in hiring of college graduates over the previous year (NACE, 2018).

For new graduates to stand out in a competitive marketplace, they must be able to demonstrate leadership skills and highlight practical experience. In addition to maintaining a strong GPA (3.0 or higher), undergraduate students should engage in extracurricular activities such as participating on a sport team, volunteering for projects, organizing events, leading a club, running for office, or managing a group or team. By doing so, students will be able to practice leadership skills introduced in coursework.

College students are improving upon their leadership activities every day. By accomplishing tasks such as homework, written papers, and tests on a regular basis, it could be argued that students are developing strong time-management, communication, and problem-solving skills, which are all traits of a good leader. This is true, but it is hard to demonstrate in an interview with future employers how these skills are a benefit.

Students may also find other leadership opportunities outside of the college campus. Leadership activities can take place in a hometown, high school, church or synagogue, work, or recreational program. Undergraduate students are encouraged to volunteer for projects that will help build their leadership capabilities, skills, and experience during both their winter and summer breaks. Even if a leadership experience happens outside of the academic campus, it can still be included on a resume or in a leadership portfolio.

A resume acts as a sales brochure highlighting the student's specific job positions,

responsibilities, dates served, awards, activities, and skill sets. A resume gives enough information to warrant an employer to conduct a screening interview, generally over the phone. If a candidate makes it to the next round or the second interview, a leadership portfolio should be brought along as well. A **leadership portfolio** is a compilation of work examples, projects, spreadsheets, and writing samples that can be used to demonstrate a candidate's leadership ability and other skills. A leadership portfolio can be as simple as a three-ring binder with relevant materials enclosed, or to a greater extreme, elevator pitch videos, individualized web sites, or sales videos posted online.

The **elevator pitch** is a one-minute sales pitch that students craft as a branding message about themselves. Information about how to tailor your elevator pitch to try and obtain an employment position can be found here (http://www.forbes.com/sites/nextavenue/2013/02/04/the-perfect-elevator-pitch-to-land-a-job/); other examples can be found on YouTube with a simple search for "elevator speeches."

The Four Cs

In its 2012 Critical Skills Survey, the American Management Association found "the ability to think critically, solve problems, innovate, and collaborate are highly valued at every level within the organization" (PR Newswire, 2013, para.1). Additionally, three of four managers and executives of the 768 surveyed said the four Cs—**critical thinking**, **communication**, **collaboration**, and **creativity**—will become even more important in the fast-paced, competitive global economy. By understanding what is needed in the workforce prior to graduation, a student can build these skills before leaving campus, or early on in his or her career.

The top-level competencies of critical thinking, communication, collaboration, and creativity are developed in individuals through experiential learning. **Experiential learning** simply means that students need to gain "real world" work experience as part of the learning process. Experiential learning is instrumental in acquiring the four Cs. But prior to developing expertise in the four Cs, young leaders must develop competencies in core skills first. The core skills associated with strong leadership include the individualized development of analytic skills, communication, delegation, interpersonal skills, organizational skills, problem solving, strategic planning, time management, tactfulness, and teamwork.

▶ Skills in Action

To illustrate common skills associated with strong leadership, this chapter will use an example of a college student who is volunteering to manage a local Little League team and how the day-to-day tasks can build leadership skills. The team has 11 players, one head coach (the college student), two assistant coaches, and parents who are actively involved in their children's athletic development.

- *Analytic skills:* These competencies are numerically or statistically based and are used to problem solve. As a coach, data such as player statistics, errors, runs batted in (RBIs), and times at bat could be used to develop a stronger team or try to create a competitive advantage.
- *Communication skills:* These competencies include speaking capability, written communication, presenting, and listening (Robles, 2012). A coach's communication skills are imperative because he or she will speak with players, parents, and league officials. Understanding how to use words and body language to communicate helps the coach transmit the correct message to the parents.

- *Delegation skills:* This denotes the coach assigning work to be completed by others. Delegating work to assistant coaches and volunteer parents displays leadership capabilities.
- *Interpersonal skills:* The ability to be sociable, nice, personable, patient, friendly, and nurturing; showing a sense of humor and empathy; and exhibiting self-control (Robles, 2012) are important traits for leaders. As a coach, strong interpersonal skills help build rapport and trust among players and parents.
- *Problem-solving skills:* These are methods and techniques used to develop and find solutions to problems. As a coach, you will need to manage problems as they arise without getting frazzled by the situation.
- *Strategic planning skills:* This area of the skill set helps an organization focus on producing effective decisions and actions that create value (Bryson, 2004). As a coach, you will need to plan the team line-ups, player positions, and batting order, while maintaining fair amounts of playing time and the desire to produce both fun and wins.
- *Time management skills:* These competencies are used in balancing multiple tasks at once and making the most of available time. As a coach, time management skills come into play when the team is practicing at multiple stations and the coach is in charge of the processes.
- *Teamwork skills:* These include being cooperative, getting along with others, and being agreeable, supportive, helpful, and collaborative (Robles, 2012). Leaders must encourage players on teams to work together, trust each other, and support each other.

By itemizing the tasks done on a baseball field—or any other practical experience—students can demonstrate how the projects they engage in have transferable skills to any type of leadership role. This itemization should be done before composing a resume so skills can be mentioned within bulleted job duties or in an overview at the top of a resume.

▶ Leadership Opportunities on Campus

During college, it is a good idea to take advantage of the opportunities made available at your institution. Many classes in sport management programs are now programming experiential-learning opportunities into the curriculum so students will experience a classroom assignment in a "real work" environment. In addition, these assignments provide an opportunity for students to begin building their resumes while in school.

Springfield College in Springfield, Massachusetts, uses approximately 80 to 100 sport management students every January to staff the Spalding Hoophall Classic, sponsored by the Basketball Hall of Fame. This national high school basketball showcase is a 5-day event during which undergraduate students work as ushers, security personnel, liaisons to teams, and supervisors. Upper-level sport management students serve as supervisors while freshmen and sophomores perform liaison, security, ushering, and media check-in duties. The tournament provides a perfect marriage of curriculum with student leadership development. Although faculty members are present at the tournament to answer questions, the student supervisors are in charge of various leadership duties, such as scheduling shifts, delegating, mentoring younger students, and helping provide an exemplary customer service experience to the many players and coaches who have traveled to Springfield. As younger students show

Faculty members mentor upper-level sport management students during the Spalding Hoophall Classic at Springfield College.

Photo provided by John Borland, courtesy of Springfield College.

proficiency in ushering, security, liaison, and media check-in tasks, they are afforded opportunities to become supervisors at future tournaments.

Not all sport management or business programs have these experiential-learning opportunities available, so students may need to initiate an opportunity if one is not readily available. Ideas and examples of leadership opportunities that students can develop for themselves on campus include: Take classes in leadership and leadership development; participate in case-study competitions; become a team captain in either a varsity sport, club sports, or intramurals; actively participate in your Student Government Association (SGA); take a leadership role in Greek life; become a student club president; volunteer to run an event for either student activities or athletics; ask your professor for extra leadership-based projects; volunteer at a local Boys and Girls Club; coach youth sports; volunteer to take the leadership role when working on group projects; become a resident assistant; or work as an orientation leader and/or give campus tours for your admissions office. The opportunities are there; students need to seek them out and get involved.

Student-Athletes

Student-athletes may have difficulty finding the time to volunteer for additional projects outside of the classroom or on the sport field. Many student-athletes dedicate 20 to 30 hours a week to their sport and simply do not have time (Brown, 2011). To gain leadership skills, student-athletes are encouraged to take on leadership roles within teams on which they play. A leadership role on a sport team may include a position as team captain, co-captain, or team manager.

Students who take on leadership roles within sport teams are shown to have similar skills to those of others who do not

participate in sport but volunteer for other activities. Leadership skills such as communication, coordination, and problem solving are developed among these athletes as they are involved in scheduling, organizing, and managing team events (Tanguay, Camp, Endres, & Torres, 2012).

Volunteering

Volunteering at events is a good way for college students to learn about the business of running professional events. The Fiesta Bowl, Federation Cup (women's tennis), Chicago Marathon, and Deutsche Bank Championship are examples of events that look for volunteers to run the event prior to and on game days. The Nichols College Sport Management program views volunteer experiences as an integral part of students' development before looking for a job. Volunteering is important because it:

- Builds students' professional experience
- Provides exposure to the inner workings of events
- Allows for networking with professionals in the sport industry
- Provides support to a local charity event
- Teaches how to work and manage volunteers
- Makes classroom learning more relevant

If your academic program does not encourage volunteering at events, it is recommended that students locate all of the major sport, recreation, and entertainment events held in the general geographic vicinity of their hometowns and reach out to offer their time, experience, and skill.

Now that this chapter has discussed the development of leadership skills and places on and off campus where these skills can be obtained, **TABLES 15.1** and **15.2** provide a summary of leadership competencies that can be developed based on the event, activity, or project in which a student is engaged.

TABLE 15.1 Leadership Skills by Event, Project, or Activity

	Analytic	Communication	Delegation	Interpersonal	Organizational	Problem Solving	Strategic Planning	Time Management	Tactfulness	Teamwork
Athletic team manager	x	x	x	x	x	x		x	x	x
Giving campus tours		x		x	x	x		x	x	
Case study competitions	x	x	x	x	x	x	x	x	x	x
Classes in leadership development		x		x	x	x	x	x	x	
Coaching youth sports	x	x	x	x	x	x	x	x	x	x
Event or student activities		x	x	x	x	x	x	x	x	x
Group projects		x	x	x	x	x	x	x	x	x
Leadership-based projects		x	x	x	x	x	x	x	x	x
Leadership position in Greek life		x	x	x	x	x	x	x	x	x
Orientation leader		x		x	x	x		x	x	x
Resident assistant		x	x	x	x	x		x	x	x
Running a radio show		x		x	x	x		x	x	
Special event or tournament for athletics	x	x	x	x	x	x	x	x	x	x
Student-athlete		x	x	x	x	x		x	x	x
Student club president	x	x	x	x	x	x	x	x	x	x
Student Government Association (SGA)	x	x	x	x	x	x	x	x	x	x
Team captain, either varsity or intramural		x	x	x	x	x		x	x	x
Volunteering at a Boys and Girls Club		x		x	x	x		x	x	x

TABLE 15.2 Leadership Skills by Academic Event, Project, or Activity

	Analytic	Communication	Delegation	Interpersonal	Organizational	Problem Solving	Strategic Planning	Time Management	Tactfulness	Teamwork
Solving case studies	X	X	X		X	X				
Working with databases	X				X	X				
Developing Excel workbooks	X				X	X				
Group project		X	X	X	X	X		X	X	X
PowerPoint presentation	X	X			X					
Giving a presentation/speech		X	X	X	X			X	X	
Reflection paper		X			X	X				
Research paper	X	X			X	X		X		
Simulation game	X		X	X	X	X	X	X		
Creating and conducting survey analysis	X	X	X	X	X	X	X	X	X	X
Volunteering at an event		X			X	X	X		X	X

▶ Internships

Ryan and Krapels (1997) define **internships** as "learning opportunities that improve job selection and provide low-cost, nearly risk-free, hands-on job training to prospective employees, while at the same time, interns contribute real, productive work" (p. 126). Internships and other experiential opportunities (hands-on work) allow students to build leadership skills and professional skills, and apply their academics to real world situations. Experiential-learning opportunities within companies or schools go by many names, which can include co-opportunities (co-ops), internship, externship, volunteerism, student teaching, or a practicum. For the purpose of our discussion, all of the above will be known as an internship.

Educators find that exposing students to real world experiences such as teaching, management issues, and leadership and administration will provide an easier and more successful transition for them into the workforce (Turner, 1993). According to Eyler (2009), "Experiential education [internships], which takes students into the community, helps students both to bridge classroom study and life in the world and to transform inert knowledge into knowledge-in-use." (p. 24). In a practical application, an internship is often an organized work situation in which a student, receiving little or no money, will volunteer his or her time at a professional sport organization and receive college credit in his or her academic program. In exchange for time and energy, students will receive practical hands-on education that may lead to enhanced job skills, leadership skills, and/or future employment.

The National Association of Colleges and Employers (NACE, 2012) reported that 61.2% of full-time internships have led to a full-time employment offer. In 2015, NACE reported results of their *Class of 2015 Student Survey*, which reinforces the fact that internships are vital in finding a leadership position in sport and setting oneself apart in the competitive job market. They found that 72.2% of those who had paid internships/co-ops with private, profit-driven companies received job offers. Only 36.6% of those who did not conduct an internship or co-op received an offer. More importantly, the difference in starting salary was about $15,000, those with internships or co-op started at $53,521 and those without, started at $38,572. (NACE, 2016).

For many students, the internship is their first experience in an office atmosphere. In addition to learning specific tasks, students are exposed to a unique organizational culture, which includes the leadership hierarchy, team dynamics, office politics, dress codes, deadlines and timelines, and practical lessons in management.

The length of an internship is dictated by one of two things, generally the amount of credits that a student needs to earn and the team or company the student works for.

A full-time internship may require between 10 and 60 hours a week or 100 to 450 hours in the semester. But some organizations might ask a student to work longer than the school requires, given the events or activities that the organization has planned during the intern's time with the organization. For example, an intern for a minor league baseball team might start in January to begin promotions for a new season but is often asked to stay during the summer season to assist with game operations.

Current trends are starting to show that sport teams, athletic departments, and companies are asking students to extend their internships to a full year, but work fewer hours per week. By doing so, internship sites are giving students more responsibilities and longer-term projects.

Who Does an Internship?

Generally, those in the college-age group secure internships. Students from any major who are willing to create an experiential education for themselves are encouraged to complete internship(s). It is not uncommon for a student to complete 3 to 4 internships during their college career. As the economy has changed, a new trend has emerged as older generations of employees, not just college-age students, are looking for internships. In a recent trend explained by Cohen (2012), **returnships** (a term trademarked by Goldman Sachs) are internships for those professionals who are resuming a career after a hiatus from work, such as a job layoff, raising a child, or taking time to take care of a sick parent. Companies such as Goldman Sachs, Sara Lee, and Sikorsky Aircraft offer short experiences to those who have been out of work and are trying to break back into the marketplace.

How Do You Find an Internship?

Internships are experiential education opportunities and can be found using a variety of methods. In today's world, it is easy to find internship listings on the Internet, through job search engines, or in specialized locations for internships like portals, such as WorkinSports.com, Teamworkonline.com, NCAA The Market, and Indeed.com. Students' first step should be to talk to their professors, along with their career services office. Depending on the size of a school, there may even be an office dedicated to internships and other practical-experience opportunities. Some academic programs have internship coordinators.

Internship seekers who are unsure of the type of internship, place of internship, or desired area in which they would like to use their time should start backward. First, identify the geographic location in which you would like to conduct an internship. Second, identify the team or organization for which you would like to work. Third, identify the type of work that you would like to do, such as game-day operations, marketing, finance, sales or sponsorship, ticketing, coaching, or public relations. Do not apply only for your dream internship. Be sure to apply for several internships. Having to pick between two or three options can be difficult, but it is better than having no options at all. **TABLE 15.3** gives examples of the types of companies, events, and leagues that offer internships. This is not an exhaustive list, just examples. Most teams post their current available internships on their web sites.

TABLE 15.3 Internship Site Examples

Potential Internship Site	Web site
Anschutz Entertainment Group	https://www.aegworldwide.com/careers/job-search
Cape Cod Baseball League	http://www.capecodbaseball.org/teams/players-interns/
Disney Professional Internships	http://disneyinterns.com
ESPN	https://espncareers.com/college/internships
International Management Group	http://img.com/
Ladies Professional Golf Association	http://www.lpga.com/careers-about/careers/internship-program
Live Nation	http://concerts.livenation.com/careers
Major League Baseball	www.mlb.com/careers
Major League Soccer	http://www.mlssoccer.com/jobs
NASCAR	www.employment.nascar.com/#/internship
National Basketball Association	www.nba.com/careers/internship_program.html

(continues)

TABLE 15.3 Internship Site Examples	(continued)
Potential Internship Site	**Web site**
National Collegiate Athletic Association	www.ncaa.org
National Football League	www.nfl.com/careers/internships
National Hockey League	http://hockeyjobs.nhl.com/teamwork/jobs
National Recreation and Park Association	www.nrpa.org
NBCUniversal	www.nbcunicareers.com/internships
Nike	https://jobs.nike.com/university
Octagon	www.octagon.com
PGA Tour	www.pgatour.com/company/internships.html
Royal Caribbean Cruises	https://www.royalcareersatsea.com/
SMG Worldwide	http://www.smgworld.com
Tough Mudder	http://tmhq.com/careers
Under Armour	https://careers.underarmour.com/
U.S. Golf Association	www.usga.org
U.S. Olympic Team	www.teamusa.org/Careers/Internship-Program.aspx
U.S. Rugby Association	www.usarugby.org/careers
U.S. Sailing	http://home.ussailing.org
U.S. Tennis Association	www.usta.com

Table 15.3 has a sample list of companies where you can find internships. There are many more companies that have great internships but are often overlooked by students. These include manufactures of sport equipment and apparel, health clubs, online sport applications, technology companies or sports outside of the traditional televised ones, such as archery, bowling, fishing, and pickleball. By expanding your search to these

alternatives, you will find you have less competition for great positions.

When do you start?

Do not wait until the last minute to begin the internship search. A 6-month window is preferable to do the search. Job postings may not be up when the student is ready to apply, but at least students can identify sites where they would like to apply and possibly talk to others who have worked at these sites.

▶ Applying for an Internship

Applying for internships takes preparation and planning. Students should have resumes and sample cover letters ready several months before they need to send out applications. These resumes and cover letters need to be vetted by both a student's career services office and the student's academic advisor. Furthermore, different cover letters and resumes need to be sent out for different job postings because each internship site is looking for different skills and competencies. Students must tailor their resumes, cover letters, and portfolios to different work sites.

The companies looking for interns for the summer, fall, or spring will indicate the position title, job description, hours, location, and other information in a job posting. These postings can usually be found on company web sites. When applying for a position, students may need to upload a resume; cover letter; and, potentially, a short video about themselves.

Using Your Career Services Office

Your career service office is one of the best places to start your internship search. They will offer a current list of internship and job opportunities; have workshops on internships, resume writing, interview tips, and will have employers on campus. If you haven't done so, make an appointment to discuss your options and the services that you can use.

Getting Hired

Bryant Richards, the director of corporate governance at Mohegan Sun Casino in Uncasville, Connecticut, asks this question of all potential interns: "What can you bring to the table that somebody else cannot?" Richards wants to know what skills, talents, and uniqueness interns have that others do not possess, and he wants to know about students' willingness to work hard (Bryant Richards, personal communication, 2013).

Richards explained how the expectations of supervisors are relatively low for interns at many sites in the hospitality and sport industries. He said, "In many cases, it does not take much for a manager to say, 'Wow,' when it comes to interns." If a student can create a "Wow" from each of the manager(s) who oversee internships, it is more likely that he or she will get better opportunities and increased responsibilities than the other interns.

In getting hired for an internship, students generally have one shot at impressing a corporate recruiter, the department head, or a manager. In many cases, the key is how students present and represent their skills and talent. By the time an applicant has been invited onto the property, the person in charge of hiring has done background research on the applicant. They have Googled you, checked your Twitter feed, searched for you on Facebook and Instagram, and have made calls to your professors.

Many of the hiring managers understand the academic programs from which interns have come. They may work with the professors there, look at the courses that students have taken, and, in some cases, have helped build the projects that students do in class. Richards said that during the interview process he looks for internship candidates to demonstrate their leadership potential, which can be illustrated by past experiences on their resumes. Richards said his organization also looks for transferable skills that Mohegan can work with because of the industry training that interns will receive.

Richards said that many times it is the simple things that occur during the internship interview that make the difference. Did an applicant show up on time? How did he or she treat the receptionist? Is the student dressed for the position? Is the student prepared for the position? Did the student do his or her homework on the company?

Richards said his organization seeks interns with burgeoning leadership skills, and he identifies these by looking for leadership roles that can be demonstrated by the students. Those roles could be in one's community, being a resident assistant, working in the admissions office on campus, or working in other team-like environments that put the students into situations in which they need to work together and make judgments quickly.

Richards pointed out that organizations, unlike academic programs, do not accept "C" work. Although a professor may accept work late with points deducted or grade assignments on a sliding scale, this situation does not exist in the workplace. Students need to get the job done right the first time. In the workforce, it is not acceptable to get a 70 on a document that is turned in to a supervisor. Getting a 70 on a work project means that your supervisor will have to redo it, and it also shows that the student did not have the skill or desire to complete work with high standards (Bryant Richards, personal communication, 2013).

"You're Fired"

It does not happen very often, but to protect yourself from being fired, you should understand the rules of employment at your internship site. Sport management professor Timothy Liptrap from Nichols College, who places more than 60 interns a year and speaks publicly on the use of social media in sport organizations, tells a story about one of his junior sport management students who was released from his internship with an NFL team due to a Twitter post. After his first day of work, the student was so excited that he Tweeted about his day.

In reality, it was not a significant post, but the student violated the NFL team's social media policy by putting the team name in a Twitter post without permission. Another student took an internship with the New York Knicks and shortly after he started, the student decorated his cubicle with Boston Celtics banners, flags, and pictures. The student was not fired, but he did receive a warning from his supervisor. Liptrap also had a student fired from a regional speedway, after he received a speeding ticket while distributing fliers while using the company car, which also doubled as the track's pace car. In addition, another student was released from a National Hockey League team after he revealed to a local reporter what he heard in a staff meeting about an impending player trade.

Students are occasionally released from internships for failing to understand the company policies, norms, or rules. Liptrap advises each student to treat the internship as an extended job interview; be professional and respectful of the organization and its staff.

Liptrap and Richards of Mohegan Sun recommend these tips for interns:

- Be the first one in the office every day and the last to leave.
- Show up on time.
- Dress appropriately for the position.
- If you say you are going to do something, follow through and do it.
- Try to solve a problem (before you ask your boss for help).
- Identify problems that your boss may not have noticed yet.
- Respect the culture of the office.
- Have loyalty to the company.
- Do it right the first time.
- Do not embarrass the college, your professor, or yourself.
- Do not embarrass your manager or boss.
- Plan ahead on projects.
- Act professionally at all times.
- Shake hands well and firmly, and make good eye contact.
- Have conversations with people of different backgrounds.

▸ Networking and Relationship Building

It has often been said in the sport industry—and probably by your professors—that finding a job comes down to whom you (or your relatives) know or, as others say, who knows you. Many young college graduates have proven this theory wrong by working hard at internships and showing off their skills, talents, and experiences. In other words, they have made themselves indispensable to organizations. This is not to say that whom you know is not important, because it is. Having a large network of friends, business colleagues, and friends of friends has opened doors to opportunities for many people, young and old.

Networking Tools

Susan Adams, the author of *Me 2.0: 4 Steps to Building Your Future*, has created a list of what she believes to be the six most important **networking** tools that newly graduated college students should use to get their first job out of college (Adams, 2012). Her list includes:

1. Create a LinkedIn profile.
2. Establish a presence on WordPress or through your own blog.
3. Get an internship as early as possible.
4. Get creative about finding a mentor.
5. Use your school's career services office.
6. Join a professional development or industry-specific group.

Networking cannot wait until after school. However, it should start when a student begins school. Getting to know professors, setting up "job shadows" at nearby organizations, attending conferences such as baseball's Winter Meetings, attending lectures on campus given by leaders, and volunteering at events and then offering your services again after the event is over to an organizer are all part of networking activities that students can pursue in school. Furthermore, at internship sites, students often make the mistake of only getting to know their supervisors. Getting to know everyone in the building and finding out their paths to their current jobs is a strategy students should employ.

▸ Mentoring

Relationship building can also be accomplished through acquiring a mentor; furthermore, if the mentor is a leader, this can be a way for a student to model leadership behavior and build leadership skills. A mentor could be one of your parents, a coach, an employer, a professor, or a friend whom you admire for their accomplishments. According to Holland, Major, and Orvis (2012), a mentor is a seasoned professional or peer who provides guidance, encouragement, and social support to help a mentee succeed in their social life, job, or career. Having a mentor aids in a student's personal and career development—in particular, when enhancing a student's leadership skills. Goulet (2012) found that there is a correlation between **mentorship** and leadership, "particularly after practicing leadership through challenging experiences, developing leaders benefit from the mentoring a more experienced person can offer" (p. 51).

In addition to developing leadership skills, acquiring and working with a mentor may lead to increased income at work. It was found that young professionals who have had a positive mentor have earned more than $7,000 a year more than their peers who did not (Fried, Lim, Mangla, Rosato, & Wang, 2013).

Finding a Mentor

A young professional may need to take a proactive approach when developing a relationship with a potential mentor. It is not uncommon to have multiple mentors for different life stages or phases within a career. Your first career mentor should be one whom you admire, respect, and believe can help you reach your next goal.

Mentorship should be seen as a two-way street. In the corporate world, the next level past mentorship is called sponsorship. A mid-level to senior-level leader in a company will sponsor a younger employee and help him or her with career decisions and leadership development, and position them for success. This model and sponsorship would consider the mentee a protégé. In a study of 4,000 sponsors and protégés, sponsors indicated that the most successful protégés are those who demonstrate trust and show loyalty. When the potential sponsors were asked about what it takes to be successful protégés, 62% said that protégés should "assume responsibility and be self-directed," 39% said they should "deliver 110%," and 34% said that protégés should "offer skill sets and bring a perspective different than mine" (Hewlett, Marshall, & Sherbin, 2011, p. 133).

▶ Getting Started at Your First Job

Essentially, college serves as a minor league. You make mistakes and grow at the same time. You gather practical experiences to put on your resume; you develop networks and acquire mentors. Once you walk across that stage and grab your diploma, and unless you have aspirations to complete a graduate degree, you have graduated to the professional ranks.

Once you start your first job, you are naturally nervous and intimidated by the people around you. You may not be quite sure about the work you need to do and how your supervisor perceives you. You may also be concerned about not embarrassing yourself. A common sense model that works in the sport industry has five basic premises; these premises are:

1. Be proactive in your work.
2. Listen more than you speak.
3. Communicate.
4. Keep up with industry trends.
5. Take responsibility for your actions.

Let's step through this model with an example. You have just started a ticket sales job at a professional basketball team. Your supervisor has been in the business for well over 20 years and has a great track record at the team and within the industry. She has an extensive network of other business professionals, as well as those in the league. As you start your first week of work, you are learning that the hours are extensive, your boss is very particular, the expectations on you are extreme, and you need to make your sales quota each month.

Be proactive in your work. Chances are that your manager is busy with work, her bosses, and other employees. You'll become a model employee if you provide your boss with information that she needs when she needs it without her having to ask you for it. Be proactive and help your boss in her job, and you will be recognized for it later on. For example, if your boss is going to a meeting with her supervisor and needs Excel spreadsheets from you, be sure to give them to her *before* she needs them.

Listen more than you speak. In your first few months at a new position, it is imperative that you listen to others. Although you may have a strong opinion on how the work should be done, it might be offensive to those who have worked there for years if you try to make changes without listening and understanding the process within the office. If you argue with your boss over the way work should be completed, keep in mind that you are perceived as being new to the office and "wet behind the ears." A helpful tip would be to take notes as you are shown a new method, process, or work that is required of you.

Communicate. Do not be afraid to ask questions and communicate with your supervisor. Many managers and supervisors would like to see you ask questions because it indicates that you are interested in the work. Asking questions helps you to understand what is being presented and shows that you are trying to give your best to the project at hand.

Keep up with industry trends. Show your leadership as you build knowledge in your field. A mistake that many professionals make is not taking time to keep up with changes in the industry. Ask your manager and fellow employees what they read to keep up with industry knowledge. To become an expert in your area, it has been shown that you will need to devote more than 10,000 hours of deliberate practice to your trade (Ericsson, Prietula, & Cokely, 2007). It has been shown "consistently and overwhelmingly, experts are always made, not born" (p. 5), and deliberate practice was a key to their success. Your deliberate practice can start your first day at work, by reading the *SportsBusiness Journal*, in-house training manuals, and current news about your industry for an hour a day. By doing so, you will become knowledgeable in the industry and a resource in the office.

Take responsibility for your actions. Be willing to take responsibility for your actions, either good or bad. The sport industry is a small industry, and people are well connected and know each other. Build your reputation on honesty, and that brand will stay with you the rest of your career. When you are with your boss and she asks you a question, answer regardless of whether it has negative consequences—but do it with diplomacy.

This common sense model of the five premises will help you to develop a foundation of being a respected leader in the sport industry.

Going back to the example of your new job in ticket sales, you will find that in order to sell tickets and gain respect from your peers and supervisor, you will need to build trust and influence. Dr. Robert Cialdini, the author of *Influence: The Psychology of Persuasion*, encourages young leaders to consider how their actions in the workplace influence those around them. Cialdini's rules, as described by Barbara Kaufman (2011), are simple:

- Tell the truth, and be consistent in your explanations; inconsistency breeds distrust.
- Encourage others to "speak truth to power" and tell the truth, no matter how unpalatable.
- Set a good example by admitting your mistakes and developing a culture that expects others to be accountable for and learn from their mistakes.
- Follow through on promises and commitments.

▶ Summary

Students have the opportunity to gain leadership skills in a variety of settings prior to completing their first internships or getting their first entry-level positions. Those leadership opportunities can be gained inside and outside of the classroom. Students can take up positions of leadership in student clubs, in volunteer organizations, on intercollegiate or club sports teams, and in Greek life, to name a few. Leadership skills can be developed and refined in this setting and should be included on students' resumes when applying for internship positions. Students should recognize that a first internship can be used as a platform to showcase work skills and also provide the best opportunity to learn from other professionals in the organization. At a student's first internship, he or she can also begin to develop leadership skills in a work setting. Finally, students should seek mentors and develop a network of professional contacts who will help support leadership development.

LEADERSHIP PERSPECTIVE

Paul Cacciatore

Paul Cacciatore is the Vice President Member Experience & Arena Operations for the Boston Celtics

Courtesy of Paul Cacciatore.

Q: How did you become interested in Sport Management and in the Celtics

At a very young age, I would accompany my dad when he would help stuff envelopes for season ticket holders of the Celtics. This was my first exposure to Sport Management. I knew early on that Sport Management was the career that I wanted and the path I was going to take. I was going to college for Sport Management and taking advantage of every experience I could, including an internship. These experiences required me to be flexible and think on my feet. At times, I had to be deliberate and detail oriented, while thinking outside of the box. For example, when I was in college and had a question for the professor, I would record the time that the material was presented. This detail-oriented approach set me apart from the other students in how I was viewed by my professor. In turn, when an opportunity came up to be the student representative on a committee that was hiring a new faculty member, I was identified as the student representative candidate. Each practical and academic opportunity opened a door to the next door and before long, I was finishing my academic career with a recommendation from the Dean of the school.

Q: What is your role in leadership?

I started with the Celtics in 1996 in Customer Service. I sold season tickets, serviced season tickets, and took care of group sales clients, among other things. I placed myself in a position where people throughout the organization viewed me as a recognizable figure. In addition, I saw a change in the industry on the horizon with more emphasis on technology, so I learned the emerging technologies in ticketing, barcoding, etc. Applying this technical knowledge in a way that supported the organization's vision made me indispensable within the organization. I advanced to become the Director of Ticket Operations, then to the Vice President of Member Experience & Arena Operations. In this current role, I am responsible for connecting the Celtics organization to the public. I am responsible for making memorable relationships for our guests. This means developing emotional connections between the Celtics organization and the public. It begins with the relationships with my employees and developing a foundation of trust. Relationships built on trust create an environment in which that we can communicate effectively, deliver services with efficiency, and, most importantly, connect with our guests on a personal level.

Q: What skills are needed to be an effective leader?
When touring the Google campus, I came across a board with six words on it and immediately wrote them down on my hand. I thought to myself that this is what my managers should be doing every day: inspiring, teaching, protecting, removing obstacles, being human, and repeating. I really believe that as a leader, if I try to do one of these daily, I can become more approachable and make a personal connection with everyone with whom I interact. One of my goals is to build future leaders and that only happens when my employees feel empowered, heard, validated, and supported. Managers need to have a sense of trust among them and with me. They also need to feel a sense of importance and purpose, which, of course, they are and they do.

Q: What lessons would you give to students on their path to being future leaders?
I would suggest that students not be afraid to be different. They should do things that set them apart from the pack. This gets them noticed in a crowded environment. When a challenge or problem arises, they need to be solution focused. They should develop a strategy to resolve the problem and present this to their leader. The leader may not use their suggestion, but they have shown effort, gone through the exercise of developing a plan, and proven themselves to be forward thinking. Every problem is a potential exercise in developing a solution and this generates empowerment in my employees.

▶ Key Terms

Collaboration

Communication

Creativity

Critical thinking

Elevator pitch

Experiential learning

Internship

Leadership portfolio

Mentorship

Networking

Returnships

▶ Discussion Questions

1. As noted in the chapter, undergraduate students can begin to develop leadership skills while in school. Consider your experiences outside of the classroom. What leadership skills have you learned and developed from those out of class experiences? What skills do you need to still develop?

2. If you were composing an elevator pitch, what would you be likely to include?

3. With which activities can you become involved while you are at school that can help you to develop your leadership skills?

4. After reading this chapter, it should be apparent how important internships have become. What kind of work would you like to pursue? Which organizations would you like to pursue?

5. Identify a person in your life whom you would consider a mentor. What have you learned from this mentor with regard to leadership skills?

▶ # References

Adams, S. (2012). 6 things you must do to get your first job after college. *Forbes*. Retrieved from http://www.forbes.com/sites/susanadams/2012/11/12/6-things-you-must-do-to-get-your-first-job-after-college

Brown, G. (2011). Second GOALS study emphasizes coach influence. *National Collegiate Athletic Association*. Retrieved from http://www.ncaa.org/wps/wcm/connect/public/NCAA/Resources/Latest+News/2011/January/Second+GOALS+study+emphasizes+coach+influence

Bryson, J. M. (2004). *Strategic planning for public and nonprofit organizations: A guide to strengthening and sustaining organizational achievement, 3rd Edition*. San Francisco, CA: Jossey-Bass.

Cision PR Newswire. (2013, February 13). American Management Association survey reveals that more than half of executives admit their employees are "average" at best. Retrieved from http://www.prnewswire.com/news-releases/american-management-association-survey-reveals-that-more-than-half-of-executives-admit-their-employees-are-average-at-best-191016351.html

Cohen, C. F. (2012). The 40-year-old intern. *Harvard Business Review, 90*(11), 21–23.

Desilver, D. (2016). More older Americans are working, and working more, than they used to. Retrieved from http://www.pewresearch.org/fact-tank/2016/06/20/more-older-americans-are-working-and-working-more-than-they-used-to/

Ericsson, K. A., Prietula, M. J., & Cokely, E. T. (2007). The making of an expert. *Harvard Business Review, 85*(7–8), 114–121, 193.

Eyler, J. (2009). The power of experiential education. *Liberal Education, 95*(4), 24–31.

Fried, C., Lim, P., Mangla, I., Rosato, D., & Wang, P. (2013). Building wealth: Best moves if you're 35 to 44. *Money, 42*(4), 68.

Goulet, L. (2012). Leadership is everybody's business. *T+D, 66*(8), 48–53.

Hewlett, S. A., Marshall, M., & Sherbin, L. (2011). The relationship you need to get right. *Harvard Business Review, 89*(10), 131–134.

Holland, J. M., Major, D. A., & Orvis, K. A. (2012). Understanding how peer mentoring and capitalization link STEM students to their majors. *Career Development Quarterly, 60*(4), 343–354.

Kaufman, B. (2011). Leadership strategies: Build your sphere of influence. *Business Strategy Series, 12*(6), 315–320.

Kavoussi, B. (2012, November 13). Jobless youths left behind as older workers fill more openings. *Huffington Post*. Retrieved from http://www.huffingtonpost.com/2012/07/06/jobs-young-people_n_1654367.html

MyCommNet. (2013, February 1). Millennial jobs report: Youth unemployment reaches 13.1 percent. *PR Newswire*. Retrieved from http://plp.acc.commnet.edu:6018/ps/i.do?id=GALE%7CA317172410&v=2.1&u=22522&it=r&p=GPS&sw=w

National Association of College and Employers (2016). Paid Interns/Co-ops See Greater Offer Rates and Salary Offers than Their Unpaid Classmates. Retrieved from http://www.naceweb.org/job-market/internships/paid-interns-co-ops-see-greater-offer-rates-and-salary-offers-than-their-unpaid-classmates/PR Newswire. (2016, March 23).

National Associate of College and Employers (2018). Employers Plan to Increase College Hiring by Almost 17 Percent. Retrieved from http://www.naceweb.org/about-us/press/2018/employers-plan-to-increase-college-hiring-by-almost-17-percent/

National Association of Colleges and Employers. (2017). Employers prefer candidates with work Experience. Retrieved from http://www.naceweb.org/talent-acquisition/candidate-selection/employers-prefer-candidates-with-work-experience/

Robles, M. M. (2012). Executive perceptions of the top 10 soft skills needed in today's workplace. *Business Communication Quarterly, 75*(4), 453–465.

Ryan, C., & Krapels, R. H. (1997). Organizations and internships. *Business Communication Quarterly, 60*(4), 126–131.

Statista (2017). Monthly youth unemployment rate in the United States from August 2016 to August 2017 (seasonally adjusted). Retrieved from https://www.statista.com/statistics/217448/seasonally-adjusted-monthly-youth-unemployment-rate-in-the-us/

Tanguay, D. M., Camp, R. R., Endres, M. L., & Torres, E. (2012). The impact of sports participation and gender on inferences drawn from resumes. *Journal of Managerial Issues, 24*(2), 191–206.

Turner, E. T. (1993). On the spot: Spontaneous learning. *Journal of Physical Education, Recreation and Dance, 64*(8), 9–11.

University of Wisconsin-Madison. (n.d.). What are Nonprofits and how are they organized? Retrieved from https://careers.ls.wisc.edu/what-are-career-communities/nonprofit-management-education/

Vernon, S. (2017). Why older workers keep staying on the job. Retrieved from https://www.cbsnews.com/news/why-older-workers-keep-staying-on-the-job/

About the Contributors

Peter Bachiochi, PhD

Peter Bachiochi is a Professor of Psychology at Eastern Connecticut State University, where he teaches courses in Industrial-Organizational Psychology at the undergraduate and graduate levels. He worked for four years at IBM in their HR Research group as a survey specialist and internal consultant. He continues to provide survey consulting services to several nonprofit organizations. His research interests include minority employee recruiting and retention, student engagement and retention, affirmative action, job satisfaction, and team leadership. He has published and presented on these topics extensively. He is an ad-hoc reviewer for the *Journal of Business and Psychology*.

Blair Browning, PhD

Blair Browning is an assistant professor in the Department of Communication at Baylor University. He teaches courses in leadership and conflict management, as well as small group communication. His research interests center on interim and transitional leadership, the influence of social media with regard to communication and sport, and communication pedagogy. His work has appeared in outlets such as *Human Relations, International Journal of Sport Communication, OD Practitioner*, and *Communication Teacher*. He received the prestigious Collins Outstanding Professor Award at Baylor in 2012.

Zack J. Damon, PhD

Zack J. Damon is an assistant professor of sport management at the University of Central Arkansas. He is also the Graduate Program Director for the Executive Masters of Arts in Sport Management online degree, which he created. His research center on investigating follower development into leaders in sport as well as how leadership influences various follower and organizational outcomes in sport organizations. Dr. Damon has published research on the previously mentioned topics and has given research presentations domestically (U.S.) and internationally.

Wendi Everton, PhD

Wendi Everton is a professor of Industrial and Organizational Psychology in the Department of Psychology at Eastern Connecticut State University. She teaches courses in statistics, research methods, and psychology of work including a course in groups and teams. Her research interests focus on the perceptions of fairness in a wide variety of organizations (including academic and sport organizations).

Emmett Gill, PhD

Dr. Gill is the director of the Student-Athlete's Human Rights Pro (SAHRP) – (a 501©4 organization dedicated to social justice for student-athletes) and an assistant professor at the North Carolina Central University (NCCU) Department of Social Work.

Prior to coming to NCCU, Emmett worked at the U.S. Military Academy Center for Enhanced Performance, where he supervised men's and women's basketball student-athletes with academic and athletic performance enhancement and Rutgers University (assistant professor). Before his work at The Center, Dr. Gill was a learning specialist with the University of Maryland football team and his caseload included eight honor roll student-athletes.

Dr. Gill's scholarship focuses on the intersection between social work and collegiate athletics. His latest work, Integrating Sports into Social Work Education, will appear in an upcoming issue of the Journal of Social Work Education.

Heidi Grappendorf, PhD

Heidi Grappendorf is an Associate Professor and Program Director in Sport Management at Western Carolina University. She previously held positions at the University of Cincinnati, North Carolina State University, Texas Tech University, Salem State University, and Webber International University.

Heidi's research involves the under representation of women and diversity in leadership. Her interests include the lack of women and diversity in sport management and leadership. She has given numerous national and international presentations. Additionally, she has authored over 30 journal articles, written seven book chapters, and has written a textbook related to women in sport leadership. Furthermore, she has served as vice president of research for the National Association for Girls and Women in Sport (NAGWS), was on the executive board of the Research Consortium, the editorial board of *Women in Sport & Physical Activity Journal*, and was a co-chair of the North American Society for

Sport Management Diversity Committee. For over 10 years, she has also been the President of Women in NASSM (WIN) within the North American Society for Sport Management (NASSM). At the university level, she has chaired the Association of Women Faculty, and the Council on the Status of Women, as well as having served on the faculty senate.

Meg Hancock, PhD

Meg Hancock is an associate professor of Sport Administration and the Chair of the Health and Sport Sciences Department at the University of Louisville (UofL). She teaches courses in sport management and leadership, athletics in higher education, and sport and social issues. Meg's research interests include gender and diversity in the workplace, sport management education, and the student athlete experience. She currently serves on the editorial boards of the *Women in Sport and Physical Activity Journal*, *Journal of Amateur Sport*, and *Journal of Athlete Development and Experience*. Prior to UofL, she worked as an assistant athletic director and an assistant dean of first-year students.

Maylon Hanold, EdD

Maylon Hanold is Director of the Master in Sport Business Leadership program at Seattle University. She teaches courses in research methods for sport, sport sociology, sport leadership, women and sport leadership, and organizational effectiveness. Her research interests lie at the intersections of leadership, sport sociology, and gender. Her leadership research focuses on the physicality of leadership as related to embodied biases, empathy as a leadership skill, authentic leadership, and leadership development. In addition, she has written about lived experiences in sport including ultrarunning, long-distance running, and transgender recreational sport experiences.

Algerian Hart, PhD

Algerian Hart is the Sport Management Graduate Coordinator and Associate Professor in the Kinesiology Department at Western Illinois University. A former elite athlete and coach, he was a recognized NCAA (National Collegiate Athletic Association) speaker for Hazing, and Drugs and Alcohol Awareness. Dr. Hart serves as Chair of the Diversity and Conference Climate Committee for the North American Society for the Sociology of Sport. He has written extensively in the areas of NCAA governed student-athlete matriculation, marginalized populations within higher education, and is the author of "The Student Athlete's Guide to College Success." He teaches courses in sport leadership, organizational behavior, and sport governance and policy.

Larena Hoeber, PhD

Dr. Larena Hoeber is a professor in the Faculty of Kinesiology & Health Studies at the University of Regina. She currently teaches courses on sport management, sport marketing, and sociology of sport at the undergraduate level, and qualitative research methods at the graduate level. Her research agenda focuses on the use of organizational theory, feminist theories, and contemporary qualitative research approaches to understand and critique the functioning of amateur sport organizations and socio-cultural issues within the sport industry. Her specific research interests are in the areas of gender, innovation, fandom, and interdisciplinary research. Dr. Hoeber has published her research in the *Journal of Sport Management; Sport Management Review; European Sport Management Quarterly; Gender, Work & Organization; Sex Roles; Qualitative Research in Sport; Exercise & Health; Leisure Studies*; and *Online Information Review.*

Orland Hoeber, PhD

Dr. Orland Hoeber is a professor in the Department of Computer Science at the University of Regina. His primary research interests are at the intersection of interactive information retrieval and information visualization. He also conducts interdisciplinary research on the process of innovation and the use of novel computer technology to support the collection and visual analysis of qualitative data in business and academic research contexts. He is a principal investigator, co-investigator, or collaborator on multiple research grants from both the Natural Sciences and Engineering Research Council of Canada (NSERC) and the Social Sciences and Humanities Research Council of Canada (SSHRC).

Mary A. Hums, PhD

Mary A. Hums was the 2009 NASSM Earle F. Zeigler Lecturer, an Erasmus Mundus Visiting International Scholar in Belgium, and represented the U.S. at the International Olympic Academy in Olympia, Greece. Dr. Hums worked the Paralympic Games in Atlanta, Salt Lake City, Athens, and Vancouver, as well as the Olympic Games in Athens. She also served as athletic Director at St. Mary-of-the-Woods College. Author/Editor of five books and numerous articles and book chapters, Hums has given over 150 presentations both domestically and abroad. She earned her Ph.D. from Ohio State University, an M.B.A. and M.A. from the University of Iowa, and a B.B.A. from the University of Notre Dame. Hums contributed to Article 30.5 of the United Nations Convention on the Rights of Persons with Disabilities and is a Research Fellow at the Institute for Human Centered Design. She is an inductee to the Indiana ASA Softball Hall of Fame.

David Legg, PhD

David Legg is a Professor and Chairperson of the Department of Health and Physical Education at Mount Royal University in Calgary,

Canada. In 2004, David was a visiting professor at Dalhousie University in Halifax, Canada, and in 2008-2009, at Deakin University in Melbourne. As a volunteer, David is the past President for the Canadian Paralympic Committee, past Board Member for the Toronto 2015 Pan Parapan American Games, and is president elect for the International Federation of Adapted Physical Activity.

Timothy Liptrap, EdD

Timothy Liptrap is an Associate Professor of Sport Management Chair of the Nichols College Sport Management program. His research interests are in social media, marketing, youth sports, and leadership development. Professionally, he was a Vice President of World TeamTennis, the National Marketing Manager of the United States Tennis Association, and named as one of the Top 40 under 40 in the Tennis Industry. In his off time, Dr. Liptrap is actively involved with his local baseball, basketball, and football programs as a coach and board member.

Jacqueline McDowell, PhD

Jacqueline McDowell, PhD, is an Assistant Professor in the Department of Recreation, Sport and Tourism at the University of Illinois at Urbana-Champaign. Dr. McDowell's research focuses on issues of diversity and inclusion in intercollegiate athletics. Her primary research interest is investigating the organizational experiences of women of color who serve in athletic administration and coaching positions and exploring how they negotiate their race and gender identities in the workplace. She is also interested in exploring the outcomes of diversity management strategies and the effectiveness of diversity initiatives in sport organizations. She teaches courses in sport ethics, human resource management, and intercollegiate athletics management.

Jennifer (Bruening) McGarry, PhD

Dr. (Bruening) McGarry has been a part of the Sport Management program at the University of Connecticut since January of 2002 after spending eight years as an athletic administrator and volleyball coach at Kenyon College in Ohio, including two years as athletic director. She serves as the Department Head of Educational Leadership and coordinates the master's and PhD programs in sport management. Dr. McGarry's research line has focused primarily on barriers and supports for underrepresented populations in sport. She is a research fellow with Northeastern University's Center for the Study of Sport in Society and the North American Society for Sport Management. Dr. McGarry is also the program founder and director for Husky Sport. Husky Sport has both a program and a research component. The program provides mentors (UConn students) as planners of sessions at community sites in Hartford, Connecticut, that emphasize exposure and access to sport and physical activity, and advocate good nutrition and healthy lifestyles. Research has focused specifically on the impact of such a program on pre-adolescent females and the impact of involvement in such a program on the college student mentors.

Nadia Moreno

Nadia Moreno is currently working as Sport for Development Officer for the A Ganar Program. Led by Partners of the Americas, A Ganar is a youth workforce development program that utilizes soccer and other team sports to help youth in Latin America and the Caribbean, ages 16 to 24, find jobs, learn entrepreneurial skills, or re-enter the formal education system. Nadia is a graduate from Emory University with a degree in Political Science and Sociology. Prior to joining A Ganar, Nadia worked with Soccer in the Streets (Atlanta, Georgia) and Fundacion Fundem (Bogota, Colombia). She has extensive experience in sport and community outreach work. Nadia is a firm believer in the power of sport to change lives.

Michael Mudrick, PhD

Michael Mudrick is an assistant professor in the Graham School of Business at York College of Pennsylvania. His research interests include sport consumer behavior, media credibility, and gender issues in sport.

Jon Welty Peachey, PhD

Jon Welty Peachey is an associate professor of sport management in the Department of Recreation, Sport and Tourism at the University of Illinois at Urbana-Champaign. He teaches courses in management of sport organizations, critical issues in sport, facility and event planning, sport finance, and organizational behavior at the undergraduate and graduate levels. His research agenda centers on sport-for-development and social change, organizational change, and developing effective and inclusive leadership strategies for sport organizations. He is a Research Fellow with the North American Society for Sport Management, serves on the editorial boards of the *Journal of Sport Management* and *Sport Management Review* among others, and is a frequent invited speaker and consultant internationally on leadership and sport-for-development. Prior to his work in academia, Dr. Welty Peachey worked as a senior administrator in the international sport field for a decade.

Brooke Page Rosenbauer

Brooke Page Rosenbauer is the Senior Technical Coordinator for Sport-for-Development at Partners of the Americas. Focusing specifically on the Caribbean region, she coordinates the "A Ganar" youth workforce development program, which uses a sport-based employability curriculum to reduce youth unemployment.

Previously, Brooke directed the Lose the Shoes campaign for Grassroot Soccer's HIV/AIDS awareness and prevention program and has over 10 years of youth coaching experience. She is the 2008 Harry S. Truman Scholar for the state of Vermont and holds a Master's of Science in International Health Policy and Management from the Heller School of Social Policy and Management at Brandeis University in Boston, Massachusetts. Brooke's main research and career interests include youth and health, specifically the use of sport and physical activity in preventing chronic disease.

Pete Schroeder, EdD

Pete Schroeder is an associate professor of Sport Management and chair of the Department of Health, Exercise, and Sports Sciences at the University of the Pacific. He earned his doctorate from the University of Missouri in Leadership and Policy Analysis and a B.S. in Exercise Science at Truman State University. He has conducted award-winning research on organizational culture in university and college sport and has published research in *Sport, Education and Society, Journal of Sport Behavior, Journal of College Student Development, and Journal of Issues in Intercollegiate Athletics*. In addition, he has presented research on international labor migration and sport management pedagogy. He is a member of the College Sport Research Institute and has consulted for multiple university athletic departments and teams.

Kathryn Shea, PhD

Kathryn Shea is the Director of the Sport Management Program at Fisher College, where she teaches courses in sport governance, venue management, sport media and public relations, and sport law. She oversees the development of the sport management curriculum and professional partnerships with sport organizations to offer students experiential learning opportunities. Shea rowed on the University of Wisconsin Varsity Women's Rowing Team and this experience led to her career in coaching, athletic administration and, ultimately, to earning her master's and doctorate at Indiana University. Her research examines the structure and efficacy of policies and on compliance in sport.

Janelle E. Wells, PhD

Janelle E. Wells is an assistant professor in the Department of Sport Management in the College of Education at Florida State University. After receiving her BBA and MBA in management and prior to earning her doctorate, Dr. Wells worked in the private sector and coached collegiate volleyball. She has taught Human Resource Management in Sport, Administration in Sport and Physical Activity, Introduction to Business Statistics, Sport and Society, Introduction to Sport Management, as well as guest lectured on Sport and Business Finance. Her research interests focus on the career development of sport leaders as well as the impact of leaders on employee selection, turnover, organizational change, and performance.

Index

Note: Page numbers followed by *f*, or *t*, indicate material in figures, or tables, respectively

L

laissez-faire leadership, 11, 22, 25, 100
Latham, Rachael, 291
leader
  authoritarian, 11
  behavior, 11
  change process, 173–174
  charismatic, 9
  definition of, 3–4
  democratic, 11
  election, 8
  emergence, 8
  environmental constraints, 174–175
  and follower relationship, 52–53
  of physical education, 226
  power. *See* power
  servant. *See* servant leader
  skills of, 232–234
  transactional. *See* transactional leaders
  transformational. *See* transformational leaders
leader-member exchange (LMX), 72–73
leadership, 43
  achievement-oriented, 13
  active listening, 99
  alignment with people, 55–56
  authentic, 33
  autocratic, 177
  charismatic, 23
  coherent, 45
  communication styles, 99–100
  competencies, 98, 98*t*
  cultural sensitivity, 99
  definition, 3–4, 56–57, 97
  democratic, 11
  directive, 13
  empowerment, 73–75
  ethical approach to, 131
  ethical decision-making, 125–130
  ethics and ethical dilemmas, 119–124
  as excellent management, 45–46
  as a function of management, 46–47
  Gen Z, 76–77
  historical and current barriers in, 266–271

history, 43–47, 118–119
humility, 79–80
importance of, 172
information accuracy, 99
knowledge of communication context, 98
laissez-faire, 11, 22, 25
and management
  defining, 48–51
  differences between, 47–49, 50*t*–51*t*, 52–54
  functions of, 57*t*
  overlap, 45
  synonymous, 44–45
millennials, 75
motivation of, 56
MTL, 77–78
narcissism, 79–80
NCAA college sports, 271–273
Ohio State Studies for, 9–10
opportunities on campus, 306–309
and organizational change, 175–177
participative, 10, 13, 100, 177
path–goal theory of, 13
paths to, 8–9
processes, 93–94
race and, 261–278
servant. *See* servant leadership
situational, 10–13
skills building, 303–305
social justice efforts, 273–275
studies, 10
styles, dynamics of, 7–8
supportive, 13
theories, 3, 9–13
traits, 9
transactional. *See* transactional leadership
transformational, 46–47, 49
trust, 98–99
types, 12, 94, 95*t*
University of Michigan Studies for, 10
vision and strategy, 54–55
women of color in sport, 275–276
leadership portfolio, 304
Legalizing Discrimination and Sport, case study, 115–116
legitimate power, 5
Lewin, K., 11
Likert, Rensis, system of management, 10

Lippitt, R., 11
Liptrap, Tim, 314
LMX. *See* leader-member exchange
LOCOG. *See* London Organising Committee of the Olympic and Paralympic Games
London Organising Committee of the Olympic and Paralympic Games (LOCOG), 288
Lopiano, Donna, 253

M

Mace, Ronald L., 293
magnitude of consequences, 127
Major League Baseball (MLB), 118, 248, 267
Major League Soccer (MLS), 248
management, 43
  historical perspective, 43–47
  leadership and
    defining, 48–51
    differences between, 47–49, 50*t*–51*t*, 52–54
    functions of, 57*t*
    overlap, 45
    processes, 56
    as synonymous, 44–45
  plan implementation, 55
manager, 43
  and subordinates relationship, 52–53
managerial determinants, 194–195
managerial grid
  Blake, 11–13, 12*f*
  Mouton, 11–13, 12*f*
Managerial Mystique, The: Restoring Leadership in Business, 46
managerial wisdom, 155*t*
Manager Manifesto, 148
Mark "Garvey" Candella, 218–220
mastery, 70–71
Mathare Youth Sports Association (MYSA), 230, 231
McCarty, Bill, 275
McGillivray, Dave, 83–84
M&E. *See* monitoring and evaluation
mentorship, 315–316
Miami Heat, 211
middle of the road management, 12